S0-BNJ-191

THE MODERN LIBRARY
of the World's Best Books

SELECTED POETRY

O F

Edmund Spenser

*The publishers will be pleased to send, upon
request, an illustrated folder listing
each volume in*

THE MODERN LIBRARY

Selected Poetry of

EDMUND
SPENSER

EDITED, WITH AN INTRODUCTION, BY

William Nelson

Professor of English, Columbia University

THE MODERN LIBRARY

NEW YORK

First Printing

© *Copyright, 1964, by Random House, Inc.*

All rights reserved under International and Pan-American Copyright Conventions. Published in New York by Random House, Inc., and simultaneously in Toronto, Canada, by Random House of Canada, Limited.

Library of Congress Catalog Card Number: 64–18940

THE MODERN LIBRARY
is published by RANDOM HOUSE, INC.
BENNETT CERF • DONALD S. KLOPFER

Manufactured in the United States of America

Contents

Introduction

To Edmund Spenser, as to sensitive men of every age, the world seemed a chaotic, discordant place, its creatures constantly at odds with each other, unwilling or unable to live in ordered peace. This apparent discord, to be sure, served the ends of the Creator, but from the limited, human point of view it was discord none the less. In England there were men so unnatural as to betray their most glorious of queens, across the Channel a nobleman sold his religion for a crown, over the Alps Antichrist claimed authority over Christ's church, in the skies planets failed to keep their even courses and the constellations of the zodiac no longer matched the astrological signs which bore their names. The time was out of joint and men perverse, and the harmony which characterized Eden before the Fall would return only after the Judgment. Yet it might exist in the imagination of an erected intelligence, figured as an ancient world of virtuous heroes, as a pastoral paradise, or as a realm of ideas, unsullied by matter. It was the function of the true poet, Renaissance critical theory declared, to portray such worlds in order to show man the sickness in which he lived and the health toward which he should strive. To this task Spenser devoted his career.

A friend of Spenser's whom we know only by the initials "E.K." undertook to introduce the "new poet" to the English public in the year 1579. His preface to *The Shepheardes Calender* contrasts that poem with the formless product of "the rakehelly rout of our ragged rhymers . . . which without learning boast, without judgment jangle, without reason rage and foam, as if some instinct of poetical spirit had newly ravished them above the meanness of common capacity." Such an advertisement presumes an audience of judgment, one which has a serious interest in poetry, is cultivated and learned enough to understand the relation of a modern work to the tradition from which it derives, and recognizes and appreciates the artistry of a work which E.K. describes as "well

grounded, finely framed, and strongly trussed up together."
And the writer so advertised must be one with the conviction
that poetry is not an unpremeditated outpouring of the spirit
but a learned vocation, deliberate in its method and in its
choice of goals.

Since learning suggests pedantry and artistry artifice, the
qualities that E.K. thought admirable may repel the reader
rather than attract him. It is in fact possible to find delight in
Spenser's poetry for reasons quite different from those offered in the introduction to *The Shepheardes Calender*. The
poet is a master of metrical effects, his flow of words is abun-
dant, his imagination warm and rich. *The Faerie Queene* can
be read half in a dream, the attention fascinated by a succession of image and incident so removed from reality that monsters seem childishly charming. If an occasional note implying
thoughtful purpose intrudes itself into such an entertainment
it can be ignored as an irrelevance or regarded as that con-
trasting discord which makes the rest delicious. But reading
The Faerie Queene or any of Spenser's poems in this way is
not unlike reading Shakespeare's plays for the excitement of
their plots.

However we may choose to read him, Spenser at least had
no desire merely "to feed youth's fancy and the flocking fry,"
as Cuddie puts it in the October eclogue of the *Calender*. Of
the literary inheritance that the Renaissance derived from
classical times there was perhaps nothing more important than
the idea that the poet, master of the sweetest art of persua-
sion, was originally responsible for the civilization of mankind and continued to be its principal inspiration to virtuous
and noble action. Horace had exalted poetry by declaring that
it was the magic of Orpheus' song that drew savage man from
the wilderness to live under law, that it was Amphion's lute
that built the city of Thebes and established its constitution.
These instances and others like them are constantly recalled
by the writers of the Renaissance. Often, to be sure, such rec-
ollection is only formal obeisance to the critical dogma of
the time; if there is a didactic purpose in many of the amorous
songs or displays of rhetorical virtuosity, it is well hidden. But
Spenser, like Milton after him, believed profoundly that the
poet's vocation was that of servant and guide to the common-
wealth.

For such a career, the inevitable model in Renaissance times
was Vergil. The appearance of *The Shepheardes Calender*
was itself a signal of Spenser's intention to follow those classical footsteps: as Vergil had tested his poetic talent in the
humble genre of the pastoral before venturing the heroic

reach of the *Aeneid,* so Spenser elected to begin with a collection of eclogues, planning even then the noble poem which
was to be his crowning achievement. To mark the fulfillment
of that plan, when the first part of *The Faerie Queene* was
published, a decade later, it began with a paraphrase of the
lines which in Renaissance editions appeared at the head of the
Aeneid ("Ille ego qui quondam . . ."):

> Lo! I, the man whose Muse whylome did maske,
> As time her taught, in lowly Shephards weeds,
> Am now enforst, a farre unfitter taske,
> For trumpets sterne to chaunge mine Oaten reeds

In these verses the readers to whom Spenser addressed himself
would have recognized the poet's daring claim to the composition of an English *Aeneid.*

Neither the *Calender* nor *The Faerie Queene* resembles its
Vergilian counterpart in the sense that Gray's odes, let us
say, are Pindaric, or Johnson's satire Juvenalian. Spenser is
less an imitator than a competitor; what he imitates is Vergil's
own rivalry with Theocritus and Homer. His object is not to
write in the manner of Vergil but rather to create for his own
time, for his own nation, and for his own traditions the equivalent of what Vergil made for his. If the Roman poet coupled
pastoral simplicity and an antiquity of virtuous heroes with a
celebration of the new golden age of Augustus, Spenser
joined in imaginative union the truth of the English countryside and the chivalry of ancient Britons with a blazon of the
glorious court of Queen Elizabeth. If Vergil challenged Homer by singing the praises of Rome, that second Troy, Spenser threw down the gage to both:

> a third kingdom yet is to arise
> Out of the Trojans scattered ofspring,
> That in all glory and great enterprise,
> Both first and second Troy shall dare to equalise.

The "great enterprise" included poetry, too. There was high
hope in the hearts of Spenser's contemporaries that their
country would match or surpass the literary achievement of
Greece and Rome. The poet Samuel Daniel chides those who
doubt:

> Or should we carelesse come behind the rest
> In powre of wordes, that go before in worth,
> When as our accents equall to the best

Is able greater wonders to bring forth:
When all that ever hotter spirits exprest
Comes bettered by the patience of the North?

And although Spenser sometimes assumes the role of humble
follower of his great predecessors, it is clear from the ambition of his works that his aim was higher.

The Shepheardes Calender illustrates both Spenser's tradi-
tionalism and his independence. As his readers opened the
book they would recognize the woodcuts in it as imitations of
those in contemporary editions of Vergil's Bucolics. In the
October eclogue they would remark that the career of the
"Romish" Tityrus—the pastoral name which Vergil used for
himself—is the measure by which that of Colin—Spenser—is
tested. But the Calender pays homage to an English Tityrus,
too, the "shepherd" Geoffrey Chaucer, and it echoes in theme
and phrase not only classical pastoral but that of Renaissance
writers in French and Latin. Instead of choosing the traditional pastoral names, Coridon, Daphnis, and the like, as most
of his contemporaries did, Spenser elects strange harsh-
sounding ones that give the impression of rusticity: Diggon
Davie, Hobbinol, Wrenock. He invents a special vocabulary
for the poem, a mixture of the rude and the antique, an experi-
ment which Sir Philip Sidney, to whom the Calender was
dedicated, thought excessively bold. Rather than some English equivalent for Vergil's hexameter, Spenser employs a
great variety of verse forms ranging from elaborate stanzaic
patterns to deliberately irregular, jagged couplets, and he
sharpens awareness of that variety by setting, for example, the
light country roundelay of Perigot and Willy next to the
grave sestine of Colin's love lament.

The range of subject matter in the Calender is equally re-
markable. Spenser draws on all of the resources which the
tradition offered him, including in his twelve eclogues the
lament of the unhappy lover, the debate between youth and
age, the song contest for a rustic prize, the celebration of a
great personage, the elegy, the complaint of the poet unre-
warded, the comment of pastoral simplicity on corrupt greed
and ambition. These "plaintive," "recreative," and "moral"
poems, as E.K. describes them, boldly contrast with each
other. But the effect is not discord, because the twelve eclogues, the many meters, and the diverse subjects are
"strongly trussed up together."

The organization of the eclogues into a unit is Spenser's
most striking innovation. The whole is structured as a calendar, each poem bearing the name of a month. In January

Colin complains to the barren ground, "Whilome thy fresh spring flowrd," and in December he echoes that complaint: "Whilome in youth, when flowrd my joyfull spring." References to the season of the year recur throughout the *Calender*, not regularly, for Spenser is no mechanical architect, but often enough to maintain a sense of the passage and circularity of time. And this temporal frame suggests the theme which binds together the disparate elements of the work, the theme of youth and age, of growth and decay, of hope and its blasting.

The calendar motif expresses itself in the realms of the lover, the priest, and the poet. Youthful love is improvidently happy, budding, rich in promise; with maturity comes the bitter pang, with age the dried-up harvest. In the days of the Biblical patriarchs and of Christ's apostles the pastor looked for no other reward than heaven; now he has become lazy, proud, hungry for lordship, careless of his flock. Vergil lived in a heroic age and had a Maecenas to nourish his talent; the time now is degenerate and no one cares for the poet. From this bad world we are asked to look back to a golden age when love was always happy, the flock was safe from Satanic wolves and foxes, the poet freely sang his lovely lays. But the view is not only to the past, nor is the end altogether the barrenness of December, though that is the prevailing note. "The time was once, and may againe retorne," says Piers of true religion. Hobbinol has found the paradise that Adam lost. And if Colin truly loved the beauty of his Rosalind, his song would not be silenced by pain but rather raised "above the starry skie," higher, perhaps, than the Vergilian summit.

Colin Clouts Come Home Againe, written more than a decade later, is a pastoral similar to *The Shepheardes Calender* in its poetic aims but more immediately pleasing because its devices are less obtrusive. The occasion for the poem was Spenser's journey from Ireland in 1589 in company with Sir Walter Ralegh to present the first three books of *The Faerie Queene* to Queen Elizabeth. In this poem the transitions are smooth, there are no shocking juxtapositions of meter, the rusticity of the vocabulary remains a flavor only, the new pastoral names, Melissa, Alexis, Marin, avoid harshness. Yet the variety of mood and matter is as wide as in the *Calender*. The tone ranges from rhapsody to bitter satire. Colin tells his wondering auditors of his voyage over the fearful sea, of incomparable England and its great Queen, of the poets and ladies of the court, of the false courtier, of love counterfeit and true, of his hopeless passion for proud Rosalind. The discourse concerns the lover, the poet, and the courtier, the last taking the place of the priest in the *Calender*. In both pastorals the grand movement is circular, the *Calender* returning from winter to winter and *Colin Clout* beginning and ending in the Irish countryside. But in this poem the poles are of place rather than time; the touchstone by which the here and now is tested is not an ancient golden age but the innocence of the shepherds to whom Colin tells his tale.

The structure of *Mother Hubberds Tale* is of another kind. Mother Hubberd tells the poet of the escapades of a fox and an ape, characters out of the satiric beast fables which were so popular in the late Middle Ages. As narrative, Spenser's *Tale* is remarkably ill-conceived: the principal characters abruptly leave one adventure for another; at the beginning of the poem they dwell in a world of men but at the end they are living among beasts; long speeches and digressive exclamations interrupt the story. The unity of the poem, however, depends not upon the narrative but upon a structure of idea. Four episodes deal successively with four estates of mankind: the peasantry, the church, the nobility, and the throne. In each of these episodes the fox and the ape gain positions of responsibility by trickery rather than by right, in each they abuse these positions for their own advantage, in each their abuse is at last discovered by a higher power. The theme, the duty of man to his calling, is stated in different ways: in the first episode it appears in the account of the malfeasance of the evil pair as responsible shepherds, in the second in the self-revealing advice given to them by the Formal Priest (the priest in form only), in the third Mother Hubberd breaks in to contrast the natures of the true and the false courtier, in the fourth the ways of a tyrant are made manifest by the actions of the usurping ape and his false counselor. But throughout the villains are counterfeits, the ape mocking man's appearance, the fox mocking man's intelligence. Or to turn the meaning about, those who seek for themselves are not men but beasts.

Muiopotmos or the Fate of the Butterflie is the most delightful and delicate of Spenser's poems, and I would not join the company of those scholars who have weighed it down with multiple meanings. Yet ideally at least delight and instruction should go together, and *Muiopotmos* is neither art for art's sake nor frivolity. Unlike *Mother Hubberds Tale*, *Muiopotmos* tells of a single action, though a slender one. A beautiful butterfly named Clarion delights himself in lordly fashion in a lush garden, falls into the web of the spider Aragnoll, struggles helplessly, and is stung to death. The tale is interrupted by two episodes imitative of Ovid's *Metamor-*

phoses. One tells how the nymph Astery was transformed by Venus into a butterfly because her companions slandered her; the other how Arachne, bitterly angry because Pallas excelled her in weaving, was turned by her own venomousness into a spider.

The stanzas which introduce the poem seem quite irrelevant to it: the poet promises to sing of a deadly battle between two armed heroes whose mutual scorn and hatred led at length to open war. These lines culminate in the exclamation:

> And is there then
> Such rancour in the harts of mightie men?

But the hatred is one-sided only, there is nothing in the poem that can be called a battle between the butterfly and the spider, no open war, and no rancorous men. The contradiction of promise by performance has led some of Spenser's critics to suppose that the work as we have it is an incomplete or careless revision of an earlier draft.

The purpose of these stanzas as I understand it is not to provide a précis of the story that follows but rather to set the tone in which it is to be read. Spenser recalls to his reader the deadly debate between Hector and the wrathful Achilles, as at the end of the poem he reminds him of the death of Turnus in the *Aeneid*, in order to announce that his genre is mock epic, the mirror in little of the great world. But the littleness is not intended, as in other mock epics, to produce an effect of contempt or ridicule. Vergil wrote of Juno's hatred of the Trojans, *"tantaene animis caelestibus irae?"* (Can such resentment dwell in heavenly breasts?) By substituting human breasts for heavenly ones, Spenser makes the same comparison, though for a different purpose, that Gloucester makes in *King Lear:* "As flies to wanton boys, are we to th'gods." From the godlike level that men hold with respect to the insect world it is possible to view dispassionately mortal felicity and lordship, to understand the fragile impermanence of innocence and beauty under the assault of the envy which they fatefully arouse. The note of rancor and envy and the words themselves ring through the poem: ladies of the court envy the color of Clarion's wings; Astery's companions envy her success in gathering flowers; Arachne's needlework is excellent beyond envy, her defeat by Pallas fills her with poisonous rancor, her descendant inherits that rancor and kills the hero. Clarion's superlative qualities produce the pride which leads to his disaster. Although he does not fall into the spider's web until the end of the poem he is already trapped when he is most happy: his "cruell fate is woven even now / Of Joves owne hand," and before he is caught in Aragnoll's threads Pallas weaves a butterfly into the border of her work. The mock-heroic opening, the episodes, the descriptions, the little tale itself all tend to the same effect, a "delightful teaching" of the tragic lesson that the destruction of felicity is implicit in felicity itself.

Spenser's overriding tendency to organize his compositions in terms of parallel and contrast is nowhere more evident than in the *Fowre Hymnes*. In his dedication to this work he says that the first two hymns of "earthly" love and beauty were written in the "greener times" of his youth, and that the last two, of "celestial" love and beauty, constitute a retractation. But they were all published together, and together they make a whole. Its structure appears most clearly when the hymns of love and the hymns of beauty are set side by side. The love which is Cupid and the love which is Christ are both creative, both all-consuming, both full of pain. In one kind of love man woos a proud lady; in the other Christ woos flinty mankind. But the earthly lover raises himself to nobility through love, while Christ "downe descended, like a most demisse / And abject thrall." And the pinnacle of happiness for love here is the connubial bed, for love there "Th'Idee of his pure glorie." The hymns to beauty present similar contrasts. Earthly beauty, figured in Venus, is derived from a "wondrous Paterne" according to which "this worlds great Workmaister" fashioned all things "as comely as he could." Spenser is deliberately vague about the "Workmaister" except that by limiting his power he rules out his identification with God. The higher beauty is represented by Sapience, seated in the bosom of God, in comparison with whom Venus seems foul. In both realms, the seeker for true beauty must first strip away the veil of appearance that hides it. But the movement of the earthly hymn is down, from that pattern kept secret from sinful eyes to the fair lady in whom it is embodied. The celestial hymn moves upward from this fair world of sense to the "Unmoving, uncorrupt" heaven beyond, at the height of which may be seen "that Soveraine Light, / From whose pure beams al perfect beauty springs."

To yoke earth and heaven in this way Spenser made use of a vocabulary of ideas drawn from the most diverse sources, from *courtoisie*, from Platonism, from Christianity. As a philosophical construct the amalgam is incoherent, even absurd. The love of the troubadours concerned itself with earth, Platonic love admitted the divine origin of earthly beauty but left the world behind in its upward climb, traditional Christianity tended to reject it altogether. As a poet rather than as a philosopher Spenser strove nevertheless to find in all of these traditions support for his conviction that human love is a good precisely because the heavenly love which it reflects is an infinite, not merely a greater good.

It is this kind of relationship between the temporal and the eternal that manifests itself in the *Epithalamion*, Spenser's magnificent celebration of his own marriage. Beginning at dawn and ending just before dawn the song is formally circumscribed by the limits of the mundane day. In these bounds are included the rich variety of moods associated with an earthly wedding: impatient expectation, humble reverence, Bacchic abandon, the fear and the delight of sexual union. But the frame breaks at the end as the hope for children leads to a prophecy of their heavenly destination. That ultimate happiness does not destroy the joy of the wedding; rather it justifies it. The same attitude finds expression in Christian terms in the 68th sonnet of the *Amoretti*, and in Platonic terms in the 72nd. In like manner, in the first book of *The Faerie Queene* the Hermit on the Hill of Contemplation explains to the Red Cross Knight that although the city of Cleopolis with its tower of earthly glory is quite dimmed by the radiance of the New Jerusalem

> Yet is Cleopolis, for earthly frame,
> The fairest peece that eie beholden can,
> And well beseemes all knights of noble name,
> That covett in th'immortall booke of fame
> To be eternized, that same to haunt,
> And doen their service to that soveraigne Dame,
> That glory does to them for guerdon graunt:
> For she is hevenly borne, and heaven may justly vaunt.

The Faerie Queene, it has been said, is easy to read but hard to understand. Its difficulty depends in part upon the fact that Spenser was in his own time a "deep" poet, addressing himself to a learned audience. More important, *The Faerie Queene* was conceived in terms of ideas about the nature of a great poem which we cannot fully recapture, ideas which are at odds with some of our basic critical assumptions. Although the exegetical literature is very extensive and indeed grows greater year by year, there is as yet no standard, generally accepted interpretation of the meaning and structure of the poem. It is therefore impossible to follow the course usually proper to an Introduction of this kind of presenting the conclusions of the scholars and critics who have studied the work.

I must therefore risk a statement of my own understanding of it. Those who are familiar with the body of Spenser criticism will recognize my indebtedness to it; they will also note, and I hope not too hastily condemn, my deviations from the tradition.

Before *The Faerie Queene* can be read on its own terms it is necessary to set aside certain false expectations about it. The Aristotelian dictum that plot is the soul of a tragedy or of an epic poem does not apply to this work. It is no more a story than Spenser's other poems. The central action is Arthur's search for Gloriana, but after we are informed that, like Sir Thopas in Chaucer's burlesque tale, he dreamed of the queen of fairies and fell in love with her, we hear almost nothing more about the matter. On one occasion, indeed, he pauses in his chase after Florimel to wish that Gloriana were as fair as she. In the course of the six books Arthur appears intermittently, rescuing the unfortunate and subduing the vile, but he is no closer to Gloriana's Cleopolis at the end of the sixth book than he was at the beginning of the first, and this is strange because he encounters many Cleopolitans who could have shown him the way. Had Spenser completed the twelve books he envisaged he might have described Arthur's arrival at the glorious city and his union with its queen. But unless the unwritten books were to be very different from those we have Spenser did not conceive of Arthur's love for Gloriana as a motor for the narrative in the sense that the goals of Vergil's Aeneas, Tasso's Godfredo, and Camoëns' da Gama determine the actions of their great poems. In fact, Arthur's dream of Gloriana is not the foundation of a plot but a figure of speech declaring the noble man's inspiring vision of heroic achievement, his "great desire of glory and of fame." And this flimsiness of plot equally characterizes the quests of the several champions who are the titular heroes of the successive books.

Yet *The Faerie Queene* is filled with stories, many of them brilliantly told. They are drawn, twisted sometimes almost unrecognizably, from the widest variety of sources imaginable, from classical myth and medieval romance, history and fable, from Vergil, Ovid, the *Golden Legend*, Chaucer's tales, the poems of Ariosto and Tasso. From these and many others Spenser borrowed not only incidents and episodes but set descriptions, exclamations, apostrophes, and moral observations. Whatever he borrowed he bent and shaped to serve the intellectual and emotional ends of his discourse, so that there can be nothing more misleading than to read his intention from that of his source. He is bound by no single technique of expression: sometimes a story or portrait is presented as an illustrative example; sometimes it must be understood as an "allegory" or extended metaphor. The adventures of the Squire of Dames provides an instance of the weakness of womankind against the wiles of a determined seducer; Amoret's heart drawn from her breast and bleeding from a wound is a rhetorical trope for her spiritual suffering. Sometimes an episode moves from the realm of example to that of metaphor without a break, as in the story of Hellenore who is seduced in "realistic" fashion by the rake Paridell and is last seen figuratively as the common mistress of a company of goatlike satyrs, the animality of her nature victorious. Technical distinctions among these kinds of statement tend merely to obscure the poet's meaning. Spenser expects of his readers not that kind of analysis but a developing recognition of the complexity of his theme from its expression in his titles, the names of his characters, the situations in which they find themselves, the figures of speech, the very music of his verse. The recognition once achieved reciprocally illuminates the meaning of the materials out of which it arises, the whole producing at once a fullness and a precision of poetic statement.

In the freedom and eclecticism of its method *The Faerie Queene* is quite unlike such great medieval allegories as the *Divina Commedia*, the *Roman de la Rose*, and *Piers Plowman*. Spenser cites as his models not these but the works of Xenophon, Homer, Vergil, Ariosto and Tasso. As Renaissance critics understood these writers they were all heroic poets (although Xenophon wrote in prose) because they created fictions describing the nature of the virtuous hero. In the explanatory preface which he wrote for the *Gerusalemme Liberata*, Tasso characterizes the genre as a compound of imitation and allegory (the translation is that of Spenser's contemporary Fairfax):

> . . . imitation regardeth the actions of man subjected to the outward senses, and about them being principally employed, seeketh to represent them with effectual and expressive phrases, such as lively set before our corporal eyes the things represented: it doth not consider the customs, affections, or discourses of the mind as they be inward, but only as they come forth thence, and being manifested in words, in deeds, or working, do accompany the action. On the other side allegory respecteth the passions, opinions, and customs, not only as they do appear, but principally in their being hidden and inward, and more obscurely doth express them with notes (as a man

may say) mystical, such as only the understanders of the nature of things can fully comprehend.

In rhetoric, the word "allegory" means merely "extended metaphor." It is rather in Tasso's sense of allegory as "the glass and figure of human life" that Spenser speaks of his poem as "a continued allegory or dark conceit." A mirror is defined not by the materials which compose it but by the function it serves. *The Faerie Queene* is an allegory because its stories, metaphors, descriptions, and direct statements are intended to probe the "hidden and inward" of man's nature.

Since the poem is unfinished it is necessary to rely on what we have of it and on Spenser's letter to Ralegh which "giveth great light to the reader" for an understanding of the structure of the whole. Its general purpose is "to fashion a gentleman or noble person in vertuous and gentle discipline"—that is, to describe or delineate a member of the ruling class who is governed both by the precepts of moral philosophy and by the chivalric code. Setting aside as matter for another great poem that aspect of the subject which concerns the public, official character of the gentleman, Spenser labors in *The Faerie Queene* to "pourtraict in Arthure, before he was king, the image of a brave knight, perfected in the twelve private morall vertues, as Aristotle hath devised." For the "more variety of the history" he divides the subject among twelve several champions, each representing a particular moral quality, with Arthur remaining as their sum, or "Magnificence." Spenser does not say, it is important to note, that he will describe the way in which virtue and gentility are inculcated by training and experience, that is, the process by which Arthur achieves perfection. *The Faerie Queene* is not primarily a *Bildungsroman*, a story of progress and development. To be sure, there are instances in the poem in which characters change as a result of what happens to them. But the emphasis throughout is on revelation, not on growth. The process by which the poem moves is one in which the reader gains a clearer and deeper understanding of the complex nature of man.

That nature is of this world and therefore a mixed thing, made up of diverse and conflicting elements, beautiful in its reflection of the divine, foul in its distortion of that image by the muddy substance of which it is made. Man retains his humanity as the world itself stands, not in a state of rest but in an unstable equilibrium of opposing forces, always in danger of collapse, and there can be no final resolution until Judgment Day solves everything. It is to these antagonisms

in the human condition that Spenser directs his reader's attention.

Always a seeker for variety, Spenser has given to each of the
books of *The Faerie Queene* a particular narrative flavor.
The Red Cross Knight is St. George of the *Golden Legend*,
Guyon a hero of classical epic, Britomart a heroine like Ariosto's Bradamante. Cambel is out of Chaucer; Artegall is a
euhemerized god of ancient myth, an Osiris or Hercules; the
story of Calidore is of the kind of Sidney's *Arcadia* and of
the Greek romances from which the *Arcadia* derives; and the
cantos of Mutabilitie suggest Ovid's *Metamorphoses*. Nevertheless, in method and in the view of life which they express
the books of *The Faerie Queene* do not differ essentially from
each other. Each presents human nature in terms of its basic
contradictions, virtue implying vice, the motive which draws
man to good capable also of drawing him to evil. Each points
the right way, at the same time emphasizing the terrible difficulty of following it. And each applies its instruction, derived from the realm of the individual, to the larger world
of Britain and of society as a whole.

In the Book of Holinesse the principal dichotomy is stated
at once in the black veil which obscures Una's sunlit beauty.
That beauty is so universally powerful that a fierce lion and
a savage race are made tame by it. But it is hidden by the
veil, which is a token of the Fall of Man, so that even the Red
Cross Knight can be misled into thinking truth false and falsehood true. In the same sense, Fradubio is misled by a foggy
mist into rejecting his Fraelissa and accepting the false Duessa.
Dark, too, is the Wood of Error, like Dante's *selva oscura* the
shadowy forest of this world, apparently full of delights yet
it "heavens light did hide." In the darkness man stumbles and
falls, and he cannot by his own powers keep to the right way.
Since it is particularly the religious man who is conscious of
his own sins the Red Cross Knight is "solemne sad" when first
we meet him; because of that disease of conscience he almost
falls victim to Sans Joy (who stands at the opposite pole
from Speranza, hope in the joy of heaven), almost succumbs
to the temptation of Despair in his own salvation, wishes for
death when he is instructed by Fidelia, and begs either to
die or to withdraw from the world after he has seen a vision
of the New Jerusalem. The paradox which makes the Knight
of Holinesse particularly vulnerable to the sin of despair, that
is, the denial of Christ's sacrifice, is given dramatic expression
in the course of the climactic battle with the Old Dragon. A
flake of fire from the monster's hell-mouth falls into his armor, the armor which is that of the Christian man described

by St. Paul in his Epistle to the Ephesians. The armor itself—
his true belief—almost destroys the knight: "That erst him
goodly armd, now most of all him harmd."

To the doom of darkness and death for the soul there is a
counter. From the Holy Book "with blood ywritt" which she
holds in one hand Fidelia preaches to the Knight not only
words that kill but also those that "rayse againe to life the
hart that she did thrill." The Book is at once the Law of the
Old Testament by which man is damned and the Promise of
the New by which he is saved. In her other hand she holds a
golden cup in which there is a deadly serpent but also the
wine and water of the communion. The saving grace of God
comes to man in his greatest need. It is manifested in the
"chance" rescues of the Knight in his battle with the Dragon,
in the quickening faith urged upon him by Una when he is
almost overcome by Error and Despair. In his battle with
Sans Joy even the false Duessa becomes an unwitting instrument of salvation. Only by that grace can the veil of delusion
be lifted. By the light of Arthur's blazing shield "all that
was not such as seemed in sight . . . did fade and suddeine
fall." In that light, the terrible Orgoglio—Pride—is discovered to be what he is, a bladder stuffed with wind, and man,
like Adam before the Fall, sees truly the world in which he
lives.

In the *Golden Legend* life of St. George, which everybody
of Spenser's time knew, the etymology of the saint's name is
given: "George is said of *geos*, which is as much to say as
'earth,' and *orge*, that is 'tilling,' so George is to say as 'tilling
the earth,' that is his flesh." The life of the saint is compared
to the labor of a peasant whose arduous tilling at length
yields the promised harvest. In the letter to Ralegh, Spenser
reminds the reader of this agricultural trope by describing
the Knight, on his first appearance at the court of Gloriana, as
a simple rustic. The legendary life of George ends with his
sainthood, but Spenser's tale does not end so. His George must
serve six years in the earthly "warlike" duty demanded by
Gloriana before he can attain the sabbath of heaven which he
desires. He has become wiser as to his own nature, and therefore less easy a prey for the powers of evil, but he will continue to sin, no doubt even to despair, since he is flesh and
therefore in the dark: "For blood can nought but sin, and
wars but sorrows yield."

George is not only a man of earth but also the patron saint
of England. He must contend, therefore, with Satanic forces
expressed in the particular of the Church of Rome, with the
hypocrisy of the mock ascetic Archimago, and with the false-

ness of Duessa, wearer of the triple crown of the papacy. In this special sense the Book of Holinesse becomes the history of the church of Britain, seduced from its original purity by the wiles of Rome, and reunited with the true faith at last by the Tudor dynasty. In another special sense, the slayer of the Old Dragon is Christ, for the life of any man destined for heaven is an *imitatio Christi,* and the conquest of the monster that besieges mankind is Christ's work. But while Spenser clearly intends these applications he does not permit them to dominate his legend of George the man, servant of Gloriana and tiller of his flesh.

As in the state of Eden Una's face is without its veil, so in an ideal world man's nature is in its proper order. Reason guides the organism; subservient to it are the emotions and appetites which men share with beasts and those "vegetative" drives necessary to the maintenance and reproduction of life. This is the state of things represented by the House of Alma in the Legend of Temperance. But that house, though beautifully fashioned, is impermanently built of a substance like "slime" and it is constantly under assault by the enemy without. The assault has as its purpose the subversion of right human nature; it is always at the point of succeeding because of the weakness of that nature.

Throughout Book II, human weakness is figured in terms of the difficulty of controlling two contradictory tendencies, one forward, life-seeking, pleasure-loving, ambitious; the other retiring, life-avoiding, morosely angry, self-destructive. Under proper rational rule neither tendency is inherently evil, Arthur's praiseworthy ambition manifesting a leaning toward the one and Sir Guyon's praiseworthy "shamefastness" a leaning toward the other. But out of control they overturn the order of nature and, usurping the authority of reason, reduce man to beast or rob him of his manhood. In the two cantos included in this selection Arthur and Guyon battle against representatives of these contrary clans. Arthur's opponent, Maleger, wears a skull as his helmet, and his pallor and his withered skin identify him as the negation of vitality. He fights by retreating, deriving his strength from his weakness. Guyon's enemy, Acrasia, on the other hand, is surrounded by everything that delights and attracts, and the poet lavishes his skill on the description of her seductive paradise. Yet in truth she is as barren and destructive a force as Maleger, for her Bower of Bliss is a trap, symbolized by the entangling golden ivy vine which is spread over it, and the Genius who presides at its gate is not the true god of generation but his contrary, the foe of life.

Although Arthur conquers Maleger and Guyon destroys
the Bower, unlike the noble spirit of Aristotle's ethic neither
hero is able to live a life completely in accordance with virtue. The idea that man, however gifted by nature and edu-
cated by experience, is finally capable of subduing his lesser
nature is not only alien to Spenser's thinking but to Christian
doctrine. For this reason the poet provides two key instances
in which the rational powers of Arthur and Guyon prove
inadequate to the challenge. In the former (Canto vii, not included in this volume), Sir Guyon rejects what most men desire, money and power. But in so doing he deprives himself
also of vital food and air, falling prey, therefore, to the negative, life-destroying tendency. Not his own strength but
God's grace must save him from this predicament. In the second instance (Canto xi, stanzas 28-30) as Arthur attempts to
bind the foul hag Impotence he is seized and overthrown by
Impatience, the uncontrolled form of ambitious reaching, and
again he can be rescued only by divinely inspired interven-
tion. In both cases, the conquest by man of one tendency
leads to his defeat by the other. These overthrows are of
course entirely "natural" and they arouse the sympathy
rather than the condemnation of the reader. They are as
natural, in fact, as sin itself, and as inevitable to man.

Political dimension is given to the Legend of Temperance
by the historical works which Arthur and Guyon read in the
chamber of memory in Alma's house (Canto x, not here
reprinted). Arthur's book tells of the turbulent history of Britain from the time of its fabled foundation by the grandson of
Aeneas "Till it reduced was to one mans governments," until,
that is, its constitution became analogous to that of a rightly
ordered human nature. The happy conclusion is not described, for Arthur's book breaks off in the middle, but we
know how it may be recognized from the volume that Guyon
reads, a history of Fairyland full of glorious accomplishment
which ends with the reign of Gloriana: "Long may'st thou
Glorian, live in glory and great powre!"

Acrasia makes humanity barren, but the motive that draws
man to the seemingly desirable may also draw him to that
which is in truth good and therefore fruitful. If there is a false
Genius who is the foe of life there is also a true one who is
its friend. Desire—that is, Cupid or cupidity—is the subject
of Book III, the Legend of Chastity. The attractive magnet
is represented by the beauty of Florimel and the wealth of
Marinell. Many fair ladies seek the latter; the former is pur-
sued by young and old, peasant and prince, vicious and virtuous. In a vile nature such as Malbecco's, hungers like these

produce nothing but sterility and self-destruction. In a gentle soul the immediate effect is also pain and waste, as it is for Scudamour and Amoret, but the result at last is generation, whether of children or of noble deeds.

Children are the work of the woman Venus; noble deeds of the maiden Diana. Their adopted children, Amoret and Belphoebe, reflect the natures of their divine foster parents but as mortals in mixed form, so that Venus's Amoret is a chaste woman while Diana's Belphoebe is a womanly maiden. The description of Belphoebe's dwelling provides a token balance to the elaborate portrayal of Amoret's Garden of Adonis; the one is the haunt of great princes, fruitful of deeds, the other the "seminary" or breeding ground of the world's creatures.

That seminary is a web of traditions too tangled for analysis here. Those familiar with Chaucer's *Parlement of Foules* and the *Roman de la Rose* will recognize in the Garden of Adonis the traditional walled pleasance fanned by gentle breezes, rich in trees, flowers, fountains, and singing birds, a symbol of the beauty, the beneficence, and the fecundity of nature. The Platonic strain is evident in the immateriality of the "babes" of the Garden, seeds of the life of this world, entities which may be identified with the "seminal reasons" that St. Augustine borrowed from Plotinus and the Stoics to provide a philosophic gloss for the Mosaic account of creation. Spenser combines these traditions to fashion a realm in which the sexual motive, free of the filth and confusion inevitable to material bodies, displays its true nature, sinless and creative. In the center of the Garden he places a symbol of this state, the Mount of Venus—the anatomical *mons veneris*—below which the boar of lust is kept safely imprisoned.

In the Garden of Adonis, "Franckly each Paramor his leman knowes." But love in this world, whatever its kind, is by no means free of uncertainty and suffering. Belphoebe inspires the love that "beareth fruit of honor" if not of children; her servant Timias, unwilling to reveal to so noble a nature his passion for her, sickens almost to death. In this relationship Spenser suggests the love of a subject for his sovereign, in particular that of Sir Walter Ralegh for Queen Elizabeth. The sexual love of Scudamour for Amoret is beset with troubles as painful. From the fierce urgency of lust, whether manifested in brute force or in the wily siege of the polished seducer, the chaste woman recoils in horror, fleeing like Florimel from noble and vile alike. Amoret remembers the tragic stories of women whom love had betrayed and abandoned, the stories distilled into the procession of the Masque of

Cupid, and it is this memory that cuts her heart and holds her prisoner.

The solution, hard to achieve, is the reconciliation of Venus and Diana. Britomart is its symbol, for she combines their qualities; she is Amoret and Belphoebe, feminine yet fearless. She rejects Marinell's wealth, for she has its essence, power, and she does not join in the pursuit of Florimel, not only because she is a woman but also because she does not "lightly" follow Beauty's chase (in the *Hymne in Honour of Beautie* Spenser tells us that "Love is not so light / As streight to burne at first beholders sight"). She falls in love, indeed, not with a superficial appearance but with the image she conjures up in the magic mirror, an ideal of virtue and strength. Even so, she is vulnerable both to Gardante, the thrust through the eyes, and to Busirane, personification of the sexual drive, but since she is strong and virginal in spirit her wounds are superficial. She is able to traverse the passionate flame which Scudamour cannot pass because like him she is bold, but unlike him she is not too bold—her sword points forward, but her shield protects her face. Her final achievement is the release of Amoret from the chain with which Busirane has bound her womanhood. It is Busirane, not Amoret, who must be held in restraint. And with Busirane not dead but forced to obey, Amoret and Scudamour can join in that pure, sexual embrace which ended the Legend of Chastity in the version published in 1590.

As in the other books, Spenser finds the reflection of his theme in the great world. The rake Paridell supplies an installment of the legendary history of Britain by telling of the sterile, bloody consequence of the false love of his ancestor Paris. Such a love destroys not only the individual but a nation as well. But the prophecy of her progeny which Merlin imparts to Britomart turns that history to point the opposing moral. Her true love, he tells her, begins with pain, "And with sharpe fits thy tender hart oppresseth sore,"

> For so must all things excellent begin;
> And eke enrooted deepe must be that Tree,
> Whose big embodied braunches shall not lin
> Till they to hevens hight forth stretched bee

and from her womb, in justification of love's pain, will spring a famous line, the rulers of Britain, until at last "a royal virgin" reigns.

Of the remaining books of *The Faerie Queene*, only passages comparable in function to the descriptions of the House of

Holinesse in Book I and the Garden of Adonis in Book III are here reprinted. The Temple of Venus in the fourth book defines the subject of the Legend of Friendship: it is the maintenance of the bond which holds together kindred, lovers, and friends. The book begins with an account of the wedding of Amoret and Scudamour and its disruption by Busirane, and it ends in expectation of the marriage of Florimel and Marinell. In the porch of Venus's temple sits Dame Concord, an aspect of the goddess herself, who is flanked by two young men, Hate, the elder, and Love, the younger and stronger. They declare Concord to be no simple harmony but the overcoming of a primal antagonism in which chaos is held in control but continues its disruptive struggle. Scudamour's abduction of Amoret illustrates the problem as it affects the lover: he must be bold to win her, but his boldness arouses the terrible fear which threatens their union and for a time destroys it. Elsewhere in the book the poet tells of Cambel and Triamond who must engage in desperate struggle before they become fast friends, of Timias and Belphoebe who can re-establish the tie which binds subject to sovereign only after a torment of mistrust and suspicion, of Britomart and Artegall who can plight their troth only after strength has conquered beauty and beauty strength. In the stanzas here reprinted, a suppliant to the goddess Venus prays for his long-sought union with his lady in words borrowed from the invocation to Lucretius's *Of the Nature of Things*, a prayer which conceives of human love in the context of those forces which hold the world together and make it fruitful. And it is such a union that is celebrated in the marriage of the Thames and the Medway, described in Canto xi, a marriage which stands for the fruitful harmony which holds together the diversity of a nation.

Britomart's strange dream in the Temple of Isis poses the central problem of the fifth book, the Legend of Justice, a problem not unlike that presented by Shakespeare's *Measure for Measure*. In a golden age there is no need for codified law since natural justice resides in men's hearts. But in this iron time civilization depends not only upon law but also upon its rigorous and cunning enforcement. Such rigor takes no note of persons; in its single concern with the general it may degenerate into ruthless cruelty, and the power which it implies may corrupt those who wield it. The counterbalance to the heartlessness of the code is "equity," that branch of justice which roots itself in the individual case. Equity too is subject to corruption, for it may turn into partiality or effeminacy, so weakening law that chaos comes again. It is such a fiery chaos that is let loose upon the world of Britomart's dream while the crocodile—the law—sleeps. Once aroused, the crocodile puts out the fire, but "swolne with pride of his owne peerlesse powre" becomes himself a threat to the state. Only when equity and law are joined in one, when Isis and Osiris, Britomart and Artegall, are wedded is true justice born.

The oppositions of Britomart's dream appear again in the trial of Duessa at the court of Mercilla (Canto ix, not included here), a thinly veiled allusion to the trial of Queen Mary of Scotland. On one side of Mercilla sits Artegall, unmoved in his judgment of Duessa's guilt, on the other Arthur, shaken at least for a time by her beauty and the regality of her station. Under Mercilla's throne is a chained lion, counterpart of the crocodile beneath the statue of Isis. When the testimony has been given and Duessa's guilt is apparent Mercilla rises, hiding a tear. She does not pronounce the sentence, partly because Queen Elizabeth avoided personal responsibility for Mary's execution, but more significantly because *The Faerie Queene* has to do with the moral struggles of the governor, not with his political acts. In the morality of a nation, as in that of an individual, true justice is terror and love, mortality and mercy, force and its qualification.

In order to assert that "courtesy" is a question of morals rather than of manners, of essential character rather than of breeding, Spenser identifies it as the free gift of the guileless, unadorned Graces whose dwelling place is made beautiful not by man's art but by "nature's skill." His subject in the sixth book is the "ground" or "root" of courtesy, the native quality that renders men attractive to others and creates, therefore, the condition necessary to the harmonious intercourse of mankind. Its negative is represented by the Blatant Beast, that which rends both innocent and guilty and poisons human relations, and by the three bad brothers, Despetto, Decetto, and Defetto: Despight (or Proud Cruelty), Deceit, and Detraction.

As often in *The Faerie Queene*, the problem to be solved is presented in the form of a paradox. The man essentially courteous is necessarily a hater of the cruel, underhanded competitiveness that disrupts the court and the civil society of which the court is the pinnacle. He is tempted, therefore, to deny his own noble nature and to withdraw to an imagined pastoral paradise, exchanging his sword for a sheep hook. Sir Calidore's error is made manifest in his colloquy with old Melibee. To Calidore's complaint against the fortune that had set him in high place, Melibee answers:

> fittest is, that all contented rest
> With that they hold: each hath his fortune in his brest.

The meaning is that man must be satisfied to accept that station in life to which his nature assigns him. But Calidore chooses to misunderstand, taking the shepherd's instruction as warrant for electing what "fortune" he wishes, and so escapes from his own nobility and his work in the world.

The crux of the moral struggle lies in Calidore's indecision as to whether his retirement among the shepherds is to be a vacation from his duties or an abandonment of them. There would have been no mischief in the former alternative. The true courtier, says the poet in *Mother Hubberds Tale*, is entitled to rest for a space after his arduous labors. In fact, the home of the Graces is Mount Acidale, the place to which Venus resorts when she is wearied with her business at Cytherea. And here the poet Colin also diverts himself from his duty, begging pardon of Gloriana to sing "one minim" of praise to his own lady.

But the book ends on a graver note. The poet, like his hero Calidore, is weary of contending with the Blatant Beast, the detractors and the slanderers of his poetry:

> Therefore do you, my rimes, keep better measure
> And seeke to please; that now is counted wise mens
> threasure.

At the conclusion of other books of *The Faerie Queene* Spenser announces a breathing space: this story will be continued elsewhere, the poetic ship must be refitted for its next voyage. But here, the resolve to "please" rather than to teach pleasingly is tantamount—for Spenser—to a declaration that he will abandon his art.

There remains, nevertheless, a fragment of "some succeeding book" of *The Faerie Queene* which was included in an edition of the poem published a decade after his death. In these "Cantos of Mutabilitie," presumably part of a Legend of Constancy, Spenser meets head on the tremendous problem of justifying this changeful, mortal world, rich in beauty and variety but full of tribulation and evil, as the work of a single, immutable, and beneficent Creator. He has touched on facets of the dilemma elsewhere in *The Faerie Queene*, notably in the third book, where Adonis, "Father of all formes," is described as "eterne in mutabilitie / And by succession made perpetuall," and in the prologue to the fifth, which laments the decay of the world from its first perfection.

In the first of these Cantos of Mutabilitie the episode of the wood god Faunus restates the theme of mundane decay. Arlo was once a paradise, but through Faunus's foolish seeking after forbidden knowledge (a parody of the sin of Adam) the "best and fairest Hill . . . Was made the most unpleasant and most ill." This unhappy change is a sign of Mutability's domination over the world, a domination which she claims extends not merely below the sphere of the moon, her traditional realm, but beyond it to the stars themselves.

But change is not merely decay and confusion. Mutability's face is so fair that Jove stays his wrath at her presumption. The procession of the elements, of the seasons and the months, of life and death which the Titaness summons to prove her claim to universal dominion proves also the various beauty of this world. And the fact that it is a procession, that variety and change are subject to "Natures Sergeant," Order, means that Mutability is not chaos though descended from Chaos on her mother's side. In fact—and here the grand paradox emerges—the incessant change which Mutability alleges in her claim to imperial rule moves in the direction of re-establishing the first perfect state of creation, that Eden we have lost:

> all things stedfastnesse do hate
> And changed be; yet, being rightly wayd,
> They are not changed from their first estate;
> But by their change their being do dilate,
> And turning to themselves at length againe,
> Do worke their owne perfection so by fate

Spenser might have derived such a solution from Plotinus, who writes in the *Enneads* (III, vii, 11):

> The lesser must always be working towards the increase of its Being, this will be its imitation of what is immediately complete, self-realized, endless without stage: only thus can its Being reproduce that of the High.

For the philosopher, by means of infinite extension in time and variation in form, the finite creature mimics the timelessness and all-inclusiveness of the Supreme. Spenser's word "dilate" seems to point directly at such a conception. But like St. Augustine, Spenser assimilated pagan philosophy to Christianity. Plotinus's mutable forever imitates the immutable.

For the poet, the process has an end, as it had a beginning; there will be a time

> when no more Change shall be,
> But stedfast rest of all things, firmely stayd
> Upon the pillours of Eternity,
> That is contrayr to Mutabilitie

Until that time the uncertain struggle continues, between order and chaos, love and hate, reason and passion, faith and self-doubt. But in the end there will be an end also of the insoluble contrarieties of the human condition, the pervasive subject of Spenser's poetry.

WILLIAM NELSON

Biographical Note

The poet was born in London in 1554 or earlier, attended the Merchant Taylors School, and in 1569 went to Pembroke College in Cambridge as a "sizar" or poor scholar. He proceeded B.A. in 1573 and M.A. in 1576. While at Cambridge he became friendly with Gabriel Harvey, a learned rhetorician who is best known today, unhappily for his reputation, as a principal butt of the satire of Thomas Nashe. In 1578 Spenser served as secretary to the bishop of Rochester, Thomas Young, who had been Master of Pembroke during the poet's residence. In the following year he entered the service of the Earl of Leicester and in a letter to Harvey described himself as in "some use of familiarity" with Leicester's nephew, Philip Sidney, to whom he dedicated *The Shepheardes Calender* (1579). He expected to be sent by Leicester to France, but in 1580, when Arthur Lord Grey de Wilton went to Ireland as newly appointed governor, Spenser accompanied him as secretary. Although Grey was recalled to England in 1582, Spenser remained in Ireland for most of his life, serving in a variety of official capacities. Probably from 1584 on, he was deputy to the clerk of the Council of Munster, the clerk being Lodowick Bryskett with whom he was on friendly terms. In 1588, he was in possession of the estate of Kilcolman, sequestered from the rebellious Irish Earl of Desmond, and the patent formally granting the land to him was passed in 1590. Sir Walter Ralegh held a huge Irish territory not far from Kilcolman, and in 1589 accompanied the poet to the court of Queen Elizabeth. The presentation of the first three books of *The Faerie Queene* followed, Spenser receiving as reward an annuity of 50 pounds for life. He seems to have quarreled with Elizabeth's chief minister, William Cecil, Lord Burghley, at about this time, although some scholars argue that the trouble had begun a decade earlier as a result of Spenser's adherence to the party of Cecil's rival for power, the Earl of Leicester. The clearest references to the poet's antagonism to the peer occur in lines 892-918 of *Mother Hubberds Tale* (pp. 513-14 below) and in the prologue to the fourth book of *The Faerie Queene* (pp. 370-71 below). Spenser's marriage to Elizabeth Boyle is celebrated in the Epithalamion which was published in 1595. This appears to have been a second marriage; an Edmund Spenser, probably the poet, had been married to Machabyas Chylde in 1579. Spenser was in England again in 1596 during which the last three books of *The Faerie Queene* were published. In October, 1598, Irish rebels sacked his castle of Kilcolman and Spenser, who had just been designated sheriff of Cork, came to England, delivering messages to the Privy Council. On January 13, 1599 he died. According to the contemporary historian Camden, he was buried in Westminster Abbey "near to Chaucer, at the charge of the Earl of Essex; his hearse being attended by poets, and mournful elegies and poems, with the pens that wrote them, thrown into the tomb."

The Dates of Publication of Spenser's Works

1569   22 verse translations of "epigrams" and "sonnets" included (without signature) in Jan van der Noot, *A Theatre wherein be represented as wel the miseries & calamities that follow the voluptuous Worldlings, As also the greate ioyes and plesures which the faithfull do enioy*

1579   *The Shepheardes Calender* (signed "Immerito")

1590   *The Faerie Queene* (the first three books)

1591   *Complaints. Containing sundrie small Poemes of the worldes vanity*. The volume comprises: *The Ruines of Time, The Teares of the Muses, Virgil's Gnat, Prosopopoia or Mother Hubberds Tale, Ruines of Rome, Muiopotmos or the Fate of the Butterflie, Visions of the Worlds Vanitie, The Visions of Bellay*, and *The Visions of Petrarch* (the last two sets of "visions" include reworkings of the translations originally published in van der Noot's *Theatre* [1569])

1591   *Daphnaida, an Elegy upon the death of the noble and vertuous Douglas Howard*

1595   *Colin Clouts Come Home Againe*. The volume also includes *Astrophel, a Pastorall Elegie upon the death of the most Noble and valorous Knight, Sir Philip Sidney* by Spenser and others.

1595   *Amoretti and Epithalamion*

1596   *The Faerie Queene* (six books)

1596   *Fowre Hymnes*

1596   *Prothalamion*

1609   *Two Cantos of Mutabilitie* (published in an edition of *The Faerie Queene*)

1633   *A View of the Present State of Ireland* (the first printing, but manuscript copies go back to the date of its composition, 1596)

(Spenser's correspondence with Gabriel Harvey was published in two volumes which appeared in 1580, *Three Proper, and wittie, familiar Letters,* and *Two Other very commendable Letters.* He contributed sonnets to the works of others published in 1592, 1595, 1596, and 1599. Some scholars attribute to him *Axiochus. A most excellent Dialogue written in Greeke by Plato the Phylosopher,* a translation of a psuedo-Platonic work signed "Edw. Spenser" and published in 1592.)

Selected Bibliography

I. COLLECTED EDITIONS

The Works, a Variorum Edition. Edited by E. Greenlaw and others. 9 vols. Baltimore: Johns Hopkins Press, 1932-1949. *Index* to the *Works.* Compiled by C. G. Osgood. Baltimore: Johns Hopkins Press, 1957. [The standard edition, with a great body of critical and textual commentary.]

The Poetical Works. Edited by J. C. Smith and E. de Selincourt. 3 vols. Oxford: Clarendon Press, 1909-1910, reprinted 1961. [Large type, textual and bibliographical notes.]

The Poetical Works. Edited by J. C. Smith and E. de Selincourt. 1 vol. New York: Oxford University Press, 1912. [Textual notes, glossary, critical introduction by E. de Selincourt.]

The Complete Poetical Works. Edited by R. E. Neil Dodge. 1 vol. Boston: Houghton Mifflin, 1908. [Biographical introduction, glossary, notes.]

II. SCHOLARLY AND CRITICAL COMMENT

Arthos, John, *On the Poetry of Spenser and the Form of Romances.* London: Allen and Unwin, 1956. [A study of the poems against the background of medieval romance and Italian epic romance.]

Bennett, Josephine Waters, *The Evolution of The Faerie Queene.* Chicago: University of Chicago Press, 1942. Reprinted, New York: Burt Franklin, 1960. [An investigation of the process by which the poem came to be written.]

Bradner, Leicester, *Edmund Spenser and The Faerie Queene.* Chicago: University of Chicago Press, 1948.

Davis, B. E. C., *Edmund Spenser, a Critical Study.* Cambridge, 1933.

Freeman, Rosemary, *Edmund Spenser.* London, for the British Council and the National Book League: Longmans, Green, 1957.

Frye, Northrop, "The Structure of Imagery in The Faerie Queene." *University of Toronto Quarterly*, xxx, 2 January, 1961, 109-127.

Hamilton, A. C., *The Structure of Allegory in The Faerie Queene*. Oxford: Clarendon Press, 1961.

Hough, Graham Goulden, *A Preface to The Faerie Queene*. New York: Norton, 1963.

Judson, A. C., *The Life of Edmund Spenser*. Baltimore: Johns Hopkins Press, 1945. [The most detailed biography.]

Lewis, C. S., *The Allegory of Love*. New York: Oxford University Press, 1936. [A study of allegorical methods and conventions from late classical times, with particular emphasis on the method of *The Faerie Queene*.]

Mueller, W. R. (ed.), *Spenser's Critics: Changing Currents in Literary Taste*. Syracuse, N. Y.: Syracuse University Press, 1959.

Mueller, W. R. and D. C. Allen (eds.), *That Soueraine Light: Essays in Honor of Edmund Spenser 1552-1952*. Baltimore: Johns Hopkins Press, 1952. [Essays by various authors.]

Nelson, W. (ed.), *Form and Convention in the Poetry of Edmund Spenser: Selected Papers from the English Institute*. New York and London: Columbia University Press, 1961.

Nelson, W. *The Poetry of Edmund Spenser, a Study*. New York: Columbia University Press, 1963.

Parker, M. P., *The Allegory of The Faerie Queene*. Oxford: Clarendon Press, 1960.

Renwick, W. L., *Edmund Spenser: An Essay on Renaissance Poetry*. New York: Longmans, Green, 1925.

Watkins, W. B. C., *Shakespeare and Spenser*. Princeton: Princeton University Press, 1950. Reprinted, Cambridge, Mass.: Walker de Berry, 1961. [A study of the two writers in terms of themes common to both.]

III. REFERENCE BOOKS

Carpenter, F. I., *A Reference Guide to Edmund Spenser*. Chicago, 1923. Reprinted, Gloucester, Mass.: Peter Smith, 1950. Supplement by D. F. Atkinson. Baltimore: Johns Hopkins Press, 1937, and by Waldo F. McNeir, and Foster Provost, *Annotated Bibliography of Edmund Spenser, 1937-1960*. Pittsburgh: Duquesne University Press, 1962.

Johnson, F. R., *A Critical Bibliography of the Works Printed before 1700*. Baltimore, 1933.

Osgood, C. G., *A Concordance to the Poems of Edmund Spenser*. Carnegie Institute of Washington, 1915.

Wurtsbaugh, J., *Two Centuries of Spenserian Scholarship*. Baltimore, 1936.

A NOTE ON THE TEXT AND GLOSSARY

The text of this edition is based upon that of R. Morris and John W. Hales, first published as The Globe Edition in 1869 and very frequently reprinted. A number of minor corrections have been made with the assistance of the meticulous listing of variants provided by the editors of the great variorum edition of *The Works of Edmund Spenser*, published by the Johns Hopkins Press. The practice of the Morris and Hales edition of relying upon the 1590 printing for the text of the first three books of *The Faerie Queene* has been retained. It is at least likely that Spenser's spelling is more closely approximated in the 1590 edition than in the 1596.

The glossary makes no pretense to completeness. I have tried to explain on the pages where they occur those words which seem likely to confuse or mislead the modern reader. In addition, a brief glossary of frequently repeated Spenserian usages is printed on pp. 611-12.

THE
Faerie Queene

THE

Faerie Queene

THE FIRST THREE BOOKS OF *The Faerie Queene* were entered in the Stationers' Register on December 1, 1589 and published early in the following year. The poet had been at work on the poem for a decade, and at least as early as 1588 a manuscript copy of some part of it circulated in England. According to his account in *Colin Clouts Come Home Againe* he presented *The Faerie Queene* to Elizabeth in October, 1589, following his introduction to her by Sir Walter Ralegh. He was rewarded with an annuity of 50 pounds for life. The published work was dedicated to the queen and included sonnets addressed to the great ladies and gentlemen of the court as well as a letter to Sir Walter Ralegh explaining the purpose and method of the poem (see below, pages 449-53).

The fourth, fifth, and sixth books, together with a second edition of the first three, were published in 1596. In this edition the letter to Ralegh does not appear and a new ending is supplied to the third book. The Cantos of Mutabilitie were first printed after the poet's death, in an edition of *The Faerie Queene* dated 1609.

THE FAERIE QVEENE

DISPOSED INTO TWELUE BOOKS,

FASHIONING

XII. MORALL VERTUES.

TO
THE MOST HIGH,
MIGHTIE
And
MAGNIFICENT
EMPRESSE RENOVV-
MED FOR PIETIE, VER-
TVE, AND ALL GRATIOVS
GOVERNMENT ELIZABETH BY
THE GRACE OF GOD QVEENE
OF ENGLAND FRAVNCE AND
IRELAND AND OF VIRGI-
NIA, DEFENDOVR OF THE
FAITH, &c. HER MOST
HVMBLE SERVAVNT
EDMVND SPENSER
DOTH IN ALL HV-
MILITIE DEDI-
CATE, PRE-
SENT
AND CONSECRATE THESE
HIS LABOVRS TO LIVE
VVITH THE ETERNI-
TIE OF HER
FAME.

THE FIRST BOOK OF

THE FAERIE QUEENE

Contayning the Legend of the Knight of the
Red Crosse, or of Holinesse.

I

Lo! I, THE MAN whose Muse whylome did maske,
As time her taught, in lowly Shephards weeds,
Am now enforst, a farre unfitter taske,
For trumpets sterne to chaunge mine Oaten reeds,
And sing of Knights and Ladies gentle deeds;
Whose praises having slept in silence long,
Me, all too meane, the sacred Muse areeds
To blazon broade emongst her learned throng:
Fierce warres and faithful loves shall moralize my song.

I I

Helpe then, O holy virgin! chiefe of nyne,
Thy weaker Novice to performe thy will;
Lay forth out of thine everlasting scryne
The antique rolles, which there lye hidden still,
Of Faerie knights, and fayrest Tanaquill,
Whom that most noble Briton Prince so long
Sought through the world, and suffered so much ill,
That I must rue his undeserved wrong:
O, helpe thou my weake wit, and sharpen my dull tong!

I I I

And thou, most dreaded impe of highest Jove,
Faire Venus sonne, that with thy cruell dart

I, 7   areeds: counsels   III, 1   impe: child
II, 3   scryne: archive

At that good knight so cunningly didst rove,
That glorious fire it kindled in his hart;
Lay now thy deadly Heben bowe apart,
And with thy mother mylde come to mine ayde;
Come, both; and with you bring triumphant Mart,
In loves and gentle jollities arraid,
After his murdrous spoyles and bloudie rage allayd.

I V

And with them eke, O Goddesse heavenly
Mirrour of grace and Majestie divine,
Great Ladie of the greatest Isle, whose light bright!
Like Phoebus lampe throughout the world doth shine,
Shed thy faire beames into my feeble eyne,
And raise my thoughtes, too humble and too vile,
To thinke of that true glorious type of thine,
The argument of mine afflicted stile:
The which to heare vouchsafe, O dearest dread, a-while!

CANTO I.

The Patrone of true Holinesse
Foule Errour doth defeate:
Hypocrisie, him to entrappe,
Doth to his home entreate.

I

A GENTLE Knight was pricking on the plaine,
Ycladd in mightie armes and silver shielde,
Wherein old dints of deepe woundes did remaine,
The cruell markes of many' a bloody fielde;
Yet armes till that time did he never wield.
His angry steede did chide his foming bitt,
As much disdayning to the curbe to yield:
Full jolly knight he seemd, and faire did sitt,
As one for knightly giusts and fierce encounters fitt.

I I

And on his brest a bloodie Crosse he bore,
The deare remembrance of his dying Lord,
For whose sweete sake that glorious badge he wore,
And dead, as living, ever him ador'd:
Upon his shield the like was also scor'd,
For soveraine hope which in his helpe he had.

I, I   gentle: noble   I, I   pricking: riding

Right faithfull true he was in deede and word,
But of his cheere did seeme too solemne sad;
Yet nothing did he dread, but ever was ydrad.

I I I

Upon a great adventure he was bond,
That greatest Gloriana to him gave,
(That greatest Glorious Queene of Faery lond)
To winne him worshippe, and her grace to have,
Which of all earthly thinges he most did crave:
And ever as he rode his hart did earne
To prove his puissance in battell brave
Upon his foe, and his new force to learne,
Upon his foe, a Dragon horrible and stearne.

I V

A lovely Ladie rode him faire beside,
Upon a lowly Asse more white then snow,
Yet she much whiter; but the same did hide
Under a vele, that wimpled was full low;
And over all a blacke stole shee did throw:
As one that inly mournd, so was she sad,
And heavie sate upon her palfrey slow;
Seemed in heart some hidden care she had,
And by her, in a line, a milkewhite lambe she lad.

V

So pure and innocent, as that same lambe,
She was in life and every vertuous lore;
And by descent from Royall lynage came
Of ancient Kinges and Queenes, that had of yore
Their scepters stretcht from East to Westerne shore,
And all the world in their subjection held;
Till that infernall feend with foule uprore
Forwasted all their land, and them expeld;
Whom to avenge she had this Knight from far compeld.

V I

Behind her farre away a Dwarfe did lag,
That lasie seemd, in being ever last,
Or wearied with bearing of her bag
Of needments at his backe. Thus as they past,
The day with cloudes was suddeine overcast,
And angry Jove an hideous storme of raine
Did poure into his Lemans lap so fast,

II, 8 cheere: countenance   III, 6 earne: yearn

That everie wight to shrowd it did constrain;
And this faire couple eke to shroud themselves were fain.

v i i

Enforst to seeke some covert nigh at hand,
A shadie grove not farr away they spide,
That promist ayde the tempest to withstand;
Whose loftie trees, yclad with sommers pride,
Did spred so broad, that heavens light did hide,
Not perceable with power of any starr:
And all within were pathes and alleies wide,
With footing worne, and leading inward farr.
Faire harbour that them seems, so in they entred ar.

v i i i

And foorth they passe, with pleasure forward led,
Joying to heare the birdes sweete harmony,
Which, therein shrouded from the tempest dred,
Seemd in their song to scorne the cruell sky.
Much can they praise the trees so straight and hy,
The sayling Pine; the Cedar proud and tall;
The vine-propp Elme; the Poplar never dry;
The builder Oake, sole king of forrests all;
The Aspine good for staves; the Cypresse funerall;

i x

The Laurell, meed of mightie Conquerours
And Poets sage; the Firre that weepeth still:
The Willow, worne of forlorne Paramours;
The Eugh, obedient to the benders will;
The Birch for shaftes; the Sallow for the mill;
The Mirrhe sweete-bleeding in the bitter wound;
The warlike Beech; the Ash for nothing ill;
The fruitful Olive; and the Platane round;
The carver Holme; the Maple seeldom inward sound.

x

Led with delight, they thus beguile the way,
Untill the blustring storme is overblowne;
When, weening to returne whence they did stray,
They cannot finde that path, which first was showne,
But wander too and fro in waies unknowne,
Furthest from end then, when they neerest weene,
That makes them doubt their wits be not their owne:
So many pathes, so many turnings seene,
That which of them to take in diverse doubt they been.

VIII, 5   can: did

X I

At last resolving forward still to fare,
Till that some end they finde, or in or out,
That path they take that beaten seemd most bare,
And like to lead the labyrinth about;
Which when by tract they hunted had throughout,
At length it brought them to a hollowe cave
Amid the thickest woods. The Champion stout
Eftsoones dismounted from his courser brave,
And to the Dwarfe a while his needless spere he gave.

X I I

'Be well aware,' quoth then that Ladie milde,
'Least suddaine mischiefe ye too rash provoke:
The danger hid, the place unknowne and wilde,
Breedes dreadfull doubts. Oft fire is without smoke,
And perill without show: therefore your stroke,
Sir Knight, with-hold, till further tryall made.'
'Ah Ladie,' (sayd he) 'shame were to revoke
The forward footing for an hidden shade:
Vertue gives her selfe light through darknesse for to wade.'

X I I I

'Yea but' (quoth she) 'the perill of this place
I better wot then you: though nowe too late
To wish you backe returne with foule disgrace,
Yet wisedome warnes, whilest foot is in the gate,
To stay the steppe, ere forced to retrate.
This is the wandring wood, this *Errours* den,
A monster vile, whom God and man does hate:
Therefore I read beware.' 'Fly, fly!' (quoth then
The fearefull Dwarfe) 'this is no place for living men.'

X I V

But, full of fire and greedy hardiment,
The youthfull Knight could not for ought be staide;
But forth unto the darksom hole he went,
And looked in: his glistring armor made
A litle glooming light, much like a shade;
By which he saw the ugly monster plaine,
Halfe like a serpent horribly displaide,
But th'other halfe did womans shape retaine,
Most lothsom, filthie, foule, and full of vile disdaine.

X V

And, as she lay upon the durtie ground,
Her huge long taile her den all overspred,

Yet was in knots and many boughtes upwound,
Pointed with mortall sting. Of her there bred
A thousand yong ones, which she dayly fed,
Sucking upon her poisnous dugs; each one
Of sundrie shapes, yet all ill-favored:
Soone as that uncouth light upon them shone,
Into her mouth they crept, and suddain all were gone.

X V I

Their dam upstart out of her den effraide,
And rushed forth, hurling her hideous taile
About her cursed head; whose folds displaid
Were stretcht now forth at length without entraile.
She lookt about, and seeing one in mayle,
Armed to point, sought backe to turne againe;
For light she hated as the deadly bale,
Ay wont in desert darknes to remaine,
Where plain none might her see, nor she see any plaine.

X V I I

Which when the valiant Elfe perceiv'd, he lept
As Lyon fierce upon the flying pray,
And with his trenchand blade her boldly kept
From turning backe, and forced her to stay:
Therewith enrag'd she loudly gan to bray,
And turning fierce her speckled taile advaunst,
Threatning her angrie sting, him to dismay;
Who, nought aghast, his mightie hand enhaunst:
The stroke down from her head unto her shoulder glaunst.

X V I I I

Much daunted with that dint her sence was dazd;
Yet kindling rage her selfe she gathered round,
And all attonce her beastly bodie raizd
With doubled forces high above the ground:
Tho, wrapping up her wrethed sterne arownd,
Lept fierce upon his shield, and her huge traine
All suddenly about his body wound,
That hand or foot to stirr he strove in vaine.
God helpe the man so wrapt in Errours endlesse traine!

X I X

His Lady, sad to see his sore constraint,
Cride out, 'Now, now, Sir knight, shew what ye bee;

xv, 3 boughtes: coils	xvii, 8 enhaunst: raised
xvi, 4 entraile: coiling	xviii, 9 traine: tail, treachery

Add faith unto your force, and be not faint;
Strangle her, els she sure will strangle thee.'
That when he heard, in great perplexitie,
His gall did grate for griefe and high disdaine;
And, knitting all his force, got one hand free,
Wherewith he grypt her gorge with so great paine,
That soone to loose her wicked bands did her constraine.

x x

Therewith she spewd out of her filthie maw
A floud of poyson horrible and blacke,
Full of great lumps of flesh and gobbets raw,
Which stunck so vildly, that it forst him slacke
His grasping hold, and from her turne him backe.
Her vomit full of bookes and papers was, —
With loathly frogs and toades, which eyes did lacke,
And creeping sought way in the weedy gras:
Her filthie parbreake all the place defiled has.

x x i

As when old father Nilus gins to swell
With timely pride above the Aegyptian vale
His fattie waves doe fertile slime outwell,
And overflow each plaine and lowly dale:
But, when his later spring gins to avale,
Huge heapes of mudd he leaves, wherin there breed
Ten thousand kindes of creatures, partly male
And partly femall, of his fruitful seed;
Such ugly monstrous shapes elswher may no man reed.

x x i i

The same so sore annoyed has the knight,
That, welnigh choked with the deadly stinke,
His forces faile, ne can no lenger fight:
Whose corage when the feend perceivd to shrinke,
She poured forth out of her hellish sinke
Her fruitfull cursed spawne of serpents small,
Deformed monsters, fowle, and blacke as inke,
Which swarming all about his legs did crall,
And him encombred sore, but could not hurt at all.

x x i i i

As gentle shepheard in sweete eventide,
When ruddy Phebus gins to welke in west,

xx, 9   parbreake: vomit   xxi, 5   avale: ebb
xxi, 3   fattie: muddy, rich   xxiii, 2   welke: fade

High on an hill, his flocke to vewen wide,
Markes which doe byte their hasty supper best;
A cloud of cumbrous gnattes doe him molest,
All striving to infixe their feeble stinges,
That from their noyance he no where can rest;
But with his clownish hands their tender wings
He brusheth oft, and oft doth mar their murmurings.

X X I V

Thus ill bestedd, and fearefull more of shame
Then of the certeine perill he stood in,
Halfe furious unto his foe he came,
Resolvd in minde all suddenly to win,
Or soone to lose, before he once would lin;
And stroke at her with more then manly force,
That from her body, full of filthie sin,
He raft her hatefull heade without remorse:
A streame of cole-black blood forth gushed from her corse.

X X V

Her scattered brood, soone as their Parent deare
They saw so rudely falling to the ground,
Groning full deadly, all with troublous feare
Gathred themselves about her body round,
Weening their wonted entrance to have found
At her wide mouth; but being there withstood,
They flocked all about her bleeding wound,
And sucked up their dying mothers bloud,
Making her death their life, and eke her hurt their good.

X X V I

That detestable sight him much amazde,
To see th' unkindly Impes, of heaven accurst,
Devoure their dam; on whom while so he gazd,
Having all satisfide their bloudy thurst,
Their bellies swolne he saw with fulnesse burst,
And bowels gushing forth: well worthy end
Of such as drunke her life the which them nurst!
Now needeth him no lenger labour spend,
His foes have slaine themselves, with whom he should con-
	tend.

X X V I I

His Lady, seeing all that chaunst from farre,
Approcht in hast to greet his victorie;

XXIV, 5   lin: cease

And saide, 'Faire knight, borne under happie starre,
Who see your vanquisht foes before you lye,
Well worthie be you of that Armory,
Wherein ye have great glory wonne this day,
And proov'd your strength on a strong enimie,
Your first adventure: many such I pray,
And henceforth ever wish that like succeed it may!'

XXVIII

Then mounted he upon his Steede againe,
And with the Lady backward sought to wend.
That path he kept which beaten was most plaine,
Ne ever would to any byway bend,
But still did follow one unto the end,
The which at last out of the wood them brought.
So forward on his way (with God to frend)
He passed forth, and new adventure sought:
Long way he traveiled before he heard of ought.

XXIX

At length they chaunst to meet upon the way
An aged Sire, in long blacke weedes yclad,
His feete all bare, his beard all hoarie gray,
And by his belt his booke he hanging had;
Sober he seemde, and very sagely sad,
And to the ground his eyes were lowly bent,
Simple in shew, and voide of malice bad;
And all the way he prayed as he went,
And often knockt his brest, as one that did repent.

XXX

He faire the knight saluted, louting low,
Who faire him quited, as that courteous was;
And after asked him, if he did know
Of straunge adventures, which abroad did pas.
'Ah! my dear sonne,' (quoth he) 'how should, alas!
Silly old man, that lives in hidden cell,
Bidding his beades all day for his trespas,
Tydings of warre and worldly trouble tell?
With holy father sits not with such thinges to mell.

XXXI

'But if of daunger, which hereby doth dwell,
And homebredd evil ye desire to heare,
Of a straunge man I can you tidings tell,

xxx, 6　silly: simple　　　　　　　xxx, 9　mell: meddle

That wasteth all this countrie, farre and neare.'
'Of such,' (saide he,) 'I chiefly doe inquere,
And shall thee well rewarde to shew the place,
In which that wicked wight his dayes doth weare;
For to all knighthood it is foule disgrace,
That such a cursed creature lives so long a space.'

X X X I I

'Far hence' (quoth he) 'in wastfull wildernesse
His dwelling is, by which no living wight
May ever passe, but thorough great distresse.'
'Now,' (saide the Ladie,) 'draweth toward night,
And well I wote, that of your later fight
Ye all forwearied be; for what so strong,
But, wanting rest, will also want of might?
The Sunne, that measures heaven all day long,
At night doth baite his steedes the Ocean waves emong.

X X X I I I

'Then with the Sunne take, Sir, your timely rest,
And with new day new worke at once begin:
Untroubled night, they say, gives counsell best.'
'Right well, Sir knight, ye have advised bin,'
Quoth then that aged man: 'the way to win
Is wisely to advise; now day is spent:
Therefore with me ye may take up your In
For this same night.' The knight was well content;
So with that godly father to his home they went.

X X X I V

A litle lowly Hermitage it was,
Downe in a dale, hard by a forests side,
Far from resort of people that did pas
In traveill to and froe: a litle wyde
There was an holy chappell edifyde,
Wherein the Hermite dewly wont to say
His holy thinges each morne and eventyde:
Thereby a christall streame did gently play,
Which from a sacred fountaine welled forth alway.

X X X V

Arrived there, the litle house they fill,
Ne looke for entertainment where none was;
Rest is their feast, and all thinges at their will:
The noblest mind the best contentment has.

With faire discourse the evening so they pas;
For that olde man of pleasing wordes had store,
And well could file his tongue as smooth as glas:
He told of Saintes and Popes, and evermore
He strowd an *Ave-Mary* after and before.

X X X V I

The drouping night thus creepeth on them fast;
And the sad humor loading their eyeliddes,
As messenger of Morpheus, on them cast
Sweet slombring deaw, the which to sleep them biddes.
Unto their lodgings then his guestes he riddes:
Where when all drownd in deadly sleepe he findes,
He to his studie goes; and there amiddes
His magick bookes, and artes of sundrie kindes,
He seekes out mighty charmes to trouble sleepy minds.

X X X V I I

Then choosing out few words most horrible,
(Let none them read) thereof did verses frame;
With which, and other spelles like terrible,
He bad awake blacke Plutoes griesly Dame;
And cursed heven; and spake reprochful shame
Of highest God, the Lord of life and light:
A bold bad man, that dar'd to call by name
Great Gorgon, prince of darknes and dead night;
At which Cocytus quakes, and Styx is put to flight.

X X X V I I I

And forth he cald out of deepe darknes dredd
Legions of Sprights, the which, like litle flyes
Fluttring about his ever-damned hedd,
Awaite whereto their service he applyes,
To aide his friendes, or fray his enimies.
Of those he chose out two, the falsest twoo,
And fittest for to forge true-seeming lyes:
The one of them he gave a message too,
The other by him selfe staide, other worke to doo.

X X X I X

He, making speedy way through spersed ayre,
And through the world of waters wide and deepe,
To Morpheus house doth hastily repaire.
Amid the bowels of the earth full steepe,
And low, where dawning day doth never peepe,

XXXVI, 2   sad: heavy

His dwelling is; there Tethys his wet bed
Doth ever wash, and Cynthia still doth steepe
In silver deaw his ever-drouping hed,
Whiles sad Night over him her mantle black doth spred.

X L

Whose double gates he findeth locked fast,
The one faire fram'd of burnisht Yvory,
The other all with silver overcast;
And wakeful dogges before them farre doe lye,
Watching to banish Care their enimy,
Who oft is wont to trouble gentle Sleepe.
By them the Sprite doth passe in quietly,
And unto Morpheus comes, whom drowned deepe
In drowsie fit he findes: of nothing he takes keepe.

X L I

And more to lulle him in his slumber soft,
A trickling streame from high rock tumbling downe,
And ever-drizling raine upon the loft,
Mixt with a murmuring winde, much like the sowne
Of swarming Bees, did cast him in a swowne.
No other noyse, nor peoples troublous cryes,
As still are wont t'annoy the walled towne,
Might there be heard; but carelesse Quiet lyes
Wrapt in eternall silence farre from enimyes.

X L I I

The Messenger approching to him spake;
But his waste wordes retournd to him in vaine:
So sound he slept, that nought mought him awake.
Then rudely he him thrust, and pusht with paine,
Whereat he gan to stretch; but he againe
Shooke him so hard, that forced him to speake.
As one then in a dreame, whose dryer braine
Is tost with troubled sights and fancies weake,
He mumbled soft, but would not all his silence breake.

X L I I I

The Sprite then gan more boldly him to wake,
And threatned unto him the dreaded name
Of Hecate: whereat he gan to quake,
And, lifting up his lompish head, with blame
Halfe angrie asked him, for what he came.
'Hether' (quoth he,) 'me Archimago sent,

XLII, 7   dryer: barren

He that the stubborne Sprites can wisely tame,
He bids thee to him send for his intent
A fit false dreame, that can delude the sleepers sent.'

X L I V

The God obayde; and, calling forth straight way
A diverse Dreame out of his prison darke,
Delivered it to him, and downe did lay
His heavie head, devoide of careful carke;
Whose sences all were straight benumbd and starke.
He, backe returning by the Yvorie dore,
Remounted up as light as chearefull Larke;
And on his litle winges the dreame he bore
In hast unto his Lord, where he him left afore.

X L V

Who all this while, with charmes and hidden artes,
Had made a Lady of that other Spright,
And fram'd of liquid ayre her tender partes,
So lively and so like in all mens sight,
That weaker sence it could have ravisht quight:
The maker selfe, for all his wondrous witt,
Was nigh beguiled with so goodly sight.
Her all in white he clad, and over it
Cast a black stole, most like to seeme for Una fit.

X L V I

Now, when that ydle dreame was to him brought,
Unto that Elfin knight he bad him fly,
Where he slept soundly void of evil thought,
And with false shewes abuse his fantasy,
In sort as he him schooled privily:
And that new creature, borne without her dew,
Full of the makers guyle, with usage sly
He taught to imitate that Lady trew,
Whose semblance she did carrie under feigned hew.

X L V I I

Thus, well instructed, to their worke they haste;
And, comming where the knight in slomber lay,
The one upon his hardie head him plaste,
And made him dreame of loves and lustfull play,
That nigh his manly hart did melt away,
Bathed in wanton blis and wicked joy.
Then seemed him his Lady by him lay,

And to him playnd, how that false winged boy
Her chaste hart had subdewd to learne Dame Pleasures toy.

XLVIII

And she her selfe, of beautie soveraigne Queene,
Fayre Venus, seemde unto his bed to bring
Her, whom he, waking, evermore did weene
To bee the chastest flowre that aye did spring
On earthly braunch, the daughter of a king,
Now a loose Leman to vile service bound:
And eke the Graces seemed all to sing,
Hymen Iö Hymen! dauncing all around;
Whylst freshest Flora her with Yvie girlond crownd.

XLIX

In this great passion of unwonted lust,
Or wonted feare of doing ought amis,
He starteth up, as seeming to mistrust
Some secret ill, or hidden foe of his.
Lo! there before his face his Ladie is,
Under blacke stole hyding her bayted hooke;
And as halfe blushing offred him to kis,
With gentle blandishment and lovely looke,
Most like that virgin true which for her knight him took.

L

All cleane dismayd to see so uncouth sight,
And half enraged at her shamelesse guise,
He thought have slaine her in his fierce despight;
But hastie heat tempring with sufferance wise,
He stayde his hand; and gan himselfe advise
To prove his sense, and tempt her faigned truth.
Wringing her hands, in wemens pitteous wise,
Tho can she weepe, to stirre up gentle ruth
Both for her noble blood, and for her tender youth.

LI

And sayd, 'Ah Sir, my liege Lord, and my love,
Shall I accuse the hidden cruell fate,
And mightie causes wrought in heaven above,
Or the blind God that doth me thus amate,
For hoped love to winne me certaine hate?
Yet thus perforce he bids me do, or die.
Die is my dew; yet rew my wretched state,
You, whom my hard avenging destinie
Hath made judge of my life or death indifferently.

L I I

'Your owne deare sake forst me at first to leave
My fathers kingdom'—There she stopt with teares;
Her swollen hart her speech seemd to bereave,
And then againe begonne; 'My weaker yeares,
Captiv'd to fortune and frayle worldly feares,
Fly to your fayth for succour and sure ayde:
Let me not die in languor and long teares.'
'Why, Dame,' (quoth he,) 'what hath ye thus dismayd?
What frayes ye, that were wont to comfort me affrayd?'

L I I I

'Love of your selfe,' she saide, 'and deare constraint,
Lets me not sleepe, but waste the wearie night
In secret anguish and unpittied plaint,
Whiles you in carelesse sleepe are drowned quight.'
Her doubtfull words made that redoubted knight
Suspect her truth: yet since no' untruth he knew,
Her fawning love with foule disdainefull spight
He would not shend; but said, 'Deare dame, I rew,
That for my sake unknowne such griefe unto you grew.

L I V

'Assure your selfe, it fell not all to ground;
For all so deare as life is to my hart,
I deeme your love, and hold me to you bound:
Ne let vaine feares procure your needlesse smart,
Where cause is none; but to your rest depart.'
Not all content, yet seemd she to appease
Her mournefull plaintes, beguiled of her art,
And fed with words that could not chose but please:
So, slyding softly forth, she turnd as to her ease.

L V

Long after lay he musing at her mood,
Much griev'd to thinke that gentle Dame so light,
For whose defence he was to shed his blood.
At last, dull wearines of former fight
Having yrockt asleepe his irkesome spright,
That troublous dreame gan freshly tosse his braine
With bowres, and beds, and ladies deare delight:
But, when he saw his labour all was vaine,
With that misformed spright he backe returnd againe.

LIII, 5   doubtfull: ambiguous

CANTO II.

*The guilefull great Enchaunter parts
The Redcrosse Knight from Truth:
Into whose stead faire falshood steps,
And workes him woefull ruth.*

I

B Y THIS THE Northerne wagoner had set
His sevenfold teme behind the stedfast starre
That was in Ocean waves yet never wet,
But firme is fixt, and sendeth light from farre
To al that in the wide deepe wandring arre;
And chearefull Chaunticlere with his note shrill
Had warned once, that Phoebus fiery carre
In hast was climbing up the Easterne hill,
Full envious that night so long his roome did fill:

I I

When those accursed messengers of hell,
That feigning dreame, and that faire-forged Spright,
Came to their wicked maister, and gan tel
Their bootelesse paines, and ill succeeding night:
Who, all in rage to see his skilfull might
Deluded so, gan threaten hellish paine,
And sad Proserpines wrath, them to affright:
But, when he saw his threatning was but vaine,
He cast about, and searcht his baleful bokes againe.

I I I

Eftsoones he tooke that miscreated faire,
And that false other Spright, on whom he spred
A seeming body of the subtile aire,
Like a young Squire, in loves and lusty-hed
His wanton daies that ever loosely led,
Without regard of armes and dreaded fight:
Those twoo he tooke, and in a secrete bed,
Covered with darkenes and misdeeming night,
Them both together laid to joy in vaine delight.

I V

Forthwith he runnes with feigned faithfull hast
Unto his guest, who, after troublous sights
And dreames, gan now to take more sound repast;
Whom suddenly he wakes with fearful frights,

As one aghast with feends or damned sprights,
And to him cals; 'Rise, rise! unhappy Swaine,
That here wex old in sleepe, whiles wicked wights
Have knit themselves in Venus shameful chaine:
Come, see where your false Lady doth her honor staine.'

v

All in amaze he suddenly up start
With sword in hand, and with the old man went;
Who soone him brought into a secret part,
Where that false couple were full closely ment
In wanton lust and leud enbracement:
Which when he saw, he burnt with gealous fire;
The eie of reason was with rage yblent,
And would have slaine them in his furious ire,
But hardly was restreined of that aged sire.

v i

Retourning to his bed in torment great,
And bitter anguish of his guilty sight,
He could not rest; but did his stout heart eat,
And wast his inward gall with deepe despight,
Yrkesome of life, and too long lingring night.
At last faire Hesperus in highest skie
Had spent his lampe, and brought forth dawning light:
Then up he rose, and clad him hastily:
The dwarfe him brought his steed; so both away do fly.

v i i

Now when the rosy fingred Morning faire,
Weary of aged Tithones saffron bed,
Had spred her purple robe through deawy aire,
And the high hils Titan discovered,
The royall virgin shooke off drousy-hed;
And, rising forth out of her baser bowre,
Lookt for her knight, who far away was fled,
And for her dwarfe, that wont to wait each howre:
Then gan she wail and weepe to see that woeful stowre.

v i i i

And after him she rode, with so much speede
As her slowe beast could make; but all in vaine,
For him so far had borne his light-foot steede,
Pricked with wrath and fiery fierce disdaine,

v, 4   ment: mingled   vii, 9   stowre: misfortune
v, 7   yblent: blinded

That him to follow was but fruitlesse paine:
Yet she her weary limbes would never rest;
But every hil and dale, each wood and plaine,
Did search, sore grieved in her gentle brest,
He so ungently left her, whome she loved best.

I X

But subtill Archimago, when his guests
He saw divided into double parts,
And Una wandring in woods and forrests,
Th' end of his drift, he praisd his divelish arts,
That had such might over true meaning harts;
Yet rests not so, but other meanes doth make,
How he may worke unto her further smarts;
For her he hated as the hissing snake,
And in her many troubles did most pleasure take.

x

He then devisde himselfe how to disguise;
For by his mighty science he could take
As many formes and shapes in seeming wise,
As ever Proteus to himselfe could make:
Sometime a fowle, sometime a fish in lake,
Now like a foxe, now like a dragon fell;
That of himselfe he ofte for feare would quake,
And oft would flie away. O! who can tell
The hidden powre of herbes, and might of Magick spel?

X I

But now seemde best the person to put on
Of that good knight, his late beguiled guest:
In mighty armes he was yclad anon,
And silver shield; upon his coward brest
A bloody crosse, and on his craven crest
A bounch of heares discolourd diversly.
Full jolly knight he seemde, and wel addrest;
And when he sate upon his courser free,
Saint George himselfe ye would have deemed him to be.

X I I

But he, the knight whose semblaunt he did beare,
The true Saint George, was wandred far away,
Still flying from his thoughts and gealous feare:
Will was his guide, and griefe led him astray.

XII, 4 will: appetite, inclination, often distinguished from "wit," the rational faculty

At last him chaunst to meete upon the way
A faithlesse Sarazin, all armde to point,
In whose great shield was writ with letters gay
Sans foy; full large of limbe and every joint
He was, and cared not for God or man a point.

X I I I

Hee had a faire companion of his way,
A goodly Lady clad in scarlot red,
Purfled with gold and pearle of rich assay;
And like a Persian mitre on her hed
Shee wore, with crowns and owches garnished,
The which her lavish lovers to her gave.
Her wanton palfrey all was overspred
With tinsell trappings, woven like a wave,
Whose bridle rung with golden bels and bosses brave.

X I V

With faire disport, and courting dalliaunce,
She intertainde her lover all the way;
But, when she saw the knight his speare advaunce,
She soone left off her mirth and wanton play,
And bad her knight addresse him to the fray,
His foe was nigh at hand. He, prickte with pride
And hope to winne his Ladies hearte that day,
Forth spurred fast: adowne his coursers side
The red bloud trickling staind the way, as he did ride.

X V

The knight of the Redcrosse, when him he spide
Spurring so hote with rage dispiteous,
Gan fairely couch his speare, and towards ride.
Soone meete they both, both fell and furious,
That, daunted with theyr forces hideous,
Their steeds doe stagger, and amazed stand;
And eke themselves, too rudely rigorous,
Astonied with the stroke of their owne hand,
Doe backe rebutte, and ech to other yealdeth land.

X V I

As when two rams, stird with ambitious pride,
Fight for the rule of the rich fleeced flocke,
Their horned fronts so fierce on either side
Doe meete, that, with the terror of the shocke,
Astonied, both stand sencelesse as a blocke,

XIII, 5   owches: brooches

Forgetfull of the hanging victory:
So stood these twaine, unmoved as a rocke,
Both staring fierce, and holding idely
The broken reliques of their former cruelty.

XVII

The Sarazin, sore daunted with the buffe,
Snatcheth his sword, and fiercely to him flies;
Who well it wards, and quyteth cuff with cuff:
Each others equall puissaunce envies,
And through their iron sides with cruell spies
Does seeke to perce; repining courage yields
No foote to foe: the flashing fier flies,
As from a forge, out of their burning shields;
And streams of purple bloud new die the verdant fields.

XVIII

'Curse on that Cross,' (quoth then the Sarazin,)
'That keepes thy body from the bitter fitt!
Dead long ygoe, I wote, thou haddest bin,
Had not that charme from thee forwarned itt:
But yet I warne thee now assured sitt,
And hide thy head.' Therewith upon his crest
With rigor so outrageous he smitt,
That a large share it hewd out of the rest,
And glauncing downe his shield from blame him fairly blest.

XIX

Who, thereat wondrous wroth, the sleeping spark
Of native vertue gan eftsoones revive;
And at his haughty helmet making mark,
So hugely stroke, that it the steele did rive,
And cleft his head. He, tumbling downe alive,
With bloudy mouth his mother earth did kis,
Greeting his grave: his grudging ghost did strive
With the fraile flesh; at last it flitted is,
Whither the soules doe fly of men that live amis.

XX

The Lady, when she saw her champion fall
Like the old ruines of a broken towre,
Staid not to waile his woefull funerall,
But from him fled away with all her powre;
Who after her as hastily gan scowre,

XVIII, 2 fitt: mortal crisis   XVIII, 9 blest: saved
XVIII, 4 forwarned: forfended

Bidding the dwarfe with him to bring away
The Sarazins shield, signe of the conqueroure.
Her soone he overtooke, and bad to stay;
For present cause was none of dread her to dismay.

X X I

Shee turning backe, with ruefull countenaunce,
Cride, 'Mercy, mercy, Sir, vouchsafe to show
On silly Dame, subject to hard mischaunce,
And to your mighty wil!' Her humblesse low,
In so ritch weedes, and seeming glorious show,
Did much emmove his stout heroïcke heart;
And said, 'Deare dame, your suddein overthrow
Much rueth me; but now put feare apart,
And tel both who ye be, and who that tooke your part.'

X X I I

Melting in teares, then gan shee thus lament.
'The wretched woman, whom unhappy howre
Hath now made thrall to your commandement,
Before that angry heavens list to lowre,
And fortune false betraide me to thy powre,
Was (O! what now availeth that I was?)
Borne the sole daughter of an Emperour,
He that the wide West under his rule has,
And high hath set his throne where Tiberis doth pas.

X X I I I

'He, in the first flowre of my freshest age,
Betrothed me unto the onely haire
Of a most mighty king, most rich and sage:
Was never Prince so faithfull and so faire,
Was never Prince so meeke and debonaire;
But ere my hoped day of spousall shone,
My dearest Lord fell from high honors staire
Into the hands of hys accursed fone,
And cruelly was slaine; that shall I ever mone.

X X I V

'His blessed body, spoild of lively breath,
Was afterward, I know not how, convaid,
And fro me hid: of whose most innocent death
When tidings came to mee, unhappy maid,
O, how great sorrow my sad soule assaid!
Then forth I went his woefull corse to find,
And many yeares throughout the world I straid,

A virgin widow, whose deepe wounded mind
With love long time did languish, as the striken hind.

X X V

'At last it chaunced this proud Sarazin
To meete me wandring; who perforce me led
With him away, but yet could never win
The Fort, that Ladies hold in soveraigne dread.
There lies he now with foule dishonor dead,
Who, whiles he livde, was called proud Sans foy,
The eldest of three brethren; all three bred
Of one bad sire, whose youngest is Sans joy;
And twixt them both was born the bloudy bold Sans loy.

X X V I

'In this sad plight, friendlesse, unfortunate,
Now miserable I Fidessa, dwell,
Craving of you, in pitty of my state,
To doe none ill, if please ye not doe well.'
He in great passion al this while did dwell,
More busying his quicke eies her face to view,
Then his dull eares to heare what shee did tell;
And said, 'faire lady, hart of flint would rew
The undeserved woes and sorrowes, which ye shew.

X X V I I

'Henceforth in safe assuraunce may ye rest,
Having both found a new friend you to aid,
And lost an old foe that did you molest;
Better new friend then an old foe is said.'
With chaunge of chear the seeming simple maid
Let fal her eien, as shamefast, to the earth,
And yeelding soft, in that she nought gainsaid,
So forth they rode, he feining seemely merth,
And shee coy lookes: so dainty, they say, maketh derth.

X X V I I I

Long time they thus together traveiled;
Til, weary of their way, they came at last
Where grew two goodly trees, that faire did spred
Their armes abroad, with gray mosse overcast;
And their greene leaves, trembling with every blast,
Made a calme shadowe far in compasse round:
The fearefull shepheard, often there aghast,

xxvii, 9   dainty . . . maketh derth: scarcity enhances value

Under them never sat, ne wont there sound
His mery oaten pipe, but shund th' unlucky ground.

XXIX

But this good knight, soone as he them can spie,
For the coole shade him thither hastly got:
For golden Phoebus, now ymounted hie,
From fiery wheeles of his faire chariot
Hurled his beame so scorching cruell hot,
That living creature mote it not abide;
And his new Lady it endured not.
There they alight, in hope themselves to hide
From the fierce heat, and rest their weary limbs a tide.

XXX

Faire seemely pleasaunce each to other makes,
With goodly purposes, there as they sit;
And in his falsed fancy he her takes
To be the fairest wight that lived yit;
Which to expresse he bends his gentle wit:
And, thinking of those braunches greene to frame
A girlond for her dainty forehead fit,
He pluckt a bough; out of whose rifte there came
Smal drops of gory bloud, that trickled down the same.

XXXI

Therewith a piteous yelling voice was heard,
Crying, 'O! spare with guilty hands to teare
My tender sides in this rough rynd embard;
But fly, ah! fly far hence away, for feare
Least to you hap that happened to me heare,
And to this wretched Lady, my deare love;
O, too deare love, love bought with death too deare!'
Astond he stood, and up his heare did hove;
And with that suddein horror could no member move.

XXXII

At last whenas the dreadfull passion
Was overpast, and manhood well awake,
Yet musing at the straunge occasion,
And doubting much his sence, he thus bespake:
'What voice of damned Ghost from Limbo lake,
Or guilefull spright wandring in empty aire,
Both which fraile men doe oftentimes mistake,
Sends to my doubtful eares these speaches rare,
And ruefull plaints, me bidding guiltlesse blood to spare?'

XXXIII

Then, groning deep; 'Nor damned Ghost,' (quoth he,)
'Nor guileful sprite to thee these words doth speake;
But once a man, Fradubio, now a tree;
Wretched man, wretched tree! whose nature weake
A cruell witch, her cursed will to wreake,
Hath thus transformd, and plast in open plaines,
Where Boreas doth blow full bitter bleake,
And scorching Sunne does dry my secret vaines;
For though a tree I seme, yet cold and heat me paines.'

XXXIV

'Say on, Fradubio, then, or man or tree,'
Quoth then the Knight; 'by whose mischievous arts
Art thou misshaped thus, as now I see?
He oft finds med'cine who his griefe imparts,
But double griefs afflict concealing harts,
As raging flames who striveth to suppresse.'
'The author then,' (said he) 'of all my smarts,
Is one Duessa, a false sorceresse,
That many errant knights hath broght to wretchednesse.

XXXV

'In prime of youthly yeares, when corage hott
The fire of love, and joy of chevalree,
First kindled in my brest, it was my lott
To love this gentle Lady, whome ye see
Now not a Lady, but a seeming tree;
With whome, as once I rode accompanyde,
Me chaunced of a knight encountred bee,
That had a like faire Lady by his syde;
Lyke a faire Lady, but did fowle Duessa hyde.

XXXVI

'Whose forged beauty he did take in hand
All other Dames to have exceeded farre:
I in defence of mine did likewise stand,
Mine, that did then shine as the Morning starre.
So both to batteill fierce arraunged arre,
In which his harder fortune was to fall
Under my speare: such is the dye of warre.
His Lady, left as a prise martiall,
Did yield her comely person to be at my call.

X X X V I I

'So doubly lov'd of ladies, unlike faire,
Th' one seeming such, the other such indeede,
One day in doubt I cast for to compare
Whether in beauties glorie did exceede:
A Rosy girlond was the victors meede.
Both seemde to win, and both seemde won to bee,
So hard the discord was to be agreede.
Frælissa was as faire as faire mote bee,
And ever false Duessa seemde as faire as shee.

X X X V I I I

'The wicked witch, now seeing all this while
The doubtfull ballaunce equally to sway,
What not by right she cast to win by guile;
And by her hellish science raisd streight way
A foggy mist that overcast the day,
And a dull blast, that breathing on her face
Dimmed her former beauties shining ray,
And with foule ugly forme did her disgrace:
Then was she fayre alone, when none was faire in place.

X X X I X

'Then cride she out, "Fye, fye! deformed wight,
'Whose borrowed beautie now appeareth plaine
'To have before bewitched all mens sight:
'O! leave her soone, or let her soone be slaine."
Her loathly visage viewing with disdaine,
Eftsoones I thought her such as she me told,
And would have kild her; but with faigned paine
The false witch did my wrathfull hand withhold:
So left her, where she now is turned to treen mould.

X L

'Thensforth I tooke Duessa for my Dame,
And in the witch unweeting joyd long time,
Ne ever wist but that she was the same;
Till on a day (that day is everie Prime,
When Witches wont do penance for their crime,)
I chaunst to see her in her proper hew,
Bathing her selfe in origane and thyme:
A filthy foule old woman I did vew,
That ever to have toucht her I did deadly rew.

xxxix, 9   treen: wooden   xxxix, 9   mould: form, body

X L I

'Her neather partes misshapen, monstruous,
Were hidd in water, that I could not see;
But they did seeme more foule and hideous,
Then womans shape man would beleeve to bee.
Thensforth from her most beastly companie
I gan refraine, in minde to slipp away,
Soone as appeard safe opportunitie:
For danger great, if not assurd decay,
I saw before mine eyes, if I were knowne to stray.

X L I I

'The divelish hag by chaunges of my cheare
Perceiv'd my thought; and, drownd in sleepie night,
With wicked herbes and oyntments did besmeare
My body all, through charmes and magicke might,
That all my senses were bereaved quight:
Then brought she me into this desert waste,
And by my wretched lovers side me pight;
Where now, enclosd in wooden wals full faste,
Banisht from living wights, our wearie daies we waste.'

X L I I I

'But how long time,' said then the Elfin knight,
'Are you in this misformed hous to dwell?'
'We may not chaunge,' (quoth he,) 'this evill plight,
Till we be bathed in a living well:
That is the terme prescribed by the spell.'
'O! how,' sayd he, 'mote I that well out find,
That may restore you to your wonted well?'
'Time and suffised fates to former kynd
Shall us restore: none else from hence may us unbynd.'

X L I V

The false Duessa, now Fidessa hight,
Heard how in vaine Fradubio did lament,
And knew well all was true. But the good knight,
Full of sad feare and ghastly dreriment,
When all this speech the living tree had spent,
The bleeding bough did thrust into the ground,
That from the blood he might be innocent,
And with fresh clay did close the wooden wound:
Then, turning to his Lady, dead with feare her fownd.

XLIII, 8   kynd: nature

X L V

Her seeming dead he fownd with feigned feare,
As all unweeting of that well she knew;
And paynd himselfe with busie care to reare
Her out of carelesse swowne. Her eyelids blew,
And dimmed sight, with pale and deadly hew,
At last she up gan lift: with trembling cheare
Her up he tooke, (too simple and too trew)
And oft her kist. At length, all passed feare,
He set her on her steede, and forward forth did beare.

CANTO III.

Forsaken Truth long seekes her love,
And makes the Lyon mylde;
Marres blind Devotions mart, and fals
In hand of leachour vylde.

I

Nought is there under heav'ns wide hollownesse,
That moves more deare compassion of mind,
Then beautie brought t'unworthie wretchednesse
Through envies snares, or fortunes freakes unkind.
I, whether lately through her brightnes blynd,
Or through alleageance, and fast fealty,
Which I do owe unto all womankynd,
Feele my hart perst with so great agony,
When such I see, that all for pitty I could dy.

I I

And now it is empassioned so deepe,
For fairest Unaes sake, of whom I sing,
That my frayle eies these lines with teares do steepe,
To thinke how she through guyleful handeling,
Though true as touch, though daughter of a king,
Though faire as ever living wight was fayre,
Though nor in word nor deede ill meriting,
Is from her knight divorced in despayre.
And her dew loves deryv'd to that vile witches shayre.

I I I

Yet she, most faithfull Ladie, all this while
Forsaken, wofull, solitarie mayd,

XLV, 4   blew: leaden-colored   II, 5   touch: touchstone

Far from all peoples preace, as in exile,
In wildernesse and wastfull deserts strayd,
To seeke her knight; who, subtily betrayd
Through that late vision which th'Enchaunter wrought,
Had her abandoned. She, of nought affrayd,
Through woods and wastnes wide him daily sought;
Yet wished tydinges none of him unto her brought.

I V

One day, nigh wearie of the yrkesome way,
From her unhastie beast she did alight;
And on the grasse her dainty limbs did lay
In secrete shadow, far from all mens sight:
From her fayre head her fillet she undight,
And layd her stole aside. Her angels face,
As the great eye of heaven, shyned bright,
And made a sunshine in the shady place;
Did never mortall eye behold such heavenly grace.

V

It fortuned, out of the thickest wood
A ramping Lyon rushed suddeinly,
Hunting full greedy after salvage blood.
Soone as the royall virgin he did spy,
With gaping mouth at her ran greedily,
To have attonce devourd her tender corse;
But to the pray when as he drew more ny,
His bloody rage aswaged with remorse,
And, with the sight amazd, forgat his furious forse.

V I

In stead thereof he kist her wearie feet,
And lickt her lilly hands with fawning tong,
As he her wronged innocence did weet.
O, how can beautie maister the most strong,
And simple truth subdue avenging wrong!
Whose yielded pryde and proud submission,
Still dreading death, when she had marked long,
Her hart gan melt in great compassion;
And drizling teares did shed for pure affection.

V I I

'The Lyon, Lord of everie beast in field,'
Quoth she, 'his princely puissance doth abate,
And mightie proud to humble weake does yield,

vi, 3   weet: understand

Forgetfull of the hungry rage, which late
Him prickt, in pittie of my sad estate:
But he, my Lyon, and my noble Lord,
How does he find in cruell hart to hate
Her, that him lov'd, and ever most adord
As the God of my life? why hath he me abhord?'

    V I I I

Redounding teares did choke th' end of her plaint,
Which softly ecchoed from the neighbour wood;
And, sad to see her sorrowfull constraint,
The kingly beast upon her gazing stood:
With pittie calmd downe fell his angry mood.
At last, in close hart shutting up her payne,
Arose the virgin, borne of heavenly brood,
And to her snowy Palfrey got agayne,
To seeke her strayed Champion if she might attayne.

    I X

The Lyon would not leave her desolate,
But with her went along, as a strong gard
Of her chast person, and a faythfull mate
Of her sad troubles and misfortunes hard:
Still, when she slept, he kept both watch and ward;
And, when she wakt, he wayted diligent,
With humble service to her will prepard:
From her fayre eyes he tooke commandement,
And ever by her lookes conceived her intent.

    X

Long she thus traveiled through deserts wyde,
By which she thought her wandring knight shold pas,
Yet never shew of living wight espyde;
Till that at length she found the troden gras,
In which the tract of peoples footing was,
Under the steepe foot of a mountaine hore:
The same she followes, till at last she has
A damzel spyde, slow footing her before,
That on her shoulders sad a pot of water bore.

    X I

To whom approching she to her gan call,
To weet if dwelling place were nigh at hand;
But the rude wench her answerd nought at all:
She could not heare, nor speake, nor understand;

VIII, I   redounding: overflowing

Till, seeing by her side the Lyon stand,
With suddeine feare her pitcher downe she threw,
And fled away: for never in that land
Face of fayre Lady she before did vew,
And that dredd Lyons looke her cast in deadly hew.

X I I

Full fast she fled, ne ever lookt behynd,
As if her life upon the wager lay;
And home she came, whereas her mother blynd
Sate in eternall night: nought could she say;
But, suddeine catching hold, did her dismay
With quaking hands, and other signes of feare:
Who, full of ghastly fright and cold affray,
Gan shut the dore. By this arrived there
Dame Una, weary Dame, and entrance did requere:

X I I I

Which when none yielded, her unruly Page
With his rude clawes the wicket open rent,
And let her in; where, of his cruell rage
Nigh dead with feare, and faint astonishment,
Shee found them both in darksome corner pent;
Where that old woman day and night did pray
Upon her beads, devoutly penitent:
Nine hundred *Pater nosters* every day,
And thrise nine hundred *Aves* she was wont to say.

X I V

And to augment her painefull penaunce more,
Thrise every weeke in ashes shee did sitt,
And next her wrinkled skin rough sackecloth wore,
And thrise three times did fast from any bitt;
But now, for feare her beads she did forgett:
Whose needlesse dread for to remove away,
Faire Una framed words and count'naunce fitt;
Which hardly doen, at length she gan them pray,
That in their cotage small that night she rest her may.

X V

The day is spent; and commeth drowsie night,
When every creature shrowded is in sleepe.
Sad Una downe her laies in weary plight,
And at her feete the Lyon watch doth keepe:
In stead of rest she does lament and weepe,
For the late losse of her deare loved knight,

And sighes, and grones, and evermore does steepe
Her tender brest in bitter teares all night;
All night she thinks too long, and often lookes for light.

X V I

Now when Aldeboran was mounted hye
Above the shinie Cassiopeias chaire,
And all in deadly sleepe did drowned lye
One knocked at the dore, and in would fare:
He knocked fast, and often curst, and sware,
That ready entraunce was not at his call;
For on his backe a heavy load he bare
Of nightly stelths, and pillage severall,
Which he had got abroad by purchas criminall.

X V I I

He was, to weete, a stout and sturdy thiefe,
Wont to robbe churches of their ornaments,
And poore mens boxes of their due reliefe,
Which given was to them for good intents:
The holy Saints of their rich vestiments
He did disrobe, when all men carelesse slept,
And spoild the Priests of their habiliments;
Whiles none the holy things in safety kept,
Then he by conning sleights in at the window crept.

X V I I I

And all that he by right or wrong could find,
Unto this house he brought, and did bestow
Upon the daughter of this woman blind,
Abessa, daughter of Corceca slow,
With whom he whoredome usd, that few did know,
And fed her fatt with feast of offerings,
And plenty, which in all the land did grow:
Ne spared he to give her gold and rings;
And now he to her brought part of his stolen things.

X I X

Thus, long the dore with rage and threats he bett,
Yet of those fearfull women none durst rize.
The Lyon frayed them, him in to lett.
He would no lenger stay him to advize,
But open breakes the dore in furious wize,
And entring is, when that disdainfull beast,
Encountring fierce, him suddein doth surprize;

XIX, 4   advize: consider

And, seizing cruell clawes on trembling brest,
Under his Lordly foot him proudly hath supprest.

X X

Him booteth not resist, nor succour call,
His bleeding hart is in the vengers hand;
Who streight him rent in thousand peeces small,
And quite dismembred hath: the thirsty land
Dronke up his life; his corse left on the strand.
His fearefull freends weare out the wofull night,
Ne dare to weepe, nor seeme to understand
The heavie hap which on them is alight;
Affraid least to themselves the like mishappen might.

X X I

Now when broad day the world discovered has,
Up Una rose, up rose the lyon eke;
And on their former journey forward pas,
In waies unknowne, her wandring knight to seeke,
With paines far passing that long wandring Greeke,
That for his love refused deitye.
Such were the labours of this Lady meeke,
Still seeking him, that from her still did flye;
Then furthest from her hope, when most she weened nye.

X X I I

Soone as she parted thence, the fearfull twayne,
That blind old woman, and her daughter dear,
Came forth; and, finding Kirkrapine there slayne,
For anguish great they gan to rend their heare,
And beat their brests, and naked flesh to teare:
And when they both had wept and wayld their fill,
Then forth they ran, like two amazed deare,
Halfe mad through malice and revenging will,
To follow her that was the causer of their ill.

X X I I I

Whome overtaking, they gan loudly bray,
With hollow houling, and lamenting cry;
Shamefully at her rayling all the way,
And her accusing of dishonesty,
That was the flowre of faith and chastity:
And still, amidst her rayling, she did pray
That plagues, and mischiefes, and long misery,
Might fall on her, and follow all the way,
And that in endlesse error she might ever stray.

XXIV

But, when she saw her prayers nought prevaile,
Shee backe retourned with some labour lost:
And in the way, as shee did weepe and waile,
A knight her mett in mighty armes embost,
Yet knight was not for all his bragging bost;
But subtill Archimag, that Una sought
By traynes into new troubles to have toste:
Of that old woman tidings he besought,
If that of such a Lady shee could tellen ought.

XXV

Therewith she gan her passion to renew,
And cry, and curse, and raile, and rend her heare,
Saying, that harlott she too lately knew,
That causd her shed so many a bitter teare;
And so forth told the story of her feare.
Much seemed he to mone her haplesse chaunce,
And after for that Lady did inquere;
Which being taught, he forward gan advaunce
His fair enchaunted steed, and eke his charmed launce.

XXVI

Ere long he came where Una traveild slow,
And that wilde champion wayting her besyde;
Whome seeing such, for dread hee durst not show
Him selfe too nigh at hand, but turned wyde
Unto an hil; from whence when she him spyde,
By his like seeming shield her knight by name
She weend it was, and towards him gan ride:
Approaching nigh she wist it was the same;
And with faire fearefull humblesse towards him shee came:

XXVII

And weeping said, 'Ah, my long lacked Lord,
Where have ye bene thus long out of my sight?
Much feared I to have bene quite abhord,
Or ought have done, that ye displeasen might,
That should as death unto my deare heart light:
For since mine eie your joyous sight did mis,
My chearefull day is turnd to chearelesse night,
And eke my night of death the shadow is;
But welcome now, my light, and shining lampe of blis!'

XXIV, 4 embost: enclosed   XXVII, 5 deare: loving

XXVIII

He thereto meeting said, 'My dearest Dame,
Far be it from your thought, and fro my wil,
To thinke that knighthood I so much should shame,
As you to leave that have me loved stil,
And chose in Faery court, of meere goodwil,
Where noblest knights were to be found on earth.
The earth shall sooner leave her kindly skil
To bring forth fruit, and make eternal derth,
Then I leave you, my liefe, yborn of hevenly berth.

XXIX

'And sooth to say, why I lefte you so long,
Was for to seeke adventure in straunge place;
Where, Archimago said, a felon strong
To many knights did daily worke disgrace;
But knight he now shall never more deface:
Good cause of mine excuse, that mote ye please
Well to accept, and evermore embrace
My faithfull service, that by land and seas
Have vowd you to defend. Now then, your plaint appease.'

XXX

His lovely words her seemd due recompence
Of all her passed paines: one loving howre
For many yeares of sorrow can dispence;
A dram of sweete is worth a pound of sowre.
Shee has forgott how many a woeful stowre
For him she late endurd; she speakes no more
Of past: true is, that true love hath no powre
To looken backe; his eies be fixt before.
Before her stands her knight, for whom she toyld so sore

XXXI

Much like, as when the beaten marinere,
That long hath wandred in the Ocean wide,
Ofte soust in swelling Tethys saltish teare;
And long time having tand his tawney hide
With blustring breath of Heaven, that none can bide,
And scorching flames of fierce Orions hound;
Soone as the port from far he has espide,
His chearfull whistle merily doth sound,
And Nereus crownes with cups; his mates him pledg around.

XXVIII, 7   kindly: natural

XXXII

Such joy made Una, when her knight she found;
And eke th' enchaunter joyous seemde no lesse
Then the glad marchant, that does vew from ground
His ship far come from watrie wildernesse;
He hurles out vowes, and Neptune oft doth blesse.
So forth they past; and all the way they spent
Discoursing of her dreadful late distresse,
In which he askt her, what the Lyon ment;
Who told her all that fell, in journey as she went.

XXXIII

They had not ridden far, when they might see
One pricking towards them with hastie heat,
Full strongly armd, and on a courser free
That through his fiersnesse fomed all with sweat,
And the sharpe yron did for anger eat,
When his hot ryder spurd his chauffed side:
His looke was sterne, and seemed still to threat
Cruell revenge, which he in hart did hyde;
And on his shield *Sansloy* in bloody lines was dyde.

XXXIV

When nigh he drew unto this gentle payre,
And saw the Red-crosse which the knight did beare,
He burnt in fire; and gan eftsoones prepare
Himselfe to batteill with his couched speare.
Loth was that other, and did faint through feare,
To taste th' untryed dint of deadly steele:
But yet his Lady did so well him cheare,
That hope of new good hap he gan to feele;
So bent his speare, and spurd his horse with yron heele.

XXXV

But that proud Paynim forward came so ferce
And full of wrath, that, with his sharphead speare,
Through vainly crossed shield he quite did perce;
And, had his staggering steed not shronke for feare,
Through shield and body eke he should him beare:
Yet, so great was the puissance of his push,
That from his sadle quite he did him beare.
He, tombling rudely downe, to ground did rush,
And from his gored wound a well of bloud did gush.

X X X V I

Dismounting lightly from his loftie steed,
He to him lept, in minde to reave his life,
And proudly said; 'Lo! there the worthie meed
Of him that slew Sansfoy with bloody knife:
Henceforth his ghost, freed from repining strife,
In peace may passen over Lethe lake;
When mourning altars, purgd with enimies life,
The black infernall Furies doen aslake:
Life from Sansfoy thou tookst, Sansloy shall from thee take.'

X X X V I I

Therewith in haste his helmet gan unlace,
Till Una cride, 'O! hold that heavie hand,
Deare Sir, what ever that thou be in place:
Enough is, that thy foe doth vanquisht stand
Now at thy mercy: Mercy not withstand;
For he is one the truest knight alive,
Though conquered now he lye on lowly land;
And, whilest him fortune favour, fayre did thrive
In bloudy field; therefore, of life him not deprive.'

X X X V I I I

Her piteous wordes might not abate his rage,
But, rudely rending up his helmet, would
Have slayne him streight; but when he sees his age,
And hoarie head of Archimago old,
His hasty hand he doth amased hold,
And halfe ashamed wondred at the sight:
For that old man well knew he, though untold,
In charmes and magick to have wondrous might,
Ne ever wont in field, ne in round lists, to fight:

X X X I X

And said, 'Why Archimago, lucklesse syre,
What doe I see? what hard mishap is this,
That hath thee hether brought to taste mine yre?
Or thine the fault, or mine the error is,
In stead of foe to wound my friend amis?'
He answered nought, but in a traunce still lay,
And on those guilefull dazed eyes of his
The cloude of death did sit. Which doen away,
He left him lying so, ne would no lenger stay:

XXXVII, 3   place: rank

X L

But to the virgin comes; who all this while
Amased stands, her selfe so mockt to see
By him, who has the guerdon of his guile,
For so misfeigning her true knight to bee:
Yet is she now in more perplexitie,
Left in the hand of that same Paynim bold,
From whom her booteth not at all to flie:
Who, by her cleanly garment catching hold,
Her from her Palfrey pluckt, her visage to behold.

X L I

But her fiers servant, full of kingly aw
And high disdaine, whenas his soveraine Dame
So rudely handled by her foe he saw,
With gaping jawes full greedy at him came,
And, ramping on his shield, did weene the same
Have reft away with his sharp rending clawes:
But he was stout, and lust did now inflame
His corage more, that from his griping pawes
He hath his shield redeemd, and forth his swerd he drawes.

X L I I

O! then, too weake and feeble was the forse
Of salvage beast his puissance to withstand;
For he was strong, and of so mightie corse,
As ever wielded speare in warlike hand,
And feates of armes did wisely understand.
Eft soones he perced through his chaufed chest
With thrilling point of deadly yron brand,
And launcht his Lordly hart: with death opprest
He ror'd aloud, whiles life forsooke his stubborne brest.

X L I I I

Who now is left to keepe the forlorne maid
From raging spoile of lawlesse victors will?
Her faithfull gard remov'd, her hope dismaid,
Her selfe a yielded pray to save or spill:
He now, Lord of the field, his pride to fill,
With foule reproches and disdaineful spight
Her vildly entertaines; and, will or nill,
Beares her away upon his courser light:
Her prayers nought prevaile, his rage is more of might.

XLII, 7   thrilling: piercing

XLIV

And all the way, with great lamenting paine,
And piteous plaintes, she filleth his dull eares,
That stony hart could riven have in twaine;
And all the way she wetts with flowing teares;
But he, enrag'd with rancor, nothing heares.
Her servile beast yet would not leave her so,
But followes her far off, ne ought he feares
To be partaker of her wandring woe;
More mild in beastly kind then that her beastly foe.

CANTO IV.

To sinfull hous of Pryde Duessa
Guydes the faithfull knight;
Where, brothers death to wreak, Sansjoy
Doth chaleng him to fight.

I

YOUNG KNIGHT whatever, that dost armes professe,
And through long labours huntest after fame,
Beware of fraud, beware of fickelenesse,
In choice, and chaunge of thy deare-loved Dame;
Least thou of her believe too lightly blame,
And rash misweening doe thy hart remove:
For unto knight there is no greater shame
Then lightnesse and inconstancie in love:
That doth this Redcrosse knights ensample plainly prove.

II

Who, after that he had faire Una lorne,
Through light misdeeming of her loialtie;
And false Duessa in her sted had borne,
Called Fidess', and so supposd to be,
Long with her traveild; till at last they see
A goodly building bravely garnished;
The house of mightie Prince it seemd to be,
And towards it a broad high way that led,
All bare through peoples feet which thether traveiled.

III

Great troupes of people traveild thetherward
Both day and night, of each degree and place;
But few returned, having scaped hard,

With balefull beggery, or foule disgrace;
Which ever after in most wretched case,
Like loathsome lazars, by the hedges lay.
Thether Duessa badd him bend his pace,
For she is wearie of the toilsom way,
And also nigh consumed is the lingring day.

IV

A stately Pallace built of squared bricke,
Which cunningly was without morter laid,
Whose wals were high, but nothing strong nor thick,
And golden foile all over them displaid,
That purest skye with brightnesse they dismaid:
High lifted up were many loftie towres,
And goodly galleries far over laid,
Full of faire windowes and delightful bowres:
And on the top a Diall told the timely howres.

V

It was a goodly heape for to behould,
And spake the praises of the workmans witt;
But full great pittie, that so faire a mould
Did on so weake foundation ever sitt:
For on a sandie hill, that still did flitt
And fall away, it mounted was full hie,
That every breath of heaven shaked itt:
And all the hinder partes, that few could spie,
Were ruinous and old, but painted cunningly.

VI

Arrived there, they passed in forth right;
For still to all the gates stood open wide:
Yet charge of them was to a Porter hight,
Cald Malvenù, who entrance none denide:
Thence to the hall, which was on every side
With rich array and costly arras dight.
Infinite sortes of people did abide
There waiting long, to win the wished sight
Of her, that was the Lady of that Pallace bright.

VII

By them they passe, all gazing on them round,
And to the Presence mount; whose glorious vew
Their frayle amazed senses did confound:
In living Princes court none ever knew
Such endlesse richesse, and so sumpteous shew;

Ne Persia selfe, the nourse of pompous pride,
Like ever saw. And there a noble crew
Of Lords and Ladies stood on every side,
Which with their presence fayre the place much beautifide.

V I I I

High above all a cloth of State was spred,
And a rich throne, as bright as sunny day;
On which there sate, most brave embellished
With royall robes and gorgeous array,
A mayden Queene that shone as Titans ray,
In glistring gold and perelesse pretious stone;
Yet her bright blazing beautie did assay
To dim the brightnesse of her glorious throne,
As envying her selfe, that too exceeding shone:

I X

Exceeding shone, like Phoebus fayrest childe,
That did presume his fathers fyrie wayne,
And flaming mouthes of steedes, unwonted wilde,
Through highest heaven with weaker hand to rayne:
Proud of such glory and advancement vayne,
While flashing beames do daze his feeble eyen,
He leaves the welkin way most beaten playne,
And, rapt with whirling wheeles, inflames the skyen
With fire not made to burne, but fayrely for to shyne.

X

So proud she shyned in her princely state,
Looking to heaven, for earth she did disdayne,
And sitting high, for lowly she did hate:
Lo! underneath her scornefull feete was layne
A dreadfull Dragon with an hideous trayne;
And in her hand she held a mirrhour bright,
Wherein her face she often vewed fayne,
And in her selfe-lov'd semblance took delight;
For she was wondrous faire, as any living wight.

X I

Of griesly Pluto she the daughter was,
And sad Proserpina, the Queene of hell;
Yet did she thinke her pearelesse worth to pas
That parentage, with pride so did she swell;
And thundring Jove, that high in heaven doth dwell
And wield the world, she claymed for her syre,
Or if that any else did Jove excell;

For to the highest she did still aspyre,
Or, if ought higher were than that, did it desyre.

X I I

And proud Lucifera men did her call,
That made her selfe a Queene, and crownd to be;
Yet rightfull kingdome she had none at all,
Ne heritage of native soveraintie;
But did usurpe with wrong and tyrannie
Upon the scepter which she now did hold:
Ne ruld her Realme with lawes, but pollicie,
And strong advizement of six wisards old,
That, with their counsels bad, her kingdome did uphold.

X I I I

Soone as the Elfin knight in presence came,
And false Duessa, seeming Lady fayre,
A gentle Husher, Vanitie by name,
Made rowme, and passage for them did prepaire:
So goodly brought them to the lowest stayre
Of her high throne; where they, on humble knee
Making obeysaunce, did the cause declare,
Why they were come her roiall state to see,
To prove the wide report of her great Majestee.

X I V

With loftie eyes, halfe loth to looke so lowe,
She thancked them in her disdainefull wise;
Ne other grace vouchsafed them to showe
Of Princesse worthy; scarse them bad arise.
Her Lordes and Ladies all this while devise
Themselves to setten forth to straungers sight:
Some frounce their curled heare in courtly guise;
Some prancke their ruffes; and others trimly dight
Their gay attyre; each others greater pride does spight.

X V

Goodly they all that knight doe entertayne,
Right glad with him to have increast their crew;
But to Duess' each one himselfe did payne
All kindnesse and faire courtesie to shew,
For in that court whylome her well they knew:
Yet the stout Faery mongst the middest crowd
Thought all their glorie vaine in knightly vew,
And that great Princesse too exceeding prowd,
That to strange knight no better countenance allowd.

X V I

Suddein upriseth from her stately place
The roiall Dame, and for her coche doth call:
All hurtlen forth; and she, with princely pace,
As faire Aurora in her purple pall
Out of the East the dawning day doth call.
So forth she comes; her brightnes brode doth blaze.
The heapes of people, thronging in the hall,
Doe ride each other upon her to gaze:
Her glorious glitterand light doth all mens eies amaze.

X V I I

So forth she comes, and to her coche does clyme,
Adorned all with gold and girlonds gay,
That seemd as fresh as Flora in her prime;
And strove to match, in roiall rich array,
Great Junoes golden chayre; the which, they say,
The gods stand gazing on, when she does ride
To Joves high hous through heavens bras-paved way,
Drawne of fayre Pecocks, that excell in pride,
And full of Argus eyes their tayles dispredden wide.

X V I I I

But this was drawne of six unequall beasts,
On which her six sage Counsellours did ryde,
Taught to obay their bestiall beheasts,
With like conditions to their kindes applyde:
Of which the first, that all the rest did guyde,
Was sluggish Idlenesse, the nourse of sin;
Upon a slouthfull Asse he chose to ryde,
Arayd in habit blacke, and amis thin,
Like to an holy Monck, the service to begin.

X I X

And in his hand his Portesse still he bare,
That much was worne, but therein little redd;
For of devotion he had little care,
Still drownd in sleepe, and most of his daies dedd:
Scarse could he once uphold his heavie hedd,
To looken whether it were night or day.
May seeme the wayne was very evill ledd,
When such an one had guiding of the way,
That knew not whether right he went, or else astray.

xviii, 8 amis: amice, a loose gar-   xix, 1 Portesse: breviary
ment

x x

From worldly cares himselfe he did esloyne,
And greatly shunned manly exercise;
From everie worke he chalenged essoyne,
For contemplation sake: yet otherwise
His life he led in lawlesse riotise,
By which he grew to grievous malady;
For in his lustlesse limbs, through evill guise,
A shaking fever raignd continually.
Such one was Idlenesse, first of this company.

x x i

And by his side rode loathsome Gluttony,
Deformed creature, on a filthie swyne.
His belly was upblowne with luxury,
And eke with fatnesse swollen were his eyne;
And like a Crane his necke was long and fyne
With which he swallowed up excessive feast,
For want whereof poore people oft did pyne:
And all the way, most like a brutish beast,
He spued up his gorge, that all did him deteast.

x x i i

In greene vine leaves he was right fitly clad,
For other clothes he could not weare for heate;
And on his head an yvie girland had,
From under which fast trickled downe the sweat.
Still as he rode he somewhat still did eat,
And in his hand did beare a bouzing can,
Of which he supt so oft, that on his seat
His dronken corse he scarse upholden can:
In shape and life more like a monster then a man.

x x i i i

Unfit he was for any worldly thing,
And eke unhable once to stirre or go;
Not meet to be of counsell to a king,
Whose mind in meat and drinke was drowned so,
That from his frend he seeldome knew his fo.
Full of diseases was his carcas blew,
And a dry dropsie through his flesh did flow,
Which by misdiet daily greater grew.
Such one was Gluttony, the second of that crew.

xx, 1   esloyne: keep aloof
xx, 3   essoyne: excuse

xxii, 6   bouzing can: drinking cup
xxiii, 6   blew: livid

XXIV

And next to him rode lustfull Lechery
Upon a bearded Gote, whose rugged heare,
And whally eies (the signe of gelosy,)
Was like the person selfe whom he did beare:
Who rough, and blacke, and filthy, did appeare,
Unseemely man to please faire Ladies eye;
Yet he of Ladies oft was loved deare,
When fairer faces were bid standen by:
O! who does know the bent of womens fantasy?

XXV

In a greene gowne he clothed was full faire,
Which underneath did hide his filthinesse;
And in his hand a burning hart he bare,
Full of vaine follies and new fanglenesse:
For he was false, and fraught with ficklenesse,
And learned had to love with secret lookes;
And well could daunce, and sing with ruefulnesse;
And fortunes tell, and read in loving bookes,
And thousand other waies to bait his fleshly hookes.

XXVI

Inconstant man, that loved all he saw,
And lusted after all that he did love;
Ne would his looser life be tide to law,
But joyd weake wemens hearts to tempt, and prove,
If from their loyall loves he might them move:
Which lewdnes fild him with reprochfull pain
Of that foule evill, which all men reprove,
That rotts the marrow, and consumes the braine.
Such one was Lechery, the third of all this traine.

XXVII

And greedy Avarice by him did ride,
Uppon a Camell loaden all with gold:
Two iron coffers hong on either side,
With precious metall full as they might hold;
And in his lap an heap of coine he told;
For of his wicked pelfe his God he made,
And unto hell him selfe for money sold:
Accursed usury was all his trade,
And right and wrong ylike in equall ballaunce waide.

XXIV, 3   whally eies: wall-eyes

XXVIII

His life was nigh unto deaths dore yplaste;
And thred-bare cote, and cobled shoes, hee ware;
Ne scarse good morsell all his life did taste,
But both from backe and belly still did spare,
To fill his bags, and richesse to compare:
Yet childe ne kinsman living had he none
To leave them to; but thorough daily care
To get, and nightly feare to lose his owne,
He led a wretched life, unto himselfe unknowne.

XXIX

Most wretched wight, whom nothing might suffise;
Whose greedy lust did lacke in greatest store;
Whose need had end, but no end covetise;
Whose welth was want, whose plenty made him pore;
Who had enough, yett wished ever more;
A vile disease: and eke in foote and hand
A grievous gout tormented him full sore,
That well he could not touch, nor goe, nor stand.
Such one was Avarice, the fourth of this faire band.

XXX

And next to him malicious Envy rode
Upon a ravenous wolfe, and still did chaw
Between his cankred teeth a venemous tode,
That all the poison ran about his chaw;
But inwardly he chawed his owne maw
At neighbours welth, that made him ever sad,
For death it was, when any good he saw;
And wept, that cause of weeping none he had;
But when he heard of harme he wexed wondrous glad.

XXXI

All in a kirtle of discolourd say
He clothed was, ypaynted full of eies;
And in his bosome secretly there lay
An hatefull Snake, the which his taile uptyes
In many folds, and mortall sting implyes.
Still as he rode he gnasht his teeth to see
Those heapes of gold with griple Covetyse;
And grudged at the great felicitee
Of proud Lucifera, and his owne companee.

XXVIII, 5   compare: acquire   XXXI, 1   say: fine-textured cloth
XXXI, 1   discolourd: many-colored   XXXI, 7   griple: grasping

XXXII

He hated all good workes and vertuous deeds,
And him no lesse, that any like did use;
And who with gratious bread the hungry feeds,
His almes for want of faith he doth accuse.
So every good to bad he doth abuse;
And eke the verse of famous Poets witt
He does backebite, and spightfull poison spues
From leprous mouth on all that ever writt.
Such one vile Envy was, that fifte in row did sitt.

XXXIII

And him beside rides fierce revenging Wrath,
Upon a Lion, loth for to be led;
And in his hand a burning brond he hath,
The which he brandisheth about his hed:
His eies did hurle forth sparcles fiery red,
And stared sterne on all that him beheld;
As ashes pale of hew, and seeming ded;
And on his dagger still his hand he held,
Trembling through hasty rage when choler in him sweld.

XXXIV

His ruffin raiment all was staind with blood
Which he had spilt, and all to rags yrent,
Through unadvized rashnes woxen wood;
For of his hands he had no governement,
Ne car'd for blood in his avengement:
But, when the furious fitt was overpast,
His cruel facts he often would repent;
Yet, wilfull man, he never would forecast
How many mischieves should ensue his heedlesse hast.

XXXV

Full many mischiefes follow cruell Wrath:
Abhorred bloodshed, and tumultuous strife,
Unmanly murder, and unthrifty scath,
Bitter despight, with rancours rusty knife,
And fretting griefe, the enemy of life:
All these, and many evils moe haunt ire,
The swelling Splene, and Frenzy raging rife,
The shaking Palsey, and Saint Fraunces fire.
Such one was Wrath, the last of this ungodly tire.

XXXIV, 3   wood: mad   XXXIV, 7   facts: deeds

XXXVI

And, after all, upon the wagon beame,
Rode Sathan with a smarting whip in hand,
With which he forward lasht the laesy teme,
So oft as Slowth still in the mire did stand.
Huge routs of people did about them band,
Showting for joy; and still before their way
A foggy mist had covered all the land;
And, underneath their feet, all scattered lay
Dead sculls and bones of men whose life had gone astray.

XXXVII

So forth they marchen in this goodly sort,
To take the solace of the open aire,
And in fresh flowring fields themselves to sport:
Emongst the rest rode that false Lady faire,
The foule Duessa, next unto the chaire
Of proud Lucifer', as one of the traine:
But that good knight would not so nigh repaire,
Him selfe estraunging from their joyaunce vaine,
Whose fellowship seemd far unfitt for warlike swaine.

XXXVIII

So, having solaced themselves a space
With pleasaunce of the breathing fields yfed,
They backe retourned to the princely Place;
Whereas an errant knight in armes ycled,
And heathnish shield, wherein with letters red,
Was writt *Sansjoy*, they new arrived find:
Enflam'd with fury and fiers hardy hed,
He seemd in hart to harbour thoughts unkind,
And nourish bloody vengeaunce in his bitter mind.

XXXIX

Who, when the shamed shield of slaine Sansfoy
He spide with that same Faery champions page,
Bewraying him that did of late destroy
His eldest brother; burning all with rage,
He to him lept, and that same envious gage
Of victors glory from him snacht away:
But th' Elfin knight, which ought that warlike wage,
Disdaind to loose the meed he wonne in fray;
And, him rencountring fierce, reskewd the noble pray.

XXXIX, 5 envious: enviable   XXXIX, 7 ought: owned

X L

Therewith they gan to hurtlen greedily,
Redoubted battaile ready to darrayne,
And clash their shields, and shake their swerds on hy,
That with their sturre they troubled all the traine;
Till that great Queene, upon eternall paine
Of high displeasure that ensewen might,
Commaunded them their fury to refraine;
And, if that either to that shield had right,
In equall lists they should the morrow next it fight.

X L I

'Ah dearest Dame,' quoth then the Paynim bold,
'Pardon the error of enraged wight,
Whome great griefe made forgett the raines to hold
Of reasons rule, to see this recreaunt knight,
No knight, but treachour full of false despight
And shameful treason, who through guile hath slayn
The prowest knight that ever field did fight,
Even stout Sansfoy, (O who can then refrayn?)
Whose shield he beares renverst, the more to heap disdayn.

X L I I

'And, to augment the glorie of his guile,
His dearest love, the faire Fidessa, loe!
Is there possessed of the traytour vile;
Who reapes the harvest sowen by his foe,
Sowen in bloodie field, and bought with woe:
That brothers hand shall dearely well requight,
So be, O Queene! you equall favour showe.'
Him litle answerd th' angry Elfin knight;
He never meant with words, but swords, to plead his right:

X L I I I

But threw his gauntlet, as a sacred pledge
His cause in combat the next day to try:
So been they parted both, with harts on edge
To be aveng'd each on his enimy.
That night they pas in joy and jollity,
Feasting and courting both in bowre and hall;
For Steward was excessive Gluttony,
That of his plenty poured forth to all:
Which doen, the Chamberlain, Slowth, did to rest them call.

XL, 2 darrayne: wage

X L I V

Now whenas darkesome night had all displayd
Her coleblacke curtein over brightest skye;
The warlike youthes, on dayntie couches layd,
Did chace away sweet sleepe from sluggish eye,
To muse on meanes of hoped victory.
But whenas Morpheus had with leaden mace
Arrested all that courtly company,
Uprose Duessa from her resting place,
And to the Paynims lodging comes with silent pace.

X L V

Whom broad awake she findes, in troublous fitt,
Fore-casting how his foe he might annoy;
And him amoves with speaches seeming fitt:
'Ah deare Sansjoy, next dearest to Sansfoy,
Cause of my new griefe, cause of my new joy;
Joyous to see his ymage in mine eye,
And greevd to thinke how foe did him destroy,
That was the flowre of grace and chevalrye;
Lo! his Fidessa, to thy secret faith I flye.'

X L V I

With gentle wordes he can her fayrely greet,
And bad say on the secrete of her hart:
Then, sighing soft; 'I learne that litle sweet
Oft tempred is,' (quoth she,) 'with muchell smart:
For since my brest was launcht with lovely dart
Of deare Sansfoy, I never joyed howre,
But in eternall woes my weaker hart
Have wasted, loving him with all my powre,
And for his sake have felt full many an heavie stowre.

X L V I I

'At last, when perils all I weened past,
And hop'd to reape the crop of all my care,
Into new woes unweeting I was cast
By this false faytor, who unworthie ware
His worthie shield, whom he with guilefull snare
Entrapped slew, and brought to shamefull grave:
Me, silly maid, away with him he bare,
And ever since hath kept in darksome cave,
For that I would not yeeld that to Sansfoy I gave.

XLVI, 1   can: did

XLVIII

'But since faire Sunne hath sperst that lowring clowd,
And to my loathed life now shewes some light,
Under your beames I will me safely shrowd
From dreaded storme of his disdainfull spight:
To you th' inheritance belonges by right
Of brothers prayse, to you eke longes his love.
Let not his love, let not his restlesse spright,
Be unreveng'd that calles to you above
From wandring Stygian shores, where it doth endlesse move.'

XLIX

Thereto said he, 'Faire Dame, be nought dismaid
For sorrowes past; their griefe is with them gone:
Ne yet of present perill be affraid,
For needlesse feare did never vantage none;
And helplesse hap it booteth not to mone.
Dead is Sansfoy, his vitall paines are past,
Though greeved ghost for vengeance deep do grone:
He lives that shall him pay his dewties last,
And guiltie Elfin blood shall sacrifice in hast.'

L

'O! but I feare the fickle freakes,' (quoth shee)
'Of fortune false, and oddes of armes in field.'
'Why, dame,' (quoth he) 'what oddes can ever bee,
Where both doe fight alike, to win or yield?'
'Yea, but,' (quoth she) 'he beares a charmed shield,
And eke enchaunted armes, that none can perce:
Ne none can wound the man that does them wield.'
'Charmd or enchaunted,' answerd he then ferce,
'I no whitt reck; ne you the like need to reherce.

LI

'But, faire Fidessa, sithens fortunes guile,
Or enimies powre, hath now captived you,
Returne from whence ye came, and rest a while,
Till morrow next that I the Elfe subdew,
And with Sansfoyes dead dowry you endew.'
'Ay me! that is a double death,' (she said)
'With proud foes sight my sorrow to renew,
Where ever yet I be, my secret aide
Shall follow you.' So, passing forth, she him obaid.

XLIX, 5   helplesse: beyond help

CANTO V.

The faithfull knight in equall field
Subdewes his faithlesse foe;
Whom false Duessa saves, and for
His cure to hell does goe.

I

THE NOBLE HART that harbours vertuous thought,
And is with childe of glorious great intent,
Can never rest, untill it forth have brought
Th'eternall brood of glorie excellent:
Such restlesse passion did all night torment
The flaming corage of that Faery knight,
Devizing how that doughtie turnament
With greatest honour he atchieven might:
Still did he wake, and still did watch for dawning light.

I I

At last, the golden Orientall gate
Of greatest heaven gan to open fayre;
And Phoebus, fresh as brydegrome to his mate,
Came dauncing forth, shaking his deawie hayre.
And hurld his glistring beams through gloomy ayre.
Which when the wakeful Elfe perceiv'd, streightway,
He started up, and did him selfe prepayre
In sunbright armes, and battailous array;
For with that Pagan proud he combatt will that day.

I I I

And forth he comes into the commune hall;
Where earely waite him many a gazing eye,
To weet what end to straunger knights may fall.
There many Minstrales maken melody,
To drive away the dull melancholy;
And many Bardes, that to the trembling chord
Can tune their timely voices cunningly;
And many Chroniclers, that can record
Old loves, and warres for Ladies doen by many a Lord.

I V

Soone after comes the cruell Sarazin,
In woven maile all armed warily;
And sternly lookes at him, who not a pin
Does care for looke of living creatures eye.

They bring them wines of Greece and Araby,
And daintie spices fetch from furthest Ynd,
To kindle heat of corage privily;
And in the wine a solemne oth they bynd
T'observe the sacred lawes of armes that are assynd.

V

At last forth comes that far renowmed Queene:
With royall pomp and princely majestie
She is ybrought unto a paled greene,
And placed under stately canapee,
The warlike feates of both those knights to see.
On th' other side in all mens open vew
Duessa placed is, and on a tree
Sansfoy his shield is hangd with bloody hew;
Both those the lawrell girlonds to the victor dew.

V I

A shrilling trompett sownded from on hye,
And unto battaill bad them selves addresse:
Their shining shieldes about their wrestes they tye,
And burning blades about their heades doe blesse,
The instruments of wrath and heavinesse.
With greedy force each other doth assayle,
And strike so fiercely, that they do impresse
Deepe dinted furrowes in the battred mayle:
The yron walles to ward their blowes are weak and fraile.

V I I

The Sarazin was stout and wondrous strong,
And heaped blowes like yron hammers great;
For after blood and vengeance he did long:
The knight was fiers, and full of youthly heat,
And doubled strokes, like dreaded thunders threat;
For all for praise and honour he did fight.
Both stricken stryke, and beaten both doe beat,
That from their shields forth flyeth firie light,
And hewen helmets deepe shew marks of eithers might.

V I I I

So th' one for wrong, the other strives for right.
As when a Gryfon, seized of his pray,
A Dragon fiers encountreth in his flight,
Through widest ayre making his ydle way,

v, 3   paled: fenced   vi, 4   blesse: brandish

That would his rightfull ravine rend away:
With hideous horror both together smight,
And souce so sore that they the heavens affray;
The wise Southsayer, seeing so sad sight,
Th' amazed vulgar telles of warres and mortall fight.

                    I X

So th' one for wrong, the other strives for right,
And each to deadly shame would drive his foe:
The cruell steele so greedily doth bight
In tender flesh, that streames of blood down flow;
With which the armes, that earst so bright did show,
Into a pure vermillion now are dyde.
Great ruth in all the gazers harts did grow,
Seeing the gored woundes to gape so wyde,
That victory they dare not wish to either side.

                    x

At last the Paynim chaunst to cast his eye,
His suddein eye flaming with wrathfull fyre,
Upon his brothers shield, which hong thereby:
Therewith redoubled was his raging yre,
And said; 'Ah! wretched sonne of wofull syre,
Doest thou sit wayling by blacke Stygian lake,
Whylest here thy shield is hanged for victors hyre?
And, sluggish german, doest thy forces slake
To after-send his foe, that him may overtake?

                    X I

'Goe, caytive Elfe, him quickly overtake,
And soone redeeme from his long-wandring woe:
Goe, guiltie ghost, to him my message make,
That I his shield have quit from dying foe.'
Therewith upon his crest he stroke him so,
That twise he reeled, readie twise to fall:
End of the doubtfull battaile deemed tho
The lookers on; and lowd to him gan call
The false Duessa, 'Thine the shield, and I, and all!'

                    X I I

Soone as the Faerie heard his Ladie speake,
Out of his swowning dreame he gan awake;
And quickning faith, that earst was woxen weake,

viii, 5   ravine: prey   x, 8   german: brother
viii, 7   souce: swoop

The creeping deadly cold away did shake:
Tho mov'd with wrath, and shame, and Ladies sake,
Of all attonce he cast avengd to be,
And with so' exceeding furie at him strake,
That forced him to stoupe upon his knee:
Had he not stouped so, he should have cloven bee.

X I I I

And to him said; 'Goe now, proud Miscreant,
Thyselfe thy message do to german deare;
Alone he, wandring, thee too long doth want:
Goe say, his foe thy shield with his doth beare.'
Therewith his heavie hand he high gan reare,
Him to have slaine; when lo! a darkesome clowd
Upon him fell: he no where doth appeare,
But vanisht is. The Elfe him calls alowd,
But answer none receives; the darknes him does shrowd.

X I V

In haste Duessa from her place arose,
And to him running said; 'O! prowest knight,
That ever Ladie to her love did chose,
Let now abate the terrour of your might,
And quench the flame of furious despight,
And bloodie vengeance: lo! th' infernall powres,
Covering your foe with cloud of deadly night,
Have borne him hence to Plutoes balefull bowres:
The conquest yours; I yours; the shield, and glory yours.'

X V

Not all so satisfide, with greedy eye
He sought all round about, his thristy blade
To bathe in blood of faithlesse enimy;
Who all that while lay hid in secret shade.
He standes amazed how he thence should fade:
At last the trumpets Triumph sound on hie;
And running Heralds humble homage made,
Greeting him goodly with new victorie,
And to him brought the shield, the cause of enmitie.

X V I

Wherewith he goeth to that soveraine Queene;
And falling her before on lowly knee,
To her makes present of his service seene:
Which she accepts with thankes and goodly gree,

xvi, 3   seene: skilled   xvi, 4   gree: gratitude

Greatly advauncing his gay chevalree:
So marcheth home, and by her takes the knight,
Whom all the people followe with great glee,
Shouting, and clapping all their hands on hight,
That all the ayre it fills, and flyes to heaven bright.

X V I I

Home is he brought, and layd in sumptuous bed,
Where many skilfull leaches him abide
To salve his hurts, that yet still freshly bled.
In wine and oyle they wash his woundes wide,
And softly gan embalme on everie side:
And all the while most heavenly melody
About the bed sweet musicke did divide,
Him to beguile of griefe and agony:
And all the while Duessa wept full bitterly.

X V I I I

As when a wearie traveiler, that strayes
By muddy shore of broad seven-mouthed Nile,
Unweeting of the perillous wandring wayes,
Doth meete a cruell craftie Crocodile,
Which, in false griefe hyding his harmefull guile,
Doth weepe full sore, and sheddeth tender teares;
The foolish man, that pities all this while
His mournefull plight, is swallowed up unwares,
Forgetfull of his owne that mindes an others cares.

X I X

So wept Duessa untill eventyde,
That shyning lampes in Joves high house were light;
Then forth she rose, ne lenger would abide,
But comes unto the place where th' Hethen knight,
In slombring swownd, nigh voyd of vitall spright,
Lay cover'd with inchaunted cloud all day:
Whom when she found, as she him left in plight,
To wayle his wofull case she would not stay,
But to the Easterne coast of heaven makes speedy way:

X X

Where griesly Night, with visage deadly sad,
That Phoebus chearefull face durst never vew,
And in a foule blacke pitchy mantle clad,
She findes forth comming from her darksome mew,
Where she all day did hide her hated hew.

XVII, 7   divide: perform

Before the dore her yron charet stood,
Already harnessed for journey new,
And cole blacke steedes yborne of hellish brood,
That on their rusty bits did champ as they were wood.

X X I

Who when she saw Duessa, sunny bright,
Adornd with gold and jewels shining cleare,
She greatly grew amazed at the sight,
And th' unacquainted light began to feare,
For never did such brightnes there appeare;
And would have backe retyred to her cave,
Untill the witches speach she gan to heare,
Saying; 'Yet, O thou dreaded Dame! I crave
Abyde, till I have told the message which I have.'

X X I I

She stayd; and foorth Duessa gan proceede:
'O! thou most auncient Grandmother of all.
More old then Jove, whom thou at first didst breede,
Or that great house of Gods caelestiall,
Which wast begot in Daemogorgons hall,
And sawst the secrets of the world unmade.
Why suffredst thou thy Nephewes deare to fall,
With Elfin sword most shamefully betrade?
Lo! where the stout Sansjoy doth sleepe in deadly shade.

X X I I I

'And him before, I saw with bitter eyes
The bold Sansfoy shrinck underneath his speare:
And now the pray of fowles in field he lyes,
Nor wayld of friends, nor layd on groning beare,
That whylome was to me too dearely deare.
O! what of gods then boots it to be borne,
If old Aveugles sonnes so evill heare?
Or who shall not great Nightes children scorne,
When two of three her Nephewes are so fowle forlorne?

X X I V

'Up, then! up, dreary Dame, of darknes Queene!
Go, gather up the reliques of thy race;
Or else goe them avenge, and let be seene
That dreaded Night in brightest day hath place,
And can the children of fayre light deface.'
Her feeling speaches some compassion mov'd

XXII, 7 Nephewes: descendants

In hart, and chaunge in that great mothers face:
Yet pitty in her hart was never prov'd
Till then, for evermore she hated, never lov'd:

X X V

And said, 'Deare daughter, rightly may I rew
The fall of famous children borne of mee,
And good successes which their foes ensew:
But who can turne the stream of destinee,
Or breake the chayne of strong necessitee,
Which fast is tyde to Joves eternall seat?
The sonnes of Day he favoureth, I see,
And by my ruines thinkes to make them great:
To make one great by others losse is bad excheat.

X X V I

'Yet shall they not escape so freely all,
For some shall pay the price of others guilt;
And he the man that made Sansfoy to fall,
Shall with his owne blood price that he hath spilt.
But what art thou, that telst of Nephews kilt?'
'I, that do seeme not I, Duessa ame,'
Quoth she, 'how ever now, in garments gilt
And gorgeous gold arayd, I to thee came,
Duessa I, the daughter of Deceipt and Shame.'

X X V I I

Then, bowing downe her aged backe, she kist
The wicked witch, saying, 'In that fayre face
Tho false resemblaunce of Deceipt, I wist,
Did closely lurke; yet so true-seeming grace
It carried, that I scarse in darksome place
Could it discerne, though I the mother bee
Of falshood, and roote of Duessaes race.
O welcome, child! whom I have longd to see,
And now have seene unwares. Lo! now I goe with thee.'

X X V I I I

Then to her yron wagon she betakes,
And with her beares the fowle welfavourd witch.
Through mirkesome aire her ready way she makes:
Her twyfold Teme, of which two blacke as pitch,
And two were browne, yet each to each unlich,
Did softly swim away, ne ever stamp
Unlesse she chaunst their stubborne mouths to twitch;

xxv, 9   excheat: gain   xxvi, 4   price: pay for

Then, foming tarre, their bridles they would champ,
And trampling the fine element would fiercely ramp.

X X I X

So well they sped, that they be come at length
Unto the place whereas the Paynim lay,
Devoid of outward sence and native strength,
Coverd with charmed cloud from vew of day,
And sight of men, since his late luckelesse fray.
His cruell wounds, with cruddy bloud congeald,
They binden up so wisely as they may,
And handle softly, till they can be heald:
So lay him in her charett, close in night conceald.

X X X

And, all the while she stood upon the ground,
The wakefull dogs did never cease to bay,
As giving warning of th' unwonted sound,
With which her yron wheeles did them affray,
And her darke griesly looke them much dismay;
The messenger of death, the ghastly owle,
With drery shriekes did also her bewray;
And hungry wolves continually did howle
At her abhorred face, so filthy and so fowle.

X X X I

Thence turning backe in silence softe they stole,
And brought the heavy corse with easy pace
To yawning gulfe of deepe Avernus hole.
By that same hole an entraunce, darke and bace,
With smoake and sulphur hiding all the place,
Descends to hell: there creature never past,
That backe retourned without heavenly grace;
But dreadfull Furies, which their chaines have brast,
And damned sprights sent forth to make ill men aghast.

X X X I I

By that same way the direfull dames doe drive
Their mournefull charett, fild with rusty blood,
And downe to Plutoes house are come bilive:
Which passing through, on every side them stood
The trembling ghosts with sad amazed mood,
Chattring their iron teeth, and staring wide
With stony eies; and all the hellish brood

XXXII, 3   bilive: speedily

Of feends infernall flockt on every side,
To gaze on erthly wight that with the Night durst ride.

X X X I I I

They pas the bitter waves of Acheron,
Where many soules sit wailing woefully,
And come to fiery flood of Phlegeton,
Whereas the damned ghosts in torments fry,
And with sharp shrilling shriekes doe bootlesse cry,
Cursing high Jove, the which them thither sent.
The house of endlesse paine is built thereby,
In which ten thousand sorts of punishment
The cursed creatures doe eternally torment.

X X X I V

Before the threshold dreadfull Cerberus
His three deformed heads did lay along,
Curled with thousand adders venemous,
And lilled forth his bloody flaming tong:
At them he gan to reare his bristles strong,
And felly gnarre, untill Dayes enemy
Did him appease; then downe his taile he hong,
And suffered them to passen quietly;
For she in hell and heaven had power equally.

X X X V

There was Ixion turned on a wheele,
For daring tempt the Queene of heaven to sin;
And Sisyphus an huge round stone did reele
Against an hill, ne might from labour lin;
There thristy Tantalus hong by the chin;
And Tityus fed a vultur on his maw;
Typhoeus joynts were stretched on a gin;
Theseus condemned to endlesse slouth by law;
And fifty sisters water in leake vessels draw.

X X X V I

They all, beholding worldly wights in place,
Leave off their worke, unmindfull of their smart,
To gaze on them; who forth by them doe pace,
Till they be come unto the furthest part;
Where was a Cave ywrought by wondrous art.
Deepe, darke, uneasy, dolefull, comfortlesse,
In which sad Æsculapius far apart

xxxv, 4   lin: cease   xxxv, 7   gin: machine

Emprisond was in chaines remedilesse;
For that Hippolytus rent corse he did redresse.

X X X V I I

Hippolytus a jolly huntsman was,
That wont in charett chace the foming bore:
He all his Peeres in beauty did surpas,
But Ladies love as losse of time forbore:
His wanton stepdame loved him the more;
But, when she saw her offred sweets refusd,
Her love she turnd to hate, and him before
His father fierce of treason false accusd,
And with her gealous termes his open eares abusd:

X X X V I I I

Who, all in rage, his Sea-god syre besought
Some cursed vengeaunce on his sonne to cast.
From surging gulf two Monsters streight were brought,
With dread whereof his chacing steedes aghast
Both charett swifte and huntsman overcast:
His goodly corps, on ragged cliffs yrent,
Was quite dismembred, and his members chast
Scattered on every mountaine as he went,
That of Hippolytus was lefte no moniment.

X X X I X

His cruell step-dame, seeing what was donne,
Her wicked daies with wretched knife did end,
In death avowing th' innocence of her sonne.
Which hearing, his rash syre began to rend
His heare, and hasty tong that did offend:
Tho, gathering up the reliques of his smart,
By Dianes meanes, who was Hippolyts frend,
Them brought to Aesculape, that by his art
Did heale them all againe, and joyned every part.

X L

Such wondrous science in mans witt to rain
When Jove avizd, that could the dead revive,
And fates expired could renew again,
Of endlesse life he might him not deprive,
But unto hell did thrust him downe alive,
With flashing thunderbolt ywounded sore:
Where, long remaining, he did alwaies strive
Himselfe with salves to health for to restore,
And slake the heavenly fire that raged evermore.

X L I

There auncient Night arriving did alight
From her nigh weary wayne, and in her armes
To Aesculapius brought the wounded knight:
Whome having softly disaraid of armes,
Tho gan to him discover all his harmes,
Beseeching him with prayer and with praise,
If either salves, or oyles, or herbes, or charmes,
A fordonne wight from dore of death mote raise,
He would at her request prolong her nephews daies.

X L I I

'Ah Dame,' (quoth he) 'thou temptest me in vaine,
To dare the thing, which daily yet I rew,
And the old cause of my continued paine
With like attempt to like end to renew.
Is not enough, that, thrust from heaven dew,
Here endlesse penaunce for one fault I pay,
But that redoubled crime with vengeaunce new
Thou biddest me to eeke? Can Night defray
The wrath of thundring Jove, that rules both night and day?'

X L I I I

'Not so,' (quoth she) 'but, sith that heavens king
From hope of heaven hath thee excluded quight,
Why fearest thou, that canst not hope for thing;
And fearest not that more thee hurten might,
Now in the powre of everlasting Night?
Goe to then, O thou far renowmed sonne
Of great Apollo! shew thy famous might
In medicine, that els hath to thee wonne
Great pains, and greater praise, both never to be donne.'

X L I V

Her words prevaild: And then the learned leach
His cunning hand gan to his wounds to lay,
And all things els the which his art did teach:
Which having seene, from thence arose away
The mother of dredd darknesse, and let stay
Aveugles sonne there in the leaches cure;
And, backe retourning, took her wonted way
To ronne her timely race, whilst Phoebus pure
In westerne waves his weary wagon did recure.

XLII, 8   eeke: add to

X L V

The false Duessa, leaving noyous Night,
Returnd to stately pallace of Dame Pryde:
Where when she came, she found the Faery knight
Departed thence; albee his woundes wyde
Not throughly heald unready were to ryde.
Good cause he had to hasten thence away;
For on a day his wary Dwarfe had spyde
Where in a dungeon deepe huge nombers lay
Of caytive wretched thralls, that wayled night and day:

X L V I

A ruefull sight as could be seene with eie,
Of whom he learned had in secret wise
The hidden cause of their captivitie;
How mortgaging their lives to Covetise,
Through wastfull Pride and wanton Riotise,
They were by law of that proud Tyrannesse,
Provokt with Wrath and Envyes false surmise,
Condemned to that Dongeon mercilesse,
Where they should live in wo, and dye in wretchednesse.

X L V I I

There was that great proud king of Babylon,
That would compell all nations to adore,
And him as onely God to call upon;
Till, through celestiall doome thrown out of dore,
Into an Oxe he was transformed of yore.
There also was king Croesus, that enhaunst
His hart too high through his great richesse store;
And proud Antiochus, the which advaunst
His cursed hand gainst God, and on his altares daunst.

X L V I I I

And them long time before, great Nimrod was,
That first the world with sword and fire warrayd;
And after him old Ninus far did pas
In princely pomp, of all the world obayd.
There also was that mightie Monarch layd
Low under all, yet above all in pride,
That name of native syre did fowle upbrayd,
And would as Ammons sonne be magnifide,
Till, scornd of God and man, a shamefull death he dide.

X L I X

All these together in one heape were throwne,
Like carkases of beastes in butchers stall.
And in another corner wide were strowne
The Antique ruins of the Romanes fall:
Great Romulus, the Grandsyre of them all;
Proud Tarquin, and too lordly Lentulus;
Stout Scipio, and stubborne Hanniball;
Ambitious Sylla, and sterne Marius;
High Caesar, great Pompey, and fiers Antonius.

L

Amongst these mightie men were wemen mixt,
Proud wemen, vaine, forgetfull of their yoke:
The bold Semiramis, whose sides transfixt
With sonnes own blade her fowle reproches spoke:
Fayre Sthenoboea, that her selfe did choke
With wilfull chord for wanting of her will;
High minded Cleopatra, that with stroke
Of Aspes sting her selfe did stoutly kill;
And thousands moe the like that did that dongeon fill.

L I

Besides the endlesse routes of wretched thralles,
Which thither were assembled day by day
From all the world, after their wofull falles,
Through wicked pride and wasted welthes decay.
But most of all, which in that dongeon lay,
Fell from high Princes courtes, or Ladies bowres,
Where they in ydle pomp, or wanton play,
Consumed had their goods and thriftlesse howres,
And lastly thrown themselves into these heavy stowres.

L I I

Whose case whenas the carefull Dwarfe had tould,
And made ensample of their mournfull sight
Unto his Maister, he no lenger would
There dwell in perill of like painefull plight,
But earely rose; and, ere that dawning light
Discovered had the world to heaven wyde,
He by a privy Posterne tooke his flight,
That of no envious eyes he mote be spyde:
For, doubtlesse, death ensewd if any him descryde.

L I I I

Scarse could he footing find in that fowle way,
For many corses, like a great Lay-stall,
Of murdred men, which therein strowed lay
Without remorse or decent funerall;
Which al through that great Princesse pride did fall,
And came to shamefull end. And them besyde,
Forth ryding underneath the castell wall,
A Donghill of dead carcases he spyde:
The dreadfull spectacle of that sad house of Pryde.

CANTO VI.

From lawlesse lust by wondrous grace
Fayre Una is releast:
Whom salvage nation does adore,
And learnes her wise beheast.

I

As when a ship, that flyes fayre under sayle,
An hidden rocke escaped hath unwares,
That lay in waite her wrack for to bewaile,
The Marriner yet halfe amazed stares
At perill past, and yet in doubt ne dares
To joy at his foolhappie oversight:
So doubly is distrest twixt joy and cares
The dreadlesse corage of this Elfin knight,
Having escapt so sad ensamples in his sight.

I I

Yet sad he was, that his too hastie speed
The fayre Duess' had forst him leave behind;
And yet more sad, that Una, his deare dreed,
Her truth had staynd with treason so unkind:
Yet cryme in her could never creature find;
But for his love, and for her own selfe sake,
She wandred had from one to other Ynd,
Him for to seeke, ne ever would forsake,
Till her unwares the fiers Sansloy did overtake:

I I I

Who, after Archimagoes fowle defeat,
Led her away into a forest wilde;

LIII, 2   Lay-stall: refuse heap   II, 4   unkind: unnatural

And, turning wrathfull fyre to lustfull heat,
With beastly sin thought her to have defilde,
And made the vassall of his pleasures vilde.
Yet first he cast by treatie, and by traynes
Her to persuade that stubborne fort to yilde:
For greater conquest of hard love he gaynes,
That workes it to his will, then he that it constraines.

         I V

With fawning wordes he courted her a while;
And, looking lovely and oft sighing sore,
Her constant hart did tempt with diverse guile:
But wordes, and lookes, and sighes she did abhore;
As rock of Diamond stedfast evermore.
Yet for to feed his fyrie lustfull eye,
He snatcht the vele that hong her face before:
Then gan her beautie shyne as brightest skye,
And burnt his beastly hart t'efforce her chastitye.

         V

So when he saw his flatt'ring artes to fayle,
And subtile engines bett from batteree;
With greedy force he gan the fort assayle,
Whereof he weend possessed soone to bee,
And win rich spoile of ransackt chastitee.
Ah heavens! that doe this hideous act behold,
And heavenly virgin thus outraged see,
How can ye vengeance just so long withhold,
And hurle not flashing flames upon that Paynim bold?

         V I

The pitteous mayden, carefull, comfortlesse,
Does throw out thrilling shriekes, and shrieking cryes,
The last vaine helpe of wemens great distresse,
And with loud plaintes importuneth the skyes,
That molten starres doe drop like weeping eyes;
And Phoebus. flying so most shamefull sight,
His blushing face in foggy cloud implyes,
And hydes for shame. What witt of mortal wight
Can now devise to quitt a thrall from such a plight?

         V I I

Eternal providence, exceeding thought,
Where none appeares can make her selfe a way.
A wondrous way it for this Lady wrought,
From Lyons clawes to pluck the gryped pray.

Her shrill outcryes and shrieks so loud did bray,
That all the woodes and forestes did resownd:
A troupe of Faunes and Satyres far away
Within the wood were dauncing in a rownd,
Whiles old Sylvanus slept in shady arber sownd:

VIII

Who, when they heard that pitteous strained voice,
In haste forsooke their rurall meriment,
And ran towardes the far rebownded noyce,
To weet what wight so loudly did lament.
Unto the place they come incontinent:
Whom when the raging Sarazin espyde,
A rude, mishapen, monstrous rablement,
Whose like he never saw, he durst not byde,
But got his ready steed, and fast away gan ryde.

I X

The wyld woodgods, arrived in the place,
There find the virgin, doolfull, desolate,
With ruffled rayments, and fayre blubbred face,
As her outrageous foe had left her late;
And trembling yet through feare of former hate.
All stand amazed at so uncouth sight,
And gin to pittie her unhappie state:
All stand astonied at her beautie bright,
In their rude eyes unworthie of so wofull plight.

X

She, more amazd, in double dread doth dwell;
And every tender part for feare does shake.
As when a greedy Wolfe, through honger fell,
A seely Lamb far from the flock does take,
Of whom he meanes his bloody feast to make,
A Lyon spyes fast running towards him,
The innocent pray in hast he does forsake;
Which, quitt from death, yet quakes in every lim
With chaunge of feare, to see the Lyon looke so grim.

X I

Such fearefull fitt assaid her trembling hart,
Ne word to speake, ne joynt to move, she had;
The salvage nation feele her secret smart,
And read her sorrow in her count'nance sad;
Their frowning forheades, with rough hornes yclad,

And rustick horror, all asyde doe lay;
And, gently grenning, shew a semblance glad
To comfort her; and, feare to put away,
Their backward bent knees teach her humbly to obay.

X I I

The doubtfull Damzell dare not yet committ
Her single person to their barbarous truth;
But still twixt feare and hope amazd does sitt,
Late learnd what harme to hasty trust ensu'th.
They, in compassion of her tender youth,
And wonder of her beautie soverayne,
Are wonne with pitty and unwonted ruth;
And, all prostrate upon the lowly playne,
Doe kisse her feete, and fawne on her with count'nance fayne.

X I I I

Their harts she ghesseth by their humble guise,
And yieldes her to extremitie of time:
So from the ground she fearelesse doth arise,
And walketh forth without suspect of crime.
They, all as glad as birdes of joyous Pryme,
Thence lead her forth, about her dauncing round,
Shouting, and singing all a shepheards ryme;
And with greene braunches strowing all the ground,
Do worship her as Queene with olive girlond cround.

X I V

And all the way their merry pipes they sound,
That all the woods with doubled Eccho ring;
And with their horned feet doe weare the ground,
Leaping like wanton kids in pleasant Spring.
So towards old Sylvanus they her bring;
Who, with the noyse awaked, commeth out
To weet the cause, his weake steps governing
And aged limbs on cypresse stadle stout,
And with an yvie twyne his waste is girt about.

X V

Far off he wonders what them makes so glad;
Or Bacchus merry fruit they did invent,
Or Cybeles franticke rites have made them mad:
They, drawing nigh, unto their God present
That flowre of fayth and beautie excellent.

xiv, 8   stadle: staff   xv, 2   invent: find

The God himselfe, vewing that mirrhour rare,
Stood long amazd, and burnt in his intent:
His owne fayre Dryope now he thinkes not faire,
And Pholoe fowle, when her to this he doth compaire.

XVI

The woodborne people fall before her flat,
And worship her as Goddesse of the wood;
And old Sylvanus selfe bethinkes not what
To thinke of wight so fayre, but gazing stood
In doubt to deeme her borne of earthly brood:
Sometimes dame Venus selfe he seemes to see;
But Venus never had so sober mood:
Sometimes Diana he her takes to be,
But misseth bow and shaftes, and buskins to her knee.

XVII

By vew of her he ginneth to revive
His ancient love, and dearest Cyparisse;
And calles to mind his pourtraiture alive,
How fayre he was, and yet not fayre to this;
And how he slew with glauncing dart amisse
A gentle Hynd, the which the lovely boy
Did love as life, above all worldly blisse;
For griefe whereof the lad n'ould after joy,
But pynd away in anguish and selfe-wild annoy.

XVIII

The wooddy nymphes, faire Hamadryades,
Her to behold do thither runne apace;
And all the troupe of light-foot Naiades
Flocke all about to see her lovely face;
But, when they vewed have her heavenly grace,
They envy her in their malitious mind,
And fly away for feare of fowle disgrace:
But all the Satyres scorne their woody kind,
And henceforth nothing faire but her on earth they find.

XIX

Glad of such lucke, the luckelesse lucky mayd
Did her content to please their feeble eyes,
And long time with that salvage people stayd,
To gather breath in many miseryes.
During which time her gentle wit she plyes
To teach them truth, which worship her in vaine,
And made her th' Image of Idolatryes;

But when their bootlesse zeale she did restrayne
From her own worship, they her Asse would worship fayn.

X X

It fortuned, a noble warlike knight
By just occasion to that forrest came
To seeke his kindred, and the lignage right
From whence he tooke his weldeserved name:
He had in armes abroad wonne muchell fame,
And fild far landes with glorie of his might:
Plaine, faithfull, true, and enimy of shame,
And ever lov'd to fight for Ladies right;
But in vaine glorious frayes he litle did delight.

X X I

A Satyres sonne, yborne in forrest wyld,
By straunge adventure as it did betyde,
And there begotten of a Lady myld,
Fayre Thyamis, the daughter of Labryde;
That was in sacred bandes of wedlocke tyde
To Therion, a loose unruly swayne,
Who had more joy to raunge the forrest wyde,
And chase the salvage beast with busie payne,
Then serve his Ladies love, and waste in pleasures vayne.

X X I I

The forlorne mayd did with loves longing burne,
And could not lacke her lovers company;
But to the woods she goes, to serve her turne,
And seeke her spouse that from her still does fly,
And followes other game and venery:
A Saytre chaunst her wandring for to finde;
And, kindling coles of lust in brutish eye,
The loyall linkes of wedlocke did unbinde,
And made her person thrall unto his beastly kind.

X X I I I

So long in secret cabin there he held
Her captive to his sensuall desyre,
Till that with timely fruit her belly sweld,
And bore a boy unto that salvage syre:
Then home he suffred her for to retyre,
For ransome leaving him the late-borne childe;
Whom, till to ryper yeares he gan aspyre,
He nousled up in life and manners wilde,
Emongst wild beastes and woods, from lawes of men exilde.

XXIV

For all he taught the tender ymp was but
To banish cowardize and bastard feare:
His trembling hand he would him force to put
Upon the Lyon and the rugged Beare;
And from the she Beares teats her whelps to teare;
And eke wyld roring Buls he would him make
To tame, and ryde their backes, not made to beare;
And the Robuckes in flight to overtake,
That everie beast for feare of him did fly, and quake.

XXV

Thereby so fearlesse and so fell he grew,
That his own syre, and maister of his guise,
Did often tremble at his horrid vew;
And oft, for dread of hurt, would him advise
The angry beastes not rashly to despise,
Nor too much to provoke; for he would learne
The Lyon stoup to him in lowly wise,
(A lesson hard) and make the Libbard sterne
Leave roaring, when in rage he for revenge did earne.

XXVI

And for to make his powre approved more,
Wyld beastes in yron yokes he would compell;
The spotted Panther, and the tusked Bore,
The Pardale swift, and the Tigre cruell,
The Antelope, and Wolfe both fiers and fell;
And them constraine in equall teme to draw.
Such joy he had their stubborne harts to quell,
And sturdie courage tame with dreadfull aw,
That his beheast they feared as a tyrans law.

XXVII

His loving mother came upon a day
Unto the woodes, to see her little sonne;
And chaunst unwares to meet him in the way,
After his sportes and cruell pastime donne;
When after him a Lyonesse did runne,
That roaring all with rage did lowd requere
Her children deare, whom he away had wonne:
The Lyon whelpes she saw how he did beare,
And lull in rugged armes withouten childish feare.

XXVIII

The fearefull Dame all quaked at the sight,
And turning backe gan fast to fly away;

Untill, with love revokt from vaine affright,
She hardly yet perswaded was to stay,
And then to him these womanish words gan say:
'Ah Satyrane, my dearling and my joy,
For love of me leave off this dreadfull play;
To dally thus with death is no fit toy:
Go, find some other play-fellowes, mine own sweet boy.'

X X I X

In these and like delightes of bloody game
He trayned was, till ryper years he raught;
And there abode, whylst any beast of name
Walkt in that forrest, whom he had not taught
To feare his force: and then his courage haught
Desyrd of forreine foemen to be knowne,
And far abroad for straunge adventures sought;
In which his might was never overthrowne;
But through al Faery lond his famous worth was blown.

X X X

Yet evermore it was his manner faire,
After long labours and adventures spent,
Unto those native woods for to repaire,
To see his syre and ofspring auncient.
And now he thither came for like intent;
Where he unwares the fairest Una found,
Straunge Lady in so straunge habiliment,
Teaching the Satyres, which her sat around,
Trew sacred lore, which from her sweet lips did redound.

X X X I

He wondred at her wisedome hevenly rare,
Whose like in womens witt he never knew;
And, when her curteous deeds he did compare,
Gan her admire, and her sad sorrowes rew,
Blaming of Fortune, which such troubles threw.
And joyd to make proofe of her cruelty
On gentle Dame, so hurtlesse and so trew:
Thenceforth he kept her goodly company,
And learnd her discipline of faith and verity.

X X X I I

But she, all vowd unto the Redcrosse Knight,
His wandring perill closely did lament,
Ne in this new acquaintaunce could delight;
But her deare heart with anguish did torment,
And all her witt in secret counsels spent,

How to escape. At last in privy wise
To Satyrane she shewed her intent;
Who, glad to gain such favour, gan devise,
How with that pensive Maid he best might thence arise.

XXXIII

So on a day, when Satyres all were gone
To do their service to Sylvanus old,
The gentle virgin, left behinde alone,
He led away with corage stout and bold.
Too late it was to Satyres to be told,
Or ever hope recover her againe:
In vaine he seeks that having cannot hold.
So fast he carried her with carefull paine,
That they the woods are past, and come now to the plaine.

XXXIV

The better part now of the lingring day
They traveild had, whenas they far espide
A weary wight forwandring by the way;
And towards him they gan in haste to ride,
To weete of newes that did abroad betide,
Or tidings of her knight of the Redcrosse;
But he them spying gan to turne aside
For feare, as seemd, or for some feigned losse:
More greedy they of newes fast towards him do crosse.

XXXV

A silly man, in simple weeds forworne,
And soild with dust of the long dried way;
His sandales were with toilsome travell torne,
And face all tand with scorching sunny ray,
As he had traveild many a sommers day
Through boyling sands of Arabie and Ynde,
And in his hand a Jacobs staffe, to stay
His weary limbs upon; and eke behind
His scrip did hang, in which his needments he did bind.

XXXVI

The knight, approching nigh, of him inquerd
Tidings of warre, and of adventures new;
But warres, nor new adventures, none he herd.
Then Una gan to aske, if ought he knew,
Or heard abroad of that her champion trew,
That in his armour bare a croslet red?
'Ay me! Deare dame,' (quoth he) 'well may I rew

To tell the sad sight which mine eies have red;
These eies did see that knight both living and eke ded.'

X X X V I I

That cruell word her tender hart so thrild,
That suddein cold did ronne through every vaine,
And stony horrour all her sences fild
With dying fitt, that downe she fell for paine.
The knight her lightly reared up againe,
And comforted with curteous kind reliefe:
Then, wonne from death, she bad him tellen plaine
The further processe of her hidden griefe:
The lesser pangs can beare who hath endur'd the chief.

X X X V I I I

Then gan the Pilgrim thus: 'I chaunst this day,
This fatall day that shall I ever rew,
To see two knights, in travell on my way,
(A sory sight) arraung'd in batteill new,
Both breathing vengeaunce, both of wrathfull hew.
My-fearefull flesh did tremble at their strife,
To see their blades so greedily imbrew,
That, dronke with blood, yet thristed after life:
What more? The Redcrosse knight was slain with Paynim
knife.'

X X X I X

'Ah! dearest Lord,' (quoth she) 'how might that bee,
And he the stoutest knight that ever wonne?'
'Ah! dearest dame,' (quoth hee) 'how might I see
The thing that might not be, and yet was donne?'
'Where is,' (said Satyrane) 'that Paynims sonne,
That him of life, and us of joy, hath refte?'
'Not far away,' (quoth he) 'he hence doth wonne,
Foreby a fountaine, where I late him lefte
Washing his bloody wounds, that through the steele were
cleft.'

X L

Therewith the knight thence marched forth in hast,
Whiles Una, with huge heavinesse opprest,
Could not for sorrow follow him so fast;
And soone he came, as he the place had ghest,
Whereas that Pagan proud him selfe did rest
In secret shadow by a fountaine side:

XXXIX, 2 wonne: lived   XXXIX, 7 wonne: dwell

Even he it was, that earst would have supprest
Faire Una; whom when Satyrane espide,
With foule reprochfull words he boldly him defide.

X L I

And said; 'Arise, thou cursed Miscreaunt,
That hast with knightlesse guile, and trecherous train,
Faire knighthood fowly shamed, and doest vaunt
That good knight of the Redcrosse to have slain:
Arise, and with like treason now maintain
Thy guilty wrong, or els thee guilty yield.'
The Sarazin, this hearing, rose amain,
And, catching up in hast his three-square shield
And shining helmet, soone him buckled to the field.

X L I I

And, drawing nigh him, said; 'Ah! misborn Elfe,
In evill houre thy foes thee hither sent
Anothers wrongs to wreak upon thy selfe:
Yet ill thou blamest me for having blent
My name with guile and traiterous intent:
That Redcrosse knight, perdie, I never slew:
But had he beene where earst his armes were lent,
Th'enchaunter vaine his errour should not rew:
But thou his errour shalt, I hope, now proven trew.'

X L I I I

Therewith they gan, both furious and fell,
To thunder blowes, and fiersly to assaile
Each other, bent his enimy to quell,
That with their force they perst both plate and maile,
And made wide furrowes in their fleshes fraile,
That it would pitty any living eie.
Large floods of blood adowne their sides did raile,
But floods of blood could not them satisfie:
Both hongred after death; both chose to win, or die.

X L I V

So long they fight, and full revenge pursue,
That, fainting, each themselves to breathen lett,
And, ofte refreshed, battell oft renue.
As when two Bores, with rancling malice mett,
Their gory sides fresh bleeding fiercely frett;
Til breathlesse both themselves aside retire,

xli, 8   three-square: triangular   xliii, 7   raile: flow
xlii, 4   blent: stained

Where foming wrath their cruell tuskes they whett,
And trample th' earth, the whiles they may respire,
Then backe to fight againe, new breathed and entire.

X L V

So fiersly, when these knights had breathed once,
They gan to fight retourne, increasing more
Their puissant force, and cruell rage attonce,
With heaped strokes more hugely then before;
That with their drery wounds, and bloody gore,
They both, deformed, scarsely could bee known.
By this, sad Una fraught with anguish sore,
Led with their noise which through the aire was thrown,
Arriv'd wher they in erth their fruitles blood had sown.

X L V I

Whom all so soone as that proud Sarazin
Espide, he gan revive the memory
Of his leud lusts, and late attempted sin,
And lefte the doubtfull battell hastily,
To catch her, newly offred to his eie,
But Satyrane, with strokes him turning, staid,
And sternely bad him other businesse plie
Then hunt the steps of pure unspotted Maid:
Wherewith he al enrag'd these bitter speaches said.

X L V I I

'O foolish faeries soone! what fury mad
Hath thee incenst to hast thy dolefull fate?
Were it not better I that Lady had
Then that thou hadst repented it too late?
Most sencelesse man he, that himselfe doth hate,
To love another: Lo! then, for thine ayd,
Here take thy lovers token on thy pate.'
So they to fight; the whiles the royall Mayd
Fledd farre away, of that proud Paynim sore afrayd.

X L V I I I

But that false Pilgrim, which that leasing told,
Being in deed old Archimage, did stay
In secret shadow all this to behold;
And much rejoyced in their bloody fray:
But, when he saw the Damsell passe away,
He left his stond, and her pursewd apace,
In hope to bring her to her last decay.

XLVIII, 1   leasing: lie

But for to tell her lamentable cace,
And eke this battels end, will need another place.

CANTO VII.

The Redcrosse knight is captive made
By Gyaunt proud opprest:
Prince Arthure meets with Una great-
ly with those newes distrest.

I

What man so wise, what earthly witt so ware,
As to discry the crafty cunning traine,
By which deceipt doth maske in visour faire,
And cast her coulours, died deepe in graine,
To seeme like truth, whose shape she well can faine,
And fitting gestures to her purpose frame,
The guiltlesse man with guile to entertaine?
Great maistresse of her art was that false Dame,
The false Duessa, cloked with Fidessaes name.

I I

Who when, returning from the drery Night,
She fownd not in that perilous hous of Pryde,
Where she had left the noble Redcrosse knight,
Her hoped pray, she would no lenger byde,
But forth she went to seeke him far and wide.
Ere long she fownd, whereas he wearie sate
To reste him selfe foreby a fountaine syde,
Disarmed all of yron-coted Plate;
And by his side his steed the grassy forage ate.

I I I

Hee feedes upon the cooling shade, and bayes
His sweatie forehead in the breathing wynd,
Which through the trembling leaves full gently playes,
Wherein the chearefull birds of sundry kynd
Doe chaunt sweet musick to delight his mynd.
The witch approching gan him fayrely greet,
And with reproch of carelesnes unkynd
Upbrayd, for leaving her in place unmeet,
With fowle words tempring faire, soure gall with hony sweet.

I V

Unkindnesse past, they gan of solace treat,
And bathe in pleasaunce of the joyous shade,

Which shielded them against the boyling heat,
And with greene boughes decking a gloomy glade,
About the fountaine like a girlond made;
Whose bubbling wave did ever freshly well,
Ne ever would through fervent sommer fade:
The sacred Nymph, which therein wont to dwell,
Was out of Dianes favor, as it then befell.

       v

The cause was this: one day, when Phœbe fayre
With all her band was following the chace,
This nymph, quite tyr'd with heat of scorching ayre,
Satt downe to rest in middest of the race:
The goddesse wroth gan fowly her disgrace,
And badd the waters, which from her did flow,
Be such as she her selfe was then in place.
Thenceforth her waters wexed dull and slow,
And all that drinke thereof do faint and feeble grow.

       v i

Hereof this gentle knight unweeting was;
And lying downe upon the sandie graile,
Dronke of the streame, as cleare as christall glas:
Eftsoones his manly forces gan to fayle,
And mightie strong was turnd to feeble frayle.
His chaunged powres at first them selves not felt,
Till crudled cold his corage gan assayle,
And cheareful blood in fayntnes chill did melt,
Which like a fever fit through all his bodie swelt.

       v i i

Yet goodly court he made still to his Dame,
Pourd out in loosnesse on the grassy grownd,
Both carelesse of his healthe, and of his fame;
Till at the last he heard a dreadfull sownd,
Which through the wood loud bellowing did rebownd,
That all the earth for terror seemd to shake,
And trees did tremble. Th' Elfe, therewith astownd,
Upstarted lightly from his looser make,
And his unready weapons gan in hand to take.

       v i i i

But ere he could his armour on him dight,
Or gett his shield, his monstrous enimy
With sturdie steps came stalking in his sight,

vi, 2   graile: gravel   vi, 9   swelt: burned
vi, 7   crudled: curdled   vii, 8   make: mate

An hideous Geaunt, horrible and hye,
That with his tallnesse seemd to threat the skye;
The ground eke groned under him for dreed:
His living like saw never living eye,
Ne durst behold: his stature did exceed
The hight of three the tallest sonnes of mortall seed.

I X

The greatest Earth his uncouth mother was,
And blustring Æolus his boasted syre;
Who with his breath, which through the world doth pas,
Her hollow womb did secretly inspyre,
And fild her hidden caves with stormie yre,
That she conceiv'd; and trebling the dew time
In which the wombes of wemen doe expyre,
Brought forth this monstrous masse of earthly slyme,
Puft up with emptie wynd, and fild with sinfull cryme.

x

So growen great, through arrogant delight
Of th' high descent whereof he was yborne,
And through presumption of his matchlesse might,
All other powres and knighthood he did scorne.
Such now he marcheth to this man forlorne,
And left to losse; his stalking steps are stayde
Upon a snaggy Oke, which he had torne
Out of his mothers bowelles, and it made
His mortall mace, wherewith his foemen he dismayde.

X I

That, when the knight he spyde, he gan advaunce
With huge force and insupportable mayne,
And towardes him with dreadfull fury praunce;
Who haplesse, and eke hopelesse, all in vaine
Did to him pace sad battaile to darrayne,
Disarmd, disgraste, and inwardly dismayde;
And eke so faint in every joynt and vayne,
Through that fraile fountain which him feeble made,
That scarsely could he weeld his bootlesse single blade.

X I I

The Geaunt strooke so maynly mercilesse,
That could have overthrowne a stony towre;
And, were not hevenly grace that did him blesse,
He had beene pouldred all as thin as flowre:

XI, 2   mayne: strength

But he was wary of that deadly stowre,
And lightly lept from underneath the blow:
Yet so exceeding was the villeins powre,
That with the winde it did him overthrow,
And all his sences stound that still he lay full low.

X I I I

As when that divelish yron Engin, wrought
In deepest Hell, and framd by Furies skill,
With windy Nitre and quick Sulphur fraught,
And ramd with bollet rownd, ordaind to kill,
Conceiveth fyre, the heavens it doth fill
With thundring noyse, and all the ayre doth choke,
That none can breath, nor see, nor heare at will,
Through smouldry cloud of duskish stincking smoke;
That th' only breath him daunts, who hath escapt the stroke.

X I V

So daunted when the Geaunt saw the knight,
His heavie hand he heaved up on hye,
And him to dust thought to have battred quight,
Until Duessa loud to him gan crye,
'O great Orgoglio! greatest under skye,
O! hold thy mortall hand for Ladies sake;
Hold for my sake, and doe him not to dye,
But vanquisht thine eternall bondslave make,
And me, thy worthy meed, unto thy Leman take.'

X V

He hearkned, and did stay from further harmes,
To gayne so goodly guerdon as she spake:
So willingly she came into his armes,
Who her as willingly to grace did take,
And was possessed of his newfound make.
Then up he tooke the slombred sencelesse corse,
And, ere he could out of his swowne awake,
Him to his castle brought with hastie forse,
And in a Dongeon deepe him threw without remorse.

X V I

From that day forth Duessa was his deare,
And highly honourd in his haughtie eye:
He gave her gold and purple pall to weare,
And triple crowne set on her head full hye,
And her endowd with royall majestye.
Then, for to make her dreaded more of men,

And peoples hartes with awfull terror tye,
A monstrous beast ybredd in filthy fen
He chose, which he had kept long time in darksom den.

X V I I

Such one it was, as that renowmed Snake
Which great Alcides in Stremona slew,
Long fostred in the filth of Lerna lake:
Whose many heades, out budding ever new,
Did breed him endlesse labor to subdew.
But this same Monster much more ugly was,
For seven great heads out of his body grew,
An yron brest, and back of scaly bras,
And all embrewd in blood his eyes did shine as glas.

X V I I I

His tayle was stretched out in wondrous length,
That to the hous of hevenly gods it raught:
And with extorted powre, and borrow'd strength,
The everburning lamps from thence it braught,
And prowdly threw to ground, as things of naught;
And underneath his filthy feet did tread
The sacred thinges, and holy heastes foretaught.
Upon this dreadfull Beast with sevenfold head
He sett the false Duessa, for more aw and dread.

X I X

The wofull Dwarfe, which saw his maisters fall
Whiles he had keeping of his grasing steed,
And valiant knight become a caytive thrall,
When all was past, tooke up his forlorne weed;
His mightie Armour, missing most at need;
His silver shield, now idle, maisterlesse;
His poynant speare that many made to bleed,
The rueful moniments of heavinesse;
And with them all departes to tell his great distresse.

X X

He had not travaild long, when on the way
He wofull Lady, wofull Una, met,
Fast flying from that Paynims greedy pray,
Whilest Satyrane him from pursuit did let.
Who when her eyes she on the Dwarf had set,
And saw the signes that deadly tydinges spake,
She fell to ground for sorrowfull regret,

XIX, 7   poynant: keen   xx, 4   let: prevent

And lively breath her sad brest did forsake;
Yet might her pitteous hart be seene to pant and quake.

X X I

The messenger of so unhappie newes
Would faine have dyde: dead was his hart within,
Yet outwardly some little comfort shewes.
At last, recovering hart, he does begin
To rubb her temples, and to chaufe her chin,
And everie tender part does tosse and turne:
So hardly he the flitted life does win
Unto her native prison to retourne;
Then gins her grieved ghost thus to lament and mourne:

X X I I

'Ye dreary instruments of dolefull sight,
That doe this deadly spectacle behold,
Why doe ye lenger feed on loathed light,
Or liking find to gaze on earthly mould,
Sith cruell fates the carefull threds unfould,
The which my life and love together tyde?
Now let the stony dart of sencelesse cold
Perce to my hart, and pas through everie side,
And let eternall night so sad sight fro me hyde.

X X I I I

'O lightsome day! the lampe of highest Jove,
First made by him mens wandring wayes to guyde,
When darknesse he in deepest dongeon drove,
Henceforth thy hated face for ever hyde,
And shut up heavens windowes shyning wyde;
For earthly sight can nought but sorrow breed,
And late repentance which shall long abyde:
Mine eyes no more on vanitie shall feed,
But seeled up with death shall have their deadly meed.'

X X I V

Then downe againe she fell unto the ground,
But he her quickly reared up againe:
Thrise did she sinke adowne in deadly swownd,
And thrise he her reviv'd with busie paine.
At last when life recover'd had the raine,
And over-wrestled his strong enimy,
With foltring tong, and trembling everie vaine,
'Tell on,' (quoth she) 'the wofull Tragedy,
The which these reliques sad present unto mine eye.

X X V

'Tempestuous fortune hath spent all her spight,
And thrilling sorrow throwne his utmost dart:
Thy sad tong cannot tell more heavy plight
Then that I feele, and harbour in mine hart:
Who hath endur'd the whole can beare ech part.
If death it be, it is not the first wound
That launched hath my brest with bleeding smart.
Begin, and end the bitter balefull stound;
If lesse then that I feare, more favour I have found.'

X X V I

Then gan the Dwarfe the whole discourse declare;
The subtile traines of Archimago old;
The wanton loves of false Fidessa fayre,
Bought with the blood of vanquisht Paynim bold;
The wretched payre transformd to treën mould;
The house of Pryde, and perilles round about;
The combat which he with Sansjoy did hould;
The lucklesse conflict with the Gyaunt stout,
Wherein captiv'd, of life or death he stood in doubt.

[margin, handwritten:] Summary of RCK's adventures

X X V I I

She heard with patience all unto the end,
And strove to maister sorrowfull assay,
Which greater grew the more she did contend,
And almost rent her tender hart in tway,
And love fresh coles unto her fire did lay;
For greater love, the greater is the losse.
Was never Lady loved dearer day
Then she did love the knight of the Redcrosse,
For whose deare sake so many troubles her did tosse.

X X V I I I

At last when fervent sorrow slaked was,
She up arose, resolving him to find
Alive or dead; and forward forth doth pas,
All as the Dwarfe the way to her assynd;
And evermore, in constant carefull mind,
She fedd her wound with fresh renewed bale.
Long tost with stormes, and bet with bitter wind,
High over hills, and lowe adowne the dale,
She wandred many a wood, and measurd many a vale.

XXVII, 2   assay: tribulation

X X I X

At last she chaunced by good hap to meet
A goodly knight, faire marching by the way,
Together with his Squyre, arayed meet:
His glitterand armour shined far away,
Like glauncing light of Phœbus brightest ray;
From top to toe no place appeared bare,
That deadly dint of steele endanger may.
Athwart his brest a bauldrick brave he ware,
That shind, like twinkling stars, with stones most pretious
　　　rare.

X X X

And in the midst thereof one pretious stone
Of wondrous worth, and eke of wondrous mights,
Shapt like a Ladies head, exceeding shone,
Like Hesperus emongst the lesser lights,
And strove for to amaze the weaker sights:
Thereby his mortall blade full comely hong
In yvory sheath, ycarv'd with curious slights,
Whose hilts were burnisht gold, and handle strong
Of mother perle; and buckled with a golden tong.

X X X I

His haughtie Helmet, horrid all with gold,
Both glorious brightnesse and great terrour bredd:
For all the crest a Dragon did enfold
With greedie pawes, and over all did spredd
His golden winges: his dreadfull hideous hedd,
Close couched on the bever, seemd to throw
From flaming mouth bright sparckles fiery redd,
That suddeine horrour to faint hartes did show;
And scaly tayle was stretcht adowne his back full low.

X X X I I

Upon the top of all his loftie crest,
A bounch of heares discolourd diversly,
With sprincled pearle and gold full richly drest,
Did shake, and seemd to daunce for jollity,
Like to an almond tree ymounted hye
On top of greene Selinis all alone,
With blossoms brave bedecked daintily;
Whose tender locks do tremble every one
At everie little breath that under heaven is blowne.

XXXIII

His warlike shield all closely cover'd was,
Ne might of mortall eye be ever seene;
Not made of steele, nor of enduring bras,
Such earthly mettals soon consumed beene,
But all of Diamond perfect pure and cleene
It framed was, one massy entire mould,
Hewen out of Adamant rocke with engines keene,
That point of speare it never percen could,
Ne dint of direfull sword divide the substance would.

XXXIV

The same to wight he never wont disclose,
But whenas monsters huge he would dismay,
Or daunt unequall armies of his foes,
Or when the flying heavens he would affray;
For so exceeding shone his glistring ray,
That Phœbus golden face it did attaint,
As when a cloud his beames doth over-lay;
And silver Cynthia wexed pale and faynt,
As when her face is staynd with magicke arts constraint.

XXXV

No magicke arts hereof had any might,
Nor bloody wordes of bold Enchaunters call;
But all that was not such as seemd in sight
Before that shield did fade, and suddeine fall:
And when him list the raskall routes appall,
Men into stones therewith he could transmew,
And stones to dust, and dust to nought at all;
And, when him list the prouder lookes subdew,
He would them gazing blind, or turne to other hew.

XXXVI

Ne let it seeme that credence this exceedes;
For he that made the same was knowne right well
To have done much more admirable deedes.
It Merlin was, which whylome did excell
All living wightes in might of magicke spell:
Both shield and sword, and armour all he wrought
For this young Prince, when first to armes he fell;
But, when he dyde, the Faery Queene it brought
To Faerie lond, where yet it may be seene, if sought:

xxxv, 5   raskall: base

XXXVII

A gentle youth, his dearely loved Squire,
His speare of heben wood behind him bare,
Whose harmeful head, thrise heated in the fire,
Had riven many a brest with pikehead square:
A goodly person, and could menage faire
His stubborne steed with curbed canon bitt,
Who under him did trample as the aire,
And chauft that any on his backe should sitt:
The yron rowels into frothy fome he bitt.

XXXVIII

Whenas this knight nigh to the Lady drew,
With lovely court he gan her entertaine;
But, when he heard her answers loth, he knew
Some secret sorrow did her heart distraine;
Which to allay, and calme her storming paine,
Faire feeling words he wisely gan display,
And for her humor fitting purpose faine,
To tempt the cause it selfe for to bewray,
Wherewith enmovd, these bleeding words she gan to say.

XXXIX

'What worlds delight, or joy of living speach,
Can hart, so plungd in sea of sorrowes deep,
And heaped with so huge misfortunes, reach?
The carefull cold beginneth for to creep,
And in my heart his yron arrow steep,
Soone as I thinke upon my bitter bale.
Such helplesse harmes yts better hidden keep,
Then rip up griefe where it may not availe:
My last left comfort is my woes to weepe and waile.'

XL

'Ah Lady deare,' quoth then the gentle knight,
'Well may I ween your griefe is wondrous great;
For wondrous great griefe groneth in my spright,
Whiles thus I heare you of your sorrowes treat.
But, woefull Lady, let me you intrete,
For to unfold the anguish of your hart:
Mishaps are maistred by advice discrete,
And counsell mitigates the greatest smart:
Found never help who never would his hurts impart.'

XXXVII, 2   heben: ebony   XXXVIII, 4   distraine: distress

X L I

'O, but,' (quoth she) 'great griefe will not be tould,
And can more easily be thought then said.'
'Right so,' (quoth he) 'but he that never would
Could never: will to might gives greatest aid.'
'But griefe,' (quoth she) 'does greater grow displaid,
If then it find not helpe, and breeds despaire.'
'Despaire breeds not,' (quoth he) 'where faith is staid.'
'No faith so fast,' (quoth she) 'but flesh does paire.'
'Flesh may empaire,' (quoth he) 'but reason can repaire.'

X L I I

His goodly reason, and well-guided speach,
So deepe did settle in her gracious thought,
That her perswaded to disclose the breach
Which love and fortune in her heart had wrought;
And said; 'Faire Sir, I hope good hap hath brought
You to inquere the secrets of my griefe,
Or that your wisedome will direct my thought,
Or that your prowesse can me yield reliefe:
Then, heare the story sad, which I shall tell you briefe.

X L I I I

'The forlorne Maiden, whom your eies have seene
The laughing stocke of fortunes mockeries,
Am th' onely daughter of a King and Queene,
Whose parents deare, whiles equal destinies
Did ronne about, and their felicities
The favourable heavens did not envy,
Did spred their rule through all the territories,
Which Phison and Euphrates floweth by,
And Gehons golden waves doe wash continually:

X L I V

'Till that their cruell cursed enemy,
An huge great Dragon, horrible in sight,
Bred in the loathly lakes of Tartary,
With murdrous ravine, and devouring might,
Their kingdome spoild, and countrey wasted quight:
Themselves, for feare into his jawes to fall,
He forst to castle strong to take their flight;
Where, fast embard in mighty brasen wall,
He has them now fowr years besiegd to make them thrall.

XLI, 8   paire: impair

XLV

'Full many knights, adventurous and stout,
Have enterpriz'd that Monster to subdew.
From every coast that heaven walks about,
Have thither come the noble Martial crew
That famous harde atchievements still pursew;
Yet never any could that girlond win,
But all still shronke, and still he greater grew:
All they, for want of faith, or guilt of sin,
The pitteous pray of his fiers cruelty have bin.

XLVI

'At last, yled with far reported praise,
Which flying fame throughout the world had spred,
Of doughty knights, whom Faery land did raise,
That noble order hight of maidenhed,
Forthwith to court of Gloriane I sped,
Of Gloriane, great Queene of glory bright,
Whose kingdomes seat Cleopolis is red;
There to obtaine some such redoubted knight,
That Parents deare from tyrants powre deliver might.

XLVII

'Yt was my chaunce (my chaunce was faire and good)
There for to find a fresh unproved knight;
Whose manly hands imbrewd in guilty blood
Had never beene, ne ever by his might
Had throwne to ground the unregarded right:
Yet of his prowesse proofe he since hath made
(I witnes am) in many a cruell fight;
The groning ghosts of many one dismaide
Have felt the bitter dint of his avenging blade.

XLVIII

'And ye, the forlorne reliques of his powre,
His biting sword, and his devouring speare,
Which have endured many a dreadfull stowre,
Can speake his prowesse that did earst you beare,
And well could rule; now he hath left you heare
To be the record of his ruefull losse,
And of my dolefull disaventurous deare.
O! heavie record of the good Redcrosse,
Where have yee left your lord that could so well you tosse?

XLVIII, 7   deare: injury

X L I X

'Well hoped I, and faire beginnings had,
That he my captive languor should redeeme:
Till, all unweeting, an Enchaunter bad
His sence abusd, and made him to misdeeme
My loyalty, not such as it did seeme,
That rather death desire then such despight.
Be judge, ye heavens, that all things right esteeme,
How I him lov'd, and love with all my might.
So thought I eke of him, and think I thought aright.

L

'Thenceforth me desolate he quite forsooke,
To wander where wilde fortune would me lead,
And other bywaies he himselfe betooke,
Where never foote of living wight did tread,
That brought not backe the balefull body dead:
In which him chaunced false Duessa meete,
Mine onely foe, mine onely deadly dread;
Who with her witchcraft, and misseeming sweete,
Inveigled him to follow her desires unmeete.

L I

'At last, by subtile sleights she him betraid
Unto his foe, a Gyaunt huge and tall;
Who him disarmed, dissolute, dismaid,
Unwares surprised, and with mighty mall
The monster mercilesse him made to fall,
Whose fall did never foe before behold:
And now in darkesome dungeon, wretched thrall,
Remedilesse for aie he doth him hold.
This is my cause of griefe, more great then may be told.'

L I I

Ere she had ended all she gan to faint:
But he her comforted, and faire bespake:
'Certes, Madame, ye have great cause of plaint;
That stoutest heart, I weene, could cause to quake:
But be of cheare, and comfort to you take;
For till I have acquitt your captive knight,
Assure your selfe I will you not forsake.'
His chearefull words reviv'd her chearelesse spright,
So forth they went, the Dwarfe them guiding ever right.

LI, 4   mall: club

CANTO VIII.

Faire virgin, to redeeme her deare,
Brings Arthure to the fight:
Who slayes the Gyaunt, wounds the beast,
And strips Duessa quight.

I

Ay me! how many perils doe enfold
The righteous man, to make him daily fall,
Were not that heavenly grace doth him uphold,
And stedfast truth acquite him out of all.
Her love is firme, her care continuall,
So oft as he, through his own foolish pride
Or weaknes, is to sinfull bands made thrall:
Els should this Redcrosse knight in bands have dyde,
For whose deliverance she this Prince doth thither guyd.

I I

They sadly traveild thus, untill they came
Nigh to a castle builded strong and hye:
Then cryde the Dwarfe, 'Lo! yonder is the same,
In which my Lord, my liege, doth lucklesse ly
Thrall to that Gyaunts hatefull tyranny:
Therefore, deare Sir, your mightie powres assay.'
The noble knight alighted by and by
From loftie steed, and badd the Ladie stay
To see what end of fight should him befall that day.

I I I

So with his Squire, th' admirer of his might,
He marched forth towardes that castle wall,
Whose gates he fownd fast shutt, ne living wight
To warde the same, nor answere commers call.
Then tooke that Squire an horne of bugle small,
Which hong adowne his side in twisted gold
And tasselles gay. Wyde wonders over all
Of that same hornes great virtues weren told,
Which had approved bene in uses manifold.

I V

Was never wight that heard that shrilling sownd,
But trembling feare did feel in every vaine:
Three miles it might be easy heard arownd,

III, 5　bugle: wild ox

And Ecchoes three aunswer'd it selfe againe:
No false enchauntment, nor deceiptfull traine,
Might once abide the terror of that blast,
But presently was void and wholly vaine:
No gate so strong, no locke so firme and fast,
But with that percing noise flew open quite, or brast.

V

The same before the Geaunts gate he blew,
That all the castle quaked from the grownd,
And every dore of freewill open flew.
The Gyaunt selfe, dismaied with that sownd,
Where he with his Duessa dalliaunce fownd,
In hast came rushing forth from inner bowre,
With staring countenance sterne, as one astownd,
And staggering steps, to weet what suddein stowre
Had   wrought   that   horror   strange,   and   dar'd   his   dreaded
      powre.

V I

And after him the proud Duessa came,
High mounted on her many headed beast,
And every head with fyrie tongue did flame,
And every head was crowned on his creast,
And bloody mouthed with late cruell feast.
That when the knight beheld, his mightie shild
Upon his manly arme he soone addrest,
And at him fiersly flew, with corage fild,
And eger greedinesse through every member thrild.

V I I

Therewith the Gyant buckled him to fight,
Inflamd with scornefull wrath and high disdaine,
And lifting up his dreadfull club on hight,
All armd with ragged snubbes and knottie graine,
Him thought at first encounter to have slaine.
But wise and wary was that noble Pere;
And, lightly leaping from so monstrous maine,
Did fayre avoide the violence him nere:
It booted nought to thinke such thunderbolts to beare.

V I I I

Ne shame he thought to shonne so hideous might:
The ydle stroke, enforcing furious way,
Missing the marke of his misaymed sight,
Did fall to ground, and with his heavy sway

So deepely dinted in the driven clay,
That three yardes deepe a furrow up did throw.
The sad earth, wounded with so sore assay,
Did grone full grievous underneath the blow,
And trembling with strange feare did like an erthquake show.

I X

As when almightie Jove, in wrathfull mood,
To wreake the guilt of mortall sins is bent,
Hurles forth his thundring dart with deadly food
Enrold in flames, and smouldring dreriment,
Through riven cloudes and molten firmament,
The fiers threeforked engin, making way,
Both loftie towres and highest trees hath rent,
And all that might his angry passage stay;
And, shooting in the earth, castes up a mount of clay.

X

His boystrous club, so buried in the grownd,
He could not rearen up againe so light,
But that the Knight him at advantage fownd;
And, whiles he strove his combred clubbe to quight
Out of the earth, with blade all burning bright
He smott off his left arme, which like a block
Did fall to ground, depriv'd of native might:
Large streames of blood out of the truncked stock
Forth gushed, like fresh water streame from riven rocke.

X I

Dismayed with so desperate deadly wound,
And eke impatient of unwonted payne,
He loudly brayd with beastly yelling sownd,
That all the fieldes rebellowed againe.
As great a noyse, as when in Cymbrian plaine
An heard of Bulles, whom kindly rage doth sting,
Doe for the milky mothers want complaine,
And fill the fieldes with troublous bellowing:
The neighbor woods arownd with hollow murmur ring.

X I I

That when his deare Duessa heard, and saw
The evil stownd that daungerd her estate,
Unto his aide she hastily did draw
Her dreadfull beast; who, swolne with blood of late,
Came ramping forth with proud presumpteous gate,
And threatned all his heades like flaming brandes.

But him the Squire made quickly to retrate,
Encountring fiers with single sword in hand:
And twixt him and his Lord did like a bulwarke stand.

X I I I

The proud Duessa, full of wrathfull spight,
And fiers disdaine to be affronted so,
Enforst her purple beast with all her might,
That stop out of the way to overthroe,
Scorning the let of so unequall foe:
But nathemore would that corageous swayne
To her yeeld passage gainst his Lord to goe,
But with outrageous strokes did him restraine,
And with his body bard the way atwixt them twaine.

X I V

Then tooke the angrie witch her golden cup,
Which still she bore, replete with magick artes;
Death and despeyre did many thereof sup,
And secret poyson through their inner partes,
Th' eternall bale of heavie wounded harts:
Which, after charmes and some enchauntments said,
She lightly sprinkled on his weaker partes:
Therewith his sturdie corage soon was quayd,
And all his sences were with suddein dread dismayd.

X V

So downe he fell before the cruell beast,
Who on his neck his bloody clawes did seize,
That life nigh crusht out of his panting brest:
No powre he had to stirre, nor will to rize.
That when the carefull knight gan well avise,
He lightly left the foe with whom he fought,
And to the beast gan turne his enterprise,
For wondrous anguish in his hart it wrought,
To see his loved Squyre into such thraldom brought:

X V I

And, high advauncing his blood-thirstie blade,
Stroke one of those deformed heades so sore,
That of his puissaunce proud ensample made:
His monstrous scalpe downe to his teeth it tore,
And that misformed shape misshaped more.
A sea of blood gusht from the gaping wownd,
That her gay garments staynd with filthy gore,

XIV, 2   still: always   XIV, 8   quayd: subdued

And overflowed all the field arownd,
That over shoes in blood he waded on the grownd.

X V I I

Thereat he rored for exceeding paine,
That to have heard great horror would have bred;
And scourging th' emptie ayre with his long trayne,
Through great impatience of his grieved hed,
His gorgeous ryder from her loftie sted
Would have cast downe, and trodd in durty myre,
Had not the Gyaunt soone her succoured;
Who, all enrag'd with smart and frantick yre,
Came hurtling in full fiers, and forst the knight retyre.

X V I I I

The force, which wont in two to be disperst,
In one alone left hand he now unites,
Which is through rage more strong then both were erst;
With which his hideous club aloft he dites,
And at his foe with furious rigor smites,
That strongest Oake might seeme to overthrow.
The stroke upon his shield so heavie lites,
That to the ground it doubleth him full low:
What mortall wight could ever beare so monstrous blow?

X I X

And in his fall his shield, that covered was,
Did loose his vele by chaunce, and open flew;
The light whereof, that hevens light did pas,
Such blazing brightnesse through the ayer threw,
That eye mote not the same endure to vew.
Which when the Gyaunt spyde with staring eye,
He downe let fall his arme, and soft withdrew
His weapon huge, that heaved was on hye
For to have slain the man, that on the ground did lye.

X X

And eke the fruitfull-headed beast, amazd
At flashing beames of that sunshiny shield,
Became stark blind, and all his sences dazd,
That downe he tumbled on the durtie field,
And seemd himselfe as conquered to yield.
Whom when his maistresse proud perceiv'd to fall,
Whiles yet his feeble feet for faintnesse reeled,
Unto the Gyaunt lowdly she gan call;
'O! helpe, Orgoglio; helpe! or els we perish all.'

X X I

At her so pitteous cry was much amoov'd
Her champion stout; and for to ayde his frend,
Againe his wonted angry weapon proov'd,
But all in vaine, for he has redd his end
In that bright shield, and all their forces spend
Them selves in vaine: for, since that glauncing sight,
He hath no powre to hurt, nor to defend,
As where th' Almighties lightning brond does light,
It dimmes the dazed eyen, and daunts the sences quight.

X X I I

Whom when the Prince, to batteill new addrest
And threatning high his dreadfull stroke, did see,
His sparkling blade about his head he blest,
And smote off quite his right leg by the knee,
That downe he tombled; as an aged tree,
High growing on the top of rocky clift,
Whose hartstrings with keene steele nigh hewen be;
The mightie trunck, halfe rent with ragged rift,
Doth roll adowne the rocks, and fall with fearefull drift.

X X I I I

Or as a Castle, reared high and round,
By subtile engins and malitious slight
Is undermined from the lowest ground,
And her foundation forst, and feebled quight,
At last downe falles; and with her heaped hight
Her hastie ruine does more heavie make,
And yields it selfe unto the victours might.
Such was this Gyaunts fall, that seemd to shake
The stedfast globe of earth, as it for feare did quake.

X X I V

The knight, then lightly leaping to the pray,
With mortall steele him smot againe so sore,
That headlesse his unweldy bodie lay,
All wallowd in his owne fowle bloody gore,
Which flowed from his wounds in wondrous store.
But, soone as breath out of his brest did pas,
That huge great body, which the Gyaunt bore,
Was vanisht quite; and of that monstrous mas
Was nothing left, but like an emptie blader was.

X X V

Whose grievous fall when false Duessa spyde,
Her golden cup she cast unto the ground,
And crowned mitre rudely threw asyde:
Such percing griefe her stubborne hart did wound,
That she could not endure that dolefull stound
But leaving all behind her fled away:
The light-foot Squyre her quickly turnd around,
And, by hard meanes enforcing her to stay,
So brought unto his Lord as his deserved pray.

X X V I

The roiall Virgin which beheld from farre,
In pensive plight and sad perplexitie,
The whole atchievement of this doubtfull warre,
Came running fast to greet his victorie,
With sober gladnesse and myld modestie;
And with sweet joyous cheare him thus bespake:
'Fayre braunch of noblesse, flowre of chevalrie,
That with your worth the world amazed make,
How shall I quite the paynes ye suffer for my sake?

X X V I I

'And you, fresh budd of vertue springing fast,
Whom these sad eyes saw nigh unto deaths dore,
What hath poore Virgin for such perill past
Wherewith you to reward? Accept therefore
My simple selfe, and service evermore:
And he that high does sit, and all things see
With equall eye, their merites to restore,
Behold what ye this day have done for mee,
And what I cannot quite, requite with usuree.

X X V I I I

'But sith the heavens, and your faire handeling,
Have made you master of the field this day,
Your fortune maister eke with governing,
And, well begonne, end all so well, I pray!
Ne let that wicked woman scape away;
For she it is, that did my Lord bethrall,
My dearest Lord, and deepe in dongeon lay,
Where he his better dayes hath wasted all:
O heare, how piteous he to you for ayd does call!'

X X I X

Forthwith he gave in charge unto his Squyre,
That scarlot whore to keepen carefully;
Whyles he himselfe with greedie great desyre
Into the Castle entred forcibly,
Where living creature none he did espye.
Then gan he lowdly through the house to call,
But no man car'd to answere to his crye:
There raignd a solemne silence over all;
Nor voice was heard, nor wight was seene in bowre or hall.

X X X

At last, with creeping crooked pace forth came
An old old man, with beard as white as snow,
That on a staffe his feeble steps did frame,
And guyde his wearie gate both too and fro,
For his eye sight him fayled long ygo;
And on his arme a bounch of keyes he bore,
The which unused rust did overgrow:
Those were the keyes of every inner dore;
But he could not them use, but kept them still in store.

X X X I

But very uncouth sight was to behold,
How he did fashion his untoward pace;
For as he forward moovd his footing old,
So backward still was turnd his wrincled face:
Unlike to men, who ever, as they trace,
Both feet and face one way are wont to lead.
This was the auncient keeper of that place,
And foster father of the Gyaunt dead;
His name Ignaro did his nature right aread.

X X X I I

His reverend heares and holy gravitee
The knight much honord, as beseemed well;
And gently askt, where all the people bee,
Which in that stately building wont to dwell:
Who answerd him full soft, *he could not tell.*
Again he askt, where that same knight was layd.
Whom great Orgoglio with his puissaunce fell
Had made his caytive thrall: againe he sayde,
He could not tell; ne ever other answere made.

XXXI, 1   uncouth: strange   XXXII, 8   caytive: captive

X X X I I I

Then asked he, which way he in might pas?
He could not tell, againe he answered.
Thereat the courteous knight displeased was,
And said; 'Old syre, it seemes thou hast not red
How ill it sits with that same silver hed,
In vaine to mocke, or mockt in vaine to bee:
But if thou be, as thou art pourtrahed
With natures pen, in ages grave degree,
Aread in graver wise what I demaund of thee.'

X X X I V

His answere likewise was, *he could not tell*:
Whose sencelesse speach, and doted ignorance,
Whenas the noble Prince had marked well,
He ghest his nature by his countenance,
And calmd his wrath with goodly temperance.
Then, to him stepping, from his arme did reach
Those keyes, and made himselfe free enterance.
Each dore he opened without any breach,
There was no barre to stop, nor foe him to empeach.

X X X V

There all within full rich arayd he found,
With royall arras, and resplendent gold,
And did with store of every thing abound,
That greatest Princes presence might behold.
But all the floore (too filthy to be told)
With blood of guiltlesse babes, and innocents trew,
Which there were slaine as sheepe out of the fold,
Defiled was, that dreadfull was to vew;
And sacred ashes over it was strowed new.

X X X V I

And there beside of marble stone was built
An Altare, carv'd with cunning ymagery,
On which trew Christians blood was often spilt,
And holy Martyres often doen to dye
With cruell malice and strong tyranny:
Whose blessed sprites, from underneath the stone,
To God for vengeance cryde continually;
And with great griefe were often heard to grone,
That hardest heart would bleede to hear their piteous mone.

X X X V I I

Through every rowme he sought, and everie bowr,
But no where could he find that wofull thrall:
At last he came unto an yron doore,
That fast was lockt, but key found not at all
Emongst that bounch to open it withall;
But in the same a little grate was pight,
Through which he sent his voyce, and lowd did call
With all his powre, to weet if living wight
Were housed therewithin, whom he enlargen might.

X X X V I I I

Therewith an hollow, dreary, murmuring voyce
These pitteous plaintes and dolours did resound:
'O! who is that, which bringes me happy choyce
Of death, that here lye dying every stound,
Yet live perforce in balefull darkenesse bound?
For now three Moones have changed thrice their hew,
And have been thrice hid underneath the ground,
Since I the heavens chearefull face did vew.
O! welcome thou, that doest of death bring tydings trew.'

X X X I X

Which when that Champion heard, with percing point
Of pitty deare his hart was thrilled sore:
And trembling horrour ran through every joynt,
For ruth of gentle knight so fowle forlore:
Which shaking off, he rent that yron dore
With furious force and indignation fell;
Where entred in, his foot could find no flore,
But all a deepe descent, as darke as hell,
That breathed ever forth a filthie banefull smell.

X L

But nether darkenesse fowle, nor filthy bands,
Nor noyous smell, his purpose could withhold,
(Entire affection hateth nicer hands)
But that with constant zele and corage bold,
After long paines and labors manifold,
He found the meanes that Prisoner up to reare;
Whose feeble thighes, unable to uphold
His pined corse, him scarse to light could beare;
A ruefull spectacle of death and ghastly drere.

XL, 3   nicer: fastidious

X L I

His sad dull eies, deepe sunck in hollow pits,
Could not endure th' unwonted sunne to view;
His bare thin cheekes for want of better bits,
And empty sides deceived of their dew,
Could make a stony hart his hap to rew;
His rawbone armes, whose mighty brawned bowrs
Were wont to rive steele plates, and helmets hew,
Were clene consum'd; and all his vitall powres
Decayd, and al his flesh shronk up like withered flowres.

X L I I

Whome when his Lady saw, to him she ran
With hasty joy: to see him made her glad,
And sad to view his visage pale and wan,
Who earst in flowres of freshest youth was clad.
Tho, when her well of teares she wasted had,
She said; 'Ah dearest Lord! what evill starre
On you hath frownd, and pourd his influence bad,
That of your selfe ye thus berobbed arre,
And this misseeming hew your manly looks doth marre?

X L I I I

'But welcome now, my Lord in wele or woe,
Whose presence I have lackt too long a day:
And fie on Fortune, mine avowed foe,
Whose wrathful wreakes them selves doe now alay:
And for these wronges shall treble penaunce pay
Of treble good: good growes of evils priefe.'
The chearelesse man, whom sorrow did dismay,
Had no delight to treaten of his griefe;
His long endured famine needed more reliefe.

X L I V

'Faire Lady,' then said that victorious knight,
'The things, that grievous were to doe, or beare,
Them to renew, I wote, breeds no delight,
Best musicke breeds delight in loathing eare:
But th' only good that growes of passed feare
Is to be wise, and ware of like agein.
This daies ensample hath this lesson deare
Deepe written in my heart with yron pen,
That blisse may not abide in state of mortall men.

XLI, 3 bits: food   XLI, 6 bowrs: muscles

X L V

'Henceforth, Sir knight, take to you wonted strength,
And maister these mishaps with patient might.
Loe! where your foe lies stretcht in monstrous length;
And loe! that wicked woman in your sight,
The roote of all your care and wretched plight,
Now in your powre, to let her live, or die.'
'To doe her die,' (quoth Una) 'were despight,
And shame t'avenge so weake an enimy;
But spoile her of her scarlot robe, and let her fly.'

X L V I

So, as she bad, that witch they disaraid,
And robd of roiall robes, and purple pall.
And ornaments that richly were displaid;
Ne spared they to strip her naked all.
Then, when they had despoyld her tire and call,
Such as she was their eies might her behold,
That her misshaped parts did them appall:
A loathly, wrinckled hag, ill favoured, old,
Whose secret filth good manners biddeth not be told.

X L V I I

Her crafty head was altogether bald,
And, as in hate of honorable eld,
Was overgrowne with scurfe and filthy scald;
Her teeth out of her rotten gummes were feld,
And her sowre breath abhominably smeld;
Her dried dugs, lyke bladders lacking wind,
Hong downe, and filthy matter from them weld;
Her wrizled skin, as rough as maple rind,
So scabby was that would have loathd all womankind.

X L V I I I

Her neather parts, the shame of all her kind,
My chaster Muse for shame doth blush to write;
But at her rompe she growing had behind
A foxes taile, with dong all fowly dight;
And eke her feete most monstrous were in sight;
For one of them was like an Eagles claw,
With griping talaunts armd to greedy fight,
The other like a beares uneven paw,
More ugly shape yet never living creature saw.

XLVI, 2   pall: rich cloth   XLVI, 5   call: head-dress

XLIX

Which when the knights beheld amazd they were,
And wondred at so fowle deformed wight.
'Such then,' (said Una,) 'as she seemeth here,
Such is the face of falshood: such the sight
Of fowle Duessa, when her borrowed light
Is laid away, and counterfesaunce knowne.'
Thus when they had the witch disrobed quight,
And all her filthy feature open showne,
They let her goe at will, and wander waies unknowne.

L

Shee, flying fast from heavens hated face,
And from the world that her discovered wide,
Fled to the wastfull wildernesse apace,
From living eies her open shame to hide,
And lurkt in rocks and caves, long unespide.
But that faire crew of knights, and Una faire,
Did in that castle afterwards abide,
To rest them selves, and weary powres repaire;
Where store they fownd of al that dainty was and rare.

CANTO IX.

His loves and lignage Arthure tells:
The knights knitt friendly bands:
Sir Trevisan flies from Despeyre,
Whom Redcros knight withstands.

I

O GOODLY golden chayne, wherewith yfere
The vertues linked are in lovely wize;
And noble mindes of yore allyed were,
In brave poursuitt of chevalrous emprize,
That none did others safety despize,
Nor aid envy to him in need that stands;
But friendly each did others praise devize,
How to advaunce with favourable hands,
As this good Prince redeemd the Redcrosse knight from
bands.

II

Who when their powres, empayrd through labor long,
With dew repast they had recured well,

1, 1   yfere: in company

And that weake captive wight now wexed strong,
Them list no lenger there at leasure dwell,
But forward fare as their adventures fell:
But, ere they parted, Una faire besought
That straunger knight his name and nation tell;
Least so great good, as he for her had wrought,
Should die unknown, and buried be in thankles thought.

I I I

'Faire virgin,' (said the Prince,) 'yee me require
A thing without the compas of my witt;
For both the lignage, and the certein Sire,
From which I sprong, from mee are hidden yitt;
For all so soone as life did me admitt
Into this world, and shewed hevens light,
From mothers pap I taken was unfitt,
And streight deliver'd to a Fary knight,
To be upbrought in gentle thewes and martiall might.

I V

'Unto Old Timon he me brought bylive;
Old Timon, who in youthful yeares hath beene
In warlike feates th' expertest man alive,
And is the wisest now on earth I weene:
His dwelling is low in a valley greene,
Under the foot of Rauran mossy hore,
From whence the river Dee, as silver cleene,
His tombling billowes rolls with gentle rore;
There all my daies he trained mee up in vertuous lore.

V

'Thither the great magicien Merlin came,
As was his use, ofttimes to visitt mee,
For he had charge my discipline to frame,
And Tutors nouriture to oversee.
Him oft and oft I askt in privity,
Of what loines and what lignage I did spring;
Whose aunswere bad me still assured bee,
That I was sonne and heire unto a king,
As time in her just term the truth to light should bring.'

V I

'Well worthy impe,' said then the Lady gent,
'And Pupill fitt for such a Tutors hand!
But what adventure, or what high intent,

III, 9   thewes: manners

Hath brought you hither into Faery land,
Aread, Prince Arthure, crowne of Martiall band?'
'Full hard it is,' (quoth he) 'to read aright
The course of heavenly cause, or understand
The secret meaning of th' eternall might,
That rules mens waies, and rules the thoughts of living wight.

v i i

'For whether he, through fatal deepe foresight,
Me hither sent for cause to me unghest;
Or that fresh bleeding wound, which day and night
Whilome doth rancle in my riven brest,
With forced fury following his behest,
Me hither brought by wayes yet never found,
You to have helpt I hold my selfe yet blest.'
'Ah! courteous Knight,' (quoth she) 'what secret wound
Could ever find to grieve the gentlest hart on ground?'

v i i i

'Dear Dame,' (quoth he) 'you sleeping sparkes awake,
Which, troubled once, into huge flames will grow;
Ne ever will their fervent fury slake,
Till living moysture into smoke do flow,
And wasted life doe lye in ashes low:
Yet sithens silence lesseneth not my fire,
But, told, it flames; and, hidden, it does glow,
I will revele what ye so much desire.
Ah, Love! lay down thy bow, the whiles I may respyre.

i x

'It was in freshest flowre of youthly yeares,
When corage first does creepe in manly chest,
Then first the cole of kindly heat appeares
To kindle love in every living brest:
But me had warnd old Timons wise behest,
Those creeping flames by reason to subdew,
Before their rage grew to so great unrest,
As miserable lovers use to rew,
Which still wex old in woe, whiles wo stil wexeth new.

x

'That ydle name of love, and lovers life,
As losse of time, and vertues enimy,
I ever scornd, and joyd to stirre up strife,
In middest of their mournfull Tragedy;
Ay wont to laugh when them I heard to cry,

And blow the fire which them to ashes brent:
Their God himselfe, grievd at my libertie,
Shott many a dart at me with fiers intent;
But I them warded all with wary government.

X I

'But all in vaine: no fort can be so strong,
Ne fleshly brest can armed be so sownd,
But will at last be wonne with battrie long,
Or unawares at disavantage fownd.
Nothing is sure that growes on earthly grownd;
And who most trustes in arme of fleshly might,
And boastes in beauties chaine not to be bownd,
Doth soonest fall in disaventrous fight,
And yeeldes his caytive neck to victours most despight.

X I I

'Ensample make of him your haplesse joy,
And of my selfe now mated, as ye see;
Whose prouder vaunt that proud avenging boy
Did soone pluck downe, and curbd my libertee.
For on a day, prickt forth with jollitee
Of looser life and heat of hardiment,
Raunging the forest wide on courser free,
The fields, the floods, the heavens, with one consent,
Did seeme to laugh on me, and favour mine intent.

X I I I

'Forwearied with my sportes, I did alight
From loftie steed, and downe to sleepe me layd,
The verdant gras my couch did goodly dight,
And pillow was my helmett fayre displayd;
Whiles every sence the humour sweet embayd,
And slombring soft my hart did steale away,
Me seemed, by my side a royall Mayd
Her daintie limbes full softly down did lay:
So fayre a creature yet saw never sunny day.

X I V

'Most goodly glee and lovely blandishment
She to me made, and badd me love her deare;
For dearely sure her love was to me bent,
As, when just time expired, should appeare.
But whether dreames delude, or true it were,
Was never hart so ravisht with delight,

XII, 2   mated: overcome   XIII, 5   embayd: bathed

Ne living man like wordes did ever heare,
As she to me delivered all that night;
And at her parting said, She Queene of Faeries hight.

        x v

'When I awoke, and found her place devoyd,
And nought but pressed gras where she had lyen,
I sorrowed all so much as earst I joyd,
And washed all her place with watry eyen.
From that day forth I lov'd that face divyne;
From that day forth I cast in carefull mynd,
To seek her out with labor and long tyne,
And never vowd to rest till her I fynd:
Nyne monethes I seek in vain, yet ni'll that vow unbynd.'

        x v i

Thus as he spake, his visage wexed pale,
And chaunge of hew great passion did bewray;
Yett still he strove to cloke his inward bale,
And hide the smoke that did his fire display,
Till gentle Una thus to him gan say:
'O happy Queene of Faeries! that hast fownd,
Mongst many, one that with his prowesse may
Defend thine honour, and thy foes confownd.
True loves are often sown, but seldom grow on grownd.'

        x v i i

'Thine, O! then,' said the gentle Redcrosse knight,
'Next to that Ladies love, shalbe the place,
O fayrest virgin! full of heavenly light,
Whose wondrous faith, exceeding earthly race,
Was firmest fixt in myne extremest case.
And you, my Lord, the Patrone of my life,
Of that great Queene may well gaine worthie grace,
For onely worthie you through prowes priefe,
Yf living man mote worthie be to be her liefe.'

        x v i i i

So diversly discoursing of their loves,
The golden Sunne his glistring head gan shew,
And sad remembraunce now the Prince amoves
With fresh desire his voyage to pursew;
Als Una earnd her traveill to renew.
Then those two knights, fast friendship for to bynd,
And love establish each to other trew,

xv, 7   tyne: grief

Gave goodly gifts, the signes of gratefull mynd,
And eke, as pledges firme, right hands together joynd.

X I X

Prince Arthur gave a boxe of Diamond sure,
Embowd with gold and gorgeous ornament,
Wherein were closd few drops of liquor pure,
Of wondrous worth, and vertue excellent,
That any wownd could heale incontinent.
Which to requite, the Redcrosse knight him gave
A booke, wherein his Saveours testament
Was writt with golden letters rich and brave:
A worke of wondrous grace, and hable soules to save.

X X

Thus beene they parted; Arthur on his way
To seeke his love, and th' other for to fight
With Unaes foe, that all her realme did pray.
But she, now weighing the decayed plight
And shrunken synewes of her chosen knight,
Would not a while her forward course pursew,
Ne bring him forth in face of dreadfull fight,
Till he recovered had his former hew;
For him to be yet weake and wearie well she knew.

X X I

So as they traveild, lo! they gan espy
An armed knight towards them gallop fast,
That seemed from some feared foe to fly,
Or other griesly thing that him aghast.
Still as he fledd his eye was backward cast,
As if his feare still followed him behynd:
Als flew his steed as he his bandes had brast,
And with his winged heels did tread the wynd,
As he had beene a fole of Pegasus his kynd.

X X I I

Nigh as he drew, they might perceive his head
To bee unarmd, and curld uncombed heares
Upstaring stiffe, dismaid with uncouth dread:
Nor drop of blood in all his face appeares,
Nor life in limbe; and, to increase his feares,
In fowle reproch of knighthoodes fayre degree,
About his neck an hempen rope he weares,
That with his glistring armes does ill agree;
But he of rope or armes has now no memoree.

XXIII

The Redcrosse knight toward him crossed fast,
To weet what mister wight was so dismayd.
There him he findes all sencelesse and aghast,
That of him selfe he seemd to be afrayd;
Whom hardly he from flying forward stayd,
Till he these wordes to him deliver might:
'Sir knight, aread who hath ye thus arayd,
And eke from whom make ye this hasty flight?
For never knight I saw in such misseeming plight.'

XXIV

He answerd nought at all; but adding new
Feare to his first amazment, staring wyde
With stony eyes and hartlesse hollow hew,
Astonisht stood, as one that had aspyde
Infernall furies with their chaines untyde.
Him yett againe, and yett againe, bespake
The gentle knight; who nought to him replyde;
But, trembling every joynt, did inly quake,
And foltring tongue, at last, these words seemd forth to
    shake;

XXV

'For Gods deare love, Sir knight, doe me not stay;
For loe! he comes, he comes fast after mee.'
Eft looking back would faine have runne away;
But he him forst to stay, and tellen free
The secrete cause of his perplexitie:
Yet nathemore by his bold hartie speach
Could his blood frosen hart emboldened bee,
But through his boldnes rather feare did reach;
Yett, forst, at last he made through silence suddein breach.

XXVI

'And am I now in safetie sure,' (quoth he)
'From him that would have forced me to dye?
And is the point of death now turnd fro mee,
That I may tell this haplesse history?'
'Fear nought,' (quoth he) 'no daunger now is nye.'
'Then shall I you recount a ruefull cace,'
(Said he) 'the which with this unlucky eye
I late beheld; and, had not greater grace
Me reft from it, had bene partaker of the place.

XXIII, 2   mister: kind of

XXVII

'I lately chaunst (Would I had never chaunst!)
With a fayre knight to keepen companee,
Sir Terwin hight, that well himselfe advaunst
In all affayres, and was both bold and free,
But not so happy as mote happy bee:
He lov'd, as was his lot, a Lady gent,
That him againe lov'd in the least degree;
For she was proud, and of too high intent,
And joyd to see her lover languish and lament:

XXVIII

'From whom retourning sad and comfortlesse,
As on the way together we did fare,
We met that villen, (God from him me blesse!)
That cursed wight, from whom I scapt whyleare,
A man of hell that calls himselfe Despayre:
Who first us greets, and after fayre areedes
Of tydinges straunge, and of adventures rare:
So creeping close, as Snake in hidden weedes,
Inquireth of our states, and of our knightly deedes.

XXIX

'Which when he knew, and felt our feeble harts
Embost with bale, and bitter byting griefe,
Which love had launched with his deadly darts,
With wounding words, and termes of foule repriefe,
He pluckt from us all hope of dew reliefe,
That earst us held in love of lingring life;
Then hopelesse, hartlesse, gan the cunning thiefe
Perswade us dye, to stint all further strife:
To me he lent this rope, to him a rusty knife.

XXX

'With which sad instrument of hasty death,
That wofull lover, loathing lenger light,
A wyde way made to let forth living breath:
But I, more fearefull or more lucky wight,
Dismayd with that deformed dismall sight,
Fledd fast away, halfe dead with dying feare;
Ne yet assur'd of life by you, Sir knight,
Whose like infirmity like chaunce may beare;
But God you never let his charmed speaches heare!'

XXXI

'How may a man,' (said he) 'with idle speach
Be wonne to spoyle the Castle of his health?'
'I wote,' (quoth he) 'whom tryall late did teach,
That like would not for all this worldes wealth.
His subtile tong like dropping honny mealt'h
Into the heart, and searcheth every vaine;
That, ere one be aware, by secret stealth
His powre is reft, and weaknes doth remaine.
O! never, Sir, desire to try his guilefull traine.'

XXXII

'Certes,' (sayd he) 'hence shall I never rest,
Till I that treachours art have heard and tryde:
And you, Sir knight, whose name mote I request,
Of grace do me unto his cabin guyde.'
'I, that hight Trevisan,' (quoth he) 'will ryde
Against my liking backe to doe you grace:
But nor for gold nor glee will I abyde
By you, when ye arrive in that same place;
For lever had I die then see his deadly face.'

XXXIII

Ere long they come where that same wicked wight
His dwelling has, low in an hollow cave,
For underneath a craggy cliff ypight,
Darke, dolefull, dreary, like a greedy grave,
That still for carrion carcases doth crave:
On top whereof ay dwelt the ghastly Owle,
Shrieking his balefull note, which ever drave
Far from that haunt all other chearefull fowle,
And all about it wandring ghostes did wayle and howle.

XXXIV

And all about old stockes and stubs of trees,
Whereon nor fruit nor leafe was ever seene,
Did hang upon the ragged rocky knees;
On which had many wretches hanged beene,
Whose carcases were scattred on the greene,
And throwne about the cliffs. Arrived there,
That bare-head knight, for dread and dolefull teene,
Would faine have fled, ne durst approchen neare;
But th' other forst him staye, and comforted in feare.

X X X V

That darkesome cave they enter, where they find
That cursed man, low sitting on the ground,
Musing full sadly in his sullein mind:
His griesie lockes, long growen and unbound,
Disordred hong about his shoulders round,
And hid his face, through which his hollow eyne
Lookt deadly dull, and stared as astound;
His raw-bone cheekes, through penurie and pine,
Were shronke into his jawes, as he did never dyne.

X X X V I

His garment, nought but many ragged clouts,
With thornes together pind and patched was,
The which his naked sides he wrapt abouts;
And him beside there lay upon the gras
A dreary corse, whose life away did pas,
All wallowd in his own yet luke-warme blood,
That from his wound yet welled fresh, alas!
In which a rusty knife fast fixed stood,
And made an open passage for the gushing blood.

X X X V I I

Which piteous spectacle, approving trew
The wofull tale that Trevisan had told,
Whenas the gentle Redcrosse knight did vew,
With firie zeale he burnt in courage bold
Him to avenge before his blood were cold,
And to the villein sayd; 'Thou damned wight,
The authour of this fact we here behold,
What justice can but judge against thee right,
With thine owne blood to price his blood, here shed in sight?'

X X X V I I I

'What franticke fit,' (quoth he) 'hath thus distraught
Thee, foolish man, so rash a doome to give?
What justice ever other judgement taught,
But he should dye who merites not to live?
None els to death this man despayring drive
But his owne guiltie mind, deserving death.
Is then unjust to each his dew to give?
Or let him dye, that loatheth living breath,
Or let him die at ease, that liveth here uneath?

xxxv, 8   pine: pain   xxxvii, 9   price: pay for
xxxvii, 7   fact: deed

XXXIX

'Who travailes by the wearie wandring way,
To come unto his wished home in haste,
And meetes a flood that doth his passage stay,
Is not great grace to helpe him over past,
Or free his feet that in the myre sticke fast?
Most envious man, that grieves at neighbours good;
And fond, that joyest in the woe thou hast!
Why wilt not let him passe, that long hath stood
Upon the bancke, yet wilt thy selfe not pas the flood?

XL

'He there does now enjoy eternall rest
And happy ease, which thou doest want and crave,
And further from it daily wanderest:
What if some little payne the passage have,
That makes frayle flesh to feare the bitter wave,
Is not short payne well borne, that bringes long ease,
And layes the soule to sleepe in quiet grave?
Sleepe after toyle, port after stormie seas,
Ease after warre, death after life, does greatly please.'

XLI

The knight much wondred at his suddeine wit,
And sayd; 'The terme of life is limited,
Ne may a man prolong, nor shorten, it:
The souldier may not move from watchfull sted,
Nor leave his stand untill his Captaine bed.'
'Who life did limit by almightie doome,'
(Quoth he) 'knowes best the termes established;
And he, that points the Centonell his roome,
Doth license him depart at sound of morning droome.'

XLII

'Is not his deed, what ever thing is donne
In heaven and earth? Did not he all create
To die againe? All ends that was begonne:
Their times in his eternall booke of fate
Are written sure, and have their certein date.
Who then can strive with strong necessitie,
That holds the world in his still chaunging state,
Or shunne the death ordaynd by destinie?
When houre of death is come, let none aske whence, nor why.

XLI, I   suddeine: sharp

X L I I I

'The lenger life, I wote, the greater sin;
The greater sin, the greater punishment:
All those great battels, which thou boasts to win
Through strife, and blood-shed, and avengement,
Now praysd, hereafter deare thou shalt repent;
For life must life, and blood must blood, repay.
Is not enough thy evill life forespent?
For he that once hath missed the right way,
The further he doth goe, the further he doth stray.

X L I V

'Then doe no further goe, no further stray,
But here ly downe, and to thy rest betake,
Th' ill to prevent, that life ensewen may;
For what hath life that may it loved make,
And gives not rather cause it to forsake?
Feare, sicknesse, age, losse, labour, sorrow, strife,
Payne, hunger, cold that makes the hart to quake,
And ever fickle fortune rageth rife;
All which, and thousands mo, do make a loathsome life.

X L V

'Thou, wretched man, of death hast greatest need,
If in true ballaunce thou wilt weigh thy state;
For never knight, that dared warlike deed,
More luckless dissaventures did amate:
Witnes the dungeon deepe, wherein of late
Thy life shutt up for death so oft did call;
And though good lucke prolonged hath thy date,
Yet death then would the like mishaps forestall,
Into the which hereafter thou maist happen fall.

X L V I

'Why then doest thou, O man of sin! desire
To draw thy dayes forth to their last degree?
Is not the measure of thy sinfull hire
High heaped up with huge iniquitee,
Against the day of wrath to burden thee?
Is not enough, that to this Lady mild
Thou falsed hast thy faith with perjuree,
And sold thy selfe to serve Duessa vild,
With whom in all abuse thou hast thy selfe defild?

XLV, 4   amate: dismay

XLVII

'Is not he just, that all this doth behold
From highest heven, and beares an equall eie?
Shall he thy sins up in his knowledge fold,
And guilty be of thine impietie?
Is not his lawe, Let every sinner die;
Die shall all flesh? What then must needs be donne,
Is it not better to doe willinglie,
Then linger till the glas be all out ronne?
Death is the end of woes: die soone, O faeries sonne!'

XLVIII

The knight was much enmoved with his speach,
That as a swords poynt through his hart did perse,
And in his conscience made a secrete breach,
Well knowing trew all that he did reherse,
And to his fresh remembraunce did reverse
The ugly vew of his deformed crimes;
That all his manly powres it did disperse,
As he were charmed with inchaunted rimes;
That oftentimes he quakt, and fainted oftentimes.

XLIX

In which amazement when the Miscreaunt
Perceived him to waver, weake and fraile,
Whiles trembling horror did his conscience daunt,
And hellish anguish did his soule assaile;
To drive him to despaire, and quite to quaile,
Hee shewd him, painted in a table plaine,
The damned ghosts that doe in torments waile,
And thousand feends that doe them endlesse paine
With fire and brimstone, which for ever shall remaine

L

The sight whereof so throughly him dismaid,
That nought but death before his eies he saw,
And ever burning wrath before him laid,
By righteous sentence of th' Almighties law.
Then gan the villein him to overcraw,
And brought unto him swords, ropes, poison, fire,
And all that might him to perdition draw;
And bad him choose what death he would desire;
For death was dew to him that had provokt Gods ire.

L I

But, whenas none of them he saw him take,
He to him raught a dagger sharpe and keene,
And gave it him in hand: his hand did quake
And tremble like a leafe of Aspin greene,
And troubled blood through his pale face was seene
To come and goe with tidings from the heart,
As it a ronning messenger had beene.
At last, resolv'd to work his finall smart,
He lifted up his hand, that backe againe did start.

L I I

Which whenas Una saw, through every vaine
The crudled cold ran to her well of life,
As in a swowne: but, soone reliv'd againe,
Out of his hand she snatcht the cursed knife,
And threw it to the ground, enraged rife,
And to him said; 'Fie, fie, faint hearted Knight!
What meanest thou by this reprochfull strife?
Is this the battaile which thou vauntst to fight
With that fire-mouthed Dragon, horrible and bright?

L I I I

'Come; come away, fraile, feeble, fleshly wight,
Ne let vaine words bewitch thy manly hart,
Ne divelish thoughts dismay thy constant spright:
In heavenly mercies hast thou not a part?
Why shouldst thou then despeire, that chosen art?
Where justice growes, there grows eke greater grace,
The which doth quench the brond of hellish smart,
And that accurst hand-writing doth deface.
Arise, sir Knight; arise, and leave this cursed place.'

L I V

So up he rose, and thence amounted streight.
Which when the carle beheld, and saw his guest
Would safe depart, for all his subtile sleight,
He chose an halter from among the rest,
And with it hong him selfe, unbid, unblest.
But death he could not worke himselfe thereby,
For thousand times he so him selfe had drest,
Yet nathelesse it could not doe him die,
Till he should die his last, that is, eternally.

LII, 2   crudled: curdled   LIV, 5   unbid: without prayer

CANTO X.

Her faithfull knight faire Una brings
To house of Holinesse;
Where he is taught repentaunce, and
The way to hevenly blesse.

I

W HAT MAN IS HE, that boasts of fleshly might
And vaine assuraunce of mortality,
Which, all so soone as it doth come to fight
Against spirituall foes, yields by and by,
Or from the fielde most cowardly doth fly!
Ne let the man ascribe it to his skill,
That thorough grace hath gained victory:
If any strength we have, it is to ill,
But all the good is Gods, both power and eke will.

I I

By that which lately hapned Una saw
That this her knight was feeble, and too faint;
And all his sinewes woxen weake and raw,
Through long enprisonment, and hard constraint,
Which he endured in his late restraint,
That yet he was unfitt for bloody fight.
Therefore, to cherish him with diets daint,
She cast to bring him where he chearen might,
Till he recovered had his late decayed plight.

I I I

There was an auncient house nor far away,
Renowmd throughout the world for sacred love
And pure unspotted life: so well, they say,
It governd was, and guided evermore,
Through wisedome of a matrone grave and hore;
Whose onely joy was to relieve the needes
Of wretched soules, and helpe the helpelesse pore:
All night she spent in bidding of her bedes,
And all the day in doing good and godly deedes.

I V

Dame Cælia men did her call, as thought
From heaven to come, or thither to arise;
The mother of three daughters, well upbrought
In goodly thewes, and godly exercise:

IV, 4   thewes: manners

The eldest two, most sober, chast, and wise,
Fidelia and Speranza, virgins were;
Though spousd, yet wanting wedlocks solemnize;
But faire Charissa to a lovely fere
Was linked, and by him had many pledges dere.

V

Arrived there, the dore they find fast lockt,
For it was warely watched night and day,
For feare of many foes; but, when they knockt,
The Porter opened unto them streight way.
He was an aged syre, all hory gray,
With lookes full lowly cast, and gate full slow,
Wont on a staffe his feeble steps to stay,
Hight Humiltá. They passe in, stouping low;
For streight and narrow was the way which he did show.

V I

Each goodly thing is hardest to begin;
But, entred in, a spatious court they see,
Both plaine and pleasaunt to be walked in;
Where them does meete a francklin faire and free,
And entertaines with comely courteous glee;
His name was Zele, that him right well became:
For in his speaches and behaveour hee
Did labour lively to expresse the same,
And gladly did them guide, till to the Hall they came.

V I I

There fayrely them receives a gentle Squyre,
Of myld demeanure and rare courtesee,
Right cleanly clad in comely sad attyre;
In word and deede that shewd great modestee,
And knew his good to all of each degree,
Hight Reverence. He them with speaches meet
Does faire entreat; no courting nicetee,
But simple trew, and eke unfained sweet,
As might become a Squyre so great persons to greet.

V I I I

And afterwardes them to his Dame he leades,
That aged Dame, the Lady of the place,
Who all this while was busy at her beades;
Which doen, she up arose with seemely grace,

---

iv, 8   fere: mate   vii, 5   knew his good: knew how
v, 9   streight: restricted   to behave

And toward them full matronely did pace.
Where, when that fairest Una she beheld,
Whom well she knew to spring from hevenly race,
Her heart with joy unwonted inly sweld,
As feeling wondrous comfort in her weaker eld:

I X

And, her embracing, said; 'O happy earth,
Whereon thy innocent feet doe ever tread!
Most vertuous virgin, borne of hevenly berth,
That, to redeeme thy woefull parents head
From tyrans rage and ever-dying dread,
Hast wandred through the world now long a day,
Yett ceassest not thy weary soles to lead;
What grace hath thee now hither brought this way?
Or doen thy feeble feet unweeting hither stray?

X

'Straunge thing it is an errant knight to see
Here in this place; or any other wight,
That hither turnes his steps. So few there bee,
That chose the narrow path, or seeke the right:
All keepe the broad high way, and take delight
With many rather for to goe astray,
And be partakers of their evill plight,
Then with a few to walke the rightest way.
O foolish men! why hast ye to your own decay?'

X I

'Thy selfe to see, and tyred limbes to rest,
O matrone sage,' (quoth she) 'I hither came;
And this good knight his way with me addrest,
Ledd with thy prayses, and broad-blazed fame,
That up to heven is blowne.' The auncient Dame
Him goodly greeted in her modest guyse,
And enterteynd them both, as best became,
With all the court'sies that she could devyse,
Ne wanted ought to shew her bounteous or wise.

X I I

Thus as they gan of sondrie thinges devise,
Loe! two most goodly virgins came in place,
Ylinked arme in arme in lovely wise:
With countenance demure, and modest grace,
They numbred even steps and equall pace;
Of which the eldest, that Fidelia hight,

Like sunny beames threw from her Christall face
That could have dazd the rash beholders sight,
And round about her head did shine like hevens light.

XIII

She was araied all in lilly white,
And in her right hand bore a cup of gold,
With wine and water fild up to the hight,
In which a Serpent did himselfe enfold,
That horrour made to all that did behold;
But she no whitt did chaunge her constant mood:
And in her other hand she fast did hold
A booke, that was both signd and seald with blood;
Wherein darke things were writt, hard to be understood.

XIV

Her younger sister, that Speranza hight,
Was clad in blew, that her beseemed well;
Not all so chearefull seemed she of sight,
As was her sister: whether dread did dwell
Or anguish in her hart, is hard to tell.
Upon her arme a silver anchor lay,
Whereon she leaned ever, as befell;
And ever up to heven, as she did pray,
Her stedfast eyes were bent, ne swarved other way.

XV

They, seeing Una, towardes her gan wend,
Who them encounters with like courtesee;
Many kind speeches they betweene them spend,
And greatly joy each other for to see:
Then to the knight with shamefast modestie
They turne themselves, at Unaes meeke request,
And him salute with well beseeming glee;
Who faire them quites, as him beseemed best,
And goodly gan discourse of many a noble gest.

XVI

Then Una thus: 'But she, your sister deare,
The deare Charissa, where is she become?
Or wants she health, or busie is elswhere?'
'Ah! no,' said they, 'but forth she may not come;
For she of late is lightned of her wombe,
And hath encreast the world with one sonne more,
That her to see should be but troublesome.'

xv, 9   gest: action

'Indeed,' (quoth she) 'that should her trouble sore;
But thankt be God, and her encrease so evermore!'

X V I I

Then said the aged Cælia, 'Deare dame,
And you, good Sir, I wote that of youre toyle
And labors long, through which ye hither came,
Ye both forwearied be: therefore, a whyle
I read you rest, and to your bowres recoyle.'
Then called she a Groome, that forth him ledd
Into a goodly lodge, and gan despoile
Of puissant armes, and laid in easie bedd:
His name was meeke Obedience, rightfully aredd.

X V I I I

Now when their wearie limbes with kindly rest,
And bodies were refresht with dew repast,
Fayre Una gan Fidelia fayre request,
To have her knight into her schoolehous plaste,
That of her heavenly learning he might taste,
And heare the wisedom of her wordes divine.
She graunted; and that knight so much agraste,
That she him taught celestiall discipline,
And opened his dull eyes, that light mote in them shine.

X I X

And that her sacred Booke, with blood ywritt,
That none could reade except she did them teach,
She unto him disclosed every whitt;
And heavenly documents thereout did preach,
That weaker witt of man could never reach;
Of God; of grace; of justice; of free-will;
That wonder was to heare her goodly speach:
For she was hable with her wordes to kill,
And rayse againe to life the hart that she did thrill.

X X

And, when she list poure out her larger spright,
She would commaund the hasty Sunne to stay,
Or backward turne his course from hevens hight:
Sometimes great hostes of men she could dismay;
Dry-shod to passe she parts the flouds in tway;
And eke huge mountaines from their native seat
She would commaund themselves to beare away,

xvii, 5   bowres: bed-chambers   xix, 9   thrill: pierce
xviii, 7   agraste: graced

And throw in raging sea with roaring threat.
Almightie God her gave such powre and puissaunce great.

X X I

The faithfull knight now grew in little space,
By hearing her, and by her sisters lore,
To such perfection of all hevenly grace,
That wretched world he gan for to abhore,
And mortall life gan loath as thing forlore,
Greevd with remembrance of his wicked wayes,
And prickt with anguish of his sinnes so sore,
That he desirde to end his wretched dayes:
So much the dart of sinfull guilt the soule dismayes.

X X I I

But wise Speranza gave him comfort sweet,
And taught him how to take assured hold
Upon her silver anchor, as was meet;
Els had his sinnes, so great and manifold,
Made him forget all that Fidelia told.
In this distressed doubtfull agony,
When him his dearest Una did behold
Disdeining life, desiring leave to dye,
She found her selfe assayld with great perplexity;

X X I I I

And came to Cælia to declare her smart;
Who, well acquainted with that commune plight,
Which sinfull horror workes in wounded hart,
Her wisely comforted all that she might,
With goodly counsell and advisement right;
And streightway sent with carefull diligence,
To fetch a Leach, the which had great insight
In that disease of grieved conscience,
And well could cure the same: His name was Patience.

X X I V

Who, comming to that sowle-diseased knight,
Could hardly him intreat to tell his grief:
Which knowne, and all that noyd his heavie spright
Well searcht, eftsoones he gan apply relief
Of salves and med'cines, which had passing prief;
And thereto added wordes of wondrous might.
By which to ease he him recured brief,
And much aswag'd the passion of his plight,
That he his paine endur'd, as seeming now more light.

X X V

But yet the cause and root of all his ill,
Inward corruption and infected sin,
Not purg'd nor heald, behind remained still,
And festring sore did ranckle yett within,
Close creeping twixt the marow and the skin:
Which to extirpe, he laid him privily
Downe in a darksome lowly place far in,
Whereas he meant his corrosives to apply,
And with streight diet tame his stubborne malady.

X X V I

In ashes and sackcloth he did array
His daintie corse, proud humors to abate;
And dieted with fasting every day,
The swelling of his woundes to mitigate;
And made him pray both earely and eke late:
And ever, as superfluous flesh did rott,
Amendment readie still at hand did wayt,
To pluck it out with pincers fyrie whott,
That soone in him was lefte no one corrupted jott.

X X V I I

And bitter Penaunce, with an yron whip,
Was wont him once to disple every day:
And sharp Remorse his hart did prick and nip,
That drops of blood thence like a well did play:
And sad Repentance used to embay
His blamefull body in salt water sore,
The filthy blottes of sin to wash away.
So in short space they did to health restore
The man that would not live, but erst lay at deathes dore.

X X V I I I

In which his torment often was so great,
That like a Lyon he would cry and rore,
And rend his flesh, and his owne synewes eat.
His owne deare Una, hearing evermore
His ruefull shriekes and gronings, often tore
Her guiltlesse garments and her goolden heare,
For pitty of his payne and anguish sore:
Yet all with patience wisely she did beare,
For well she wist his cryme could els be never cleare.

xxvii, 2   disple: discipline

XXIX

Whom, thus recover'd by wise Patience
And trew Repentaunce, they to Una brought,
Who, joyous of his cured conscience,
Him dearely kist, and fayrely eke besought
Himselfe to chearish, and consuming thought
To put away out of his carefull brest.
By this Charissa, late in child-bed brought,
Was woxen strong, and left her fruitfull nest:
To her fayre Una brought this unacquainted guest.

XXX

She was a woman in her freshest age,
Of wondrous beauty, and of bounty rare,
With goodly grace and comely personage,
That was on earth not easie to compare;
Full of great love, but Cupids wanton snare
As hell she hated; chaste in worke and will:
Her necke and brests were ever open bare,
That ay thereof her babes might sucke their fill;
The rest was all in yellow robes arayed still.

XXXI

A multitude of babes about her hong,
Playing their sportes, that joyd her to behold;
Whom still she fed whiles they were weake and young,
But thrust them forth still as they wexed old:
And on her head she wore a tyre of gold,
Adornd with gemmes and owches wondrous fayre,
Whose passing price uneath was to be told:
And by her syde there sate a gentle payre,
Of turtle doves, she sitting in an yvory chayre.

XXXII

The knight and Una entring fayre her greet,
And bid her joy of that her happy brood;
Who them requites with court'sies seeming meet,
And entertaynes with friendly chearefull mood.
Then Una her besought, to be so good
As in her vertuous rules to schoole her knight,
Now after all his torment well withstood
In that sad house of Penaunce, where his spright
Had past the paines of hell and long-enduring night.

XXXIII

She was right joyous of her just request;
And taking by the hand that Faeries sonne,
Gan him instruct in everie good behest,
Of love, and righteousnes, and well to donne;
And wrath and hatred warely to shonne,
That drew on men Gods hatred and his wrath,
And many soules in dolours had fordonne:
In which when him she well instructed hath,
From thence to heaven she teacheth him the ready path.

XXXIV

Wherein his weaker wandring steps to guyde,
An auncient matrone she to her does call,
Whose sober lookes her wisedome well descryde:
Her name was Mercy; well knowne over-all
To be both gratious and eke liberall:
To whom the carefull charge of him she gave,
To leade aright, that he should never fall
In all his waies through this wide worldes wave;
That Mercy in the end his righteous soule might save.

XXXV

The godly Matrone by the hand him beares
Forth from her presence, by a narrow way,
Scattred with bushy thornes and ragged breares,
Which still before him she remov'd away,
That nothing might his ready passage stay:
And ever, when his feet encombred were,
Or gan to shrinke, or from the right to stray,
She held him fast, and firmely did upbeare,
As carefull Nourse her child from falling oft does reare.

XXXVI

Eftsoones unto an holy Hospitall,
That was foreby the way, she did him bring;
In which seven Bead-men, that had vowed all
Their life to service of high heavens King,
Did spend their daies in doing godly thing.
Their gates to all were open evermore,
That by the wearie way were traveiling;
And one sate wayting ever them before,
To call in commers-by that needy were and pore.

XXXVII

The first of them, that eldest was and best,
Of all the house had charge and governement,
As Guardian and Steward of the rest.
His office was to give entertainement
And lodging unto all that came and went;
Not unto such as could him feast againe,
And double quite for that he on them spent;
But such as want of harbour did constraine:
Those for Gods sake his dewty was to entertaine.

XXXVIII

The second was as Almner of the place:
His office was the hungry for to feed,
And thristy give to drinke; a worke of grace.
He feard not once himselfe to be in need,
Ne car'd to hoord for those whom he did breede;
The grace of God he layd up still in store,
Which as a stocke he left unto his seede.
He had enough; what need him care for more?
And had he lesse, yet some he would give to the pore.

XXXIX

The third had of their wardrobe custody,
In which were not rich tyres, nor garments gay,
The plumes of pride, and winges of vanity,
But clothes meet to keepe keene cold away,
And naked nature seemely to aray;
With which bare wretched wights he dayly clad,
The images of God in earthly clay;
And, if that no spare clothes to give he had,
His owne cote he would cut, and it distribute glad.

X L

The fourth appointed by his office was
Poore prisoners to relieve with gratious ayd,
And captives to redeeme with price of bras
From Turkes and Sarazins, which them had stayd:
And though they faulty were, yet well he wayd,
That God to us forgiveth every howre
Much more then that why they in bands were layd:
And he, that harrowd hell with heavie stowre,
The faulty soules from thence brought to his heavenly bowre.

X L I

The fift had charge sick persons to attend,
And comfort those in point of death which lay;
For them most needeth comfort in the end,
When sin, and hell, and death, doe most dismay
The feeble soule departing hence away.
All is but lost, that living we bestow,
If not well ended at our dying day.
O man! have mind of that last bitter throw;
For as the tree does fall, so lyes it ever low.

X L I I

The sixt had charge of them now being dead,
In seemely sort their corses to engrave,
And deck with dainty flowres their brydall bed,
That to their heavenly spouse both sweet and brave
They might appeare, when he their soules shall save.
The wondrous workmanship of Gods owne mould,
Whose face he made all beastes to feare, and gave
All in his hand, even dead we honour should.
Ah, dearest God, me graunt, I dead be not defould!

X L I I I

The seventh, now after death and buriall done,
Had charge the tender Orphans of the dead
And wydowes ayd, least they should be undone:
In face of judgement he their right would plead,
Ne ought the powre of mighty men did dread
In their defence; nor would for gold or fee
Be wonne their rightfull causes downe to tread;
And, when they stood in most necessitee,
He did supply their want, and gave them ever free.

X L I V

There when the Elfin knight arrived was,
The first and chiefest of the seven, whose care
Was guests to welcome, towardes him did pas;
Where seeing Mercie, that his steps upbare
And alwaies led, to her with reverence rare
He humbly louted in meeke lowlinesse,
And seemely welcome for her did prepare:
For of their order she was Patronesse,
Albe Charissa were their chiefest founderesse.

XLI, 8   throw: throe

XLV

There she awhile him stayes, himselfe to rest,
That to the rest more hable he might bee;
During which time, in every good behest,
And godly worke of Almes and charitee,
Shee him instructed with great industree.
Shortly therein so perfect he became,
That, from the first unto the last degree,
His mortall life he learned had to frame
In holy righteousnesse, without rebuke or blame.

XLVI

Thence forward by that painfull way they pas
Forth to an hill that was both steepe and hy,
On top whereof a sacred chappell was,
And eke a litle Hermitage thereby,
Wherein an aged holy man did lie,
That day and night said his devotion,
Ne other worldly busines did apply:
His name was hevenly Contemplation;
Of God and goodnes was his meditation.

XLVII

Great grace that old man to him given had;
For God he often saw from heavens hight:
All were his earthly eien both blunt and bad,
And through great age had lost their kindly sight,
Yet wondrous quick and persaunt was his spright,
As Eagles eie that can behold the Sunne.
That hill they scale with all their powre and might,
That his fraile thighes, nigh weary and fordonne,
Gan faile; but by her helpe the top at last he wonne.

XLVIII

There they doe finde that godly aged Sire,
With snowy lockes adowne his shoulders shed;
As hoary frost with spangles doth attire
The mossy braunches of an Oke halfe ded.
Each bone might through his body well be red
And every sinew seene, through his long fast:
For nought he car'd his carcas long unfed;
His mind was full of spiritual repast,
And pyn'd his flesh to keepe his body low and chast.

XLIX

Who, when these two approching he aspide,
At their first presence grew agrieved sore,
That forst him lay his hevenly thoughts aside;
And had he not that Dame respected more,
Whom highly he did reverence and adore,
He would not once have moved for the knight.
They him saluted, standing far afore,
Who, well them greeting, humbly did requight,
And asked to what end they clomb that tedious hight?

L

'What end,' (quoth she) 'should cause us take such paine,
But that same end, which every living wight
Should make his marke high heaven to attaine?
Is not from hence the way, that leadeth right
To that most glorious house, that glistreth bright
With burning starres and everliving fire,
Whereof the keies are to thy hand behight
By wise Fidelia? Shee doth thee require,
To shew it to this knight, according his desire.'

LI

'Thrise happy man,' said then the father grave,
'Whose staggering steps thy steady hand doth lead,
And shewes the way his sinfull soule to save!
Who better can the way to heaven aread
Then thou thyselfe, that was both borne and bred
In hevenly throne, where thousand Angels shine?
Thou doest the praiers of the righteous sead
Present before the majesty divine,
And his avenging wrath to clemency incline.

LII

'Yet, since thou bidst, thy pleasure shalbe donne.
Then come, thou man of earth, and see the way,
That never yet was seene of Faeries sonne;
That never leads the traveiler astray,
But after labors long and sad delay,
Brings them to joyous rest and endlesse blis.
But first thou must a season fast and pray,
Till from her bands the spright assoiled is,
And have her strength recur'd from fraile infirmitis.'

L I I I

That done, he leads him to the highest Mount,
Such one as that same mighty man of God,
That blood-red billowes, like a walled front,
On either side disparted with his rod,
Till that his army dry-foot through them yod,
Dwelt forty daies upon; where, writt in stone
With bloody letters by the hand of God,
The bitter doome of death and balefull mone
He did receive, whiles flashing fire about him shone:

L I V

Or like that sacred hill, whose head full hie,
Adornd with fruitfull Olives all arownd,
Is, as it were for endlesse memory
Of that deare Lord who oft thereon was fownd,
For ever with a flowring girlond crownd:
Or like that pleasaunt Mount, that is for ay
Through famous Poets verse each where renownd,
On which the thrise three learned Ladies play
Their hevenly notes, and make full many a lovely lay.

L V

From thence, far off he unto him did shew
A little path that was both steepe and long,
Which to a goodly Citty led his vew,
Whose wals and towres were builded high and strong
Of perle and precious stone, that earthly tong
Cannot describe, nor wit of man can tell;
Too high a ditty for my simple song.
The Citty of the greate king hight it well,
Wherein eternall peace and happinesse doth dwell.

L V I

As he thereon stood gazing, he might see
The blessed Angels to and fro descend
From highest heven in gladsome companee,
And with great joy into that Citty wend,
As commonly as frend does with his frend.
Whereat he wondred much, and gan enquere,
What stately building durst so high extend
Her lofty towres unto the starry sphere,
And what unknowen nation there empeopled were?

L V I I

'Faire Knight,' (quoth he) 'Hierusalem that is,
The new Hierusalem, that God has built
For those to dwell in that are chosen his,
His chosen people, purg'd from sinful guilt
With pretious blood, which cruelly was spilt
On cursed tree, of that unspotted lam,
That for the sinnes of al the world was kilt:
Now are they Saints all in that Citty sam,
More dear unto their God then younglings to their dam.'

L V I I I

'Til now,' said then the knight, 'I weened well,
That great Cleopolis, where I have beene,
In which that fairest Faery Queene doth dwell,
The fairest citty was that might be seene;
And that bright towre, all built of christall clene,
Panthea, seemd the brightest thing that was;
But now by proofe all otherwise I weene,
For this great Citty that does far surpas,
And this bright Angels towre quite dims that towre of glas.'

L I X

'Most trew,' then said the holy aged man;
'Yet is Cleopolis, for earthly frame,
The fairest peece that eie beholden can,
And well beseemes all knights of noble name,
That covett in th' immortall booke of fame
To be eternized, that same to haunt,
And doen their service to that soveraigne Dame,
That glory does to them for guerdon graunt:
For she is hevenly borne, and heaven may justly vaunt.

L X

'And thou, faire ymp, sprong out from English race,
How ever now accompted Elfins sonne,
Well worthy doest thy service for her grace,
To aide a virgin desolate, foredonne;
But when thou famous victory hast wonne,
And high emongst all knights hast hong thy shield,
Thenceforth the suitt of earthly conquest shonne,
And wash thy hands from guilt of bloody field:
For blood can nought but sin, and wars but sorrows yield.

LVII, 8   sam: together

LXI

'Then seek this path that I to thee presage,
Which after all to heaven shall thee send;
Then peaceably thy painefull pilgrimage
To yonder same Hierusalem doe bend,
Where is for thee ordaind a blessed end:
For thou, emongst those Saints whom thou doest see,
Shalt be a Saint, and thine owne nations frend
And Patrone: thou *Saint George* shalt called bee,
Saint George of mery *England*, the signe of victoree.'

LXII

'Unworthy wretch,' (quoth he) 'of so great grace,
How dare I thinke such glory to attaine?'
'These, that have it attaynd, were in like cace,
As wretched men, and lived in like paine.'
'But deeds of armes must I at last be faine
And Ladies love to leave, so dearely bought?'
'What need of armes, where peace doth ay remaine,'
(Said he) 'and bitter battailes all are fought?
As for loose loves, they'are vaine, and vanish into nought.'

LXIII

'O! let me not,' (quoth he) 'then turne againe
Backe to the world, whose joyes so fruitlesse are;
But let me heare for aie in peace remaine,
Or streightway on that last long voiage fare,
That nothing may my present hope empare.'
'That may not be,' (said he) 'ne maist thou yitt
Forgoe that royal maides bequeathed care,
Who did her cause into thy hand committ,
Till from her cursed foe thou have her freely quitt.'

LXIV

'Then shall I soone,' (quoth he) 'so God me grace,
Abett that virgins cause disconsolate,
And shortly backe returne unto this place,
To walke this way in Pilgrims poore estate.
But now aread, old father, why of late
Didst thou behight me borne of English blood,
Whom all a Faeries sonne doen nominate?'
'That word shall I,' (said he) 'avouchen good,
Sith to thee is unknowne the cradle of thy brood.

L X V

'For, well I wote, thou springst from ancient race
Of Saxon kinges, that have with mightie hand,
And many bloody battailes fought in face,
High reard their royall throne in Britane land,
And vanquisht them, unable to withstand:
From thence a Faery thee unweeting reft,
There as thou slepst in tender swadling band,
And her base Elfin brood there for thee left:
Such, men do Chaungelings call, so chaung'd by Faeries theft.

L X V I

'Thence she thee brought into this Faery lond,
And in an heaped furrow did thee hyde;
Where thee a Ploughman all unweeting fond,
As he his toylesome teme that way did guyde,
And brought thee up in ploughmans state to byde,
Whereof Georgos he thee gave to name;
Till prickt with courage, and thy forces pryde,
To Faery court thou cam'st to seek for fame,
And prove thy puissant armes, as seemes thee best became.'

L X V I I

'O holy Sire!' (quoth he) 'how shall I quight
The many favours I with thee have fownd,
That hast my name and nation redd aright,
And taught the way that does to heaven bownd!'
This saide, adowne he looked to the grownd
To have returnd; but dazed were his eyne
Through passing brightnes, which did quite confound
His feeble sence, and too exceeding shyne.
So darke are earthly thinges compard to things divine.

L X V I I I

At last, whenas himselfe he gan to fynd,
To Una back he cast him to retyre,
Who him awaited still with pensive mynd.
Great thankes, and goodly meed, to that good syre
He thens departing gave for his paynes hyre
So came to Una, who him joyd to see;
And, after litle rest, gan him desyre
Of her adventure myndfull for to bee.
So leave they take of Cælia and her daughters three.

CANTO XI.

The knight with that old Dragon fights
Two days incessantly:
The third him overthrowes, and gayns
Most glorious victory.

I

HIGH TIME NOW gan it wex for Una fayre
To thinke of those her captive Parents deare,
And their forwasted kingdom to repayre:
Whereto whenas they now approched neare,
With hartie wordes her knight she gan to cheare,
And in her modest maner thus bespake:
'Deare knight, as deare as ever knight was deare,
That all these sorrowes suffer for my sake,
High heven behold the tedious toyle ye for me take!

I I

'Now are we come unto my native soyle,
And to the place where all our perilles dwell;
Here hauntes that feend, and does his dayly spoyle;
Therefore, henceforth, bee at your keeping well,
And ever ready for your foeman fell:
The sparke of noble corage now awake,
And strive your excellent selfe to excell:
That shall ye evermore renowmed make
Above all knights on earth, that batteill undertake.'

I I I

And pointing forth, 'Lo! yonder is,' (said she)
'The brasen towre, in which my parents deare
For dread of that huge feend emprisond be;
Whom I from far see on the walles appeare,
Whose sight my feeble soule doth greatly cheare:
And on the top of all I do espye
The watchman wayting tydings glad to heare;
That, (O my Parents!) might I happily
Unto you bring, to ease you of your misery!'

I V

With that they heard a roaring hideous sownd,
That all the ayre with terror filled wyde,
And seemd uneath to shake the stedfast ground.
Eftsoones that dreadful Dragon they espyde,

Where stretcht he lay upon the sunny side
Of a great hill, himselfe like a great hill:
But, all so soone as he from far descryde
Those glistring armes that heven with light did fill,
He rousd himselfe full blyth, and hastned them untill.

V

Then badd the knight his Lady yede aloof,
And to an hill herselfe withdraw asyde;
From whence she might behold the battailles proof,
And eke be safe from daunger far descryde.
She him obayd, and turnd a little wyde.—
Now, O thou sacred Muse! most learned Dame.
Fayre ympe of Phœbus and his aged bryde,
The Nourse of time and everlasting fame,
That warlike handes ennoblest with immortall name;

V I

O! gently come into my feeble brest;
Come gently, but not with that mightie rage,
Wherewith the martiall troupes thou doest infest,
And hartes of great Heroës doest enrage,
That nought their kindled corage may aswage:
Soone as thy dreadfull trompe begins to sownd,
The God of warre with his fiers equipage
Thou doest awake, sleepe never he so sownd;
And scared nations doest with horror sterne astownd.

V I I

Fayre Goddesse, lay that furious fitt asyde,
Till I of warres and bloody Mars doe sing,
And Bryton fieldes with Sarazin blood bedyde,
Twixt that great faery Queene and Paynim king,
That with their horror heven and earth did ring;
A worke of labour long, and endlesse prayse:
But now a while lett downe that haughtie string,
And to my tunes thy second tenor rayse,
That I this man of God his godly armes may blaze.

V I I I

By this, the dreadful Beast drew nigh to hand,
Halfe flying and halfe footing in his haste,
That with his largenesse measured much land,
And made wide shadow under his huge waste,
As mountaine doth the valley overcaste.

VI, 3   infest: infect   VII, 9   blaze: blazon, depict

Approching nigh, he reared high afore
His body monstrous, horrible, and vaste;
Which, to increase his wondrous greatnes more,
Was swoln with wrath and poyson, and with bloody gore;

I X

And over all with brasen scales was armd,
Like plated cote of steele, so couched neare
That nought mote perce; ne might his corse bee harmd
With dint of swerd, nor push of pointed speare:
Which as an Eagle, seeing pray appeare,
His aery plumes doth rouze, full rudely dight;
So shaked he, that horror was to heare:
For as the clashing of an Armor bright,
Such noyse his rouzed scales did send unto the knight.

x

His flaggy winges, when forth he did display,
Were like two sayles, in which the hollow wynd
Is gathered full, and worketh speedy way:
And eke the pennes, that did his pineons bynd,
Were like mayne-yardes with flying canvas lynd;
With which whenas him list the ayre to beat,
And there by force unwonted passage fynd,
The cloudes before him fledd for terror great,
And all the hevens stood still amazed with his threat.

X I

His huge long tayle, wownd up in hundred foldes,
Does overspred his long bras-scaly back,
Whose wreathed boughtes when ever he unfoldes,
And thick entangled knots adown does slack,
Bespotted as with shieldes of red and blacke,
It sweepeth all the land behind him farre,
And of three furlongs does but litle lacke;
And at the point two stinges in fixed arre,
Both deadly sharp, that sharpest steele exceeden farre.

X I I

But stinges and sharpest steele did far exceed
The sharpnesse of his cruel rending clawes:
Dead was it sure, as sure as death in deed,
What ever thing does touch his ravenous pawes,
Or what within his reach he ever drawes.

ix, 2 couched: disposed	x, 4 pennes: quills	
x, 1 flaggy: drooping	xi, 3 boughtes: coils	

But his most hideous head my tongue to tell
Does tremble; for his deepe devouring jawes
Wyde gaped, like the griesly mouth of hell,
Through which into his darke abysse all ravin fell.

X I I I

And, that more wondrous was, in either jaw
Three ranckes of yron teeth enraunged were,
In which yett trickling blood, and gobbets raw,
Of late devoured bodies did appeare,
That sight thereof bredd cold congealed feare;
Which to increase, and all atonce to kill,
A cloud of smoothering smoke, and sulphure seare,
Out of his stinking gorge forth steemed still,
That all the ayre about with smoke and stench did fill.

X I V

His blazing eyes, like two bright shining shieldes,
Did burne with wrath, and sparkled living fyre:
As two broad Beacons, sett in open fieldes,
Send forth their flames far off to every shyre,
And warning give that enimies conspyre
With fire and sword the region to invade:
So flam'd his eyne with rage and rancorous yre;
But far within, as in a hollow glade,
Those glaring lampes were sett that made a dreadfull shade.

X V

So dreadfully he towardes him did pas,
Forelifting up a-loft his speckled brest,
And often bounding on the brused gras,
As for great joyance of his newcome guest.
Eftsoones he gan advance his haughty crest,
As chauffed Bore his bristles doth upreare;
And shoke his scales to battaile ready drest,
That made the Redcrosse knight nigh quake for feare,
As bidding bold defyaunce to his foeman neare.

X V I

The knight gan fayrely couch his steady speare,
And fiersely ran at him with rigorous might:
The pointed steele, arriving rudely theare,
His harder hyde would nether perce nor bight,
But, glauncing by, foorth passed forward right.
Yet sore amoved with so puissaunt push,
The wrathfull beast about him turned light,

And him so rudely, passing by, did brush
With his long tayle, that horse and man to ground did rush.

X V I I

Both horse and man up lightly rose againe,
And fresh encounter towardes him addrest;
But th' ydle stroke yet backe recoyld in vaine,
And found no place his deadly point to rest.
Exceeding rage enflam'd the furious Beast,
To be avenged of so great despight;
For never felt his imperceable brest
So wondrous force from hand of living wight;
Yet had he prov'd the powre of many a puissant knight.

X V I I I

Then, with his waving wings displayed wyde,
Himselfe up high he lifted from the ground,
And with strong flight did forcibly divyde
The yielding ayre, which nigh too feeble found
Her flitting parts, and element unsound,
To beare so great a weight: he, cutting way
With his broad sayles, about him soared round;
At last, low stouping with unweldy sway,
Snatcht up both horse and man, to beare them quite away.

X I X

Long he them bore above the subject plaine,
So far as Ewghen bow a shaft may send,
Till struggling strong did him at last constraine
To let them downe before his flightes end:
As hagard hauke, presuming to contend
With hardy fowle above his hable might,
His wearie pounces all in vaine doth spend
To trusse the pray too heavy for his flight;
Which, comming down to ground, does free it selfe by fight.

X X

He so disseized of his gryping grosse,
The knight his thrillant speare againe assayd
In his bras-plated body to embosse,
And three mens strength unto the stroake he layd;
Wherewith the stiffe beame quaked as affrayd,
And glauncing from his scaly necke did glyde
Close under his left wing, then broad displayd:

xIx, 5   hagard: untamed

The percing steele there wrought a wound full wyde,
That with the uncouth smart the Monster lowdly cryde.

X X I

He cryde, as raging seas are wont to rore
When wintry storme his wrathful wreck does threat;
The rolling billowes beate the ragged shore,
As they the earth would shoulder from her seat;
And greedy gulfe does gape, as he would eat
His neighbour element in his revenge:
Then gin the blustring brethren boldly threat
To move the world from off his stedfast henge,
And boystrous battaile make, each other to avenge.

X X I I

The steely head stuck fast still in his flesh,
Till with his cruell clawes he snatcht the wood,
And quite a sunder broke. Forth flowed fresh
A gushing river of blacke gory blood,
That drowned all the land whereon he stood;
The streame thereof would drive a water-mill:
Trebly augmented was his furious mood
With bitter sence of his deepe rooted ill,
That flames of fire he threw forth from his large nosethril.

X X I I I

His hideous tayle then hurled he about,
And therewith all enwrapt the nimble thyes
Of his froth-fomy steed, whose courage stout
Striving to loose the knott that fast him tyes,
Himselfe in streighter bandes too rash implyes,
That to the ground he is perforce constraynd
To throw his ryder; who can quickly ryse
From off the earth, with durty blood distaynd,
For that reprochfull fall right fowly he disdaynd;

X X I V

And fercely tooke his trenchand blade in hand,
With which he stroke so furious and so fell,
That nothing seemd the puissaunce could withstand:
Upon his crest the hardned yron fell,
But his more hardned crest was armd so well,
That deeper dint therein it would not make;
Yet so extremely did the buffe him quell,

XXIII, 7   can: did

That from thenceforth he shund the like to take,
But when he saw them come he did them still forsake.

XXV

The knight was wroth to see his stroke beguyld,
And smot againe with more outrageous might;
But backe againe the sparcling steele recoyld,
And left not any marke where it did light,
As if in Adamant rocke it had beene pight.
The beast, impatient of his smarting wound
And of so fierce and forcible despight,
Thought with his winges to stye above the ground;
But his late wounded wing unserviceable found.

XXVI

Then full of griefe and anguish vehement,
He lowdly brayd, that like was never heard;
And from his wide devouring oven sent
A flake of fire, that flashing in his beard
Him all amazd, and almost made afeard:
The scorching flame sore swinged all his face,
And through his armour all his body seard,
That he could not endure so cruell cace,
But thought his armes to leave, and helmet to unlace.

XXVII

Not that great Champion of the antique world,
Whom famous Poetes verse so much doth vaunt,
And hath for twelve huge labours high extold,
So many furies and sharpe fits did haunt,
When him the poysoned garment did enchaunt,
When Centaures blood and bloody verses charmd;
As did this knight twelve thousand dolours daunt,
Whom fyrie steele now burnt, that erst him armd;
That erst him goodly armd, now most of all him harmd.

XXVIII

Faynt, wearie, sore, emboyled, grieved, brent,
With heat, toyle, wounds, armes, smart, and inward fire,
That never man such mischiefes did torment:
Death better were; death did he oft desire,
But death will never come when needes require.
Whom so dismayd when that his foe beheld,
He cast to suffer him no more respire,

xxv, 8   stye: rise   xxvi, 4   flake: flash

But gan his sturdy sterne about to weld,
And him so strongly stroke, that to the ground him feld.

X X I X

It fortuned, (as fayre it then befell)
Behynd his backe, unweeting, where he stood,
Of auncient time there was a springing well,
From which fast trickled forth a silver flood,
Full of great vertues, and for med'cine good:
Whylome, before that cursed Dragon got
That happy land, and all with innocent blood
Defyld those sacred waves, it rightly hot
The well of life, ne yet his vertues had forgot:

X X X

For unto life the dead it could restore,
And guilt of sinfull crimes cleane wash away;
Those that with sicknesse were infected sore
It could recure; and aged long decay
Renew, as one were borne that very day.
Both Silo this, and Jordan, did excell,
And th' English Bath, and eke the German Spau;
Ne can Cephise, nor Hebrus, match this well:
Into the same the knight back overthrowen fell.

X X X I

Now gan the golden Phœbus for to steepe
His fierie face in billowes of the west,
And his faint steedes watred in Ocean deepe,
Whiles from their journall labours they did rest;
When that infernall Monster, having kest
His wearie foe into that living well,
Gan high advaunce his broad discoloured brest
Above his wonted pitch, with countenance fell,
And clapt his yron wings as victor he did dwell.

X X X I I

Which when his pensive Lady saw from farre,
Great woe and sorrow did her soule assay,
As weening that the sad end of the warre;
And gan to highest God entirely pray
That feared chaunce from her to turne away:
With folded hands, and knees full lowly bent,
All night shee watcht, ne once adowne would lay

XXVIII, 8   sterne: tail   XXXI, 4   journall: daily

Her dainty limbs in her sad dreriment,
But praying still did wake, and waking did lament.

XXXIII

The morrow next gan earely to appeare,
That Titan rose to runne his daily race;
But earely, ere the morrow next gan reare
Out of the sea faire Titans deawy face,
Up rose the gentle virgin from her place,
And looked all about, if she might spy
Her loved knight to move his manly pace:
For she had great doubt of his safety,
Since late she saw him fall before his enimy.

XXXIV

At last she saw where he upstarted brave
Out of the well, wherein he drenched lay:
As Eagle, fresh out of the ocean wave,
Where he hath lefte his plumes all hory gray,
And deckt himselfe with fethers youthly gay,
Like Eyas hauke up mounts unto the skies,
His newly-budded pineons to assay,
And marveiles at himselfe stil as he flies:
So new this new-borne knight to battell new did rise.

XXXV

Whom when the damned feend so fresh did spy,
No wonder if he wondred at the sight,
And doubted whether his late enimy
It were, or other new supplied knight.
He now, to prove his late-renewed might,
High brandishing his bright deaw-burning blade.
Upon his crested scalp so sore did smite,
That to the scull a yawning wound it made:
The deadly dint his dulled sences all dismaid.

XXXVI

I wote not whether the revenging steele
Were hardned with that holy water dew
Wherein he fell, or sharper edge did feele,
Or his baptized hands now greater grew,
Or other secret vertue did ensew;
Els never could the force of fleshly arme,
Ne molten mettall, in his blood embrew;

xxxiv, 6   Eyas: newly fledged

For till that stownd could never wight him harme
By subtilty, nor slight, nor might, nor mighty charme.

x x x v i i

The cruell wound enraged him so sore,
That loud he yelded for exceeding paine;
As hundred ramping Lions seemd to rore,
Whom ravenous hunger did thereto constraine:
Then gan he tosse aloft his stretched traine,
And therewith scourge the buxome aire so sore,
That to his force to yielden it was faine;
Ne ought his sturdy strokes might stand afore,
That high trees overthrew, and rocks in peeces tore.

x x x v i i i

The same advauncing high above his head,
With sharpe intended sting so rude him smott,
That to the earth him drove, as stricken dead;
Ne living wight would have him life behott:
The mortall sting his angry needle shott
Quite through his shield, and in his shoulder seasd,
Where fast it stucke, ne would thereout be gott:
The griefe thereof him wondrous sore diseasd,
Ne might his rancling paine with patience be appeasd.

x x x i x

But yet, more mindfull of his honour deare
Then of the grievous smart which him did wring.
From loathed soile he can him lightly reare,
And strove to loose the far infixed sting:
Which when in vaine he tryde with struggeling,
Inflam'd with wrath, his raging blade he hefte,
And strooke so strongly, that the knotty string
Of his huge taile he quite a sonder clefte;
Five joints thereof he hewd, and but the stump him lefte.

x l

Hart cannot thinke what outrage and what cries,
With fowle enfouldred smoake and flashing fire,
The hell-bred beast threw forth unto the skies,
That all was covered with darknesse dire:
Then, fraught with rancour and engorged yre,
He cast at once him to avenge for all;
And, gathering up himselfe out of the mire

xxxvii, 6　buxome: yielding　　　　xxxviii, 4　behott: promised

With his uneven wings, did fiercely fall
Upon his sunne-bright shield, and grypt it fast withall.

X L I

Much was the man encombred with his hold,
In feare to lose his weapon in his paw,
Ne wist yett how his talaunts to unfold;
Nor harder was from Cerberus greedy jaw
To plucke a bone, then from his cruell claw
To reave by strength the griped gage away:
Thrise he assayd it from his foote to draw,
And thrise in vaine to draw it did assay;
It booted nought to thinke to robbe him of his pray.

X L I I

Tho, when he saw no power might prevaile,
His trusty sword he cald to his last aid,
Wherewith he fiersly did his foe assaile,
And double blowes about him stoutly laid,
That glauncing fire out of the yron plaid,
As sparkles from the Andvile use to fly,
When heavy hammers on the wedge are swaid:
Therewith at last he forst him to unty
One of his grasping feete, him to defend thereby.

X L I I I

The other foote, fast fixed on his shield,
Whenas no strength nor stroks mote him constraine
To loose, ne yet the warlike pledge to yield,
He smott thereat with all his might and maine,
That nought so wondrous puissaunce might sustaine:
Upon the joint the lucky steele did light,
And made such way that hewd it quite in twaine;
The paw yett missed not his minisht might,
But hong still on the shield, as it at first was pight.

X L I V

For griefe thereof and divelish despight,
From his infernall fournace forth he threw
Huge flames that dimmed all the hevens light,
Enrold in duskish smoke and brimstone blew:
As burning Aetna from his boyling stew
Doth belch out flames, and rockes in peeces broke,
And ragged ribs of mountaines molten new,

XLI, 3   talaunts: talons

Enwrapt in coleblacke clowds and filthy smoke,
That al the land with stench and heven with horror choke.

X L V

The heate whereof, and harmefull pestilence,
So sore him noyd, that forst him to retire
A little backeward for his best defence,
To save his body from the scorching fire,
Which he from hellish entrailes did expire.
It chaunst, (eternall God that chaunce did guide)
As he recoiled backeward, in the mire
His nigh foreweried feeble feet did slide,
And downe he fell, with dread of shame sore terrifide.

X L V I

There grew a goodly tree him faire beside,
Loaden with fruit and apples rosy redd,
As they in pure vermilion had been dide,
Whereof great vertues over-all were redd;
For happy life to all which thereon fedd,
And life eke everlasting did befall:
Great God it planted in that blessed stedd
With his Almighty hand, and did it call
The tree of life, the crime of our first fathers fall.

X L V I I

In all the world like was not to be fownd,
Save in that soile, where all good things did grow,
And freely sprong out of the fruitfull grownd,
As incorrupted Nature did them sow,
Till that dredd Dragon all did overthrow.
Another like faire tree eke grew thereby,
Whereof whoso did eat, eftsoones did know
Both good and ill. O mournfull memory!
That tree through one mans fault hath doen us all to dy.

X L V I I I

From that first tree forth flowd, as from a well,
A trickling streame of Balme, most soveraine
And dainty deare, which on the ground still fell,
And overflowed all the fertile plaine,
As it had deawed bene with timely raine:
Life and long health that gracious ointment gave,
And deadly wounds could heale, and reare againe

XLVI, 7   stedd: place

The senceless corse appointed for the grave:
Into that same he fell, which did from death him save.

XLIX

For nigh thereto the ever damned Beast
Durst not approch, for he was deadly made,
And al that life preserved did detest;
Yet he it oft adventur'd to invade.
By this the drouping day-light gan to fade,
And yield his rowme to sad succeeding night,
Who with her sable mantle gan to shade
The face of earth and wayes of living wight,
And high her burning torch set up in heaven bright.

L

When gentle Una saw the second fall
Of her deare knight, who, weary of long fight
And faint through losse of blood, moov'd not at all,
But lay, as in a dreame of deepe delight,
Besmeard with pretious Balme, whose vertuous might
Did heale his woundes, and scorching heat alay;
Againe she stricken was with sore affright,
And for his safetie gan devoutly pray,
And watch the noyous night, and wait for joyous day.

LI

The joyous day gan early to appeare;
And fayre Aurora from the deawy bed
Of aged Tithone gan herselfe to reare
With rosy cheekes, for shame as blushing red:
Her golden locks for hast were loosely shed
About her eares, when Una her did marke
Clymbe to her charet, all with flowers spred,
From heven high to chace the chearelesse darke;
With mery note her lowd salutes the mounting larke.

LII

Then freshly up arose the doughty knight,
All healed of his hurts and woundes wide,
And did himselfe to battaile ready dight;
Whose early foe awaiting him beside
To have devourd, so soone as day he spyde,
When now he saw himselfe so freshly reare,
As if late fight had nought him damnifyde,
He woxe dismaid, and gan his fate to feare:
Nathlesse with wonted rage he him advaunced neare.

L I I I

And in his first encounter, gaping wyde,
He thought attonce him to have swallowd quight,
And rusht upon him with outragious pryde;
Who him rencountring fierce, as hauke in flight,
Perforce rebutted backe. The weapon bright,
Taking advantage of his open jaw,
Ran through his mouth with so importune might,
That deepe emperst his darksom hollow maw,
And, back retyrd, his life blood forth with all did draw.

L I V

So downe he fell, and forth his life did breath,
That vanisht into smoke and cloudes swift;
So downe he fell, that th' earth him underneath
Did grone, as feeble so great load to lift;
So downe he fell, as an huge rocky clift,
Whose false foundacion waves have washt away,
With dreadfull poyse is from the mayneland rift,
And rolling downe great Neptune doth dismay:
So downe he fell, and like an heaped mountaine lay.

L V

The knight him selfe even trembled at his fall,
So huge and horrible a masse it seemd;
And his deare Lady, that beheld it all,
Durst not approch for dread which she misdeemd;
But yet at last, whenas the direfull feend
She saw not stirre, off-shaking vaine affright
She nigher drew, and saw that joyous end:
Then God she praysd, and thankt her faithfull knight,
That had atchievde so great a conquest by his might.

CANTO XII.

Fayre Una to the Redcrosse Knight
Betrouthed is with joy:
Though false Duessa, it to barre,
Her false sleightes doe imploy.

I

BEHOLD! I see the haven nigh at hand
To which I meane my wearie course to bend;

LIV, 7   poyse: weight

Vere the maine shete, and beare up with the land,
The which afore is fayrly to be kend,
And seemeth safe from storms that may offend;
There this fayre virgin wearie of her way
Must landed bee, now at her journeyes end;
There eke my feeble barke a while may stay,
Till mery wynd and weather call her thence away.

I I

Scarsely had Phœbus in the glooming East
Yett harnessed his fyrie-footed teeme,
Ne reard above the earth his flaming creast,
When the last deadly smoke aloft did steeme,
That signe of last outbreathed life did seeme
Unto the watchman on the castle-wall;
Who thereby dead that balefull Beast did deeme,
And to his Lord and Lady lowd gan call,
To tell how he had seene the Dragons fatall fall.

I I I

Uprose with hasty joy, and feeble speed,
That aged Syre, the Lord of all that land,
And looked forth, to weet if trew indeed
Those tydinges were, as he did understand:
Which whenas trew by tryall he out fond,
He badd to open wyde his brasen gate,
Which long time had beene shut, and out of hond
Proclaymed joy and peace through all his state;
For dead now was their foe, which them forrayed late.

I V

Then gan triumphant Trompets sownd on hye,
That sent to heven the ecchoed report
Of their new joy, and happie victory
Gainst him, that had them long opprest with tort,
And fast imprisoned in sieged fort.
Then all the people, as in solemne feast,
To him assembled with one full consort,
Rejoycing at the fall of that great beast,
From whose eternall bondage now they were release.

V

Forth came that auncient Lord, and aged Queene,
Arayd in antique robes downe to the grownd,
And sad habiliments right well beseene:

IV, 4   tort: wrong

A noble crew about them waited rownd
Of sage and sober peres, all gravely gownd;
Whom far before did march a goodly band
Of tall young men, all hable armes to sownd;
But now they laurell braunches bore in hand,
Glad signe of victory and peace in all their land.

V I

Unto that doughtie Conquerour they came,
And him before themselves prostrating low,
Their Lord and Patrone loud did him proclame,
And at his feet their lawrell boughes did throw.
Soone after them, all dauncing on a row,
The comely virgins came, with girlands dight,
As fresh as flowres in medow greene doe grow
When morning deaw upon their leaves doth light;
And in their handes sweet Timbrels all upheld on hight.

V I I

And them before the fry of children yong
Their wanton sportes and childish mirth did play,
And to the Maydens sownding tymbrels song
In well attuned notes a joyous lay,
And made delightful musick all the way,
Untill they came where that faire virgin stood:
As fayre Diana in fresh sommers day
Beholdes her nymphes enraung'd in shady wood,
Some wrestle, some do run, some bathe in christall flood.

V I I I

So she beheld those maydens meriment
With chearefull vew; who, when to her they came,
Themselves to ground with gracious humblesse bent,
And her ador'd by honorable name,
Lifting to heven her everlasting fame:
Then on her head they sett a girlond greene,
And crowned her twixt earnest and twixt game:
Who, in her self-resemblance well beseene,
Did seeme, such as she was, a goodly maiden Queene.

I X

And after all the raskall many ran,
Heaped together in rude rablement,
To see the face of that victorious man,

VII, 2   wanton: careless   IX, I   many: company
IX, I   raskall: base

Whom all admired as from heaven sent,
And gazd upon with gaping wonderment;
But when they came where that dead Dragon lay,
Stretcht on the ground in monstrous large extent,
The sight with ydle feare did them dismay,
Ne durst approch him nigh to touch, or once assay.

x

Some feard, and fledd; some feard, and well it faynd;
One, that would wiser seeme then all the rest,
Warnd him not touch, for yet perhaps remaynd
Some lingring life within his hollow brest,
Or in his wombe might lurke some hidden nest
Of many Dragonettes, his fruitfull seede:
Another saide, that in his eyes did rest
Yet sparckling fyre, and badd thereof take heed;
Another said, he saw him move his eyes indeed.

X I

One mother, whenas her foolehardy chyld
Did come too neare, and with his talants play,
Halfe dead through feare, her litle babe revyld,
And to her gossibs gan in counsell say;
'How can I tell, but that his talants may
Yet scratch my sonne, or rend his tender hand?'
So diversly them selves in vaine they fray;
Whiles some more bold to measure him nigh stand,
To prove how many acres he did spred of land.

X I I

Thus flocked all the folke him rownd about;
The whiles that hoarie king, with all his traine,
Being arrived where that champion stout
After his foes defeasaunce did remaine,
Him goodly greetes, and fayre does entertayne
With princely gifts of yvory and gold,
And thousand thankes him yeeldes for all his paine.
Then when his daughter deare he does behold,
Her dearely doth imbrace, and kisseth manifold.

X I I I

And after to his Pallace he them bringes,
With shaumes, and trompets, and with Clarions sweet;
And all the way the joyous people singes,
And with their garments strowes the paved street;

XI, 2   talants: talons

Whence mounting up, they fynd purveyaunce meet
Of all, that royall Princes court became;
And all the floore was underneath their feet
Bespredd with costly scarlott of great name,
On which they lowly sitt, and fitting purpose frame.

X I V

What needes me tell their feast and goodly guize,
In which was nothing riotous nor vaine?
What needes of dainty dishes to devize,
Of comely services, or courtly trayne?
My narrow leaves cannot in them contayne
The large discourse of roiall Princes state.
Yet was their manner then but bare and playne;
For th' antique world excesse and pryde did hate:
Such proud luxurious pompe is swollen up but late.

X V

Then, when with meates and drinkes of every kinde
Their fervent appetites they quenched had,
That auncient Lord gan fit occasion finde,
Of straunge adventures, and of perils sad
Which in his travell him befallen had,
For to demaund of his renowmed guest:
Who then with utt'rance grave, and count'nance sad,
From poynt to poynt, as is before exprest,
Discourst his voyage long, according his request.

X V I

Great pleasure, mixt with pittiful regard,
That godly King and Queene did passionate,
Whyles they his pittifull adventures heard;
That oft they did lament his lucklesse state,
And often blame the too importune fate
That heapd on him so many wrathfull wreakes;
For never gentle knight, as he of late,
So tossed was in fortunes cruell freakes:
And all the while salt teares bedeawd the hearers cheaks.

X V I I

Then sayd that royall Pere in sober wise;
'Deare Sonne, great beene the evils which ye bore
From first to last in your late enterprise,
That I note whether praise or pitty more;
For never living man, I weene, so sore

XVI, 2 passionate: express feelingly   XVII, 4 note: do not know

In sea of deadly daungers was distrest:
But since now safe ye seised have the shore,
And well arrived are, (high God be blest!)
Let us devize of ease and everlasting rest.'

x v i i i

'Ah dearest Lord!' said then that doughty knight,
'Of ease or rest I may not yet devize;
For by the faith which I to armes have plight,
I bownden am streight after this emprize,
As that your daughter can ye well advize,
Backe to retourne to that great Faery Queene,
And her to serve sixe yeares in warlike wize,
Gainst that proud Paynim king that works her teene:
Therefore I ought crave pardon, till I there have beene.'

x i x

'Unhappy falls that hard necessity,'
(Quoth he) 'the troubler of my happy peace,
And vowed foe of my felicity;
Ne I against the same can justly preace:
But since that band ye cannot now release,
Nor doen undo, (for vowes may not be vayne)
Soone as the terme of those six yeares shall cease,
Ye then shall hither backe retourne agayne,
The marriage to accomplish vowd betwixt you twayn.

x x

'Which, for my part, I covet to performe
In sort as through the world I did proclame,
That who-so kild that monster most deforme,
And him in hardy battayle overcame,
Should have mine onely daughter to his Dame,
And of my kingdom heyre apparaunt bee:
Therefore, since now to thee perteynes the same
By dew desert of noble chevalree,
Both daughter and eke kingdome lo! I yield to thee.'

x x i

Then forth he called that his daughter fayre,
The fairest Un', his onely daughter deare,
His onely daughter and his only hayre;
Who forth proceeding with sad sober cheare,
As bright as doth the morning starre appeare

xix, 4   preace: contend

Out of the East, with flaming lockes bedight,
To tell that dawning day is drawing neare,
And to the world does bring long-wished light:
So faire and fresh that Lady shewd herselfe in sight.

X X I I

So faire and fresh, as freshest flowre in May;
For she had layd her mournefull stole aside,
And widow-like sad wimple throwne away,
Wherewith her heavenly beautie she did hide,
Whiles on her wearie journey she did ride;
And on her now a garment she did weare
All lilly white, withoutten spot or pride,
That seemd like silke and silver woven neare;
But neither silke nor silver therein did appeare.

X X I I I

The blazing brightnesse of her beauties beame,
And glorious light of her sunshyny face,
To tell were as to strive against the streame:
My ragged rimes are all too rude and bace
Her heavenly lineaments for to enchace.
Ne wonder; for her own deare loved knight,
All were she daily with himselfe in place,
Did wonder much at her celestial sight:
Oft had he seene her faire, but never so faire dight.

X X I V

So fairely dight when she in presence came,
She to her Syre made humble reverence,
And bowed low, that her right well became,
And added grace unto her excellence:
Who with great wisedome and grave eloquence
Thus gan to say—But, eare he thus had sayd,
With flying speede, and seeming great pretence,
Came running in, much like a man dismayd,
A Messenger with letters, which his message sayd.

X X V

All in the open hall amazed stood
At suddeinnesse of that unwary sight,
And wondred at his breathlesse hasty mood:
But he for nought would stay his passage right,
Till fast before the king he did alight;
Where falling flat great humblesse he did make,

And kist the ground whereon his foot was pight;
Then to his handes that writt he did betake,
Which he disclosing read thus, as the paper spake:

X X V I

'To thee, most mighty king of Eden fayre,
Her greeting sends in these sad lines addrest
The wofull daughter and forsaken heyre
Of that great Emperour of all the West;
And bids thee be advized for the best,
Ere thou thy daughter linck, in holy band
Of wedlocke, to that new unknowen guest:
For he already plighted his right hand
Unto another love, and to another land.

X X V I I

'To me, sad mayd, or rather widow sad,
He was affyaunced long time before,
And sacred pledges he both gave, and had,
False erraunt knight, infamous, and forswore!
Witnesse the burning Altars, which he swore,
And guilty heavens of his bold perjury;
Which though he hath polluted oft of yore,
Yet I to them for judgement just doe fly,
And them conjure t' avenge this shamefull injury.

X X V I I I

'Therefore, since mine he is, or free or bond,
Or false or trew, or living or else dead,
Withhold, O soverayne Prince! your hasty hond
From knitting league with him, I you aread;
Ne weene my right with strength adowne to tread,
Through weaknesse of my widowhed or woe;
For truth is strong her rightfull cause to plead,
And shall finde friends, if need requireth soe.
So bids thee well to fare, Thy neither friend nor foe,
                                              Fidessa.'

X X I X

When he these bitter byting wordes had red,
The tydings straunge did him abashed make,
That still he sate long time astonished,
As in great muse, ne word to creature spake.
At last his solemn silence thus he brake,
With doubtfull eyes fast fixed on his guest:

'Redoubted knight, that for myne only sake
Thy life and honor late adventurest,
Let nought be hid from me that ought to be exprest.

x x x

'What meane these bloody vowes and idle threats,
Throwne out from womanish impatient mynd?
What hevens? what altars? what enraged heates,
Here heaped up with termes of love unkynd,
My conscience cleare with guilty bands would bynd?
High God be witnesse that I guiltlesse ame;
But if yourselfe, Sir knight, ye faulty fynd,
Or wrapped be in loves of former Dame,
With cryme doe not it cover, but disclose the same.'

x x x i

To whom the Redcrosse knight this answere sent:
'My Lord, my king, be nought hereat dismayd,
Till well ye wote by grave intendiment,
What woman, and wherefore, doth me upbrayd
With breach of love and loialty betrayd.
It was in my mishaps, as hitherward
I lately traveild, that unwares I strayd
Out of my way, through perils straunge and hard,
That day should faile me ere I had them all declard.

x x x i i

'There did I find, or rather I was fownd
Of this false woman that Fidessa hight,
Fidessa hight the falsest Dame on grownd,
Most false Duessa, royall richly dight,
That easy was t' inveigle weaker sight:
Who by her wicked arts and wylie skill,
Too false and strong for earthly skill or might,
Unwares me wrought unto her wicked will,
And to my foe betrayd when least I feared ill.'

x x x i i i

Then stepped forth the goodly royall Mayd,
And on the ground herselfe prostrating low,
With sober countenance thus to him sayd:
'O! pardon me, my soveraine Lord, to show
The secret treasons, which of late I know
To have bene wrought by that false sorceresse:
Shee, onely she, it is, that earst did throw

This gentle knight into so great distresse,
That death him did awaite in daily wretchednesse.

X X X I V

'And now it seemes, that she suborned hath
This crafty messenger with letters vaine,
To worke new woe and improvided scath,
By breaking of the band betwixt us twaine;
Wherein she used hath the practicke paine
Of this false footman, clokt with simplenesse,
Whome if ye please for to discover plaine,
Ye shall him Archimago find, I ghesse,
The falsest man alive: who tries, shall find no lesse.'

X X X V

The king was greatly moved at her speach;
And, all with suddein indignation fraight,
Bad on that Messenger rude hands to reach.
Eftsoones the Gard, which on his state did wait,
Attacht that faytor false, and bound him strait,
Who seeming sorely chauffed at his band,
As chained beare whom cruell dogs doe bait,
With ydle force did faine them to withstand,
And often semblaunce made to scape out of their hand.

X X X V I

But they him layd full low in dungeon deepe,
And bound him hand and foote with yron chains;
And with continual watch did warely keepe.
Who then would thinke that by his subtile trains
He could escape fowle death or deadly pains?
Thus, when that Princes wrath was pacifide,
He gan renew the late forbidden bains,
And to the knight his daughter deare he tyde
With sacred rites and vowes for ever to abyde.

X X X V I I

His owne two hands the holy knotts did knitt,
That none but death for ever can divide;
His owne two hands, for such a turne most fitt,
The housling fire did kindle and provide,
And holy water thereon sprinckled wide;
At which the bushy Teade a groome did light,
And sacred lamp in secret chamber hide,

xxxiv, 5   practicke: crafty   xxxvii, 6   Teade: torch
xxxvii, 4   housling: sacramental

Where it should not be quenched day nor night,
For feare of evil fates, but burnen ever bright.

XXXVIII

Then gan they sprinckle all the posts with wine,
And made great feast to solemnize that day:
They all perfumde with frankincense divine,
And precious odours fetcht from far away,
That all the house did sweat with great aray:
And all the while sweete Musicke did apply
Her curious skill the warbling notes to play,
To drive away the dull Melancholy;
The whiles one sung a song of love and jollity.

XXXIX

During the which there was an heavenly noise
Heard sownd through all the Pallace pleasantly,
Like as it had bene many an Angels voice
Singing before th' eternall majesty,
In their trinall triplicities on hye:
Yett wist no creature whence that hevenly sweet
Proceeded, yet each one felt secretly
Himselfe thereby refte of his sences meet,
And ravished with rare impression in his sprite.

XL

Great joy was made that day of young and old,
And solemne feast proclaymd throughout the land,
That their exceeding merth may not be told:
Suffice it heare by signes to understand
The usuall joyes at knitting of loves band.
Thrise happy man the knight himselfe did hold,
Possessed of his Ladies hart and hand;
And ever, when his eie did her behold,
His heart did seeme to melt in pleasures manifold.

XLI

Her joyous presence, and sweet company,
In full content he there did long enjoy;
Ne wicked envy, ne vile gealosy,
His deare delights were hable to annoy:
Yet, swimming in that sea of blisfull joy,
He nought forgott how he whilome had sworne,
In case he could that monstrous beast destroy,
Unto his Faery Queene backe to retourne;
The which he shortly did, and Una left to mourne.

XLII

Now, strike your sailes, yee jolly Mariners,
For we be come unto a quiet rode,
Where we must land some of our passengers,
And light this weary vessell of her lode:
Here she a while may make her safe abode,
Till she repaired have her tackles spent,
And wants supplide; and then againe abroad
On the long voiage whereto she is bent:
Well may she speede, and fairely finish her intent!

THE SECOND BOOK OF

THE FAERIE QUEENE

Contayning the Legend of Sir Guyon,
or of Temperaunce.

I

RIGHT WELL I WOTE, most mighty Soveraine,
That all this famous antique history
Of some th' aboundance of an ydle braine
Will judged be, and painted forgery,
Rather then matter of just memory;
Sith none that breatheth living aire does know
Where is that happy land of Faery,
Which I so much doe vaunt, yet no where show,
But vouch antiquities, which no body can know.

I I

But let that man with better sence advize,
That of the world least part to us is red;
And daily how through hardy enterprize
Many great Regions are discovered,
Which to late age were never mentioned.
Who ever heard of th' Indian Peru?
Or who in venturous vessell measured
The Amazons huge river, now found trew?
Or fruitfullest Virginia who did ever vew?

III

Yet all these were, when no man did them know,
Yet have from wisest ages hidden beene;
And later times thinges more unknowne shall show.
Why then should witlesse man so much misweene,
That nothing is but that which he hath seene?
What if within the Moones fayre shining spheare,
What if in every other starre unseene
Of other worldes he happily should heare,
He wonder would much more; yet such to some appeare.

IV

Of faery lond yet if he more inquyre,
By certein signes, here sett in sondrie place,
He may it fynd; ne let him then admyre,
But yield his sence to bee too blunt and bace,
That no'te without an hound fine footing trace.
And thou, O fayrest Princesse under sky!
In this fayre mirrhour maist behold thy face,
And thine owne realmes in lond of Faery,
And in this antique ymage thy great auncestry.

V

The which O! pardon me thus to enfold
In covert vele, and wrap in shadowes light,
That feeble eyes your glory may behold,
Which ells could not endure those beames bright,
But would bee dazled with exceeding light.
O! pardon, and vouchsafe with patient eare
The brave adventures of this faery knight,
The good Sir Guyon, gratiously to heare;
In whom great rule of Temp'raunce goodly doth appeare.

[*Early in the Legend of Temperance Sir Guyon, accompanied by his faithful guide, the Palmer, chances upon the dying lady Amavia. She has stabbed herself in grief over the death of her husband Mortdant, victim of the enchantments of the witch Acrasia. Their child Ruddymane plays on her body. Taking up the bloody-handed baby, Guyon swears vengeance. Later, he and Prince Arthur fight their way through an army of besiegers into the House of Alma where they are fairly entertained. The eleventh canto tells of Arthur's conquest of Maleger, chief of the besieging force, the twelfth of Guyon's fulfillment of his pledged vengeance.*]

III, 8   happily: by chance   IV, 3   admyre: wonder

CANTO XI.

The enimies of Temperaunce
Besiege her dwelling place:
Prince Arthure them repelles, and fowle
Maleger doth deface.

I

WHAT WARRE SO CRUEL, or what siege so sore,
As that which strong affections doe apply
Against the forte of reason evermore,
To bring the sowle into captivity?
Their force is fiercer through infirmity
Of the fraile flesh, relenting to their rage,
And exercise most bitter tyranny
Upon the partes brought into their bondage:
No wretchednesse is like to sinfull vellenage.

I I

But in a body which doth freely yeeld
His partes to reasons rule obedient,
And letteth her that ought the scepter weeld,
All happy peace and goodly government
Is setled there in sure establishment.
There Alma, like a virgin Queene most bright,
Doth florish in all beautie excellent;
And to her guestes doth bounteous banket dight,
Attempred goodly well for health and for delight.

I I I

Early, before the Morne with cremosin ray
The windowes of bright heaven opened had,
Through which into the world the dawning day
Might looke, that maketh every creature glad,
Uprose Sir Guyon, in bright armour clad,
And to his purposd journey him prepar'd:
With him the Palmer eke in habit sad
Him selfe addrest to that adventure hard:
So to the rivers syde they both together far'd:

I V

Where them awaited ready at the ford
The Ferriman, as Alma had behight,
With his well-rigged bote: They goe abord,

1, 6   relenting: giving way*

And he eftsoones gan launch his barke forthright.
Ere long they rowed were quite out of sight,
And fast the land behynd them fled away.
But let them pas, whiles wind and wether right
Doe serve their turnes: here I a while must stay,
To see a cruell fight doen by the prince this day.

v

For all so soone as Guyon thence was gon
Upon his voyage with his trustie guyde,
That wicked band of villeins fresh begon
That castle to assaile on every side,
And lay strong siege about it far and wyde.
So huge and infinite their numbers were,
That all the land they under them did hyde;
So fowle and ugly, that exceeding feare
Their visages imprest when they approched neare.

v i

Them in twelve troupes their Captein did dispart,
And round about in fittest steades did place,
Where each might best offend his proper part,
And his contrary object most deface,
As every one seem'd meetest in that cace.
Seven of the same against the Castle gate
In strong entrenchments he did closely place,
Which with incessaunt force and endlesse hate
They battred day and night, and entraunce did awate.

v i i

The other five five sondry wayes he sett
Against the five great Bulwarkes of that pyle,
And unto each a Bulwarke did arrett,
T' assayle with open force or hidden guyle,
In hope thereof to win victorious spoile.
They all that charge did fervently apply
With greedie malice and importune toyle,
And planted there their huge artillery,
With which they dayly made most dreadfull battery.

v i i i

The first troupe was a monstrous rablement
Of fowle misshapen wightes, of which some were
Headed like Owles, with beckes uncomely bent;
Others like Dogs; others like Gryphons dreare;

VII, 3   arrett: entrust

And some had wings, and some had clawes to teare:
And every one of them had Lynces eyes;
And every one did bow and arrowes beare.
All those were lawlesse lustes, currupt envyes,
And covetous aspects, all cruell enimyes.

I X

Those same against the bulwarke of the Sight
Did lay strong siege and battailous assault,
Ne once did yield it respitt day nor night;
But soone as Titan gan his head exault,
And soone againe as he his light withhault,
Their wicked engins they against it bent;
That is, each thing by which the eyes may fault:
But two then all more huge and violent,
Beautie and Money, they that Bulwarke sorely rent.

X

The second Bulwarke was the Hearing sence,
Gainst which the second troupe assignment makes;
Deformed creatures, in straunge difference,
Some having heads like Harts, some like to Snakes,
Some like wilde Bores late rouzd out of the brakes:
Slaunderous reproches, and fowle infamies,
Leasinges, backbytinges, and vain-glorious crakes,
Bad counsels, prayses, and false flatteries:
All those against that fort did bend their batteries.

X I

Likewise that same third Fort, that is the Smell,
Of that third troupe was cruelly assayd;
Whose hideous shapes were like to feendes of hell,
Some like to houndes, some like to Apes, dismayd,
Some like to Puttockes, all in plumes arayd;
All shap't according their conditions:
For by those ugly formes weren pourtrayd
Foolish delights, and fond abusions,
Which doe that sence besiege with light illusions.

X I I

And that fourth band which cruell battry bent
Against the fourth Bulwarke, that is the Taste,
Was, as the rest, a grysie rablement;

VIII, 8   envyes: desires   XI, 5   Puttockes: buzzards
x, 7   crakes: boasts

Some mouth'd like greedy Oystriges; some faste
Like loathly Toades; some fashioned in the waste
Like swine: for so deformd is luxury,
Surfeat, misdiet, and unthriftie waste,
Vaine feastes, and ydle superfluity:
All those this sences Fort assayle incessantly.

X I I I

But the fift troupe, most horrible of hew
And ferce of force, is dreadfull to report;
For some like Snailes, some did like spyders shew,
And some like ugly Urchins thick and short:
Cruelly they assayed that fift Fort,
Armed with dartes of sensuall Delight,
With stinges of carnall lust, and strong effort
Of feeling pleasures, with which day and night
Against that same fift bulwarke they continued fight.

X I V

Thus these twelve troupes with dreadfull puissaunce
Against that Castle restlesse siege did lay,
And evermore their hideous Ordinaunce
Upon the Bulwarkes cruelly did play,
That now it gan to threaten neare decay:
And evermore their wicked Capitayn
Provoked them the breaches to assay,
Sometimes with threats, sometimes with hope of gayn,
Which by the ransack of that peece they should attayn.

X V

On th' other syde, th' assieged Castles ward
Their stedfast stonds did mightily maintaine,
And many bold repulse and many hard
Atchievement wrought, with perill and with payne,
That goodly frame from ruine to sustaine:
And those two brethren Gyauntes did defend
The walles so stoutly with their sturdie mayne,
That never entraunce any durst pretend,
But they to direfull death their groning ghosts did send.

X V I

The noble Virgin, Ladie of the Place,
Was much dismayed with that dreadful sight,
For never was she in so evill cace,
Till that the Prince, seeing her wofull plight,

XII, 4   faste: faced

Gan her recomfort from so sad affright,
Offring his service, and his dearest life
For her defence against that Carle to fight,
Which was their chiefe and th' authour of that strife:
She him remercied as the Patrone of her life.

XVII

Eftsoones himselfe in glitterand armes he dight,
And his well proved weapons to him hent;
So, taking courteous congé, he behight
Those gates to be unbar'd, and forth he went.
Fayre mote he thee, the prowest and most gent,
That ever brandished bright steele on hye!
Whome soone as that unruly rablement
With his gay Squyre issewing did espye,
They reard a most outrageous dreadfull yelling cry:

XVIII

And therewithall attonce at him let fly
Their fluttring arrowes, thicke as flakes of snow,
And round about him flocke impetuously,
Like a great water flood, that tombling low
From the high mountaines, threates to overflow
With suddein fury all the fertile playne,
And the sad husbandmans long hope doth throw
Adowne the streame, and all his vowes make vayne;
Nor bounds nor banks his headlong ruine may sustayne.

XIX

Upon his shield their heaped hayle he bore,
And with his sword disperst the raskall flockes,
Which fled asonder, and him fell before;
As withered leaves drop from their dryed stockes,
When the wroth Western wind does reave their locks:
And underneath him his courageous steed,
The fierce Spumador, trode them downe like docks;
The fierce Spumador, borne of heavenly seed,
Such as Laomedon of Phœbus race did breed.

XX

Which suddeine horrour and confused cry
When as their Capteine heard, in haste he yode
The cause to weet, and fault to remedy:
Upon a Tygre swift and fierce he rode,
That as the winde ran underneath his lode,

XVII, 5   thee: prosper   XIX, 7   docks: weeds

Whiles his long legs nigh raught unto the ground.
Full large he was of limbe, and shoulders brode,
But of such subtile substance and unsound,
That like a ghost he seem'd whose grave-clothes were un-
    bound:

X X I

And in his hand a bended bow was seene,
And many arrowes under his right side,
All deadly daungerous, all cruell keene,
Headed with flint, and fethers bloody dide;
Such as the Indians in their quivers hide:
Those could he well direct and streight as line,
And bid them strike the marke which he had eyde;
Ne was there salve, ne was there medicine,
That mote recure their wounds; so inly they did tine.

X X I I

As pale and wan as ashes was his looke,
His body leane and meagre as a rake,
And skin all withered like a dryed rooke;
Thereto as cold and drery as a snake,
That seemd to tremble evermore and quake;
All in a canvas thin he was bedight,
And girded with a belt of twisted brake:
Upon his head he wore an Helmet light,
Made of a dead mans skull, that seemd a ghastly sight.

X X I I I

Maleger was his name; and after him
There follow'd fast at hand two wicked Hags,
With hoary lockes all loose, and visage grim:
Their feet unshod, their bodies wrapt in rags,
And both as swift on foot as chased Stags;
And yet the one her other legge had lame,
Which with a staffe, all full of litle snags,
She did support, and Impotence her name.
But th' other was Impatience, arm'd with raging flame.

X X I V

Soone as the Carle from far the Prince espyde
Glistring in armes and warlike ornament,
His Beast he felly prickt on either syde,
And his mischievous bow full readie bent,
With which at him a cruell shaft he sent:

xxi, 9   tine: suffer   xxii, 7   brake: bracken

But he was warie, and it warded well
Upon his shield, that it no further went,
But to the ground the idle quarrell fell:
Then he another and another did expell.

X X V

Which to prevent the Prince his mortall speare
Soone to him raught, and fierce at him did ride,
To be avenged of that shot whyleare;
But he was not so hardy to abide
That bitter stownd, but turning quicke aside
His light-foot beast, fled fast away for feare:
Whom to poursue the Infant after hide
So fast as his good Courser could him beare;
But labour lost it was to weene approch him neare.

X X V I

For as the winged wind his Tigre fled,
That vew of eye could scarse him overtake,
Ne scarse his feet on ground were seene to tred:
Through hils and dales he speedy way did make,
Ne hedge ne ditch his readie passage brake;
And in his flight the villein turn'd his face
(As wonts the Tartar by the Caspian lake,
Whenas the Russian him in fight does chace)
Unto his Tygres taile, and shot at him apace.

X X V I I

Apace he shot, and yet he fled apace,
Still as the greedy knight nigh to him drew;
And oftentimes he would relent his pace,
That him his foe more fiercely should poursew:
But when his uncouth manner he did vew,
He gan avize to follow him no more,
But keepe his standing, and his shaftes eschew,
Untill he quite had spent his perlous store,
And then assayle him fresh, ere he could shift for more.

X X V I I I

But that lame Hag, still as abroad he strew
His wicked arrowes, gathered them againe,
And to him brought, fresh batteill to renew;
Which he espying cast her to restraine
From yielding succour to that cursed Swaine,
And her attaching thought her hands to tye;
But soone as him dismounted on the plaine

That other Hag did far away espye
Binding her sister, she to him ran hastily;

X X I X

And catching hold of him, as downe he lent,
Him backeward overthrew, and downe him stayd
With their rude handes and gryesly graplement;
Till that the villein, comming to their ayd,
Upon him fell, and lode upon him layd:
Full litle wanted but he had him slaine,
And of the battell balefull end had made,
Had not his gentle Squire beheld his paine,
And commen to his reskew, ere his bitter bane.

X X X

So greatest and most glorious thing on ground
May often need the helpe of weaker hand;
So feeble is mans state, and life unsound,
That in assuraunce it may never stand,
Till it dissolved be from earthly band.
Proofe be thou, Prince, the prowest man alyve,
And noblest borne of all in Britayne land;
Yet thee fierce Fortune did so nearely drive,
That, had not grace thee blest, thou shouldest not survive.

X X X I

The Squyre arriving fiercely in his armes
Snatcht first the one, and then the other Jade,
His chiefest letts and authors of his harmes,
And them perforce withheld with threatned blade,
Least that his Lord they should behinde invade;
The whiles the Prince, prickt with reprochful shame,
As one awakte out of long slombring shade,
Revivyng thought of glory and of fame,
United all his powres to purge him selfe from blame.

X X X I I

Like as a fire, the which in hollow cave
Hath long bene underkept and down supprest,
With murmurous disdayne doth inly rave,
And grudge in so streight prison to be prest,
At last breakes forth with furious unrest,
And strives to mount unto his native seat;
All that did earst it hinder and molest,
Yt now devoures with flames and scorching heat,
And carries into smoake with rage and horror great.

X X X I I I

So mightely the Briton Prince him rouzd
Out of his holde, and broke his caytive bands;
And as a Beare, whom angry curres have touzd,
Having off-shakt them and escapt their hands,
Becomes more fell, and all that him withstands
Treads down and overthrowes. Now had the Carle
Alighted from his Tigre, and his hands
Discharged of his bow and deadly quar'le,
To seize upon his foe flatt lying on the marle.

X X X I V

Which now him turnd to disavantage deare;
For neither can he fly, nor other harme,
But trust unto his strength and manhood meare,
Sith now he is far from his monstrous swarme,
And of his weapons did himselfe disarme.
The knight, yet wrothfull for his late disgrace,
Fiercely advaunst his valorous right arme,
And him so sore smott with his yron mace,
That groveling to the ground he fell, and fild his place.

X X X V

Wel weened hee that field was then his owne,
And all his labor brought to happy end;
When suddein up the villeine overthrowne
Out of his swowne arose, fresh to contend,
And gan him selfe to second battaill bend,
As hurt he had not beene. Thereby there lay
An huge great stone, which stood upon one end,
And had not bene removed many a day;
Some land-marke seemd to bee, or signe of sundry way:

X X X V I

The same he snatcht, and with exceeding sway
Threw at his foe, whe was right well aware
To shonne the engin of his meant decay;
It booted not to thinke that throw to beare,
But grownd he gave, and lightly lept areare:
Eft fierce retourning, as a faulcon fayre,
That once hath failed of her souse full neare,
Remounts againe into the open ayre,
And unto better fortune doth her selfe prepayre.

XXXIII, 8 quar'le: square-headed arrow XXXIV, 9 fild: defiled
XXXVI, 7 souse: swoop

X X X V I I

So brave retourning, with his brandisht blade
He to the Carle him selfe agayn addrest,
And strooke at him so sternely, that he made
An open passage through his riven brest,
That halfe the steele behind his backe did rest;
Which drawing backe, he looked evermore
When the hart blood should gush out of his chest,
Or his dead corse should fall upon the flore;
But his dead corse upon the flore fell nathemore.

X X X V I I I

Ne drop of blood appeared shed to bee,
All were the wownd so wide and wonderous
That through his carcas one might playnly see.
Halfe in amaze with horror hideous,
And halfe in rage to be deluded thus,
Again through both the sides he strooke him quight,
That made his spright to grone full piteous;
Yet nathemore forth fled his groning spright,
But freshly, as at first, prepard himselfe to fight.

X X X I X

Thereat he smitten was with great affright,
And trembling terror did his hart apall;
Ne wist he what to thinke of that same sight,
Ne what to say, ne what to doe at all:
He doubted least it were some magicall
Illusion that did beguile his sense,
Or wandring ghost that wanted funerall,
Or aery spirite under false pretence,
Or hellish feend raysd up through divelish science.

X L

His wonder far exceeded reasons reach,
That he began to doubt his dazeled sight,
And oft of error did himselfe appeach:
Flesh without blood, a person without spright,
Wounds without hurt, a body without might,
That could doe harme, yet could not harmed bee,
That could not die, yet seemd a mortall wight,
That was most strong in most infirmitee;
Like did he never heare, like did he never see.

X L I

Awhile he stood in this astonishment,
Yet would he not for all his great dismay

Give over to effect his first intent,
And th' utmost meanes of victory assay,
Or th' utmost yssew of his owne decay.
His owne good sword Mordure, that never fayld
At need till now, he lightly threw away,
And his bright shield that nought him now avayld;
And with his naked hands him forcibly assayld.

X L I I

Twixt his two mighty armes him up he snatcht,
And crusht his carcas so against his brest,
That the disdainfull sowle he thence dispatcht,
And th' ydle breath all utterly exprest.
Tho, when he felt him dead, adowne he kest
The lumpish corse unto the sencelesse grownd;
Adowne he kest it with so puissant wrest,
That backe againe it did alofte rebownd,
And gave against his mother earth a gronefull sownd.

X L I I I

As when Joves harnesse-bearing Bird from hye
Stoupes at a flying heron with proud disdayne,
The stone-dead quarrey falls so forciblye,
That yt rebownds against the lowly playne,
A second fall redoubling backe agayne.
Then thought the Prince all peril sure was past,
And that he victor onely did remayne;
No sooner thought, then that the Carle as fast
Gan heap huge strokes on him, as ere he down was cast.

X L I V

Nigh his wits end then woxe th' amazed knight,
And thought his labor lost, and travell vayne,
Against this lifelesse shadow so to fight:
Yet life he saw, and felt his mighty mayne,
That, whiles he marveild still, did still him payne;
Forthy he gan some other wayes advize,
How to take life from that dead-living swayne,
Whom still he marked freshly to arize
From th' earth, and from her womb new spirits to reprize.

X L V

He then remembred well, that had bene sayd,
How th' Earth his mother was, and first him bore,
She eke, so often as his life decayd,
Did life with usury to him restore,
And reysd him up much stronger then before,

So soone as he unto her wombe did fall:
Therefore to grownd he would him cast no more,
Ne him committ to grave terrestriall,
But beare him farre from hope of succour usuall.

X L V I

Tho up he caught him twixt his puissant hands,
And having scruzd out of his carrion corse
The lothfull life, now loosd from sinfull bands,
Upon his shoulders carried him perforse
Above three furlongs, taking his full course
Until he came unto a standing lake;
Him thereinto he threw without remorse,
Ne stird, till hope of life did him forsake:
So end of that Carles dayes and his owne paynes did make.

X L V I I

Which when those wicked Hags from far did spye,
Like two mad dogs they ran about the lands,
And th' one of them with dreadfull yelling crye,
Throwing away her broken chaines and bands,
And having quencht her burning fier-brands,
Hedlong her selfe did cast into that lake;
But Impotence with her owne wilfull hands
One of Malegers cursed darts did take,
So ryv'd her trembling hart, and wicked end did make.

X L V I I I

Thus now alone he conquerour remaines:
Tho, cumming to his Squyre that kept his steed,
Thought to have mounted; but his feeble vaines
Him faild thereto, and served not his need,
Through losse of blood which from his wounds did bleed,
That he began to faint, and life decay:
But his good Squyre, him helping up with speed,
With stedfast hand upon his horse did stay,
And led him to the Castle by the beaten way.

X L I X

Where many Groomes and Squyres ready were
To take him from his steed full tenderly:
And eke the fayrest Alma mett him there
With balme, and wine, and costly spicery,
To comfort him in his infirmity.
Eftesoones shee causd him up to be convayd,

And of his armes despoyled easily
In sumptuous bed shee made him to be layd:
And al the while his wounds were dressing by him stayd.

CANTO XII.

Guyon, by Palmers governaunce,
Passing through perilles great,
Doth overthrow the Bowre of blis,
And Acrasy defeat.

I

Now GINNES this goodly frame of Temperaunce
Fayrely to rise, and her adorned hed
To pricke of highest prayse forth to advaunce,
Formerly grounded and fast setteled
On firme foundation of true bountyhed:
And this brave knight, that for this vertue fightes,
Now comes to point of that same perilous sted,
Where Pleasure dwelles in sensuall delights,
Mongst thousand dangers, and ten thousand Magick mights.

I I

Two dayes now in that sea he sayled has,
Ne ever land beheld, ne living wight,
Ne ought save perill still as he did pas:
Tho, when appeared the third Morrow bright
Upon the waves to spred her trembling light,
An hideous roring far away they heard,
That all their sences filled with affright;
And streight they saw the raging surges reard
Up to the skyes, that them of drowning made affeard.

I I I

Said then the Boteman, 'Palmer, stere aright,
And keepe an even course; for yonder way
We needes must pas (God doe us well acquight!)
That is the Gulfe of Greedinesse, they say,
That deepe engorgeth all this worldes pray;
Which having swallowd up excessively,
He soone in vomit up againe doth lay,
And belcheth forth his superfluity,
That all the seas for feare doe seeme away to fly.

I V

'On thother syde an hideous Rocke is pight
Of mightie Magnes stone, whose craggie clift
Depending from on high, dreadfull to sight,
Over the waves his rugged armes doth lift,
And threatneth downe to throw his ragged rift
On whoso cometh nigh; yet nigh it drawes
All passengers, that none from it can shift:
For, whiles they fly that Gulfes devouring jawes,
They on this rock are rent, and sunck in helples wawes.'

v

Forward they passe, and strongly he then rowes,
Untill they nigh unto that Gulfe arryve,
Where streame more violent and greedy growes:
Then he with all his puisaunce doth stryve
To strike his oares, and mightily doth drive
The hollow vessell through the threatfull wave;
Which, gaping wide to swallow them alyve
In th' huge abysse of his engulfing grave,
Doth rore at them in vaine, and with great terrour rave.

V I

They, passing by, that grisely mouth did see
Sucking the seas into his entralles deepe,
That seemd more horrible then hell to bee,
Or that darke dreadfull hole of Tartare steepe
Through which the damned ghosts doen often creepe
Backe to the world, bad livers to torment:
But nought that falles into this direfull deepe
Ne that approcheth nigh the wyde descent,
May backe retourne, but is condemned to be drent.

V I I

On th'other side they saw that perilous Rocke,
Threatning it selfe on them to ruinate,
On whose sharp cliftes the ribs of vessels broke;
And shivered ships, which had beene wrecked late,
Yet stuck with carkases exanimate
Of such, as having all their substance spent
In wanton joyes and lustes intemperate,
Did afterwards make shipwrack violent
Both of their life and fame, for ever fowly blent.

IV, 2   Magnes: magnet   VII, 9   blent: stained

V I I I

Forthy this hight The Rocke of vile Reproch,
A daungerous and detestable place,
To which nor fish nor fowle did once approch,
But yelling Meawes, with Seagulles hoars and bace,
And Cormoyraunts, with birds of ravenous race,
Which still sat waiting on that wastfull clift
For spoile of wretches, whose unhappy cace,
After lost credit and consumed thrift,
At last them driven hath to this despairefull drift.

I X

The Palmer, seeing them in safetie past,
Thus saide; 'Behold th' ensamples in our sights
Of lustfull luxurie and thriftlesse wast.
What now is left of miserable wightes,
Which spent their looser daies in leud delightes,
But shame and sad reproch, here to be red
By these rent reliques, speaking their ill plightes?
Let all that live hereby be counselled
To shunne Rocke of Reproch, and it as death to dred!'

x

So forth they rowed; and that Ferryman
With his stiffe oares did brush the sea so strong,
That the hoare waters from his frigot ran,
And the light bubles daunced all along,
Whiles the salt brine out of the billowes sprong.
At last far off they many Islandes spy
On every side floting the floodes emong:
Then said the knight; 'Lo! I the land descry;
Therefore, old Syre, thy course doe thereunto apply.'

X I

'That may not bee,' said then the Ferryman,
'Least wee unweeting hap to be fordonne;
For those same Islands, seeming now and than,
Are not firme land, nor any certein wonne,
But stragling plots which to and fro doe ronne
In the wide waters: therefore are they hight
The Wandring Islands. Therefore doe them shonne;
For they have ofte drawne many a wandring wight
Into most deadly daunger and distressed plight.

VIII, I   Forthy: therefore

X I I

'Yet well they seeme to him, that farre doth vew,
Both faire and fruitfull, and the grownd dispred
With grassy greene of delectable hew;
And the tall trees with leaves appareled
Are deckt with blossoms dyde in white and red,
That mote the passengers thereto allure;
But whosoever once hath fastened
His foot thereon, may never it recure,
But wandreth evermore uncertein and unsure.

X I I I

'As th' Isle of Delos whylome, men report,
Amid th' Aegæan sea long time did stray,
Ne made for shipping any certeine port,
Till that Latona traveiling that way,
Flying from Junoes wrath and hard assay,
Of her fayre twins was there delivered,
Which afterwards did rule the night and day:
Thenceforth it firmely was established,
And for Apolloes temple highly herried.'

X I V

They to him hearken, as beseemeth meete,
And passe on forward: so their way does ly,
That one of those same Islands, which doe fleet
In the wide sea, they needes must passen by
Which seemd so sweet and pleasaunt to the eye,
That it would tempt a man to touchen there:
Upon the banck they sitting did espy
A daintie damsell dressing of her heare,
By whom a little skippet floting did appeare.

X V

She, them espying, loud to them can call,
Bidding them nigher draw unto the shore,
For she had cause to busie them withall;
And therewith lowdly laught: But nathemore
Would they once turne, but kept on as afore:
Which when she saw, she left her lockes undight,
And running to her boat withouten ore,
From the departing land it launched light,
And after them did drive with all her power and might.

XVI

Whom overtaking, she in merry sort
Them gan to bord, and purpose diversly;
Now faining dalliaunce and wanton sport,
Now throwing forth lewd wordes immodestly;
Till that the Palmer gan full bitterly
Her to rebuke for being loose and light:
Which not abiding, but more scornfully
Scoffing at him that did her justly wite,
She turnd her bote about, and from them rowed quite.

XVII

That was the wanton Phædria, which late
Did ferry him over the Idle lake:
Whom nought regarding they kept on their gate,
And all her vaine allurements did forsake;
When them the wary Boteman thus bespake:
'Here now behoveth us well to avyse,
And of our safety good heede to take;
For here before a perlous passage lyes,
Where many Mermayds haunt making false melodies:

XVIII

'But by the way there is a great Quicksand,
And a whirlepoole of hidden jeopardy;
Therefore, Sir Palmer, keepe an even hand,
For twixt them both the narrow way doth ly.'
Scarse had he saide, when hard at hand they spy
That quicksand nigh with water covered;
But by the checked wave they did descry
It plaine, and by the sea discoloured:
It called was the quickesand of Unthriftyhed.

XIX

They, passing by, a goodly Ship did see
Laden from far with precious merchandize,
And bravely furnished as ship might bee,
Which through great disaventure, or mesprize,
Her selfe had ronne into that hazardize;
Whose mariners and merchants with much toyle
Labour'd in vaine to have recur'd their prize,
And the rich wares to save from pitteous spoyle;
But neither toyle nor traveill might her backe recoyle.

XVI, 2   bord: jest with

X X

On th' other side they see that perilous Poole,
That called was the Whirlepoole of decay;
In which full many had with haplesse doole
Beene suncke, of whom no memorie did stay:
Whose circled waters rapt with whirling sway,
Like to a restlesse wheele, still ronning round,
Did covet, as they passed by that way,
To draw their bote within the utmost bound
Of his wide Labyrinth, and then to have them dround.

X X I

But th' heedful Boteman strongly forth did stretch
His brawnie armes, and all his bodie straine,
That th' utmost sandy breach they shortly fetch,
Whiles the dredd daunger does behind remaine.
Suddeine they see from midst of all the Maine
The surging waters like a mountaine rise,
And the great sea, puft up with proud disdaine,
To swell above the measure of his guise,
As threatning to devoure all that his powre despise.

X X I I

The waves come rolling, and the billowes rore
Outragiously, as they enraged were,
Or wrathfull Neptune did them drive before
His whirling charet for exceeding feare;
For not one puffe of winde there did appeare,
That all the three thereat woxe much afrayd,
Unweeting what such horrour straunge did reare.
Eftsoones they saw an hideous hoast arrayd
Of huge Sea monsters, such as living sence dismayd:

X X I I I

Most ugly shapes and horrible aspects,
Such as Dame Nature selfe mote feare to see,
Or shame that ever should so fowle defects
From her most cunning hand escaped bee;
All dreadfull pourtraicts of deformitee:
Spring-headed Hydraes; and sea-shouldring Whales;
Great whirlpooles which all fishes make to flee;
Bright Scolopendraes arm'd with silver scales;
Mighty Monoceros with immeasured tayles;

xx, 3   doole: grief
xxiii, 6   Spring-headed: having heads that spring afresh

XXIV

The dreadful Fish that hath deserv'd the name
Of Death, and like him lookes in dreadfull hew;
The griesly Wasserman, that makes his game
The flying ships with swiftnes to pursew:
The horrible Sea-satyre, that doth shew
His fearefull face in time of greatest storme;
Huge Ziffius, whom Mariners eschew
No lesse then rockes, (as travellers informe)
And greedy Rosmarines with visages deforme.

XXV

All these, and thousand thousands many more,
And more deformed Monsters thousand fold,
With dreadfull noise and hollow rombling rore
Came rushing, in the fomy waves enrold,
Which seem'd to fly for feare them to behold.
Ne wonder, if these did the knight appall;
For all that here on earth we dreadfull hold,
Be but as bugs to fearen babes withall,
Compared to the creatures in the seas entrall.

XXVI

'Feare nought,' then saide the Palmer well aviz'd,
'For these same Monsters are not these in deed,
But are into these fearefull shapes disguiz'd
By that same wicked witch, to worke us dreed,
And draw from on this journey to proceed.'
Tho lifting up his vertuous staffe on hye,
He smote the sea, which calmed was with speed,
And all that dreadfull Armie fast gan flye
Into great Tethys bosome, where they hidden lye.

XXVII

Quit from that danger forth their course they kept;
And as they went they heard a ruefull cry
Of one that wayld and pittifully wept,
That through the sea resounding plaints did fly:
At last they in an Island did espy
A seemely Maiden sitting by the shore,
That with great sorrow and sad agony
Seemed some great misfortune to deplore,
And lowd to them for succour called evermore.

xxv, 8   bugs: bugbears

x x v i i i

Which Guyon hearing streight his Palmer bad
To stere the bote towards that dolefull Mayd,
That he might know and ease her sorrow sad;
Who, him avizing better, to him sayd:
'Faire Sir, be not displeasd if disobayd:
For ill it were to hearken to her cry,
For she is inly nothing ill apayd;
But onely womanish fine forgery,
Your stubborne hart t'affect with fraile infirmity.

x x i x

'To which when she your courage hath inclind
Through foolish pitty, then her guilefull bayt
She will embosome deeper in your mind,
And for your ruine at the last awayt.'
The Knight was ruled, and the Boteman strayt
Held on his course with stayed stedfastnesse,
Ne ever shroncke, ne ever sought to bayt
His tyred armes for toylesome wearinesse,
But with his oares did sweepe the watry wildernesse.

x x x

And now they nigh approched to the sted
Whereas those Mermayds dwelt: it was a still
And calmy bay, on th' one side sheltered
With the brode shadow of an hoarie hill;
On th' other side an high rocke toured still,
That twixt them both a pleasaunt port they made,
And did like an halfe Theatre fulfill:
There those five sisters had continuall trade,
And usd to bath themselves in that deceiptfull shade.

x x x i

They were faire Ladies, till they fondly striv'd
With th' Heliconian maides for maystery;
Of whom they, over-comen, were depriv'd
Of their proud beautie, and th' one moyity
Transformd to fish for their bold surquedry;
But th' upper halfe their hew retayned still,
And their sweet skill in wonted melody;
Which ever after they abusd to ill,
T' allure weake traveillers, whom gotten they did kill.

xxviii, 7   apayd: pleased   xxxi, 5   surquedry: presumption

X X X I I

So now to Guyon, as he passed by,
Their pleasaunt tunes they sweetly thus applyde:
'O thou fayre sonne of gentle Faery,
That art in mightie armes most magnifyde
Above all knights that ever batteill tryde,
O! turne thy rudder hitherward awhile
Here may thy storme-bett vessell safely ryde,
This is the Port of rest from troublous toyle,
The worldes sweet In from paine and wearisome turmoyle.'

X X X I I I

With that the rolling sea, resounding soft,
In his big base them fitly answered;
And on the rocke the waves breaking aloft
A solemne Meane unto them measured;
The whiles sweet Zephyrus lowd whisteled
His treble, a straunge kinde of harmony,
Which Guyons senses softly tickeled,
That he the boteman bad row easily,
And let him heare some part of their rare melody.

X X X I V

But him the Palmer from that vanity
With temperate advice discounselled,
That they it past, and shortly gan descry
The land to which their course they leveled;
When suddeinly a grosse fog over-spred
With his dull vapour all that desert has,
And heavens chearefull face enveloped,
That all things one, and one as nothing was,
And this great Universe seemd one confused mas.

X X X V

Thereat they greatly were dismayd, ne wist
How to direct theyr way in darkenes wide,
But feard to wander in that wastefull mist,
For tombling into mischiefe unespide:
Worse is the daunger hidden then descride.
Suddeinly an innumerable flight
Of harmefull fowles about them fluttering cride,
And with their wicked wings them ofte did smight,
And sore annoyed, groping in that griesly night.

X X X V I

Even all the nation of unfortunate
And fatall birds about them flocked were,
Such as by nature men abhorre and hate;
The ill-faste Owle, deaths dreadfull messengere;
The hoars Night-raven, trump of dolefull drere;
The lether-winged Batt, dayes enimy;
The ruefull Strich, still waiting on the bere;
The whistler shrill, that whoso heares doth dy;
The hellish Harpyes, prophets of sad destiny.

X X X V I I

All those, and all that els does horror breed,
About them flew, and fild their sayles with feare:
Yet stayd they not, but forward did proceed,
Whiles th' one did row, and th' other stifly steare;
Till that at last the weather gan to cleare,
And the faire land it selfe did playnly sheow.
Said then the Palmer; 'Lo! where does appeare
The sacred soile where all our perills grow.
Therfore, Sir knight, your ready arms about you throw.'

X X X V I I I

He hearkned, and his armes about him tooke,
The whiles the nimble bote so well her sped,
That with her crooked keele the land she strooke:
Then forth the noble Guyon sallied,
And his sage Palmer that him governed;
But th' other by his bote behind did stay.
They marched fayrly forth, of nought ydred,
Both firmely armd for every hard assay,
With constancy and care, gainst daunger and dismay.

X X X I X

Ere long they heard an hideous bellowing
Of many beasts, that roard outrageously,
As if that hungers poynt or Venus sting
Had them enraged with fell surquedry:
Yet nought they feard, but past on hardily,
Untill they came in vew of those wilde beasts,
Who all attonce, gaping full greedily,
And rearing fercely their upstaring crests,
Ran towards to devoure those unexpected guests.

X L

But soone as they approcht with deadly threat,
The Palmer over them his staffe upheld,
His mighty staffe, that could all charmes defeat.
Eftesoones their stubborne corages were queld,
And high advaunced crests downe meekely feld;
Instead of fraying, they them selves did feare,
And trembled as them passing they beheld:
Such wondrous powre did in that staffe appeare,
All monsters to subdew to him that did it beare.

X L I

Of that same wood it fram'd was cunningly,
Of which Caduceus whilome was made,
Caduceus, the rod of Mercury,
With which he wonts the Stygian realmes invade
Through ghastly horror and eternall shade:
Th' infernall feends with it he can asswage,
And Orcus tame, whome nothing can persuade,
And rule the Furyes when they most doe rage.
Such vertue in his staffe had eke this Palmer sage.

X L I I

Thence passing forth, they shortly doe arryve
Whereas the Bowre of Blisse was situate;
A place pickt out by choyce of best alyve,
That natures worke by art can imitate:
In which whatever in this worldly state
Is sweete and pleasing unto living sense,
Or that may dayntest fantasy aggrate,
Was poured forth with plentifull dispence,
And made there to abound with lavish affluence.

X L I I I

Goodly it was enclosed rownd about,
As well their entred guestes to keep within,
As those unruly beasts to hold without;
Yet was the fence thereof but weake and thin:
Nought feard theyr force that fortilage to win,
But wisedomes powre, and temperaunces might,
By which the mightiest things efforced bin:
And eke the gate was wrought of substaunce light,
Rather for pleasure then for battery or fight.

X L I V

Yt framed was of precious yvory,
That seemd a worke of admirable witt;
And therein all the famous history
Of Jason and Medæa was ywritt;
Her mighty charmes, her furious loving fitt;
His goodly conquest of the golden fleece,
His falsed fayth, and love too lightly flitt;
The wondred Argo, which in venturous peece
First through the Euxine seas bore all the flowr of Greece.

X L V

Ye might have seene the frothy billowes fry
Under the ship as thorough them she went,
That seemd the waves were into yvory,
Or yvory into the waves were sent;
And otherwhere the snowy substaunce sprent
With vermell, like the boyes blood therein shed,
A piteous spectacle did represent;
And otherwhiles, with gold besprinkeled,
Yt seemd th'enchaunted flame which did Crëusa wed.

X L V I

All this and more might in that goodly gate
Be red, that ever open stood to all
Which thither came; but in the Porch there sate
A comely personage of stature tall,
And semblaunce pleasing, more then naturall,
That traveilers to him seemd to entize:
His looser garment to the ground did fall,
And flew about his heeles in wanton wize,
Not fitt for speedy pace, or manly exercize.

X L V I I

They in that place him Genius did call:
Not that celestiall powre, to whom the care
Of life, and generation of all
That lives, perteines in charge particulare,
Who wondrous things concerning our welfare,
And straunge phantomes doth lett us ofte foresee,
And ofte of secret ill bids us beware:
That is our Selfe, whom though we do not see,
Yet each doth in him selfe it well perceive to bee.

XLIV, 8   wondred: wonderful   XLIV, 8   peece: vessel

X L V I I I

Therefore a God him sage Antiquity
Did wisely make, and good Agdistes call;
But this same was to that quite contrary,
The foe of life, that good envyes to all,
That secretly doth us procure to fall
Through guilefull semblants which he makes us see:
He of this Gardin had the governall,
And Pleasures porter was devizd to bee,
Holding a staffe in hand for more formalitee.

X L I X

With diverse flowres he daintily was deckt,
And strowed rownd about; and by his side
A mighty Mazer bowle of wine was sett,
As if it had to him bene sacrifide,
Wherewith all new-come guests he gratyfide:
So did he eke Sir Guyon passing by;
But he his ydle curtesie defide,
And overthrew his bowle disdainfully,
And broke his staffe with which he charmed semblants sly.

L

Thus being entred, they behold arownd
A large and spacious plaine, on evry side
Strowed with pleasauns; whose fayre grassy grownd
Mantled with greene, and goodly beautifide
With all the ornaments of Floraes pride,
Wherewith her mother Art, as halfe in scorne
Of niggard Nature, like a pompous bride
Did decke her, and too lavishly adorne,
When forth from virgin bowre she comes in th' early morne.

L I

Therewith the Heavens alwayes joviall
Lookte on them lovely, still in stedfast state,
Ne suffred storme nor frost on them to fall,
Their tender buds or leaves to violate;
Nor scorching heat, nor cold intemperate,
T' afflict the creatures which therein did dwell;
But the milde ayre with season moderate
Gently attempred, and disposd so well,
That still it breathed forth sweet spirit and holesom smell:

L I I

More sweet and holesome then the pleasaunt hill
Of Rhodope, on which the Nimphe that bore
A gyaunt babe herselfe for griefe did kill;
Or the Thessalian Tempe, where of yore
Fayre Daphne Phœbus hart with love did gore;
Or Ida, where the Gods lov'd to repayre,
When ever they their heavenly bowres forlore;
Or sweet Parnasse, the haunt of Muses fayre;
Or Eden selfe, if ought with Eden mote compayre.

L I I I

Much wondred Guyon at the fayre aspect
Of that sweet place, yet suffred no delight
To sincke into his sence, nor mind affect,
But passed forth, and lookt still forward right,
Brydling his will and maystering his might,
Till that he came unto another gate;
No gate, but like one, being goodly dight
With bowes and braunches, which did broad dilate
Their clasping armes in wanton wreathings intricate:

L I V

So fashioned a Porch with rare device.
Archt over head with an embracing vine,
Whose bounches hanging downe seemd to entice
All passers by to taste their lushious wine,
And did them selves into their hands incline,
As freely offering to be gathered;
Some deepe empurpled as the Hyacine,
Some as the Rubine laughing sweetely red,
Some like faire Emeraudes, not yet well ripened.

L V

And them amongst some were of burnisht gold,
So made by art to beautify the rest,
Which did themselves emongst the leaves enfold,
As lurking from the vew of covetous guest,
That the weake boughes, with so rich load opprest
Did bow adowne as overburdened.
Under that Porch a comely dame did rest
Clad in fayre weedes but fowle disordered,
And garments loose that seemd unmeet for womanhed.

L V I

In her left hand a Cup of gold she held,
And with her right the riper fruit did reach,
Whose sappy liquor, that with fulnesse sweld,
Into her cup she scruzd with daintie breach
Of her fine fingers, without fowle empeach,
That so faire winepresse made the wine more sweet:
Thereof she usd to give to drinke to each,
Whom passing by she happened to meet:
It was her guise all Straungers goodly so to greet.

L V I I

So she to Guyon offred it to tast,
Who, taking it out of her tender hond,
The cup to ground did violently cast,
That all in peeces it was broken fond,
And with the liquor stained all the lond:
Whereat Excesse exceedingly was wroth,
Yet no'te the same amend, ne yet withstond,
But suffered him to passe, all were she loth;
Who, nought regarding her displeasure, forward goth.

L V I I I

There the most daintie Paradise on ground
It selfe doth offer to his sober eye,
In which all pleasures plenteously abownd,
And none does others happinesse envye;
The painted flowres, the trees upshooting hye,
The dales for shade, the hilles for breathing space,
The trembling groves, the christall running by,
And, that which all faire workes doth most aggrace,
The art which all that wrought appeared in no place.

L I X

One would have thought, (so cunningly the rude
And scorned partes were mingled with the fine)
That nature had for wantonesse ensude
Art, and that Art at nature did repine;
So striving each th' other to undermine,
Each did the others worke more beautify;
So diff'ring both in willes agreed in fine:

LVI, 3   sappy: juicy   LIX, 7   fine: end
LIX, 3   ensude: imitated

So all agreed, through sweete diversity,
This Gardin to adorne with all variety.

L X

And in the midst of all a fountaine stood,
Of richest substance that on earth might bee,
So pure and shiny that the silver flood
Through every channell running one might see;
Most goodly it with curious ymageree
Was overwrought, and shapes of naked boyes,
Of which some seemd with lively jollitee
To fly about, playing their wanton toyes,
Whylest others did them selves embay in liquid joyes.

L X I

And over all of purest gold was spred
A trayle of yvie in his native hew;
For the rich metall was so coloured,
That wight who did not well avis'd it vew
Would surely deeme it to bee yvie trew:
Low his lascivious armes adown did creepe,
That themselves dipping in the silver dew
Their fleecy flowres they fearefully did steepe,
Which drops of Christall seemd for wantones to weep.

L X I I

Infinit streames continually did well
Out of this fountaine, sweet and faire to see,
The which into an ample laver fell,
And shortly grew to so great quantitie,
That like a litle lake it seemd to bee;
Whose depth exceeded not three cubits hight,
That through the waves one might the bottom see,
All pav'd beneath with Jaspar shining bright,
That seemd the fountaine in that sea did sayle upright.

L X I I I

And all the margent round about was sett
With shady Laurell trees, thence to defend
The sunny beames which on the billowes bett,
And those which therein bathed mote offend.
As Guyon hapned by the same to wend,
Two naked Damzelles he therein espyde,
Which therein bathing seemed to contend
And wrestle wantonly, ne car'd to hyde
Their dainty partes from vew of any which them eyd.

L X I V

Sometimes the one would lift the other quight
Above the waters, and then downe againe
Her plong, as over-maystered by might,
Where both awhile would covered remaine,
And each the other from to rise restraine;
The whiles their snowy limbes, as through a vele,
So through the christall waves appeared plaine:
Then suddeinly both would themselves unhele,
And th' amarous sweet spoiles to greedy eyes revele.

L X V

As that faire Starre, the messenger of morne,
His deawy face out of the sea doth reare;
Or as the Cyprian goddesse, newly borne
Of th' Ocean's fruitfull froth, did first appeare:
Such seemed they, and so their yellow heare
Christalline humor dropped downe apace.
Whom such when Guyon saw, he drew him neare,
And somewhat gan relent his earnest pace;
His stubborne brest gan secret pleasaunce to embrace.

L X V I

The wanton Maidens, him espying, stood
Gazing awhile at his unwonted guise;
Then th' one her selfe low ducked in the flood,
Abasht that her a straunger did avise;
But thother rather higher did arise,
And her two lilly paps aloft displayd,
And all that might his melting hart entyse
To her delights she unto him bewrayd;
The rest hidd underneath him more desirous made.

L X V I I

With that the other likewise up arose,
And her faire lockes, which formerly were bownd
Up in one knott, she low adowne did lose,
Which flowing low and thick her cloth'd arownd,
And th' yvorie in golden mantle gownd:
So that faire spectacle from him was reft,
Yet that which reft it no lesse faire was fownd.
So hidd in lockes and waves from lookers theft,
Nought but her lovely face she for his looking left.

LXIV, 8   unhele: uncover

L X V I I I

Withall she laughed, and she blusht withall,
That blushing to her laughter gave more grace,
And laughter to her blushing, as did fall.
Now when they spyde the knight to slacke his pace
Them to behold, and in his sparkling face
The secrete signes of kindled lust appeare,
Their wanton meriments they did encreace,
And to him beckned to approch more neare,
And shewd him many sights that corage cold could reare.

L X I X

On which when gazing him the Palmer saw,
He much rebukt those wandring eyes of his,
And counseld well him forward thence did draw.
Now are they come nigh to the Bowre of blis,
Of her fond favorites so nam'd amis,
When thus the Palmer: 'Now, Sir, well avise;
For here the end of all our traveill is:
Here wonnes Acrasia, whom we must surprise,
Els she will slip away, and all our drift despise.

L X X

Eftsoones they heard a most melodious sound,
Of all that mote delight a daintie eare,
Such as attonce might not on living ground,
Save in this Paradise, be heard elsewhere:
Right hard it was for wight which did it heare,
To read what manner musicke that mote bee:
For all that pleasing is to living eare
Was there consorted in one harmonee;
Birdes, voices, instruments, windes, waters, all agree:

L X X I

The joyous birdes, shrouded in chearefull shade
Their notes unto the voice attempred sweet;
Th' Angelicall soft trembling voyces made
To th' instruments divine respondence meet;
The silver sounding instruments did meet
With the base murmure of the waters fall;
The waters fall with difference discreet,
Now soft, now loud, unto the wind did call;
The gentle warbling wind low answered to all.

LXIX, 7   traveill: labor   LXXI, 7   discreet: distinct
LXXI, 7   difference: variation

L X X I I

There, whence that Musick seemed heard to bee,
Was the faire Witch her selfe now solacing
With a new Lover, whom, through sorceree
And witchcraft, she from farre did thither bring:
There she had him now laid aslombering
In secret shade after long wanton joyes,
Whilst round about them pleasauntly did sing
Many faire Ladies and lascivious boyes,
That ever mixt their song with light licentious toyes.

L X X I I I

And all that while right over him she hong
With her false eyes fast fixed in his sight,
As seeking medicine whence she was stong,
Or greedily depasturing delight;
And oft inclining downe, with kisses light
For feare of waking him, his lips bedewd,
And through his humid eyes did sucke his spright,
Quite molten into lust and pleasure lewd;
Wherewith she sighed soft, as if his case she rewd.

L X X I V

The whiles some one did chaunt this lovely lay:
Ah! see, whoso fayre thing doest faine to see,
In springing flowre the image of thy day.
Ah! see the Virgin Rose, how sweetly shee
Doth first peepe foorth with bashfull modestee,
That fairer seemes the lesse ye see her may.
Lo! see soone after how more bold and free
Her bared bosome she doth broad display;
Lo! see soone after how she fades and falls away.

L X X V

So passeth, in the passing of a day,
Of mortall life the leafe, the bud, the flowre;
Ne more doth florish after first decay,
That earst was sought to deck both bed and bowre
Of many a lady', and many a Paramowre.
Gather therefore the Rose whilest yet is prime,
For soone comes age that will her pride deflowre;
Gather the Rose of love whilest yet is time,
Whilest loving thou mayst loved be with equall crime.

LXXV, 9   crime: sin

L X X V I

He ceast; and then gan all the quire of birdes
Their diverse notes t'attune unto his lay,
As in approvaunce of his pleasing wordes.
The constant payre heard all that he did say,
Yet swarved not, but kept their forward way
Through many covert groves and thickets close,
In which they creeping did at last display
That wanton Lady with her lover lose,
Whose sleepie head she in her lap did soft dispose.

L X X V I I

Upon a bed of Roses she was layd,
As faint through heat, or dight to pleasant sin;
And was arayd, or rather disarayd,
All in a vele of silke and silver thin,
That hid no whit her alablaster skin,
But rather shewd more white, if more might bee:
More subtile web Arachne cannot spin;
Nor the fine nets, which oft we woven see
Of scorched deaw, do not in th' ayre more lightly flee.

L X X V I I I

Her snowy brest was bare to ready spoyle
Of hungry eies, which n'ote therewith be fild;
And yet, through languour of her late sweet toyle,
Few drops, more cleare then Nectar, forth distild,
That like pure Orient perles adowne it trild;
And her faire eyes, sweet smyling in delight,
Moystened their fierie beames, with which she thrild
Fraile harts, yet quenched not; like starry light,
Which, sparckling on the silent waves, does seeme more
    bright.

L X X I X

The young man, sleeping by her, seemd to be
Some goodly swayne of honorable place,
That certes it great pitty was to see
Him his nobility so fowle deface:
A sweet regard and amiable grace,
Mixed with manly sternesse, did appeare,
Yet sleeping, in his well proportiond face;
And on his tender lips the downy heare
Did now but freshly spring, and silken blossoms beare.

L X X X

His warlike Armes, the ydle instruments
Of sleeping praise, were hong upon a tree;
And his brave shield, full of old moniments,
Was fowly ras't, that none the signes might see:
Ne for them ne for honour cared hee,
Ne ought that did to his advauncement tend;
But in lewd loves, and wastfull luxuree,
His dayes, his goods, his bodie, he did spend:
O horrible enchantment, that him so did blend!

L X X X I

The noble Elfe and carefull Palmer drew
So nigh them, minding nought but lustfull game,
That suddein forth they on them rusht, and threw
A subtile net, which only for the same
The skilfull Palmer formally did frame:
So held them under fast; the whiles the rest
Fled all away for feare of fowler shame.
The faire Enchauntresse, so unwares opprest,
Tryde all her arts and all her sleights thence out to wrest.

L X X X I I

And eke her lover strove, but all in vaine;
For that same net so cunningly was wound,
That neither guile nor force might it distraine.
They tooke them both, and both them strongly bound
In captive bandes, which there they readie found:
But her in chaines of adamant he tyde;
For nothing else might keepe her safe and sound:
But Verdant (so he hight) he soone untyde,
And counsell sage in steed thereof to him applyde.

L X X X I I I

But all those pleasaunt bowres, and Pallace brave,
Guyon broke downe with rigour pittilesse;
Ne ought their goodly workmanship might save
Them from the tempest of his wrathfulnesse,
But that their blisse he turn'd to balefulnesse.
Their groves he feld; their gardins did deface;
Their arbers spoyle; their Cabinets suppresse;
Their banket houses burne; their buildings race;
And, of the fayrest late, now made the fowlest place.

LXXXIII, 7 Cabinets: bowers   LXXXIII, 8 race: raze

LXXXIV

Then led they her away, and eke that knight
They with them led, both sorrowfull and sad.
The way they came, the same retourn'd they right,
Till they arrived where they lately had
Charm'd those wild-beasts that rag'd with furie mad;
Which, now awaking, fierce at them gan fly,
As in their mistresse reskew whom they lad;
But them the Palmer soone did pacify.
Then Guyon askt, what meant those beastes which there did
    ly?

LXXXV

Sayd he; 'These seeming beasts are men indeed,
Whom this Enchauntresse hath transformed thus;
Whylome her lovers, which her lustes did feed,
Now turned into figures hideous,
According to their mindes like monstruous.'
'Sad end,' (quoth he) 'of life intemperate,
And mourneful meed of joyes delicious!
But, Palmer, if it mote thee so aggrate,
Let them returned be unto their former state.'

LXXXVI

Streight way he with his vertuous staffe them strooke,
And streight of beastes they comely men became;
And stared ghastly; some for inward shame,
And some for wrath to see their captive Dame:
But one above the rest in speciall
That had an hog beene late, hight Grylle by name,
Repyned greatly, and did him miscall
That had from hoggish forme him brought to naturall.

LXXXVII

Saide Guyon; 'See the mind of beastly man,
That hath so soone forgot the excellence
Of his creation, when he life began,
That now he chooseth with vile difference
To be a beast, and lacke intelligence!'
To whom the Palmer thus: 'The donghill kinde
Delightes in filth and fowle incontinence:
Let Gryll be Gryll, and have his hoggish minde;
But let us hence depart whilest wether serves and winde.'

THE THIRDE BOOKE OF

THE FAERIE QUEENE

Contayning the Legend of Britomartis,
or of Chastity.

I

It FALLS ME here to write of Chastity,
The fayrest vertue, far above the rest:
For which what needes me fetch from Faery
Forreine ensamples it to have exprest?
Sith it is shrined in my Soveraines brest,
And formd so lively in each perfect part,
That to all Ladies, which have it profest,
Need but behold the pourtraict of her hart;
If pourtrayd it might bee by any living art.

I I

But living art may not least part expresse,
Nor life-resembling pencill it can paynt:
All were it Zeuxis or Praxiteles,
His dædale hand would faile and greatly faynt,
And her perfections with his error taynt:
Ne Poets witt, that passeth Painter farre
In picturing the parts of beauty daynt,
So hard a workemanship adventure darre,
For fear, through want of words, her excellence to marre.

II, 8   darre: dare

III

How then shall I, Apprentice of the skill
That whilome in divinest wits did rayne,
Presume so high to stretch mine humble quill?
Yet now my luckelesse lott doth me constrayne
Hereto perforce. But, O dredd Soverayne!
Thus far-forth pardon, sith that choicest witt
Cannot your glorious pourtraict figure playne,
That I in colourd showes may shadow itt,
And antique praises unto present persons fitt.

IV

But if in living colours, and right hew,
Thy selfe thou covet to see pictured,
Who can it doe more lively, or more trew,
Then that sweete verse, with Nectar sprinckeled,
In which a gracious servaunt pictured
His Cynthia, his heavens fayrest light?
That with his melting sweetnes ravished,
And with the wonder of her beames bright,
My sences lulled are in slomber of delight.

V

But let that same delitious Poet lend
A little leave unto a rusticke Muse
To sing his mistresse prayse; and let him mend,
If ought amis her liking may abuse:
Ne let his fayrest Cynthia refuse
In mirrours more then one her selfe to see;
But either Gloriana let her chuse,
Or in Belphœbe fashioned to bee;
In th' one her rule, in th' other her rare chastitee.

CANTO I.

*Guyon encountreth Britomart:
Fayre Florimell is chaced:
Duessaes traines and Malecas-
taes champions are defaced.*

I

THE FAMOUS Briton Prince and Faery knight,
After long wayes and perilous paines endur'd,
Having their weary limbes to perfect plight

Restord, and sory wounds right well recur'd,
Of the faire Alma greatly were procur'd
To make there lenger sojourne and abode;
But when thereto they might not be allur'd,
From seeking praise and deeds of armes abrode,
They courteous congé tooke, and forth together yode.

I I

But the captiv'd Acrasia he sent,
Because of traveill long, a nigher way,
With a strong gard, all reskew to prevent,
And her to Faery court safe to convay;
That her for witnes of his hard assay
Unto his Faery Queene he might present:
But he him selfe betooke another way,
To make more triall of his hardiment,
And seek adventures as he with Prince Arthure went.

I I I

Long so they traveiled through wastefull wayes,
Where daungers dwelt, and perils most did wonne,
To hunt for glory and renowmed prayse.
Full many Countreyes they did overronne,
From the uprising to the setting Sunne,
And many hard adventures did atchieve;
Of all the which they honour ever wonne,
Seeking the weake oppressed to relieve,
And to recover right for such as wrong did grieve.

I V

At last, as through an open plaine they yode,
They spide a knight that towards pricked fayre;
And him beside an aged Squire there rode,
That seemd to couch under his shield three-square,
As if that age badd him that burden spare,
And yield it those that stouter could it wield.
He them espying gan him selfe prepare,
And on his arme addresse his goodly shield
That bore a Lion passant in a golden field.

V

Which seeing, good Sir Guyon deare besought
The Prince of grace to let him ronne that turne.
He graunted: then the Faery quickly raught
His poynant speare, and sharply gan to spurne

IV, 4   three-square: triangular

His fomy steed, whose fiery feete did burne
The verdant gras as he thereon did tread;
Ne did the other backe his foote returne,
But fiercely forward came withouten dread,
And bent his dreadful speare against the others head.

V I

They beene ymett, and both theyr points arriv'd;
But Guyon drove so furious and fell,
That seemd both shield and plate it would have riv'd;
Nathelesse it bore his foe not from his sell,
But made him stagger, as he were not well:
But Guyon selfe, ere well he was aware,
Nigh a speares length behind his crouper fell;
Yet in his fall so well him selfe he bare,
That mischievous mischaunce his life and limbs did spare.

V I I

Great shame and sorrow of that fall he tooke;
For never yet, sith warlike armes he bore
And shivering speare in bloody field first shooke,
He fownd him selfe dishonored so sore.
Ah! gentlest knight, that ever armor bore,
Let not thee grieve dismounted to have beene,
And brought to grownd that never wast before:
For not thy fault, but secret powre unseene:
That speare enchaunted was which layd thee on the greene.

V I I I

But weenedst thou what wight thee overthrew,
Much greater griefe and shamefuller regrett
For thy hard fortune then thou wouldst renew,
That of a single damzell thou wert mett
On equall plaine, and there so hard besett:
Even the famous Britomart it was,
Whom straunge adventure did from Britayne sett
To seeke her lover (love far sought alas!)
Whose image shee had seene in Venus looking glas.

I X

Full of disdainefull wrath he fierce uprose
For to revenge that fowle reprochefull shame,
And snatching his bright sword began to close
With her on foot, and stoutly forward came:
Dye rather would he then endure that same.
Which when his Palmer saw, he gan to feare

His toward perill, and untoward blame,
Which by that new rencounter he should reare;
For death sate on the point of that enchaunted speare:

          X

And hasting towards him gan fayre perswade
Not to provoke misfortune, nor to weene
His speares default to mend with cruell blade;
For by his mightie Science he had seene
The secrete vertue of that weapon keene,
That mortall puissaunce mote not withstond.
Nothing on earth mote alwaies happy beene:
Great hazard were it, and adventure fond,
To loose long gotten honour with one evill hond.

          X I

By such good meanes he him discounselled
From prosecuting his revenging rage:
And eke the Prince like treaty handeled,
His wrathfull will with reason to aswage;
And laid the blame, not to his carriage,
But to his starting steed that swarv'd asyde,
And to the ill purveyaunce of his page,
That had his furnitures not firmely tyde.
So is his angry corage fayrly pacifyde.

          X I I

Thus reconcilement was betweene them knitt,
Through goodly temperaunce and affection chaste;
And either vowd with all their power and witt
To let not others honour be defaste
Of friend or foe, who ever it embaste;
Ne armes to beare against the others syde:
In which accord the Prince was also plaste,
And with that golden chaine of concord tyde.
So goodly all agreed they forth yfere did ryde.

          X I I I

O! goodly usage of those antique tymes,
In which the sword was servaunt unto right;
When not for malice and contentious crymes,
But all for prayse, and proofe of manly might,
The martiall brood accustomed to fight:
Then honour was the meed of victory,
And yet the vanquished had no despight.

XII, 5   embaste: dishonored

Let later age that noble use envy,
Vyle rancor to avoid and cruel surquedry.

X I V

Long they thus traveiled in friendly wise,
Through countreyes waste, and eke well edifyde,
Seeking adventures hard, to exercise
Their puissaunce, whylome full dernly tryde.
At length they came into a forest wyde,
Whose hideous horror and sad trembling sownd,
Full griesly seemd: Therein they long did ryde,
Yet tract of living creature none they fownd,
Save Beares, Lyons, and Buls, which romed them arownd.

X V

All suddenly out of the thickest brush,
Upon a milkwhite Palfrey all alone,
A goodly Lady did foreby them rush,
Whose face did seeme as cleare as Christall stone,
And eke, through feare, as white as whales bone:
Her garments all were wrought of beaten gold,
And all her steed with tinsell trappings shone,
Which fledd so fast that nothing mote him hold,
And scarse them leasure gave her passing to behold.

X V I

Still as she fledd her eyes she backward threw,
As fearing evill that poursewd her fast;
And her faire yellow locks behind her flew,
Loosely disperst with puff of every blast:
All as a blazing starre doth farre outcast
His hearie beames, and flaming lockes dispredd,
At sight whereof the people stand aghast;
But the sage wisard telles, as he has redd,
That it importunes death and dolefull dreryhedd.

X V I I

So as they gazed after her a whyle,
Lo! where a griesly foster forth did rush,
Breathing out beastly lust her to defyle:
His tyreling Jade he fiersly forth did push
Through thicke and thin, both over banck and bush,
In hope her to attaine by hooke or crooke,
That from his gory sydes the blood did gush.

XIII, 9   surquedry: arrogance   XVII, 2   foster: forester
XIV, 4   dernly: grievously

Large were his limbes, and terrible his looke,
And in his clownish hand a sharp bore speare he shooke.

X V I I I

Which outrage when those gentle knights did see,
Full of great envy and fell gealosy
They stayd not to avise who first should bee,
But all spurd after, fast as they mote fly,
To reskew her from shamefull villany.
The Prince and Guyon equally bylive
Her selfe pursewd, in hope to win thereby
Most goodly meede, the fairest Dame alive:
But after the foule foster Timias did strive.

X I X

The whiles faire Britomart, whose constant mind
Would not so lightly follow beauties chace,
Ne reckt of Ladies Love, did stay behynd,
And them awayted there a certaine space,
To weet if they would turne backe to that place;
But when she saw them gone she forward went,
As lay her journey, through that perlous Pace,
With stedfast corage and stout hardiment:
Ne evil thing she feard, ne evill thing she ment.

X X

At last, as nigh out of the wood she came,
A stately Castle far away she spyde,
To which her steps directly she did frame.
That Castle was most goodly edifyde,
And plaste for pleasure nigh that forrest syde:
But faire before the gate a spatious playne,
Mantled with greene, it selfe did spredden wyde,
On which she saw six knights, that did darrayne
Fiers battaill against one with cruell might and mayne.

X X I

Mainely they all attonce upon him laid,
And sore beset on every side arownd,
That nigh he breathlesse grew, yet nought dismaid,
Ne ever to them yielded foot of grownd,
All had he lost much blood through many a wownd,
But stoutly dealt his blowes, and every way,
To which he turned in his wrathfull stownd,

xviii, 2   envy: emulation   xxi, 1   Mainely: strongly
xix, 7   Pace: tract

Made them recoile, and fly from dredd decay,
That none of all the six before him durst assay.

X X I I

Like dastard Curres that, having at a bay
The salvage beast embost in wearie chace,
Dare not adventure on the stubborne pray,
Ne byte before, but rome from place to place
To get a snatch when turned is his face.
In such distresse and doubtfull jeopardy
When Britomart him saw, she ran apace
Unto his reskew, and with earnest cry
Badd those same six forbeare that single enimy.

X X I I I

But to her cry they list not lenden eare,
Ne ought the more their mightie strokes surceasse.
But gathering him rownd about more neare,
Their direfull rancour rather did encreasse;
Till that she rushing through the thickest preasse
Perforce disparted their compacted gyre,
And soone compeld to hearken unto peace.
Tho gan she myldly of them to inquyre
The cause of their dissention and outrageous yre.

X X I V

Whereto that single knight did answere frame:
'These six would me enforce by oddes of might
To chaunge my liefe, and love another Dame;
That death me liefer were then such despight,
So unto wrong to yield my wrested right:
For I love one, the truest one on grownd,
Ne list me chaunge; she th' Errant Damzell hight;
For whose deare sake full many a bitter stownd
I have endurd, and tasted many a bloody wownd.'

X X V

'Certes,' (said she) 'then beene ye sixe to blame,
To weene your wrong by force to justify;
For knight to leave his Lady were great shame
That faithfull is, and better were to dy.
All losse is lesse, and lesse the infamy,
Then losse of love to him that loves but one:
Ne may love be compeld by maistery;

xxII, 2　embost: hard pressed　　　xxIII, 6　gyre: circle

For soone as maistery comes sweet Love anone
Taketh his nimble winges, and soone away is gone.'

X X V I

Then spake one of those six; 'There dwelleth here
Within this castle wall a Lady fayre,
Whose soveraine beautie hath no living pere;
Thereto so bounteous and so debonayre,
That never any mote with her compayre:
She hath ordaind this law, which we approve,
That every knight which doth this way repayre,
In case he have no Lady nor no love,
Shall doe unto her service, never to remove:

X X V I I

'But if he have a Lady or a Love,
Then must he her forgoe with fowle defame,
Or els with us by dint of sword approve,
That she is fairer then our fairest Dame;
As did this knight, before ye hither came.'
'Perdy,' (said Britomart) 'the choise is hard;
But what reward had he that overcame?'
'He should advaunced bee to high regard,'
(Said they) 'and have our Ladies love for his reward.

X X V I I I

'Therefore aread, Sir, if thou have a love.'
'Love hath I sure,' (quoth she) 'but Lady none;
Yet will I not fro mine own love remove,
Ne to your Lady will I service done,
But wreake your wronges wrought to this knight alone,
And prove his cause.' With that, her mortall speare
She mightily aventred towards one,
And downe him smot ere well aware he weare;
Then to the next she rode, and downe the next did beare.

X X I X

Ne did she stay till three on ground she layd
That none of them himselfe could reare againe:
The fourth was by that other knight dismayd,
All were he wearie of his former paine;
That now there do but two of six remaine,
Which two did yield before she did them smight.
'Ah!' (said she then) 'now may ye all see plaine,
That truth is strong, and trew love most of might,
That for his trusty servaunts doth so strongly fight.'

XXX

'Too well we see,' (saide they) 'and prove too well
Our faulty weakenes, and your matchlesse might:
Forthy, faire Sir, yours be the Damozell,
Which by her owne law to yourt lot doth light,
And we your liegemen faith unto you plight.'
So underneath her feet their swords they mard,
And, after, her besought, well as they might,
To enter in and reape the dew reward.
She graunted; and then in they all together far'd.

XXXI

Long were it to describe the goodly frame,
And stately port of Castle Joyeous,
(For so that Castle hight by commun name)
Where they were entertaynd with courteous
And comely glee of many gratious
Faire Ladies, and of many a gentle knight,
Who, through a Chamber long and spacious,
Eftsoones them brought unto their Ladies sight,
That of them cleeped was the Lady of Delight.

XXXII

But for to tell the sumptuous aray
Of that great chamber should be labour lost;
For living wit, I weene, cannot display
The roiall riches and exceeding cost
Of every pillour and of every post,
Which all of purest bullion framed were,
And with great perles and pretious stones embost;
That the bright glister of their beames cleare
Did sparckle forth great light, and glorious did appeare.

XXXIII

These stranger knights, through passing, forth were led
Into an inner rowme, whose royaltee
And rich purveyance might uneath be red;
Mote Princes place be seeme so deckt to bee.
Which stately manner whenas they did see,
The image of superfluous riotize,
Exceeding much the state of meane degree,
They greatly wondred whence so sumptuous guize
Might be maintaynd, and each gan diversely devize.

xxx, 6   mard: dishonored (?)   xxxi, 9   cleeped: named

XXXIV

The wals were round about appareiled
With costly clothes of Arras and of Toure;
In which with cunning hand was pourtrahed
The love of Venus and her Paramoure,
The fayre Adonis, turned to a flowre,
A worke of rare device and wondrous wit.
First did it shew the bitter balefull stowre,
Which her essayd with many a fervent fit,
When first her tender hart was with his beautie smit.

XXXV

Then with what sleights and sweet allurements she
Entyst the Boy, as well that art she knew,
And wooed him her Paramoure to bee,
Now making girlonds of each flowre that grew
To crowne his golden lockes with honour dew;
Now leading him into a secret shade
From his Beauperes, and from bright heavens vew,
Where him to sleepe she gently would perswade,
Or bathe him in a fountaine by some covert glade:

XXXVI

And whilst he slept she over him would spred
Her mantle, colour'd like the starry skyes,
And her soft arme lay underneath his hed,
And with ambrosiall kisses bathe his eyes;
And whilst he bath'd with her two crafty spyes
She secretly would search each daintie lim,
And throw into the well sweet Rosemaryes,
And fragrant violets, and Paunces trim;
And ever with sweet Nectar she did sprinkle him.

XXXVII

So did she steale his heedelesse hart away,
And joyd his love in secret unespyde:
But for she saw him bent to cruell play,
To hunt the salvage beast in forrest wyde,
Dreadfull of daunger that mote him betyde,
She oft and oft adviz'd him to refraine
From chase of greater beastes, whose brutish pryde
Mote breede him scath unwares: but all in vaine;
For who can shun the chance that dest'ny doth ordaine.

XXXIV, 2   clothes: cloths, tapestries   XXXV, 7   Beauperes: companions

XXXVIII

Lo! where beyond he lyeth languishing,
Deadly engored of a great wilde Bore;
And by his side the Goddesse groveling
Makes for him endlesse mone, and evermore
With her soft garment wipes away the gore
Which staynes his snowy skin with hatefull hew:
But, when she saw no helpe might him restore,
Him to a dainty flowre she did transmew,
Which in that cloth was wrought as if it lively grew.

XXXIX

So was that chamber clad in goodly wize:
And rownd about it many beds were dight,
As whylome was the antique worldes guize,
Some for untimely ease, some for delight,
As pleased them to use that use it might;
And all was full of Damzels and of Squyres
Dauncing and reveling both day and night,
And swimming deepe in sensuall desyres;
And Cupid still emongest them kindled lustfull fyres.

XL

And all the while sweet Musicke did divide
Her looser notes with Lydian harmony;
And all the while sweet birdes thereto applide
Their daintie layes and dulcet melody,
Ay caroling of love and jollity,
That wonder was to heare their trim consort.
Which when those knights beheld, with scornefull eye
They sdeigned such lascivious disport,
And loath'd the loose demeanure of that wanton sort.

XLI

Thence they were brought to that great Ladies vew,
Whom they found sitting on a sumptuous bed
That glistred all with gold and glorious shew,
As the proud Persian Queenes accustomed.
She seemd a woman of great bountihed,
And of rare beautie, saving that askaunce
Her wanton eyes, ill signes of womanhed,
Did roll too lightly, and too often glaunce,
Without regard of grace or comely amenaunce.

XL, 1   divide: perform

XLII

Long worke it were, and needlesse, to devize
Their goodly entertainement and great glee.
She caused them be led in courteous wize
Into a bowre, disarmed for to be,
And cheared well with wine and spiceree:
The Redcrosse Knight was soon disarmed there;
But the brave Mayd would not disarmed bee,
But onely vented up her umbriere,
And so did let her goodly visage to appere.

XLIII

As when fayre Cynthia, in darkesome night,
Is in a noyous cloud enveloped,
Where she may finde the substance thin and light,
Breakes forth her silver beames, and her bright hed
Discovers to the world discomfited:
Of the poore traveiler that went astray
With thousand blessings she is heried.
Such was the beautie and the shining ray,
With which fayre Britomart gave light unto the day.

XLIV

And eke those six, which lately with her fought,
Now were disarmd, and did them selves present
Unto her vew, and company unsought;
For they all seemed courteous and gent,
And all sixe brethren, borne of one parent,
Which had them traynd in all civilitee,
And goodly taught to tilt and turnament:
Now were they liegmen to this Ladie free,
And her knights service ought, to hold of her in fee.

XLV

The first of them by name Gardantè hight,
A jolly person, and of comely vew;
The second was Parlantè, a bold knight;
And next to him Jocantè did ensew;
Basciantè did him selfe most courteous shew;
But fierce Bacchantè seemd too fell and keene;
And yett in armes Noctantè greater grew:
All were faire knights, and goodly well beseene;
But to faire Britomart they all but shadowes beene.

XLIII, 7   heried: praised   XLIV, 9   ought: owed

X L V I

For shee was full of amiable grace
And manly terror mixed therewithall;
That as the one stird up affections bace,
So th' other did mens rash desires apall,
And hold them backe that would in error fall:
As hee that hath espide a vermeill Rose,
To which sharp thornes and breres the way forstall,
Dare not for dread his hardy hand expose,
But wishing it far off his ydle wish doth lose.

X L V I I

Whom when the Lady saw so faire a wight,
All ignorant of her contrary sex,
(For shee her weend a fresh and lusty knight,)
Shee greatly gan enamoured to wex
And with vaine thoughts her falsed fancy vex:
Her fickle hart conceived hasty fyre,
Like sparkes of fire which fall in sclender flex,
That shortly brent into extreme desyre,
And ransackt all her veines with passion entyre.

X L V I I I

Eftsoones shee grew to great impatience,
And into termes of open outrage brust,
That plaine discovered her incontinence;
Ne reckt shee who her meaning did mistrust,
For she was given all to fleshly lust,
And poured forth in sensuall delight,
That all regard of shame she had discust,
And meet respect of honor putt to flight:
So shamelesse beauty soone becomes a loathly sight.

X L I X

Faire Ladies, that to love captived arre,
And chaste desires doe nourish in your mind,
Let not her fault your sweete affections marre,
Ne blott the bounty of all womankind,
'Mongst thousands good one wanton Dame to find:
Emongst the Roses grow some wicked weeds:
For this was not to love, but lust, inclind;
For love does alwaies bring forth bounteous deeds,
And in each gentle hart desire of honor breeds.

XLVII, 7　flex: flax	XLVIII, 4　mistrust: suspect
XLVIII, 2　outrage: excess	XLVIII, 7　discust: shaken off

L

Nought so of love this looser Dame did skill,
But as a cole to kindle fleshly flame,
Giving the bridle to her wanton will,
And treading under foote her honest name:
Such love is hate, and such desire is shame.
Still did she rove at her with crafty glaunce
Of her false eies, that at her hart did ayme,
And told her meaning in her countenaunce;
But Britomart dissembled it with ignoraunce.

L I

Supper was shortly dight, and downe they satt;
Where they were served with all sumptuous fare,
Whiles fruitfull Ceres and Lyæus fatt
Pourd out their plenty without spight or spare.
Nought wanted there that dainty was and rare,
And aye the cups their bancks did overflow;
And aye betweene the cups she did prepare
Way to her love, and secret darts did throw;
But Britomart would not such guilfull message know.

L I I

So, when they slaked had the fervent heat
Of appetite with meates of every sort,
The Lady did faire Britomart entreat
Her to disarme, and with delightfull sport
To loose her warlike limbs and strong effort;
But when shee mote not thereunto be wonne,
(For shee her sexe under that straunge purport
Did use to hide, and plaine apparaunce shonne)
In playner wise to tell her grievaunce she begonne.

L I I I

And all attonce discovered her desire
With sighes, and sobs, and plaints, and piteous griefe,
The outward sparkes of her inburning fire;
Which spent in vaine, at last she told her briefe,
That but if she did lend her short reliefe
And doe her comfort, she mote algates dye:
But the chaste damzell, that had never priefe
Of such malengine and fine forgerye,
Did easely beleeve her strong extremitye.

LII, 2   meates: food   LIII, 8   malengine: deceit
LIII, 6   algates: altogether

L I V

Full easy was for her to have beliefe,
Who by self-feeling of her feeble sexe,
And by long triall of the inward griefe
Wherewith imperious love her hart did vexe,
Could judge what paines doe loving harts perplexe.
Who meanes no guile be guiled soonest shall,
And to faire semblaunce doth light faith annexe:
The bird that knowes not the false fowlers call,
Into his hidden nett full easely doth fall.

L V

Forthy she would not in discourteise wise
Scorne the faire offer of good will profest;
For great rebuke it is love to despise,
Or rudely sdeigne a gentle harts request,
But with faire countenaunce, as beseemed best,
Her entertaynd: nath'lesse shee inly deemd
Her love too light, to wooe a wandring guest,
Which she misconstruing, thereby esteemd
That from like inward fire that outward smoke had steemd.

L V I

Therewith a while she her flit fancy fedd,
Till she mote winne fit time for her desire;
But yet her wound still inward freshly bledd,
And through her bones the false instilled fire
Did spred it selfe, and venime close inspire.
Tho were the tables taken all away;
And every knight, and every gentle Squire,
Gan choose his Dame with *Bascimano* gay,
With whom he ment to make his sport and courtly play.

L V I I

Some fell to daunce, some fel to hazardry,
Some to make love, some to make meryment,
As diverse witts to diverse things apply;
And all the while faire Malecasta bent
Her crafty engins to her close intent.
By this th' eternall lampes, wherewith high Jove
Doth light the lower world, were halfe yspent,
And the moist daughters of huge Atlas strove
Into the Ocean deepe to drive their weary drove.

LVI, 8   *Bascimano:* kissing of the hand

L V I I I

High time it seemed then for everie wight
Them to betake unto their kindly rest:
Eftesoones long waxen torches weren light
Unto their bowres to guyden every guest.
Tho, when the Britonesse saw all the rest
Avoided quite, she gan her selfe despoile,
And safe committ to her soft fethered nest,
Wher through long watch, and late daies weary toile,
She soundly slept, and carefull thoughts did quite assoile.

L I X

Now whenas all the world in silence deepe
Yshrowded was, and every mortall wight
Was drowned in the depth of deadly sleepe;
Faire Malecasta, whose engrieved spright
Could find no rest in such perplexed plight,
Lightly arose out of her wearie bed,
And, under the blacke vele of guilty Night,
Her with a scarlott mantle covered
That was with gold and Ermines faire enveloped.

L X

Then panting softe, and trembling every joynt,
Her fearfull feete towards the bowre she mov'd,
Where she for secret purpose did appoynt
To lodge the warlike maide, unwisely loov'd;
And, to her bed approching, first she proov'd
Whether she slept or wakte: with her softe hand
She softely felt if any member moov'd,
And lent her wary eare to understand
If any puffe of breath or signe of sence shee fond.

L X I

Which whenas none she fond, with easy shifte,
For feare least her unwares she should abrayd,
Th' embroder'd quilt she lightly up did lifte,
And by her side her selfe she softly layd,
Of every finest fingers touch affrayd;
Ne any noise she made, ne word she spake,
But inly sigh'd. At last the royall Mayd
Out of her quiet slomber did awake,
And chaunged her weary side the better ease to take.

LVIII, 9   assoile: dispel   LXI, 2   abrayd: awake

L X I I

Where feeling one close couched by her side,
She lightly lept out of her filed bedd,
And to her weapon ran, in minde to gride
The loathed leachour. But the Dame, halfe dedd
Through suddein feare and ghastly drerihedd,
Did shrieke alowd, that through the hous it rong,
And the whole family, therewith adredd,
Rashly out of their rouzed couches sprong,
And to the troubled chamber all in armes did throng.

L X I I I

And those six knights, that ladies Champions
And eke the Redcrosse knight ran to the stownd.
Halfe armd and halfe unarmd, with them attons:
Where when confusedly they came, they fownd
Their lady lying on the sencelesse grownd:
On thother side they saw the warlike Mayd
Al in her snow-white smocke, with locks unbownd,
Threatning the point of her avenging blaed;
That with so troublous terror they were all dismayd.

L X I V

About their Ladye first they flockt arownd;
Whom having laid in comfortable couch,
Shortly they reard out of her frosen swownd;
And afterwardes they gan with fowle reproch
To stirre up strife, and troublous contecke broch:
But by ensample of the last dayes losse,
None of them rashly durst to her approch,
Ne in so glorious spoile themselves embosse:
Her succourd eke the Champion of the bloody Crosse.

L X V

But one of those six knights, Gardantè hight,
Drew out a deadly bow and arrow keene,
Which forth he sent, with felonous despight
And fell intent, against the virgin sheene:
The mortall steele stayd not till it was seene
To gore her side; yet was the wound not deepe,
But lightly rased her soft silken skin,
That drops of purple blood thereout did weepe,
Which did her lilly smock with staines of vermeil steep.

LXII, 2   filed: defiled   LXII, 8   Rashly: hurriedly
LXII, 3   gride: pierce   LXIV, 5   contecke: strife

LXVI

Wherewith enrag'd she fiercely at them flew,
And with her flaming sword about her layd,
That none of them foule mischiefe could eschew,
But with her dreadfull strokes were all dismayd:
Here, there, and every where, about her swayd
Her wrathfull steele, that none mote it abyde;
And eke the Redcrosse knight gave her good ayd,
Ay joyning foot to foot, and syde to syde;
That in short space their foes they have quite terrifyde.

LXVII

Tho, whenas all were put to shamefull flight,
The noble Britomartis her arayd,
And her bright armes about her body dight.
For nothing would she lenger there be stayd,
Where so loose life, and so ungentle trade,
Was usd of knightes and Ladies seeming gent:
So earely, ere the grosse Earthes gryesy shade
Was all disperst out of the firmament,
They tooke their steeds, and forth upon their journey went.

CANTO II.

The Redcrosse knight to Britomart
Describeth Artegall:
The wondrous myrrhour, by which she
In love with him did fall.

I

Here have i cause in men just blame to find,
That in their proper praise too partiall bee,
And not indifferent to woman kind,
To whom no share in armes and chevalree
They doe impart, ne maken memoree
Of their brave gestes and prowesse martiall:
Scarse do they spare to one, or two, or three,
Rowme in their writtes; yet the same writing small
Does all their deedes deface, and dims their glories all.

II

But by record of antique times I finde
That wemen wont in warres to beare most sway,

LXVII, 7   gryesy: grim

And to all great exploites them selves inclind,
Of which they still the girlond bore away;
Till envious Men, fearing their rules decay,
Gan coyne streight lawes to curb their liberty:
Yet sith they warlike armes have laide away,
They have exceld in artes and pollicy,
That now we foolish men that prayse gin eke t'envy.

I I I

Of warlike puissaunce in ages spent,
Be thou, faire Britomart, whose prayse I wryte;
But of all wisedom bee thou precedent,
O soveraine Queene! whose prayse I would endyte,
Endite I would as dewtie doth excyte;
But ah! my rymes too rude and rugged arre,
When in so high an object they do lyte,
And, striving fit to make, I feare, doe marre:
Thy selfe thy prayses tell, and make them knowen farre.

I V

She, traveiling with Guyon, by the way
Of sondry thinges faire purpose gan to find,
T'abridg their journey long, and lingring day;
Mongst which it fell into that Fairies mind
To aske this Briton Maid, what uncouth wind
Brought her into those partes, and what inquest
Made her dissemble her disguised kind?
Faire Lady she him seemd, like Lady drest,
But fairest knight alive, when armed was her brest.

v

Thereat she sighing softly had no powre
To speake a while, ne ready answere make,
But with hart-thrilling throbs and bitter stowre,
As if she had a fever fitt, did quake,
And every daintie limbe with horrour shake;
And ever and anone the rosy red
Flasht through her face, as it had beene a flake
Of lightning through bright heven fulmined:
At last, the passion past, she thus him answered.

V I

'Faire Sir, I let you weete, that from the howre
I taken was from nourses tender pap,
I have been trained up in warlike stowre,

II, 6   streight: strict

To tossen speare and shield, and to affrap
The warlike ryder to his most mishap:
Sithence I loathed have my life to lead,
As Ladies wont, in pleasures wanton lap,
To finger the fine needle and nyce thread,
Me lever were with point of foemans speare be dead.

V I I

'All my delight on deedes of armes is sett,
To hunt out perilles and adventures hard,
By sea, by land, where so they may be mett,
Onely for honour and for high regard,
Without respect of richesse or reward:
For such intent into these partes I came,
Withouten compasse or withouten card,
Far fro my native soyle, that is by name
The greater Brytayne, here to seek for praise and fame.

V I I I

'Fame blazed hath, that here in Faery lond
Doe many famous knightes and Ladies wonne,
And many straunge adventures to bee fond,
Of which great worth and worship may be wonne;
Which to prove, I this voyage have begonne.
But mote I weet of you, right courteous knight,
Tydings of one that hath unto me donne
Late foule dishonour and reprochfull spight,
The which I seeke to wreake, and Arthegall he hight.'

I X

The worde gone out she backe againe would call,
As her repenting so to have missayd,
But that he, it uptaking ere the fall,
Her shortly answered: 'Faire martiall Mayd,
Certes ye misavised beene t' upbrayd
A gentle knight with so unknightly blame;
For, weet ye well, of all that ever playd
At tilt or tourney, or like warlike game,
The noble Arthegall hath ever borne the name.

X

'Forthy great wonder were it, if such shame
Should ever enter in his bounteous thought,
Or ever doe that mote deserven blame:
The noble corage never weeneth ought

VII, 7   card: chart

That may unworthy of it selfe be thought.
Therefore, faire Damzell, be ye well aware,
Least that too farre ye have your sorrow sought:
You and your countrey both I wish welfare,
And honour both; for each of other worthy are.'

X I

The royall Maid woxe inly wondrous glad,
To heare her Love so highly magnifyde;
And joyd that ever she affixed had
Her hart on knight so goodly glorifyde,
How ever finely she it faind to hyde.
The loving mother, that nine monethes did beare
In the deare closett of her painefull syde
Her tender babe, it seeing safe appeare,
Doth not so much rejoyce as she rejoyced theare.

X I I

But to occasion him to further talke,
To feed her humor with his pleasing style,
Her list in stryfull termes with him to balke,
And thus replyde: 'How ever, Sir, ye fyle
Your courteous tongue his prayses to compyle,
It ill beseemes a knight of gentle sort,
Such as ye have him boasted, to beguyle
A simple maide, and worke so hainous tort,
In shame of knighthood, as I largely can report.

X I I I

'Let bee therefore my vengeaunce to disswade,
And read where I that faytour false may find.'
'Ah! but if reason faire might you perswade
To slake your wrath, and mollify your mind'
(Said he) 'perhaps ye should it better find:
For hardie thing it is, to weene by might
That man to hard conditions to bind,
Or ever hope to match in equall fight,
Whose prowesse paragone saw never living wight.

X I V

'Ne soothlich is it easie for to read
Where now on earth, or how, he may be fownd;
For he ne wonneth in one certeine stead,
But restlesse walketh all the world arownd,

---

xii, 3   stryfull: contentious   xiii, 2   faytour: villain
xii, 3   balke: bandy words

Ay doing thinges that to his fame redownd,
Defending Ladies cause and Orphans right,
Whereso he heares that any doth confownd
Them comfortlesse through tyranny or might:
So is his soveraine honour raisde to hevens hight.'

X V

His feeling wordes her feeble sence much pleased,
And softly sunck into her molten hart:
Hart that is inly hurt is greatly eased
With hope of thing that may allegge his smart;
For pleasing wordes are like to Magick art,
That doth the charmed Snake in slomber lay.
Such secrete ease felt gentle Britomart,
Yet list the same efforce with faind gainesay;
So dischord ofte in Musick makes the sweeter lay:—

X V I

And sayd; 'Sir knight, these ydle termes forbeare;
And, sith it is uneath to finde his haunt,
Tell me some markes by which he may appeare,
If chaunce I him encounter paravaunt;
For perdy one shall other slay, or daunt:
What shape, what shield, what armes, what steed, what stedd,
And what so else his person most may vaunt.'
All which the Redcrosse knight to point aredd,
And him in everie part before her fashioned.

X V I I

Yet him in everie part before she knew,
However list her now her knowledge fayne,
Sith him whylome in Britayne she did vew,
To her revealed in a mirrhour playne;
Whereof did grow her first engraffed payne,
Whose root and stalke so bitter yet did taste,
That but the fruit more sweetnes did contayne,
Her wretched dayes in dolour she mote waste,
And yield the pray of love to lothsome death at last.

X V I I I

By straunge occasion she did him behold,
And much more straungely gan to love his sight,
As it in bookes hath written beene of old.
In Deheubarth, that now South-wales is hight,
What time king Ryence raign'd and dealed right,

xvii, 5 engraffed: implanted

The great Magitien Merlin had deviz'd,
By his deepe science and hell-dreaded might,
A looking glasse, right wondrously aguiz'd,
Whose vertues through the wyde worlde soone were solem-
    niz'd.

X I X

It vertue had to shew in perfect sight
Whatever thing was in the world contaynd,
Betwixt the lowest earth and hevens hight,
So that it to the looker appertaynd:
Whatever foe had wrought, or frend had faynd,
Therein discovered was, ne ought mote pas,
Ne ought in secret from the same remaynd;
Forthy it round and hollow shaped was,
Like to the world itselfe, and seemd a world of glas.

X X

Who wonders not, that reades so wonderous worke?
But who does wonder, that has red the Towre
Wherein th' Aegyptian Phao long did lurke
From all mens vew, that none might her discoure,
Yet she might all men vew out of her bowre?
Great Ptolomæe it for his lemans sake
Ybuilded all of glasse, by Magicke powre,
And also it impregnable did make;
Yet when his love was false he with a peaze it brake.

X X I

Such was the glassy globe that Merlin made,
And gave unto king Ryence for his gard,
That never foes his kingdome might invade,
But he it knew at home before he hard
Tydings thereof, and so them still debar'd.
It was a famous Present for a Prince,
And worthy worke of infinite reward,
That treasons could bewray, and foes convince:
Happy this Realme, had it remayned ever since!

X X I I

One day it fortuned fayre Britomart
Into her fathers closet to repayre;
For nothing he from her reserv'd apart,
Being his onely daughter and his hayre;

xviii, 8   aguiz'd: fashioned   xxi, 8   convince: conquer
xx, 9   peaze: blow

Where when she had espyde that mirrhour fayre,
Her selfe awhile therein she vewd in vaine:
Tho, her avizing of the vertues rare
Which thereof spoken were, she gan againe
Her to bethinke of that mote to her selfe pertaine.

X X I I I

But as if falleth, in the gentlest harts
Imperious Love hath highest set his throne,
And tyrannizeth in the bitter smarts
Of them that to him buxome are and prone:
So thought this Mayd (as maydens use to done)
Whom fortune for her husband would allot:
Not that she lusted after any one,
For she was pure from blame of sinfull blott;
Yet wist her life at last must lincke in that same knot.

X X I V

Eftsoones there was presented to her eye
A comely knight, all arm'd in complete wize,
Through whose bright ventayle, lifted up on hye,
His manly face, that did his foes agrize,
And frends to termes of gentle truce entize,
Lookt forth, as Phœbus face out of the east
Betwixt two shady mountaynes doth arize:
Portly his person was, and much increast
Through his Heroicke grace and honorable gest.

X X V

His crest was covered with a couchant Hownd,
And all his armour seemd of antique mould,
But wondrous massy and assured sownd,
And round about yfretted all with gold,
In which there written was, with cyphres old,
Achilles armes, which Arthegall did win:
And on his shield enveloped sevenfold
He bore a crowned little Ermelin,
That deckt the azure field with her fayre pouldred skin.

X X V I

The Damzell well did vew his Personage
And liked well, ne further fastned not,
But went her way; ne her unguilty age
Did weene, unwares, that her unlucky lot

XXIII, 4 buxome: compliant   XXIV, 9 gest: action
XXIV, 4 agrize: terrify

Lay hidden in the bottome of the pot.
Of hurt unwist most daunger doth redound;
But the false Archer, which that arrow shot
So slyly that she did not feele the wound,
Did smyle full smoothly at her weetlesse wofull stound.

XXVII

Thenceforth the fether in her lofty crest,
Ruffed of love, gan lowly to availe;
And her prowd portaunce and her princely gest,
With which she earst tryumphed, now did quaile:
Sad, solemne, sowre, and full of fancies fraile,
She woxe; yet wist she nether how, nor why.
She wist not, silly Mayd, what she did aile,
Yet wist she was not well at ease perdy;
Yet thought it was not love, but some melancholy.

XXVIII

So soone as Night had with her pallid hew
Defaste the beautie of the shyning skye,
And refte from men the worldes desired vew,
She with her Nourse adowne to sleepe did lye;
But sleepe full far away from her did fly:
In stead thereof sad sighes and sorrowes deepe
Kept watch and ward about her warily,
That nought she did but wayle, and often steepe
Her dainty couch with teares which closely she did weepe.

XXIX

And if that any drop of slombring rest
Did chaunce to still into her weary spright,
When feeble nature felt her selfe opprest,
Streight-way with dreames, and with fantastick sight
Of dreadfull things, the same was put to flight;
That oft out of her bed she did astart,
As one with vew of ghastly feends affright:
Tho gan she to renew her former smart,
And thinke of that fayre visage written in her hart.

XXX

One night, when she was tost with such unrest,
Her aged Nourse, whose name was Glaucè hight,
Feeling her leape out of her loathed nest,
Betwixt her feeble armes her quickly keight,
And downe againe her in her warme bed dight:

XXVII, 2 availe: drop down   XXX, 4 keight: caught

'Ah! my deare daughter, ah! my dearest dread,
What uncouth fit,' (sayd she) 'what evill plight
Hath thee opprest, and with sad drearyhead
Chaunged thy lively cheare, and living made thee dead?

x x x i

'For not of nought these suddein ghastly feares
All night afflict thy naturall repose;
And all the day, when as thine equall peares
Their fit disports with faire delight doe chose,
Thou in dull corners doest thy selfe inclose;
Ne tastest Princes pleasures, ne doest spred
Abroad thy fresh youths fayrest flowre, but lose
Both leafe and fuite, both too untimely shed,
As one in wilfull bale for ever buried.

x x x i i

'The time that mortall men their weary cares
Do lay away, and all wilde beastes do rest,
And every river eke his course forbeares,
Then doth this wicked evill thee infest,
And rive with thousand throbs thy thrilled brest:
Like an huge Aetn' of deepe engulfed gryefe,
Sorrow is heaped in thy hollow chest,
Whence foorth it breakes in sighes and anguish ryfe,
As smoke and sulphure mingled with confused stryfe.

x x x i i i

'Ay me! how much I feare least love it bee!
But if that love it be, as sure I read
By knowen signes and passions which I see,
Be it worthy of thy race and royall sead,
Then I avow, by this most sacred head
Of my deare foster childe, to ease thy griefe
And win thy will: Therefore away doe dread;
For death nor daunger from thy dew reliefe
Shall me debarre: tell me therefore, my liefest liefe!'

x x x i v

So having sayd, her twixt her armes twaine
Shee streightly straynd, and colled tenderly;
And every trembling joynt and every vaine
Shee softly felt, and rubbed busily,
To doe the frosen cold away to fly;

xxx, 6   dread: revered one   xxxiv, 2   colled: embraced
xxxii, 5   thrilled: pierced

And her faire deawy eies with kisses deare
Shee ofte did bathe, and ofte againe did dry;
And ever her importund not to feare
To let the secret of her hart to her appeare.

x x x v

The Damzell pauzd; and then thus fearfully:
'Ah! Nurse, what needeth thee to eke my payne?
Is not enough that I alone doe dye,
But it must doubled bee with death of twaine?
For nought for me but death there doth remaine.'
'O daughter deare!' (said she) 'despeire no whit;
For never sore but might a salve obtaine:
That blinded God, which hath ye blindly smit,
Another arrow hath your lovers hart to hit.'

x x x v i

'But mine is not' (quoth she) 'like other wownd;
For which no reason can finde remedy.'
'Was never such, but mote the like be fownd,'
(Said she) 'and though no reason may apply
Salve to your sore, yet love can higher stye
Then reasons reach, and oft hath wonders donne.'
'But neither God of love nor God of skye
Can doe' (said she) 'that which cannot be donne.'
'Things ofte impossible' (quoth she) 'seeme, ere begonne.'

x x x v i i

'These idle wordes' (said she) 'doe nought aswage
My stubborne smart, but more annoiaunce breed:
For no, no usuall fire, no usuall rage
Yt is, O Nourse! which on my life doth feed,
And sucks the blood which from my hart doth bleed:
But since thy faithful zele lets me not hyde
My crime, (if crime it be) I will it reed.
Nor Prince nor pere it is, whose love hath gryde
My feeble brest of late, and launched this wound wyde.

x x x v i i i

'Nor man it is, nor other living wight,
For then some hope I might unto me draw;
But th' only shade and semblant of a knight,
Whose shape or person yet I never saw,
Hath me subjected to loves cruell law:

xxxvii, 8 gryde: pierced

The same one day, as me misfortune led,
I in my fathers wondrous mirrhour saw,
And, pleased with that seeming goodly-hed,
Unwares the hidden hooke with baite I swallowed.

x x x i x

'Sithens it hath infixed faster hold
Within my bleeding bowells, and so sore
Now ranckleth in this same fraile fleshly mould,
That all my entrailes flow with poisnous gore,
And th' ulcer groweth daily more and more;
Ne can my ronning sore finde remedee,
Other then my hard fortune to deplore,
And languish, as the leafe faln from the tree,
Till death make one end of my daies and miseree!'

x l

'Daughter,' (said she) 'what need ye be dismayd?
Or why make ye such Monster of your minde?
Of much more uncouth thing I was affrayd,
Of filthy lust, contrary unto kinde;
But this affection nothing straunge I finde;
For who with reason can you aye reprove
To love the semblaunt pleasing most your minde,
And yield your heart whence ye cannot remove?
No guilt in you, but in the tyranny of love.

x l i

'Not so th' Arabian Myrrhe did set her mynd,
Nor so did Biblis spend her pining hart;
But lov'd their native flesh against al kynd,
And to their purpose used wicked art:
Yet playd Pasiphaë a more monstrous part,
That lov'd a Bul, and learnd a beast to bee.
Such shamefull lustes who loaths not, which depart
From course of nature and of modestee?
Sweete love such lewdnes bands from his faire companee.

x l i i

'But thine, my Deare, (welfare thy heart, my deare!)
Though straunge beginning had, yet fixed is
On one that worthy may perhaps appeare;
And certes seemes bestowed not amis:
Joy thereof have thou and eternall blis!'
With that, upleaning on her elbow weake,

Her alablaster brest she soft did kis,
Which all that while shee felt to pant and quake,
As it an Earth-quake were: at last she thus bespake.

X L I I I

'Beldame, your words doe worke me litle ease;
For though my love be not so lewdly bent
As those ye blame, yet may it nought appease
My raging smart, ne ought my flame relent,
But rather doth my helpelesse griefe augment;
For they, how ever shamefull and unkinde,
Yet did possesse their horrible intent;
Short end of sorrowes they therby did finde;
So was their fortune good, though wicked were their minde.

X L I V

'But wicked fortune mine, though minde be good,
Can have no ende nor hope of my desire,
But feed on shadowes whiles I die for food,
And like a shadowe wexe, whiles with entire
Affection I doe languish and expire,
I, fonder then Cephisus foolish chyld,
Who, having vewed in a fountaine shere
His face, was with the love thereof beguyld;
I, fonder, love a shade, the body far exyld.'

X L V

'Nought like,' (quoth shee) 'for that same wretched boy
Was of him selfe the ydle Paramoure,
Both love and lover, without hope of joy,
For which he faded to a watry flowre:
But better fortune thine, and better howre,
Which lov'st the shadow of a warlike knight;
No shadow but a body hath in powre:
That body, wheresoever that it light,
May learned be by cyphers, or by Magicke might.

X L V I

'But if thou may with reason yet represse
The growing evill, ere it strength have gott,
And thee abandond wholy do possesse,
Against it strongly strive, and yield thee nott
Til thou in open fielde adowne be smott:
But if the passion mayster thy fraile might,
So that needs love or death must bee thy lott,

Then, I avow to thee, by wrong or right
To compas thy desire, and find that loved knight.'

XLVII

Her chearefull words much cheard the feeble spright
Of the sicke virgin, that her downe she layd
In her warme bed to sleepe, if that she might;
And the old-woman carefully displayd
The clothes about her round with busy ayd;
So that at last a litle creeping sleepe
Surprisd her sence: Shee, therewith well apayd,
The dronken lamp down in the oyl did steepe,
And sett her by to watch, and sett her by to weepe.

XLVIII

Earely, the morrow next, before that day
His joyous face did to the world revele,
They both uprose and tooke their ready way
Unto the Church, their praiers to appele
With great devotion, and with little zele:
For the faire Damzel from the holy herse
Her love-sick hart to other thoughts did steale;
And that old Dame said many an idle verse,
Out of her daughters hart fond fancies to reverse.

XLIX

Retourned home, the royall Infant fell
Into her former fitt; for-why no powre
Nor guidaunce of herselfe in her did dwell:
But th' aged Nourse, her calling to her bowre,
Had gathered Rew, and Savine, and the flowre
Of Camphora, and Calamint, and Dill;
All which she in a earthen Pot did poure,
And to the brim with Coltwood did it fill,
And many drops of milk and blood through it did spill.

L

Then, taking thrise three heares from off her head,
Them trebly breaded in a threefold lace,
And round about the Pots mouth bound the thread;
And, after having whispered a space
Certein sad words with hollow voice and bace,
Shee to the virgin sayd, thrise sayd she itt;
'Come daughter, come; come, spit upon my face;

xLVII, 7 apayd: pleased

Spitt thrise upon me, thrise upon me spitt;
Th' uneven nomber for this busines is most fitt.'

L I

That sayd, her rownd about she from her turnd,
She turned her contrary to the Sunne;
Thrise she her turnd contrary, and returnd
All contrary; for she the right did shunne;
And ever what she did was streight undonne.
So thought she to undoe her daughters love;
But love, that is in gentle brest begonne,
No ydle charmes so lightly may remove:
That well can witnesse who by tryall it does prove.

L I I

Ne ought it mote the noble Mayd avayle,
Ne slake the fury of her cruell flame,
But that shee still did waste, and still did wayle,
That, through long languour and hart-burning brame,
She shortly like a pyned ghost became
Which long hath waited by the Stygian strond.
That when old Glaucè saw, for feare least blame
Of her miscarriage should in her be fond,
She wist not how t'amend, nor how it to withstond.

CANTO III.

Merlin bewrayes to Britomart
The state of Arthegall:
And shews the famous Progeny,
Which from them springen shall.

I

Most sacred fyre, that burnest mightily
In living brests, ykindled first above
Emongst th' eternall spheres and lamping sky,
And thence pourd into men, which men call Love!
Not that same, which doth base affections move
In brutish mindes, and filthy lust inflame,
But that sweete fit that doth true beautie love,
And choseth vertue for his dearest Dame,
Whence spring all noble deedes and never dying fame:

I I

Well did Antiquity a God thee deeme,
That over mortall mindes hast so great might,

To order them as best to thee doth seeme,
And all their actions to direct aright:
The fatall purpose of divine foresight
Thou doest effect in destined descents,
Through deepe impression of thy secret might,
And stirredst up th' Heroës high intents,
Which the late world admyres for wondrous moniments.

I I I

But thy dredd dates in none doe triumph more,
Ne braver proofe in any of thy powre
Shewd'st thou, then in this royall Maid of yore,
Making her seeke an unknowne Paramoure,
From the worlds end, through many a bitter stowre:
From whose two loynes thou afterwardes did rayse
Most famous fruites of matrimoniall bowre,
Which through the earth have spredd their living prayse,
That fame in tromp of gold eternally displayes.

I V

Begin then, O my dearest sacred Dame!
Daughter of Phœbus and of Memorye,
That doest ennoble with immortall name
The warlike Worthies, from antiquitye,
In thy great volume of Eternitye:
Begin, O Clio! and recount from hence
My glorious Soveraines goodly auncestrye,
Till that by dew degrees, and long protense,
Thou have it lastly brought unto her Excellence.

V

Full many wayes within her troubled mind
Old Glaucè cast to cure this Ladies griefe;
Full many waies she sought, but none could find,
Nor herbes, nor charmes, nor counsel, that is chiefe
And choicest med'cine for sick harts reliefe:
Forthy great care she tooke, and greater feare,
Least that it should her turne to fowle repriefe
And sore reproch, when so her father deare
Should of his dearest daughters hard misfortune heare.

V I

At last she her avisde, that he which made
That mirrhour, wherein the sicke Damosell
So straungely vewed her straunge lovers shade,

II, 5   fatall: fated   IV, 8   protense: duration

To weet, the learned Merlin, well could tell
Under what coast of heaven the man did dwell,
And by what means his love might best be wrought:
For, though beyond the Africk Ismael
Or th' Indian Peru he were, she thought
Him forth through infinite endevour to have sought.

V I I

Forthwith them selves disguising both in straunge
And base atyre, that none might them bewray,
To Maridunum, that is now by chaunge
Of name Cayr-Merdin cald, they tooke their way:
There the wise Merlin whylome wont (they say)
To make his wonne, low underneath the ground,
In a deepe delve, farre from the vew of day,
That of no living wight he mote be found,
When so he counseld with his sprights encompast round.

V I I I

And, if thou ever happen that same way
To traveill, go to see that dreadful place.
It is an hideous hollow cave (they say)
Under a Rock that lyes a litle space
From the swift Barry, tombling downe apace
Emongst the woody hilles of Dynevowre:
But dare thou not, I charge, in any cace
To enter into that same balefull Bowre,
For feare the cruell Feendes should thee unwares devowre:

I X

But standing high aloft low lay thine eare,
And there such ghastly noyse of yron chaines
And brasen Caudrons thou shalt rombling heare,
Which thousand sprights with long enduring paines
Doe tosse, that it will stonn thy feeble braines;
And oftentimes great grones, and grievous stownds,
When too huge toile and labour them constraines,
And oftentimes loud strokes and ringing sowndes
From under that deepe Rock most horribly rebowndes.

X

The cause, some say, is this: A litle whyle
Before that Merlin dyde, he did intend
A brasen wall in compas to compyle
About Cairmardin, and did it commend
Unto these Sprights to bring to perfect end:

During which worke the Lady of the Lake,
Whom long he lov'd, for him in hast did send;
Who, thereby forst his workemen to forsake,
Them bownd till his retourne their labour not to slake.

        X I

In the meane time, through that false Ladies traine
He was surprisd, and buried under beare,
Ne ever to his worke returnd againe:
Nath'lesse those feends may not their work forbeare,
So greatly his commandement they feare,
But there doe toyle and traveile day and night
Untill that brasen wall they up doe reare;
For Merlin had in Magick more insight
Then ever him before, or after, living wight:

        X I I

For he by wordes could call out of the sky
Both Sunne and Moone, and make them him obay;
The Land to sea, and sea to maineland dry,
And darksom night he eke could turne to day:
Huge hostes of men he could alone dismay,
And hostes of men of meanest thinges could frame,
When so him list his enimies to fray;
That to this day, for terror of his fame,
The feends do quake when any him to them does name.

        X I I I

And, sooth, men say that he was not the sonne
Of mortall Syre or other living wight,
But wondrously begotten, and begonne
By false illusion of a guilefull Spright
On a faire Lady Nonne, that whilome hight
Matilda, daughter to Pubidius,
Who was the lord of Mathraval by right,
And coosen unto king Ambrosius;
Whence he indued was with skill so merveilous.

        X I V

They, here arriving, staid awhile without,
Ne durst adventure rashly in to wend,
But of their first intent gan make new dout,
For dread of daunger which it might portend;
Untill the hardy Mayd (with love to frend)
First entering, the dreadfull Mage there fownd

XI, 2 beare: tomb

Deepe busied bout worke of wondrous end,
And writing straunge characters in the grownd,
With which the stubborne feendes he to his service bownd.

X V

He nought was moved at their entraunce bold,
For of their comming well he wist afore;
Yet list them bid their businesse to unfold,
As if ought in this world in secrete store
Were from him hidden, or unknowne of yore.
Then Glaucè thus: 'Let not it thee offend,
That we thus rashly through thy darksom dore
Unwares have prest; for either fatall end,
Or other mightie cause, us two did hither send.'

X V I

He bad tell on; and then she thus began.
'Now have three Moones with borrowd brothers light
Thrise shined faire, and thrise seemd dim and wan,
Sith a sore evill, which this virgin bright
Tormenteth and doth plonge in dolefull plight,
First rooting tooke; but what thing it mote bee,
Or whence it sprong, I can not read aright:
But this I read, that, but if remedee
Thou her afford, full shortly I her dead shall see.'

X V I I

Therewith th' Enchaunter softly gan to smyle
At her smooth speeches, weeting inly well
That she to him dissembled womanish guyle,
And to her said: 'Beldame, by that ye tell
More needed of leach-crafte hath your Damozell,
Then of my skill: who helpe may have elsewhere,
In vaine seekes wonders out of Magick spell.'
Th' old woman wox half blanck those wordes to heare,
And yet was loth to let her purpose plaine appeare;

X V I I I

And to him said: 'Yf any leaches skill,
Or other learned meanes, could have redrest
This my deare daughters deepe engraffed ill,
Certes I should be loth thee to molest;
But this sad evill, which doth her infest,
Doth course of naturall cause farre exceed,

XVIII, 3   engraffed: implanted

And housed is within her hollow brest,
That either seemes some cursed witches deed,
Or evill spright, that in her doth such torment breed.'

X I X

The wisard could no lenger beare her bord,
But, brusting forth in laughter, to her sayd:
'Glaucè, what needes this colourable word
To cloke the cause that hath it selfe bewrayd?
Ne ye, fayre Britomartis, thus arayd,
More hidden are then Sunne in cloudy vele;
Whom thy good fortune, having fate obayd,
Hath hither brought for succour to appele;
The which the powres to thee are pleased to revele.'

X X

The doubtfull Mayd, seeing her selfe descryde,
Was all abasht, and her pure yvory
Into a cleare Carnation suddeine dyde;
As fayre Aurora, rysing hastily,
Doth by her blushing tell that she did lye
All night in old Tithonus frozen bed,
Whereof she seemes ashamed inwardly:
But her olde Nourse was nought dishartened,
But vauntage made of that which Merlin had ared;

X X I

And sayd; 'Sith then thou knowest all our griefe,
(For what doest not thou knowe?) of grace I pray,
Pitty our playnt, and yield us meet reliefe.'
With that the Prophet still awhile did stay,
And then his spirite thus gan foorth display:
'Most noble Virgin, that by fatall lore
Hast learn'd to love, let no whit thee dismay
The hard beginne that meetes thee in the dore,
And with sharpe fits thy tender hart oppresseth sore:

X X I I

'For so must all things excellent begin;
And eke enrooted deepe must be that Tree,
Whose big embodied braunches shall not lin
Till they to hevens hight forth stretched bee:
For from thy wombe a famous Progenee

xix, 1   bord: idle tale   xxii, 3   lin: stop
xxi, 6   fatall: fated

Shall spring out of the auncient Trojan blood,
Which shall revive the sleeping memoree
Of those same antique Peres, the hevens brood,
Which Greeke and Asian rivers stayned with their blood.

XXIII

'Renowmed kings, and sacred Emperours,
Thy fruitfull Ofspring, shall from thee descend;
Brave Captaines, and most mighty warriours,
That shall their conquests through all lands extend,
And their decayed kingdomes shall amend:
The feeble Britons, broken with long warre,
They shall upreare, and mightily defend
Against their forren foe that commes from farre,
Till universall peace compound all civill jarre.

XXIV

'It was not, Britomart, thy wandring eye
Glauncing unwares in charmed looking glas,
But the streight course of hevenly destiny,
Led with eternall providence, that has
Guyded thy glaunce, to bring his will to pas:
Ne is thy fate, ne is thy fortune ill,
To love the prowest knight that ever was.
Therefore submit thy wayes unto his will,
And doe by all dew meanes thy destiny fulfill.'

XXV

'But read,' (saide Glaucè) 'thou Magitian,
What meanes shall she out seeke, or what waies take?
How shall she know, how shall she finde the man?
Or what needes her to toyle, sith fates can make
Way for themselves their purpose to pertake?'
Then Merlin thus: 'Indeede the fates are firme,
And may not shrinck, though all the world do shake;
Yet ought mens good endevours them confirme,
And guyde the heavenly causes to their constant terme.

XXVI

'The man, whom heavens have ordaynd to bee
The spouse of Britomart, is Arthegall:
He wonneth in the land of Fayeree,
Yet is no Fary borne, ne sib at all
To Elfes, but sprong of seed terrestriall,
And whylome by false Faries stolne away,

XXVI, 4   sib: related

Whyles yet in infant cradle he did crall;
Ne other to himselfe is knowne this day,
But that he by an Elfe was gotten of a Fay:

X X V I I

'But sooth he is the sonne of Gorloïs,
And brother unto Cador, Cornish king;
And for his warlike feates renowmed is,
From where the day out of the sea doth spring,
Untill the closure of the Evening:
From thence him, firmely bound with faithfull band,
To this his native soyle thou backe shalt bring,
Strongly to ayde his countrey to withstand
The powre of forreine Paynims which invade thy land.

X X V I I I

'Great ayd thereto his mighty puissaunce
And dreaded name shall give in that sad day;
Where also proofe of thy prow valiaunce
Thou then shalt make, t' increase thy lovers pray.
Long time ye both in armes shall beare great sway,
Till thy wombes burden thee from them do call,
And his last fate him from thee take away;
Too rathe cut off by practise criminall
Of secrete foes, that him shall make in mischiefe fall.

X X I X

'With thee yet shall he leave, for memory
Of his late puissaunce, his ymage dead,
That living him in all activity
To thee shall represent. He, from the head
Of his coosen Constantius, without dread
Shall take the crowne that was his fathers right,
And therewith crowne himselfe in th' others stead:
Then shall he issew forth with dreadfull might
Against his Saxon foes in bloody field to fight.

X X X

'Like as a Lyon that in drowsie cave
Hath long time slept, himselfe so shall he shake;
And comming forth shall spred his banner brave
Over the troubled South, that it shall make
The warlike Mertians for feare to quake:
Thrise shall he fight with them, and twise shall win;

xxviii, 8   rathe: soon

But the third time shall fayre accordaunce make:
And, if he then with victorie can lin,
He shall his dayes with peace bring to his earthly In.

X X X I

'His sonne, hight Vortipore, shall him succeede
In kingdome, but not in felicity:
Yet shall he long time warre with happy speed,
And with great honour many batteills try;
But at the last to th' importunity
Of froward fortune shall be forst to yield:
But his sonne Malgo shall full mightily
Avenge his fathers losse with speare and shield,
And his proud foes discomfit in victorious field.

X X X I I

'Behold the man! and tell me, Britomart,
If ay more goodly creature thou didst see?
How like a Gyaunt in each manly part
Beares he himselfe with portly majestee,
That one of th' old Heroës seemes to bee!
He the six Islands, comprovinciall
In auncient times unto great Britainee,
Shall to the same reduce, and to him call
Their sondry kings to do their homage severall.

X X X I I I

'All which his sonne Careticus awhile
Shall well defend, and Saxons powre suppresse;
Untill a straunger king, from unknowne soyle
Arriving, him with multitude oppresse;
Great Gormond, having with huge mightinesse
Ireland subdewd, and therein fixt his throne,
Like a swift Otter, fell through emptinesse,
Shall overswim the sea, with many one
Of his Norveyses, to assist the Britons fone.

X X X I V

'He in his furie all shall overronne,
And holy Church with faithlesse handes deface,
That thy sad people, utterly fordonne,
Shall to the utmost mountaines fly apace.
Was never so great waste in any place,
Nor so fowle outrage doen by living men;
For all thy Citties they shall sacke and race,

And the greene grasse that groweth they shall bren,
That even the wilde beast shall dy in starved den.

X X X V

'Whiles thus thy Britons doe in languour pine,
Proud Etheldred shall from the North arise,
Serving th' ambitious will of Augustine,
And, passing Dee, with hardy enterprise
Shall backe repulse the valiaunt Brockwell twise,
And Bangor with massacred Martyrs fill,
But the third time shall rew his foolhardise:
For Cadwan, pittying his peoples ill,
Shall stoutly him defeat, and thousand Saxons kill.

X X X V I

'But after him, Cadwallin mightily
On his sonne Edwin all those wrongs shall wreake;
Ne shall availe the wicked sorcery
Of false Pellite his purposes to breake,
But him shall slay, and on a gallowes bleak
Shall give th' enchaunter his unhappy hire.
Then shall the Britons, late dismayd and weake,
From their long vassalage gin to respire,
And on their Paynim foes avenge their ranckled ire.

X X X V I I

'Ne shall he yet his wrath so mitigate,
Till both the sonnes of Edwin he have slayne,
Offricke and Osricke, twinnes unfortunate,
Both slaine in battaile upon Layburne playne,
Together with the king of Louthiane,
Hight Adin, and the king of Orkeny,
Both joynt partakers of their fatall payne:
But Penda, fearefull of like desteny,
Shall yield him selfe his liegeman, and sweare fealty.

X X X V I I I

'Him shall he make his fatall Instrument
T' afflict the other Saxons unsubdewd;
He marching forth with fury insolent
Against the good king Oswald, who indewd
With heavenly powre, and by Angels reskewd,
Al holding crosses in their hands on hye,
Shall him defeate withouten blood imbrewd:
Of which that field, for endlesse memory,
Shall Hevenfield be cald to all posterity.

XXXIX

'Whereat Cadwallin wroth shall forth issew,
And an huge hoste into Northumber lead,
With which he godly Oswald shall subdew,
And crowne with martiredome his sacred head:
Whose brother Oswin, daunted with like dread,
With price of silver shall his kingdome buy;
And Penda, seeking him adowne to tread,
Shall tread adowne, and doe him fowly dye;
But shall with guifts his Lord Cadwallin pacify.

XL

'Then shall Cadwallin die; and then the raine
Of Britons eke with him attonce shall dye;
Ne shall the good Cadwallader, with paine
Or powre, be hable it to remedy,
When the full time, prefixt by destiny,
Shal be expird of Britons regiment:
For heven it selfe shall their successe envy,
And them with plagues and murrins pestilent
Consume, till all their warlike puissaunce be spent.

XLI

Yet after all these sorrowes, and huge hills
Of dying people, during eight yeares space,
Cadwallader, not yielding to his ills,
From Armoricke, where long in wretched cace
He liv'd, retourning to his native place,
Shal be by vision staide from his intent:
For th' heavens have decreëd to displace
The Britons for their sinnes dew punishment
And to the Saxons over-give their government.

XLII

'Then woe, and woe, and everlasting woe,
Be to the Briton babe that shal be borne
To live in thraldome of his fathers foe!
Late king, now captive; late lord, now forlorne;
The worlds reproch; the cruell victors scorne;
Banisht from princely bowre to wastefull wood!
O! who shal helpe me to lament and mourne
The royall seed, the antique Trojan blood,
Whose empire lenger here then ever any stood?'

XLIII

The Damzell was full deepe empassioned
Both for his griefe, and for her peoples sake,
Whose future woes so plaine he fashioned;
And, sighing sore, at length him thus bespake:
'Ah! but will hevens fury never slake,
Nor vengeaunce huge relent it selfe at last?
Will not long misery late mercy make,
But shall their name for ever be defaste,
And quite from off the earth their memory be raste?'

XLIV

'Nay but the terme' (sayd he) 'is limited,
That in this thraldome Britons shall abide;
And the just revolution measured
That they as Straungers shal be notifide:
For twise fowre hundreth yeares shalbe supplide,
Ere they to former rule restor'd shal bee,
And their importune fates all satisfide:
Yet, during this their most obscuritee,
Their beames shall ofte breake forth, that men them faire
      may see.

XLV

'For Rhodoricke, whose surname shal be Great,
Shall of him selfe a brave ensample shew,
That Saxon kinges his friendship shall intreat;
And Howell Dha shall goodly well indew
The salvage minds with skill of just and trew:
Then Griffyth Conan also shall upreare
His dreaded head, and the old sparkes renew
Of native corage, that his foes shall feare,
Least back againe the kingdom he from them should beare.

XLVI

'Ne shall the Saxons selves all peaceably
Enjoy the crowne, which they from Britons wonne
First ill, and after ruled wickedly;
For, ere two hundred yeares be full outronne,
There shall a Raven, far from rising Sunne,
With his wide wings upon them fiercely fly,
And bid his faithlesse chickens overronne

XLIV, 4   notifide: known

The fruitfull plaines, and with fell cruelty
In their avenge tread downe the victors surquedry.

X L V I I

'Yet shall a third both these and thine subdew.
There shall a Lion from the sea-bord wood
Of Neustria come roring, with a crew
Of hungry whelpes, his battailous bold brood,
Whose clawes were newly dipt in cruddy blood,
That from the Daniske Tyrants head shall rend
Th' usurped crowne, as if that he were wood,
And the spoile of the countrey conquered
Emongst his young ones shall divide with bountyhed.

X L V I I I

'Tho, when the terme is full accomplishid,
There shall a sparke of fire, which hath long-while
Bene in his ashes raked up and hid,
Bee freshly kindled in the fruitfull Ile
Of Mona, where it lurked in exile;
Which shall breake forth into bright burning flame,
And reach into the house that beares the stile
Of roiall majesty and soveraine name:
So shall the Briton blood their crowne agayn reclame.

X L I X

'Thenceforth eternall union shall be made
Betweene the nations different afore,
And sacred Peace shall lovingly persuade
The warlike minds to learne her goodly lore,
And civile armes to exercise no more:
Then shall a royall Virgin raine, which shall
Stretch her white rod over the Belgicke shore,
And the great Castle smite so sore withall,
That it shall make him shake, and shortly learne to fall.

L

'But yet the end is not.'—There Merlin stayd,
As overcomen of the spirites powre,
Or other ghastly spectacle dismayd,
That secretly he saw, yet note discoure:
Which suddein fitt, and halfe extatick stoure,
When the two fearefull wemen saw, they grew
Greatly confused in behaveoure.

XLVII, 7 wood: mad   L, 4 discoure: reveal

At last, the fury past, to former hew
Hee turnd againe, and chearfull looks as earst did shew.

L I

Then, when them selves they well instructed had
Of all that needed them to be inquird,
They both, conceiving hope of comfort glad,
With lighter hearts unto their home retird;
Where they in secret counsell close conspird,
How to effect so hard an enterprize,
And to possesse the purpose they desird:
Now this, now that, twixt them they did devize,
And diverse plots did frame to maske in strange disguise.

L I I

At last the Nourse in her foolhardy wit
Conceiv'd a bold devise, and thus bespake:
'Daughter, I deeme that counsel aye most fit,
That of the time doth dew advauntage take.
Ye see that good king Uther now doth make
Strong warre upon the Paynim brethren, hight
Octa and Oza, whome hee lately brake
Beside Cayr Verolame in victorious fight,
That now all Britany doth burne in armes bright.

L I I I

'That, therefore, nought our passage may empeach,
Let us in feigned armes our selves disguize,
And our weake hands (need makes good schollers) teach
The dreadful speare and shield to exercize:
Ne certes, daughter, that same warlike wize,
I weene, would you misseeme; for ye beene tall,
And large of limbe t' achieve an hard emprize;
Ne ought ye want but skil, which practize small
Wil bring, and shortly make you a mayd Martiall.

L I V

'And, sooth, it ought your corage much inflame
To heare so often, in that royall hous,
From whence, to none inferior, ye came,
Bards tell of many wemen valorous,
Which have full many feats adventurous
Performd, in paragone of proudest men:
The bold Bunduca, whose victorious

LIV, 1   corage: spirit

Exployts made Rome to quake; stout Guendolen;
Renowmed Martia; and redoubted Emmilen.

L V

'And, that which more then all the rest may sway,
Late dayes ensample, which these eyes beheld:
In the last field before Menevia,
Which Uther with those forrein Pagans held,
I saw a Saxon Virgin, the which feld
Great Ulfin thrise upon the bloody playne;
And, had not Carados her hand withheld
From rash revenge, she had him surely slayne:
Yet Carados himselfe from her escapt with payne.'

L V I

'Ah! read,' (quoth Britomart) 'how is she hight?'
'Fayre Angela' (quoth she) 'men do her call,
No whit lesse fayre then terrible in fight:
She hath the leading of a Martiall
And mightie people, dreaded more then all
The other Saxons, which doe, for her sake
And love, themselves of her name *Angles* call.
Therefore, faire Infant, her ensample make
Unto thy selfe, and equall corage to thee take.'

L V I I

Her harty wordes so deepe into the mynd
Of the yong Damzell sunke, that great desire
Of warlike armes in her forthwith they tynd,
And generous stout courage did inspyre,
That she resolv'd, unweeting to her Syre,
Advent'rous knighthood on her selfe to don;
And counseld with her Nourse her Maides attyre
To turne into a massy habergeon,
And bad her all things put in readinesse anon.

L V I I I

Th' old woman nought that needed did omit,
But all thinges did conveniently purvay.
It fortuned (so time their turne did fitt)
A band of Britons, ryding on forray
Few dayes before, had gotten a great pray
Of Saxon goods; emongst the which was seene
A goodly Armour, and full rich aray,
Which long'd to Angela, the Saxon Queene,
All fretted round with gold, and goodly wel beseene.

L I X

The same, with all the other ornaments,
King Ryence caused to be hanged hy
In his chiefe Church, for endlesse moniments
Of his successe and gladfull victory:
Of which her selfe avising readily.
In th' evening late old Glaucè thither led
Faire Britomart, and, that same Armory
Downe taking, her therein appareled
Well as she might, and with brave bauldrick garnished.

L X

Beside those armes there stood a mightie speare,
Which Bladud made by Magick art of yore,
And usd the same in batteill aye to beare;
Sith which it had beene here preserv'd in store,
For his great virtues proved long afore:
For never wight so fast in sell could sit,
But him perforce unto the ground it bore.
Both speare she tooke and shield which hong by it;
Both speare and shield of great powre, for her purpose fit.

L X I

Thus when she had the virgin all arayd,
Another harnesse which did hang thereby
About her selfe she dight, that the yong Mayd
She might in equall armes accompany,
And as her Squyre attend her carefully.
Tho to their ready Steedes they clombe full light,
And through back waies, that none might them espy,
Covered with secret cloud of silent night,
Themselves they forth convaid, and passed forward right.

L X I I

Ne rested they, till that to Faery lond
They came, as Merlin them directed late:
Where, meeting with this Redcrosse Knight, she fond
Of diverse thinges discourses to dilate,
But most of Arthegall and his estate.
At last their wayes so fell, that they mote part:
Then each to other, well affectionate,
Friendship professed with unfained hart.
The Redcrosse Knight diverst, but forth rode Britomart.

LX, 6   sell: saddle

CANTO IV.

Bold Marinell of Britomart
Is throwne on the Rich strond:
Faire Florimell of Arthure is
Long followed, but not fond.

I

WHERE IS THE Antique glory now become,
That whylome wont in wemen to appeare?
Where be the brave atchievements doen by some?
Where be the batteilles, where the shield and speare,
And all the conquests which them high did reare,
That matter made for famous Poets verse,
And boastfull men so oft abasht to heare?
Beene they all dead, and laide in dolefull herse,
Or doen they onely sleepe, and shall againe reverse?

I I

If they be dead, then woe is me therefore;
But if they sleepe, O let them soone awake!
For all too long I burne with envy sore
To heare the warlike feates which Homere spake
Of bold Penthesilee, which made a lake
Of Greekish blood so ofte in Trojan plaine;
But when I reade, how stout Debora strake
Proud Sisera, and how Camill' hath slaine
The huge Orsilochus, I swell with great disdaine.

I I I

Yet these, and all that els had puissaunce,
Cannot with noble Britomart compare,
As well for glorie of great valiaunce,
As for pure chastitee and vertue rare,
That all her goodly deedes doe well declare.
Well worthie stock, from which the branches sprong
That in late yeares so faire a blossome bare,
As thee, O Queene! the matter of my song,
Whose lignage from this Lady I derive along.

I V

Who when, through speaches with the Redcrosse Knight,
She learned had th' estate of Arthegall,
And in each point her selfe informd aright,

II, 9   disdaine: indignation

A friendly league of love perpetuall
She with him bound, and Congé tooke withall:
Then he forth on his journey did proceede,
To seeke adventures which mote him befall,
And win him worship through his warlike deed,
Which alwaies of his paines he made the chiefest meed.

V

But Britomart kept on her former course,
Ne ever dofte her armes, but all the way
Grew pensive through that amarous discourse,
By which the Redcrosse knight did earst display
Her lovers shape and chevalrous aray:
A thousand thoughts she fashiond in her mind,
And in her feigning fancie did pourtray
Him such as fittest she for love could find,
Wise, warlike, personable, courteous, and kind.

V I

With such selfe-pleasing thoughts her wound she fedd,
And thought so to beguile her grievous smart;
But so her smart was much more grievous bredd,
And the deepe wound more deep engord her hart,
That nought but death her dolour mote depart.
So forth she rode, without repose or rest,
Searching all lands and each remotest part,
Following the guydance of her blinded guest,
Till that to the sea-coast at length she her addrest.

V I I

There she alighted from her light-foot beast,
And sitting downe upon the rocky shore,
Badd her old Squyre unlace her lofty creast:
Tho having vewd awhile the surges hore
That gainst the craggy clifts did loudly rore,
And in their raging surquedry disdaynd
That the fast earth affronted them so sore,
And their devouring covetize restraynd;
Thereat she sighed deepe, and after thus complaynd.

V I I I

'Huge sea of sorrow and tempestuous griefe,
Wherein my feeble barke is tossed long
Far from the hoped haven of reliefe,
Why doe thy cruel billowes beat so strong;
And thy moyst mountaines each on others throng,

Threatning to swallow up my fearefull lyfe?
O! doe thy cruell wrath and spightfull wrong
At length allay, and stint thy stormy strife,
Which in these troubled bowels raignes and rageth ryfe.

I X

'For els my feeble vessell, crazd and crackt
Through thy strong buffets and outrageous blowes,
Cannot endure, but needes it must be wrackt
On the rough rocks, or on the sandy shallowes,
The whiles that love it steres, and fortune rowes:
Love, my lewd Pilott, hath a restlesse minde;
And fortune, Boteswaine, no assurance knowes;
But saile withouten starres gainst tyde and winde:
How can they other doe, sith both are bold and blinde?

x

'Thou God of windes, that raignest in the seas,
That raignest also in the Continent,
At last blow up some gentle gale of ease,
The which may bring my ship, ere it be rent,
Unto the gladsome port of her intent.
Then, when I shall my selfe in safety see,
A table, for eternall moniment
Of thy great grace and my great jeopardee,
Great Neptune, I avow to hallow unto thee!'

X I

Then sighing softly sore, and inly deepe,
She shut up all her plaint in privy griefe
For her great courage would not let her weepe,
Till that old Glaucè gan with sharpe repriefe
Her to restraine, and give her good reliefe
Through hope of those, which Merlin had her told
Should of her name and nation be chiefe,
And fetch their being from the sacred mould
Of her immortall womb, to be in heaven enrold.

X I I

Thus as she her recomforted, she spyde
Where far away one, all in armour bright,
With hasty gallop towards her did ryde.
Her dolour soone she ceast, and on her dight
Her Helmet, to her Courser mounting light;
Her former sorrow into suddein wrath,

x, 7   table: tablet

Both coosen passions of distroubled spright,
Converting, forth she beates the dusty path:
Love and despight attonce her courage kindled hath.

X I I I

As, when a foggy mist hath overcast
The face of heven, and the cleare ayre engroste,
The world in darkenes dwels; till that at last
The watry Southwinde, from the seabord coste
Upblowing, doth disperse the vapour lo'ste,
And poures it selfe forth in a stormy showre:
So the fayre Britomart, having disclo'ste
Her clowdy care into a wrathfull stowre,
The mist of griefe dissolv'd did into vengeance powre.

X I V

Eftsoones, her goodly shield addressing fayre,
That mortall speare she in her hand did take,
And unto battaill did her selfe prepayre.
The knight, approching, sternely her bespake:
'Sir knight, that doest thy voyage rashly make
By this forbidden way in my despight,
Ne doest by others death ensample take,
I read thee soone retyre, whiles thou hast might,
Least afterwards it be too late to take thy flight.'

X V

Ythrild with deepe disdaine of his proud threat,
She shortly thus: 'Fly they, that need to fly;
Wordes fearen babes. I meane not thee entreat
To passe, but maugre thee will passe or dy.'
Ne lenger stayd for th' other to reply,
But with sharpe speare the rest made dearly knowne.
Strongly the straunge knight ran, and sturdily
Strooke her full on the brest, that made her downe
Decline her head, and touch her crouper with her crown.

X V I

But she againe him in the shield did smite
With so fierce furie and great puissaunce,
That, through his three-square scuchin percing quite
And through his mayled hauberque, by mischaunce
The wicked steele through his left side did glaunce.
Him so transfixed she before her bore

XIII, 5   lo'ste: loosed, set free   xv, I   Ythrild: pierced
XIII, 7   disclo'ste: revealed   xvi, 3   three-square: triangular -

Beyond his croupe, the length of all her launce;
Till, sadly soucing on the sandy shore,
He tombled on an heape, and wallowd in his gore.

X V I I

Like as the sacred Oxe that carelesse stands,
With gilden hornes and flowry girlonds crownd,
Proud of his dying honor and deare bandes,
Whiles th' altars fume with frankincense arownd,
All suddeinly, with mortall stroke astownd,
Doth groveling fall, and with his streaming gore
Distaines the pillours and the holy grownd,
And the faire flowres that decked him afore:
So fell proud Marinell upon the pretious shore.

X V I I I

The martiall Mayd stayd not him to lament,
But forward rode, and kept her ready way
Along the strond; which, as she over-went,
She saw bestrowed all with rich aray
Of pearles and pretious stones of great assay,
And all the gravell mixt with golden owre:
Whereat she wondred much, but would not stay
For gold, or perles, or pretious stones, an howre,
But them despised all; for all was in her powre.

X I X

Whiles thus he lay in deadly stonishment,
Tydings hereof came to his mothers eare:
His mother was the blacke-browd Cymoënt,
The daughter of great Nereus, which did beare
This warlike sonne unto an earthly peare,
The famous Dumarin; who, on a day
Finding the Nymph asleepe in secret wheare,
As he by chaunce did wander that same way,
Was taken with her love, and by her closely lay.

X X

There he this knight of her begot, whom borne
She, of his father, Marinell did name;
And in a rocky cave, as wight forlorne,
Long time she fostred up, till he became
A mighty man at armes, and mickle fame
Did get through great adventures by him donne:

xvi, 8   sadly: heavily

For never man he suffred by that same
Rich strond to travell, whereas he did wonne,
But that he must do battail with the Sea-nymphes sonne.

X X I

An hundred knights of honorable name
He had subdew'd, and them his vassals made
That through all Faerie lond his noble fame
Now blazed was, and feare did all invade,
That none durst passen through that perilous glade:
And to advaunce his name and glory more,
Her Sea-god syre she dearely did perswade
T' endow her sonne with threasure and rich store
Bove all the sonnes that were of earthly wombes ybore.

X X I I

The God did graunt his daughters deare demaund,
To doen his Nephew in all riches flow;
Eftsoones his heaped waves he did commaund
Out of their hollow bosome forth to throw
All the huge threasure, which the sea below
Had in his greedy gulfe devoured deepe,
And him enriched through the overthrow
And wreckes of many wretches, which did weepe
And often wayle their wealth, which he from them did keepe.

X X I I I

Shortly upon that shore there heaped was
Exceeding riches and all pretious things,
The spoyle of all the world; that it did pas
The wealth of th' East, and pompe of Persian kings:
Gold, amber, yvorie, perles, owches, rings,
And all that els was pretious and deare,
The sea unto him voluntary brings;
That shortly he a great Lord did appeare,
As was in all the lond of Faery, or else wheare.

X X I V

Thereto he was a doughty dreaded knight,
Tryde often to the scath of many Deare,
That none in equall armes him matchen might:
The which his mother seeing gan to feare
Least his too haughtie hardines might reare
Some hard mishap in hazard of his life.
Forthy she oft him counseld to forbeare

The bloody batteill and to stirre up strife,
But after all his warre to rest his wearie knife.

x x v

And, for his more assuraunce, she inquir'd
One day of Proteus by his mighty spell
(For Proteus was with prophecy inspir'd)
Her deare sonnes destiny to her to tell,
And the sad end of her sweet Marinell:
Who, through foresight of his eternall skill,
Bad her from womankind to keepe him well,
For of a woman he should have much ill;
A virgin straunge and stout him should dismay or kill.

x x v i

Forthy she gave him warning every day
The love of women not to entertaine;
A lesson too too hard for living clay
From love in course of nature to refraine.
Yet he his mothers lore did well retaine,
And ever from fayre Ladies love did fly;
Yet many Ladies fayre did oft complaine,
That they for love of him would algates dy:
Dy, who so list for him, he was loves enimy.

x x v i i

But ah! who can deceive his destiny,
Or weene by warning to avoyd his fate?
That, when he sleepes in most security
And safest seemes, him soonest doth amate,
And findeth dew effect or soone or late;
So feeble is the powre of fleshly arme.
His mother bad him wemens love to hate,
For she of womans force did feare no harme;
So, weening to have arm'd him, she did quite disarme.

x x v i i i

This was that woman, this that deadly wownd,
That Proteus prophecide should him dismay;
The which his mother vainely did expownd
To be hart-wownding love, which should assay
To bring her sonne unto his last decay.
So ticle be the termes of mortall state,
And full of subtile sophismes, which doe play
With double sences, and with false debate,
T' approve the unknowen purpose of eternall fate.

XXIX

Too trew the famous Marinell it fownd,
Who, through late triall, on that wealthy Strond
Inglorious now lies in sencelesse swownd,
Through heavy stroke of Britomartis hond.
Which when his mother deare did understond,
And heavy tidings heard, whereas she playd
Amongst her watry sisters by a pond,
Gathering sweete daffadillyes, to have made
Gay girlonds from the Sun their forheads fayr to shade;

XXX

Eftesoones both flowres and girlonds far away
Shee flong, and her faire deawy lockes yrent;
To sorrow huge she turnd her former play,
And gamesom merth to grievous dreriment:
Shee threw her selfe downe on the Continent,
Ne word did speake, but lay as in a swowne,
Whiles all her sisters did for her lament
With yelling outcries, and with shrieking sowne;
And every one did teare her girlond from her crowne.

XXXI

Soone as shee up out of her deadly fitt
Arose, shee bad her charett to be brought;
And all her sisters that with her did sitt
Bad eke attonce their charetts to be sought:
Tho, full of bitter griefe and pensife thought,
She to her wagon clombe; clombe all the rest,
And forth together went with sorow fraught.
The waves, obedient to theyr beheast,
Them yielded ready passage, and their rage surceast.

XXXII

Great Neptune stoode amazed at their sight,
Whiles on his broad rownd backe they softly slid,
And eke him selfe mournd at their mournful plight,
Yet wist not what their wailing ment; yet did,
For great compassion of their sorow, bid
His mighty waters to them buxome bee:
Eftesoones the roaring billowes still abid,
And all the griesly Monsters of the See
Stood gaping at their gate, and wondred them to see.

xxx, 5 Continent: earth

X X X I I I

A teme of Dolphins raunged in aray
Drew the smooth charett of sad Cymoent:
They were all taught by Triton to obay
To the long raynes at her commaundement:
As swifte as swallowes on the waves they went,
That their brode flaggy finnes no fome did reare,
Ne bubling rowndell they behinde them sent.
The rest, of other fishes drawen weare,
Which with their finny oars the swelling sea did sheare.

X X X I V

Soone as they bene arriv'd upon the brim
Of the Rich Strond, their charets they forlore,
And let their temed fishes softly swim
Along the margent of the fomy shore,
Least they their finnes should bruze, and surbate sore
Their tender feete upon the stony grownd:
And comming to the place, where all in gore
And cruddy blood enwallowed they fownd
The lucklesse Marinell lying in deadly swownd.

X X X V

His mothers swowned thrise, and the third time
Could scarce recovered bee out of her paine:
Had she not beene devoide of mortall slime,
Shee should not then have been relyv'd againe;
But, soone as life recovered had the raine,
Shee made so piteous mone and deare wayment,
That the hard rocks could scarse from tears refraine;
And all her sister Nymphes with one consent
Supplide her sobbing breaches with sad complement.

X X X V I

'Deare image of my selfe, (she sayd) 'that is
The wretched sonne of wretched mother borne,
Is this thine high advauncement? O! is this
Th' immortall name, with which thee, yet unborne,
Thy Grandsire Nereus promist to adorne?
Now lyest thou of life and honor refte;
Now lyest thou a lumpe of earth forlorne;
Ne of thy late life memory is lefte,
Ne can thy irrevocable desteny bee wefte.

xxxiii, 6   flaggy: drooping   xxxv, 9   breaches: interruptions
xxxiii, 7   rowndell: circle   xxxvi, 9   wefte: avoided
xxxiv, 5   surbate: bruise

XXXVII

'Fond Proteus, father of false prophecis!
And they more fond that credit to thee give!
Not this the worke of womans hand ywis,
That so deepe wound through these deare members drive.
I feared love; but they that love doe live,
But they that dye doe nether love nor hate:
Nath'lesse to thee thy folly I forgive;
And to my selfe, and to accursed fate,
The guilt I doe ascribe: deare wisedom bought too late!

XXXVIII

'O! what availes it of immortall seed
To beene ybredd and never borne to dye?
Farre better I it deeme to die with speed
Then waste in woe and waylfull miserye:
Who dyes, the utmost dolor doth abye;
But who that lives is lefte to waile his losse:
So life is losse, and death felicity:
Sad life worse than glad death; and greater crosse
To see frends grave, then dead the grave self to engrosse.

XXXIX

'But if the heavens did his dayes envie,
And my short blis maligne, yet mote they well
Thus much afford me, ere that he did die,
That the dim eies of my deare Marinell
I mote have closed, and him bed farewell,
Sith other offices for mother meet
They would not graunt——
Yett, maulgre them, farewell, my sweetest sweet!
Farewell, my sweetest sonne, sith we no more shall meet!'

X L

Thus when they all had sorowed their fill,
They softly gan to search his griesly wownd:
And, that they might him handle more at will,
They him disarmd; and, spredding on the grownd
Their watchet mantles frindgd with silver rownd,
They softly wipt away the gelly blood
From th' orifice; which having well upbownd,
They pourd in soveraine balme and nectar good,
Good both for erthly med'cine and for hevenly food.

XXXVIII, 9 engrosse: take possession of XL, 5 watchet: light or pale blue

X L I

Tho when the lilly handed Liagore
(This Liagore whilome had learned skill
In leaches craft, by great Apolloes lore,
Sith her whilome upon high Pindus hill
He loved, and at last her wombe did fill
With hevenly seed, whereof wise Pæon sprong)
Did feele his pulse, shee knew there staied still
Some litle life his feeble sprites emong;
Which to his mother told, despeyre she from her flong.

X L I I

Tho, up him taking in their tender hands,
They easely unto her charett beare:
Her teme at her commaundement quiet stands,
Whiles they the corse into her wagon reare,
And strowe with flowres the lamentable beare.
Then all the rest into their coches clim,
And through the brackish waves their passage sheare;
Upon great Neptunes necke they softly swim,
And to her watry chamber swiftly carry him.

X L I I I

Deepe in the bottome of the sea her bowre
Is built of hollow billowes heaped hye,
Like to thicke clouds that threat a stormy showre,
And vauted all within, like to the Skye,
In which the Gods doe dwell eternally:
There they him laide in easy couch well dight,
And sent in haste for Tryphon, to apply
Salves to his wounds, and medicines of might;
For Tryphon of sea gods the soveraine leach is hight.

X L I V

The whiles the Nymphes sitt all about him rownd,
Lamenting his mishap and heavy plight:
And ofte his mother, vewing his wide wownd,
Cursed the hand that did so deadly smight
Her dearest sonne, her dearest harts delight:
But none of all those curses overtooke
The warlike Maide, th' ensample of that might;
But fairely well shee thryvd, and well did brooke
Her noble deeds, ne her right course for ought forsooke.

xLIV, 8   brooke: profit by

X L V

Yet did false Archimage her still pursew,
To bring to passe his mischievous intent,
Now that he had her singled from the crew
Of courteous knights, the Prince and Faery gent,
Whom late in chace of beauty excellent
Shee lefte, pursewing that same foster strong,
Of whose fowle outrage they impatient,
And full of firy zele, him followed long,
To reskew her from shame, and to revenge her wrong.

X L V I

Through thick and thin, through mountains and through
    playns,
Those two great champions did attonce pursew
The fearefull damzell with incessant payns;
Who from them fled, as light-foot hare from vew
Of hunter swifte and sent of howndes trew.
At last they came unto a double way;
Where, doubtfull which to take, her to reskew,
Themselves they did dispart, each to assay
Whether more happy were to win so goodly pray.

X L V I I

But Timias, the Princes gentle Squyre,
That Ladies love unto his Lord forlent,
And with proud envy and indignant yre
After that wicked foster fiercely went:
So beene they three three sondry wayes ybent;
But fayrest fortune to the Prince befell,
Whose chaunce it was, that soone he did repent,
To take that way in which that Damozell
Was fledd afore, affraid of him as feend of hell.

X L V I I I

At last of her far off he gained vew.
Then gan he freshly pricke his fomy steed,
And ever as he nigher to her drew,
So evermore he did increase his speed,
And of each turning still kept wary heed:
Alowd to her he oftentimes did call,
To doe away vaine doubt and needlesse dreed:
Full myld to her he spake, and oft let fall
Many meeke wordes to stay and comfort her withall.

XLVI, 9   Whether: which

XLIX

But nothing might relent her hasty flight,
So deepe the deadly feare of that foule swaine
Was earst impressed in her gentle spright.
Like as a fearefull Dove, which through the raine
Of the wide ayre her way does cut amaine,
Having farre off espyde a Tassell gent,
Which after her his nimble winges doth straine,
Doubleth her hast for feare to bee for-hent,
And with her pineons cleaves the liquid firmament.

L

With no lesse hast, and eke with no lesse dreed,
That fearefull Ladie fledd from him, that ment
To her no evill thought nor evill deed;
Yet former feare of being fowly shent
Carried her forward with her first intent:
And though, oft looking backward, well she vewde
Her selfe freed from that foster insolent,
And that it was a knight which now her sewde,
Yet she no less the knight feard then that villein rude.

LI

His uncouth shield and straunge armes her dismayd,
Whose like in Faery lond were seldom seene,
That fast she from him fledd, no lesse afrayd
Then of wilde beastes if she had chased beene;
Yet he her followd still with corage keene
So long, that now the golden Hesperus
Was mounted high in top of heaven sheene,
And warnd his other brethren joyeous
To light their blessed lamps in Joves eternall hous.

LII

All suddeinly dim wox the dampish ayre,
And griesly shadowes covered heaven bright,
That now with thousand starres was decked fayre:
Which when the Prince beheld, a lothfull sight,
And that perforce, for want of lenger light,
He mote surceasse his suit, and lose the hope
Of his long labour, he gan fowly wyte
His wicked fortune that had turnd aslope,
And cursed night that reft from him so goodly scope.

xlix, 6   Tassell gent: male falcon   lii, 8   aslope: awry
lii, 7   wyte: blame   lii, 9   scope: object of desire

L I I I

Tho, when her wayes he could no more descry,
But to and fro at disaventure strayd;
Like as a ship, whose Lodestar suddeinly
Covered with clouds her Pilott hath dismayd;
His wearisome pursuit perforce he stayd,
And from his loftie steed dismounting low
Did let him forage. Downe himselfe he layd
Upon the grassy ground to sleepe a throw:
The cold earth was his couch, the hard steele his pillow.

L I V

But gentle Sleepe envyde him any rest:
In stead thereof sad sorrow and disdaine
Of his hard hap did vexe his noble brest,
And thousand Fancies bett his ydle brayne
With their light wings, the sights of semblants vaine.
Oft did he wish that Lady faire mote bee
His Faery Queene, for whom he did complaine,
Or that his Faery Queene were such as shee;
And ever hasty Night he blamed bitterlie.

L V

'Night! thou foule Mother of annoyaunce sad,
Sister of heavie death, and nourse of woe,
Which wast begot in heaven, but for thy bad
And brutish shape thrust downe to hell below,
Where, by the grim floud of Cocytus slow,
Thy dwelling is in Herebus black hous,
(Black Herebus, thy husband, is the foe
Of all the Gods,) where thou ungratious
Halfe of thy dayes doest lead in horrour hideous.

L V I

'What had th' eternall Maker need of thee
The world in his continuall course to keepe,
That doest all thinges deface, ne lettest see
The beautie of his worke? Indeed, in sleepe
The slouthfull body that doth love to steepe
His lustlesse limbes, and drowne his baser mind,
Doth praise thee oft, and oft from Stygian deepe
Calles thee his goddesse, in his errour blind,
And great Dame Natures handmaide chearing every kind.

L V I I

'But well I wote, that to an heavy hart
Thou art the roote and nourse of bitter cares,
Breeder of new, renewer of old smarts:
Instead of rest thou lendest rayling teares;
Instead of sleepe thou sendest troublous feares
And dreadfull visions, in the which alive
The dreary image of sad death appeares:
So from the wearie spirit thou doest drive
Desired rest, and men of happiness deprive.

L V I I I

'Under thy mantle black there hidden lye
Light-shonning thefte, and traiterous intent,
Abhorred bloodshed, and vile felony,
Shamefull deceipt, and daunger imminent,
Fowle horror, and eke hellish dreriment:
All these, I wote, in thy protection bee,
And light doe shonne for feare of being shent;
For light ylike is loth'd of them and thee:
And all that lewdnesse love doe hate the light to see.

L I X

'For day discovers all dishonest wayes,
And sheweth each thing as it is in deed:
The prayses of high God he faire displayes,
And his large bountie rightly doth areed:
Dayes dearest children be the blessed seed
Which darknesse shall subdue and heaven win:
Truth is his daughter; he her first did breed
Most sacred virgin without spot of sinne.
Our life is day, but death with darknesse doth begin.

L X

'O! when will day then turne to me againe,
And bring with him his long expected light?
O Titan! hast to reare thy joyous waine;
Speed thee to spred abroad thy beames bright,
And chace away this too long lingring night;
Chase her away, from whence she came, to hell:
She, she it is, that hath me done despight:
There let her with the damned spirits dwell,
And yield her rowme to day that can it governe well.'

L X I

Thus did the Prince that wearie night outweare
In restlesse anguish and unquiet paine;
And earely, ere the morrow did upreare
His deawy head out of the Ocean maine,
He up arose, as halfe in great disdaine,
And clombe unto his steed. So forth he went
With heavy look and lumpish pace, that plaine
In him bewraid great grudge and maltalent:
His steed eke seemd t' apply his steps to his intent.

CANTO V.

Prince Arthur heares of Florimell:
Three fosters Timias wound;
Belphebe findes him almost dead,
And reareth out of sownd.

I

Wonder it is to see in diverse mindes
How diversly love doth his pageaunts play,
And shewes his powre in variable kindes:
The baser wit, whose ydle thoughts alway
Are wont to cleave unto the lowly clay,
It stirreth up to sensuall desire,
And in lewd slouth to wast his carelesse day;
But in brave sprite it kindles goodly fire,
That to all high desert and honour doth aspire.

I I

Ne suffereth it uncomely idlenesse
In his free thought to build her sluggish nest,
Ne suffereth it thought of ungentlenesse
Ever to creepe into his noble brest;
But to the highest and the worthiest
Lifteth it up that els would lowly fall:
It lettes not fall, it lettes it not to rest;
It lettes not scarse this Prince to breath at all,
But to his first poursuit him forward still doth call.

I I I

Who long time wandred through the forest wyde
To finde some issue thence; till that at last

LXI, 8   maltalent: ill will   Argument, 4   sownd: swoon

He met a Dwarfe that seemed terrifyde
With some late perill which he hardly past,
Or other accident which him aghast;
Of whom he asked, whence he lately came,
And whither now he traveiled so fast?
For sore he swat, and, ronning through that same
Thicke forest, was bescracht and both his feet nigh lame.

I V

Panting for breath, and almost out of hart,
The Dwarfe him answerd; 'Sir, ill mote I stay
To tell the same; I lately did depart
From Faery court, where I have many a day
Served a gentle Lady of great sway
And high accompt through out all Elfin land,
Who lately left the same, and tooke this way.
Her now I seeke; and if ye understand
Which way she fared hath, good Sir, tell out of hand.'

v

'What mister wight,' (saide he) 'and how arayd?'
'Royally clad' (quoth he) 'in cloth of gold,
As meetest may beseeme a noble mayd:
Her faire lockes in rich circlet be enrold,
A fayrer wight did never Sunne behold;
And on a Palfrey rydes more white then snow,
Yet she her selfe is whiter manifold.
The surest signe, whereby ye may her know,
Is that she is the fairest wight alive, I trow.'

V I

'Now certes, swaine,' (said he) 'such one, I weene,
Fast flying through this forest from her fo,
A foule ill-favoured foster, I have seene:
Her selfe, well as I might, I reskewd tho,
But could not stay, so fast she did foregoe,
Carried away with wings of speedy feare.'
'Ah, dearest God!' (quoth he) 'that is great woe,
And wondrous ruth to all that shall it heare:
But can ye read, Sir, how I may her finde, or where?'

V I I

'Perdy, me lever were to weeten that,'
(Saide he) 'then ransome of the richest knight,

---

iii, 8　swat: sweated　　　　　　vii, 1　lever: rather
v, 1　mister: kind of

Or all the good that ever yet I gat:
But froward fortune, and too forward Night,
Such happinesse did, maulgre, to me spight,
And fro me reft both life and light attone.
But, Dwarfe, aread what is that Lady bright
That through this forest wandreth thus alone?
For of her errour straunge I have great ruth and mone.'

V I I I

'That Ladie is,' (quoth he) 'where so she bee,
The bountiest virgin and most debonaire
That ever living eye, I weene, did see.
Lives none this day that may with her compare
In stedfast chastitie and vertue rare,
The goodly ornaments of beautie bright;
And is ycleped Florimell the fayre,
Faire Florimell belov'd of many a knight,
Yet she loves none but one, that Marinell is hight.

I X

'A Sea-nymphes sonne, that Marinell is hight,
Of my deare Dame is loved dearely well:
In other none, but him, she sets delight;
All her delight is set on Marinell,
But he sets nought at all by Florimell;
For Ladies love his mother long ygoe
Did him, they say, forwarne through sacred spell:
But fame now flies, that of a forreine foe
He is yslaine, which is the ground of all our woe.

X

'Five daies there be since he (they say) was slaine,
And fowre, since Florimell the Court forwent,
And vowed never to returne againe,
Till him alive or dead she did invent.
Therefore, faire Sir, for love of knighthood gent,
And honour of trew Ladies, if ye may
By your good counsell, or bold hardiment,
Or succour her, or me direct the way,
Do one or other good, I you most humbly pray.

X I

'So may ye gaine to you full great renowme
Of all good Ladies through the worlde so wide,
And haply in her hart finde highest rowme

vii, 9   errour: wandering   x, 4   invent: find

Of whom ye seeke to be most magnifide;
At least eternall meede shall you abide.'
To whom the Prince: 'Dwarfe, comfort to thee take,
For, till thou tidings learne what her betide,
I here avow thee never to forsake.
Ill weares he armes, that nill them use for Ladies sake.'

X I I

So with the Dwarfe he back retourn'd againe,
To seeke his Lady where he mote her finde;
But by the way he greatly gan complaine
The want of his good Squire late lefte behinde,
For whom he wondrous pensive grew in minde,
For doubt of daunger which mote him betide;
For him he loved above all mankinde,
Having him trew and faithfull ever tride.
And bold, as ever Squyre that waited by knights side:

X I I I

Who all this while full hardly was assayd
Of deadly daunger, which to him betidd;
For, whiles his Lord pursewd that noble Mayd,
After that foster fowle he fiercely ridd
To bene avenged of the shame he did
To that faire Damzell: Him he chaced long
Through the thicke woods wherein he would have hid
His shamefull head from his avengement strong,
And oft him threatned death for his outrageous wrong.

X I V

Nathlesse the villein sped himselfe so well,
Whether through swiftnesse of his speedie beast,
Or knowledge of those woods where he did dwell,
That shortly he from daunger was releast,
And out of sight escaped at the least:
Yet not escaped from the dew reward
Of his bad deedes, which daily he increast,
Ne ceased not, till him oppressed hard
The heavie plague that for such leachours is prepard.

X V

For soone as he was vanisht out of sight,
His coward courage gan emboldned bee,
And cast t' avenge him of that fowle despight
Which he had borne of his bold enimee:

xv, 2　courage: spirit

Tho to his brethren came, for they were three
Ungratious children of one gracelesse syre,
And unto them complayned how that he
Had used beene of that foolehardie Squyre:
So them with bitter words he stird to bloodie yre.

X V I

Forthwith themselves with their sad instruments
Of spoyle and murder they gan arme bylive,
And with him foorth into the forrest went
To wreake the wrath, which he did earst revive
In their sterne brests, on him which late did drive
Their brother to reproch and shamefull flight;
For they had vow'd that never he alive
Out of that forest should escape their might:
Vile rancour their rude harts had fild with such despight.

X V I I

Within that wood there was a covert glade,
Foreby a narrow foord, to them well knowne,
Through which it was uneath for wight to wade;
And now by fortune it was overflowne.
By that same way they knew that Squyre unknowne
Mote algates passe: forthy themselves they set
There in await with thicke woods overgrowne,
And all the while their malice they did whet
With cruell threats his passage through the ford to let.

X V I I I

It fortuned, as they devised had:
The gentle Squyre came ryding that same way,
Unweeting of their wile and treason bad,
And through the ford to passen did assay;
But that fierce foster, which late fled away,
Stoutly foorth stepping on the further shore,
Him boldly bad his passage there to stay,
Till he had made amends, and full restore
For all the damage which he had him doen afore.

X I X

With that at him a quiv'ring dart he threw,
With so fell force, and villeinous despite,
That through his haberjeon the forkehead flew,
And through the linked mayles empierced quite,

xvi, 1   sad: grievous
xvi, 2   bylive: quickly
                     xvii, 9   let: prevent

But had no powre in his soft flesh to bite.
That stroke the hardy Squire did sore displease,
But more that him he could not come to smite;
For by no meanes the high banke he could sease,
But labour'd long in that deepe ford with vaine disease.

x x

And still the foster with his long bore-speare
Him kept from landing at his wished will.
Anone one sent out of the thicket neare
A cruell shaft, headed with deadly ill,
And fethered with an unlucky quill:
The wicked steele stayd not till it did light
In his left thigh, and deepely did it thrill:
Exceeding griefe that wound in him empight,
But more that with his foes he could not come to fight.

x x i

At last, through wrath and vengeaunce making way,
He on the bancke arryvd with mickle payne,
Where the third brother him did sore assay,
And drove at him with all his might and mayne
A forest-bill, which both his hands did strayne;
But warily he did avoide the blow,
And with his speare requited him againe,
That both his sides were thrilled with the throw,
And a large streame of blood out of the wound did flow.

x x i i

He, tombling downe, with gnashing teeth did bite
The bitter earth, and bad to lett him in
Into the balefull house of endlesse night,
Where wicked ghosts doe waile their former sin.
Tho gan the battaile freshly to begin;
For nathemore for that spectacle bad
Did th' other two their cruell vengeaunce blin,
But both attonce on both sides him bestad,
And load upon him layd his life for to have had.

x x i i i

Tho when that villayn he aviz'd, which late
Affrighted had the fairest Florimell,
Full of fiers fury and indignant hate
To him he turned, and with rigor fell

xxi, 5   forest-bill: a digging or pruning tool
xxii, 7   blin: cease from

Smote him so rudely on the Pannikell,
That to the chin he clefte his head in twaine.
Downe on the ground his carkas groveling fell:
His sinfull sowle with desperate disdaine
Out of her fleshly ferme fled to the place of paine.

x x i v

That seeing, now the only last of three
Who with that wicked shafte him wounded had,
Trembling with horror, as that did foresee
The fearefull end of his avengement sad,
Through which he follow should his brethren bad,
His bootelesse bow in feeble hand upcaught,
And therewith shott an arrow at the lad;
Which, fayntly fluttering, scarce his helmet raught,
And glauncing fel to ground, but him annoyed naught.

x x v

With that he would have fled into the wood;
But Timias him lightly overhent,
Right as he entring was into the flood,
And strooke at him with force so violent,
That headlesse him into the foord he sent:
The carcas with the streame was carried downe,
But th' head fell backeward on the Continent;
So mischief fel upon the meaners crowne.
They three be dead with shame, the Squire lives with re-
nowne.

x x v i

He lives, but takes small joy of his renowne;
For of that cruell wound he bled so sore,
That from his steed he fell in deadly swowne:
Yet still the blood forth gusht in so great store,
That he lay wallowd all in his owne gore.
Now God thee keepe, thou gentlest squire alive,
Els shall thy loving Lord thee see no more;
But both of comfort him thou shalt deprive,
And eke thy selfe of honor which thou didst atchive.

x x v i i

Providence hevenly passeth living thought,
And doth for wretched mens reliefe make way;
For loe! great grace or fortune thither brought

xxiii, 5   Pannikell: brain-pan   xxv, 7   Continent: earth
xxiii, 9   ferme: enclosure

Comfort to him that comfortlesse now lay.
In those same woods ye well remember may
How that a noble hunteresse did wonne,
Shee, that base Braggadochio did affray,
And make him fast out of the forest ronne;
Belphœbe was her name, as faire as Phœbus sunne.

X X V I I I

She on a day, as shee pursewd the chace
Of some wilde beast, which with her arrowes keene
She wounded had, the same along did trace
By tract of blood, which she had freshly seene
To have besprinckled all the grassy greene:
By the great persue which she there perceav'd,
Well hoped shee the beast engor'd had beene,
And made more haste the life to have bereav'd;
But ah! her expectation greatly was deceav'd.

X X I X

Shortly she came whereas that wofull Squire,
With blood deformed, lay in deadly swownd;
In whose faire eyes, like lamps of quenched fire,
The Christall humor stood congealed rownd;
His locks, like faded leaves fallen to grownd,
Knotted with blood in bounches rudely ran;
And his sweete lips, on which before that stownd
The bud of youth to blossome faire began.
Spoild of their rosy red were woxen pale and wan.

X X X

Saw never living eie more heavy sight,
That could have made a rocke of stone to rew.
Or rive in twaine: which when that Lady bright,
Besides all hope, with melting eies did view,
All suddeinly abasht shee chaunged hew,
And with sterne horror backward gan to start;
But when shee better him beheld shee grew
Full of soft passion and unwonted smart:
The point of pitty perced through her tender hart.

X X X I

Meekely shee bowed downe, to weete if life
Yett in his frosen members did remaine;
And, feeling by his pulses beating rife
That the weake sowle her seat did yett retaine,
She cast to comfort him with busie paine.

His double folded necke she reard upright,
And rubd his temples and each trembling vaine;
His mayled haberjeon she did undight,
And from his head his heavy burganet did light.

XXXII

Into the woods thenceforth in haste shee went,
To seeke for hearbes that mote him remedy;
For shee of herbes had great intendiment,
Taught of the Nymphe which from her infancy
Her nourced had in trew Nobility:
There, whether yt divine Tobacco were,
Or Panachæa, or Polygony,
Shee fownd, and brought it to her patient deare,
Who al this while lay bleeding out his hartblood neare.

XXXIII

The soveraine weede betwixt two marbles plaine
Shee pownded small, and did in peeces bruze:
And then atweene her lily handes twaine
Into his wound the juice thereof did scruze;
And round about, as she could well it uze,
The flesh therewith shee suppled and did steepe,
T' abate all spasme, and soke the swelling bruze;
And, after having searcht the intuse deepe,
She with her scarf did bind the wound from cold to keepe.

XXXIV

By this he had sweet life recur'd agayne,
And, groning inly deepe, at last his eies,
His watry eies drizling like deawy rayne,
He up gan lifte toward the azure skies,
From whence descend all hopelesse remedies:
Therewith he sigh'd; and, turning him aside,
The goodly Maide, ful of divinities
And gifts of heavenly grace, he by him spide,
Her bow and gilden quiver lying him beside.

XXXV

'Mercy, deare Lord!' (said he) 'what grace is this
That thou hast shewed to me sinfull wight,
To send thine Angell from her bowre of blis
To comfort me in my distressed plight.
Angell, or Goddesse doe I call thee right?

XXXII, 3 intendiment: understanding
XXXIV, 5 hopelesse: unhoped for

What service may I doe unto thee meete,
That hast from darkenes me returnd to light,
And with thy hevenly salves and med'cines sweete
Hast drest my sinfull wounds? I kisse thy blessed feete.'

x x x v i

Thereat she blushing said; 'Ah! gentle Squire,
Nor Goddesse I, nor Angell; but the Mayd
And daughter of a woody Nymphe, desire
No service but thy safety and ayd;
Which if thou gaine, I shal be well apayd.
Wee mortall wights, whose lives and fortunes bee,
To commun accidents stil open layd,
Are bownd with commun bond of fraïltee,
To succor wretched wights whom we captived see.'

x x x v i i

By this her Damzells, which the former chace
Had undertaken after her, arryv'd,
As did Belphœbe, in the bloody place,
And thereby deemd the beast had bene depriv'd
Of life, whom late their ladies arrow ryv'd:
Forthy the bloody tract they followd fast,
And every one to ronne the swiftest stryv'd;
But two of them the rest far overpast,
And where their Lady was arrived at the last.

x x x v i i i

Where when they saw that goodly boy with blood
Defowled, and their Lady dresse his wownd,
They wondred much; and shortly understood
How him in deadly case theyr Lady fownd,
And reskewed out of the heavy stownd.
Eftsoones his warlike courser, which was strayd
Farre in the woodes whiles that he lay in swownd,
She made those Damzels search; which being stayd,
They did him set thereon, and forth with them convayd.

x x x i x

Into that forest farre they thence him led,
Where was their dwelling, in a pleasant glade
With mountaines rownd about environed,
And mightie woodes which did the valley shade
And like a stately Theatre it made,
Spreading it selfe into a spatious plaine:
And in the midst a little river plaide

Emongst the pumy stones, which seemd to plaine
With gentle murmure that his cours they did restraine.

X L

Beside the same a dainty place there lay,
Planted with mirtle trees and laurells greene,
In which the birds song many a lovely lay
Of Gods high praise, and of their loves sweet teene,
As it an earthly Paradize had beene:
In whose enclosed shadow there was pight
A faire Pavilion, scarcely to bee seene,
The which was al within most richly dight,
That greatest Princes liking it mote well delight.

X L I

Thither they brought that wounded Squyre, and layd
In easie couch his feeble limbes to rest.
He rested him awhile; and then the Mayd
His readie wound with better salves new drest:
Daily she dressed him, and did the best
His grievous hurt to guarish, that she might;
That shortly she his dolour hath redrest,
And his foule sore reduced to faire plight:
It she reduced, but himselfe destroyed quight.

X L I I

O foolish physick, and unfruitfull paine,
That heales up one, and makes another wound!
She his hurt thigh to him recurd againe,
But hurt his hart, the which before was sound,
Through an unwary dart, which did rebownd
From her faire eyes and gratious countenaunce.
What bootes it him from death to be unbownd,
To be captived in endlesse duraunce
Of sorrow and despeyre without aleggeaunce!

X L I I I

Still as his wound did gather, and grow hole,
So still his hart woxe sore, and health decayd:
Madnesse to save a part, and lose the whole!
Still whenas he beheld the heavenly Mayd,
Whiles dayly playsters to his wownd she layd,
So still his Malady the more increast,
The whiles her matchlesse beautie him dismayd.

XLI, 6 guarish: heal   XLII, 9 aleggeaunce: alleviation

Ah God! what other could he do at least,
But love so fayre a Lady that his life releast?

X L I V

Long while he strove in his corageous brest
With reason dew the passion to subdew,
And love for to dislodge out of his nest:
Still when her excellencies he did vew,
Her soveraine bountie and celestiall hew,
The same to love he strongly was constraynd:
But when his meane estate he did revew,
He from such hardy boldnesse was restraynd,
And of his lucklesse lott and cruell love thus playnd:

X L V

'Unthankfull wretch,' (said he) 'is this the meed,
With which her soverain mercy thou doest quight?
Thy life she saved by her gratious deed;
But thou doest weene with villeinous despight
To blott her honour, and her heavenly light.
Dye rather, dye, then so disloyally
Deeme of her high desert, or seeme so light:
Fayre death it is, to shonne more shame, to dy;
Dye rather, dy, then ever love disloyally.

X L V I

'But if to love disloyalty it bee,
Shall I then hate her that from deathes dore
Me brought? ah, farre be such reproch fro mee!
What can I lesse doe then her love therefore,
Sith I her dew reward cannot restore?
Dye rather, dye, and dying doe her serve;
Dying her serve, and living her adore,
Thy life she gave, thy life she doth deserve:
Dye rather, dye, then ever from her service swerve.

X L V I I

'But, foolish boy, what bootes thy service bace
To her to whom the hevens doe serve and sew?
Thou, a meane Squyre of meeke and lowly place;
She, hevenly borne and of celestiall hew.
How then? of all love taketh equall vew;
And doth not highest God vouchsafe to take
The love and service of the basest crew?
If she will not, dye meekly for her sake:
Dye rather, dye, then ever so faire love forsake!'

XLVIII

Thus warreid he long time against his will;
Till that through weakenesse he was forst at last
To yield himselfe unto the mightie ill,
Which, as a victour proud, gan ransack fast
His inward partes, and all his entrayles wast,
That neither blood in face nor life in hart
It left, but both did quite drye up and blast;
As percing levin, which the inner part
Of every thing consumes, and calcineth by art.

XLIX

Which seeing fayre Belphœbe gan to feare,
Least that his wound were inly well not heald,
Or that the wicked steele empoysned were:
Litle shee weend that love he close conceald.
Yet still he wasted, as the snow congeald
When the bright sunne his beams theron doth beat:
Yet never he his hart to her reveald;
But rather chose to dye for sorow great,
Then with dishonorable termes her to entreat.

L

She, gracious Lady, yet no paines did spare
To doe him ease, or doe him remedy.
Many Restoratives of vertues rare,
And costly Cordialles she did apply,
To mitigate his stubborne malady:
But that sweet Cordiall; which can restore
A love-sick hart, she did to him envy;
To him, and to all th' unworthy world forlore
She did envy that soveraine salve in secret store.

L I

That daintie Rose, the daughter of her Morne,
More deare then life she tendered, whose flowre
The girlond of her honour did adorne:
Ne suffred she the Middayes scorching powre,
Ne the sharp Northerne wind thereon to showre;
But lapped up her silken leaves most chayre,
When so the froward skye began to lowre;
But, soone as calmed was the christall ayre,
She did it fayre dispred and let to florish fayre.

XLVIII, 1   warreid: struggled   LI, 6   chayre: dear
XLVIII, 8   levin: lightning

L I I

Eternall God, in his almightie powre,
To make ensample of his heavenly grace,
In Paradize whylome did plant this flowre;
Whence he it fetcht out of her native place,
And did in stocke of earthly flesh enrace,
That mortall men her glory should admyre.
In gentle Ladies breste and bounteous race
Of woman kind it fayrest Flowre doth spyre,
And beareth fruit of honour and all chast desyre.

L I I I

Fayre ympes of beautie, whose bright shining beames
Adorne the world with like to heavenly light,
And to your willes both royalties and Reames
Subdew, through conquest of your wondrous might,
With this fayre flowre your goodly girlonds dight,
Of chastity and vertue virginall,
That shall embellish more your beautie bright,
And crowne your heades with heavenly coronall,
Such as the Angels weare before Gods tribunall!

L I V

To your faire selves a faire ensample frame
Of this faire virgin, this Belphebe fayre;
To whom, in perfect love and spotlesse fame
Of chastitie, none living may compayre:
Ne poysnous Envy justly can empayre
The prayse of her fresh flowring Maydenhead;
Forthy she standeth on the highest stayre
Of th' honorable stage of womanhead,
That Ladies all may follow her ensample dead.

L V

In so great prayse of stedfast chastity
Nathlesse she was so courteous and kynde,
Tempred with grace and goodly modesty,
That seemed those two vertues strove to fynd
The higher place in her Heroick mynd:
So striving each did other more augment,
And both encrease the prayse of woman kynde,
And both encrease her beautie excellent:
So all did make in her a perfect complement.

LII, 5   enrace: implant   LIII, I   ympes: children
LII, 8   spyre: cause to shoot

CANTO VI.

The birth of fayre Belphœbe and
Of Amorett is told:
The Gardins of Adonis fraught
With pleasures manifold.

I

WELL MAY I WEENE, faire Ladies, all this while
Ye wonder how this noble Damozell
So great perfections did in her compile,
Sith that in salvage forests she did dwell,
So farre from court and royall Citadell,
The great schoolmaistresse of all courtesy:
Seemeth that such wilde woodes should far expell
All civile usage and gentility,
And gentle sprite deforme with rude rusticity.

I I

But to this faire Belphœbe in her berth
The hevens so favorable were and free,
Looking with myld aspect upon the earth
In th' Horoscope of her nativitee,
That all the gifts of grace and chastitee
On her they poured forth of plenteous horne:
Jove laught on Venus from his soverayne see,
And Phœbus with faire beames did her adorne,
And all the Graces rockt her cradle being borne.

I I I

Her berth was of the wombe of Morning dew,
And her conception of the joyous Prime;
And all her whole creation did her shew
Pure and unspotted from all loathly crime
That is ingenerate in fleshly slime.
So was this virgin borne, so was she bred;
So was she trayned up from time to time
In all chaste vertue and true bounti-hed,
Till to her dew perfection she were ripened.

I V

Her mother was the faire Chrysogonee,
The daughter of Amphisa, who by race
A Faerie was, yborne of high degree.
She bore Belphœbe; she bore in like cace

Fayre Amoretta in the second place:
These two were twinnes, and twixt them two did share
The heritage of all celestiall grace:
That all the rest it seemd they robbed bare
Of bounty, and of beautie, and all vertues rare.

V

It were a goodly storie to declare
By what straunge accident faire Chrysogone
Conceiv'd these infants, and how them she bare
In this wilde forrest wandring all alone,
After she had nine moneths fulfild and gone:
For not as other wemens commune brood
They were enwombed in the sacred throne
Of her chaste bodie; nor with commune food,
As other wemens babes, they sucked vitall blood:

V I

But wondrously they were begot and bred
Through influence of th' hevens fruitfull ray
As it in antique bookes is mentioned.
It was upon a Sommers shinie day,
When Titan faire his beames did display,
In a fresh fountaine, far from all mens vew,
She bath'd her brest the boyling heat t'allay;
She bath'd with roses red and violets blew,
And all the sweetest flowers that in the forrest grew:

V I I

Till faint through yrkesome wearines, adowne
Upon the grassy ground her selfe she layd
To sleepe, the whiles a gentle slombring swowne
Upon her fell, all naked bare displayd.
The sunbeames bright upon her body playd,
Being through former bathing mollifide,
And pierst into her wombe, where they embayd
With so sweet sence and secret powre unspide,
That in her pregnant flesh they shortly fructifide.

V I I I

Miraculous may seeme to him that reades
So straunge ensample of conception.
But reason teacheth that the fruitfull seades
Of all things living, through impression
Of the sunbeames in moyst complexion,

VII, 7 embayd: suffused

Doe life conceive and quickned are by kynd:
So, after Nilus inundation.
Infinite shapes of creatures men doe fynd
Informed in the mud on which the Sunne hath shynd.

I X

Great father he of generation
Is rightly cald, th' authour of life and light;
And his faire sister for creation
Ministreth matter fit, which, tempred right
With heate and humour, breedes the living wight.
So sprong these twinnes in womb of Chrysogone;
Yet wist she nought thereof, but sore affright,
Wondred to see her belly so upblone,
Which still increast till she her terme had full outgone.

X

Whereof conceiving shame and foule disgrace,
Albe her guiltlesse conscience her cleard,
She fled into the wildernesse a space,
Till that unweeldy burden she had reard.
And shund dishonor which as death she feard:
Where, wearie of long traveill, downe to rest
Her selfe she set, and comfortably cheard:
There a sad cloud of sleepe her overkest,
And seized every sence with sorrow sore opprest.

X I

It fortuned, faire Venus having lost
Her little sonne, the winged god of love,
Who, for some light displeasure which him crost,
Was from her fled as flit as ayery Dove,
And left her blissfull bowre of joy above:
(So from her often he had fled away,
When she for ought him sharpely did reprove,
And wandred in the world in straunge aray,
Disguiz'd in thousand shapes, that none might him bewray.)

X I I

Him for to seeke, she left her heavenly hous,
The house of goodly formes and faire aspect,
Whence all the world derives the glorious
Features of beautie, and all shapes select,
With which high God his workmanship hath deckt;
And searched everie way through which his wings
Had borne him, or his tract she mote detect:

She promist kisses sweet, and sweeter things,
Unto the man that of him tydings to her brings.

X I I I

First she him sought in Court, where most he us'd
Whylome to haunt, but there she found him not:
But many there she found which sore accus'd
His falshood, and with fowle infamous blot
His cruell deedes and wicked wyles did spot:
Ladies and Lordes she everywhere mote heare
Complayning, how with his empoysned shot
Their wofull harts he wounded had whyleare
And so had left them languishing twixt hope and feare.

X I V

She then the Cities sought from gate to gate,
And everie one did aske, did he him see?
And everie one her answerd, that too late
He had him seene, and felt the crueltee
Of his sharpe dartes and whot artilleree:
And every one threw forth reproches rife
Of his mischievous deedes, and sayd that hee
Was the disturber of all civill life,
The enimy of peace, and authour of all strife.

X V

Then in the countrey she abroad him sought,
And in the rurall cottages inquir'd;
Where also many plaintes to her were brought,
How he their heedelesse harts with love had fir'd,
And his false venim through their veines inspir'd:
And eke the gentle Shepheard swaynes, which sat
Keeping their fleecy flockes as they were hyr'd,
She sweetly heard complaine, both how and what
Her sonne had to them doen; yet she did smile thereat.

X V I

But when in none of all these she him got,
She gan avize where els he mote him hyde:
At last she her bethought that she had not
Yet sought the salvage woods and forests wyde,
In which full many lovely Nymphes abyde;
Mongst whom might be that he did closely lye,
Or that the love of some of them him tyde:
Forthy she thither cast her course t' apply,
To search the secret haunts of Dianes company.

XVII

Shortly unto the wastefull woods she came,
Whereas she found the Goddesse with her crew,
After late chace of their embrewed game,
Sitting beside a fountaine in a rew;
Some of them washing with the liquid dew
From off their dainty limbs the dusty sweat
And soyle, which did deforme their lively hew;
Others lay shaded from the scorching heat,
The rest upon her person gave attendance great.

XVIII

She, having hong upon a bough on high
Her bow and painted quiver, had unlaste
Her silver buskins from her nimble thigh,
And her lanck loynes ungirt, and brests unbraste,
After her heat the breathing cold to taste:
Her golden lockes, that late in tresses bright
Embreaded were for hindring of her haste,
Now loose about her shoulders hong undight,
And were with sweet Ambrosia all besprinckled light.

XIX

Soone as she Venus saw behind her backe,
She was asham'd to be so loose surpriz'd;
And woxe halfe wroth against her damzels slacke,
That had not her thereof before aviz'd,
But suffred her so carelessly disguiz'd
Be overtaken. Soone her garments loose
Upgath'ring, in her bosome she compriz'd
Well as she might, and to the Goddesse rose;
Whiles all her Nymphes did like a girlond her enclose.

XX

Goodly she gan faire Cytherea greet,
And shortly asked her, what cause her brought
Into that wildernesse for her unmeet,
From her sweete bowres, and beds with pleasures fraught?
That suddein chaunge she straunge adventure thought.
To whom halfe weeping she thus answered;
That she her dearest sonne Cupido sought,
Who in his frowardnes from her was fled,
That she repented sore to have him angered.

XVII, 3   embrewed: blood-stained   XVIII, 7   for: to prevent

X X I

Thereat Diana gan to smile, in scorne
Of her vaine playnt, and to her scoffing sayd:
'Great pitty sure that ye be so forlorne
Of your gay sonne, that gives ye so good ayd
To your disports: ill mote ye bene apayd.'
But she was more engrieved, and replide;
'Faire sister, ill beseemes it to upbrayd
A dolefull heart with so disdainfull pride:
The like that mine may be your paine another tide.

X X I I

'As you in woods and wanton wildernesse
Your glory sett to chace the salvage beasts,
So my delight is all in joyfulnesse,
In beds, in bowres, in banckets, and in feasts:
And ill becomes you, with your lofty creasts,
To scorne the joy that Jove is glad to seeke:
We both are bownd to follow heavens beheasts,
And tend our charges with obeisaunce meeke.
Spare, gentle sister, with reproch my paine to eeke;

X X I I I

'And tell me, if that ye my sonne have heard
To lurke emongst your Nimphes in secret wize,
Or keepe their cabins: much I am affeard
Least he like one of them him selfe disguize,
And turne his arrowes to their exercize.
So may he long him selfe full easie hide;
For he is faire and fresh in face and guize
As any Nimphe; (let not it be envide.)'
So saying, every Nimph full narrowly shee eide.

X X I V

But Phœbe therewith sore was angered,
And sharply saide: 'Goe, Dame; goe, seeke your boy,
Where you him lately lefte, in Mars his bed:
He comes not here; we scorne his foolish joy,
Ne lend we leisure to his idle toy:
But if I catch him in this company,
By Stygian lake I vow, whose sad annoy
The Gods doe dread, he dearly shall abye:
Ile clip his wanton wings, that he no more shall flye.'

XXII, 9   eeke: add to

X X V

Whom whenas Venus saw so sore displeased,
Shee inly sory was, and gan relent
What shee had said; so her she soone appeasd
With surged words and gentle blandishment,
Which as a fountaine from her sweete lips went,
And welled goodly forth, that in short space
She was well pleasd, and forth her damzells sent
Through all the woods, to search from place to place,
If any tract of him or tidings they mote trace.

X X V I

To search the God of love her Nimphes she sent
Throughout the wandring forest every where:
And after them her selfe eke with her went
To seeke the fugitive both farre and nere.
So long they sought, till they arrived were
In that same shady covert whereas lay
Faire Crysogone in slombry traunce whilere;
Who in her sleepe (a wondrous thing to say)
Unwares had borne two babes, as faire as springing day.

X X V I I

Unwares she them conceivd, unwares she bore:
She bore withouten paine, that she conceiv'd
Withouten pleasure; ne her need implore
Lucinaes aide: which when they both perceiv'd,
They were through wonder nigh of sence berev'd,
And gazing each on other nought bespake.
At last they both agreed her seeming griev'd
Out of her heavie swowne not to awake
But from her loving side the tender babes to take.

X X V I I I

Up they them tooke; each one a babe uptooke,
And with them carried to be fostered.
Dame Phœbe to a Nymphe her babe betooke
To be upbrought in perfect Maydenhed,
And, of her selfe, her name Belphœbe red:
But Venus hers thence far away convayd,
To be upbrought in goodly womanhed;
And, in her litle loves stead, which was strayd,
Her Amoretta cald, to comfort her dismayd.

X X I X

Shee brought her to her joyous Paradize,
Wher most she wonnes when she on earth does dwell;
So faire a place as Nature can devize:
Whether in Paphos, or Cytheron hill,
Or it in Gnidus bee. I wote not well;
But well I wote by triall, that this same
All other pleasaunt places doth excell,
And called is by her lost lovers name,
The Gardin of Adonis, far renowmd by fame.

X X X

In that same Gardin all the goodly flowres,
Wherewith dame Nature doth her beautify,
And decks the girlonds of her Paramoures,
Are fetcht: there is the first seminary
Of all things that are borne to live and dye,
According to their kynds. Long worke it were
Here to account the endlesse progeny
Of all the weeds that bud and blossome there;
But so much as doth need must needs be counted here.

X X X I

It sited was in fruitfull soyle of old,
And girt in with two walls on either side;
The one of yron, the other of bright gold,
That none might thorough breake, nor overstride.
And double gates it had which opened wide,
By which both in and out men moten pas:
Th' one faire and fresh, the other old and dride.
Old Genius the porter of them was.
Old Genius, the which a double nature has.

X X X I I

He letteth in, he letteth out to wend
All that to come into the world desire:
A thousand thousand naked babes attend
About him day and night, which doe require
That he with fleshly weeds would them attire:
Such as him list, such as eternall fate
Ordained hath, he clothes with sinfull mire,
And sendeth forth to live in mortall state,
Till they agayn returne backe by the hinder gate.

xxx, 8   weeds: plants   xxxii, 5   weeds: clothes

XXXIII

After that they againe retourned beene,
They in that Gardin planted bee agayne,
And grow afresh, as they had never seene
Fleshly corruption, nor mortall payne.
Some thousand yeares so doen they there remayne,
And then of him are clad with other hew,
Or sent into the chaungefull world agayne,
Till thither they retourne where first they grew:
So, like a wheele, arownd they ronne from old to new.

XXXIV

Ne needs there Gardiner to sett or sow,
To plant or prune; for of their owne accord
All things, as they created were, doe grow,
And yet remember well the mighty word
Which first was spoken by th' Almighty Lord,
That bad them to increase and multiply:
Ne doe they need with water of the ford.
Or of the clouds, to moysten their roots dry;
For in themselves eternall moisture they imply.

XXXV

Infinite shapes of creatures there are bred,
And uncouth formes, which none yet ever knew:
And every sort is in a sondry bed
Sett by it selfe, andranckt in comely rew;
Some fitt for reasonable sowles t' indew;
Some made for beasts, some made for birds to weare;
And all the fruitfull spawne of fishes hew
In endlesse rancks along enraunged were,
That seemd the Ocean could not containe them there.

XXXVI

Daily they grow, and daily forth are sent
Into the world, it to replenish more;
Yet is the stocke not lessened nor spent,
But still remaines in everlasting store,
As it at first created was of yore:
For in the wide wombe of the world there lyes
In hatefull darknes and in deepe horrore,
An huge eternall Chaos, which supplyes
The substaunces of natures fruitfull progenyes.

XXXVII

All things from thence doe their first being fetch,
And borrow matter whereof they are made
Which, whenas forme and feature it does ketch,
Becomes a body, and doth then invade
The state of life out of the griesly shade.
That substaunce is eterne, and bideth so;
Ne when the life decayes and forme does fade,
Doth it consume and into nothing goe,
But chaunged is, and often altred to and froe.

XXXVIII

The substaunce is not chaungd nor altered,
But th' only forme and outward fashion;
For every substaunce is conditioned
To chaunge her hew, and sondry formes to don,
Meet for her temper and complexion:
For formes are variable, and decay
By course of kinde and by occasion;
And that faire flowre of beautie fades away,
As doth the lilly fresh before the sunny ray.

XXXIX

Great enimy to it, and to all the rest
That in the Gardin of Adonis springs,
Is wicked Tyme; who with his scyth addrest
Does mow the flowring herbes and goodly things,
And all their glory to the ground downe flings,
Where they do wither, and are fowly mard:
He flyes about, and with his flaggy winges
Beates downe both leaves and buds without regard,
Ne ever pitty may relent his malice hard.

XL

Yet pitty often did the gods relent,
To see so faire thinges mard and spoiled quight;
And their great mother Venus did lament
The losse of her deare brood, her deare delight:
Her hart was pierst with pitty at the sight,
When walking through the Gardin them she saw,
Yet no'te she find redresse for such despight:
For all that lives is subject to that law;
All things decay in time, and to their end doe draw.

XXXIX, 7 flaggy: drooping

X L I

But were it not that Time their troubler is,
All that in this delightfull Gardin growes
Should happy bee, and have immortall blis:
For here all plenty and all pleasure flowes;
And sweete love gentle fitts emongst them throwes,
Without fell rancor or fond gealosy.
Franckly each Paramor his leman knowes,
Each bird his mate; ne any does envy
Their goodly meriment and gay felicity.

X L I I

There is continuall Spring, and harvest there
Continuall, both meeting at one tyme;
For both the boughes doe laughing blossoms beare,
And with fresh colours decke the wanton Pryme,
And eke attonce the heavy trees they clyme,
Which seeme to labour under their fruites lode:
The whiles the joyous birdes make their pastyme
Emongst the shady leaves, their sweet abode,
And their trew loves without suspition tell abrode.

X L I I I

Right in the middest of that Paradise
There stood a stately Mount, on whose round top
A gloomy grove of mirtle trees did rise,
Whose shady boughes sharp steele did never lop,
Nor wicked beastes their tender buds did crop,
But like a girlond compassed the hight;
And from their fruitfull sydes sweet gum did drop,
That all the ground, with pretious deaw bedight,
Threw forth most dainty odours and most sweet delight.

X L I V

And in the thickest covert of that shade
There was a pleasaunt Arber, not by art
But of the trees owne inclination made,
Which knitting their rancke braunches, part to part,
With wanton yvie twine entrayld athwart,
And Eglantine and Caprifole emong,
Fashiond above within their inmost part,
That nether Phœbus beams could through them throng,
Nor Aeolus sharp blast could worke them any wrong.

XLII, 4 **wanton:** luxuriant   XLII, 4 Pryme: spring

X L V

And all about grew every sort of flowre,
To which sad lovers were transformde of yore;
Fresh Hyacinthus, Phœbus paramoure
And dearest love;
Foolish Narcisse, that likes the watry shore;
Sad Amaranthus, made a flowre but late,
Sad Amaranthus, in whose purple gore
Me seemes I see Amintas wretched fate,
To whom sweet Poets verse hath given endlesse date.

X L V I

There wont fayre Venus often to enjoy
Her deare Adonis joyous company,
And reape sweet pleasure of the wanton boy:
There yet, some say, in secret he does ly,
Lapped in flowres and pretious spycery,
By her hid from the world, and from the skill
Of Stygian Gods, which doe her love envy;
But she her selfe, when ever that she will,
Possesseth him, and of his sweetnesse takes her fill.

X L V I I

And sooth, it seemes, they say; for he may not
For ever dye, and never buried bee
In balefull night where all thinges are forgot:
All be he subject to mortalitie,
Yet is eterne in mutabilitie,
And by succession made perpetuall,
Transformed oft, and chaunged diverslie;
For him the Father of all formes they call:
Therefore needs mote he live, that living gives to all.

X L V I I I

There now he liveth in eternall blis,
Joying his goddesse, and of her enjoyd;
Ne feareth he henceforth that foe of his,
Which with his cruell tuske him deadly cloyd:
For that wilde Bore, the which him once annoyd,
She firmely hath emprisoned for ay,
That her sweet love his malice mote avoyd,
In a strong rocky Cave, which is, they say,
Hewen underneath that Mount, that none him losen may.

XLVIII, 4 cloyd: gored   XLVIII, 5 annoyd: harmed

XLIX

There now he lives in everlasting joy,
With many of the Gods in company
Which thither haunt, and with the winged boy,
Sporting him selfe in safe felicity:
Who when he hath with spoiles and cruelty
Ransackt the world, and in the wofull harts
Of many wretches set his triumphes hye,
Thither resortes, and, laying his sad dartes
Asyde, with faire Adonis playes his wanton partes.

L

And his trew love faire Psyche with him playes,
Fayre Psyche to him lately reconcyld,
After long troubles and unmeet upbrayes
With which his mother Venus her revyld,
And eke himselfe her cruelly exyld:
But now in stedfast love and happy state
She with him lives, and hath him borne a chyld,
Pleasure, that doth both gods and men aggrate,
Pleasure, the daughter of Cupid and Psyche late.

L I

Hither great Venus brought this infant fayre,
The younger daughter of Chrysogonee,
And unto Psyche with great trust and care
Committed her, yfostered to bee
And trained up in trew feminitee:
Who no lesse carefully her tendered
Then her owne daughter Pleasure, to whom shee
Made her companion, and her lessoned
In all the lore of love, and goodly womanhead.

L I I

In which when she to perfect ripenes grew,
Of grace and beautie noble Paragone,
She brought her forth into the worldes vew,
To be th' ensample of true love alone,
And Lodestarre of all chaste affection
To all fayre Ladies that doe live on grownd.
To Faery court she came; where many one
Admyrd her goodly haveour, and fownd
His feeble hart wide launched with loves cruel wownd.

XLIX, 8   sad: grievous

L I I I

But she to none of them her love did cast,
Save to the noble knight Sir Scudamore.
To whom her loving hart she linked fast
In faithfull love, t' abide for evermore;
And for his dearest sake endured sore
Sore trouble of an hainous enimy,
Who her would forced have to have forlore
Her former love and stedfast loialty,
As ye may elswhere reade that ruefull history.

L I V

But well I weene, ye first desire to learne
What end unto that fearefull Damozell,
Which fledd so fast from that same foster stearne
Whom with his brethren Timias slew, befell:
That was, to weet, the goodly Florimell;
Who wandring for to seeke her lover deare,
Her lover deare, her dearest Marinell,
Into misfortune fell, as ye did heare,
And from Prince Arthure fled with wings of idle feare.

CANTO VII.

The witches sonne loves Florimell:
She flyes; he faines to dy.
Satyrane save the Squyre of Dames
From Gyaunts tyranny.

I

LIKE AS AN Hynd forth singled from the heard,
That hath escaped from a ravenous beast,
Yet flyes away of her owne feete afeard,
And every leafe, that shaketh with the least
Murmure of winde, her terror hath encreast;
So fledd fayre Florimell from her vaine feare,
Long after she from perill was releast:
Each shade she saw, and each noyse she did heare,
Did seeme to be the same which she escapt wileare.

I I

All that same evening she in flying spent,
And all that night her course continewed,
Ne did she let dull sleepe once to relent,

Nor wearinesse to slack her hast, but fled
Ever alike, as if her former dred
Were hard behind, her ready to arrest;
And her white Palfrey, having conquered
The maistring raines out of her weary wrest,
Perforce her carried where ever he thought best.

   I I I

So long as breath and hable puissaunce
Did native corage unto him supply,
His pace he freshly forward did advaunce,
And carried her beyond all jeopardy;
But nought that wanteth rest can long aby:
He, having through incessant traveill spent
His force, at last perforce adowne did ly,
Ne foot could further move. The Lady gent
Thereat was suddein strook with great astonishment;

   I V

And, forst t' alight, on foot mote algates fare
A traveiler unwonted to such way:
Need teacheth her this lesson hard and rare,
That fortune all in equall launce doth sway,
And mortall miseries doth make her play.
So long she traveild, till at length she came
To an hilles side, which did to her bewray
A litle valley subject to the same,
All coverd with thick woodes that quite it overcame.

   V

Through the tops of the high trees she did descry
A litle smoke, whose vapour thin and light
Reeking aloft uprolled to the sky:
Which chearefull signe did send unto her sight
That in the same did wonne some living wight.
Eftsoones her steps she thereunto applyd,
And came at last in weary wretched plight
Unto the place, to which her hope did guyde,
To finde some refuge there, and rest her wearie syde.

   V I

There in a gloomy hollow glen she found
A little cottage, built of stickes and reedes
In homely wize, and wald with sods around;
In which a witch did dwell, in loathly weedes

IV, 8 subject: beneath

And wilfull want, all carelesse of her needes;
So choosing solitarie to abide
Far from all neighbours, that her divelish deedes
And hellish arts from people she might hide,
And hurt far off unknowne whom ever she envide.

VII

The Damzell there arriving entred in;
Where sitting on the flore the Hag she found
Busie (as seem'd) about some wicked gin:
Who, soone as she beheld that suddein stound,
Lightly upstarted from the dustie ground,
And with fell looke and hollow deadly gaze
Stared on her awhile, as one astound,
Ne had one word to speake for great amaze,
But shewd by outward signes that dread her sence did daze.

VIII

At last, turning her feare to foolish wrath,
She askt, what devill had her thither brought,
And who she was, and what unwonted path
Had guided her, unwelcomed, unsought?
To which the Damzell, full of doubtfull thought,
Her mildly answer'd: 'Beldame, be not wroth
With silly Virgin, by adventure brought
Unto your dwelling, ignorant and loth,
That crave but rowme to rest while tempest overblo'th.'

IX

With that adowne out of her christall eyne
Few trickling teares she softly forth let fall,
That like to orient perles did purely shyne
Upon her snowy cheeke; and therewithall
She sighed soft, that none so bestiall
Nor salvage hart, but ruth of her sad plight
Would make to melt, or pitteously appall;
And that vile Hag, all were her whole delight
In mischiefe, was much moved at so pitteous sight;

X

And gan recomfort her in her rude wyse,
With womanish compassion of her plaint,
Wiping the teares from her suffused eyes,
And bidding her sit downe, to rest her faint
And wearie limbes awhile. She, nothing quaint

VII, 3 gin: stratagem　　　　　　x, 5 quaint: fastidious

Nor 'sdeignfull of so homely fashion,
Sith brought she was now to so hard constraint,
Sate downe upon the dusty ground anon;
As glad of that small rest as Bird of tempest gon.

X I

Tho gan she gather up her garments rent,
And her loose lockes to dight in order dew
With golden wreath and gorgeous ornament;
Whom such whenas the wicked Hag did vew,
She was astonisht at her heavenly hew,
And doubted her to deeme an earthly wight,
But or some Goddesse, or of Dianes crew,
And thought her to adore with humble spright:
T' adore thing so divine as beauty were but right.

X I I

This wicked woman had a wicked sonne,
The comfort of her age and weary dayes,
A laesy loord, for nothing good to donne,
But stretched forth in ydlenesse alwayes,
Ne ever cast his mind to covet prayse,
Or ply himselfe to any honest trade,
But all the day before the sunny rayes
He us'd to slug, or sleepe in slothfull shade:
Such laesinesse both lewd and poore attonce him made.

X I I I

He, comming home at undertime, there found
The fayrest creature that he ever saw
Sitting beside his mother on the ground;
The sight whereof did greatly him adaw,
And his base thought with terrour and with aw
So inly smot, that as one, which hath gaz'd
On the bright Sunne unwares, doth soone withdraw
His feeble eyne, with too much brightnes daz'd,
So stared he on her, and stood long while amaz'd.

X I V

Softly at last he gan his mother aske,
What mister wight that was, and whence deriv'd,
That in so straunge disguizement there did maske,
And by what accident she there arriv'd?
But she, as one nigh of her wits depriv'd,

xii, 3   loord: lout   xiv, 2   mister: kind of
xiii, i   undertime: midday

With nought but ghastly lookes him answered;
Like to a ghost, that lately is reviv'd
From Stygian shores where late it wandered:
So both at her, and each at other wondered.

x v

But the fayre Virgin was so meeke and myld,
That she to them vouchsafed to embace
Her goodly port, and to their senses vyld
Her gentle speach applyde, that in short space
She grew familiare in that desert place.
During which time the Chorle, through her so kind
And courteise use, conceiv'd affection bace,
And cast to love her in his brutish mind:
No love, but brutish lust, that was so beastly tind.

x v i

Closely the wicked flame his bowels brent,
And shortly grew into outrageous fire;
Yet had he not the hart, nor hardiment,
As unto her to utter his desire;
His caytive thought durst not so high aspire:
But with soft sighes and lovely semblaunces
He ween'd that his affection entire
She should aread; many resemblaunces
To her he made, and many kinde remembraunces.

x v i i

Oft from the forrest wildings he did bring,
Whose sides empurpled were with smyling red;
And oft young birds, which he had taught to sing,
His maistresse praises sweetly caroled:
Girlonds of flowres sometimes for her faire hed
He fine would dight; sometimes the squirrell wild
He brought to her in bands, as conquered
To be her thrall, his fellow-servant vild:
All which she of him tooke with countenance meeke and mild.

x v i i i

But, past a while, when she fit season saw
To leave that desert mansion, she cast
In secret wize herselfe thence to withdraw,
For feare of mischiefe, which she did forecast
Might by the witch or by her sonne compast.

xv, 9   tind: kindled
xvi, 8   resemblaunces: shows of affection
xvii, 1   wildings: crab apples

Her wearie Palfrey, closely as she might,
Now well recovered after long repast,
In his proud furnitures she freshly dight,
His late miswandred wayes now to remeasure right.

X I X

And earely, ere the dawning day appear'd,
She forth issewed, and on her journey went:
She went in perill, of each noyse affeard,
And of each shade that did it selfe present;
For still she feared to be overhent
Of that vile hag, or her uncivile sonne;
Who when, too late awaking, well they kent
That their fayre guest was gone, they both begonne
To make exceeding mone, as they had been undonne.

X X

But that lewd lover did the most lament
For her depart, that ever man did heare:
He knockt his brest with desperate intent,
And scratcht his face, and with his teeth did teare
His rugged flesh, and rent his ragged heare;
That his sad mother, seeing his sore plight,
Was greatly woe begon, and gan to feare
Least his fraile senses were emperisht quight,
And love to frenzy turnd, sith love is franticke hight.

X X I

All wayes shee sought him to restore to plight,
With herbs, with charms, with counsel, and with teares;
But tears, nor charms, nor herbs, nor counsell, might
Asswage the fury which his entrails teares:
So strong is passion that no reason heares.
Tho when all other helpes she saw to faile,
She turnd her selfe backe to her wicked leares;
And by her divelish arts thought to prevaile
To bringe her backe againe, or worke her finall bale.

X X I I

Eftesoones out of her hidden cave she cald
An hideous beast of horrible aspect,
That could the stoutest corage have appald;
Monstrous, mishapt, and all his backe was spect
With thousand spots of colours queint elect,

XXI, 7   leares: lore   XXII, 5   queint elect: strangely
                                      chosen

Thereto so swifte that it all beasts did pas:
Like never yet did living eie detect;
But likest it to an Hyena was,
That feeds on wemens flesh as others feede on gras.

X X I I I

It forth she cald, and gave it streight in charge
Through thicke and thin her to poursew apace,
Ne once to stay to rest, or breath at large,
Till her he had attaind and brought in place,
Or quite devourd her beauties scornefull grace.
The Monster, swifte as word that from her went,
Went forth in haste, and did her footing trace
So sure and swiftly, through his perfect sent
And passing speede, that shortly he her overhent.

X X I V

Whom when the fearefull Damzell nigh espide,
No need to bid her fast away to flie:
That ugly shape so sore her terrifide,
That it she shund no lesse then dread to die;
And her flitt palfrey did so well apply
His nimble feet to her conceived feare,
That whilest his breath did strength to him supply,
From peril free he away her did beare;
But when his force gan faile his pace gan wex areare.

X X V

Which whenas she perceiv'd, she was dismayd
At that same last extremity ful sore,
And of her safety greatly grew afrayd.
And now she gan approch to the sea shore,
As it befell, that she could flie no more,
But yield herselfe to spoile of greedinesse:
Lightly she leaped, as a wight forlore,
From her dull horse, in desperate distresse,
And to her feet betooke her doubtfull sickernesse.

X X V I

Not halfe so fast the wicked Myrrha fled
From dread of her revenging fathers hond;
Nor halfe so fast to save her maydenhed
Fled fearfull Daphne on th' Ægæan strond,
As Florimell fled from that Monster yond,
To reach the sea ere she of him were raught:

xxv, 9   doubtfull: unsafe   xxvi, 6   raught: reached
xxv, 9   sickernesse: safety

For in the sea to drowne herselfe she fond,
Rather then of the tyrant to be caught:
Thereto fear gave her wings, and need her corage taught.

X X V I I

It fortuned (high God did so ordaine)
As shee arrived on the roring shore,
In minde to leape into the mighty maine,
A little bote lay hoving her before,
In which there slept a fisher old and pore,
The whiles his nets were drying on the sand.
Into the same shee lept, and with the ore
Did thrust the shallop from the floting strand:
So safety fownd at sea which she fownd not at land.

X X V I I I

The Monster, ready on the pray to sease,
Was of his forward hope deceived quight;
Ne durst assay to wade the perlous seas,
But greedily long gaping at the sight,
At last in vaine was forst to turne his flight,
And tell the idle tidings to his Dame:
Yet, to avenge his divelish despight,
He sett upon her Palfrey tired lame,
And slew him cruelly ere any reskew came.

X X I X

And, after having him embowelled
To fill his hellish gorge, it chaunst a knight
To passe that way, as forth he traveiled:
Yt was a goodly Swaine, and of great might,
As ever man that bloody field did fight;
But in vain sheows, that wont yong knights bewitch,
And courtly services, tooke no delight;
But rather joyd to bee then seemen sich,
For both to be and seeme to him was labor lich.

X X X

It was to weete the good Sir Satyrane,
That raungd abrode to seeke adventures wilde,
As was his wont, in forest and in plaine:
He was all armd in rugged steele unfilde,
As in the smoky forge it was compilde,
And in his Scutchin bore a Satyres hedd.
He comming present, where the Monster vilde

XXVI, 7   fond: tried

Upon that milke-white Palfreyes carcas fedd,
Unto his reskew ran, and greedily him spedd.

X X X I

There well perceivd he that it was the horse
Whereon faire Florimell was wont to ride,
That of that feend was rent without remorse:
Much feared he least ought did ill betide
To that faire Maide, the flowre of wemens pride;
For her he dearely loved, and in all
His famous conquests highly magnifide:
Besides, her golden girdle, which did fall
From her in flight, he fownd, that did him sore apall.

X X X I I

Full of sad feare and doubtfull agony
Fiercely he flew upon that wicked feend,
And with huge strokes and cruell battery
Him forst to leave his pray, for to attend
Him selfe from deadly daunger to defend:
Full many wounds in his corrupted flesh
He did engrave, and muchell blood did spend,
Yet might not doe him die: but aie more fresh
And fierce he still appeard, the more he did him thresh.

X X X I I I

He wist not how him to despoile of life,
Ne how to win the wished victory,
Sith him he saw still stronger grow through strife,
And him selfe weaker through infirmity.
Greatly he grew enrag'd, and furiously
Hurling his sword away he lightly lept
Upon the beast, that with great cruelty
Rored and raged to be underkept;
Yet he perforce him held, and strokes upon him hept.

X X X I V

As he that strives to stop a suddein flood,
And in strong bancks his violence enclose,
Forceth it swell above his wonted mood,
And largely overflow the fruitfull plaine,
That all the countrey seemes to be a Maine,
And the rich furrowes flote, all quite fordonne:
The wofull husbandman doth lowd complaine
To see his whole yeares labor lost so soone,
For which to God he made so many an idle boone:

x x x v

So him he held, and did through might amate.
So long he held him, and him bett so long,
That at the last his fiercenes gan abate,
And meekely stoup unto the victor strong:
Who, to avenge the implacable wrong
Which he supposed donne to Florimell,
Sought by all meanes his dolor to prolong,
Sith dint of steele his carcas could not quell;
His maker with her charmes had framed him so well.

x x x v i

The golden ribband, which that virgin wore
About her sclender waste, he tooke in hand,
And with it bownd the beast, that lowd did rore
For great despight of that unwonted band,
Yet dared not his victor to withstand,
But trembled like a lambe fled from the pray;
And all the way him followd on the strand,
As he had long bene learned to obay;
Yet never learned he such service till that day.

x x x v i i

Thus as he led the Beast along the way,
He spide far off a mighty Giauntesse
Fast flying, on a Courser dapled gray,
From a bold knight that with great hardinesse
Her hard pursewd, and sought for to suppresse.
She bore before her lap a dolefull Squire,
Lying athwart her horse in great distresse,
Fast bounden hand and foote with cords of wire,
Whom she did meane to make the thrall of her desire.

x x x v i i i

Which whenas Satyrane beheld, in haste
He lefte his captive Beast at liberty,
And crost the nearest way, by which he cast
Her to encounter ere she passed by;
But she the way shund nathemore forthy,
But forward gallopt fast; which when he spyde,
His mighty speare he couched warily,
And at her ran: she, having him descryde,
Her selfe to fight addrest, and threw her lode aside.

xxxv, 1   amate: subdue

XXXIX

Like as a Goshauke, that in foote doth beare
A trembling Culver, having spide on hight
An Eagle that with plumy wings doth sheare
The subtile ayre stouping with all his might,
The quarry throwes to ground with fell despight,
And to the batteill doth her selfe prepare:
So ran the Geauntesse unto the fight,
Her fyrie eyes with furious sparkes did stare,
And with blasphemous bannes high God in peeces tare.

XL

She caught in hand an huge great yron mace,
Wherewith she many had of life depriv'd;
But, ere the stroke could seize his aymed place,
His speare amids her sun-brode shield arriv'd:
Yet nathemore the steele asonder riv'd,
All were the beame in bignes like a mast,
Ne her out of the stedfast sadle driv'd;
But, glauncing on the tempred metall, brast
In thousand shivers, and so forth beside her past.

XLI

Her Steed did stagger with that puissaunt strooke;
But she no more was moved with that might
Then it had lightened on an aged Oke,
Or on the marble Pillour that is pight
Upon the top of Mount Olympus hight,
For the brave youthly Champions to assay
With burning charet wheeles it nigh to smite;
But who that smites it mars his joyous play,
And is the spectacle of ruinous decay.

XLII

Yet, therewith sore enrag'd, with sterne regard
Her dreadfull weapon she to him addrest,
Which on his helmet martelled so hard
That made him low incline his lofty crest,
And bowd his battred visour to his brest:
Wherewith he was so stund that he n'ote ryde,
But reeled to and fro from east to west,
Which when his cruell enimy espyde,
She lightly unto him adjoyned syde to syde;

XXXIX, 9 bannes: curses   XLII, 3 martelled: hammered

XLIII

And, on his collar laying puissaunt hand,
Out of his wavering seat him pluckt perforse,
Perforse him pluckt, unable to withstand
Or helpe himselfe; and laying thwart her horse,
In loathly wise like to a carrion corse,
She bore him fast away. Which when the knight
That her pursewed saw, with great remorse
He nere was touched in his noble spright,
And gan encrease his speed as she encreast her flight.

XLIV

Whom when as nigh approching she espyde,
She threw away her burden angrily;
For she list not the batteill to abide,
But made her selfe more light away to fly:
Yet her the hardy knight pursewd so nye
That almost in the backe he oft her strake;
But still, when him at hand she did espy,
She turnd, and semblaunce of faire fight did make,
But, when he stayd, to flight againe she did her take.

XLV

By this the good Sir Satyrane gan wake
Out of his dreame that did him long entraunce,
And, seeing none in place, he gan to make
Exceeding mone, and curst that cruell chaunce
Which reft from him so faire a chevisaunce.
At length he spyde whereas that wofull Squyre,
Whom he had reskewed from captivaunce
Of his strong foe, lay tombled in the myre,
Unable to arise, or foote or hand to styre.

XLVI

To whom approching, well he mote perceive
In that fowle plight a comely personage
And lovely face, made fit for to deceive
Fraile Ladies hart with loves consuming rage,
Now in the blossome of his freshest age.
He reard him up and loosd his yron bands,
And after gan inquire his parentage,
And how he fell into the Gyaunts hands,
And who that was which chaced her along the lands.

XLVII

Then trembling yet through feare the Squire bespake:
'That Geauntesse Argantè is behight,
A daughter of the Titans which did make
Warre against heven, and heaped hils on hight
To scale the skyes and put Jove from his right:
Her syre Typhoeus was; who, mad through merth,
And dronke with blood of men slaine by his might,
Through incest her of his owne mother Earth
Whylome begot, being but halfe twin of that berth:

XLVIII

'For at that berth another Babe she bore;
To weet, the mightie Ollyphant, that wrought
Great wreake to many errant knights of yore,
And many hath to foule confusion brought.
These twinnes, men say, (a thing far passing thought)
While in their mothers wombe enclosd they were,
Ere they into the lightsom world were brought,
In fleshly lust were mingled both yfere,
And in that monstrous wise did to the world appere.

XLIX

'So liv'd they ever after in like sin,
Gainst natures law and good behaveoure;
But greatest shame was to that maiden twin,
Who, not content so fowly to devoure
Her native flesh and staine her brothers bowre,
Did wallow in all other fleshly myre,
And suffred beastes her body to deflowre,
So whot she burned in that lustfull fyre;
Yet all that might not slake her sensuall desyre:

L

'But over all the countrie she did raunge
To seeke young men to quench her flaming thrust,
And feed her fancy with delightfull chaunge:
Whom so she fittest findes to serve her lust,
Through her maine strength, in which she most doth trust,
She with her bringes into a secret Ile,
Where in eternall bondage dye he must,
Or be the vassall of her pleasures vile,
And in all shamefull sort him selfe with her defile.

XLVIII, 8   yfere: together

L I

'Me, seely wretch, she so at vauntage caught,
After she long in waite for me did lye,
And meant unto her prison to have brought,
Her lothsom pleasure there to satisfye;
That thousand deathes me lever were to dye
Then breake the vow that to faire Columbell
I plighted have, and yet keepe stedfastly.
As for my name, it mistreth not to tell:
Call me the Squyre of Dames; that me beseemeth well.

L I I

'But that bold knight, whom ye pursuing saw
That Geauntesse, is not such as she seemd,
But a faire virgin that in martiall law
And deedes of armes above all Dames is deemd,
And above many knightes is eke esteemd
For her great worth: She Palladine is hight.
She you from death, you me from dread, redeemd;
Ne any may that Monster match in fight,
But she, or such as she, that is so chaste a wight.'

L I I I

'Her well beseemes that Quest,' (quoth Satyrane)
'But read, thou Squyre of Dames, what vow is this,
Which thou upon thy selfe hast lately ta'ne?'
'That shall I you recount,' (quoth he) 'ywis,
So be ye pleasd to pardon all amis.
That gentle Lady whom I love and serve,
After long suit and wearie servicis,
Did aske me, how I could her love deserve,
And how she might be sure that I would never swerve?

L I V

'I, glad by any meanes her grace to gaine,
Badd her commaund my life to save or spill.
Eftsoones she badd me, with incessaunt paine
To wander through the world, abroad at will,
And every where, where with my power or skill
I might doe service unto gentle Dames,
That I the same should faithfully fulfill;
And at the twelve monethes end should bring their names
And pledges, as the spoiles of my victorious games.

LI, 8   mistreth: is necessary

L V

'So well I to faire Ladies service did,
And found such favour in their loving hartes,
That ere the yeare his course had compassid,
Thre hundred pledges for my good desartes,
And thrice three hundred thanks for my good partes,
I with me brought, and did to her present:
Which when she saw, more bent to eke my smartes
Then to reward my trusty true intent,
She gan for me devise a grievous punishment;

L V I

'To weet, that I my traveill should resume,
And with like labour walke the world arownd,
Ne ever to her presence should presume,
Till I so many other Dames had fownd,
The which, for all the suit I could propownd,
Would me refuse their pledges to afford,
But did abide for ever chaste and sownd.'
'Ah! gentle Squyre,' (quoth he) 'tell at one word,
How many fownd'st thou such to put in thy record?'

L V I I

'Indeed, Sir knight,' (said he) 'one word may tell
All that I ever fownd so wisely stayd,
For onely three they were disposd so well;
And yet three yeares I now abrode have strayd,
To fynd them out.' 'Mote I,' (then laughing sayd
The knight) 'inquire of thee what were those three,
The which thy proffred curtesie denayd?
Or ill they seemed sure avizd to bee,
Or brutishly brought up, that nev'r did fashions see.'

L V I I I

'The first which then refused me,' (said hee)
'Certes was but a common Courtisane;
Yet flat refusd to have adoe with mee,
Because I could not give her many a Jane.'
(Thereat full hartely laughed Satyrane.)
'The second was an holy Nunne to chose,
Which would not let me be her Chappellane,
Because she knew, she said, I would disclose
Her counsell, if she should her trust in me repose.

LVIII, 4 Jane: coin

L I X

'The third a Damzell was of low degree,
Whom I in countrey cottage fownd by chaunce:
Full litle weened I that chastitee
Had lodging in so meane a maintenaunce;
Yet was she fayre, and in her countenaunce
Dwelt simple truth in seemely fashion.
Long thus I woo'd her with due observaunce,
In hope unto my pleasure to have won;
But was as far at last, as when I first begon.

L X

'Safe her, I never any woman found
That chastity did for it selfe embrace,
But were for other causes firme and sound;
Either for want of handsome time and place,
Or else for feare of shame and fowle disgrace.
Thus am I hopelesse ever to attaine
My Ladies love in such a desperate case,
But all my dayes am like to waste in vaine,
Seeking to match the chaste with th' unchaste Ladies traine.'

L X I

'Perdy' (sayd Satyrane) 'thou Squyre of Dames,
Great labour fondly hast thou hent in hand,
To get small thankes, and therewith many blames,
That may emongst Alcides labours stand.'
Thence backe returning to the former land,
Where late he left the Beast he overcame,
He found him not; for he had broke his band,
And was returnd againe unto his Dame,
To tell what tydings of fayre Florimell became.

CANTO VIII.

The Witch creates a snowy La-
dy like to Florimell;
Who wrong'd by Carle, by Proteus sav'd,
Is sought by Paridell.

I

So oft as I this history record,
My heart doth melt with meere compassion,

1, 2 meere: pure

To thinke how causelesse, of her owne accord,
This gentle Damzell, whom I write upon,
Should plonged be in such affliction
Without all hope of comfort or reliefe;
That sure, I weene, the hardest hart of stone
Would hardly finde to aggravate her griefe;
For misery craves rather mercy then repriefe.

I I

But that accursed Hag, her hostesse late,
Had so enranckled her malitious hart,
That she desyrd th' abridgement of her fate,
Or long enlargement of her painefull smart.
Now when the Beast, which by her wicked art
Late foorth she sent, she backe retourning spyde
Tyde with her golden girdle; it a part
Of her rich spoyles whom he had earst destroyd
She weend, and wondrous gladnes to her hart applyde.

I I I

And, with it ronning hast'ly to her sonne,
Thought with that sight him much to have reliv'd
Who, thereby deeming sure the thing as donne,
His former griefe with furie fresh reviv'd
Much more then earst, and would have algates riv'd
The hart out of his brest: for sith her dedd
He surely dempt, himselfe he thought depriv'd
Quite of all hope wherewith he long had fedd
His foolish malady, and long time had misledd.

I V

With thought whereof exceeding mad he grew,
And in his rage his mother would have slaine,
Had she not fled into a secret mew,
Where she was wont her Sprightes to entertaine,
The maisters of her art: there was she faine
To call them all in order to her ayde,
And them conjure, upon eternall paine,
To counsell her, so carefully dismayd,
How she might heale her sonne whose senses were decayd.

v

By their advice, and her owne wicked wit,
She there deviz'd a wondrous worke to frame,
Whose like on earth was never framed yit;

III, 5　riv'd: torn

That even Nature selfe envide the same,
And grudg'd to see the counterfet should shame
The thing it selfe: In hand she boldly tooke
To make another like the former Dame,
Another Florimell, in shape and looke
So lively and so like, that many it mistooke.

V I

The substance, whereof she the body made,
Was purest snow in massy mould congeald,
Which she had gathered in a shady glade
Of the Riphœan hils, to her reveald
By errant Sprights, but from all men conceald:
The same she tempred with fine Mercury
And virgin wex that never yet was seald,
And mingled them with perfect vermily;
That like a lively sanguine it seemed to the eye.

V I I

Instead of eyes two burning lampes she set
In silver sockets, shyning like the skyes,
And a quicke moving Spirit did arret
To stirre and roll them like to womens eyes:
Instead of yellow lockes she did devyse
With golden wyre to weave her curled head;
Yet golden wyre was not so yellow thryse
As Florimells fayre heare: and, in the stead
Of life, she put a Spright to rule the carcas dead;

V I I I

A wicked Spright, yfraught with fawning guyle
And fayre resemblance above all the rest,
Which with the Prince of Darkenes fell somewhyle
From heavens blis and everlasting rest:
Him needed not instruct which way were best
Him selfe to fashion likest Florimell,
Ne how to speake, ne how to use his gest;
For he in counterfesaunce did excell,
And all the wyles of wemens wits knew passing well.

I X

Him shaped thus she deckt in garments gay,
Which Florimell had left behind her late;
That who so then her saw would surely say
It was her selfe whom it did imitate,

vii, 6   wyre: metallic thread   viii, 7   gest: deportment

Or fayrer then her selfe, if ought algate
Might fayrer be. And then she forth her brought
Unto her sonne that lay in feeble state;
Who seeing her gan streight upstart, and thought
She was the Lady selfe whom he so long had sought.

x

Tho fast her clipping twixt his armes twayne,
Extremely joyed in so happy sight,
And soone forgot his former sickely payne:
But she, the more to seeme such as she hight,
Coyly rebutted his embracement light;
Yet still, with gentle countenaunce, retain'd
Enough to hold a foole in vaine delight.
Him long she so with shadowes entertain'd,
As her Creatresse had in charge to her ordain'd.

x i

Till on a day, as he disposed was
To walke the woodes with that his Idole faire,
Her to disport and idle time to pas
In th' open freshnes of the gentle aire,
A knight that way there chaunced to repaire;
Yet knight he was not, but a boastfull swaine
That deedes of armes had ever in despaire,
Proud Braggadocchio, that in vaunting vaine
His glory did repose, and credit did maintaine.

x i i

He, seeing with that Chorle so faire a wight,
Decked with many a costly ornament,
Much merveiled thereat, as well he might,
And thought that match a fowle disparagement:
His bloody speare eftesoones he boldly bent
Against the silly clowne, who dead through feare
Feil streight to ground in great astonishment.
'Villein,' (sayd he) 'this Lady is my deare;
Dy, if thou it gainesay: I will away her beare.'

x i i i

The fearefull Chorle durst not gainesay nor dooe,
But trembling stood, and yielded him the pray;
Who, finding litle leasure her to wooe
On Tromparts steed her mounted without stay,
And without reskew led her quite away.

xii, 6   clowne: peasant

Proud man himselfe then Braggadochio deem'd,
And next to none after that happy day,
Being possessed of that spoyle, which seem'd
The fairest wight on ground, and most of men esteem'd.

X I V

But, when hee saw him selfe free from poursute,
He gan make gentle purpose to his Dame
With termes of love and lewdnesse dissolute;
For he could well his glozing speaches frame
To such vaine uses that him best became:
But she thereto would lend but light regard,
As seeming sory that she ever came
Into his powre, that used her so hard
To reave her honor, which she more than life prefard.

X V

Thus as they two of kindnes treated long,
There them by chaunce encountred on the way
An armed knight upon a courser strong,
Whose trampling feete upon the hollow lay
Seemed to thunder, and did nigh affray
That Capons corage: yet he looked grim,
And faynd to cheare his lady in dismay,
Who seemd for feare to quake in every lim,
And her to save from outrage meekely prayed him.

X V I

Fiercely that straunger forward came: and, nigh
Approching, with bold words and bitter threat
Bad that same boaster, as he mote, on high,
To leave to him that lady for excheat,
Or bide him batteill without further treat.
That challenge did too peremptory seeme,
And fild his senses with abashment great;
Yet seeing nigh him jeopardy extreme,
He it dissembled well, and light seemd to esteeme,

X V I I

Saying, 'Thou foolish knight, that weenst with words
To steale away that I with blowes have wonne,
And brought through points of many perilous swords:
But if thee list to see thy Courser ronne,
Or prove thy selfe, this sad encounter shonne,
And seeke els without hazard of thy hedd.'

xv, 1   kindnes: love   xv, 4   lay: lea

At those prowd words that other knight begonne
To wex exceeding wroth, and him aredd
To turne his steede about, or sure he should be dedd.

X V I I I

'Sith then,' (said Braggadochio) 'needes thou wilt
Thy daies abridge through proofe of puissaunce,
Turne we our steeds; that both in equall tilt
May meete againe, and each take happy chaunce.'
This said, they both a furlongs mountenaunce
Retird their steeds, to ronne in even race;
But Braggadochio, with his bloody launce,
Once having turnd, no more returnd his face,
But lefte his love to losse, and fled him selfe apace.

X I X

The knight, him seeing flie, had no regard
Him to poursew, but to the lady rode;
And having her from Trompart lightly reard,
Upon his Courser sett the lovely lode,
And with her fled away without abode.
Well weened he, that fairest Florimell
It was with whom in company he yode,
And so her selfe did alwaies to him tell;
So made him thinke him selfe in heven that was in hell.

X X

But Florimell her selfe was far away,
Driven to great distresse by fortune straunge,
And taught the carefull Mariner to play,
Sith late mischaunce had her compeld to chaunge
The land for sea, at randon there to raunge:
Yett there that cruell Queene avengeresse,
Not satisfyde so far her to estraunge
From courtly blis and wonted happinesse,
Did heape on her new waves of weary wretchednesse.

X X I

For being fled into the fishers bote
For refuge from the Monsters cruelty,
Long so she on the mighty maine did flote,
And with the tide drove forward carelesly;
For th' ayre was milde and cleared was the skie,
And all his windes Dan Aeolus did keepe
From stirring up their stormy enmity,

xx, 3   carefull: full of care

As pittying to see her waile and weepe:
But all the while the fisher did securely sleepe.

X X I I

At last when droncke with drowsinesse he woke,
And saw his drover drive along the streame,
He was dismayd; and thrise his brest he stroke,
For marveill of that accident extreame:
But when he saw that blazing beauties beame,
Which with rare light his bote did beautifye,
He marveild more, and thought he yet did dreame
Not well awakte; or that some extasye
Assotted had his sence, or dazed was his eye.

X X I I I

But when her well avizing hee perceiv'd
To be no vision nor fantasticke sight,
Great comfort of her presence he conceiv'd,
And felt in his old corage new delight
To gin awake, and stir his frosen spright:
Tho rudely askte her, how she thither came?
'Ah!' (sayd she) 'father, I note read aright
What hard misfortune brought me to this same;
Yet am I glad that here I now in safety ame.

X X I V

'But thou, good man, sith far in sea we bee,
And the great waters gin apace to swell,
That now no more we can the mayn-land see,
Have care, I pray, to guide the cock-bote well,
Least worse on sea then us on land befell.'
Thereat th' old man did nought but fondly grin,
And saide his boat the way could wisely tell;
But his deceiptfull eyes did never lin
To looke on her faire face and marke her snowy skin.

X X V

The sight whereof in his congealed flesh
Infixt such secrete sting of greedy lust,
That the drie withered stocke it gan refresh,
And kindled heat that soone in flame forth brust:
The driest wood is soonest burnt to dust.
Rudely to her he lept, and his rough hond
Where ill became him rashly would have thrust;

XXII, 2   drover: fishing boat   XXIV, 8   lin: cease

But she with angry scorne did him withstond,
And shamefully reproved for his rudenes fond.

X X V I

But he, that never good nor maners knew,
Her sharpe rebuke full litle did esteeme;
Hard is to teach an old horse amble trew:
The inward smoke, that did before but steeme,
Broke into open fire and rage extreme;
And now he strength gan adde unto his will,
Forcyng to doe that did him fowle misseeme.
Beastly he threwe her downe, ne car'd to spill
Her garments gay with scales of fish that all did fill.

X X V I I

The silly virgin strove him to withstand
All that she might, and him in vaine revild:
Shee strugled strongly both with foote and hand
To save her honor from that villaine vilde,
And cride to heven, from humane help exild.
O! ye brave knights, that boast this Ladies love,
Where be ye now, when she is nigh defild
Of filthy wretch? well may she you reprove
Of falsehood or of slouth, when most it may behove.

X X V I I I

But if that thou, Sir Satyran, didst weete,
Or thou, Sir Peridure, her sory state,
How soone would yee assemble many a fleete,
To fetch from sea that ye at land lost late!
Towres, citties, kingdomes, ye would ruinate
In your avengement and despiteous rage,
Ne ought your burning fury mote abate;
But if Sir Calidore could it presage,
No living creature could his cruelty asswage.

X X I X

But sith that none of all her knights is nye,
See how the heavens, of voluntary grace
And soveraine favor towards chastity,
Doe succor send to her distressed cace;
So much high God doth innocence embrace.
It fortuned, whilest thus she stifly strove,
And the wide sea importuned long space
With shrilling shriekes, Proteus abrode did rove,
Along the fomy waves driving his finny drove.

x x x

Proteus is Shepheard of the seas of yore,
And hath the charge of Neptunes mighty heard;
An aged sire with head all frory hore,
And sprinckled frost upon his deawy beard:
Who when those pittifull outcries he heard
Through all the seas so ruefully resownd,
His charett swifte in hast he thither steard,
Which with a teeme of scaly Phocas bownd
Was drawne upon the waves that fomed him arownd.

x x x i

And comming to that Fishers wandring bote,
That went at will withouten card or sayle,
He therein saw that yrkesome sight, which smote
Deepe indignation and compassion frayle
Into his hart attonce: streight did he hayle
The greedy villein from his hoped pray,
Of which he now did very litle fayle,
And with his staffe, that drives his heard astray,
Him bett so sore, that life and sence did much dismay.

x x x i i

The whiles the pitteous Lady up did ryse,
Ruffled and fowly raid with filthy soyle,
And blubbred face with teares of her faire eyes:
Her heart nigh broken was with weary toyle,
To save her selfe from that outrageous spoyle;
But when she looked up, to weet what wight
Had her from so infamous fact assoyld,
For shame, but more for feare of his grim sight,
Downe in her lap she hid her face, and lowdly shright.

x x x i i i

Her selfe not saved yet from daunger dredd
She thought, but chaung'd from one to other feare:
Like as a fearefull partridge, that is fledd
From the sharpe hauke which her attached neare,
And fals to ground to seeke for succor theare,
Whereas the hungry Spaniells she does spye
With greedy jawes her ready for to teare:
In such distresse and sad perplexity
Was Florimell, when Proteus she did see her by.

xxxi, 2   card: chart   xxxi, 5   hayle: drag

XXXIV

But he endevored with speaches milde
Her to recomfort, and accourage bold,
Bidding her feare no more her foeman vilde,
Nor doubt himselfe; and who he was her told:
Yet all that could not from affright her hold,
Ne to recomfort her at all prevayld;
For her faint hart was with the frosen cold
Benumbd so inly, that her wits nigh fayld,
And all her sences with abashment quite were quayld.

XXXV

Her up betwixt his rugged hands he reard,
And with his frory lips full softly kist,
Whiles the cold ysickles from his rough beard
Dropped adowne upon her yvory brest:
Yet he him selfe so busily addrest,
That her out of astonishment he wrought;
And out of that same fishers filthy nest
Removing her, into his charet brought,
And there with many gentle termes her faire besought.

XXXVI

But that old leachour, which with bold assault
That beautie durst presume to violate,
He cast to punish for his hainous fault:
Then tooke he him, yet trembling sith of late,
And tyde behind his charet, to aggrate
The virgin whom he had abusde so sore;
So drag'd him through the waves in scornfull state,
And after cast him up upon the shore;
But Florimell with him unto his bowre he bore.

XXXVII

His bowre is in the bottom of the maine,
Under a mightie rocke, gainst which doe rave
The roring billowes in their proud disdaine,
That with the angry working of the wave
Therein is eaten out an hollow cave,
That seemes rough Masons hand with engines keene
Had long while laboured it to engrave:
There was his wonne; ne living wight was seene
Save one old Nymph, hight Panopè, to keepe it cleane.

XXXVIII

Thither he brought the sory Florimell,
And entertained her the best he might,
And Panopè her entertaind eke well,
As an immortall mote a mortall wight,
To winne her liking unto his delight:
With flattering wordes he sweetly wooed her,
And offered faire guiftes t' allure her sight;
But she both offers and the offerer
Despysde, and all the fawning of the flatterer.

XXXIX

Dayly he tempted her with this or that,
And never suffred her to be at rest;
But evermore she him refused flat,
And all his fained kindnes did detest,
So firmely she had sealed up her brest.
Sometimes he boasted that a God he hight,
But she a mortall creature loved best:
Then he would make him selfe a mortall wight;
But then she said she lov'd none, but a Faery knight.

XL

Then like a Faerie knight him selfe he drest,
For every shape on him he could endew;
Then like a king he was to her exprest,
And offred kingdoms unto her in vew,
To be his Leman and his Lady trew:
But when all this he nothing saw prevaile,
With harder meanes he cast her to subdew,
And with sharpe threates her often did assayle;
So thinking for to make her stubborne corage quayle.

XLI

To dreadfull shapes he did him selfe transforme;
Now like a Gyaunt; now like to a feend;
Then like a Centaure; then like to a storme
Raging within the waves: thereby he weend
Her will to win unto his wished eend;
But when with feare, nor favour, nor with all
He els could doe, he saw him selfe esteemd,
Downe in a Dongeon deepe he let her fall,
And threatned there to make her his eternall thrall.

X L I I

Eternall thraldome was to her more liefe
Then losse of chastitie, or chaunge of love:
Dye had she rather in tormenting griefe
Then any should of falsenesse her reprove,
Or loosenes, that she lightly did remove.
Most vertuous virgin! glory be thy meed,
And crowne of heavenly prayse with Saintes above,
Where most sweet hymmes of this thy famous deed
Are still emongst them song, that far my rymes exceed.

X L I I I

Fit song of Angels caroled to bee!
But yet whatso my feeble Muse can frame
Shal be t' advance thy goodly chastitee
And to enroll thy memorable name
In th' heart of every honourable Dame,
That they thy vertuous deedes may imitate,
And be partakers of thy endlesse fame.
Yt yrkes me leave thee in this wofull state,
To tell of Satyrane where I him left of late.

X L I V

Who having ended with that Squyre of Dames
A long discourse of his adventures vayne,
The which himselfe then Ladies more defames,
And finding not th' Hyena to be slayne,
With that same Squyre retourned back againe
To his first way. And, as they forward went,
They spyde a knight fayre pricking on the playne,
As if he were on some adventure bent,
And in his port appeared manly hardiment.

X L V

Sir Satyrane him towardes did addresse,
To weet what wight he was, and what his quest,
And, comming nigh, eftsoones he gan to gesse,
Both by the burning hart which on his brest
He bare, and by the colours in his crest,
That Paridell it was. Tho to him yode,
And him saluting as beseemed best,
Gan first inquire of tydinges farre abrode,
And afterwardes on what adventure now he rode.

XLIV, 3   then: than

XLVI

Who thereto answering said: 'The tydinges bad,
Which now in Faery court all men doe tell,
Which turned hath great mirth to mourning sad,
Is the late ruine of proud Marinell,
And suddein parture of faire Florimell
To find him forth: and after her are gone
All the brave knightes that doen in armes excell
To savegard her ywandred all alone:
Emongst the rest my lott (unworthy) is to be one.'

XLVII

'Ah! gentle knight,' (said then Sir Satyrane)
'Thy labour all is lost, I greatly dread,
That hast a thanklesse service on thee ta'ne,
And offrest sacrifice unto the dead:
For dead, I surely doubt, thou maist aread
Henceforth for ever Florimell to bee;
That all the noble knights of Maydenhead,
Which her ador'd, may sore repent with mee,
And all faire Ladies may for ever sory bee.'

XLVIII

Which wordes when Paridell had heard, his hew
Gan greatly chaunge and seemd dismaid to bee;
Then said: 'Fayre Sir, how may I weene it trew,
That ye doe tell in such uncerteintee?
Or speake ye of report, or did ye see
Just cause of dread, that makes ye doubt so sore?
For, perdie, elles how mote it ever bee,
That ever hand should dare for to engore
Her noble blood? The hevens such crueltie abhore.'

XLIX

'These eyes did see that they will ever rew
T' have seene,' (quoth he) 'when as a monstrous beast
The Palfrey whereon she did travell slew,
And of his bowels made his bloody feast:
Which speaking token sheweth at the least
Her certeine losse, if not her sure decay:
Besides, that more suspicion encreast,
I found her golden girdle cast astray,
Distaynd with durt and blood, as relique of the pray.'

XLVII, 5   doubt: fear

L

'Ay me!' (said Paridell) 'the signes be sadd;
And, but God turne the same to good sooth-say,
That Ladies safetie is sore to be dradd.
Yet will I not forsake my forward way,
Till triall doe more certeine truth bewray.'
'Faire Sir,' (quoth he) 'well may it you succeed!
Ne long shall Satyrane behind you stay,
But to the rest, which in this Quest proceed,
My labour adde, and be partaker of their speed.'

L I

'Ye noble knights,' (said then the Squyre of Dames)
'Well may yee speede in so praiseworthy payne!
But sith the Sunne now ginnes to slake his beames
In deawy vapours of the westerne mayne,
And lose the teme out of his weary wayne,
Mote not mislike you also to abate
Your zealous hast, till morrow next againe
Both light of heven and strength of men relate:
Which if ye please, to yonder castle turne your gate.'

L I I

That counsell pleased well: so all yfere
Forth marched to a Castle them before;
Where soone arryving they restrained were
Of ready entraunce, which ought evermore
To errant knights be commune: wondrous sore
Thereat displeasd they were, till that young Squyre
Gan them informe the cause, why that same dore
Was shut to all which lodging did desyre:
The which to let you weet will further time requyre.

CANTO IX.

Malbecco will no straunge knights host,
For peevish gealosy.
Paridell giusts with Britomart:
Both shew their auncestry.

I

REDOUBTED KNIGHTS, and honorable Dames,
To whom I levell all my labours end,
Right sore I feare, least with unworthie blames

This odious argument my rymes should shend,
Or ought your goodly patience offend,
Whiles of a wanton Lady I doe write,
Which with her loose incontinence doth blend
The shyning glory of your soveraine light;
And knighthood fowle defaced by a faithlesse knight.

I I

But never let th' ensample of the bad
Offend the good; for good, by paragone
Of evill, may more notably be rad,
As white seemes fayrer macht with blacke attone;
Ne all are shamed by the fault of one:
For lo! in heven, whereas all goodnes is,
Emongst the Angels, a whole legione
Of wicked Sprightes did fall from happy blis;
What wonder then if one, of women all, did mis?

I I I

Then listen, Lordings, if ye list to weet
The cause why Satyrane and Paridell
Mote not be entertaynd, as seemed meet,
Into that Castle, (as that Squyre does tell.)
'Therein a cancred crabbed Carle does dwell,
That has no skill of Court nor courtesie,
Ne cares what men say of him, ill or well;
For all his dayes he drownes in privitie,
Yet has full large to live and spend at libertie.

I V

'But all his minde is set on mucky pelfe,
To hoord up heapes of evill gotten masse.
For which he others wrongs, and wreckes himselfe:
Yet is he lincked to a lovely lasse,
Whose beauty doth her bounty far surpasse;
The which to him both far unequall yeares,
And also far unlike conditions has;
For she does joy to play emongst her peares,
And to be free from hard restraynt and gealous feares.

V

'But he is old, and withered like hay,
Unfit faire Ladies service to supply:
The privie guilt whereof makes him alway
Suspect her truth, and keepe continuall spy

Upon her with his other blincked eye,
Ne suffreth he resort of living wight
Approch to her, ne keepe her company.
But in close bowre her mewes from all mens sight,
Depriv'd of kindly joy and naturall delight.

V I

'Malbecco he, and Hellenore she hight;
Unfitly yokt together in one teeme.
That is the cause why never any knight
Is suffred here to enter, but he seeme
Such as no doubt of him he neede misdeeme.'
Thereat Sir Satyrane gan smyle, and say;
'Extremely mad the man I surely deeme,
That weenes with watch and hard restraynt to stay
A womans will, which is disposd to go astray.

V I I

'In vaine he feares that which he cannot shonne;
For who wotes not, that womans subtiltyes
Can guylen Argus, when she list misdonne?
It is not yron bandes, nor hundred eyes,
Nor brasen walls, nor many wakefull spyes,
That can withhold her wilfull wandring feet;
But fast goodwill, with gentle courtesyes,
And timely service to her pleasures meet,
May her perhaps containe, that else would algates fleet.'

V I I I

'Then is he not more mad,' (sayd Paridell)
'That hath himselfe unto such service sold,
In dolefull thraldome all his dayes to dwell?
For sure a foole I doe him firmely hold,
That loves his fetters, thought they were of gold.
But why doe wee devise of others ill,
Whyles thus we suffer this same dotard old
To keepe us out in scorne, of his owne will,
And rather do not ransack all, and him selfe kill?'

I X

'Nay, let us first' (sayd Satyrane) 'entreat
The man by gentle meanes to let us in,
And afterwardes affray with cruell threat,
Ere that we to efforce it doe begin:
Then, if all fayle, we will by force it win.

v, 5   blincked: blinking

And eke reward the wretch for his mesprise,
As may be worthy of his haynous sin.'
That counsell pleasd: then Paridell did rise
And to the Castle gate approcht in quiet wise.

x

Whereat soft knocking entrance he desyrd.
The good man selfe, which then the Porter playd,
Him answered, that all were now retyrd
Unto their rest, and all the keyes convayd
Unto their maister, who in bed was layd,
That none him durst awake out of his dreme;
And therefore them of patience gently prayd.
Then Paridell began to chaunge his theme,
And threatned him with force and punishment extreme:

x i

But all in vaine, for nought mote him relent.
And now so long before the wicket fast
They wayted, that the night was forward spent,
And the faire welkin fowly overcast
Gan blowen up a bitter stormy blast,
With showre and hayle so horrible and dred,
That this faire many were compeld at last
To fly for succour to a little shed,
The which beside the gate for swyne was ordered.

x i i

It fortuned, soone after they were gone,
Another knight, whom tempest thither brought,
Came to that Castle, and with earnest mone,
Like as the rest, late entrance deare besought:
But, like so as the rest, he prayd for nought;
For flatly he of entrance was refusd.
Sorely thereat he was displeased, and thought
How to avenge himselfe so sore abusd,
And evermore the Carle of courtesie accusd.

x i i i

But, to avoyde th' intollerable stowre,
He was compeld to seeke some refuge neare,
And to that shed, to shrowd him from the showre,
He came, which full of guests he found whyleare,
So as he was not let to enter there:
Whereat he gan to wex exceeding wroth,

XI, 7 many: company

And swore that he would lodge with them yfere,
Or them dislodge, all were they liefe or loth;
And so defyde them each, and so defyde them both.

X I V

Both were full loth to leave that needfull tent,
And both full loth in darkenesse to debate;
Yet both full liefe him lodging to have lent,
And both full liefe his boasting to abate:
But chiefely Paridell his hart did grate
To heare him threaten so despightfully,
As if he did a dogge in kenell rate
That durst not barke; and rather had he dy
Then, when he was defyde, in coward corner ly.

X V

Tho hastily remounting to his steed
He forth issew'd: like as a boystrous winde,
Which in th' earthes hollow caves hath long ben hid
And shut up fast within her prisons blind,
Makes the huge element, against her kinde,
To move and tremble as it were aghast,
Untill that it an issew forth may finde:
Then forth it breakes, and with his furious blast
Confounds both land and seas, and skyes doth overcast.

X V I

Their steel-hed speares they strongly coucht, and met
Together with impetuous rage and forse,
That with the terrour of their fierce affret
They rudely drove to ground both man and horse,
That each awhile lay like a sencelesse corse.
But Paridell sore brused with the blow
Could not arise the counterchaunge to scorse,
Till that young Squyre him reared from below;
Then drew he his bright sword, and gan about him throw.

X V I I

But Satyrane forth stepping did them stay,
And with faire treaty pacifide their yre.
Then, when they were accorded from the fray,
Against that Castles Lord they gan conspire,
To heape on him dew vengeaunce for his hire.
They beene agreed; and to the gates they goe
To burn the same with unquenchable fire,

XVI, 3   affret: encounter   XVI, 7   scorse: exchange

And that uncurteous Carle, their commune foe,
To doe fowle death to die, or wrap in grievous woe.

X V I I I

Malbecco, seeing them resolvd indeed
To flame the gates, and hearing them to call
For fire in earnest, ran with fearfull speed,
And to them calling from the castle wall,
Besought them humbly him to beare withall,
As ignorant of servants bad abuse
And slacke attendaunce unto straungers call.
The knights were willing all things to excuse,
Though nought belev'd, and entraunce late did not refuse.

X I X

They beene ybrought into a comely bowre,
And servd of all things that mote needfull bee;
Yet secretly their hoste did on them lowre,
And welcomde more for feare then charitee;
But they dissembled what they did not see,
And welcomed themselves. Each gan undight
Their garments wett, and weary armour free,
To dry them selves by Vulcanes flaming light,
And eke their lately bruzed parts to bring in plight.

X X

And eke that straunger knight emonst the rest
Was for like need enforst to disaray:
Tho, whenas vailed was her lofty crest,
Her golden locks, that were in trammells gay
Upbounden, did them selves adowne display
And raught unto her heeles; like sunny beames,
That in a cloud their light did long time stay,
Their vapour vaded, shewe their golden gleames,
And through the persant aire shoote forth their azure streames.

X X I

Shee also dofte her heavy haberjeon,
Which the faire feature of her limbs did hyde;
And her well-plighted frock, which she did won
To tucke about her short when she did ryde,
Shee low let fall, that flowd from her lanck syde
Downe to her foot with carelesse modestee.
Then of them all she plainly was espyde

xvii, 9   wrap: envelop
xx, 8   vaded: vanished

xxi, 5   lanck: slender

To be a woman-wight, unwist to bee,
The fairest woman-wight that ever eie did see.

XXII

Like as Bellona (being late returnd
From slaughter of the Giaunts conquered;
Where proud Encelade, whose wide nosethrils burnd
With breathed flames, like to a furnace redd,
Transfixed with her speare downe tombled dedd
From top of Hemus by him heaped hye;)
Hath loosd her helmet from her lofty hedd,
And her Gorgonian shield gins to untye
From her lefte arme, to rest in glorious victorye.

XXIII

Which whenas they beheld, they smitten were
With great amazement of so wondrous sight;
And each on other, and they all on her,
Stood gazing, as if suddein great affright
Had them surprizd. At last, avizing right
Her goodly personage and glorious hew,
Which they so much mistooke, they tooke delight
In their first error, and yett still anew
With wonder of her beauty fed their hongry vew.

XXIV

Yet note their hongry vew be satisfide,
But seeing still the more desir'd to see,
And ever firmely fixed did abide
In contemplation of divinitee:
But most they mervaild at her chevalree
And noble prowesse, which they had approv'd,
That much they faynd to know who she mote bee;
Yet none of all them her thereof amov'd;
Yet every one her likte, and every one her lov'd.

XXV

And Paridell, though partly discontent
With his late fall and fowle indignity,
Yet was soone wonne his malice to relent,
Through gratious regard of her faire eye,
And knightly worth which he too late did try,
Yet tried did adore. Supper was dight;
Then they Malbecco prayd of courtesy,
That of his lady they might have the sight
And company at meat, to doe them more delight.

XXVI

But he, to shifte their curious request,
Gan causen why she could not come in place;
Her crased helth, her late recourse to rest,
And humid evening ill for sicke folkes cace;
But none of those excuses could take place,
Ne would they eate till she in presence came.
Shee came in presence with right comely grace,
And fairely them saluted, as became,
And shewd her selfe in all a gentle courteous Dame.

XXVII

They sate to meat; and Satyrane his chaunce
Was her before, and Paridell beside;
But he him selfe sate looking still askaunce
Gainst Britomart, and ever closely eide
Sir Satyrane, that glaunces might not glide:
But his blinde eie, that sided Paridell,
All his demeasnure from his sight did hide:
On her faire face so did he feede his fill,
And sent close messages of love to her at will.

XXVIII

And ever and anone, when none was ware,
With speaking lookes, that close embassage bore,
He rov'd at her, and told his secret care
For all that art he learned had of yore;
Ne was she ignoraunt of that leud lore,
But in his eye his meaning wisely redd,
And with the like him aunswerd evermore.
Shee sent at him one fyrie dart, whose hedd
Empoisned was with privy lust and gealous dredd.

XXIX

He from that deadly throw made no defence,
But to the wound his weake heart opened wyde:
The wicked engine through false influence
Past through his eies, and secretly did glyde
Into his heart, which it did sorely gryde.
But nothing new to him was that same paine,
Ne paine at all; for he so ofte had tryde
The powre thereof, and lov'd so oft in vaine,
That thing of course he counted love to entertaine

xxvi, 2   causen: explain   xxix, 5   gryde: pierce
xxvi, 3   crased: impaired

x x x

Thenceforth to her he sought to intimate
His inward griefe, by meanes to him well knowne:
Now Bacchus fruit out of the silver plate
He on the table dasht, as overthrowne,
Or of the fruitfull liquor overflowne;
And by the dauncing bubbles did divine,
Or therein write to lett his love be showne;
Which well she redd out of the learned line:
A sacrament prophane in mistery of wine.

x x x i

And, when so of his hand the pledge she raught,
The guilty cup she fained to mistake,
And in her lap did shed her idle draught,
Shewing desire her inward flame to slake.
By such close signes they secret way did make
Unto their wils, and one eies watch escape:
Two eies him needeth, for to watch and wake,
Who lovers will deceive. Thus was the ape,
By their faire handling, put into Malbeccoes cape.

x x x i i

Now, when of meats and drinks they had their fill,
Purpose was moved by that gentle Dame
Unto those knights adventurous, to tell
Of deeds of armes which unto them became,
And every one his kindred and his name.
Then Paridell, in whom a kindly pride
Of gratious speach and skill his words to frame
Abounded, being glad of so fitte tide
Him to commend to her, thus spake, of al well eide.

x x x i i i

'Troy, that art now nought but an idle name,
And in thine ashes buried low dost lie,
Though whilome far much greater then thy fame,
Before that angry Gods and cruell skie
Upon thee heapt a direfull destinie;
What boots it boast thy glorious descent,
And fetch from heven thy great genealogie,
Sith all thy worthie prayses being blent
Their ofspring hath embaste, and later glory shent?

xxxii, 6   kindly: natural   xxxiii, 9   shent: disgraced
xxxiii, 8   blent: stained

XXXIV

'Most famous Worthy of the world, by whome
That warre was kindled which did Troy inflame,
And stately towres of Ilion whilome
Brought unto balefull ruine, was by name
Sir Paris far renowmd through noble fame;
Who, through great prowesse and bold hardinesse,
From Lacedæmon fetcht the fayrest Dame
That ever Greece did boast, or knight possesse,
Whom Venus to him gave for meed of worthinesse;

XXXV

'Fayre Helene, flowre of beautie excellent,
And girlond of the mighty Conquerours,
That madest many Ladies deare lament
The heavie losse of their brave Paramours,
Which they far off beheld from Trojan toures,
And saw the fieldes of faire Scamander strowne
With carcases of noble warrioures
Whose fruitlesse lives were under furrow sowne.
And Xanthus sandy bankes with blood all overflowne.

XXXVI

'From him my linage I derive aright.
Who long before the ten yeares siege of Troy,
Whiles yet on Ida he a shepeheard hight,
On faire Oenone got a lovely boy,
Whom, for remembrance of her passed joy,
She, of his Father, Parius did name;
Who, after Greekes did Priams realme destroy,
Gathered the Trojan reliques sav'd from flame,
And with them sayling thence to th' isle of Paros came.

XXXVII

'That was by him cald Paros, which before
Hight Nausa: there he many yeares did raine,
And built Nausicle by the Pontick shore;
The which he dying lefte next in remaine
To Paridas his sonne,
From whom I Paridell by kin descend:
But, for faire ladies love and glories gaine,
My native soile have lefte, my dayes to spend
In seewing deeds of armes, my lives and labors end.'

XXXVII, 9   seewing: following

XXXVIII

Whenas the noble Britomart heard tell
Of Trojan warres and Priams citie sackt,
The ruefull story of Sir Paridell,
She was empassiond at that piteous act,
With zelous envy of Greekes cruell fact
Against that nation, from whose race of old
She heard that she was lineally extract;
For noble Britons sprong from Trojans bold,
And Troynovant was built of old Troyes ashes cold.

XXXIX

Then, sighing soft awhile, at last she thus:
'O lamentable fall of famous towne!
Which raignd so many yeares victorious,
And of all Asie bore the soveraine crowne,
In one sad night consumd and throwen downe.
What stony hart, that heares thy haplesse fate,
Is not empierst with deepe compassiowne,
And makes ensample of mans wretched state,
That floures so fresh at morne, and fades at evening late?

XL

'Behold, Sir, how your pitifull complaint
Hath fownd another partner of your payne;
For nothing may impresse so deare constraint
As countries cause, and commune foes disdayne.
But if it should not grieve you backe agayne
To turne your course, I would to heare desyre
What to Aeneas fell; sith that men sayne
He was not in the cities wofull fyre
Consum'd, but did him selfe to safety retyre.'

XLI

'Anchyses sonne, begott of Venus fayre,'
Said he, 'out of the flames for safegard fled,
And with a remnant did to sea repayre;
Where he through fatall errour long was led
Full many yeares, and weetlesse wandered
From shore to shore emongst the Lybick sandes,
Ere rest he fownd. Much there he suffered,
And many perilles past in forreine landes,
To save his people sad from victours vengefull handes.

xxxviii, 5   fact: deed   xli, 4   errour: wandering, mistake
xli, 4   fatall: fated

XLII

'At last in Latium he did arryve,
Where he with cruell warre was entertaind
Of th' inland folke, which sought him backe to drive,
Till he with old Latinus was constraind
To contract wedlock, (so the fates ordaind)
Wedlocke contract in blood, and eke in blood
Accomplished, that many deare complaind:
The rivall slaine, the victour, through the flood
Escaped hardly, hardly praisd his wedlock good.

XLIII

'Yet, after all, he victour did survive,
And with Latinus did the kingdom part;
But after, when both nations gan to strive
Into their names the title to convart,
His sonne Iülus did from thence depart
With all the warlike youth of Trojans bloud,
And in long Alba plast his throne apart;
Where faire it florished and long time stoud,
Till Romulus, renewing it, to Rome remoud.'

XLIV

'There; there,' (said Britomart) 'afresh appeard
The glory of the later world to spring,
And Troy againe out of her dust was reard
To sitt in second seat of soveraine king
Of all the world, under her governing.
But a third kingdom yet is to arise
Out of the Trojans scattered ofspring,
That in all glory and great enterprise,
Both first and second Troy shall dare to equalise.

XLV

'It Troynovant is hight, that with the waves
Of wealthy Thamis washed is along,
Upon whose stubborne neck, (whereat he raves
With roring rage, and sore him selfe does throng)
That all men feare to tempt his billowes strong,
She fastned hath her foot; which stands so hy,
That it a wonder of the world is song
In forreine landes; and all which passen by,
Beholding it from farre, doe thinke it threates the skye.

XLV, 2   wealthy: thriving

XLVI

'The Trojan Brute did first that citie fownd,
And Hygate made the meare thereof by West,
And Overt gate by North: that is the bownd
Toward the land; two rivers bownd the rest.
So huge a scope at first him seemed best,
To be the compasse of his kingdomes seat:
So huge a mind could not in lesser rest,
Ne in small meares containe his glory great,
That Albion had conquered first by warlike feat.'

XLVII

'Ah! fairest Lady knight,' (said Paridell)
'Pardon, I pray, my heedlesse oversight,
Who had forgot that whylome I heard tell
From aged Mnemon; for my wits beene light.
Indeed he said, (if I remember right)
That of the antique Trojan stocke there grew
Another plant, that raught to wondrous hight,
And far abroad his mightie braunches threw
Into the utmost Angle of the world he knew.

XLVIII

'For that same Brute, whom much he did advaunce
In all his speach, was Sylvius his sonne,
Whom having slain through luckles arrowes glaunce,
He fled for feare of that he had misdonne,
Or els for shame, so fowle reproch to shonne,
And with him ledd to sea an youthly trayne;
Where wearie wandring they long time did wonne,
And many fortunes prov'd in th' Ocean mayne,
And great adventures found, that now were long to sayne.

XLIX

'At last by fatall course they driven were
Into an Island spatious and brode,
The furthest North that did to them appeare:
Which, after rest, they, seeking farre abrode,
Found it the fittest soyle for their abode,
Fruitfull of all thinges fitt for living foode,
But wholy waste and void of peoples trode,
Save an huge nation of the Geaunts broode
That fed on living flesh, and dronck mens vitall blood.

XLVI, 8   meares: boundaries

L

'Whom he, through wearie wars and labours long,
Subdewd with losse of many Britons bold:
In which the great Goemagot of strong
Corineus, and Coulin of Debon old,
Were overthrowne and laide on th' earth full cold,
Which quaked under their so hideous masse;
A famous history to bee enrold
In everlasting moniments of brasse,
That all the antique Worthies merits far did passe.

L I

'His worke great Troynovant, his worke is eke
Faire Lincolne, both renowmed far away;
That who from East to West will endlong seeke,
Cannot two fairer Cities find this day,
Except Cleopolis: so heard I say
Old Mnemon. Therefore, Sir, I greet you well
Your countrey kin; and you entyrely pray
Of pardon for the strife, which late befell
Betwixt us both unknowne.' So ended Paridell.

L I I

But all the while that he these speeches spent,
Upon his lips hong faire Dame Hellenore
With vigilant regard and dew attent,
Fashioning worldes of fancies evermore
In her fraile witt, that now her quite forlore:
The whiles unwares away her wondring eye
And greedy eares her weake hart from her bore;
Which he perceiving, ever privily,
In speaking many false belgardes at her let fly.

L I I I

So long these knights discoursed diversly
Of straunge affaires, and noble hardiment,
Which they had past with mickle jeopardy.
That now the humid night was farforth spent,
And hevenly lampes were halfendeale ybrent:
Which th' old man seeing wel, who too long thought
Every discourse, and every argument,
Which by the houres he measured, besought
Them go to rest. So all unto their bowres were brought.

LII, 9   belgardes: loving looks

CANTO X.

Paridell rapeth Hellenore:
  Malbecco her poursewes;
Fynds emongst Satyres, whence with him
  To turne she doth refuse.

I

THE MORROW NEXT, SO SOONE as Phœbus Lamp
Bewrayed had the world with early light,
And fresh Aurora had the shady damp
Out of the goodly heven amoved quight,
Faire Britomart and that same Faery knight
Uprose, forth on their journey for to wend:
But Paridell complaynd, that his late fight
With Britomart so sore did him offend,
That ryde he could not, till his hurts he did amend.

I I

So foorth they far'd; but he behind them stayd,
Maulgre his host, who grudged grievously
To house a guest that would be needes obayd,
And of his owne him lefte not liberty:
Might wanting measure moveth surquedry.
Two things he feared, but the third was death;
That fiers youngmans unruly maystery;
His money, which he lov'd as living breath;
And his faire wife, whom honest long he kept uneath.

I I I

But patience perforce, he must abie
What fortune and his fate on him will lay;
Fond is the feare that findes no remedie:
Yet warily he watcheth every way,
By which he feareth evill happen may;
So th' evill thinkes by watching to prevent:
Ne doth he suffer her, nor night nor day,
Out of his sight her selfe once to absent:
So doth he punish her, and eke him selfe torment.

I V

But Paridell kept better watch then hee,
A fit occasion for his turne to finde.
False love! why do men say thou canst not see,

II, 9 uneath: with difficulty   III, 3 Fond: foolish

And in their foolish fancy feigne thee blinde,
That with thy charmes the sharpest sight doest binde,
And to thy will abuse? Thou walkest free,
And seest every secret of the minde;
Thou seest all, yet none at all sees thee:
All that is by the working of thy Deitee.

v

So perfect in that art was Paridell,
That he Malbeccoes halfen eye did wyle;
His halfen eye he wiled wondrous well,
And Hellenors both eyes did eke beguyle,
Both eyes and hart attonce, during the whyle
That he there sojourned his woundes to heale;
That Cupid selfe, it seeing, close did smyle
To weet how he her love away did steale,
And bad that none their joyous treason should reveale.

v i

The learned lover lost no time nor tyde
That least avantage mote to him afford,
Yet bore so faire a sayle, that none espyde
His secret drift, till he her layd abord.
When so in open place and commune bord
He fortun'd her to meet, with commune speach
He courted her; yet bayted every word,
That his ungentle hoste n'ote him appeach
Of vile ungentlenesse, or hospitages breach.

v i i

But when apart (if ever her apart)
He found, then his false engins fast he plyde,
And all the sleights unbosomd in his hart:
He sigh'd, he sobd, he swownd, he perdy dyde,
And cast himselfe on ground her fast besyde:
Tho, when againe he him bethought to live,
He wept, and wayld, and false laments belyde,
Saying, but if she Mercie would him give,
That he mote algates dye, yet did his death forgive.

v i i i

And otherwhyles with amorous delights
And pleasing toyes he would her entertaine;
Now singing sweetly to surprize her sprights,
Now making layes of love and lovers paine,

VI, 7 bayted: abated

Bransles, Ballads, virelayes, and verses vaine;
Oft purposes, oft riddles, he devysd,
And thousands like which flowed in his braine,
With which he fed her fancy, and entysd
To take to his new love, and leave her old despysd.

I X

And every where he might, and everie while,
He did her service dewtifull, and sewd
At hand with humble pride and pleasing guile:
So closely yet, that none but she it vewd,
Who well perceived all, and all indewd.
Thus finely did he his false nets dispred,
With which he many weake harts had subdewd
Of yore, and many had ylike misled:
What wonder then, if she were likewise carried?

x

No fort so fensible, no wals so strong,
But that continuall battery will rive,
Or daily siege, through dispurvayaunce long
And lacke of reskewes, will to parley drive;
And Peece, that unto parley eare will give,
Will shortly yield it selfe, and will be made
The vassall of the victors will bylive:
That stratageme had oftentimes assayd
This crafty Paramoure, and now it plaine display'd:

x I

For through his traines he her intrapped hath,
That she her love and hart hath wholy sold
To him, without regard of gaine or scath,
Or care of credite, or of husband old,
Whom she hath vow'd to dub a fayre Cucquold.
Nought wants but time and place, which shortly shee
Devized hath, and to her lover told.
It pleased well: So well they both agree:
So readie rype to ill ill wemens counsels bee!

x I I

Darke was the Evening, fit for lovers stealth,
When chaunst Malbecco busie be elsewhere,
She to his closet went, where all his wealth
Lay hid; thereof she countlesse summes did reare,

ix, 5　indewd: took in　　　　x, 7　bylive: quickly
x, 1　fensible: fortified

The which she meant away with her to beare;
The rest she fyr'd, for sport, or for despight:
As Hellene, when she saw aloft appeare
The Trojane flames and reach to hevens hight,
Did clap her hands, and joyed at that dolefull sight.

XIII

This second Helene, fayre Dame Hellenore,
The whiles her husband ran with sory haste
To quench the flames which she had tyn'd before,
Laught at his foolish labour spent in waste,
And ran into her lovers armes right fast;
Where streight embraced she to him did cry
And call alowd for helpe, ere helpe were past;
For lo! that Guest did beare her forcibly,
And meant to ravish her, that rather had to dy.

XIV

The wretched man hearing her call for ayd,
And ready seeing him with her to fly,
In his disquiet mind was much dismayd:
But when againe he backeward cast his eye,
And saw the wicked fire so furiously
Consume his hart, and scorch his Idoles face,
He was therewith distressed diversely,
Ne wist he how to turne, nor to what place:
Was never wretched man in such a wofull cace.

XV

Ay when to him she cryde, to her he turnd,
And left the fire; love money overcame:
But, when he marked how his money burnd,
He left his wife; money did love disclame:
Both was he loth to loose his loved Dame,
And loth to leave his liefest pelfe behinde;
Yet, sith he n'ote save both, he sav'd that same
Which was the dearest to his dounghill minde,
The God of his desire, the joy of misers blinde.

XVI

Thus whilest all things in troublous uprore were,
And all men busie to suppresse the flame,
The loving couple neede no reskew feare,
But leasure had and liberty to frame
Their purpost flight, free from all mens reclame;

XIII, 3   tyn'd: kindled

And Night, the patronesse of love-stealth fayre,
Gave them safe conduct, till to end they came.
So beene they gone yfere, a wanton payre
Of lovers loosely knit, where list them to repayre.

X V I I

Soone as the cruell flames yslaked were,
Malbecco, seeing how his losse did lye,
Out of the flames which he had quencht whylere,
Into huge waves of griefe and gealosye
Full deepe emplonged was, and drowned nye
Twixt inward doole and felonous despight:
He rav'd, he wept, he stampt, he lowd did cry,
And all the passions that in man may light
Did him attonce oppresse, and vex his caytive spright.

X V I I I

Long thus he chawd the cud of inward griefe,
And did consume his gall with anguish sore:
Still when he mused on his late mischiefe,
Then still the smart thereof increased more,
And seemd more grievous then it was before.
At last when sorrow he saw booted nought,
Ne griefe might not his love to him restore,
He gan devise how her he reskew mought:
Ten thousand wayes he cast in his confused thought.

X I X

At last resolving, like a Pilgrim pore,
To search her forth where so she might be fond,
And bearing with him treasure in close store,
The rest he leaves in ground: So takes in hond
To seeke her endlong both by sea and lond.
Long he her sought, he sought her far and nere,
And every where that he mote understond
Of knights and ladies any meetings were;
And of each one he mett he tidings did inquere.

X X

But all in vaine: his woman was too wise
Ever to come into his clouch againe,
And hee too simple ever to surprise
The jolly Paridell, for all his paine.
One day, as hee forpassed by the plaine
With weary pace, he far away espide
A couple, seeming well to be his twaine,

Which hoved close under a forest side,
As if they lay in wait, or els them selves did hide.

X X I

Well weened hee that those the same mote bee,
And as he better did their shape avize,
Him seemed more their maner did agree;
For th' one was armed all in warlike wize,
Whom to be Paridell he did devize;
And th' other, al yclad in garments light
Discolourd like to womanish disguise,
He did resemble to his lady bright;
And ever his faint hart much earned at the sight;

X X I I

And ever faine he towards them would goe,
But yet durst not for dread approchen nie,
But stood aloofe, unweeting what to doe;
Till that prickt forth with loves extremity
That is the father of fowle gealosy,
He closely nearer crept the truth to weet:
But, as he nigher drew, he easily
Might scerne that it was not his sweetest sweet,
Ne yet her Belamour, the partner of his sheet:

X X I I I

But it was scornefull Braggadochio,
That with his servant Trompart hoverd there,
Sith late he fled from his too earnest foe:
Whom such whenas Malbecco spyed clere,
He turned backe, and would have fled arere,
Till Trompart, ronning hastely, him did stay,
And bad before his soveraine Lord appere.
That was him loth, yet durst he not gainesay,
And comming him before low louted on the lay.

X X I V

The Boaster at him sternely bent his browe,
As if he could have kild him with his looke,
That to the ground him meekely made to bowe,
And awfull terror deepe into him strooke,
That every member of his body quooke.
Said he, 'Thou man of nought, what doest thou here
Unfitly furnisht with thy bag and booke,

xxiii, 9   lay: lea

Where I expected one with shield and spere
To prove some deeds of armes upon an equall pere?'

x x v

The wretched man at his imperious speach
Was all abasht, and low prostrating said:
'Good sir, let not my rudenes be no breach
Unto your patience, ne be ill ypaid;
For I unwares this way by fortune straid,
A silly Pilgrim driven to distresse,
That seeke a Lady'—There he suddein staid,
And did the rest with grievous sighes suppresse,
While teares stood in his eies, few drops of bitternesse.

x x v i

'What Lady, man?' (said Trompart) 'take good hart,
And tell thy griefe, if any hidden lye:
Was never better time to shew thy smart
Then now that noble succor is thee by,
That is the whole worlds commune remedy.'
That chearful word his weak heart much did cheare,
And with vaine hope his spirits faint supply,
That bold he sayd; 'O most redoubted Pere!
Vouchsafe with mild regard a wretches cace to heare.'

x x v i i

Then sighing sore, 'It is not long,' (saide hee)
'Sith I enjoyd the gentlest Dame alive;
Of whom a knight, no knight at all perdee,
But shame of all that doe for honor strive,
By treacherous deceipt did me deprive:
Through open outrage he her bore away,
And with fowle force unto his will did drive;
Which al good knights, that armes doe bear this day,
Are bownd for to revenge, and punish if they may.

x x v i i i

'And you, most noble Lord, that can and dare
Redresse the wrong of miserable wight,
Cannot employ your most victorious speare
In better quarell then defence of right,
And for a Lady gainst a faithlesse knight:
So shall your glory bee advaunced much,
And all faire Ladies magnify your might,

xxv, 4   ypaid: pleased

And eke my selfe, albee I simple such,
Your worthy paine shall wel reward with guerdon rich.'

x x i x

With that out of his bouget forth he drew
Great store of treasure, therewith him to tempt;
But he on it lookt scornefully askew,
As much disdeigning to be so misdempt,
Or a war-monger to be basely nempt;
And sayd; 'Thy offers base I greatly loth,
And eke thy words uncourteous and unkempt:
I tread in dust thee and thy money both,
That, were it not for shame'—So turned from him wroth.

x x x

But Trompart, that his maistres humor knew
In lofty looks to hide an humble minde,
Was inly tickled with that golden vew.
And in his eare him rownded close behinde:
Yet stoupt he not, but lay still in the winde,
Waiting advauntage on the pray to sease,
Till Trompart, lowly to the grownd inclinde,
Besought him his great corage to appease,
And pardon simple man that rash did him displease.

x x x i

Big looking like a doughty Doucepere,
At last he thus; 'Thou clod of vilest clay,
I pardon yield, and with thy rudenes beare;
But weete henceforth, that all that golden pray,
And all that els the vaine world vaunten may,
I loath as doung, ne deeme my dew reward:
Fame is my meed, and glory vertues pay:
But minds of mortall men are muchell mard
And mov'd amisse with massy mucks unmeet regard.

x x x i i

'And more: I graunt to thy great misery
Gratious respect; thy wife shall backe be sent:
And that vile knight, who ever that he bee,
Which hath thy lady reft and knighthood shent,
By Sanglamort my sword, whose deadly dent
The blood hath of so many thousands shedd,

XXIX, 5   war-monger: mercenary   XXXI, 1   Doucepere: one of Charle-
XXIX, 5   nempt: named   magne's twelve peers

I sweare, ere long shall dearely it repent;
Ne he twixt heven and earth shall hide his hedd,
But soone he shal be fownd, and shortly doen be dedd.'

XXXIII

The foolish man thereat woxe wondrous blith,
As if the word so spoken were halfe donne,
And humbly thanked him a thousand sith
That had from death to life him newly wonne.
Tho forth the Boaster marching brave begonne
His stolen steed to thunder furiously,
As if he heaven and hell would over-ronne,
And all the world confound with cruelty;
That much Malbecco joyed in his jollity.

XXXIV

Thus long they three together traveiled,
Through many a wood and many an uncouth way,
To seeke his wife that was far wandered:
But those two sought nought but the present pray,
To weete, the treasure which he did bewray,
On which their eies and harts were wholly sett,
With purpose how they might it best betray;
For, sith the howre that first he did them lett
The same behold, therewith their keene desires were whett.

XXXV

It fortuned, as they together far'd,
They spide where Paridell came pricking fast
Upon the plaine; the which him selfe prepar'd
To guist with that brave straunger knight a cast,
As on adventure by the way he past.
Alone he rode without his Paragone;
For, having filcht her bells, her up he cast
To the wide world, and lett her fly alone:
He nould be clogd. So had he served many one.

XXXVI

The gentle Lady, loose at random lefte,
The greene-wood long did walke, and wander wide
At wilde adventure, like a forlorne wefte;
Till on a day the Satyres her espide
Straying alone withouten groome or guide:
Her up they tooke, and with them home her ledd,
With them as housewife ever to abide,

XXXVI, 3   wefte: waif

To milk their gotes, and make them cheese and bredd;
And every one as commune good her handeled,

XXXVII

That shortly she Malbecco has forgott,
And eke Sir Paridell, all were he deare;
Who from her went to seeke another lott,
And now by fortune was arrived here,
Where those two guilers with Malbecco were.
Soone as the old man saw Sir Paridell,
He fainted, and was almost dead with feare,
Ne word he had to speake his griefe to tell,
But to him louted low, and greeted goodly well;

XXXVIII

And, after, asked him for Hellenore:
'I take no keepe of her,' (sayd Paridell)
'She wonneth in the forrest there before.'
So forth he rode as his adventure fell;
The whiles the Boaster from his loftie sell
Faynd to alight, something amisse to mend;
But the fresh Swayne would not his leasure dwell,
But went his way: whom when he passed kend,
He up remounted light, and after faind to wend.

XXXIX

'Perdy, nay,' (said Malbecco) 'shall ye not;
But let him passe as lightly as he came:
For litle good of him is to be got,
And mickle perill to bee put to shame.
But let us goe to seeke my dearest Dame,
Whom he hath left in yonder forest wyld;
For of her safety in great doubt I ame,
Least salvage beastes her person have despoyld:
Then all the world is lost, and we in vaine have toyld.'

XL

They all agree, and forward them addresse:
'Ah! but,' (said crafty Trompart) 'weete ye well,
That yonder in that wastefull wildernesse
Huge monsters haunt, and many dangers dwell;
Dragons, and Minotaures, and feendes of hell,
And many wilde woodmen which robbe and rend
All traveilers: therefore advise ye well
Before ye enterprise that way to wend:
One may his journey bring too soone to evill end.'

X L I

Malbecco stopt in great astonishment,
And with pale eyes fast fixed on the rest,
Their counsell crav'd in daunger imminent.
Said Trompart; 'You, that are the most opprest
With burdein of great treasure, I thinke best
Here for to stay in safetie behynd:
My Lord and I will search the wide forest.'
That counsell pleased not Malbeccoes mynd,
For he was much afraid him selfe alone to fynd.

X L I I

'Then is it best,' (said he) 'that ye doe leave
Your treasure here in some security,
Either fast closed in some hollow greave,
Or buried in the ground from jeopardy,
Till we returne againe in safety:
As for us two, least doubt of us ye have,
Hence farre away we will blyndfolded ly,
Ne privy bee unto your treasures grave.'
It pleased; so he did. Then they march forward brave.

X L I I I

Now, when amid the thickest woodes they were,
They heard a noyse of many bagpipes shrill,
And shrieking Hububs them approching nere,
Which all the forest did with horrour fill.
That dreadfull sound the bosters hart did thrill
With such amazment, that in hast he fledd,
Ne ever looked back for good or ill;
And after him eke fearefull Trompart spedd:
The old man could not fly, but fell to ground half dedd.

X L I V

Yet afterwardes, close creeping as he might,
He in a bush did hyde his fearefull hedd.
The jolly Satyres, full of fresh delight,
Came dauncing forth, and with them nimbly ledd
Faire Helenore with girlonds all bespredd,
Whom their May-lady they had newly made:
She, proude of that new honour which they redd,
And of their lovely fellowship full glade,
Daunst lively, and her face did with a Lawrell shade.

X L V

The silly man that in the thickett lay
Saw all this goodly sport, and grieved sore;
Yet durst he not against it doe or say,
But did his hart with bitter thoughts engore,
To see th' unkindnesse of his Hellenore.
All day they daunced with great lusty-hedd,
And with their horned feet the greene gras wore,
The whiles their Gotes upon the brouzes fedd,
Till drouping Phœbus gan to hyde his golden hedd.

X L V I

Tho up they gan their mery pypes to trusse,
And all their goodly heardes did gather rownd;
But every Satyre first did give a busse
To Hellenore; so busses did abound.
Now gan the humid vapour shed the grownd
With perly deaw, and th' Earthes gloomy shade
Did dim the brightnesse of the welkin rownd,
That every bird and beast awarned made
To shrowd themselves, whiles sleepe their sences did invade.

X L V I I

Which when Malbecco saw, out of the bush
Upon his handes and feete he crept full light,
And like a Gote emongst the Gotes did rush;
That, through the helpe of his faire hornes on hight,
And misty dampe of misconceyving night,
And eke through likenesse of his gotish beard,
He did the better counterfeite aright:
So home he marcht emongst the horned heard,
That none of all the Satyres him espyde or heard.

X L V I I I

At night, when all they went to sleepe, he vewd
Whereas his lovely wife emongst them lay,
Embraced of a Satyre rough and rude,
Who all the night did minde his joyous play:
Nine times he heard him come and aloft ere day,
That all his hart with gealosy did swell;
But yet that nights ensample did bewray
That not for nought his wife them loved so well,
When one so oft a night did ring his matins bell.

XLV, 8   brouzes: twigs   XLVI, 3   busse: kiss

X L I X

So closely as he could he to them crept,
When wearie of their sport to sleepe they fell,
And to his wife, that now full soundly slept,
He whispered in her eare, and did her tell
That it was he which by her side did dwell;
And therefore prayd her wake to heare him plaine.
As one out of a dreame not waked well
She turnd her, and returned backe againe;
Yet her for to awake he did the more constraine.

L

At last with irkesom trouble she abrayd;
And then perceiving that it was indeed
Her old Malbecco, which did her upbrayd
With loosenesse of her love and loathly deed,
She was astonisht with exceeding dreed,
And would have wakt the Satyre by her syde;
But he her prayd, for mercy or for meed,
To save his life, ne let him be descryde,
But hearken to his lore, and all his counsell hyde.

L I

Tho gan he her perswade to leave that lewd
And loathsom life, of God and man abhord,
And home returne, where all should be renewd
With perfect peace and bandes of fresh accord,
And she receivd againe to bed and bord,
As if no trespas ever had beene donne:
But she it all refused at one word,
And by no meanes would to his will be wonne,
But chose emongst the jolly Satyres still to wonne.

L I I

He wood her till day-spring he espyde,
But all in vaine; and then turnd to the heard,
Who butted him with hornes on every syde,
And trode downe in the durt, where his hore beard
Was fowly dight, and he of death afeard.
Early, before the heavens fairest light
Out of the ruddy East was fully reard,
The heardes out of their foldes were loosed quight,
And he emongst the rest crept forth in sory plight.

L, 1   abrayd: awoke

L I I I

So soone as he the Prison-dore did pas,
He ran as fast as both his feet could beare,
And never looked who behind him was,
Ne scarsely who before: like as a Beare,
That creeping close amongst the hives to reare
An hony-combe, the wakefull dogs espy,
And him assayling sore his carkas teare,
That hardly he with life away does fly,
Ne stayes, till safe him selfe he see from jeopardy.

L I V

Ne stayd he, till he came unto the place
Where late his treasure he entombed had;
Where when he found it not, (for Trompart bace
Had it purloyned for his maister bad)
With extreme fury he became quite mad,
And ran away, ran with him selfe away;
That who so straungely had him seene bestadd,
With upstart haire and staring eyes dismay,
From Limbo lake him late escaped sure would say.

L V

High over hilles and over dales he fledd,
As if the wind him on his winges had borne;
Ne banck nor bush could stay him, when he spedd
His nimble feet, as treading still on thorne:
Griefe, and despight, and gealosy, and scorne,
Did all the way him follow hard behynd;
And he himselfe himselfe loath'd so forlorne,
So shamefully forlorne of womankynd,
That, as a Snake, still lurked in his wounded mynd.

L V I

Still fled he forward, looking backward still;
Ne stayd his fight nor fearefull agony,
Till that he came unto a rocky hill
Over the sea suspended dreadfully,
That living creature it would terrify
To looke adowne, or upward to the hight:
From thence he threw him selfe despiteously,
All desperate of his fore-damned spright,
That seemd no help for him was left in living sight.

L V I I

But through long anguish and selfe-murdring thought,
He was so wasted and forpined quight,
That all his substance was consum'd to nought,
And nothing left but like an aery Spright,
That on the rockes he fell so flit and light,
Thet he thereby receiv'd no hurt at all;
But chaunced on a craggy cliff to light,
Whence he with crooked clawes so long did crall,
That at the last he found a cave with entrance small.

L V I I I

Into the same he creepes, and thenceforth there
Resolv'd to build his balefull mansion
In drery darkenes and continuall feare
Of that rocks fall, which ever and anon
Threates with huge ruine him to fall upon,
That he dare never sleepe, but that one eye
Still ope he keepes for that occasion;
Ne ever rests he in tranquillity,
The roring billowes beat his bowre so boystrously.

L I X

Ne ever is he wont on ought to feed
But todes and frogs, his pasture poysonous,
Which in his cold complexion doe breed
A filthy blood, or humour rancorous,
Matter of doubt and dread suspitious,
That doth with curelesse care consume the hart,
Corrupts the stomacke with gall vitious,
Cros-cuts the liver with internall smart,
And doth transfixe the soule with deathes eternall dart.

L X

Yet can he never dye, but dying lives,
And doth himselfe with sorrow new sustaine,
That death and life attonce unto him gives,
And painefull pleasure turnes to pleasing paine.
There dwels he ever, miserable swaine,
Hatefull both to him selfe and every wight;
Where he, through privy griefe and horrour vaine,
Is woxen so deform'd that he has quight
Forgot he was a man, and Gelosy is hight.

CANTO XI.

Britomart chaceth Ollyphant;
Findes Scudamour distrest:
Assayes the house of Busyrane,
Where loves spoyles are exprest.

I

O HATEFULL HELLISH SNAKE! what furie furst
Brought thee from balefull house of Proserpine,
Where in her bosome she thee long had nurst,
And fostred up with bitter milke of tine,
Fowle Gealosy! that turnest love divine
To joylesse dread and mak'st the loving hart
With hatefull thoughts to languish and to pine,
And feed it selfe with selfe-consuming smart?
Of all the passions in the mind thou vilest art!

I I

O! let him far be banished away,
And in his stead let Love for ever dwell;
Sweete Love, that doth his golden wings embay
In blessed Nectar and pure Pleasures well,
Untroubled of vile feare or bitter fell.
And ye, faire Ladies, that your kingdomes make
In th' harts of men, them governe wisely well.
And of faire Britomart ensample take,
That was as trew in love as Turtle to her make.

I I I

Who with Sir Satyrane, as earst ye red,
Forth ryding from Malbeccoes hostlesse hous,
Far off aspyde a young man, the which fled
From an huge Geaunt, that with hideous
And hatefull outrage long him chaced thus;
It was that Ollyphant, the brother deare
Of that Argantè vile and vitious,
From whom the Squyre of Dames was reft whylere;
This all as bad as she, and worse, if worse ought were.

I V

For as the sister did in feminine
And filthy lust exceede all womankinde,

I, 4   tine: affliction
II, 5   fell: rancor

II, 9   Turtle: dove

So he surpassed his sex masculine,
In beastly use, all that I ever finde:
Whom when as Britomart beheld behinde
The fearfull boy so greedily poursew,
She was emmoved in her noble minde,
T' employ her puissaunce to his reskew,
And pricked fiercely forward where she did him vew.

v

Ne was Sir Satyrane her far behinde,
But with like fiercenesse did ensew the chace.
Whom when the Gyaunt saw, he soone resinde
His former suit, and from them fled apace:
They after both, and boldly bad him bace,
And each did strive the other to outgoe;
But he them both outran a wondrous space,
For he was long, and swift as any Roe,
And now made better speed t' escape his feared foe,

v i

It was not Satyrane, whom he did feare,
But Britomart the flowre of chastity;
For he the powre of chaste hands might not beare,
But alwayes did their dread encounter fly:
And now so fast his feet he did apply,
That he has gotten to a forrest neare,
Where he is shrowded in security.
The wood they enter and search everie where,
They searched diversely, so both divided were.

v i i

Fayre Britomart so long him followed,
That she at last came to a fountaine sheare,
By which there lay a knight all wallowed
Upon the grassy ground, and by him neare
His haberjeon, his helmet, and his speare:
A little off his shield was rudely throwne,
On which the winged boy in colours cleare
Depeincted was, full easie to be knowne,
And he thereby, where ever it in field was showne.

v i i i

His face upon the grownd did groveling ly,
As if he had beene slombring in the shade;
That the brave Mayd would not for courtesy

v, 5   bad him bace: challenged him

Out of his quiet slomber him abrade,
Nor seeme too suddeinly him to invade.
Still as she stood, she heard with grievous throb
Him grone, as if his hart were peeces made,
And with most painfull pangs to sigh and sob,
That pitty did the Virgins hart of patience rob.

I X

At last forth breaking into bitter plaintes
He sayd; 'O soverayne Lord! that sit'st on hye
And raignst in blis emongst thy blessed Saintes,
How suffrest thou such shamefull cruelty
So long unwreaked of thine enimy?
Or hast thou, Lord, of good mens cause no heed?
Or doth thy justice sleepe and silent ly?
What booteth then the good and righteous deed,
If goodnesse find no grace, nor righteousnes no meed?

x

'If good find grace, and righteousnes reward,
Why then is Amoret in caytive band,
Sith that more bounteous creature never far'd
On foot upon the face of living land?
Or if that hevenly justice may withstand
The wrongfull outrage of unrighteous men,
Why then is Busirane with wicked hand
Suffred, these seven monethes day, in secret den
My Lady and my love so cruelly to pen!

X I

'My Lady and my love is cruelly pend
In dolefull darkenes from the vew of day,
Whilest deadly torments doe her chast brest rend,
And the sharpe steele doth rive her hart in tway,
All for she Scudamore will not denay.
Yet thou, vile man, vile Scudamore, art sound,
Ne canst her ayde, ne caust her foe dismay;
Unworthy wretch to tread upon the ground,
For whom so faire a Lady feeles so sore a wound!'

X I I

There an huge heape of singults did oppresse
His strugling soule, and swelling throbs empeach
His foltring toung with pangs of drerinesse,
Choking the remnant of his plaintife speach,

x, 2   caytive: captive   XII, I   singults: sighs

As if his dayes were come to their last reach:
Which when she heard, and saw the ghastly fit
Threatning into his life to make a breach,
Both with great ruth and terrour she was smit,
Fearing least from her cage the wearie soule would flit.

X I I I

Tho stouping downe she him amoved light;
Who, therewith somewhat starting, up gan looke,
And seeing him behind a stranger knight,
Whereas no living creature he mistooke,
With great indignaunce he that sight forsooke,
And, downe againe himselfe disdainfully
Abjecting, th' earth with his faire forhead strooke:
Which the bold Virgin seeing gan apply
Fit medcine to his griefe, and spake thus courtesly:—

X I V

'Ah gentle knight! whose deepe conceived griefe
Well seemes t' exceede the powre of patience,
Yet, if that hevenly grace some goode reliefe
You send, submit you to high providence;
And ever in your noble hart prepense,
That all the sorrow in the world is lesse
Then vertues might and values confidence;
For who nill bide the burden of distresse,
Must not here thinke to live; for life is wretchednesse.

X V

'Therefore, faire Sir, doe comfort to you take,
And freely read what wicked felon so
Hath outrag'd you, and thrald your gentle make.
Perhaps this hand may helpe to ease your woe,
And wreake your sorrow on your cruell foe;
At least it faire endevour will apply.'
Those feeling words so neare the quicke did goe,
That up his head he reared easily,
And, leaning on his elbowe, these few words lett fly.

X V I

'What boots it plaine that cannot be redrest,
And sow vaine sorrow in a fruitlesse eare,
Sith powre of hand, nor skill of learned brest,
Ne worldly price, cannot redeeme my deare
Out of her thraldome and continuall feare:

XIV, 5 prepense: consider

For he, the tyrant, which her hath in ward
By strong enchauntments and blacke Magicke leare,
Hath in a dungeon deepe her close embard,
And many dreadfull feends hath pointed to her gard.

XVII

'There he tormenteth her most terribly
And day and night afflicts with mortall paine,
Because to yield him love she doth deny,
Once to me yold, not to be yolde againe:
But yet by torture he would her constraine
Love to conceive in her disdainfull brest;
Till so she doe, she must in doole remaine,
Ne may by living meanes be thence relest:
What boots it then to plaine and cannot be redrest?'

XVIII

With this sad hersall of his heavy stresse
The warlike Damzell was empassiond sore,
And sayd; 'Sir knight, your cause is nothing lesse
Then is your sorrow certes, if not more;
For nothing so much pitty doth implore
As gentle Ladyes helplesse misery:
But yet, if please ye listen to my lore,
I will, with proofe of last extremity,
Deliver her fro thence, or with her for you dy.'

XIX

'Ah! gentlest knight alive,' (sayd Scudamore)
'What huge heroicke magnanimity
Dwells in thy bounteous brest! what couldst thou more,
If shee were thine, and thou as now am I?
O! spare thy happy daies, and them apply
To better boot; but let me die that ought:
More is more losse; one is enough to dy.'
'Life is not lost,' (said she) 'for which is bought
Endlesse renowm, that, more then death, is to be sought.'

XX

Thus shee at length persuaded him to rise,
And with her wend to see what new successe
Mote him befall upon new enterprise.
His armes, which he had vowed to disprofesse,
She gathered up and did about him dresse,
And his forwandred steed unto him gott:

XVI, 7   leare: lore

So forth they both yfere make their progresse,
And march not past the mountenaunce of a shott,
Till they arriv'd whereas their purpose they did plott.

X X I

There they dismounting drew their weapons bold,
And stoutly came unto the Castle gate,
Whereas no gate they found them to withhold,
Nor ward to waite at morne and evening late;
But in the Porch, that did them sore amate,
A flaming fire, ymixt with smouldry smoke
And stinking sulphure, that with griesly hate
And dreadfull horror did all entraunce choke,
Enforced them their forward footing to revoke.

X X I I

Greatly thereat was Britomart dismayd,
Ne in that stownd wist how her selfe to beare;
For daunger vaine it were to have assayd
That cruell element, which all things feare,
Ne none can suffer to approchen neare:
And, turning backe to Scudamour, thus sayd:
'What monstrous enmity provoke we heare?
Foolhardy as th' Earthes children, the which made
Batteill against the Gods, so we a God invade.

X X I I I

'Daunger without discretion to attempt
Inglorious and beastlike is: therefore, Sir knight,
Aread what course of you is safest dempt,
And how we with our foe may come to fight.'
'This is' (quoth he) 'the dolorous despight,
Which earst to you I playnd: for neither may
This fire be quencht by any witt or might,
Ne yet by any meanes remov'd away;
So mighty be th' enchauntments which the same do stay.

X X I V

'What is there ells but cease these fruitlesse paines,
And leave me to my former languishing?
Faire Amorett must dwell in wicked chaines,
And Scudamore here die with sorrowing.'
'Perdy not so,' (saide shee) 'for shameful thing
Yt were t' abandon noble chevisaunce
For shewe of perill, without venturing:

xxiv, 6   chevisaunce: enterprise

Rather let try extremities of chaunce,
Then enterprised praise for dread to disavaunce.'

X X V

Therewith, resolv'd to prove her utmost might,
Her ample shield she threw before her face,
And her swords point directing forward right
Assayld the flame; the which eftesoones gave place,
And did it selfe divide with equall space,
That through she passed, as a thonder bolt
Perceth the yielding ayre, and doth displace
The soring clouds into sad showres ymolt;
So to her yold the flames, and did their force revolt.

X X V I

Whom whenas Scudamour saw past the fire
Safe and untoucht, he likewise gan assay
With greedy will and envious desire,
And bad the stubborne flames to yield him way:
But cruell Mulciber would not obay
His threatfull pride, but did the more augment
His mighty rage, and with imperious sway
Him forst, (maulgre) his fercenes to relent,
And backe retire, all scorcht and pittifully brent.

X X V I I

With huge impatience he inly swelt,
More for great sorrow that he could not pas
Then for the burning torment which he felt;
That with fell woodnes he effierced was,
And wilfully him throwing on the gras
Did beat and bounse his head and brest ful sore:
The whiles the Championesse now entred has
The utmost rowme, and past the foremost dore;
The utmost rowme abounding with all precious store:

X X V I I I

For round about the walls yclothed were
With goodly arras of great majesty,
Woven with gold and silke, so close and nere
That the rich metall lurked privily,
As faining to be hidd from envious eye;
Yet here, and there, and every where, unwares
It shewd it selfe and shone unwillingly;

XXVII, 4 woodnes: madness   XXVII, 4 effierced: maddened

Like a discolourd Snake, whose hidden snares
Through the greene gras his long bright burnisht back de-
    clares.

x x i x

And in those Tapets weren fashioned
Many faire pourtraicts, and many a faire feate;
And all of love, and al of lusty-hed,
As seemed by their semblaunt, did entreat:
And eke all Cupids warres they did repeate,
And cruell battailes, which he whilome fought
Gainst all the Gods to make his empire great;
Besides the huge massacres, which he wrought
On mighty kings and kesars into thraldome brought.

x x x

Therein was writt how often thondring Jove
Had felt the point of his hart-percing dart,
And, leaving heavens kingdome, here did rove
In straunge disguize, to slake his scalding smart;
Now, like a Ram, faire Helle to pervart,
Now, like a Bull, Europa to withdraw:
Ah! how the fearefull Ladies tender hart
Did lively seeme to tremble, when she saw
The huge seas under her t' obay her servaunts law.

x x x i

Soone after that, into a golden showre
Him selfe he chaung'd, faire Danaë to vew;
And through the roofe of her strong brasen towre
Did raine into her lap an hony dew;
The whiles her foolish garde, that litle knew
Of such deceipt, kept th' yron dore fast bard,
And watcht that none should enter nor issew:
Vaine was the watch, and bootlesse all the ward,
Whenas the God to golden hew him selfe transfard.

x x x i i

Then was he turnd into a snowy Swan,
To win faire Leda to his lovely trade:
O wondrous skill! and sweet wit of the man,
That her in daffadillies sleeping made
From scorching heat her daintie limbes to shade;
Whiles the proud Bird, ruffing his fethers wyde
And brushing his faire brest, did her invade:

She slept; yet twixt her eielids closely spyde
How towards her he rusht, and smiled at his pryde.

XXXIII

Then shewd it how the Thebane Semelee,
Deceivd of gealous Juno, did require
To see him in his soverayne majestee
Armd with his thunderbolts and lightning fire,
Whens dearely she with death bought her desire.
But faire Alcmena better match did make,
Joying his love in likenes more entire:
Three nights in one, they say, that for her sake
He then did put, her pleasures lenger to partake.

XXXIV

Twise was he seene in soaring Eagles shape,
And with wide winges to beat the buxome ayre:
Once, when he with Asterie did scape;
Againe, when as the Trojane boy so fayre
He snatcht from Ida hill, and with him bare:
Wondrous delight it was there to behould
How the rude Shepheards after him did stare,
Trembling through feare least down he fallen should,
And often to him calling to take surer hould:

XXXV

In Satyres shape Antiopa he snatcht;
And like a fire, when he Aegin' assayd:
A shepeheard, when Mnemosyne he catcht;
And like a Serpent to the Thracian mayd.
Whyles thus on earth great Jove these pageaunts playd,
The winged boy did thrust into his throne,
And scoffing thus unto his mother sayd:
'Lo! now the hevens obey to me alone,
And take me for their Jove, whiles Jove to earth is gone.'

XXXVI

And thou, faire Phœbus, in thy colours bright
Wast there enwoven, and the sad distresse
In which that boy thee plonged, for despight
That thou bewray'dst his mothers wantonnesse,
When she with Mars was meynt in joyfulnesse;
Forthy he thrild thee with a leaden dart
To love faire Daphne, which thee loved lesse;

XXXVI, 5 meynt: mingled

Lesse she thee lov'd then was thy just desart,
Yet was thy love her death, and her death was thy smart.

XXXVII

So lovedst thou the lusty Hyacinct;
So lovedst thou the faire Coronis deare;
Yet both are of thy haplesse hand extinct,
Yet both in flowres doe live, and love thee beare,
The one a Paunce, the other a sweet-breare:
For griefe whereof, ye mote have lively seene
The God himselfe rending his golden heare,
And breaking quite his garlond ever greene,
With other signes of sorrow and impatient teene.

XXXVIII

Both for those two, and for his owne deare sonne,
The sonne of Climene, he did repent;
Who, bold to guide the charet of the Sunne,
Himselfe in thousand peeces fondly rent,
And all the world with flashing fire brent;
So like, that all the walles did seeme to flame:
Yet cruell Cupid, not herewith content,
Forst him eftsoones to follow other game,
And love a Shephards daughter for his dearest Dame.

XXXIX

He loved Isse for his dearest Dame,
And for her sake her cattell fedd awhile,
And for her sake a cowheard vile became
The servant of Admetus, cowheard vile,
Whiles that from heaven he suffered exile.
Long were to tell each other lovely fitt;
Now, like a Lyon hunting after spoile;
Now, like a stag; now, like a faulcon flit:
All which in that faire arras was most lively writ.

X L

Next unto him was Neptune pictured,
In his divine resemblance wondrous lyke:
His face was rugged, and his hoarie hed
Dropped with brackish deaw: his threeforkt Pyke
He stearnly shooke, and therewith fierce did stryke
The raging billowes, that on every syde

xxxvii, 9 teene: grief xxxix, 6 fitt: part of the song (or story)

They trembling stood, and made a long broad dyke,
That his swift charet might have passage wyde
Which foure great Hippodames did draw in temewise tyde.

X L I

His seahorses did seeme to snort amayne,
And from their nosethrilles blow the brynie streame,
That made the sparckling waves to smoke agayne,
And flame with gold; but the white fomy creame
Did shine with silver, and shoot forth his beame.
The God himselfe did pensive seeme and sad,
And hong adowne his head as he did dreame;
For privy love his brest empierced had,
Ne ought but deare Bisaltis ay could make him glad.

X L I I

He loved eke Iphimedia deare,
And Aeolus faire daughter, Arnè hight,
For whom he turnd him selfe into a Steare,
And fedd on fodder to beguile her sight.
Also to win Deucalions daughter bright,
He turnd him selfe into a Dolphin fayre;
And like a winged horse he tooke his flight
To snaky-locke Medusa to repayre,
On whom he got faire Pegasus that flitteth in the ayre.

X L I I I

Next Saturne was, (but who would ever weene
That sullein Saturne ever weend to love?
Yet love is sullein, and Saturnlike seene,
As he did for Erigone it prove)
That to a Centaure did him selfe transmove.
So proov'd it eke that gratious God of wine,
When for to compasse Philliras hard love,
He turned himselfe into a fruitfull vine,
And into her faire bosome made his grapes decline.

X L I V

Long were to tell the amorous assayes,
And gentle pangues, with which he maked meeke
The mightie Mars, to learne his wanton playes;
How oft for Venus, and how often eek
For many other Nymphes, he sore did shreek, ·
With womanish teares, and with unwarlike smarts,
Privily moystening his horrid cheeke:

There was he painted full of burning dartes,
And many wide woundes launched through his inner partes.

X L V

Ne did he spare (so cruell was the Elfe)
His owne deare mother, (ah! why should he so?)
Ne did he spare sometime to pricke himselfe,
That he might taste the sweet consuming woe,
Which he had wrought to many others moe.
But, to declare the mournfull Tragedyes
And spoiles wherewith he all the ground did strow,
More eath to number with how many eyes
High heven beholdes sad lovers nightly theeveryes.

X L V I

Kings, Queenes, Lords, Ladies, knights, and Damsels gent,
Were heap'd together with the vulgar sort,
And mingled with the raskall rablement,
Without respect of person or of port,
To shew Dan Cupids powre and great effort:
And round about a border was entrayld
Of broken bowes and arrowes shivered short;
And a long bloody river through them rayld,
So lively and so like that living sence it fayld.

X L V I I

And at the upper end of that faire rowne
There was an Altar built of pretious stone
Of passing valew and of great renowme,
On which there stood an Image all alone
Of massy gold, which with his owne light shone:
And winges it had with sondry colours dight,
More sondry colours then the proud Pavone
Beares in his boasted fan, or Iris bright,
When her discolourd bow she spreds through hevens hight.

X L V I I I

Blyndfold he was; and in his cruell fist
A mortall bow and arrowes keene did hold,
With which he shot at randon, when him list,
Some headed with sad lead, some with pure gold;
(Ah man! beware how thou those dartes behold.)
A wounded Dragon under him did ly,
Whose hideous tayle his lefte foot did enfold,

xlvi, 5   Dan: master, sir   xlvii, 9   discolourd: many-colored
xlvi, 8   rayld: flowed

And with a shaft was shot through either eye,
That no man forth might draw, ne no man remedye.

X L I X

And underneath his feet was written thus,
Unto the Victor of the Gods this bee:
And all the people in that ample hous
Did to that image bowe their humble knee,
And oft committed fowle Idolatree.
That wondrous sight faire Britomart amazd,
Ne seeing could her wonder satisfie,
But ever more and more upon it gazd,
The whiles the passing brightnes her fraile sences dazd.

L

Tho, as she backward cast her busie eye
To search each secrete of that goodly sted,
Over the dore thus written she did spye,
Bee bold: she oft and oft it over-red,
Yet could not find what sence it figured:
But what so were therein or writ or ment,
She was no whit thereby discouraged
From prosecuting of her first intent,
But forward with bold steps into the next roome went.

L I

Much fayrer then the former was that roome,
And richlier by many partes arayd;
For not with arras made in painefull loome,
But with pure gold it all was overlayd,
Wrought with wilde Antickes, which their follies playd
In the rich metall as they living were.
A thousand monstrous formes therein were made,
Such as false love doth oft upon him weare;
For love in thousand monstrous formes doth oft appeare.

L I I

And all about the glistring walles were hong
With warlike spoiles and with victorious prayes
Of mightie Conquerours and Captaines strong,
Which were whilome captived in their dayes
To cruell love, and wrought their owne decayes.
Their swerds and speres were broke, and hauberques rent,
And their proud girlonds of tryumphant bayes
Troden in dust with fury insolent,
To shew the victors might and mercilesse intent.

L I I I

The warlike Mayd, beholding earnestly
The goodly ordinaunce of this rich Place,
Did greatly wonder; ne could satisfy
Her greedy eyes with gazing a long space:
But more she mervaild that no footings trace
Nor wight appeard, but wastefull emptinesse
And solemne silence over all that place:
Straunge thing it seem'd, that none was to possesse
So rich purveyaunce, ne them keepe with carefulnesse.

L I V

And, as she lookt about, she did behold
How over that same dore was likewise writ,
Be bolde, be bolde, and every where, *Be bold;*
That much she muz'd, yet could not construe it
By any ridling skill, or commune wit.
At last she spyde at that rowmes upper end
Another yron dore, on which was writ,
Be not too bold; whereto though she did bend
Her earnest minde, yet wist not what it might intend.

L V

Thus she there wayted untill eventyde,
Yet living creature none she saw appeare,
And now sad shadowes gan the world to hyde
From mortall vew, and wrap in darkenes dreare;
Yet nould she d'off her weary armes, for feare
Of secret daunger, ne let sleepe oppresse
Her heavy eyes with natures burdein deare,
But drew her selfe aside in sickernesse,
And her wel-pointed wepons did about her dresse.

CANTO XII.

The maske of Cupid, and th' enchant-
ed Chamber are displayd;
Whence Britomart redeemes faire A-
moret through charmes decayd.

I

THo, whenas chearelesse Night ycovered had
Fayre heaven with an universall clowd,
That every wight dismayd with darkenes sad

In silence and in sleepe themselves did shrowd,
She heard a shrilling Trompet sound alowd,
Signe of nigh battaill, or got victory:
Nought therewith daunted was her courage prowd,
But rather stird to cruell enmity,
Expecting ever when some foe she might descry.

I I

With that an hideous storme of winde arose,
With dreadfull thunder and lightning atwixt,
And an earthquake, as if it streight would lose
The worlds foundations from his centre fixt:
A direfull stench of smoke and sulphure mixt
Ensewd, whose noyaunce fild the fearefull sted
From the fourth howre of night untill the sixt;
Yet the bold Britonesse was nought ydred,
Though much emmov'd, but stedfast still persevered.

I I I

All suddeinly a stormy whirlwind blew
Throughout the house, that clapped every dore,
With which that yron wicket open flew,
As it with mighty levers had bene tore;
And forth yssewd, as on the readie flore
Of some Theatre, a grave personage
That in his hand a braunch of laurell bore,
With comely haveour and count'nance sage,
Yclad in costly garments fit for tragicke Stage.

I V

Proceeding to the midst he stil did stand,
As if in minde he somewhat had to say;
And to the vulgare beckning with his hand,
In signe of silence, as to heare a play,
By lively actions he gan bewray
Some argument of matter passioned:
Which doen, he backe retyred soft away,
And, passing by, his name discovered,
Ease, on his robe in golden letters cyphered.

V

The noble Mayd still standing all this vewd,
And merveild at his straunge intendiment,
With that a joyous fellowship issewd
Of Minstrales making goodly meriment,

II, 6   sted: place

With wanton Bardes, and Rymers impudent.
All which together song full chearefully
A lay of loves delight with sweet concent:
After whom marcht a jolly company,
In manner of a maske, enranged orderly.

V I

The whiles a most delitious harmony
In full straunge notes was sweetly heard to sound,
That the rare sweetnesse of the melody
The feeble sences wholy did confound,
And the frayle soule in deepe delight nigh drownd:
And, when it ceast, shrill trompets lowd did bray,
That their report did far away rebound;
And, when they ceast, it gan againe to play,
The whiles the maskers marched forth in trim aray.

V I I

The first was Fansy, like a lovely Boy
Of rare aspect, and beautie without peare,
Matchable ether to that ympe of Troy,
Whom Jove did love and chose his cup to beare;
Or that same daintie lad, which was so deare
To great Alcides, that, when as he dyde,
He wailed womanlike with many a teare,
And every wood and every valley wyde
He filld with Hylas name; the Nymphes eke Hylas cryde.

V I I I

His garment nether was of silke nor say,
But paynted plumes in goodly order dight,
Like as the sunburnt Indians do aray
Their tawney bodies in their proudest plight:
As those same plumes so seemd he vaine and light,
That by his gate might easily appeare;
For still he far'd as dauncing in delight,
And in his hand a windy fan did beare,
That in the ydle ayre he mov'd still here and theare.

I X

And him beside marcht amorous Desyre,
Who seemd of ryper yeares then th' other Swayne,
Yet was that other swayne this elders syre,
And gave him being, commune to them twayne:
His garment was disguysed very vayne,

v, 7 concent: harmony

And his embrodered Bonet sat awry:
Twixt both his hands few sparks he close did strayne,
Which still he blew and kindled busily,
That soone they life conceiv'd, and forth in flames did fly.

x

Next after him went Doubt, who was yclad
In a discolour'd cote of straunge disguyse,
That at his backe a brode Capuccio had,
And sleeves dependaunt Albanesè-wyse:
He lookt askew with his mistrustfull eyes,
And nycely trode, as thornes lay in his way,
Or that the flore to shrinke he did avyse;
And on a broken reed he still did stay
His feeble steps, which shrunck when hard thereon he lay.

x i

With him went Daunger, cloth'd in ragged weed
Made of Beares skin, that him more dreadfull made;
Yet his owne face was dreadfull, ne did need
Straunge horrour to deforme his griesly shade:
A net in th' one hand, and a rusty blade
In th' other was; this Mischiefe, that Mishap:
With th' one his foes he threatned to invade,
With th' other he his friends ment to enwrap;
For whom he could not kill he practizd to entrap.

x i i

Next him was Feare, all arm'd from top to toe,
Yet thought himselfe not safe enough thereby,
But feard each shadow moving too or froe;
And, his owne armes when glittering he did spy
Or clashing heard, he fast away did fly,
As ashes pale of hew, and winged heeld,
And evermore on Daunger fixt his eye,
Gainst whom he alwayes bent a brasen shield,
Which his right hand unarmed fearefully did wield.

x i i i

With him went Hope in rancke, a handsome Mayd,
Of chearefull looke and lovely to behold:
In silken samite she was light arayd,
And her fayre lockes were woven up in gold:
She always smyld, and in her hand did hold
An holy-water-sprinckle, dipt in deowe,

x, 6 nycely: delicately   xi, 8 enwrap: involve

With which she sprinckled favours manifold
On whom she list, and did great liking sheowe,
Great liking unto many, but true love to feowe.

X I V

And after them Dissemblaunce and Suspect
Marcht in one rancke, yet an unequall paire;
For she was gentle and of milde aspect,
Courteous to all and seeming debonaire,
Goodly adorned and exceeding faire:
Yet was that all but paynted and pourloynd,
And her bright browes were deckt with borrowed haire;
Her deeds were forged, and her words false coynd,
And alwaies in her hand two clewes of silke she twynd.

X V

But he was fowle, ill favoured, and grim,
Under his eiebrowes looking still askaunce;
And ever, as Dissemblaunce laught on him,
He lowrd on her with daungerous eyeglaunce,
Shewing his nature in his countenaunce:
His rolling eies did never rest in place,
But walkte each where for feare of hid mischaunce,
Holding a lattis still before his face,
Through which he still did peep as forward he did pace.

X V I

Next him went Griefe and Fury, matcht yfere;
Griefe all in sable sorrowfully clad,
Downe hanging his dull head with heavy chere,
Yet inly being more then seeming sad:
A paire of Pincers in his hand he had,
With which he pinched people to the hart,
That from thenceforth a wretched life they ladd,
In wilfull languor and consuming smart,
Dying each day with inward wounds of dolours dart.

X V I I

But Fury was full ill appareiled
In rags, that naked nigh she did appeare,
With ghastly looks and dreadfull drerihed;
And from her backe her garments she did teare,
And from her head ofte rente her snarled heare:
In her right hand a firebrand shee did tosse
About her head, still roming here and there;

As a dismayed Deare in chace embost,
Forgetfull of his safety, hath his right way lost.

X V I I I

After them went Displeasure and Pleasaunce,
He looking lompish and full sullein sad,
And hanging downe his heavy countenaunce;
She chearfull, fresh, and full of joyaunce glad,
As if no sorrow she ne felt ne drad;
That evill matched paire they seemd to bee:
An angry Waspe th' one in a viall had,
Th' other in hers an hony-laden Bee.
Thus marched these six couples forth in faire degree.

X I X

After all these there marcht a most faire Dame,
Led of two grysie Villeins, th' one Despight,
The other cleped Cruelty by name:
She, dolefull Lady, like a dreary Spright
Cald by strong charmes out of eternall night,
Had Deathes owne ymage figurd in her face,
Full of sad signes, fearfull to living sight;
Yet in that horror shewd a seemely grace,
And with her feeble feete did move a comely pace.

X X

Her brest all naked, as nett yvory
Without adorne of gold or silver bright,
Wherewith the Craftesman wonts it beautify,
Of her dew honour was despoyled quight;
And a wide wound therein (O ruefull sight!)
Entrenched deep with knyfe accursed keene,
Yet freshly bleeding forth her fainting spright,
(The worke of cruell hand) was to be seene,
That dyde in sanguine red her skin all snowy cleene.

X X I

At that wide orifice her trembling hart
Was drawne forth, and in silver basin layd,
Quite through transfixed with a deadly dart,
And in her blood yet steeming fresh embayd:
And those two villeins, which her steps upstayd,
When her weake feete could scarcely her sustaine,

xvii, 8   embost: hard pressed   xxi, 4   embayd: bathed
xx, 1   nett: pure

And fading vitall powres gan to fade,
Her forward still with torture did constraine,
And evermore encreased her consuming paine.

X X I I

Next after her, the winged God him selfe
Came riding on a Lion ravenous,
Taught to obay the menage of that Elfe
That man and beast with powre imperious
Subdeweth to his kingdome tyrannous.
His blindfold eies he bad awhile unbinde,
That his proud spoile of that same dolorous
Faire Dame he might behold in perfect kinde;
Which seene, he much rejoyced in his cruell minde.

X X I I I

Of which ful prowd, him selfe up rearing hye
He looked round about with sterne disdayne,
And did survay his goodly company;
And, marshalling the evill-ordered trayne,
With that the darts which his right hand did straine
Full dreadfully he shooke, that all did quake,
And clapt on hye his coulourd winges twaine,
That all his many it affraide did make:
Tho, blinding him againe, his way he forth did take.

X X I V

Behinde him was Reproch, Repentaunce, Shame;
Reproch the first, Shame next, Repent behinde:
Repentaunce feeble, sorrowfull, and lame;
Reproch despightfull, carelesse, and unkinde;
Shame most ill-favour'd, bestiall, and blinde:
Shame lowrd, Repentaunce sighd, Reproch did scould;
Reproch sharpe stings, Repentaunce whips entwinde,
Shame burning brond-yrons in her hand did hold:
All three to each unlike, yet all made in one mould.

X X V

And after them a rude confused rout
Of persons flockt, whose names is hard to read:
Emongst them was sterne Strife, and Anger stout;
Unquiet Care, and fond Unthriftyhead;
Lewd Losse of Time, and Sorrow seeming dead;
Inconstant Chaunge, and false Disloyalty;
Consuming Riotise, and guilty Dread

XXIII, 8   many: company

Of heavenly vengeaunce; faint Infirmity;
Vile Poverty; and, lastly, Death with infamy.

XXVI

There were full many moe like maladies,
Whose names and natures I note readen well;
So many moe, as there be phantasies
In wavering wemens witt, that none can tell,
Or paines in love, or punishments in hell:
All which disguized marcht in masking wise
About the chamber by the Damozell;
And then returned, having marched thrise,
Into the inner rowme from whence they first did rise.

XXVII

So soone as they were in, the dore streightway
Fast locked, driven with that stormy blast
Which first it opened, and bore all away.
Then the brave Maid, which al this while was plast
In secret shade, and saw both first and last,
Issewed forth, and went unto the dore
To enter in, but fownd it locked fast:
It vaine she thought with rigorous uprore
For to efforce, when charmes had closed it afore.

XXVIII

Where force might not availe, there sleights and art
She cast to use, both fitt for hard emprize:
Forthy from that same rowme not to depart
Till morrow next shee did her selfe avize,
When that same Maske againe should forth arize.
The morrowe next appeard with joyous cheare,
Calling men to their daily exercize:
Then she, as morrow fresh, her selfe did reare
Out of her secret stand that day for to outweare.

XXIX

All that day she outwore in wandering
And gazing on that Chambers ornament,
Till that againe the second evening
Her covered with her sable vestiment,
Wherewith the worlds faire beautie she hath blent:
Then, when the second watch was almost past,
That brasen dore flew open, and in went
Bold Britomart, as she had late forecast,
Nether of ydle showes, nor of false charmes aghast.

x x x

So soone as she was entred, rownd about
Shee cast her eies to see what was become
Of all those persons which she saw without:
But lo! they streight were vanisht all and some;
Ne living wight she saw in all that roome,
Save that same woefull Lady, both whose hands
Were bounden fast, that did her ill become,
And her small waste girt rownd with yron bands
Upon a brasen pillour, by the which she stands.

x x x i

And her before the vile Enchaunter sate,
Figuring straunge characters of his art:
With living blood he those characters wrate,
Dreadfully dropping from her dying hart,
Seeming transfixed with a cruell dart;
And all perforce to make her him to love.
Ah! who can love the worker of her smart?
A thousand charmes he formerly did prove,
Yet thousand charmes could not her stedfast hart remove.

x x x i i

Soone as that virgin knight he saw in place,
His wicked bookes in hast he overthrew,
Not caring his long labours to deface;
And, fiercely running to that Lady trew,
A murderous knife out of his pocket drew,
The which he thought, for villeinous despight,
In her tormented bodie to embrew:
But the stout Damzell, to him leaping light,
His cursed hand withheld and maistered his might.

x x x i i i

From her, to whom his fury first he ment,
The wicked weapon rashly he did wrest,
And, turning to herselfe, his fell intent,
Unwares it strooke into her snowie chest,
That litle drops empurpled her faire brest.
Exceeding wroth therewith the virgin grew,
Albe the wound were nothing deepe imprest,
And fiercely forth her mortall blade she drew,
To give him the reward for such vile outrage dew.

XXXIV

So mightily she smote him, that to ground
He fell halfe dead: next stroke him should have slaine,
Had not the Lady, which by him stood bound,
Dernly unto her called to abstaine
From doing him to dy. For else her paine
Should be remedilesse; sith none but hee
Which wrought it could the same recure againe.
Therewith she stayd her hand, loth stayd to bee;
For life she him envyde, and long'd revenge to see:

XXXV

And to him said: 'Thou wicked man, whose meed
For so huge mischiefe and vile villany
Is death, or if that ought doe death exceed;
Be sure that nought may save thee from to dy
But if that thou this Dame do presently
Restore unto her health and former state:
This doe, and live, els dye undoubtedly.'
He, glad of life, that lookt for death but late,
Did yield him selfe right willing to prolong his date:

XXXVI

And, rising up, gan streight to over-looke
Those cursed leaves, his charmes back to reverse.
Full dreadfull thinges out of that balefull booke
He red, and measur'd many a sad verse,
That horrour gan the virgins hart to perse,
And her faire locks up stared stiffe on end,
Hearing him those same bloody lynes reherse;
And, all the while he red, she did extend
Her sword high over him, if ought he did offend.

XXXVII

Anon she gan perceive the house to quake,
And all the dores to rattle round about:
Yet all that did not her dismaied make,
Nor slack her threatfull hand for daungers dout:
But still with stedfast eye and courage stout
Abode, to weet what end would come of all.
At last that mightie chaine, which round about
Her tender waste was wound, adowne gan fall,
And that great brasen pillour broke in peeces small.

XXXIV, 4   Dernly: grievously

XXXVIII

The cruell steele, which thrild her dying hart,
Fell softly forth, as of his owne accord,
And the wyde wound, which lately did dispart
Her bleeding brest, and riven bowels gor'd,
Was closed up, as it had not beene bor'd;
And every part to safety full sownd,
As she were never hurt, was soone restord.
Tho, when she felt her selfe to be unbownd
And perfect hole, prostrate she fell unto the grownd.

XXXIX

Before faire Britomart she fell prostrate,
Saying; 'Ah noble knight! what worthy meede
Can wretched Lady, quitt from wofull state,
Yield you in lieu of this your gracious deed?
Your vertue selfe her owne reward shall breed,
Even immortal prayse and glory wyde,
Which I your vassall, by your prowesse freed,
Shall through the world make to be notifyde,
And goodly well advaunce that goodly well was tryde.'

X L

But Britomart, uprearing her from grownd,
Said: 'Gentle Dame, reward enough I weene,
For many labours more then I have found,
This, that in safetie now I have you seene,
And meane of your deliverance have beene.
Henceforth, faire Lady, comfort to you take,
And put away remembrance of late teene;
Insted thereof, know that your loving Make
Hath no lesse griefe endured for your gentle sake.'

X L I

She much was cheard to heare him mentiond,
Whom of all living wightes she loved best.
Then laid the noble Championesse strong hond
Upon th' enchaunter which had her distrest
So sore, and with foule outrages opprest.
With that great chaine, wherewith not long ygoe
He bound that pitteous Lady prisoner, now relest,
Himselfe she bound, more worthy to be so,
And captive with her led to wretchednesse and wo.

XLII

Returning back, those goodly rowmes, which erst
She saw so rich and royally arayd,
Now vanisht utterly and cleane subverst
She found, and all their glory quite decayd;
That sight of such a chaunge her much dismayd
Thence forth descending to that perlous porch
Those dreadfull flames she also found delayd
And quenched quite like a consumed torch,
That erst all entrers wont so cruelly to scorch.

XLIII

More easie issew now then entrance late
She found; for now that fained dreadfull flame,
Which chokt the porch of that enchaunted gate
And passage bard to all that thither came,
Was vanisht quite, as it were not the same,
And gave her leave at pleasure forth to passe.
Th' Enchaunter selfe, which all that fraud did frame
To have efforst the love of that faire lasse,
Seeing his worke now wasted, deepe engrieved was.

XLIV

But when the Victoresse arrived there
Where late she left the pensife Scudamore
With her own trusty Squire, both full of feare,
Neither of them she found where she them lore:
Thereat her noble hart was stonisht sore:
But most faire Amoret, whose gentle spright
Now gan to feede on hope, which she before
Conceived had, to see her own deare knight,
Being thereof beguyld, was fild with new affright.

XLV

But he, sad man, when he had long in drede
Awayted there for Britomarts returne,
Yet saw her not, nor signe of her good speed,
His expectation to despaire did turne,
Misdeeming sure that her those flames did burne;
And therefore gan advize with her old Squire,
Who her deare nourslings losse no lesse did mourne,
Thence to depart for further aide t'enquire:
Where let them wend at will, whilest here I doe respire.

[*The following stanzas concluded the Legend of Chastity in
the first (three-book) edition of 1590. In the six-book edition
of 1596 they were replaced by stanzas xliii-xlv above.*]

43.

At last she came unto the place, where late
  She left Sir Scudamour in great distresse,
  Twixt dolour and despight halfe desperate,
  Of his loues succour, of his owne redresse,
  And of the hardie Britomarts successe:
  There on the cold earth him now thrown she found,
  In wilfull anguish and dead heauinesse,
  And to him cald; whose voices knowen sound
Soon as he heard, himself he reared light from ground.

44.

There did he see, that most on earth him joyd,
  His dearest loue, the comfort of his dayes.
  Whose too long absence him had sore annoyd,
  And wearied his life with dull delayes.
  Straight he upstarted from the loathed layes,
  And to her ran with hasty egernesse,
  Like as a Deare, that greedily embayes
  In the cool soile, after long thirstinesse,
Which he in chace endured hath, now nigh breathlesse.

45.

Lightly he clipt her twixt his armes twaine,
  And streightly did embrace her body bright,
  Her body, late the prison of sad paine,
  Now the sweet lodge of loue and deare delight:
  But she, faire Lady, overcommen quight
  Of huge affection, did in pleasure melt,
  And in sweete ravishment pourd out her spright.
  No word they spake, nor earthly thing they felt,
But like two senceles stocks in long embracement dwelt.

46.

Had ye them seene, ye would have surely thought
  That they had beene that faire Hermaphrodite,
  Which that rich Romane of white marble wrought,
  And in his costly Bath causd to bee site.
  So seemd those two, as growne together quite,
  That Britomart, halfe envying their blesse,
  Was much empassiond in her gentle sprite,

And to her selfe oft wisht like happinesse:
In vain she wisht, that fate n'ould let her yet possesse.

47.

Thus doe those louers, with sweet countervayle,
  Each other of loues bitter fruit despoile.
  But now my teme begins to faint and fayle,
  All woxen weary of their journall toyle:
  Therefore I will their sweatie yokes assoyle
  At this same furrowes end, till a new day;
  And ye, faire Swayns, after your long turmoyle,
  Now cease your worke, and at your pleasure play:
Now cease your work; tomorrow is an holy day.

THE FOURTH BOOKE OF

THE FAERIE QUEENE

Containing the Legend of Cambel and Triamond, or of Friendship.

I

THE RUGGED FORHEAD, that with grave foresight
Welds kingdomes causes and affaires of state,
My looser rimes (I wote) doth sharply wite
For praising love as I have done of late,
And magnifying lovers deare debate;
By which fraile youth is oft to follie led,
Through false allurement of that pleasing baite,
That better were in vertues discipled,
Then with vaine poemes weeds to have their fancies fed.

I I

Such ones ill judge of love that cannot love,
Ne in their frosen hearts feele kindly flame:
Forthy they ought not thing unknowne reprove,
Ne naturall affection faultlesse blame
For fault of few that have abusd the same;
For it of honor and all vertue is
The roote, and brings forth glorious flowres of fame,

I, 2 Welds: manages	I, 3 wite: blame
I, 2 causes: business	II, 2 kindly: natural

That crowne true lovers with immortall blis,
The meed of them that love, and do not live amisse.

I I I

Which who so list looke backe to former ages,
And call to count the things that then were donne,
Shall find that all the workes of those wise sages,
And brave exploits which great Heroës wonne,
In love were either ended or begunne:
Witnesse the father of Philosophie,
Which to his Critias, shaded oft from sunne,
Of love full manie lessons did apply,
The which these Stoicke censours cannot well deny.

I V

To such therefore I do not sing at all;
But to that sacred Saint my soveraigne Queene,
In whose chast brest all bountie naturall
And treasures of true love enlocked beene,
Bove all her sexe that ever yet was seene.
To her I sing of love, that loveth best,
And best is lov'd of all alive, I weene,
To her this song most fitly is addrest,
The Queene of love, and Prince of peace from heaven blest.

V

Which that she may the better deigne to heare,
Do thou, dred infant, Venus dearling dove,
From her high spirit chase imperious feare,
And use of awfull Majestie remove.
Insted thereof with drops of melting love,
Deawd with ambrosiall kisses, by thee gotten
From thy sweete smyling mother from above,
Sprinckle her heart, and haughtie courage soften,
That she may hearke to love, and reade this lesson often.

[*At the beginning of the fourth book the reader learns that Busirane's abduction of Amoret took place on the night of her wedding to Scudamour. The vile hag Ate tells Scudamour that his bride and her rescuer Britomart have been seen kissing each other and sleeping together, and it is not until he discovers that Britomart is a woman that his jealous rage is turned into restored faith. Husband and wife are not reunited, however. In the canto that follows, Scudamour, now sure of Amoret's purity, recounts to Britomart, Arthur, and a group of other knights the story of how he first won her.*]

CANTO X.

Scudamour doth his conquest tell
Of vertuous Amoret:
Great Venus Temple is describ'd;
And lovers life forth set.

I

TRUE HE IT SAID, what ever man it sayd,
That love with gall and hony doth abound;
But if the one be with the other wayd,
For every dram of hony therein found
A pound of gall doth over it redound:
That I too true by triall have approved;
For since the day that first with deadly wound
My heart was launcht, and learned to have loved,
I never joyed howre, but still with care was moved.

I I

'And yet such grace is given them from above,
That all the cares and evill which they meet
May nought at all their setled mindes remove,
But seeme, gainst common sence, to them most sweet;
As bosting in their martyrdome unmeet.
So all that ever yet I have endured
I count as naught, and tread downe under feet,
Since of my love at length I rest assured,
That to disloyalty she will not be allured.

I I I

'Long were to tell the travell and long toile
Through which this shield of love I late have wonne,
And purchased this peerelesse beauties spoile,
That harder may be ended, then begonne:
But since ye so desire, your will be donne.
Then hearke, ye gentle knights and Ladies free,
My hard mishaps that ye may learne to shonne;
For though sweet love to conquer glorious bee,
Yet is the paine thereof much greater then the fee.

I V

'What time the fame of this renowmed prise
Flew first abroad, and all mens eares possest,
I, having armes then taken, gan avise

III, 6   free: noble

To winne me honour by some noble gest,
And purchase me some place amongst the best.
I boldly thought, (so young mens thoughts are bold)
That this same brave emprize for me did rest,
And that both shield and she whom I behold
Might be my lucky lot; sith all by lot we hold.

v

'So on that hard adventure forth I went,
And to the place of perill shortly came:
That was a temple faire and auncient,
Which of great mother Venus bare the name,
And farre renowmed through exceeding fame,
Much more then that which was in Paphos built,
Or that in Cyprus, both long since this same,
Though all the pillours of the one were guilt,
And all the others pavement were with yvory spilt.

v i

'And it was seated in an Island strong,
Abounding all with delices most rare,
And wall'd by nature gainst invaders wrong,
That none mote have accesse, nor inward fare,
But by one way that passage did prepare.
It was a bridge ybuilt in goodly wize
With curious Corbes and pendants graven faire,
And, arched all with porches, did arize
On stately pillours fram'd after the Doricke guize.

v i i

'And for defence thereof on th' other end
There reared was a castle faire and strong
That warded all which in or out did wend,
And flancked both the bridges sides along,
Gainst all that would it faine to force or wrong:
And therein wonned twenty valiant Knights,
All twenty tride in warres experience long;
Whose office was against all manner wights
By all meanes to maintaine that castels ancient rights.

v i i i

'Before that Castle was an open plaine,
And in the midst thereof a piller placed;
On which this shield, of many sought in vaine,

iv, 4   gest: action   vi, 7   curious: elaborate
v, 9   spilt: lavishly adorned (?)   vi, 7   Corbes: corbels

The shield of Love, whose guerdon me hath graced,
Was hangd on high with golden ribbands laced;
And in the marble stone was written this,
With golden letters goodly well enchaced;
Blessed the man that well can use his blis:
Whose ever be the shield, faire Amoret be his.

I X

'Which when I red, my heart did inly earne,
And pant with hope of that adventures hap:
Ne stayed further newes thereof to learne,
But with my speare upon the shield did rap,
That all the castle ringed with the clap.
Streight forth issewd a Knight all arm'd to proofe,
And bravely mounted to his most mishap:
Who, staying nought to question from aloofe,
Ran fierce at me that fire glaunst from his horses hoofe.

X

'Whom boldly I encountred (as I could)
And by good fortune shortly him unseated.
Eftsoones outsprung two more of equall mould;
But I them both with equall hap defeated.
So all the twenty I likewise entreated,
And left them groning there upon the plaine:
Then, preacing to the pillour, I repeated
The read thereof for guerdon of my paine,
And taking downe the shield with me did it retaine.

X I

'So forth without impediment I past,
Till to the Bridges utter gate I came;
The which I found sure lockt and chained fast.
I knockt, but no man aunswred me by name;
I cald, but no man answered to my clame:
Yet I persever'd still to knocke and call,
Till at the last I spide within the same
Where one stood peeping through a crevis small,
To whom I cald aloud, halfe angry therewithall.

X I I

'That was to weet the Porter of the place,
Unto whose trust the charge thereof was lent:
His name was Doubt, that had a double face,
Th' one forward looking, th' other backeward bent,

IX, I earne: yearn

Therein resembling Janus auncient
Which hath in charge the ingate of the yeare:
And evermore his eyes about him went,
As if some proved perill he did feare,
Or did misdoubt some ill whose cause did not appeare.

x i i i

'On th' one side he, on th' other sate Delay,
Behinde the gate that none her might espy;
Whose manner was all passengers to stay
And entertaine with her occasions sly:
Through which some lost great hope unheedily,
Which never they recover might againe;
And others, quite excluded forth, did ly
Long languishing there in unpittied paine,
And seeking often entraunce afterwards in vaine.

x i v

'Me when as he had privily espide
Bearing the shield which I had conquerd late,
He kend it streight, and to me opened wide.
So in I past, and streight he closd the gate:
But being in, Delay in close awaite
Caught hold on me, and thought my steps to stay,
Feigning full many a fond excuse to prate,
And time to steale, the threasure of mans day,
Whose smallest minute lost no riches render may.

x v

'But by no meanes my way I would forslow
For ought that ever she could doe or say;
But from my lofty steede dismounting low
Past forth on foote, beholding all the way
The goodly workes, and stones of rich assay,
Cast into sundry shapes by wondrous skill,
That like on earth no where I recken may:
And underneath, the river rolling still
With murmure soft, that seem'd to serve the workmans will.

x v i

'Thence forth I passed to the second gate,
The Gate of Good Desert, whose goodly pride
And costly frame were long here to relate.
The same to all stoode alwaies open wide;
But in the Porch did evermore abide
An hideous Giant, dreadfull to behold,

That stopt the entraunce with his spacious stride,
And with the terrour of his countenance bold
Full many did affray, that else faine enter would.

X V I I

'His name was Daunger, dreaded over-all,
Who day and night did watch and duely ward
From fearefull cowards entrance to forstall
And faint-heart-fooles, whom shew of perill hard
Could terrifie from Fortunes faire adward:
For oftentimes faint hearts, at first espiall
Of his grim face, were from approaching scard;
Unworthy they of grace, whom one deniall
Excludes from fairest hope withouten further triall.

X V I I I

'Yet many doughty warriours, often tride
In greater perils to be stout and bold,
Durst not the sternnesse of his looke abide;
But, soone as they his countenance did behold,
Began to faint, and feele their corage cold.
Againe, some other, that in hard assaies
Were cowards knowne, and litle count did hold,
Either through gifts, or guile, or such like waies,
Crept in by stouping low, or stealing of the kaies.

X I X

'But I, though meanest man of many moe,
Yet much disdaining unto him to lout,
Or creepe betweene his legs, so in to goe,
Resolv'd him to assault with manhood stout,
And either beat him in, or drive him out.
Eftsoones, advauncing that enchaunted shield,
With all my might I gan to lay about:
Which when he saw, the glaive which he did wield
He gan forthwith t'avale, and way unto me yield.

X X

'So, as I entred, I did backward looke,
For feare of harme that might lie hidden there;
And loe! his hindparts, whereof heed I tooke,
Much more deformed fearefull, ugly were,
Then all his former parts did earst appere:
For hatred, murther, treason, and despight,

XIX, 9 avale: lower

With many moe lay in ambushment there,
Awayting to entrap the warelesse wight
Which did not them prevent with vigilant foresight.

X X I

'Thus having past all perill, I was come
Within the compasse of that Islands space;
The which did seeme, unto my simple doome,
The onely pleasant and delightfull place
That ever troden was of footings trace:
For all that nature by her mother-wit
Could frame in earth, and forme of substance base,
Was there; and all that nature did omit,
Art, playing second natures part, supplyed it.

X X I I

'No tree, that is of count, in greenewood growes,
From lowest Juniper to Ceder tall,
No flowre in field, that daintie odour throwes,
And deckes his branch with blossomes overall,
But there was planted, or grew naturall:
Nor sense of man so coy and curious nice,
But there mote find to please it selfe withall;
Nor hart could wish for any queint device,
But there it present was, and did fraile sense entice.

X X I I I

'In such luxurious plentie of all pleasure,
It seem'd a second paradise to ghesse,
So lavishly enricht with Natures threasure,
That if the happie soules, which doe possesse
Th' Elysian fields and live in lasting blesse,
Should happen this with living eye to see,
They soone would loath their lesser happinesse,
And wish to life return'd againe to bee,
That in this joyous place they mote have joyance free.

X X I V

'Fresh shadowes, fit to shroud from sunny ray;
Faire lawnds, to take the sunne in season dew;
Sweet springs, in which a thousand Nymphs did play;
Soft rombling brookes, that gentle slomber drew;
High reared mounts, the lands about to vew;
Low looking dales, disloignd from common gaze;

XXIV, 2 lawnds: glades

Delightfull bowres, to solace lovers trew;
False Labyrinthes, fond runners eyes to daze;
All which by nature made did nature selfe amaze.

X X V

'And all without were walkes and alleyes dight
With divers trees enrang'd in even rankes;
And here and there were pleasant arbors pight,
And shadie seates, and sundry flowring bankes,
To sit and rest the walkers wearie shankes:
And therein thousand payres of lovers walkt,
Praysing their god, and yeelding him great thankes,
Ne ever ought but of their true loves talkt,
Ne ever for rebuke or blame of any balkt.

X X V I

'All these together by themselves did sport
Their spotlesse pleasures and sweet loves content.
But, farre away from these, another sort
Of lovers lincked in true harts consent,
Which loved not as these for like intent,
But on chast vertue grounded their desire,
Farre from all fraud or fayned blandishment;
Which, in their spirits kindling zealous fire,
Brave thoughts and noble deedes did evermore aspire.

X X V I I

"Such were great Hercules and Hyllus deare;
Trew Jonathan and David trustie tryde;
Stout Theseus and Pirithous his feare;
Pylades and Orestes by his syde;
Myld Titus and Gesippus without pryde;
Damon and Pythias, whom death could not sever:
All these, and all that ever had bene tyde
In bands of friendship, there did live for ever;
Whose lives although decay'd, yet loves decayed never.

X X V I I I

"Which when as I, that never tasted blis
Nor happie howre, beheld with gazefull eye,
I thought there was none other heaven then this;
And gan their endlesse happinesse envye,
That being free from feare and gealosye
Might frankely there their loves desire possesse;
Whilest I, through paines and perlous jeopardie,

Was forst to seeke my lifes deare patronnesse:
Much dearer be the things which come through hard distresse.

XXIX

'Yet all those sights, and all that else I saw,
Might not my steps withhold, but that forthright
Unto that purposd place I did me draw,
Where as my love was lodged day and night,
The temple of great Venus, that is hight
The Queene of beautie, and of love the mother,
There worshipped of every living wight;
Whose goodly workmanship farre past all other
That ever were on earth, all were they set together.

XXX

'Not that same famous Temple of Diane,
Whose hight all Ephesus did oversee,
And which all Asia sought with vowes prophane,
One of the worlds seven wonders sayd to bee,
Might match with this by many a degree:
Nor that which that wise King of Jurie framed
With endlesse cost to be th' Almighties see;
Nor all, that else through all the world is named
To all the heathen Gods, might like to this be clamed.

XXXI

'I, much admyring that so goodly frame,
Unto the porch approcht which open stood;
But therein sate an amiable Dame,
That seem'd to be of very sober mood,
And in her semblant shew'd great womanhood:
Strange was her tyre; for on her head a crowne
She wore, much like unto a Danisk hood,
Poudred with pearle and stone; and all her gowne
Enwoven was with gold, that raught full low adowne.

XXXII

On either side of her two young men stood,
Both strongly arm'd, as fearing one another;
Yet were they brethren both of halfe the blood,
Begotten by two fathers of one mother,
Though of contrarie natures each to other:
The one of them hight Love, the other Hate.
Hate was the elder, Love the younger brother;

xxx, 7   see: abode

Yet was the younger stronger in his state
Then th' elder, and him maystred still in all debate.

XXXIII

'Nathlesse that Dame so well them tempred both,
That she them forced hand to joyne in hand,
Albe that Hatred was thereto full loth,
And turn'd his face away, as he did stand,
Unwilling to behold that lovely band.
Yet she was of such grace and vertuous might,
That her commaundment he could not withstand,
But bit his lip for felonous despight,
And gnasht his yron tuskes at that displeasing sight.

XXXIV

'Concord she cleeped was in common reed,
Mother of blessed Peace and Friendship trew;
They both her twins, both borne of heavenly seed,
And she her selfe likewise divinely grew;
The which right well her workes divine did shew:
For strength and wealth and happinesse she lends,
And strife and warre and anger does subdew:
Of litle much, of foes she maketh friends,
And to afflicted minds sweet rest and quiet sends.

XXXV

'By her the heaven is in his course contained,
And all the world in state unmoved stands,
As their Almightie maker first ordained,
And bound them with inviolable bands;
Else would the waters overflow the lands,
And fire devoure the ayre, and hell them quight,
But that she holds them with her blessed hands.
She is the nourse of pleasure and delight,
And unto Venus grace the gate doth open right.

XXXVI

'By her I entring half dismayed was;
But she in gentle wise me entertayned,
And twixt her selfe and Love did let me pas;
But Hatred would my entrance have restrayned,
And with his club me threatned to have brayned,
Had not the Ladie with her powrefull speach
Him from his wicked will uneath refrayned;

xxxiv, 1   cleeped: called   xxxvi, 7   uneath: with difficulty
xxxv, 6   quight: requite

And th' other eke his malice did empeach,
Till I was throughly past the perill of his reach.

X X X V I I

'Into the inmost Temple thus I came,
Which fuming all with frankensence I found
And odours rising from the altars flame.
Upon an hundred marble pillors round
The roofe up high was reared from the ground,
All deckt with crownes, and chaynes, and girlands gay,
And thousand pretious gifts worth many a pound,
The which sad lovers for their vowes did pay;
And all the ground was strow'd with flowres as fresh as May.

X X X V I I I

'An hundred Altars round about were set,
All flaming with their sacrifices fire,
That with the steme thereof the Temple swet,
Which rould in clouds to heaven did aspire,
And in them bore true lovers vowes entire:
And eke an hundred brasen caudrons bright,
To bath in joy and amorous desire,
Every of which was to a damzell hight;
For all the Priests were damzels in soft linnen dight.

X X X I X

'Right in the midst the Goddesse selfe did stand
Upon an altar of some costly masse,
Whose substance was uneath to understand:
For neither pretious stone, nor durefull brasse,
Nor shining gold, nor mouldring clay it was;
But much more rare and pretious to esteeme,
Pure in aspect, and like to christall glasse,
Yet glasse was not, if one did rightly deeme;
But, being faire and brickle, likest glasse did seeme.

X L

'But it in shape and beautie did excell
All other Idoles which the heathen adore,
Farre passing that, which by surpassing skill
Phidias did make in Paphos Isle of yore,
With which that wretched Greeke, that life forlore,
Did fall in love: yet this much fairer shined,
But covered with a slender veile afore;

xxxix, 9   brickle: brittle

And both her feete and legs together twyned
Were with a snake, whose head and tail were fast combyned.

X L I

'The cause why she was covered with a vele
Was hard to know, for that her Priests the same
From peoples knowledge labour'd to concele:
But sooth it was not sure for womanish shame,
Nor any blemish which the worke mote blame;
But for, they say, she hath both kinds in one,
Both male and female, both under one name:
She syre and mother is her selfe alone,
Begets and eke conceives, ne needeth other none.

X L I I

'And all about her necke and shoulders flew
A flocke of litle loves, and sports, and joyes,
With nimble wings of gold and purple hew;
Whose shapes seem'd not like to terrestriall boyes,
But like to Angels playing heavenly toyes,
The whilest their eldest brother was away,
Cupid their eldest brother; he enjoyes
The wide kingdome of love with lordly sway,
And to his law compels all creatures to obay.

X L I I I

'And all about her altar scattered lay
Great sorts of lovers piteously complayning,
Some of their losse, some of their loves delay,
Some of their pride, some paragons disdayning,
Some fearing fraud, some fraudulently fayning,
As every one had cause of good or ill.
Amongst the rest some one, through Loves constrayning
Tormented sore, could not containe it still,
But thus brake forth, that all the temple it did fill:

X L I V

' "Great Venus! Queene of beautie and of grace,
The joy of Gods and men, that under skie
Doest fayrest shine, and most adorne thy place;
That with thy smyling looke doest pacifie
The raging seas, and makst the stormes to flie;
Thee, goddesse, thee the winds, the clouds doe feare,
And, when thou spredst thy mantle forth on hie,
The waters play, and pleasant lands appeare,
And heavens laugh, and al the world shews joyous cheare.

X L V

' "Then doth the dædale earth throw forth to thee
Out of her fruitfull lap aboundant flowres;
And then all living wights, soone as they see
The spring breake forth out of his lusty bowres,
They all doe learne to play the Paramours;
First doe the merry birds, thy prety pages,
Privily pricked with thy lustfull powres,
Chirpe loud to thee out of their leavy cages,
And thee their mother call to coole their kindly rages.

X L V I

' "Then doe the salvage beasts begin to play
Their pleasant friskes, and loath their wonted food:
The Lyons rore; the Tygres loudly bray;
The raging Buls rebellow through the wood,
And breaking forth dare tempt the deepest flood
To come where thou doest draw them with desire.
So all things else, that nourish vitall blood,
Soone as with fury thou doest them inspire,
In generation seeke to quench their inward fire.

X L V I I

' "So all the world by thee at first was made,
And dayly yet thou doest the same repayre;
Ne ought on earth that merry is and glad,
Ne ought on earth that lovely is and fayre,
But thou the same for pleasure didst prepayre:
Thou art the root of all that joyous is:
Great God of men and women, queene of th' ayre,
Mother of laughter, and welspring of blisse,
O graunt that of my love at last I may not misse!"

X L V I I I

'So did he say: but I with murmure soft,
That none might heare the sorrow of my hart,
Yet inly groning deepe and sighing oft,
Besought her to graunt ease unto my smart,
And to my wound her gratious help impart.
Whilest thus I spake, behold! with happy eye
I spyde where at the Idoles feet apart
A bevie of fayre damzels close did lye,
Wayting when as the Antheme should be sung on hye.

XLVI, 8 fury: passion

X L I X

'The first of them did seeme of ryper yeares
And graver countenance then all the rest;
Yet all the rest were eke her equall peares,
Yet unto her obayed all the best.
Her name was Womanhood; that she exprest
By her sad semblant and demeanure wyse:
For stedfast still her eyes did fixed rest,
Ne rov'd at randon, after gazers guyse,
Whose luring baytes oftimes doe heedlesse harts entyse.

L

'And next to her sate goodly Shamefastnesse,
Ne ever durst her eyes from ground upreare,
Ne ever once did looke up from her desse,
As if some blame of evill she did feare,
That in her cheekes made roses oft appeare:
And her against sweet Cherefulnesse was placed,
Whose eyes, like twinkling stars in evening cleare,
Were deckt with smyles that all sad humors chaced,
And darted forth delights the which her goodly graced.

L I

'And next to her sate sober Modestie,
Holding her hand upon her gentle hart;
And her against sate comely Curtesie,
That unto every person knew her part;
And her before was seated overthwart
Soft Silence, and submisse Obedience,
Both linckt together never to dispart;
Both gifts of God, not gotten but from thence,
Both girlonds of his Saints against their foes offence.

L I I

'Thus sate they all around in seemely rate:
And in the midst of them a goodly mayd
Even in the lap of Womanhood there sate,
The which was all in lilly white arayd,
With silver streames amongst the linnen stray'd;
Like to the Morne, when first her shyning face
Hath to the gloomy world itselfe bewray'd:
That same was fayrest Amoret in place,
Shyning with beauties light and heavenly vertues grace.

XLIX, 6   sad: sober   L, 3   desse: dais

L I I I

'Whom soone as I beheld, my hart gan throb
And wade in doubt what best were to be donne;
For sacrilege me seem'd the Church to rob,
And folly seem'd to leave the thing undonne
Which with so strong attempt I had begonne.
Tho, shaking off all doubt and shamefast feare
Which Ladies love, I heard, had never wonne
Mongst men of worth, I to her stepped neare,
And by the lilly hand her labour'd up to reare.

L I V

'Thereat that formost matrone me did blame,
And sharpe rebuke for being over bold;
Saying, it was to Knight unseemely shame
Upon a recluse Virgin to lay hold,
That unto Venus services was sold.
To whom I thus: "Nay, but it fitteth best
For Cupids man with Venus mayd to hold,
For ill your goddesse services are drest
By virgins, and her sacrifices let to rest."

L V

'With that my shield I forth to her did show,
Which all that while I closely had conceld;
On which when Cupid, with his killing bow
And cruell shafts, emblazond she beheld,
At sight thereof she was with terror queld,
And said no more: but I, which all that while
The pledge of faith, her hand, engaged held
Like warie Hynd within the weedie soyle,
For no intreatie would forgoe so glorious spoyle.

L V I

'And evermore upon the Goddesse face
Mine eye was fixt, for feare of her offence;
Whom when I saw with amiable grace
To laugh at me, and favour my pretence,
I was emboldned with more confidence;
And nought for nicenesse nor for envy sparing,
In presence of them all forth led her thence
All looking on, and like astonisht staring,
Yet to lay hand on her not one of all them daring.

LVII

'She often prayd, and often me besought,
Sometime with tender teares to let her goe,
Sometime with witching smyles; but yet, for nought
That ever she to me could say or doe,
Could she her wished freedome fro me wooe:
But forth I led her through the Temple gate,
By which I hardly past with much adoe:
But that same Ladie, which me friended late
In entrance, did me also friend in my retrate.

LVIII

'No lesse did Daunger threaten me with dread,
Whenas he saw me, maugre all his powre,
That glorious spoyle of beautie with me lead,
Then Cerberus, when Orpheus did recoure
His Leman from the Stygian Princes boure:
But evermore my shield did me defend
Against the storme of every dreadfull stoure:
Thus safely with my love I thence did wend.'
So ended he his tale, where I this Canto end.

THE FIFTH BOOKE OF

THE FAERIE QUEENE

Contayning the Legend of Artegall,
or of Justice.

I

So oft as I with state of present time
The image of the antique world compare,
When as mans age was in his freshest prime,
And the first blossome of faire vertue bare;
Such oddes I finde twixt those, and these which are,
As that, through long continuance of his course,
Me seemes the world is runne quite out of square
From the first point of his appointed sourse;
And being once amisse growes daily wourse and wourse:

I I

For from the golden age, that first was named,
It's now at earst become a stonie one;
And men themselves, the which at first were framed
Of earthly mould, and form'd of flesh and bone,
Are now transformed into hardest stone;
Such as behind their backs (so backward bred)
Were throwne by Pyrrha and Deucalione:
And if then those may any worse be red,
They into that ere long will be degendered.

I I I

Let none then blame me, if in discipline
Of vertue and of civill uses lore,

I doe not forme them to the common line
Of present dayes, which are corrupted sore,
But to the antique use which was of yore,
When good was onely for it selfe desyred,
And all men sought their owne, and none no more;
When Justice was not for most meed out-hyred,
But simple Truth did rayne, and was of all admyred.

I V

For that which all men then did vertue call,
Is now cald vice; and that which vice was hight,
Is now hight vertue, and so us'd of all:
Right now is wrong, and wrong that was is right;
As all things else in time are chaunged quight:
Ne wonder; for the heavens revolution
Is wandred farre from where it first was pight,
And so doe make contrarie constitution
Of all this lower world, toward his dissolution.

v

For who so list into the heavens looke,
And search the courses of the rowling spheares,
Shall find that from the point where they first tooke
Their setting forth, in these few thousand yeares
They all are wandred much; that plaine appeares:
For that same golden fleecy Ram, which bore
Phrixus and Helle from their stepdames feares,
Hath now forgot where he was plast of yore,
And shouldred hath the Bull which fayre Europa bore:

V I

And eke the Bull hath with his bow-bent horne
So hardly butted those two twinnes of Jove,
That they have crusht the Crab, and quite him borne
Into the great Nemæan lions grove.
So now all range, and doe at randon rove
Out of their proper places farre away,
And all this world with them amisse doe move,
And all his creatures from their course astray,
Till they arrive at their last ruinous decay.

V I I

Ne is that same great glorious lampe of light,
That doth enlumine all these lesser fyres,
In better case, ne keepes his course more right,

IV, 7   pight: set

But is miscaried with the other Spheres:
For since the terme of fourteene hundred yeres,
That learned Ptolomæe his hight did take,
He is declyned from that marke of theirs
Nigh thirtie minutes to the Southerne lake;
That makes me feare in time he will us quite forsake.

V I I I

And if to those Ægyptian wisards old,
Which in Star-read were wont have best insight,
Faith may be given, it is by them told
That since the time they first tooke the Sunnes hight,
Foure times his place he shifted hath in sight,
And twice hath risen where he now doth West,
And wested twice where he ought rise aright:
But most is Mars amisse of all the rest,
And next to him old Saturne, that was wont be best.

I X

For during Saturnes ancient raigne it's sayd
That all the world with goodnesse did abound:
All loved vertue, no man was affrayd
Of force, ne fraud in wight was to be found:
No warre was knowne, no dreadfull trompets sound;
Peace universall rayn'd mongst men and beasts,
And all things freely grew out of the ground.
Justice sate high ador'd with solemne feasts,
And to all people did divide her dred beheasts:

X

Most sacred vertue she of all the rest,
Resembling God in his imperiall might;
Whose soveraine powre is herein most exprest,
That both to good and bad he dealeth right,
And all his workes with Justice hath bedight.
That powre he also doth to Princes lend,
And makes them like himselfe in glorious sight
To sit in his own seate, his cause to end,
And rule his people right, as he doth recommend.

X I

Dread Soverayne Goddesse, that doest highest sit
In seate of judgement in th' Almighties stead,
And with magnificke might and wondrous wit
Doest to thy people righteous doome aread,

XI, 4   doome: judgment

That furthest Nations filles with awful dread,
Pardon the boldnesse of thy basest thrall,
That dare discourse of so divine a read
As thy great justice, praysed over-all,
The instrument whereof loe! here thy Artegall.

[*In Canto vi of Book IV Artegall conquers Britomart in battle but is overcome in turn by her beauty. They agree to
marry, but Artegall must first perform the task assigned to
him by Gloriana, the rescue of Eirene from the clutches of
Grantorto, the principal quest of Book V. In the course of
his adventures he fights with the proud Amazon Radigund.
As he is about to kill her he is astonished by the beauty of
her face, throws away his sword, and is made prisoner. She
dresses him in female clothing and sets him to weaving. Britomart hears of his distress and rides to the rescue. Her visit to
the temple of Isis, described below, takes place just before
she meets and kills Radigund, freeing Artegall to pursue his
quest.*]

CANTO VII.

*Britomart comes to Isis Church,
Where shee strange visions sees:
She fights with Radigund, her slaies,
And Artegall thence frees.*

I

NOUGHT IS ON EARTH more sacred or divine,
That Gods and men doe equally adore,
Then this same vertue that doth right define:
For th' hevens themselves, whence mortal men implore
Right in their wrongs, are rul'd by righteous lore
Of highest Jove, who doth true justice deale
To his inferiour Gods, and evermore
Therewith containes his heavenly Commonweale:
The skill whereof to Princes hearts he doth reveale.

I I

Well therefore did the antique world invent
That Justice was a God of soveraine grace,
And altars unto him and temples lent,
And heavenly honours in the highest place;
Calling him great Osyris, of the race
Of th' old Ægyptian Kings that whylome were,

With fayned colours shading a true case;
For that Osyris, whilest he lived here,
The justest man alive and truest did appeare.

I I I

His wife was Isis; whom they likewise made
A Goddesse of great powre and soveraynty,
And in her person cunningly did shade
That part of Justice which is Equity,
Whereof I have to treat here presently:
Unto whose temple when as Britomart
Arrived, shee with great humility
Did enter in, ne would that night depart;
But Talus mote not be admitted to her part.

I V

There she received was in goodly wize
Of many Priests, which duely did attend
Uppon the rites and daily sacrifize,
All clad in linnen robes with silver hemd;
And on their heads, with long locks comely kemd,
They wore rich Mitres shaped like the Moone,
To shew that Isis doth the Moone portend;
Like as Osyris signifies the Sunne:
For that they both like race in equall justice runne.

V

The Championesse them greeting, as she could,
Was thence by them into the Temple led;
Whose goodly building when she did behould,
Borne uppon stately pillours, all dispred
With shining gold, and arched over hed,
She wondred at the workemans passing skill,
Whose like before she never saw nor red;
And thereuppon long while stood gazing still,
But thought that she thereon could never gaze her fill.

V I

Thence forth unto the Idoll they her brought;
The which was framed all of silver fine,
So well as could with cunning hand be wrought,
And clothed all in garments made of line,
Hemd all about with fringe of silver twine:
Uppon her head she wore a Crowne of gold;
To shew that she had powre in things divine:

vi, 4   line: linen   vi, 5   twine: band

And at her feete a Crocodile was rold,
That with her wreathed taile her middle did enfold.

V I I

One foote was set uppon the Crocodile,
And on the ground the other fast did stand;
So meaning to suppresse both forged guile
And open force: and in her other hand
She stretched forth a long white sclender wand.
Such was the Goddesse; whom when Britomart
Had long beheld, her selfe uppon the land
She did prostrate, and with right humble hart
Unto her selfe her silent prayers did impart.

V I I I

To which the Idoll, as it were inclining,
Her wand did move with amiable looke,
By outward shew her inward sence desining:
Who well perceiving how her wand she shooke,
It as a token of good fortune tooke.
By this the day with dampe was overcast,
And joyous light the house of Jove forsooke;
Which when she saw her helmet she unlaste,
And by the altars side her selfe to slumber plaste.

I X

For other beds the Priests there used none,
But on their mother Earths deare lap did lie,
And bake their sides uppon the cold hard stone,
T' enure them selves to sufferaunce thereby,
And proud rebellious flesh to mortify:
For by the vow of their religion,
They tied were to stedfast chastity
And continence of life, that, all forgon,
They mote the better tend to their devotion.

X

Therefore they mote not taste of fleshly food,
Ne feed on ought the which doth bloud containe,
Ne drinke of wine; for wine, they say, is blood,
Even the bloud of Gyants, which were slaine
By thundring Jove in the Phlegrean plaine:
For which the earth (as they the story tell)
Wroth with the Gods, which to perpetuall paine

VIII, 3 desining: indicating   IX, 3 bake: harden

Had damn'd her sonnes which gainst them did rebell,
With inward griefe and malice did against them swell.

X I

And of their vitall bloud, the which was shed
Into her pregnant bosome, forth she brought
The fruitfull vine; whose liquor blouddy red,
Having the mindes of men with fury fraught,
Mote in them stirre up old rebellious thought
To make new warre against the Gods againe.
Such is the powre of that same fruit, that nought
The fell contagion may thereof restraine,
Ne within reasons rule her madding mood containe.

X I I

There did the warlike Maide her selfe repose,
Under the wings of Isis all that night;
And with sweete rest her heavy eyes did close,
After that long daies toile and weary plight:
Where whilest her earthly parts with soft delight
Of sencelesse sleepe did deeply drowned lie,
There did appeare unto her heavenly spright
A wondrous vision, which did close implie
The course of all her fortune and posteritie.

X I I I

Her seem'd, as she was doing sacrifize
To Isis, deckt with Mitre on her hed
And linnen stole after those Priestes guize,
All sodainely she saw transfigured
Her linnen stole to robe of scarlet red,
And Moone-like Mitre to a Crowne of gold;
That even she her selfe much wondered
At such a chaunge, and joyed to behold
Her selfe adorn'd with gems and jewels manifold.

X I V

And, in the midst of her felicity,
An hideous tempest seemed from below
To rise through all the Temple sodainely,
That from the Altar all about did blow
The holy fire, and all the embers strow
Uppon the ground; which, kindled privily,
Into outrageous flames unwares did grow,
That all the Temple put in jeopardy
Of flaming, and her selfe in great perplexity.

x v

With that the Crocodile, which sleeping lay
Under the Idols feete in fearelesse bowre,
Seem'd to awake in horrible dismay,
As being troubled with that stormy stowre;
And gaping greedy wide did streight devoure
Both flames and tempest: with which growen great,
And swolne with pride of his owne peerelesse powre,
He gan to threaten her likewise to eat,
But that the Goddesse with her rod him backe did beat.

x v i

Tho turning all his pride to humblesse meeke,
Him selfe before her feete he lowly threw,
And gan for grace and love of her to seeke;
Which she accepting, he so neare her drew
That of his game she soone enwombed grew,
And forth did bring a Lion of great might,
That shortly did all other beasts subdew.
With that she waked full of fearefull fright,
And doubtfully dismayd through that so uncouth sight.

x v i i

So thereuppon long while she musing lay
With thousand thoughts feeding her fantasie,
Untill she spide the lampe of lightsome day
Up-lifted in the porch of heaven hie:
Then up she rose fraught with melancholy,
And forth into the lower parts did pas,
Whereas the Priestes she found full busily
About their holy things for morrow Mas;
Whom she saluting faire, faire resaluted was:

x v i i i

But by the change of her unchearefull looke,
They might perceive she was not well in plight,
Or that some pensivenesse to heart she tooke:
Therefore thus one of them, who seem'd in sight
To be the greatest and the gravest wight,
To her bespake: 'Sir Knight, it seemes to me
That, thorough evill rest of this last night,
Or ill apayd or much dismayd ye be;
That by your change of cheare is easie for to see.'

xvi, 9   uncouth: strange   xviii, 8   apayd: pleased

X I X

'Certes,' (sayd she) 'sith ye so well have spide
The troublous passion of my pensive mind,
I will not seeke the same from you to hide;
But will my cares unfolde, in hope to find
Your aide to guide me out of errour blind.'
'Say on' (quoth he) 'the secret of your hart
For, by the holy vow which me doth bind,
I am adjur'd best counsell to impart
To all that shall require my comfort in their smart.'

X X

Then gan she to declare the whole discourse
Of all that vision which to her appeard,
As well as to her minde it had recourse.
All which when he unto the end had heard,
Like to a weake faint-hearted man he fared
Through great astonishment of that strange sight;
And, with long locks up-standing, stifly stared
Like one adawed with some dreadfull spright:
So, fild with heavenly fury, thus he her behight.

X X I

'Magnificke Virgin, that in queint disguise
Of British armes doest maske thy royall blood,
So to pursue a perillous emprize,
How couldst thou weene, through that disguized hood,
To hide thy state from being understood?
Can from th' immortall Gods ought hidden bee?
They doe thy linage, and thy Lordly brood,
They doe thy sire lamenting sore for thee,
They doe thy love forlorne in womens thraldome see.

X X I I

'The end whereof, and all the long event,
They do to thee in this same dreame discover;
For that same Crocodile doth represent
The righteous Knight that is thy faithfull lover,
Like to Osyris in all just endever:
For that same Crocodile Osyris is,
That under Isis feete doth sleepe for ever;
To shew that clemence oft, in things amis,
Restraines those sterne behests and cruell doomes of his.

xx, 8   adawed: daunted

XXIII

'That Knight shall all the troublous stormes asswage
And raging flames, that many foes shall reare
To hinder thee from the just heritage
Of thy sires Crowne, and from thy countrey deare:
Then shalt thou take him to thy loved fere,
And joyne in equall portion of thy realme;
And afterwards a sonne to him shalt beare,
That Lion-like shall shew his powre extreame.
So blesse thee God, and give thee joyance of thy dreame!'

XXIV

All which when she unto the end had heard,
She much was eased in her troublous thought,
And on those Priests bestowed rich reward;
And royall gifts of gold and silver wrought
She for a present to their Goddesse brought.
Then taking leave of them, she forward went
To seeke her love, where he was to be sought;
Ne rested till she came without relent
Unto the land of Amazons, as she was bent.

XXIII, 5   fere: mate

THE SIXTH BOOKE OF

THE FAERIE QUEENE

Contayning the Legend of Sir Calidore,
or of Courtesie.

I

THE WAIES, through which my weary steps I guyde
In this delightfull land of Faery,
Are so exceeding spacious and wyde,
And sprinckled with such sweet variety
Of all that pleasant is to eare or eye,
That I, nigh ravisht with rare thoughts delight,
My tedious travell doe forget thereby;
And, when I gin to feele decay of might,
It strength to me supplies, and chears my dulled spright.

I I

Such secret comfort and such heavenly pleasures,
Ye sacred imps, that on Parnasso dwell,
And there the keeping have of learnings threasures
Which doe all worldly riches farre excell,
Into the mindes of mortall men doe well,
And goodly fury into them infuse,
Guyde ye my footing, and conduct me well
In these strange waies where never foote did use,
Ne none can find but who was taught them by the Muse.

I I I

Revele to me the sacred noursery
Of vertue, which with you doth there remaine,

Where it in silver bowre does hidden ly
From view of men, and wicked worlds disdaine;
Since it at first was by the Gods with paine
Planted in earth, being derived at furst
From heavenly seedes of bounty soveraine,
And by them long with carefull labour nurst,
Till it to ripenesse grew, and forth to honour burst.

I V

Amongst them all growes not a fayrer flowre
Then is the bloosme of comely courtesie;
Which though it on a lowly stalke doe bowre,
Yet brancheth forth in brave nobilitie,
And spreds it selfe through all civilitie:
Of which though present age doe plenteous seeme,
Yet, being matcht with plaine Antiquitie,
Ye will them all but fayned showes esteeme,
Which carry colours faire that feeble eies misdeeme.

V

But, in the triall of true curtesie,
Its now so farre from that which then it was,
That it indeed is nought but forgerie.
Fashion'd to please the eies of them that pas,
Which see not perfect things but in a glas:
Yet is that glasse so gay, that it can blynd
The wisest sight to thinke gold that is bras;
But vertues seat is deepe within the mynd,
And not in outward shows, but inward thoughts defynd.

V I

But where shall I in all Antiquity
So faire a patterne finde, where may be seene
The goodly praise of Princely curtesie,
As in your selfe, O soveraine Lady Queene?
In whose pure minde, as in a mirrour sheene,
It showes, and with her brightnesse doth inflame
The eyes of all which thereon fixed beene,
But meriteth indeede an higher name:
Yet so from low to high uplifted is your fame.

V I I

Then pardon me, most dreaded Soveraine,
That from your selfe I doe this vertue bring,
And to your selfe doe it returne againe.

IV, 3   bowre: shelter

So from the Ocean all rivers spring,
And tribute backe repay as to their King:
Right so from you all goodly vertues well
Into the rest which round about you ring,
Faire Lords and Ladies which about you dwell,
And doe adorne your Court where courtesies excell.

[*Sir Calidore's task is the suppression of the Blatant Beast,
a monster that pours out his venom on good and bad alike.
His ceaseless pursuit leads him at length to the delightful
country described in the stanzas reprinted here. Later, in
Calidore's absence, a band of brigands descends upon this
pastoral paradise and carries off Pastorella and the other shepherds. Calidore rescues her (she is discovered to be the long-
lost daughter of a noble family) and at last subdues and
binds the Beast. But since that time the Beast has escaped.*]

C A N T O   I X.

*Calidore hostes with Meliboe,
And loves fayre Pastorell:
Coridon envies him, yet he
For ill rewards him well.*

I

Now TURNE AGAINE my teme, thou jolly swayne,
Backe to the furrow which I lately left.
I lately left a furrow, one or twayne,
Unplough'd, the which my coulter hath not cleft;
Yet seem'd the soyle both fayre and frutefull eft,
As I it past: that were too great a shame,
That so rich frute should be from us bereft;
Besides the great dishonour and defame,
Which should befall to Calidores immortall name.

I I

Great travell hath the gentle Calidore
And toyle endured, sith I left him last
Sewing the Blatant Beast; which I forbore
To finish then, for other present hast.
Full many pathes and perils he hath past,
Through hils, through dales, through forests, and through
    plaines,
In that same quest which fortune on him cast,

Which he atchieved to his owne great gaines,
Reaping eternall glorie of his restlesse paines.

I I I

So sharply he the Monster did pursew,
That day nor night he suffred him to rest,
Ne rested he himselfe, but natures dew,
For dread of daunger not to be redrest,
If he for slouth forslackt so famous quest.
Him first from court he to the citties coursed,
And from the citties to the townes him prest,
And from the townes into the countrie forsed,
And from the country back to private farmes he scorsed.

I V

From thence into the open fields he fled,
Whereas the Heardes were keeping of their neat,
And shepherds singing to their flockes that fed,
Layes of sweete love and youthes delightfull heat:
Him thether eke, for all his fearefull threat,
He followed fast, and chaced him so nie,
That to the folds, where sheepe at night doe seat,
And to the litle cots, where shepherds lie
In winters wrathfull time, he forced him to flie.

V

There on a day, as he pursew'd the chace,
He chaunst to spy a sort of shepheard groomes,
Playing on pipes and caroling apace,
The whyles their beasts there in the budded broomes
Beside them fed, and nipt the tender bloomes;
For other worldly wealth they cared nought.
To whom Sir Calidore yet sweating comes,
And them to tell him courteously besought,
If such a beast they saw, which he had thether brought.

V I

They answer'd him that no such beast they saw,
Nor any wicked feend that mote offend
Their happie flockes, nor daunger to them draw;
But if that such there were (as none they kend)
They prayd high God him farre from them to send.
Then one of them, him seeing so to sweat,
After his rusticke wise, that well he weend,

III, 9   scorsed: chased

Offred him drinke to quench his thirstie heat,
And, if he hungry were, him offred eke to eat.

VII

The knight was nothing nice, where was no need,
And tooke their gentle offer: so adowne
They prayd him sit, and gave him for to feed
Such homely what as serves the simple clowne,
That doth despise the dainties of the towne.
Tho, having fed his fill, he there besyde
Saw a faire damzell, which did weare a crowne
Of sundry flowres with silken ribbands tyde,
Yclad in home-made greene that her owne hands had dyde.

VIII

Upon a litle hillocke she was placed
Higher then all the rest, and round about
Environ'd with a girland, goodly graced,
Of lovely lasses; and them all without
The lustie shepheard swaynes sat in a rout,
The which did pype and sing her prayses dew,
And oft rejoyce, and oft for wonder shout,
As if some miracle of heavenly hew
Were downe to them descended in that earthly vew.

IX

And soothly sure she was full fayre of face,
And perfectly well shapt in every lim,
Which she did more augment with modest grace
And comely carriage of her count'nance trim,
That all the rest like lesser lamps did dim:
Who, her admiring as some heavenly wight,
Did for their soveraine goddesse her esteeme,
And, caroling her name both day and night,
The fayrest Pastorella her by name did hight.

X

Ne was there heard, ne was there shepheards swayne,
But her did honour; and eke many a one
Burnt in her love, and with sweet pleasing payne
Full many a night for her did sigh and grone:
But most of all the shepheard Coridon
For her did languish, and his deare life spend;
Yet neither she for him nor other none

vii, 1   nice: fastidious

Did care a whit, ne any liking lend:
Though meane her lot, yet higher did her mind ascend.

X I

Her whyles Sir Calidore there vewed well,
And markt her rare demeanure, which him seemed
So farre the meane of shepheards to excell,
As that he in his mind her worthy deemed
To be a Princes Paragone esteemed,
He was unwares surprisd in subtile bands
Of the blynd boy; ne thence could be redeemed
By any skill out of his cruell hands;
Caught like the bird which gazing still on others stands.

X I I

So stood he still long gazing thereupon,
Ne any will had thence to move away,
Although his quest were farre afore him gon:
But after he had fed, yet did he stay
And sate there still, untill the flying day
Was farre forth spent, discoursing diversly
Of sundry things as fell, to worke delay;
And evermore his speach he did apply
To th' heards, but meant them to the damzels fantazy.

X I I I

By this the moystie night approching fast
Her deawy humour gan on th' earth to shed,
That warn'd the shepheards to their homes to hast
Their tender flocks, now being fully fed,
For feare of wetting them before their bed.
Then came to them a good old aged syre,
Whose silver lockes bedeckt his beard and hed,
With shepheards hooke in hand, and fit attyre,
That wild the damzell rise; the day did now expyre.

X I V

He was, to weet, by common voice esteemed
The father of the fayrest Pastorell,
And of her selfe in very deede so deemed;
Yet was not so; but, as old stories tell,
Found her by fortune, which to him befell,
In th' open fields an Infant left alone;
And, taking up, brought home and noursed well

As his owne chyld; for other he had none;
That she in tract of time accompted was his owne.

X V

She at his bidding meekely did arise,
And streight unto her litle flocke did fare:
Then all the rest about her rose likewise,
And each his sundrie sheepe with severall care
Gathered together, and them homeward bare:
Whylest everie one with helping hands did strive,
Amongst themselves, and did their labours share,
To helpe faire Pastorella home to drive
Her fleecie flocke; but Coridon most helpe did give.

X V I

But Meliboee (so hight that good old man)
Now seeing Calidore left all alone,
And night arrived hard at hand, began
Him to invite unto his simple home;
Which though it were a cottage clad with lome,
And all things therein meane, yet better so
To lodge then in the salvage fields to rome.
The knight full gladly soone agreed thereto,
(Being his harts owne wish,) and home with him did go.

X V I I

There he was welcome'd of that honest syre
And of his aged Beldame homely well;
Who him besought himselfe to disattyre,
And rest himselfe till supper time befell;
By which home came the fayrest Pastorell,
After her flocke she in their fold had tyde:
And supper readie dight they to it fell
With small adoe, and nature satisfyde,
The which doth litle crave contented to abyde.

X V I I I

Tho when they had their hunger slaked well,
And the fayre mayd the table ta'ne away,
The gentle knight, as he that did excell
In courtesie and well could doe and say,
For so great kindnesse as he found that day
Gan greatly thanke his host and his good wife;
And drawing thence his speach another way,

Gan highly to commend the happie life
Which Shepheards lead, without debate or bitter strife.

X I X

'How much' (sayd he) 'more happie is the state
In which ye, father, here doe dwell at ease,
Leading a life so free and fortunate
From all the tempests of these worldly seas,
Which tosse the rest in daungerous disease;
Where warres, and wreckes, and wicked enmitie
Doe them afflict, which no man can appease;
That certes I your happinesse envie,
And wish my lot were plast in such felicitie.'

X X

'Surely, my sonne,' (then answer'd he againe)
'If happie, then it is in this intent,
That having small yet doe I not complaine
Of want, ne wish for more it to augment,
But doe my selfe with that I have content;
So taught of nature, which doth litle need
Of forreine helpes to lifes due nourishment:
The fields my food, my flocke my rayment breed;
No better doe I weare, no better doe I feed.

X X I

'Therefore I doe not any one envy,
Nor am envyde of any one therefore:
They, that have much, feare much to loose thereby,
And store of cares doth follow riches store.
The litle that I have growes dayly more
Without my care, but onely to attend it;
My lambes doe every yeare increase their score,
And my flockes father daily doth amend it.
What have I, but to praise th' Almighty that doth send it!

X X I I

'To them that list the worlds gay showes I leave,
And to great ones such follies doe forgive;
Which oft through pride do their owne perill weave,
And through ambition downe themselves doe drive
To sad decay, that might contented live.
Me, no such cares nor combrous thoughts offend,
Ne once my minds unmoved quiet grieve;
But all the night in silver sleepe I spend,
And all the day to what I list I doe attend.

X X I I I

'Sometimes I hunt the Fox, the vowed foe
Unto my Lambes, and him dislodge away;
Sometimes the fawne I practise from the Doe,
Or from the Goat her kidde, how to convay:
Another while I baytes and nets display
The birds to catch, or fishes to beguyle;
And when I wearie am, I downe doe lay
My limbes in every shade to rest from toyle,
And drinke of every brooke when thirst my throte doth
       boyle.

X X I V

'The time was once, in my first prime of yeares,
When pride of youth forth pricked my desire,
That I disdain'd amongst mine equall peares
To follow sheepe and shepheards base attire:
For further fortune then I would inquire;
And, leaving home, to roiall court I sought,
Where I did sell my selfe for yearely hire,
And in the Princes gardin daily wrought:
There I beheld such vainenesse as I never thought.

X X V

'With sight whereof soone cloyd, and long deluded
With idle hopes which them doe entertaine,
After I had ten yeares my selfe excluded
From native home, and spent my youth in vaine,
I gan my follies to my selfe to plaine,
And this sweet peace, whose lacke did then appeare:
Tho, backe returning to my sheepe againe,
I from thenceforth have learn'd to love more deare
This lowly quiet life which I inherite here.'

X X V I

Whylest thus he talkt, the knight with greedy eare
Hong still upon his melting mouth attent;
Whose sensefull words empierst his hart so neare,
That he was rapt with double ravishment,
Both of his speach, that wrought him great content,
And also of the object of his vew,
On which his hungry eye was alwayes bent;
That twixt his pleasing tongue, and her faire hew,
He lost himselfe, and like one halfe entraunced grew.

XXVII

Yet to occasion meanes to worke his mind,
And to insinuate his harts desire,
He thus replyde: 'Now surely, syre, I find,
That all this worlds gay showes, which we admire,
Be but vaine shadowes to this safe retyre
Of life, which here in lowlinesse ye lead,
Fearlesse of foes, or fortunes wrackfull yre
Which tosseth states, and under foot doth tread
The mightie ones, affrayd of every chaunges dread.

XXVIII

'That even I, which daily doe behold
The glorie of the great mongst whom I won,
And now have prov'd what happinesse ye hold
In this small plot of your dominion,
Now loath great Lordship and ambition;
And wish th' heavens so much had graced mee,
As graunt me live in like condition;
Or that my fortunes might transposed bee
From pitch of higher place unto this low degree.'

XXIX

'In vaine' (said then old Meliboe) 'doe men
The heavens of their fortunes fault accuse,
Sith they know best what is the best for them;
For they to each such fortune doe diffuse,
As they doe know each can most aptly use:
For not that which men covet most is best,
Nor that thing worst which men do most refuse;
But fittest is, that all contented rest
With that they hold: each hath his fortune in his brest.

XXX

'It is the mynd that maketh good or ill,
That maketh wretch or happie, rich or poore;
For some, that hath abundance at his will,
Hath not enough, but wants in greatest store,
And other, that hath litle, askes no more,
But in that litle is both rich and wise;
For wisedome is most riches: fooles therefore
They are which fortunes doe by vowes devize,
Sith each unto himselfe his life may fortunize.'

XXVIII, 2   won: dwell

XXXI

'Since then in each mans self' (said Calidore)
'It is to fashion his owne lyfes estate,
Give leave awhyle, good father, in this shore
To rest my barcke, which hath bene beaten late
With stormes of fortune and tempestuous fate
In seas of troubles and of toylesome paine;
That, whether quite from them for to retrate
I shall resolve, or backe to turne againe,
I may here with your selfe some small repose obtaine.

XXXII

'Not that the burden of so bold a guest
Shall chargefull be, or chaunge to you at all;
For your meane food shall be my daily feast,
And this your cabin both my bowre and hall:
Besides, for recompence hereof I shall
You well reward, and golden guerdon give,
That may perhaps you better much withall,
And in this quiet make you safer live.'
So forth he drew much gold, and toward him it drive.

XXXIII

But the good man, nought tempted with the offer
Of his rich mould, did thrust it farre away,
And thus bespake: 'Sir knight, your bounteous proffer
Be farre fro me, to whom ye ill display
That mucky masse, the cause of mens decay,
That mote empaire my peace with daungers dread;
But, if ye algates covet to assay
This simple sort of life that shepheards lead,
Be it your owne: our rudenesse to your selfe aread.'

XXXIV

So there that night Sir Calidore did dwell,
And long while after, whilest him list remaine,
Dayly beholding the faire Pastorell,
And feeding on the bayt of his owne bane:
During which time he did her entertaine
With all kind courtesies he could invent;
And every day, her companie to gaine,
When to the field she went he with her went:
So for to quench his fire he did it more augment.

x x x v

But she that never had acquainted beene
With such queint usage, fit for Queenes and Kings,
Ne ever had such knightly service seene,
But, being bred under base shepheards wings,
Had ever learn'd to love the lowly things,
Did litle whit regard his courteous guize,
But cared more for Colins carolings
Then all that he could doe, or ever devize:
His layes, his loves, his lookes, she did them all despize.

x x x v i

Which Calidore perceiving, thought it best
To chaunge the manner of his loftie looke;
And doffing his bright armes himselfe addrest
In shepheards weed; and in his hand he tooke,
Instead of steele-head speare, a shepheards hooke;
That who had seene him then, would have bethought
On Phrygian Paris by Plexippus brooke,
When he the love of fayre Oenone sought,
What time the golden apple was unto him brought.

x x x v i i

So being clad unto the fields he went
With the faire Pastorella every day,
And kept her sheepe with diligent attent,
Watching to drive the ravenous Wolfe away,
The whylest at pleasure she mote sport and play;
And every evening helping them to fold:
And otherwhiles, for need, he did assay
In his strong hand their rugged teats to hold,
And out of them to presse the milke: love so much could.

x x x v i i i

Which seeing Coridon, who her likewise
Long time had lov'd, and hop'd her love to gaine,
He much was troubled at that straungers guize,
And many gealous thoughts conceiv'd in vaine,
That this of all his labour and long paine
Should reap the harvest ere it ripened were:
That made him scoule, and pout, and oft complaine
Of Pastorell to all the shepheards there,
That she did love a stranger swayne then him more dere.

x x x i x

And ever, when he came in companie
Where Calidore was present, he would loure
And byte his lip, and even for gealousie
Was readie oft his owne heart to devoure,
Impatient of any paramoure:
Who, on the other side, did seeme so farre
From malicing, or grudging his good houre,
That all he could he graced him with her,
Ne ever shewed signe of rancour or of jarre.

x l

And oft, when Coridon unto her brought
Or litle sparrowes stolen from their nest,
Or wanton squirrels in the woods farre sought,
Or other daintie thing for her addrest,
He would commend his guift, and make the best;
Yet she no whit his presents did regard,
Ne him could find to fancie in her brest:
This new-come shepheard had his market mard.
Old love is litle worth when new is more prefard.

x l i

One day, when as the shepheard swaynes together
Were met to make their sports and merrie glee,
As they are wont in faire sunshynie weather,
The whiles their flockes in shadowes shrouded bee,
They fell to daunce: then did they all agree
That Colin Clout should pipe, as one most fit;
And Calidore should lead the ring, as hee
That most in Pastorellaes grace did sit:
Thereat frown'd Coridon, and his lip closely bit.

x l i i

But Calidore, of courteous inclination,
Tooke Coridon and set him in his place,
That he should lead the daunce, as was his fashion;
For Coridon could daunce, and trimly trace:
And when as Pastorella, him to grace,
Her flowry garlond tooke from her owne head,
And plast on his, he did it soone displace,
And did it put on Coridons instead:
Then Coridon woxe frollicke, that earst seemed dead.

xl, 8   mard: spoiled

X L I I I

Another time, when as they did dispose
To practise games and maisteries to try,
They for their Judge did Pastorella chose;
A garland was the meed of victory:
There Coridon forth stepping openly
Did chalenge Calidore to wrestling game;
For he, through long and perfect industry,
Therein well practisd was, and in the same
Thought sure t' avenge his grudge, and worke his foe great
    shame.

X L I V

But Calidore he greatly did mistake,
For he was strong and mightily stiffe pight,
That with one fall his necke he almost brake;
And had he not upon him fallen light,
His dearest joynt he sure had broken quight.
Then was the oaken crowne by Pastorell
Given to Calidore as his due right;
But he, that did in courtesie excell,
Gave it to Coridon, and said he wonne it well.

X L V

Thus did the gentle knight himselfe abeare
Amongst that rusticke rout in all his deeds,
That even they, the which his rivals were,
Could not maligne him, but commend him needs;
For courtesie amongst the rudest breeds
Good will and favour. So it surely wrought
With this faire Mayd, and in her mynde the seeds
Of perfect love did sow, that last forth brought
The fruite of joy and blisse, though long time dearely bought.

X L V I

Thus Calidore continu'd there long time
To winne the love of the faire Pastorell,
Which having got, he used without crime
Or blamefull blot; but menaged so well,
That he, of all the rest which there did dwell,
Was favoured and to her grace commended.
But what straunge fortunes unto him befell,
Ere he attain'd the point by him intended,
Shall more conveniently in other place be ended.

XLVI, 3 crime: sin

CANTO X.

*Calidore sees the Graces daunce
To Colins melody;
The whiles his Pastorell is led
Into capivity.*

I

Who now does follow the foule Blatant Beast,
Whilest Calidore does follow that faire Mayd,
Unmyndfull of his vow, and high beheast
Which by the Faery Queene was on him layd,
That he should never leave, nor be delayd
From chacing him, till he had it attchieved?
But now, entrapt of love, which him betrayd,
He mindeth more how he may be relieved
With grace from her, whose love his heart hath sore en-
  grieved.

I I

That from henceforth he meanes no more to sew
His former quest, so full of toile and paine:
Another quest, another game in vew
He hath, the guerdon of his love to gaine;
With whom he myndes for ever to remaine,
And set his rest amongst the rusticke sort,
Rather then hunt still after shadowes vaine
Of courtly favour, fed with light report
Of every blaste, and sayling alwaies in the port.

I I I

Ne certes mote he greatly blamed be
From so high step to stoupe unto so low;
For who had tasted once (as oft did he)
The happy peace which there doth overflow,
And prov'd the perfect pleasures which doe grow
Amongst poore hyndes, in hils, in woods, in dales,
Would never more delight in painted show
Of such false blisse, as there is set for stales
T' entrap unwary fooles in their eternall bales.

I V

For what hath all that goodly glorious gaze
Like to one sight which Calidore did vew?

II, 6 set his rest: take up his per-   III, 8 stales: snares
manent abode

The glaunce whereof their dimmed eies would daze,
That never more they should endure the shew
Of that sunne-shine that makes them looke askew:
Ne ought, in all that world of beauties rare,
(Save onely Glorianaes heavenly hew,
To which what can compare?) can it compare;
The which, as commeth now by course, I will declare.

V

One day, as he did raunge the fields abroad,
Whilest his faire Pastorella was elsewhere,
He chaunst to come, far from all peoples troad,
Unto a place whose pleasaunce did appere
To passe all others on the earth which were:
For all that ever was by natures skill
Devized to worke delight was gathered there,
And there by her were poured forth at fill,
As if, this to adorne, she all the rest did pill.

V I

It was an hill plaste in an open plaine,
That round about was bordered with a wood
Of matchlesse hight, that seem'd th' earth to disdaine;
In which all trees of honour stately stood,
And did all winters as in sommer bud,
Spredding pavilions for the birds to bowre,
Which in their lower braunches sung aloud:
And in their tops the soring hauke did towre,
Sitting like King of fowles in majesty and powre:

V I I

And at the foote thereof a gentle flud
His silver waves did softly tumble downe,
Unmard with ragged mosse or filthy mud;
Ne mote wylde beastes, ne mote the ruder clowne,
Thereto approch; ne filth mote therein drowne:
But Nymphes and Faeries by the bancks did sit
In the woods shade which did the waters crowne,
Keeping all noysome things away from it,
And to the waters fall tuning their accents fit.

V I I I

And on the top thereof a spacious plaine
Did spred it selfe, to serve to all delight,
Either to daunce, when they to daunce would faine,

v, 9   pill: pillage   VII, 4   clowne: peasant

Or else to course about their bases light;
Ne ought there wanted which for pleasure might
Desired be, or thence to banish bale,
So pleasauntly the hill with equall hight
Did seeme to overlooke the lowly vale;
Therefore it rightly cleeped was mount Acidale.

I X

They say that Venus, when she did dispose
Her selfe to pleasaunce, used to resort
Unto this place, and therein to repose
And rest her selfe as in a gladsome port,
Or with the Graces there to play and sport;
That even her owne Cytheron, though in it
She used most to keepe her royall court,
And in her soveraine Majesty to sit,
She in regard hereof refusde and thought unfit.

x

Unto this place when as the Elfin Knight
Approcht, him seemed that the merry sound
Of a shrill pipe he playing heard on hight,
And many feete fast thumping th' hollow ground,
That through the woods their Eccho did rebound.
He nigher drew to weete what mote it be:
There he a troupe of Ladies dauncing found
Full merrily, and making gladfull glee,
And in the midst a Shepheard piping he did see.

X I

He durst not enter into th' open greene,
For dread of them unwares to be descryde,
For breaking of their daunce, if he were seene;
But in the covert of the wood did byde,
Beholding all, yet of them unespyde.
There he did see that pleased much his sight,
That even he him selfe his eyes envyde,
An hundred naked maidens lilly white
All raunged in a ring and dauncing in delight.

X I I

All they without were raunged in a ring,
And daunced round; but in the midst of them
Three other Ladies did both daunce and sing,
The whilest the rest them round about did hemme,
And like a girlond did in compasse stemme:

And in the middest of those same three was placed
Another Damzell, as a precious gemme
Amidst a ring most richly well enchaced,
That with her goodly presence all the rest much graced.

X I I I

Looke! how the crowne, which Ariadne wore
Upon her yvory forehead, that same day
That Theseus her unto his bridale bore,
When the bold Centaures made that bloudy fray
With the fierce Lapithes which did them dismay,
Being now placed in the firmament,
Through the bright heaven doth her beames display,
And is unto the starres an ornament,
Which round about her move in order excellent.

X I V

Such was the beauty of this goodly band,
Whose sundry parts were here too long to tell;
But she that in the midst of them did stand
Seem'd all the rest in beauty to excell,
Crownd with a rosie girlond that right well
Did her beseeme: And ever, as the crew
About her daunst, sweet flowres that far did smell
And fragrant odours they uppon her threw;
But most of all those three did her with gifts endew.

X V

Those were the Graces, daughters of delight,
Handmaides of Venus, which are wont to haunt
Uppon this hill, and daunce there day and night:
Those three to men all gifts of grace do graunt;
And all that Venus in her selfe doth vaunt
Is borrowed of them. But that faire one,
That in the midst was placed paravaunt,
Was she to whom that shepheard pypt alone;
That made him pipe so merrily, as never none.

X V I

She was, to weete, that jolly Shepheards lasse,
Which piped there unto that merry rout;
That jolly shepheard, which there piped, was
Poore Colin Clout (who knowes not Colin Clout?)
He pypt apace, whilest they him daunst about.
Pype, jolly shepheard, pype thou now apace
Unto thy love that made thee low to lout:

Thy love is present there with thee in place;
Thy love is there advaunst to be another Grace.

X V I I

Much wondred Calidore at this straunge sight,
Whose like before his eye had never seene;
And standing long astonished in spright,
And rapt with pleasaunce, wist not what to weene;
Whether it were the traine of beauties Queene,
Or Nymphes, or Faeries, or enchaunted show,
With which his eyes mote have deluded beene.
Therefore, resolving what it was to know,
Out of the wood he rose, and toward them did go.

X V I I I

But, soone as he appeared to their vew,
They vanisht all away out of his sight,
And cleane were gone, which way he never knew;
All save the shepheard, who, for fell despight
Of that displeasure, broke his bag-pipe quight,
And made great mone for that unhappy turne:
But Calidore, though no lesse sory wight
For that mishap, yet seeing him to mourne,
Drew neare, that he the truth of all by him mote learne.

X I X

And, first him greeting, thus unto him spake:
'Haile, jolly shepheard, which thy joyous dayes
Here leadest in this goodly merry-make,
Frequented of these gentle Nymphes alwayes,
Which to thee flocke to heare thy lovely layes!
Tell me, what mote these dainty Damzels be,
Which here with thee doe make their pleasant playes?
Right happy thou that mayst them freely see!
But why, when I them saw, fled they away from me?'

X X

'Not I so happy,' answerd then that swaine,
'As thou unhappy, which them thence didst chace,
Whom by no meanes thou canst recall againe;
For, being gone, none can them bring in place,
But whom they of them selves list so to grace.'
'Right sory I,' (saide then Sir Calidore)
'That my ill fortune did them hence displace;

xx, 2   unhappy: unfortunate

But since things passed none may now restore,
Tell me what were they all, whose lacke thee grieves so sore?'

X X I

Tho gan that shepheard thus for to dilate:
'Then wote, thou shepheard, whatsoever thou bee,
That all those Ladies, which thou sawest late,
Are Venus Damzels, all within her fee,
But differing in honour and degree:
They all are Graces which on her depend,
Besides a thousand more which ready bee
Her to adorne, when so she forth doth wend
But those three in the midst doe chiefe on her attend.

X X I I

'They are the daughters of sky-ruling Jove,
By him begot of faire Eurynome,
The Oceans daughter, in this pleasant grove,
As he, this way comming from feastfull glee
Of Thetis wedding with Æacidee,
In sommers shade him selfe here rested weary:
The first of them hight mylde Euphrosyne,
Next faire Aglaia, last Thalia merry;
Sweete Goddesses all three, which me in mirth do cherry!

X X I I I

'These three on men all gracious gifts bestow,
Which decke the body or adorne the mynde,
To make them lovely or well-favoured show;
As comely carriage, entertainement kynde,
Sweete semblaunt, friendly offices that bynde,
And all the complements of curtesie:
They teach us how to each degree and kynde
We should our selves demeane, to low, to hie,
To friends, to foes; which skill men call Civility.

X X I V

'Therefore they alwaies smoothly seeme to smile,
That we likewise should mylde and gentle be;
And also naked are, that without guile
Or false dissemblaunce all them plaine may see,
Simple and true, from covert malice free;
And eeke them selves so in their daunce they bore,
That two of them still froward seem'd to bee,

XXI, 4   fee: service   XXII, 9   cherry: cheer

But one still towards shew'd her selfe afore;
That good should from us goe, then come, in greater store.

          x x v

'Such were those Goddesses which ye did see;
But that fourth Mayd, which there amidst them traced,
Who can aread what creature mote she bee,
Whether a creature, or a goddesse graced
With heavenly gifts from heven first enraced?
But what so sure she was, she worthy was
To be the fourth with those three other placed:
Yet was she certes but a countrey lasse;
Yet she all other countrey lasses farre did passe:

          x x v i

'So farre, as doth the daughter of the day
All other lesser lights in light excell;
So farre doth she in beautyfull array
Above all other lasses beare the bell;
Ne lesse in vertue that beseemes her well
Doth she exceede the rest of all her race;
For which the Graces, that here wont to dwell,
Have for more honor brought her to this place,
And graced her so much to be another Grace.

          x x v i i

'Another Grace she well deserves to be,
In whom so many Graces gathered are,
Excelling much the meane of her degree;
Divine resemblaunce, beauty soveraine rare,
Firme Chastity, that spight ne blemish dare:
All which she with such courtesie doth grace,
That all her peres cannot with her compare,
But quite are dimmed when she is in place:
She made me often pipe, and now to pipe apace.

          x x v i i i

'Sunne of the world, great glory of the sky,
That all the earth doest lighten with thy rayes,
Great Gloriana, greatest Majesty!
Pardon thy shepheard, mongst so many layes
As he hath sung of thee in all his dayes,
To make one minime of thy poore handmayd,
And underneath thy feete to place her prayse;
That when thy glory shall be farre displayd
To future age, of her this mention may be made!'

XXIX

When thus that shepheard ended had his speach,
Sayd Calidore: 'Now sure it yrketh mee,
That to thy blisse I made this luckelesse breach,
As now the author of thy bale to be,
Thus to bereave thy loves deare sight from thee:
But, gentle Shepheard, pardon thou my shame,
Who rashly sought that which I mote not see.'
Thus did the courteous Knight excuse his blame,
And to recomfort him all comely meanes did frame.

XXX

In such discourses they together spent
Long time, as fit occasion forth them led;
With which the Knight him selfe did much content,
And with delight his greedy fancy fed
Both of his words, which he with reason red,
And also of the place, whose pleasures rare
With such regard his sences ravished,
That thence he had no will away to fare,
But wisht that with that shepheard he mote dwelling share.

TWO CANTOS OF
MUTABILITIE:

Which, Both for Forme and Matter,
Appeare to be Parcell of
Some Following Booke of

THE FAERIE QUEENE

Under
The Legend of Constancie.

CANTO VI.

Proud Change (not pleasd in mortall things
Beneath the Moone to raigne)
Pretends as well of Gods as Men
To be the Soveraine.

I

WHAT MAN THAT SEES the ever-whirling wheele,
Of Change, the which all mortall things doth sway,
But that therby doth find, and plainly feele,
How MUTABILITY in them doth play
Her cruell sports to many mens decay?
Which that to all may better yet appeare,
I will rehearse that whylome I heard say,
How she at first her selfe began to reare

Gainst all the Gods, and th' empire sought from them to
    beare.

I I

But first, here falleth fittest to unfold
Her antique race and linage ancient,
As I have found it registred of old
In Faery Land mongst records permanent.
She was, to weet, a daughter by descent
Of those old Titans that did whylome strive
With Saturnes sonne for heavens regiment;
Whom though high Jove of kingdome did deprive,
Yet many of their stemme long after did survive:

I I I

And many of them afterwards obtain'd
Great power of Jove, and high authority:
As Hecaté, in whose almighty hand
He plac't all rule and principalitie,
To be by her disposed diversly
To Gods and men, as she them list divide;
And drad Bellona, that doth sound on hie
Warres and allarums unto Nations wide,
That makes both heaven and earth to tremble at her pride.

I V

So likewise did this Titanesse aspire
Rule and dominion to her selfe to gaine;
That as a Goddesse men might her admire,
And heavenly honors yield, as to them twaine:
And first, on earth she sought it to obtaine;
Where shee such proofe and sad examples shewed
Of her great power, to many ones great paine,
That not men onely (whom she soone subdewed)
But eke all other creatures her bad dooings rewed.

V

For she the face of earthly things so changed,
That all which Nature had establisht first
In good estate, and in meet order ranged,
She did pervert, and all their statutes burst:
And all the worlds faire frame (which none yet durst
Of Gods or men to alter or misguide)
She alter'd quite; and made them all accurst

II, 7   regiment: rule   IV, 6   sad: weighty

That God had blest, and did at first provide
In that still happy state for ever to abide.

V I

Ne shee the lawes of Nature onely brake,
But eke of Justice, and of Policie;
And wrong of right, and bad of good did make
And death for life exchanged foolishlie:
Since which all living wights have learn'd to die,
And all this world is woxen daily worse.
O pittious worke of MUTABILITY,
By which we all are subject to that curse,
And death, instead of life, have sucked from our Nurse!

V I I

And now, when all the earth she thus had brought
To her behest, and thralled to her might,
She gan to cast in her ambitious thought
T' attempt the empire of the heavens hight,
And Jove himselfe to shoulder from his right.
And first, she past the region of the ayre
And of the fire, whose substance thin and slight
Made no resistance, ne could her contraire,
But ready passage to her pleasure did prepaire.

V I I I

Thence to the Circle of the Moone she clambe,
Where Cynthia raignes in everlasting glory,
To whose bright shining palace straight she came,
All fairely deckt with heavens goodly storie;
Whose silver gates (by which there sate an hory
Old aged Sire, with hower-glasse in hand,
Hight Time,) she entred, were he liefe or sory;
Ne staide till she the highest stage had scand,
Where Cynthia did sit, that never still did stand.

I X

Her sitting on an Ivory throne shee found,
Drawne of two steeds, th' one black, the other white,
Environd with tenne thousand starres around
That duly her attended day and night;
And by her side there ran her Page, that hight
Vesper, whom we the Evening-starre intend;
That with his Torche, still twinkling like twylight,

VI, 2   Policie: statecraft   VIII, 4   storie: history

Her lightened all the way where she should wend,
And joy to weary wandring travailers did lend:

x

That when the hardy Titanesse beheld
The goodly building of her Palace bright,
Made of the heavens substance, and up-held
With thousand Crystall pillors of huge hight,
She gan to burne in her ambitious spright,
And t' envie her that in such glory raigned.
Eftsoones she cast by force and tortious might
Her to displace, and to her selfe to have gained
The kingdome of the Night, and waters by her wained.

X I

Boldly she bid the Goddesse downe descend,
And let her selfe into that Ivory throne;
For she her selfe more worthy thereof wend,
And better able it to guide alone;
Whether to men, whose fall she did bemone,
Or unto Gods, whose state she did maligne,
Or to th' infernall Powers her need give lone
Of her faire light and bounty most benigne,
Her selfe of all that rule she deemed most condigne.

X I I

But she, that had to her that soveraigne seat
By highest Jove assign'd, therein to beare
Nights burning lamp, regarded not her threat,
Ne yielded ought for favour or for feare;
But with sterne count'naunce and disdainfull cheare,
Bending her horned browes, did put her back;
And, boldly blaming her for comming there,
Bade her attonce from heavens coast to pack,
Or at her perill bide the wrathfull Thunders wrack.

X I I I

Yet nathemore the Giantesse forbare,
But boldly preacing-on raught forth her hand
To pluck her downe perforce from off her chaire;
And, there-with lifting up her golden wand,
Threatned to strike her if she did with-stand:
Where-at the starres, which round about her blazed,
And eke the Moones bright wagon still did stand,

x, 7 tortious: wrong   x, 9 wained: moved

All beeing with so bold attempt amazed,
And on her uncouth habit and sterne looke still gazed.

X I V

Mean-while the lower World, which nothing knew
Of all that chaunced heere, was darkned quite;
And eke the heavens, and all the heavenly crew
Of happy wights, now unpurvaid of light,
Were much afraid, and wondred at that sight;
Fearing least Chaos broken had his chaine,
And brought againe on them eternall night;
But chiefely Mercury, that next doth raigne,
Ran forth in haste unto the king of Gods to plaine.

X V

All ran together with a great out-cry
To Joves faire palace fixt in heavens hight;
And, beating at his gates full earnestly,
Gan call to him aloud with all their might
To know what meant that suddaine lacke of light.
The father of the Gods, when this he heard,
Was troubled much at their so strange affright,
Doubting least Typhon were againe uprear'd,
Or other his old foes that once him sorely fear'd.

X V I

Eftsoones the sonne of Maia forth he sent
Downe to the Circle of the Moone, to knowe
The cause of this so straunge astonishment,
And why she did her wonted course forslowe;
And if that any were on earth belowe
That did with charmes or Magick her molest,
Him to attache, and downe to hell to throwe;
But if from heaven it were, then to arrest
The Author, and him bring before his presence prest.

X V I I

The wingd-foot God so fast his plumes did beat,
That soone he came where-as the Titanesse
Was striving with faire Cynthia for her seat;
At whose strange sight and haughty hardinesse
He wondred much, and feared her no lesse:
Yet laying feare aside to doe his charge,
At last he bade her (with bold stedfastnesse)

XIII, 9 uncouth: strange   XVI, 4 forslowe: delay

Ceasse to molest the Moone to walke at large,
Or come before high Jove her dooings to discharge.

XVIII

And there-with-all he on her shoulder laid
His snaky-wreathed Mace, whose awfull power
Doth make both Gods and hellish fiends affraid:
Where-at the Titanesse did sternly lower,
And stoutly answer'd, that in evill hower
He from his Jove such message to her brought,
To bid her leave faire Cynthia's silver bower;
Sith shee his Jove and him esteemed nought,
No more then Cynthia's selfe; but all their kingdoms sought.

XIX

The Heavens Herald staid not to reply,
But past away, his doings to relate
Unto his Lord; who now, in th' highest sky,
Was placed in his principall Estate,
With all the Gods about him congregate:
To whom when Hermes had his message told,
It did them all exceedingly amate,
Save Jove; who, changing nought his count'nance bold,
Did unto them at length these speeches wise unfold;

XX

'Harken to mee awhile, yee heavenly Powers!
Ye may remember since th' Earths cursed seed
Sought to assaile the heavens eternall towers,
And to us all exceeding feare did breed,
But, how we then defeated all their deed,
Yee all do knowe, and them destroyed quite;
Yet not so quite, but that there did succeed
An off-spring of their bloud, which did alite
Upon the fruitfull earth, which doth us yet despise.

XXI

'Of that bad seed is this bold woman bred,
That now with bold presumption doth aspire
To thrust faire Phœbe from her silver bed,
And eke our selves from heavens high Empire,
If that her might were match to her desire,
Wherefore it now behoves us to advise
What way is best to drive her to retire,

XIX, 7 amate: dismay

Whether by open force, or counsell wise:
Areed, ye sonnes of God, as best as ye can devise.'

X X I I

So having said, he ceast; and with his brow
(His black eye-brow, whose doomefull dreaded beck,
Is wont to wield the world unto his vow,
And even the highest Powers of heaven to check)
Made signe to them in their degrees to speake,
Who straight gan cast their counsell grave and wise.
Mean-while th' Earths daughter, thogh she nought did reck
Of Hermes message, yet gan now advise
What course were best to take in this hot bold emprize.

X X I I I

Eftsoones she thus resolv'd; that whil'st the Gods
(After returne of Hermes Embassie)
Were troubled, and amongst themselves at ods,
Before they could new counsels re-allie,
To set upon them in that extasie,
And take what fortune, time, and place would lend.
So forth she rose, and through the purest sky
To Joves high Palace straight cast to ascend,
To prosecute her plot. Good on-set boads good end.

X X I V

Shee there arriving boldly in did pass;
Where all the Gods she found in counsell close,
All quite unarm'd, as then their manner was.
At sight of her they suddaine all arose
In great amaze, ne wist what way to chose:
But Jove, all fearlesse, forc't them to aby;
And in his soveraine throne gan straight dispose
Himselfe, more full of grace and Majestie,
That mote encheare his friends, and foes mote terrifie.

X X V

That when the haughty Titanesse beheld,
All were she fraught with pride and impudence,
Yet with the sight thereof was almost queld;
And, inly quaking, seem'd as reft of sense
And voyd of speech in that drad audience,
Until that Jove himselfe her selfe bespake:
'Speake, thou fraile woman, speake with confidence;

XXIII, 5   extasie: astonishment   XXIV, 6   aby: remain

Whence art thou, and what doost thou here now make?
What idle errand hast thou earths mansion to forsake?'

XXVI

She, halfe confused with his great commaund,
Yet gathering spirit of her natures pride,
Him boldly answer'd thus to his demaund:
'I am a daughter, by the mothers side,
Of her that is Grand-mother magnifide
Of all the Gods, great Earth, great Chaos child;
But by the fathers, (be it not envide)
I greater am in bloud (whereon I build)
Then all the Gods, though wrongfully from heaven exil'd.

XXVII

'For Titan (as ye all acknowledge must)
Was Saturnes elder brother by birth-right,
Both sonnes of Uranus; but by unjust
And guilefull meanes, through Corybantes slight,
The younger thrust the elder from his right:
Since which thou, Jove, injuriously hast held
The Heavens rule from Titans sonnes by might,
And them to hellish dungeons downe hast feld.
Witnesse, ye Heavens, the truth of all that I have teld!'

XXVIII

Whil'st she thus spake, the Gods, that gave good eare
To her bold words, and marked well her grace,
(Beeing of stature tall as any there
Of all the Gods, and beautifull of face
As any of the Goddesses in place,)
Stood all astonied; like a sort of steeres,
Mongst whom some beast of strange and forraine race
Unwares is chaunc't, far straying from his peeres:
So did their ghastly gaze bewray their hidden feares.

XXIX

Till, having pauz'd awhile, Jove thus bespake:
'Will never mortall thoughts ceasse to aspire
In this bold sort to Heaven claime to make,
And touch celestiall seats with earthly mire?
I would have thought that bold Procrustes hire,
Or Typhons fall, or proud Ixions paine,
Or great Prometheus tasting of our ire,

XXVII, 4   slight: sleight, trickery

Would have suffiz'd the rest for to restraine,
And warn'd all men by their example to refraine.

XXX

'But now this off-scum of that cursed fry
Dare to renew the like bold enterprize,
And chalenge th' heritage of this our skie;
Whom what should hinder, but that we likewise
Should handle as the rest of her allies,
And thunder-drive to hell?' With that, he shooke
His Nectar-deawed locks, with which the skyes
And all the world beneath for terror quooke,
And eft his burning levin-brond in hand he tooke.

XXXI

But when he looked on her lovely face,
In which faire beames of beauty did appeare
That could the greatest wrath soone turne to grace,
(Such sway doth beauty even in Heaven beare)
He staid his hand; and, having chang'd his cheare
He thus againe in milder wise began:
'But ah! if Gods should strive with flesh yfere,
Then shortly should the progeny of man
Be rooted out, if Jove should do still what he can.

XXXII

'But thee, faire Titans child, I rather weene,
Through some vaine errour, or inducement light,
To see that mortall eyes have never seene;
Or through ensample of thy sisters might,
Bellona, whose great glory thou doost spight,
Since thou hast seene her dreadfull power belowe,
Mongst wretched men (dismaide with her affright)
To bandie Crownes, and Kingdoms to bestowe:
And sure thy worth no lesse than hers doth seem to showe.

XXXIII

'But wote thou this, thou hardy Titanesse,
That not the worth of any living wight
May challenge ought in Heavens interesse;
Much less the Title of old Titans Right:
For we by conquest, of our soveraine might,
And by eternal doome of Fates decree,
Have wonne the Empire of the Heavens bright;

XXX, 9 levin-brond: flash of lightning XXXIII, 3 interesse: interest

Which to our selves we hold, and to whom wee
Shall worthy deeme partakers of our blisse to bee.

X X X I V

'Then ceasse thy idle claime, thou foolish gerle;
And seeke by grace and goodnesse to obtaine
That place, from which by folly Titan fell:
There to thou maist perhaps, if so thou faine
Have Jove thy gracious Lord and Soveraine.'
So having said, she thus to him replide:
'Ceasse, Saturnes sonne, to seeke by proffers vaine
Of idle hopes t' allure me to thy side,
For to betray my Right before I have it tride.

X X X V

'But thee, O Jove! no equall Judge I deeme
Of my desert, or of my dewfull Right:
That in thine owne behalfe maist partiall seeme:
But to the highest him, that is behight
Father of Gods and men by equall might,
To weet the God of Nature, I appeale.'
There-at Jove wexed wroth, and in his spright
Did inly grudge, yet did it well conceale;
And bade Dan Phœbus scribe her Appellation seale.

X X X V I

Eftsoones the time and place appointed were,
Where all, both heavenly Powers and earthly wights,
Before great Natures presence should appeare,
For triall of their Titles and best Rights:
That was, to weet, upon the highest hights
Of Arlo-hill (Who knowes not Arlo-hill?)
That is the highest head (in all mens sights)
Of my old father MOLE, whom Shepheards quill
Renowmed hath with hymnes fit for a rurall skill.

X X X V I I

And, were it not ill fitting for this file
To sing of hilles and woods mongst warres and Knights,
I would abate the sternenesse of my stile,
Mongst these sterne stounds to mingle soft delights;
And tell how Arlo, through Dianaes spights,
(Beeing of old the best and fairest Hill
That was in all this holy Islands hights)

xxxvii, 1   file: recital

Was made the most unpleasant and most ill:
Meane-while, O Clio! lend Calliope thy quill.

XXXVIII

Whylome when IRELAND florished in fame
Of wealths and goodnesse, far above the rest
Of all that beare the British Islands name,
The gods then us'd (for pleasure and for rest)
Oft to resort there-to, when seem'd them best,
But none of all there-in more pleasure found
Then Cynthia, that is soveraine Queene profest
Of woods and forrests which therein abound,
Sprinkled with wholsom waters more then most on ground:

XXXIX

But mongst them all, as fittest for her game,
Eyther for chace of beasts with hound or boawe,
Or for to shrowde in shade from Phœbus flame,
Or bathe in fountaines that do freshly flowe
Or from high hilles or from the dales belowe,
She chose this Arlo; where she did resort
With all her Nymphes enranged on a rowe,
With whom the woody Gods did oft consort,
For with the Nymphes the Satyres love to play and sport.

XL

Amongst the which there was a Nymph that hight
Molanna; daughter of old Father Mole,
And sister unto Mulla faire and bright,
Unto whose bed false Bregog whylome stole,
That Shepheard Colin dearely did condole,
And made her lucklesse loves well known to be:
But this Molanna, were she not so shole,
Were no lesse faire and beautifull then shee;
Yet, as she is, a fayrer flood may no man see.

XLI

For, first, she springs out of two marble Rocks,
On which a grove of Oakes high-mounted growes,
That as a girlond seemes to deck the locks
Of som faire Bride, brought forth with pompous showes
Out of her bowre, that many flowers strowes:
So through the flowry Dales she tumbling downe
Through many woods and shady coverts flowes,

XL, 7 shole: shallow

(That on each side her silver channell crowne)
Till to the Plaine she come, whose Valleyes she doth drowne.

XLII

In her sweet streames Diana used oft
(After her sweaty chace and toylesome play)
To bathe her selfe; and, after, on the soft
And downy grasse her dainty limbes to lay
In covert shade, where none behold her may,
For much she hated sight of living eye.
Foolish god Faunus, though full many a day
He saw her clad, yet longed foolishly
To see her naked mongst her Nymphes in privity.

XLIII

No way he found to compasse his desire,
But to corrupt Molanna, this her maid,
Her to discover for some secret hire:
So her with flattering words he first assaid;
And after, pleasing gifts for her purvaid,
Queene-apples, and red Cherries from the tree,
With which he her allured, and betrayd
To tell what time he might her Lady see
When she her selfe did bathe, that he might secret bee.

XLIV

There-to he promist, if shee would him pleasure
With this small boone, to quit her with a better;
To weet, that where-as shee had out of measure
Long lov'd the Fanchin, who by nought did set her.
That he would undertake for this to get her
To be his Love, and of him liked well:
Besides all which, he vow'd to be her debter
For many moe good turnes then he would tell,
The least of which this little pleasure should excell.

XLV

The simple mayd did yield to him anone;
And eft him placed where he close might view
That never any saw, save onely one,
Who, for his hire to so foole-hardy dew,
Was of his hounds devour'd in Hunters hew.
Tho, as her manner was on sunny day,
Diana, with her Nymphes about her, drew

XLV, 5   hew: guise

To this sweet spring; where, doffing her array,
She bath'd her lovely limbes, for Jove a likely pray.

X L V I

There Faunus saw that pleased much his eye,
And made his hart to tickle in his brest,
That, for great joy of some-what he did spy,
He could him not containe in silent rest;
But, breaking forth in laughter, loud profest
His foolish thought: A foolish Faune indeed,
That couldst not hold thy selfe so hidden blest,
But wouldest needs thine owne conceit areed!
Babblers unworthy been of so divine a meed.

X L V I I

The Goddesse, all abashed with that noise,
In haste forth started from the guilty brooke;
And, running straight where-as she heard his voice,
Enclos'd the bush about, and there him tooke,
Like darred Larke, not daring up to looke
On her whose sight before so much he sought.
Thence forth they drew him by the hornes, and shooke
Nigh all to peeces, that they left him nought;
And then into the open light they forth him brought.

X L V I I I

Like as an huswife, that with busie care
Thinks of her Dairy to make wondrous gaine,
Finding where-as some wicked beast unware
That breakes into her Dayr' house, there doth draine
Her creaming pannes, and frustrate all her paine,
Hath, in some snare of gin set close behind,
Entrapped him, and caught into her traine;
Then thinkes what punishment were best assign'd,
And thousand deathes deviseth in her vengefull mind.

X L I X

So did Diana and her maydens all
Use silly Faunus, now within their baile:
They mocke and scorne him, and him foule miscall;
Some by the nose him pluckt, some by the taile,
And by his goatish beard some did him haile:
Yet he (poore soule!) with patience all did beare;
For nought against their wils might countervaile:

xLVII, 5 darred: frightened   XLIX, 2 baile: custody

Ne ought he said, what ever he did heare,
But, hanging downe his head, did like a Mome appeare.

L

At length, when they had flouted him their fill,
They gan to cast what penaunce him to give.
Some would have gelt him; but that same would spill
The Wood-gods breed, which must for ever live:
Others would through the river him have drive
And ducked deepe; but that seem'd penaunce light:
But most agreed, and did this sentence give,
Him in Deares skin to clad; and in that plight
To hunt him with their hounds, him selfe save how hee might.

L I

But Cynthia's selfe, more angry then the rest,
Thought not enough to punish him in sport,
And of her shame to make a gamesome jest;
But gan examine him in straighter sort,
Which of her Nymphes, or other close consort,
Him thither brought, and her to him betraid?
He, much affeard, to her confessed short
That 'twas Molanna which her so bewraid.
Then all attonce their hands upon Molanna laid.

L I I

But him (according as they had decreed)
With a Deeres-skin they covered, and then chast
With all their hounds that after him did speed;
But he, more speedy, from them fled more fast
Then any Deere, so sore him dread aghast.
They after follow'd all with shrill out-cry,
Shouting as they the heavens would have brast;
That all the woods and dales, where he did flie,
Did ring againe, and loud re-eccho to the skie.

L I I I

So they him follow'd till they weary were;
When, back returning to Molann' againe,
They, by commaund'ment of Diana, there
Her whelm'd with stones. Yet Faunus (for her paine)
Of her beloved Fanchin did obtaine,
That her he would receive unto his bed:

XLIX, 9   Mome: blockhead   LI, 4   straighter: stricter
L, 3   gelt: castrated   LII, 7   brast: burst

So now her waves passe through a pleasant Plaine,
Till with the Fanchin she her selfe do wed,
And (both combin'd) themselves in one faire river spred.

L I V

Nath'lesse Diana, full of indignation,
Thence-forth abandond her delicious brooke,
In whose sweet streame, before that bad occasion,
So much delight to bathe her limbes she tooke:
Ne onely her, but also quite forsooke
All those faire forrests about Arlo hid;
And all that Mountaine, which doth over-looke
The richest champain that may else be rid;
And the faire Shure, in which are thousand Salmons bred.

L V

Them all, and all that she so deare did way,
Thence-forth she left; and, parting from the place,
There-on a heavy haplesse curse did lay;
To weet, that Wolves, where she was wont to space,
Should harbour'd be and all those Woods deface,
And Thieves should rob and spoile that Coast around:
Since which, those Woods, and all that goodly Chase
Doth to this day with Wolves and Thieves abound:
Which too-too true that lands in-dwellers since have found.

C A N T O   V I I.

Pealing from Jove to Nature's bar,
Bold Alteration pleades
Large Evidence: but Nature soone
Her righteous Doome areads.

I

A<small>H</small>! WHITHER DOOST thou now, thou greater Muse,
Me from these woods and pleasing forrests bring,
And my fraile spirit, (that dooth oft refuse
This too high flight, unfit for her weake wing)
Lift up aloft, to tell of heavens King
(Try soveraine Sire) his fortunate successe;
And victory in bigger notes to sing
Which he obtain'd against that Titanesse,
That him of heavens Empire sought to dispossesse?

LV, 1 way: weigh, esteem   LV, 7 Chase: hunting ground

II

Yet, sith I needs must follow thy behest,
Do thou my weaker wit with skill inspire,
Fit for this turne; and in my feeble brest
Kindle fresh sparks of that immortall fire
Which learned minds inflameth with desire
Of heavenly things: for who, but thou alone
That art yborne of heaven and heavenly Sire,
Can tell things doen in heaven so long ygone,
So farre past memory of man that may be knowne?

III

Now, at the time that was before agreed,
The gods assembled all on Arlo Hill;
As well those that are sprung of heavenly seed,
As those that all the other world do fill,
And rule both sea and land unto their will:
Onely th' infernall Powers might not appeare;
As well for horror of their count'naunce ill,
As for th' unruly fiends which they did feare;
Yet Pluto and Proserpina were present there.

IV

And thither also came all other creatures,
What-ever life or motion do retaine,
According to their sundry kinds of features,
That Arlo scarsly could them all containe,
So full they filled every hill and Plaine;
And had not Natures Sergeant (that is Order)
Them well disposed by his busie paine,
And raunged farre abroad in every border,
They would have caused much confusion and disorder.

V

Then forth issewed (great goddesse) great dame Nature
With goodly port and gracious Majesty,
Being far greater and more tall of stature
Then any of the gods or Powers on hie:
Yet certes by her face and physnomy,
Whether she man or woman inly were,
That could not any creature well descry;
For with a veile, that wimpled every where,
Her head and face was hid that mote to none appeare.

V I

That, some do say, was so by skill devized,
To hide the terror of her uncouth hew
From mortall eyes that should be sore agrized;
For that her face did like a Lion shew,
That eye of wight could not indure to view:
But others tell that it so beautious was,
And round about such beames of splendor threw,
That it the Sunne a thousand times did pass,
Ne could be seene but like an image in a glass.

V I I

That well may seemen true; for well I weene,
That this same day when she on Arlo sat,
Her garment was so bright and wondrous sheene,
That my fraile wit cannot devize to what
It to compare, nor finde like stuffe to that:
As those three sacred Saints, though else most wise,
Yet on mount Thabor quite their wits forgat,
When they their glorious Lord in strange disguise
Transfigur'd sawe; his garments so did daze their eyes.

V I I I

In a fayre Plaine upon an equall Hill
She placed was in a pavilion;
Not such as Craftes-men by their idle skill
Are wont for Princes states to fashion;
But th' Earth herselfe, of her owne motion,
Out of her fruitfull bosome made to growe
Most dainty trees, that, shooting up anon,
Did seeme to bow their bloosming heads full lowe
For homage unto her, and like a throne did showe.

I X

So hard it is for any living wight
All her array and vestiments to tell,
That old Dan Geffrey (in whose gentle spright,
The pure well head of Poesie did dwell)
In his *Foules parley* durst not with it mel,
But it transferd to Alane, who he thought
Had in his *Plaint of kinde* describ'd it well:

vi, 3   agrized: horrified
viii, 1   equall Hill: level hill, plateau
ix, 5   mel: meddle

Which who will read set forth so as it ought,
Go seek he out that Alane where he may be sought.

x

And all the earth far underneath her feete
Was dight with flowers that voluntary grew
Out of the ground, and sent forth odours sweet;
Tenne thousand mores of sundry sent and hew,
That might delight the smell, or please the view,
The which the Nymphes from all the brooks thereby
Had gathered, they at her foot-stoole threw;
That richer seem'd then any tapestry,
That Princes bowres adorne with painted imagery.

x i

And Mole himselfe, to honour her the more,
Did deck himselfe in freshest faire attire;
And his high head, that seemeth alwayes hore
With hardned frosts of former winters ire,
He with an Oaken girlond now did tire,
As if the love of some new Nymph, late seene,
Had in him kindled youthfull fresh desire,
And made him change his gray attire to greene:
Ah, gentle Mole! such joyance hath thee well beseene.

x i i

Was never so great joyance since the day
That all the gods whylome assembled were
On Hæmus hill in their divine array,
To celebrate the solemne bridall cheare
Twixt Peleus and Dame Thetis pointed there;
Where Phœbus selfe, that god of Poets hight,
They say, did sing the spousall hymne full cleere,
That all the gods were ravisht with delight
Of his celestiall song, and Musicks wondrous might.

x i i i

This great Grandmother of all creatures bred,
Great Nature, ever young, yet full of eld;
Still mooving, yet unmoved from her sted;
Unseene of any, yet of all beheld;
Thus sitting in her throne, as I have teld,
Before her came dame Mutability;
And, being lowe before her presence feld

x, 4 mores: plants   xii, 5 pointed: appointed

With meek obaysance and humilitie,
Thus gan her plaintif Plea with words to amplifie:

X I V

'To thee, O greatest Goddesse, onely great!
An humble suppliant loe! I lowely fly,
Seeking for Right, which I of thee entreat,
Who Right to all dost deale indifferently,
Damning all Wrong and tortious Injurie,
Which any of thy creatures do to other
(Oppressing them with power unequally,)
Sith of them all thou art the equall mother,
And knittest each to each, as brother unto brother.

X V

'To thee therefore of this same Jove I plaine,
And of his fellow gods that faine to be,
That challenge to themselves the whole worlds raign,
Of which the greatest part is due to me,
And heaven it selfe by heritage in Fee:
For heaven and earth I both alike do deeme,
Sith heaven and earth are both alike to thee.
And gods no more then men thou doest esteeme;
For even the gods to thee, as men to gods, do seeme.

X V I

'Then weigh, O soveraigne goddesse! by what right
These gods do claime the worlds whole soveraintie,
And that is onely dew unto thy might
Arrogate to themselves ambitiously:
As for the gods owne principality,
Which Jove usurpes unjustly, that to be
My heritage Jove's selfe cannot denie,
From my great Grandsire Titan unto mee
Deriv'd by dew descent; as is well knowen to thee.

X V I I

'Yet mauger Jove, and all his gods beside,
I do possesse the worlds most regiment;
As if ye please it into parts divide,
And every parts inholders to convent,
Shall to your eyes appeare incontinent.
And, first, the Earth (great mother of us all)

XIV, 5 tortious: wrong	XVII, 2 regiment: rule
XVII, 1 mauger: in spite of	XVII, 4 convent: convene, summon
XVII, 2 most: largest	

That only seemes unmov'd and permanent,
And unto Mutabilitie not thrall,
Yet is she chang'd in part, and eeke in generall:

XVIII

'For all that from her springs, and is ybredde,
How-ever faire it flourish for a time,
Yet see we soone decay; and, being dead,
To turne againe unto their earthly slime:
Yet, out of their decay and mortall crime,
We daily see new creatures to arize,
And of their Winter spring another Prime,
Unlike in forme, and chang'd by strange disguise:
So turne they still about, and change in restlesse wise.

XIX

'As for her tenants, that is, man and beasts,
The beasts we daily see massacred dy
As thralls and vassals unto mens beheasts;
And men themselves do change continually,
From youth to eld, from wealth to poverty,
From good to bad, from bad to worst of all:
Ne doe their bodies only flit and fly,
But eeke their minds (which they immortall call)
Still change and vary thoughts, as new occasions fall.

XX

'Ne is the water in more constant case,
Whether those same on high, or these belowe;
For th' Ocean moveth still from place to place,
And every River still doth ebbe and flowe;
Ne any Lake, that seems most still and slowe,
Ne Poole so small, that can his smoothnesse holde
When any winde doth under heaven blowe;
With which the clouds are also tost and roll'd,
Now like great Hills, and streight like sluces them unfold.

XXI

'So likewise are all watry living wights
Still tost and turned with continuall change
Never abiding in their stedfast plights:
The fish, still floting, doe at random range,
And never rest, but evermore exchange
Their dwelling places, as the streames them carrie:
Ne have the watry foules a certaine grange

Wherein to rest, ne in one stead do tarry;
But flitting still doe flie, and still their places vary.

X X I I

'Next is the Ayre; which who feeles not by sense
(For of all sense it is the middle meane)
To flit still, and with subtill influence
Of his thin spirit all creatures to maintaine
In state of life? O weake life! that does leane
On thing so tickle as th' unsteady ayre,
Which every howre is chang'd and altred cleane
With every blast that bloweth, fowle or faire:
The faire doth it prolong; the fowle doth it impaire.

X X I I I

'Therein the changes infinite beholde,
Which to her creatures every minute chaunce;
Now boyling hot, streight friezing deadly cold;
Now faire sun-shine, that makes all skip and daunce;
Streight bitter stormes, and balefull countenance
That makes them all to shiver and to shake:
Rayne, haile, and snowe do pay them sad penance,
And dreadfull thunder-claps (that make them quake)
With flames and flashing lights that thousand changes make.

X X I V

'Last is the fire; which, though it live forever,
Ne can be quenched quite, yet every day
We see his parts, so soone as they do sever,
To lose their heat and shortly to decay;
So makes himself his owne consuming pray:
Ne any living creatures doth he breed,
But all that are of others bredd doth slay;
And with their death his cruell life dooth feed;
Nought leaving but their barren ashes without seede.

X X V

'Thus all these fower (the which the ground-work bee
Of all the world and of all living wights)
To thousand sorts of Change we subject see:
Yet are they chang'd (by other wondrous slights)
Into themselves, and lose their native mights;
The Fire to Ayre, and th' Ayre to Water sheere,
And Water into Earth; yet Water fights
With Fire, and Ayre with Earth, approaching neere:
Yet all are in one body, and as one appeare.

X X V I

'So in them all raignes Mutabilitie;
How-ever these, that Gods themselves do call,
Of them do claime the rule and soverainty;
As Vesta, of the fire æthereall;
Vulcan, of this with us so usuall;
Ops, of the earth; and Juno, of the ayre;
Neptune, of seas; and Nymphes, of Rivers all:
For all those Rivers to me subject are,
And all the rest, which they usurp, be all my share.

X X V I I

'Which to approven true, as I have told,
Vouchsafe, O Goddesse! to thy presence call
The rest which doe the world in being hold;
As times and seasons of the yeare that fall:
Of all the which demand in generall,
Or judge thyselfe, by verdit of thine eye,
Whether to me they are not subject all.'
Nature did yeeld thereto; and by-and-by
Bade Order call them all before her Majesty.

X X V I I I

So forth issew'd the Seasons of the yeare.
First, lusty Spring, all dight in leaves of flowres
That freshly budded and new bloosmes did beare,
(In which a thousand birds had built their bowres
That sweetly sung to call forth Paramours)
And in his hand a javelin he did beare,
And on his head (as fit for warlike stoures)
A guilt engraven morion he did weare;
That as some did him love, so others did him feare.

X X I X

Then came the jolly Sommer, being dight
In a thin silken cassock coloured greene,
That was unlyned all, to be more light;
And on his head a girlond well beseene
He wore, from which, as he had chauffed been,
The sweat did drop; and in his hand he bore
A boawe and shaftes, as he in forrest greene
Had hunted late the Libbard or the Bore,
And now would bathe his limbes with labor heated sore.

xxvii, 8   by-and-by: immediately

X X X

Then came the Autumne all in yellow clad,
As though he joyed in his plentious store,
Laden with fruits that made him laugh, full glad
That he had banisht hunger, which to-fore
Had by the belly oft him pinched sore:
Upon his head a wreath, that was enrold
With ears of corne of every sort, he bore;
And in his hand a sickle he did holde,
To reape the ripened fruits the which the earth had yold.

X X X I

Lastly, came Winter cloathed all in frize,
Chattering his teeth for cold that did him chill;
Whil'st on his hoary beard his breath did freese,
And the dull drops, that from his purpled bill
As from a limbeck did adown distill.
In his right hand a tipped staffe he held,
With which his feeble steps he stayed still;
For he was faint with cold, and weak with eld,
That scarse his loosed limbes he hable was to weld.

X X X I I

These, marching softly, thus in order went;
And after them the Monthes all riding came.
First, sturdy March, with brows full sternly bent
And armed strongly, rode upon a Ram,
The same which over Hellespontus swam;
Yet in his hand a spade he also hent,
And in a bag all sorts of seeds ysame,
Which on the earth he strowed as he went,
And fild her wombe with fruitfull hope of nourishment.

X X X I I I

Next came fresh Aprill, full of lustyhed,
And wanton as a Kid whose horne new buds:
Upon a Bull he rode, the same which led
Europa floting through th' Argolick fluds:
His hornes were gilden all with golden studs,
And garnished with garlonds goodly dight
Of all the fairest flowres and freshest buds
Which th' earth brings forth; and wet he seem'd in sight
With waves, through which he waded for his loves delight.

xxx, 9   yold: yielded

XXXIV

Then came faire May, the fayrest mayd on ground,
Deckt all with dainties of her seasons pryde,
And throwing flowres out of her lap around:
Upon two brethrens shoulders she did ride,
The twinnes of Leda; which on eyther side
Supported her like to their soveraigne Queene:
Lord! how all creatures laught when her they spide,
And leapt and daunc't as they had ravisht beene!
And Cupid selfe about her fluttred all in greene.

XXXV

And after her came jolly June, arrayd
All in greene leaves, as he a Player were;
Yet in his time he wrought as well as playd,
That by his plough-yrons mote right well appeare.
Upon a Crab he rode, that him did beare
With crooked crawling steps an uncouth pase,
And backward yode, as Bargemen wont to fare
Bending their force contrary to their face;
Like that ungracious crew which faines demurest grace.

XXXVI

Then came hot July boyling like to fire,
That all his garments he had cast away.
Upon a Lyon raging yet with ire
He boldly rode, and made him to obay:
It was the beast that whylome did forray
The Nemæan forrest, till th' Amphytrionide
Him slew, and with his hide did him array.
Behinde his back a sithe, and by his side
Under his belt he bore a sickle circling wide.

XXXVII

The sixt was August, being rich arrayd
In garment all of gold downe to the ground;
Yet rode he not, but led a lovely Mayd
Forth by the lilly hand, the which was cround
With eares of corne, and full her hand was found:
That was the righteous Virgin, which of old
Liv'd here on earth, and plenty made abound;
But after Wrong was lov'd, and Justice solde,
She left th' unrighteous world, and was to heaven extold.

xxxvii, 9   extold: raised

XXXVIII

Next him September marched, eeke on foote,
Yet was he heavy laden with the spoyle
Of harvests riches, which he made his boot,
And him enricht with bounty of the soyle:
In his one hand, as fit for harvests toyle,
He held a knife-hook; and in th' other hand
A paire of waights, with which he did assoyle
Both more and lesse, where it in doubt did stand,
And equall gave to each as Justice duly scann'd.

XXXIX

Then came October full of merry glee;
For yet his noule was totty of the must,
Which he was treading in the wine-fats see,
And of the joyous oyle, whose gentle gust
Made him so frollick and so full of lust:
Upon a dreadfull Scorpion he did ride,
The same which by Dianaes doom unjust
Slew great Orion; and eeke by his side
He had his ploughing-share and coulter ready tyde.

XL

Next was November; he full grosse and fat
As fed with lard, and that right well might seeme;
For he had been a fatting hogs of late,
That yet his browes with sweat did reek and steem,
And yet the season was full sharp and breem:
In planting eeke he took no small delight.
Whereon he rode not easie was to deeme;
For it a dreadfull Centaure was in sight,
The seed of Saturne and faire Nais, Chiron hight.

XLI

And after him came next the chill December:
Yet he, through merry feasting which he made
And great bonfires, did not the cold remember;
His Saviour's birth his mind so much did glad.
Upon a shaggy-bearded Goat he rode,
The same wherewith Dan Jove in tender yeares,
They say, was nourisht by th' Idæan mayd;

XXXVIII, 7   assoyle: determine
XXXIX, 2   noule: head
XXXIX, 2   must: new wine

XXXIX, 3   wine-fats see: abode of
the wine vats
XL, 5   breem: cold

And in his hand a broad deepe boawle he beares,
Of which he freely drinks an health to all his peeres.

X L I I

Then came old January, wrapped well
In many weeds to keep the cold away;
Yet did he quake and quiver, like to quell,
And blowe his nayles to warme them if he may;
For they were numbd with holding all the day
An hatchet keene, with which he felled wood
And from the trees did lop the needlesse spray:
Upon an huge great Earth-pot steane he stood,
From whose wide mouth there flowed forth the Romane
    Flood.

X L I I I

And lastly came cold February, sitting
In an old wagon, for he could not ride,
Drawne of two fishes, for the season fitting,
Which through the flood before did softly slyde
And swim away: yet had he by his side
His plough and harnesse fit to till the ground,
And tooles to prune the trees, before the pride
Of hasting Prime did make them burgein round.
So past the twelve Months forth, and their dew places found.

X L I V

And after these there came the Day and Night,
Riding together both with equal pase,
Th' one on a Palfrey blacke, the other white;
But Night had covered her uncomely face
With a blacke veile, and held in hand a mace,
On top whereof the moon and stars were pight;
And sleep and darknesse round about did trace:
But Day did beare upon his scepters hight
The goodly Sun encompast all with beames bright.

X L V

Then came the Howres, faire daughters of high Jove
And timely Night; the which were all endewed
With wondrous beauty fit to kindle love;
But they were virgins all, and love eschewed
That might forslack the charge to them fore-shewed
By mighty Jove; who did them porters make
Of heavens gate (whence all the gods issued)

XLII, 3   quell: perish   XLII, 8   steane: stone

Which they did daily watch, and nightly wake
By even turnes, ne ever did their charge forsake.

X L V I

And after all came Life, and lastly Death;
Death with most grim and griesly visage seene,
Yet is he nought but parting of the breath;
Ne ought to see, but like a shade to weene,
Unbodied, unsoul'd, unheard, unseene;
But Life was like a faire young lusty boy,
Such as they faine Dan Cupid to have beene,
Full of delightfull health and lively joy,
Deckt all with flowres, and wings of gold fit to employ.

X L V I I

When these were past, thus gan the Titanesse:
'Lo! mighty mother, now be judge, and say
Whether in all thy creatures more or lesse
CHANGE doth not raign and bear the greatest sway;
For who sees not that Time on all doth pray?
But Times do change and move continually:
So nothing heere long standeth in one stay:
Wherefore this lower world who can deny
But to be subject still to Mutability?'

X L V I I I

Then thus gan Jove: 'Right true it is, that these
And all things else that under heaven dwell
Are chaung'd of Time, who doth them all disseise
Of being: But who is it (to me tell)
That Time himselfe doth move, and still compell
To keepe his course? Is not that namely wee
Which poure that vertue from our heavenly cell
That moves them all, and makes them changed be?
So them we gods do rule, and in them also thee.'

X L I X

To whom thus Mutability: 'The things,
Which we see not how they are mov'd and swayd
Ye may attribute to your selves as Kings,
And say, they by your secret powre are made:
But what we see not, who shall us perswade?
But were they so, as ye them faine to be,
Mov'd by your might and ordered by your ayde,

xlviii, 3   disseise: deprive

Yet what if I can prove, that even yee
Your selves are likewise chang'd, and subject unto mee?

L

'And first, concerning her that is the first,
Even you, faire Cynthia; whom so much ye make
Joves dearest darling, she was bred and nurst
On Cynthus hill, whence she her name did take;
Then is she mortall borne, how-so ye crake:
Besides, her face and countenance every day
We changed see and sundry formes partake,
Now hornd, now round, now bright, now browne and gray;
So that 'as changefull as the Moone' men use to say.

L I

'Next Mercury; who though he lesse appeare
To change his hew, and alwayes seeme as one,
Yet he his course doth alter every yeare,
And is of late far out of order gone.
So Venus eeke, that goodly Paragone,
Though faire all night, yet is she darke all day:
And Phœbus selfe, who lightsome is alone,
Yet is he oft eclipsed by the way,
And fills the darkned world with terror and dismay.

L I I

'Now Mars, that valiant man, is changed most;
For he sometimes so far runnes out of square,
That he his way doth seem quite to have lost,
And cleane without his usuall spheere to fare;
That even these Star-gazers stonisht are
At sight thereof, and damne their lying bookes:
So likewise grim Sir Saturne oft doth spare
His sterne aspect, and calme his crabbed lookes.
So many turning cranks these have, so many crookes.

L I I I

'But you, Dan Jove, that only constant are,
And King of all the rest, as ye doe clame,
Are you not subject eeke to this misfare?
Then, let me aske you this withouten blame;
Where were ye borne? Some say in Crete by name,
Others in Thebes, and others other-where;
But, wheresoever they comment the same,

_L_, 5 crake: boast

They all consent that ye begotten were
And borne here in this world; ne other can appeare.

L I V

'Then are ye mortall borne, and thrall to me
Unlesse the kingdome of the sky yee make
Immortall and unchangeable to be:
Besides, that power and vertue which ye spake,
That ye here worke, doth many changes take,
And your owne natures change; for each of you,
That verue have or this or that to make,
Is checkt and changed from his nature trew,
By others opposition or obliquid view.

L V

'Besides, the sundry motions of your Spheares,
So sundry wayes and fashions as clerkes faine,
Some in short space, and some in longer yeares,
What is the same but alteration plaine?
Onely the starry skie doth still remaine:
Yet do the Starres and Signes therein still move,
And even itselfe is mov'd, as wizards saine:
But all that moveth doth mutation love;
Therefore both you and them to me I subject prove.

L V I

'Then, since within this wide great Universe
Nothing doth firme and permanent appeare,
But all things tost and turned by transverse,
What then should let, but I aloft should reare
My Trophee, and from all the triumph beare?
Now judge then, (O thou greatest goddesse trew)
According as thy selfe doest see and heare,
And unto me addoom that is my dew;
That is, the rule of all, all being rul'd by you.'

L V I I

So having ended, silence long ensewed;
Ne Nature to or fro spake for a space,
But with firme eyes affixt the ground still viewed.
Meane-while all creatures, looking in her face,
Expecting th' end of this so doubtfull case,
Did hang in long suspence what would ensew,
To whether side should fall the soveraine place:

LVI, 3 by transverse: haphazardly   LVI, 4 let: prevent

At length she, looking up with chearefull view,
The silence brake, and gave her doome in speeches few.

L V I I I

'I well consider all that ye have said,
And find that all things stedfastnesse do hate
And changed be; yet, being rightly wayd,
They are not changed from their first estate;
But by their change their being do dilate,
And turning to themselves at length againe,
Do worke their owne perfection so by fate:
Then over them Change doth not rule and raigne,
But they raigne over Change, and do their states maintaine.

L I X

'Cease therefore, daughter, further to aspire,
And thee content thus to be rul'd by mee,
For thy decay thou seekst by thy desire;
But time shall come that all shall changed bee,
And from thenceforth none no more change shal see.'
So was the Titanesse put downe and whist,
And Jove confirm'd in his imperiall see.
Then was that whole assembly quite dismist,
And Natur's selfe did vanish, whither no man wist.

THE VIII. CANTO,
UNPERFITE.

I

WHEN I BETHINKE me on that speech why leare
Of Mutabilitie, and well it way,
Me seemes, that though she all unworthy were
Of the Heav'ns Rule; yet, very sooth to say,
In all things else she beares the greatest sway:
Which makes me loath this state of life so tickle,
And love of things so vaine to cast away:
Whose flowring pride, so fading and so fickle,
Short Time shall soon cut down with his consuming sickle.

I I

Then gin I thinke on that which Nature sayd,
Of that same time when no more Change shall be,
But stedfast rest of all things, firmely stayd
Upon the pillours of Eternity,

LIX, 6   whist: silenced

That is contrayr to Mutabilitie;
For all that moveth doth in Change delight:
But thence-forth all shall rest eternally
With Him that is the God of Sabaoth hight:
O! that great Sabaoth God, grant me that Sabaoths sight.

A LETTER OF THE AUTHORS

Expounding His Whole Intention in the Course of This Worke: Which, for That It Giveth Great Light to the Reader, for the Better Understanding Is Hereunto Annexed.

TO THE RIGHT NOBLE AND VALOROUS

SIR WALTER RALEIGH, KNIGHT,

Lord Wardein of the Stanneryes, and her Maiesties Liefetenaunt of the County of Cornewayll.

Sir, knowing how doubtfully all Allegories may be construed, and this booke of mine, which I have entituled the Faery Queene, being a continued Allegory, or darke conceit, I have thought good, as well as for avoyding of gealous opinions and misconstructions, as also for your better light in reading thereof, (being so by you commanded) to discover unto you the general intention and meaning, which in the whole course thereof I have fashioned, without expressing of any particular purposes, or by accidents, therein occasioned. The generall end therefore of all the booke is to fashion a gentleman or noble person in vertuous and gentle discipline: Which for that I conceived shoulde be most plausible and pleasing, being coloured with an historicall fiction, the which the most part of men delight to read, rather for variety of matter then for profite of the ensample, I chose the historye of King Arthure, as most fitte for the excellency of his person, being made famous by many mens former workes, and

*also furthest from the daunger of envy, and suspition of pres-
ent time. In which I have followed all the antique Poets historicall; first Homere, who in the Persons of Agamemnon
and Ulysses hath ensampled a good governour and a vertuous
man, the one in his Ilias, the other in his Odysseis: then
Virgil, whose like intention was to doe in the person of
Aeneas: after him Ariosto comprised them both in his Or-
lando: and lately Tasso dissevered them againe, and formed
both parts in two persons, namely that part which they in
Philosophy call Ethice, or vertues of a private man, coloured
in his Rinaldo; the other named Politice in his Godfredo.
By ensample of which excellente Poets, I labour to pourtraict
in Arthure, before he was king, the image of a brave knight,
perfected in the twelve private morall vertues, as Aristotle
hath devised; the which is the purpose of these first twelve
bookes: which if I finde to be well accepted, I may be perhaps encoraged to frame the other part of politicke vertues in his person, after that hee came to be king.*

*To some, I know, this Methode will seeme displeasaunt,
which had rather have good discipline delivered plainly
in way of precepts, or sermoned at large, as they use, then
thus clowdily enwrapped in Allegoricall devises. But such,
me seeme, should be satisfide with the use of these dayes, seeing all things accounted by their showes, and nothing esteemed of, that is not delightfull and pleasing to commune
sence. For this cause is Xenophon preferred before Plato,
for that the one, in the exquisite depth of his judgement,
formed a Commune welth, such as it should be; but the other
in the person of Cyrus, and the Persians, fashioned a governement, such as might best be: So much more profitable and
gratious is doctrine by ensample, then by rule. So have I laboured to doe in the person of Arthure: whome I conceive,
after his long education by Timon, to whom he was by
Merlin delivered to be brought up, so soone as he was borne
of the Lady Igrayne, to have seene in a dream or vision the
Faery Queen, with whose excellent beauty ravished, he
awaking resolved to seeke her out; and so being by Merlin
armed, and by Timon throughly instructed, he went to seeke
her forth in Faerye land. In that Faery Queene I meane glory
in my generall intention, but in my particular I conceive
the most excellent and glorious person of our soveraine the
Queene, and her kingdome in Faery land. And yet, in some
places els, I doe otherwise shadow her. For considering she
beareth two persons, the one of a most royall Queene or Empresse, the other of a most vertuous and beautifull Lady, this*

latter part in some places I doe expresse in Belphœbe, fashioning her name according to your owne excellent conceipt of Cynthia, (Phœbe and Cynthia being both names of Diana.) So in the person of Prince Arthure I sette forth magnificence in particular; which vertue, for that (according to Aristotle and the rest) it is the perfection of all the rest, and conteineth in it them all, therefore in the whole course I mention the deedes of Arthure applyable to that vertue, which I write of in that booke. But of the xii. other vertues, I make xii. other knights the patrones, for the more variety of the history: Of which these three bookes contayn three.

The first of the knight of the Redcrosse, in whome I expresse Holynes: The seconde of Sir Guyon, in whome I sette forth Temperaunce: The third of Britomartis, a Lady Knight, in whome I picture Chastity. But, because the beginning of the whole worke seemeth abrupte, and as depending upon other antecedents, it needs that ye know the occasion of these three knights seuerall adventures. For the Methode of a Poet historical is not such, as of an Historiographer. For an Historiographer discourseth of affayres orderly as they were donne, accounting as well the times as the actions; but a Poet thrusteth into the middest, even where it most concerneth him, and there recoursing to the thinges forepaste, and divining of thinges to come, maketh a pleasing Analysis of all.

The beginning therefore of my history, if it were to be told by an Historiographer, should be the twelfth booke, which is the last; where I devise that the Faery Queene kept her Annuall feaste xii. dayes; uppon which xii. severall dayes, the occasions of the xii. severall adventures hapned, which, being undertaken by xii. severall knights, are in these xii. books severally handled and discoursed. The first was this. In the beginning of the feast there presented him selfe a tall clownishe younge man, who falling before the Queene of Faries desired a boone (as the manner then was) which during that feast she might not refuse; which was that hee might have the atchievement of any adventure, which during that feaste should happen: that being graunted, he rested him on the floore, unfitte through his rusticity for a better place. Soone after entred a faire Ladye in mourning weedes, riding on a white Asse, with a dwarfe behind her leading a warlike steed, that bore the Armes of a knight, and his speare in the dwarfes hand. Shee, falling before the Queene of Faeries, complayned that her father and mother, an ancient King and Queene, had bene by an huge dragon many years shut up in a brasen Castle, who thence suffred them not to yssew; and therefore besought the Faery Queene to assygne her some one of her knights to take on him that exployt. Presently that clownish person, upstarting, desired that adventure: whereat the Queene much wondering, and the Lady much gainesaying, yet he earnestly importuned his desire. In the end the Lady told him, that unlesse that armour which she brought, would serve him (that is, the armour of a Christian man specified by Saint Paul, v. Ephes.) that he could not succeed in that enterprise; which being forthwith put upon him, with dewe furnitures thereunto, he seemed the goodliest man in al that company, and was well liked of the Lady. And eftesoones taking on him knighthood, and mounting on that straunge Courser, he went forth with her on that adventure: where beginneth the first booke, viz.

A gentle knight was pricking on the playne. &c.

The second day ther came in a Palmer, bearing an Infant with bloody hands, whose Parents he complained to have bene slayn by an Enchaunteresse called Acrasia; and therfore craved of the Faery Queene, to appoint him some knight to performe that adventure; which being assigned to Sir Guyon, he presently went forth with that same Palmer: which is the beginning of the second booke, and the whole subject thereof. The third day there came in a Groome, who complained before the Faery Queene, that a vile Enchaunter, called Busirane, had in hand a most faire Lady, called Amoretta, whom he kept in most grievous torment, because she would not yield him the pleasure of her body. Whereupon Sir Scudamour, the lover of that Lady, presently tooke on him that adventure. But being unable to performe it by reason of the hard Enchauntments, after long sorrow, in the end met with Britomartis, who succoured him, and reskewed his loue.

But by occasion hereof many other adventures are intermedled; but rather as Accidents then intendments: As the love of Britomart, the overthrow of Marinell, the misery of Florimell, the vertuousnes of Belphœbe, the lasciviousnes of Hellenora, and many the like.

Thus much, Sir, I have briefly overronne to direct your understanding to the wel-head of the History; that from thence gathering the whole intention of the conceit, ye may as in a handfull gripe al the discourse, which otherwise may happily seeme tedious and confused. So, humbly craving the continu-

ance of your honorable favour towards me, and th' eternall establishment of your happines, I humbly take leave.

23. Ianuary 1589,
Yours most humbly affectionate,
Ed. Spenser.

Minor Poems

THE

SHEPHEARDES CALENDER:

CONTEYNING TWELVE ÆGLOGUES,
PROPORTIONABLE

TO THE TWELVE MONETHES.
ENTITLED

To the noble and vertuous Gentleman, most worthy of
all titles both of learning and chevalrie,

MAISTER PHILIP SIDNEY.

TO HIS BOOKE.

Goe, little booke! thy selfe present,
As child whose parent is unkent,
To him that is the president
Of Noblesse and of chevalree:
And if that Envie barke at thee,
As sure it will, for succoure flee
Under the shadow of his wing;
And asked who thee forth did bring,
A shepheards swaine, saye, did thee sing
All as his straying flocke he fedde:
And, when his honor has thee redde,
Crave pardon for my hardyhedde.
But, if that any aske thy name,
Say, thou wert base-begot with blame;
For-thy thereof thou takest shame.
And, when thou art past jeopardee,
Come tell me what was sayd of mee,
And I will send more after thee.

IMMERITÔ.

THE

Shepheardes Calender

[SELECTIONS]

THE SHEPHEARDES CALENDER, dedicated by the poet to Sir Philip Sidney, was licensed for publication on December 5, 1579. The published volume includes a letter addressed to Spenser's friend, Gabriel Harvey, by the editor, "E. K.," which is dated April 10, 1579. Three of the eclogues allude, more or less clearly, to Spenser's service as secretary to John Young, Bishop of Rochester, in 1578-79. The poet appears to have left Young's service for that of the Earl of Leicester, Sidney's uncle, in the spring of 1579. Another topical allusion (in the July eclogue) concerns the suspension from his duties of Archbishop Grindal ("Algrin") in 1577.

The title of the work, as E. K. explains in his introductory letter, derives from the *Kalendar and Compost of Shepherds,* a popular almanac and compendium of useful information and moral exhortation. The original edition of Spenser's work is signed with the pen name "Immerito" (the Worthless One). It includes E. K.'s letter to Harvey advertising the merits of "the new poet" and an essay entitled "The general argument of the whole book." Each of the twelve eclogues, one for each month of the year, is illustrated with an appropriate woodcut, and for each E. K. supplies an introductory "argument" and explanatory notes.

THE
SHEPHEARDES CALENDER.

JANUARIE.

ÆGLOGA PRIMA. ARGUMENT.

IN THIS FYRST ÆGLOGUE *Colin Cloute, a shepheardes boy, complaineth him of his unfortunate love, being but newly (as semeth) enamoured of a countrie lasse called Rosalinde: with which strong affection being very sore traveled, he compareth his carefull case to the sadde season of the yeare, to the frostie ground, to the frosen trees, and to his owne winter-beaten flocke. And, lastlye, fynding himselfe robbed of all former pleasaunce and delights, hee breaketh his Pipe in peeces, and casteth him selfe to the ground.*

COLIN CLOUTE.

A SHEPEHEARDS boye, (no better doe him call,)
When Winters wastful spight was almost spent,
All in a sunneshine day, as did befall,
Led forth his flock, that had bene long ypent:
 So faynt they woxe, and feeble in the folde,
 That now unnethes their feete could them uphold.

All as the Sheepe, such was the shepheards looke,
For pale and wanne he was, (alas the while!)
May seeme he lovd, or els some care he tooke;
Well couth he tune his pipe and frame his stile: 10
 Tho to a hill his faynting flocke he ledde,
 And thus him playnd, the while his shepe there fedde.

'Ye Gods of love, that pitie lovers payne,
(If any gods the paine of lovers pitie)

6 unnethes: with difficulty   11 Tho: then

Looke from above, where you in joyes remaine,
And bowe your eares unto my dolefull dittie:
  And, Pan, thou shepheards God that once didst love,
  Pitie the paines that thou thy selfe didst prove.

'Thou barrein ground, whome winters wrath hath wasted,
Art made a myrrhour to behold my plight: 20
Whilome thy fresh spring flowrd, and after hasted
Thy sommer prowde, with Daffadillies dight;
  And now is come thy wynters stormy state,
  Thy mantle mard, wherein thou maskedst late.

'Such rage as winters reigneth in my heart,
My life-bloud friesing with unkindly cold;
Such stormy stoures do breede my balefull smart,
As if my yeare were wast and woxen old;
  And yet, alas! but now my spring begonne,
  And yet, alas! yt is already donne.   30

'You naked trees, whose shady leaves are lost,
Wherein the byrds were wont to build their bowre,
And now are clothd with mosse and hoary frost,
Instede of bloosmes, wherewith your buds did flowre;
  I see your teares that from your boughes doe raine,
  Whose drops in drery ysicles remaine.

'All so my lustfull leafe is drye and sere,
My timely buds with wayling all are wasted;
The blossome which my braunch of youth did beare
With breathed sighes is blowne away and blasted;   40
  And from mine eyes the drizling teares descend,
  As on your boughes the ysicles depend.

'Thou feeble flocke, whose fleece is rough and rent,
Whose knees are weake through fast and evill fare,
Mayst witnesse well, by thy ill governement,
Thy maysters mind is overcome with care:
  Thou weake, I wanne; thou leane, I quite forlorne:
  With mourning pyne I; you with pyning mourne.

'A thousand sithes I curse that carefull hower
Wherein I longd the neighbour towne to see.   50
And eke tenne thousand sithes I blesse the stoure
Wherein I sawe so fayre a sight as shee:

18 prove: experience
26 unkindly: unnatural
27 stoures: tumults
49 sithes: times

Yet all for naught: such sight hath bred my bane.
Ah, God! that love should breede both joy and payne!

'It is not Hobbinol wherefore I plaine,
Albee my love he seeke with dayly suit;
His clownish gifts and curtsies I disdaine,
His kiddes, his cracknelles, and his early fruit.
    Ah, foolish Hobbinol! thy gyfts bene vayne;
    Colin them gives to Rosalind againe.   60

'I love thilke lasse, (alas! why doe I love?)
And am forlorne, (alas! why am I lorne?)
Shee deignes not my good will, but doth reprove,
And of my rurall musicke holdeth scorne.
    Shepheards devise she hateth as the snake,
    And laughes the songs that Colin Clout doth make.

'Wherefore, my pype, albee rude Pan thou please,
Yet for thou pleasest not where most I would:
And thou, unlucky Muse, that wontst to ease
My musing mynd, yet canst not when thou should;   70
    Both pype and Muse shall sore the while abye.'
    So broke his oaten pype, and downe dyd lye.

By that, the welked Phoebus gan availe
His weary waine; and nowe the frosty Night
Her mantle black through heaven gan overhaile:
Which seene, the pensife boy, halfe in despight,
    Arose, and homeward drove his sonned sheepe,
    Whose hanging heads did seeme his carefull case to weepe.

COLINS EMBLEME.

Anchôra speme.

APRIL.

ÆGLOGA QUARTA. ARGUMENT.

THIS ÆGLOGUE *is purposely intended to the honor and prayse of our
most gracious sovereigne, Queene Elizabeth. The speakers herein*

58	cracknelles: biscuits	73	availe: lower
61	thilke: this	77	sonned: exposed to the sun
73	welked: faded		

be Hobbinoll and Thenott, two shepheardes: the which Hobbinoll, being before mentioned greatly to have loved Colin, is here set forth more largely, complayning him of that boyes great misadventure in Love; whereby his mynd was alienate and withdrawen not onely from him, who moste loved him, but also from all former delightes and studies, as well in pleasaunt pyping, as conning ryming and singing, and other his laudable exercises. Whereby he taketh occasion, for proofe of his more excellencie and skill in poetrie, to recorde a songe, which the sayd Colin sometime made in honor of her Majestie, whom abruptely he termeth Elysa.

THENOT. HOBBINOLL.

The. Tell me, good Hobbinoll, what garres thee greete?
   What? hath some Wolfe thy tender Lambes ytorne?
Or is thy Bagpype broke, that soundes so sweete?
   Or art thou of thy loved lasse forlorne?

Or bene thine eyes attempred to the yeare,
   Quenching the gasping furrowes thirst with rayne?
Like April shoure so stremes the trickling teares
   Adowne thy cheeke, to quenche thy thristye payne.

Hob. Nor thys, nor that, so muche doeth make me mourne,
   But for the ladde, whome long I lovd so deare,   10
Nowe loves a lasse that all his love doth scorne:
   He, plongd in payne, his tressed locks dooth teare.

Shepheards delights he dooth them all forsweare;
   Hys pleasaunt Pipe, whych made us meriment,
He wylfully hath broke, and doth forbeare
   His wonted songs, wherein he all outwent.

The. What is he for a Ladde you so lament?
   Ys love such pinching payne to them that prove?
And hath he skill to make so excellent,
   Yet hath so little skill to brydle love?   20

Hob. Colin thou kenst, the Southerne shepheardes boye;
   Him Love hath wounded with a deadly darte:
Whilome on him was all my care and joye,
   Forcing with gyfts to winne his wanton heart.

But now from me hys madding mynd is starte,
   And woes the Widdowes daughter of the glenne;

1   garres: makes   1   greete: to weep

So nowe fayre Rosalind hath bredde hys smart,
   So now his frend is chaunged for a frenne.

The. But if hys ditties bene so trimly dight,
   I pray thee, Hobbinoll, recorde some one,   30
The whiles our flockes do graze about in sight,
   And we close shrowded in thys shade alone.

Hob. Contented I: then, will I singe his laye
   Of fayre Elisa, Queene of shepheardes all,
Which once he made as by a spring he laye,
   And tuned it unto the Waters fall.

'Ye dayntye Nymphs, that in this blessed brooke
   Doe bathe your brest,
Forsake your watry bowres, and hether looke,
   At my request: 40
And eke you Virgins, that on Parnasse dwell,
Whence floweth Helicon, the learned well,
      Helpe me to blaze
      Her worthy praise,
Which in her sexe doth all excell.

'Of fayre Elisa be your silver song,
   That blessed wight,
The flowre of Virgins: may shee florish long
   In princely plight!
For shee is Syrinx daughter without spotte,   50
Which Pan, the shepheards God, of her begot:
      So sprong her grace
      Of heavenly race,
No mortall blemishe may her blotte.

'See, where she sits upon the grassie greene,
   (O seemely sight!)
Yclad in Scarlot, like a mayden Queene,
   And ermines white:
Upon her head a Cremosin coronet,
With Damaske roses and Daffadillies set: 60
      Bay leaves betweene,
      And primroses greene,
Embellish the sweete Violet.

'Tell me, have ye seene her angelick face,
   Like Phoebe fayre?

28   frenne: enemy

Her heavenly haveour, her princely grace,
   Can you well compare?
The Redde rose medled with the White yfere,
In either cheeke depeincten lively chere:
   Her modest eye,
   Her Majestie,   70
Where have you seen the like but there?

'I sawe Phoebus thrust out his golden hedde,
   Upon her to gaze:
But, when he sawe how broade her beames did spredde,
   It did him amaze.
He blusht to see another Sunne belowe,
Ne durst againe his fyrye face out showe:
   Let him, if he dare,
   His brightnesse compare   80
With hers, to have the overthrowe.

'Shewe thyselfe, Cynthia, with thy silver rayes,
   And be not abasht:
When shee the beames of her beauty displayes,
   O, how art thou dasht!
But I will not match her with Latonaes seede,
Such follie great sorrow to Niobe did breede:
   Now she is a stone,
   And makes dayly mone,
Warning all other to take heede.   90

'Pan may be proud that ever he begot
   Such a Bellibone;
And Syrinx rejoyse that ever was her lot
   To beare such an one.
Soone as my younglings cryen for the dam
To her will I offer a milkwhite Lamb:
   Shee is my goddesse plaine,
   And I her shepherds swayne,
Albee forswonck and forswatt I am.

'I see Calliope speede her to the place,   100
   Where my Goddesse shines;
And after her the other Muses trace,
   With their Violines.
Bene they not Bay braunches which they do beare,

68   medled: mixed
68   yfere: together
92   Bellibone: fair maid

99   forswonck: wearied with labor
99   forswatt: covered with sweat

All for Elisa in her hand to weare?
  So sweetely they play,
  And sing all the way,
That it a heaven is to heare.

'Lo! how finely the Graces can it foote   110
  To the Instrument:
They dauncen deffly, and singen soote,
  In their meriment.
Wants not a fourth Grace, to make the daunce even?
Let that rowme to my Lady be yeven:
  She shal be a Grace,
  To fyll the fourth place,
And reigne with the rest in heaven.

'And whither rennes this bevie of Ladies bright,
  Raunged in a rowe?
They bene all Ladyes of the lake behight,   120
  That unto her goe.
Chloris, that is the chiefest Nymph of all,
Of Olive braunches beares a Coronall:
  Olives bene for peace,
  When wars doe surcease:
Such for a Princesse bene principall.

'Ye shepheards daughters, that dwell on the greene,
  Hye you there apace:
Let none come there but that Virgins bene,
  To adorne her grace: 130
And, when you come whereas shee is in place,
See that your rudenesse doe not you disgrace:
  Binde your fillets faste,
  And gird in your waste,
For more finesse, with a tawdrie lace.

'Bring hether the Pincke and purple Cullambine,
  With Gelliflowres;
Bring Coronations, and Sops in wine,
  Worne of Paramoures:
Strowe me the ground with Daffadowndillies,   140
And Cowslips, and Kingcups, and loved Lillies:
  The pretie Pawnce,
  And the Chevisaunce,
Shall match with the fayre flowre Delice.

111 soote: sweetly 135 tawdrie lace: a silk girdle or tie

'Now ryse up, Elisa, decked as thou art
    In royall aray;
And now ye daintie Damsells may depart
    Eche one her way.
I feare I have troubled your troupes to longe:
Let dame Elisa thanke you for her song: 150
    And if you come hether
    When Damsines I gether,
I will part them all you among.'

The. And was thilk same song of Colins owne making?
    Ah, foolish Boy! that is with love yblent:
Great pittie is, he be in such taking,
    For naught caren that bene so lewdly bent.

Hob. Sicker I hold him for a greater fon,
    That loves the thing he cannot purchase.
But let us homeward, for night draweth on,   160
    And twincling starres the daylight hence chase.

THENOTS EMBLEME.

O quam te memorem Virgo!

HOBBINOLS EMBLEME.

O dea certe!

MAYE.

ÆGLOGA QUINTA. ARGUMENT.

IN THIS FIFTE ÆGLOGUE, *under the persons of two shepheards, Piers
and Palinodie, be represented two formes of pastoures or Ministers,
or the Protestant and the Catholique: whose chiefe talke standeth
in reasoning, whether the life of the one must be like the other:
with whom having shewed, that it is daungerous to mainteine any
felowship, or give too much credit to their colourable and feyned
good will, he telleth him a tale of the foxe, that, by such a counter-
poynt of craftines, deceived and devoured the credulous kiddi.*

155   yblent: blinded   158   fon: fool
158   Sicker: surely

PALINODE.   PIERS.

Palinode. Is not thilke the mery moneth of May,
When love-lads masken in fresh aray?
How falles it, then, we no merrier bene,
Ylike as others, girt in gawdy greene?
Our bloncket liveryes bene all to sadde
For thilke same season, when all is ycladd
With pleasaunce: the grownd with grasse, the Wods
With greene leaves, the bushes with bloosming buds.
Yougthes folke now flocken in every where,   10
To gather May bus-kets and smelling brere:
And home they hasten the postes to dight,
And all the Kirke pillours eare day light,
With Hawthorne buds, and swete Eglantine,
And girlonds of roses, and Sopps in wine.
Such merimake holy Saints doth queme,
But we here sitten as drownd in a dreme.
    Piers. For Younkers, Palinode, such follies fitte,
But we tway bene men of elder witt.
    Pal. Sicker this morrowe, ne lenger agoe,   20
I sawe a shole of shepeheardes outgoe
With singing, and shouting, and jolly chere:
Before them yode a lusty Tabrere,
That to the many a Horne-pype playd,
Whereto they dauncen, eche one with his mayd.
To see those folkes make such jovysaunce,
Made my heart after the pype to daunce:
Tho to the greene Wood they speeden hem all,
To fetchen home May with their musicall:
And home they bringen in a royall throne,
Crowned as king: and his Queene attone   30
Was Lady Flora, on whom did attend
A fayre flocke of Faeries, and a fresh bend
Of lovely Nymphs. (O that I were there,
To helpen the Ladyes their Maybush beare!)
Ah! Piers, bene not thy teeth on edge, to thinke
How great sport they gaynen with little swinck?
    Piers. Perdie, so farre am I from envie,
That their fondnesse inly I pitie:

4   gawdy greene: yellowish green   22   Tabrere: drum player
5   bloncket: gray   30   attone: together
5   liveryes: clothes   32   bend: band
10   bus-kets: small bushes   36   swinck: labor
15   queme: please

Those faytours little regarden their charge,
While they, letting their sheepe runne at large,   40
Passen their time, that should be sparely spent,
In lustihede and wanton meryment.
Thilke same bene shepeheardes for the Devils stedde,
That playen while their flockes be unfedde:
Well is it seene theyr sheepe bene not their owne,
That letten them runne at randon alone:
But they bene hyred for little pay
Of other, that caren as little as they
What fallen the flocke, so they han the fleece,
And get all the gayne, paying but a peece.   50
I muse, what account both these will make;
The one for the hire which he doth take,
And thother for leaving his Lords taske,
When great Pan account of shepeherdes shall aske.
  Pal. Sicker, now I see thou speakest of spight,
All for thou lackest somedele their delight.
I (as I am) had rather be envied,
All were it of my foe, then fonly pitied:
And yet, if neede were, pitied would be,
Rather then other should scorne at me: 60
For pittied is mishappe that nas remedie,
But scorned bene dedes of fond foolerie.
What shoulden shepheards other things tend,
Then, sith their God his good does them send,
Reapen the fruite thereof, that is pleasure,
The while they here liven at ease and leasure?
For, when they bene dead, their good is ygoe,
They sleepen in rest, well as other moe:
Tho with them wends what they spent in cost,
But what they left behind them is lost.   70
Good is no good, but if it be spend;
God giveth good for none other end.
  Piers. Ah! Palinodie, thou art a worldes childe:
Who touches Pitch, mought needes be defilde;
But shepheards (as Algrind used to say)
Mought not live ylike as men of the laye.
With them it sits to care for their heire,
Enaunter their heritage doe impaire.
They must provide for meanes of maintenaunce,
And to continue their wont countenaunce: 80
But shepheard must walke another way,

39	faytours: vagabonds	61	nas: has no
43	stedde: place	78	Enaunter: lest by chance
58	fonly: foolishly	80	countenaunce: position

Sike wordly sovenance he must forsay.
The sonne of his loines why should he regard
To leave enriched with that he hath spard?
Should not thilke God, that gave him that good,
Eke cherish his child, if in his wayes he stood?
For if he mislive in leudnes and lust,
Little bootes all the welth and the trust,
That his father left by inheritaunce:
All will be soone wasted with misgovernaunce;   90
But through this, and other their miscreaunce
They maken many a wrong chevisaunce,
Heaping up waves of welth and woe,
The floddes whereof shall them overflowe
Sike mens follie I cannot compare
Better then to the Apes folish care,
That is so enamoured of her young one,
(And yet, God wote, such cause hath she none)
That with her hard hold, and straight embracing,
She stoppeth the breath of her youngling.   100
So often times, when as good is meant,
Evil ensueth of wrong entent.
   The time was once, and may againe retorne,
(For ought may happen, that hath bene beforne)
When shepeheards had none inheritaunce,
Ne of land, nor fee in sufferaunce,
But what might arise of the bare sheepe,
(Were it more or lesse) which they did keepe.
Well ywis was it with shepheards thoe:
Nought having, nought feared they to forgoe;   110
For Pan himselfe was their inheritaunce,
And little them served for their mayntenaunce.
The shepheards God so wel them guided,
That of nought they were unprovided;
Butter enough, honye, milke, and whay,
And their flockes fleeces them to araye:
But tract of time, and long prosperitie,
That nource of vice, this of insolencie,
Lulled the shepheards in such securitie,
That, not content with loyall obeysaunce,   120
Some gan to gape for greedie governaunce,
And match them selfe with mighty potentates,
Lovers of Lordship, and troublers of states.

82   Sike: such
82   sovenance: care
82   forsay: renounce
92   chevisaunce: enterprise

106   fee in sufferaunce: land retained after the passing of title
109   ywis: certainly
117   tract: course

Tho gan shepheards swaines to looke aloft,
And leave to live hard, and learne to ligge soft:
Tho, under colour of shepeheards, somewhile
There crept in Wolves, full of fraude, and guile,
That often devoured their owne sheepe,
And often the shepheards that did hem keepe:
This was the first sourse of shepheards sorowe,
That now nill be quitt with baile nor borrowe.   130

   Pal. Three thinges to beare bene very burdenous,
But the fourth to forbeare is outragious:
Wemen, that of Loves longing once lust,
Hardly forbearen, but have it they must:
So when choler is inflamed with rage,
Wanting revenge, is hard to asswage:
And who can counsell a thristie soule,
With patience to forbeare the offred bowle?
But of all burdens, that a man can beare,
Most is, a fooles talke to beare and to heare.   140
I wene the Geaunt has not such a weight,
That beares on his shoulders the heavens height.
Thou findest faulte where nys to be found,
And buildest strong warke upon a weake ground:
Thou raylest on, right withouten reason,
And blamest hem much for small encheason.
How shoulden shepheardes live, if not so?
What! should they pynen in payne and woe?
Nay, say I thereto, by my deare borrowe,
If I may rest, I nill live in sorrowe.   150

   Sorrowe ne neede be hastened on,
For he will come, without calling, anone.
While times enduren of tranquillitie,
Usen we freely our felicitie;
For, when approchen the stormie stowres,
We mought with our shoulders beare of the sharpe showres;
And, sooth to sayne, nought seemeth sike strife,
That shepheardes so witen ech others life,
And layen her faults the world beforne,
The while their foes done eache of hem scorne.   160
Let none mislike of that may not be mended:
So conteck soone by concord mought be ended.

   Piers. Shepheard, I list none accordaunce make
With shepheard that does the right way forsake:

---

125   ligge: lie
131   baile nor borrowe: pledge nor
security
147   encheason: cause

150   borrowe: pledge (*here,* Christ)
159   witen: blame
163   conteck: strife

And of the twaine, if choice were to me,
Had lever my foe then my freend he be;
For what concord han light and darke sam?
Or what peace has the Lion with the Lambe?
Such faitors, when their false harts bene hidde,   170
Will doe as did the Foxe by the Kidde.
    Pal. Now, Piers, of felowship, tell us that saying:
For the Ladde can keepe both our flockes from straying.
    Piers. Thilke same Kidde (as I can well devise)
Was too very foolish and unwise;
For on a tyme, in Sommer season,
The Gate her dame, that had good reason,
Yode forth abroade unto the greene wood,
To brouze, or play, or what shee thought good:
But, for she had a motherly care   180
Of her young sonne, and wit to beware,
Shee set her youngling before her knee,
That was both fresh and lovely to see,
And full of favour as kidde mought be.
His Vellet head began to shoote out,
And his wreathed hornes gan newly sprout:
The blossomes of lust to bud did beginne,
And spring forth ranckly under his chinne.
'My Sonne,' (quoth she and with that gan weepe,
For carefull thoughts in her heart did creepe)   190
'God blesse thee, poore Orphane! as he mought me,
And send thee joy of thy jollitee.
Thy father,' (that word she spake with payne,
For a sigh had nigh rent her heart in twaine)
'Thy father, had he lived this day,
To see the braunche of his body displaie,
How would he have joyed at this sweete sight!
But ah! false Fortune such joy did him spight,
And cutte of hys dayes with untimely woe,
Betraying him into the traines of hys foe.   200
Now I, a waylfull widdowe behight,
Of my old age have this one delight,
To see thee succeede in thy fathers steade,
And florish in flowres of lusty-head:
For even so thy father his head upheld,
And so his hauty hornes did he weld.'
    Tho marking him with melting eyes,
A thrilling throbbe from her hart did aryse,

168	sam: together	200	traines: snares
177	Gate: goat	201	behight: called
178	Yode: went	208	thrilling: piercing

And interrupted all her other speache
With some old sorowe that made a newe breache: 210
Seemed shee sawe in the younglings face
The old lineaments of his fathers grace.
At last her solein silence she broke,
And gan his newe-budded beard to stroke.
'Kiddie, (quoth shee) thou kenst the great care
I have of thy health and thy welfare,
Which many wyld beastes liggen in waite
For to entrap in thy tender state:
But most the Foxe, maister of collusion:
For he has voued thy last confusion. 220
For-thy, my Kiddie, be ruld by mee,
And never give trust to his trecheree:
And, if he chaunce come when I am abroade,
Sperre the yate fast for feare of fraude:
Ne for all his worst, nor for his best,
Open the dore at his request.'
    So schooled the Gate her wanton sonne,
That answerd his mother, all should be done.
Tho went the pensife Damme out of dore,
And chaunst to stomble at the threshold flore: 230
Her stombling steppe some what her amazed,
(For such, as signes of ill luck, bene dispraised;)
Yet forth shee yode, thereat halfe aghast:
And Kiddie the dore sperred after her fast.
It was not long, after shee was gone,
But the false Foxe came to the dore anone:
Not as a Foxe, for then he had be kend,
But all as a poore pedler he did wend,
Bearing a trusse of tryfles at hys backe,
As bells, and babes, and glasses, in hys packe: 240
A Biggen he had got about his brayne,
For in his headpeace he felt a sore payne:
His hinder heele was wrapt in a clout,
For with great cold he had gotte the gout.
There at the dore he cast me downe hys pack,
And layd him downe, and groned, 'Alack! Alack!
Ah, deare Lord! and sweete Saint Charitee!
That some good body woulde once pitie mee!'
    Well heard Kiddie al this sore constraint,
And lengd to know the cause of his complaint: 250

213   solein: sad   240   babes: dolls
221   For-thy: therefore   241   Biggen: child's cap
224   Sperre: bolt   243   clout: rag
217   wanton: careless

Tho, creeping close behind the Wickets clink,
Prevelie he peeped out through a chinck,
Yet not so previlie but the Foxe him spyed;
For deceitfull meaning is double eyed.
  'Ah, good young maister!' (then gan he crye)
'Jesus blesse that sweete face I espye,
And keepe your corpse from the carefull stounds
That in my carrion carcas abounds.'
  The Kidd, pittying hys heavinesse,
Asked the cause of his great distresse,   260
And also who, and whence that he were?
  Tho he, that had well ycond his lere,
Thus medled his talke with many a teare:
'Sicke, sicke, alas! and little lack of dead,
But I be relieved by your beastlyhead.
I am a poore sheepe, albe my coloure donne,
For with long traveile I am brent in the sonne:
And, if that my Grandsire me sayd be true,
Sicker, I am very sybbe to you:
So be your goodlihead doe not disdayne   270
The base kinred of so simple swaine.
Of mercye and favour, then, I you pray
With your ayd to fore-stall my neere decay.'
  Tho out of his packe a glasse he tooke,
Wherein while Kiddie unwares did looke,
He was so enamored with the newell,
That nought he deemed deare for the jewell:
Tho opened he the dore, and in came
The false Foxe, as he were starke lame:
His tayle he clapt betwixt his legs twayne,   280
Lest he should be descried by his trayne.
  Being within, the Kidde made him good glee,
All for the love of the glasse he did see.
After his chere the Pedler can chat,
And tell many lesinges of this and that,
And how he could shewe many a fine knack:
Tho shewed his ware and opened his packe,
All save a bell, which he left behind
In the basket for the Kidde to fynd:
Which when the Kidde stooped downe to catch,   290
He popt him in, and his basket did latch:
Ne stayed he once the dore to make fast,

257   corpse: body
257   stounds: sorrows
263   medled: mixed
269   very: true

269   sybbe: kin
276   newell: novelty
284   can: did

But ranne awaye with him in all hast.
Home when the doubtfull Damme had her hyde,
She mought see the dore stand open wyde.
All agast, lowdly she gan to call
Her Kidde; but he nould answere at all:
Tho on the flore she saw the merchaundise
Of which her sonne had sette to deere a prise.
What helpe? her Kidde shee knewe well was gone: 300
Shee weeped, and wayled, and made great mone.
Such end had the Kidde, for he nould warned be
Of craft, coloured with simplicitie:
And such end, perdie, does all hem remayne,
That of such falsers freendship bene fayne.
Pal. Truly, Piers, thou art beside thy wit,
Furthest fro the marke, weening it to hit.
Now, I pray thee, lette me thy tale borrowe
For our Sir John, to say to morrowe
At the Kerke, when it is holliday;   310
For well he meanes, but little can say.
But, and if foxes bene so crafty as so,
Much needeth all shepheards hem to knowe.
Piers. Of their falshode more could I recount,
But now the bright Sunne gynneth to dismount;
And, for the deawie night now doth nye,
I hold it best for us home to hye.

PALINODES EMBLEME.

Πᾶς μεν ἄπιστος ἀπιστεῖ.

PIERS HIS EMBLEME.

Τίς δ' ἄρα πίστις ἀπίστῳ;

JUNE.

ÆGLOGA SEXTA. ARGUMENT.

THIS ÆGLOGUE *is wholly vowed to the complayning of Colins ill success in his love. For being (as is aforesaid) enamoured of a country lasse, Rosalind, and having (as seemeth) founde place in her heart, he lamenteth to his deare frend Hobbinoll, that he is nowe forsaken unfaithfully, and in his steede Menalcas, another*

294 doubtfull: fearful

shepheard, received disloyally. And this is the whole Argument of this Æglogue.

HOBBINOL.   COLIN CLOUT.

Hob. Lo! Collin, here the place whose pleasaunt syte
From other shades hath weand my wandring mynde:
Tell me, what wants me here to worke delyte?
The simple ayre, the gentle warbling wynde,
So calme, so coole, as no where else I fynde:
The grassye ground with daintye Daysies dight,
The Bramble bush, where Byrds of every kynde
To the waters fall their tunes attemper right.

    Col. O happy Hobbinoll! I blesse thy state,   10
That Paradise hast founde whych Adam lost:
Here wander may thy flocke, early or late,
Withouten dreade of Wolves to bene ytost:
Thy lovely layes here mayst thou freely boste.
But I, unhappy man! whom cruell fate
And angry Gods pursue from coste to coste,
Can nowhere fynd to shroude my lucklesse pate.

    Hob. Then, if by me thou list advised be,
Forsake the soyle that so doth thee bewitch:
Leave me those hilles where harbrough nis to see,
Nor holy-bush, nor brere, nor winding witche: 20
And to the dales resort, where shepheards ritch,
And fruictfull flocks, bene every where to see:
Here no night-ravenes lodge, more black then pitche,
Nor elvish ghosts, nor gastly owles doe flee.

But frendly Faeries, met with many Graces,
And lightfoote Nymphes, can chace the lingring Night
With Heydeguyes, and trimly trodden traces,
Whilst systers nyne, which dwell on Parnasse hight,
Doe make them musick for their more delight:
And Pan himselfe, to kisse their christall faces,   30
Will pype and daunce when Phœbe shineth bright:
Such pierlesse pleasures have we in these places.

    Col. And I, whylst youth and course of carelesse yeeres,
Did let me walke withouten lincks of love,
In such delights did joy amongst my peeres:

12   ytost: disturbed   27   Heydeguyes: country dances
20   winding witche: wych elm

But ryper age such pleasures doth reprove:
My fancye eke from former follies move
To stayed steps; for time in passing weares,
(As garments doen, which wexen old above,)
And draweth newe delightes with hoary heares.　　　　40

Tho couth I sing of love, and tune my pype
Unto my plaintive pleas in verses made:
Tho would I seeke for Queene-apples unrype,
To give my Rosalind; and in Sommer shade
Dight gaudy Girlonds was my comen trade,
To crowne her golden locks: but yeeres more rype,
And losse of her, whose love as lyfe I wayd,
Those weary wanton toyes away dyd wype.

Hob. Colin, to heare thy rymes and roundelayes,
Which thou wert wont on wastfull hylls to singe,　　　　50
I more delight then larke in Sommer dayes:
Whose Echo made the neyghbour groves to ring,
And taught the byrds, which in the lower spring
Did shroude in shady leaves from sonny rayes,
Frame to thy songe their cherefull cheriping,
Or hold theyr peace, for shame of thy swete layes.

I sawe Calliope wyth Muses moe,
Soone as thy oaten pype began to sound,
Theyr yvory Luyts and Tamburins forgoe,
And from the fountaine, where they sat around,　　　　60
Renne after hastely thy silver sound;
But, when they came where thou thy skill didst showe,
They drewe abacke, as halfe with shame confound
Shepheard to see them in theyr art outgoe.

Col. Of Muses, Hobbinol, I conne no skill,
For they bene daughters of the hyghest Jove,
And holden scorne of homely shepheards quill:
For sith I heard that Pan with Phœbus strove,
Which him to much rebuke and Daunger drove,
I never lyst presume to Parnasse hyll,　　　　70
But, pyping lowe in shade of lowly grove,
I play to please myselfe, all be it ill.

Nought weigh I who my song doth prayse or blame,
Ne strive to winne renowne, or passe the rest:
With shepheard sittes not followe flying fame,

50　wastfull: desolate　　　　　75　sittes: behoves

But feede his flocke in fields where falls hem best.
I wote my rymes bene rough, and rudely drest;
The fytter they my carefull case to frame:
Enough is me to paint out my unrest,
And poore my piteous plaints out in the same.   80

The God of shepheards, Tityrus, is dead,
Who taught me homely, as I can, to make;
He, whilst he lived, was the soveraigne head
Of shepheards all that bene with love ytake:
Well couth he wayle his Woes, and lightly slake
The flames which love within his heart had bredd,
And tell us mery tales to keepe us wake,
The while our sheepe about us safely fedde.

Nowe dead he is, and lyeth wrapt in lead,
(O! why should Death on hym such outrage showe?)   90
And all hys passing skil with him is fledde,
The fame whereof doth dayly greater growe.
But, if on me some little drops would flowe
Of that the spring was in his learned hedde,
I soone would learne these woods to wayle my woe,
And teache the trees their trickling teares to shedde.

Then should my plaints, causd of discurtesee,
As messengers of all my painfull plight,
Flye to my love, where ever that she bee,
And pierce her heart with poynt of worthy wight,   100
As shee deserves that wrought so deadly spight.
And thou, Menalcas, that by trecheree
Didst underfong my lasse to wexe so light,
Shouldest well be knowne for such thy villanee.

But since I am not as I wish I were,
Ye gentle Shepheards, which your flocks do feede,
Whether on hylls, or dales, or other where,
Beare witnesse all of thys so wicked deede:
And tell the lasse, whose flowre is woxe a weede,
And faultlesse fayth is turned to faithlesse fere,   110
That she the truest shepheards hart made bleede,
That lyves on earth, and loved her most dere.

  Hob. O, carefull Colin! I lament thy case;
Thy teares would make the hardest flint to flowe!
Ah, faithlesse Rosalind and voide of grace,

91   passing: surpassing   103   underfong: ensnare
100   wight: blame   110   fere: mate

That art the roote of all this ruthfull woe!
But now is time, I gesse, homeward to goe:
Then ryse, ye blessed Flocks, and home apace,
Least night with stealing steppes doe you forsloe,
And wett your tender Lambes that by you trace.   120

COLINS EMBLEME.

Gia speme spenta.

AUGUST.

ÆGLOGA OCTAVA. ARGUMENT.

IN THIS ÆGLOGUE *is set forth a delectable controversie, made in imitation of that in Theocritus: whereto also Virgile fashioned his third and seventh Æglogue. They choose for umpere of their strife, Cuddie, a neatheards boye; who, having ended their cause, reciteth also himselfe a proper song, whereof Colin, he sayth, was Authour.*

WILLIE.   PERIGOT.   CUDDIE.

Wil. TELL me, Perigot, what shalbe the game,
Wherefore with myne thou dare thy musick matche?
Or bene thy Bagpypes renne farre out of frame?
Or hath the Crampe thy joynts benomd with ache?
Per. Ah! Willye, when the hart is ill assayde,
How can Bagpipe or joynts be well apayd?
Wil. What the foule evill hath thee so bestadde?
   Whilom thou was peregall to the best,
And wont to make the jolly shepeheards gladde,
   With pyping and dauncing did passe the rest.   10
Per. Ah! Willye, now I have learnd a newe daunce;
My old musick mard by a newe mischaunce.
Wil. Mischiefe mought to that newe mischaunce befall,
   That so hath raft us of our meriment.
But reede me what payne doth thee so appall;
   Or lovest thou, or bene thy younglings miswent?
Per. Love hath misled both my younglings and mee:
I pyne for payne, and they my payne to see.
Wil. Perdie, and wellawaye, ill may they thrive!
   Never knew I lovers sheepe in good plight: 20

119   forsloe: hinder   6   apayd: pleased
5   assayde: affected

But, and if in rymes with me thou dare strive,
  Such fond fantsies shall soone be put to flight
Per. That shall I doe, though mochell worse I fared:
Never shall be sayde that Perigot was dared.
Wil. Then loe, Perigot, the Pledge which I plight,
  A mazer ywrought of the Maple warre,
Wherein is enchased many a fayre sight
  Of Beres and Tygres, that maken fiers warre;
And over them spred a goodly wild vine,
Entrailed with a wanton Yvie twine.   30
Thereby is a Lambe in the Wolves jawes:
  But see, how fast renneth the shepheard swayne
To save the innocent from the beastes pawes,
  And here with his shepe-hooke hath him slayne.
Tell me, such a cup hast thou ever sene?
Well mought it beseme any harvest Queene.
Per. Thereto will I pawne yonder spotted Lambe,
  Of all my flocke there nis sike another,
For I brought him up without the Dambe:
  But Colin Clout rafte me of his brother,   40
That he purchast of me in the playne field:
Sore against my will was I forst to yield.
Wil. Sicker, make like account of his brother.
  But who shall judge the wager wonne or lost?
Per. That shall yonder heardgrome, and none other,
Which over the pousse hetherward doth post.
Wil. But, for the Sunnbeame so sore doth us beate,
Were not better to shunne the scortching heate?
Per. Well agreed, Willie: then, sitte thee downe, swayne:
  Sike a song never heardest thou but Colin sing.   50
Cud. Gynne when ye lyst, ye jolly shepheards twayne:
  Sike a judge as Cuddie were for a king.
Per. It fell upon a holly eve,
Wil.   Hey, ho, hollidaye!
Per. When holy fathers wont to shrieve;
Wil.   Now gynneth this roundelay.
Per. Sitting upon a hill so hye,
Wil.   Hey, ho, the high hyll!
Per. The while my flocke did feede thereby;
Wil.   The while the shepheard selfe did spill.   60
Per. I saw the bouncing Bellibone,
Wil.   Hey, ho, Bonibell!

21 and if: if	41 playne field: open, regular con-
26 warre: protuberance on a tree	test
30 Entrailed: intertwined	46 pousse: peas
41 purchast: won	61 Bellibone: fair maid

Per. Tripping over the dale alone,
Wil. She can trippe it very well.
Per. Well decked in a frocke of gray,
Wil. Hey, ho, gray is greete!
Per. And in a Kirtle of greene saye,
Wil. The greene is for maydens meete.
Per. A chapelet on her head she wore,
Wil. Hey, ho, chapelet!   70
Per. Of sweete Violets therein was store,
Wil. She sweeter then the Violet.
Per. My sheepe did leave theyr wonted food,
Wil. Hey, ho, seely sheepe!
Per. And gazd on her as they were wood,
Wil. Woode as he that did them keepe.
Per. As the bonilasse passed bye,
Wil. Hey, ho, bonilasse!
Per. She rovde at me with glauncing eye,
Wil. As cleare as the christall glasse;   80
Per. All as the Sunnye beame so bright,
Wil. Hey, ho, the Sunne-beame!
Per. Glaunceth from Phœbus face forthright,
Wil. So love into thy hart did streame:
Per. Or as the thonder cleaves, the cloudes,
Wil. Hey, ho, the Thonder!
Per. Wherein the lightsome levin shroudes,
Wil. So cleaves thy soule asonder:
Per. Or as Dame Cynthias silver raye,
Wil. Hey, ho, the Moonelight!   90
Per. Upon the glyttering wave doth playe,
Wil. Such play is a pitteous plight.
Per. The glaunce into my heart did glide;
Wil. Hey, ho, the glyder!
Per. Therewith my soule was sharply gryde,
Wil. Such woundes soone wexen wider.
Per. Hasting to raunch the arrow out,
Wil. Hey, ho, Perigot!
Per. I left the head in my hart-roote,
Wil. It was a desperate shot.   100
Per. There it rancleth, ay more and more,
Wil. Hey, ho, the arrowe!
Per. Ne can I find salve for my sore:
Wil. Love is a curelesse sorrowe.

66	greete: weeping	87	levin: lightning
67	saye: fine cloth	95	gryde: pierced
74	seely: simple	97	raunch: pluck
75	wood: mad		

Per. And though my bale with death I bought,
Wil.   Hey, ho, heavie cheere!
Per. Yet should thilk lasse not from my thought,
Wil.   So you may buye golde to deare.
Per. But whether in paynefull love I pyne,
Wil.   Hey, ho, pinching payne!   110
Per. Or thrive in welth, she shalbe mine,
Wil.   But if thou can her obteine.
Per. And if for gracelesse greefe I dye,
Wil.   Hey, ho, gracelesse griefe!
Per. Witnesse shee slewe me with her eye,
Wil.   Let thy follye be the priefe.
Per. And you, that sawe it, simple shepe,
Wil.   Hey, ho, the fayre flocke!
Per. For priefe thereof, my death shall weepe,
Wil.   And mone with many a mocke.   120
Per. So learnd I love on a holye eve,
Wil.   Hey, ho, holidaye!
Per. That ever since my hart did greve,
Wil.   Now endeth our roundelay.
Cud. Sicker, sike a roundle never heard I none:
    Little lacketh Perigot of the best,
And Willye is not greatly overgone,
    So weren his under-songs well addrest.
Wil. Herdgrome, I fear me, thou have a squint eye:
Areede uprightly who has the victorye!   130
Cud. Fayth of my soule, I deeme ech have gayned:
For-thy let the Lambe be Willye his owne:
And for Perigot, so well hath hym payned,
    To him be the wroughten mazer alone.
Per. Perigot is well pleased with the doome:
Ne can Willye wite the witelesse herdgroome.
Wil. Never dempt more right of beautye, I weene,
The shepheard of Ida that judged beauties Queene.
Cud. But tell me, shepherds, should it not yshend
    Your roundels fresh, to heare a doolefull verse   140
Of Rosalend (who knowes not Rosalend?)
    That Colin made? ylke can I you rehearse.
Per. Now say it, Cuddie, as thou art a ladde:
With mery thing its good to medle sadde.
Wil. Fayth of my soule, thou shalt ycrouned be
    In Colins stede, if thou this song areede;
For never thing on earth so pleaseth me
    As him to heare, or matter of his deede.

130   Areede: judge   139   yshend: disgrace
136   wite: blame

Cud. Then listneth ech unto my heavy laye,
And tune your pypes as ruthful as ye may.   150

'Ye wastefull Woodes! beare witnesse of my woe,
Wherein my plaints did oftentimes resound:
Ye carelesse byrds are privie to my cryes,
Which in your songs were wont to make a part:
Thou, pleasaunt spring, hast luld me oft asleepe,
Whose streames my tricklinge teares did ofte augment.

'Resort of people doth my greefs augment,
The walled townes doe worke my greater woe;
The forest wide is fitter to resound
The hollow Echo of my carefull cryes: 160
I hate the house, since thence my love did part,
Whose waylefull want debarres myne eyes from sleepe.

'Let stremes of teares supply the place of sleepe;
Let all, that sweete is, voyd: and all that may augment
My doole, draw neare! More meete to wayle my woe
Bene the wild woddes, my sorowes to resound,
Then bedde, or bowre, both which I fill with cryes,
When I them see so waist, and fynd no part

'Of pleasure past. Here will I dwell apart
In gastfull grove therefore, till my last sleepe   170
Doe close mine eyes: so shall I not augment
With sight of such a chaunge my restlesse woe.
Helpe me, ye banefull byrds, whose shrieking sound
Ys signe of dreery death, my deadly cryes

'Most ruthfully to tune: And as my cryes
(Which of my woe cannot bewray least part)
You heare all night, when nature craveth sleepe,
Increase, so let your yrksome yells augment.
Thus all the night in plaints, the daye in woe,
I vowed have to wayst, till safe and sound   180

'She home returne, whose voyces silver sound
To cheerefull songs can chaunge my cherelesse cryes.
Hence with the Nightingale will I take part,
That blessed byrd, that spends her time of sleepe
In songs and plaintive pleas, the more taugment
The memory of hys misdeede that bred her woe.

170   gastfull: fearful

And you that feele no woe,
  When as the sound
Of these my nightly cryes
  Ye heare apart,
Let breake your sounder sleepe,
  And pitie augment.'

Per. O Colin, Colin! the shepheards joye,   190
  How I admire ech turning of thy verse!
And Cuddie, fresh Cuddie, the liefest boye,
  How dolefully his doole thou didst rehearse!
Cud. Then blowe your pypes, shepheards, til you be at
  home;
The night nigheth fast, yts time to be gone.

PERIGOT HIS EMBLEME.

Vincenti gloria victi.

WILLYES EMBLEME.

Vinto non vitto.

CUDDIES EMBLEME.

Felice chi puo.

OCTOBER.

ÆGLOGA DECIMA. ARGUMENT.

IN CUDDIE *is set out the perfecte paterne of a Poete, whiche, finding
no maintenaunce of his state and studies, complayneth of the con-
tempte of Poetrie, and the causes thereof: Specially having bene in
all ages, and even amongst the most barbarous, always of singular
accoumpt and honor, and being indede so worthy and commendable an arte; or rather no arte, but a divine gift and heavenly instinct not to bee gotten by laboure and learning, but adorned with
both; and poured into the witte by a certain* 'Ενθουσιασμòς *and
celestiall inspiration, as the Author hereof els where at large discourseth in his booke called* The English Poete, *which booke being
lately come to my hands, I mynde also by Gods grace, upon further advisement, to publish.*

192   liefest: dearest

PIERCE.   CUDDIE.

Piers. CUDDIE, for shame! hold up thy heavye head,
And let us cast with what delight to chace,
And weary thys long lingring Phœbus race.
Whilome thou wont the shepheards laddes to leade
In rymes, in ridles, and in bydding base;
Now they in thee, and thou in sleepe art dead.

Cud. Piers, I have pyped erst so long with payne,
That all mine Oten reedes bene rent and wore,
And my poore Muse hath spent her spared store,
Yet little good hath got, and much lesse gayne.   10
Such pleasaunce makes the Grashopper so poore,
And ligge so layd, when Winter doth her straine.

The dapper ditties, that I wont devise
To feede youthes fancie, and the flocking fry,
Delighten much; what I the bett for-thy?
They han the pleasure, I a sclender prise;
I beate the bush, the byrds to them doe flye:
What good thereof to Cuddie can arise?

Piers. Cuddie, the prayse is better then the price,
The glory eke much greater then the gayne: 20
O! what an honor is it, to restraine
The lust of lawlesse youth with good advice,
Or pricke them forth with pleasaunce of thy vaine,
Whereto thou list their trayned willes entice.

Soone as thou gynst to sette thy notes in frame,
O, how the rurall routes to thee doe cleave!
Seemeth thou dost their soule of sence bereave;
All as the shepheard that did fetch his dame
From Plutoes balefull bowre withouten leave,
His musicks might the hellish hound did tame.   30

Cud. So praysen babes the Peacoks spotted traine,
And wondren at bright Argus blazing eye;
But who rewards him ere the more for-thy,
Or feedes him once the fuller by a graine?

5   bydding base: the game of pris-   12   layd: subdued
oner's base   24   trayned: trapped
12   ligge: lie   33   for-thy: therefore

Sike prayse is smoke, that sheddeth in the skye;
Sike words bene wynd, and wasten soone in vayne.

Piers. Abandon, then, the base and viler clowne;
Lyft up thy selfe out of the lowly dust,
And sing of bloody Mars, of wars, of giusts;
Turne thee to those that weld the awful crowne,   40
To doubted Knights, whose woundlesse armour rusts,
And helmes unbruzed wexen dayly browne.

There may thy Muse display her fluttryng wing,
And stretch her selfe at large from East to West;
Whither thou list in fayre Elisa rest,
Or, if thee please in bigger notes to sing,
Advaunce the worthy whome shee loveth best,
That first the white beare to the stake did bring.

And, when the stubborne stroke of stronger stounds
Has somewhat slackt the tenor of thy string,   50
Of love and lustihead tho mayst thou sing,
And carroll lowde, and leade the Myllers rownde,
All were Elisa one of thilke same ring;
So mought our Cuddies name to heaven sownde.

Cud. Indeede the Romish Tityrus, I heare,
Through his Mecænas left his Oaten reede,
Whereon he earst had taught his flocks to feede,
And laboured lands to yield the timely eare,
And eft did sing of warres and deadly drede,
So as the Heavens did quake his verse to here.   60

But ah! Mecænas is yclad in claye,
And great Augustus long ygoe is dead,
And all the worthies liggen wrapt in leade,
That matter made for Poets on to play:
For ever, who in derring-doe were dreade,
The loftie verse of hem was loved aye.

But after vertue gan for age to stoope,
And mightie manhode brought a bedde of ease,
The vaunting Poets found nought worth a pease
To put in preace among the learned troupe: 70
Tho gan the streames of flowing wittes to cease,
And sonne-bright honour pend in shamefull coupe.

49   stounds: strokes   65   derring-doe: daring deeds
58   eare: harvest   70   put in preace: exercise

And if that any buddes of Poesie,
Yet of the old stocke, gan to shoote agayne,
Or it mens follies mote be forst to fayne,
And rolle with rest in rymes of rybaudrye;
Or, as it sprong, it wither must agayne:
Tom Piper makes us better melodie.

Piers. O pierlesse Poesye! where is then thy place?
If nor in Princes pallace thou doe sitt,   80
(And yet is Princes pallace the most fitt,)
Ne brest of baser birth doth thee embrace,
Then make thee winges of thine aspyring wit,
And, whence thou camst, flye backe to heaven apace.

Cud. Ah, Percy! it is all to weake and wanne,
So high to sore and make so large a flight;
Her peeced pyneons bene not so in plight:
For Colin fittes such famous flight to scanne;
He, were he not with love so ill bedight,
Would mount as high, and sing as soote as Swanne.   90

Piers. Ah, fon! for love does teach him climbe so hie,
And lyftes him up out of the loathsome myre:
Such immortal mirrhor, as he doth admire,
Would rayse ones mynd above the starry skie,
And cause a caytive corage to aspire;
For lofty love doth loath a lowly eye.

Cud. All otherwise the state of Poet stands;
For lordly love is such a Tyranne fell,
That where he rules all power he doth expell;
The vaunted verse a vacant head demaundes,   100
Ne wont with crabbed care the Muses dwell:
Unwisely weaves, that takes two webbes in hand.

Who ever casts to compasse weightye prise,
And thinkes to throwe out thondring words of threate,
Let powre in lavish cups and thriftie bitts of meate,
For Bacchus fruite is frend to Phœbus wise;
And, when with Wine the braine begins to sweate,
The nombers flowe as fast as spring doth ryse.

89	bedight: afflicted	95	corage: spirit
90	soote: sweet	105	thriftie: proper
91	fon: fool	105	bitts: mouthfuls
95	caytive: base	105	meate: food

Thou kenst not, Percie, howe the ryme should rage,
O! if my temples were distaind with wine,   110
And girt in girlonds of wild Yvie twine,
How I could reare the Muse on stately stage,
And teache her tread aloft in buskin fine,
With queint Bellona in her equipage!

But ah! my corage cooles ere it be warme:
For-thy content us in thys humble shade,
Where no such troublous tydes han us assayde;
Here we our slender pypes may safely charme.
    Piers. And, when my Gates shall han their bellies layd,
Cuddie shall have a Kidde to store his farme.   120

CUDDIES EMBLEME.

Agitante calescimus illo, &c.

DECEMBER.

ÆGLOGA DUODECIMA. ARGUMENT.

THIS ÆGLOGUE (*even as the first beganne*) *is ended with a com-
playnte of Colin to God Pan; wherein, as weary of his former
wayes, hee proportioneth his life to the foure seasons of the yeare;
comparing hys youthe to the spring time, when he was fresh and
free from loves follye. His manhoode to the sommer, which, he
sayth, was consumed with greate heate and excessive drouth,
caused throughe a Comet or blasing starre, by which hee meaneth
love; which passion is commonly compared to such flames and im-
moderate heate. His riper yeares hee resembleth to an unseasonable
harveste, wherein the fruites fall ere they be rype. His latter age to
winters chyll and frostie season, now drawing neare to his last ende.*

THE gentle shepheard satte beside a springe,
All in the shadowe of a bushye brere,
That Colin hight, which wel could pype and singe,
For he of Tityrus his songs did lere:
    There, as he satte in secreate shade alone,
    Thus gan he make of love his piteous mone.

'O soveraigne Pan! thou god of shepheards all,
Which of our tender Lambkins takest keepe,
4 lere: learn

And, when our flocks into mischaunce mought fall,
Doest save from mischiefe the unwary sheepe,   10
  Als of their maisters hast no lesse regarde
  Then of the flocks, which thou doest watch and warde;

'I thee beseche (so be thou deigne to heare
Rude ditties, tund to shepeards Oaten reede,
Or if I ever sonet song so cleare,
As it with pleasaunce mought thy fancie feede)
  Hearken awhile, from thy greene cabinet,
  The rurall song of carefull Colinet.

'Whilome in youth, when flowrd my joyfull spring,
Like Swallow swift I wandred here and there;   20
For heate of heedlesse lust me so did sting,
That I of doubted daunger had no feare:
  I went the wastefull woodes and forest wide,
  Withouten dreade of Wolves to bene espyed.

'I wont to raunge amydde the mazie thickette,
And gather nuttes to make me Christmas game,
And joyed oft to chace the trembling Pricket,
Or hunt the hartlesse hare til shee were tame.
  What wreaked I of wintrye ages waste?—
  Tho deemed I my spring would ever laste.   30

'How often have I scaled the craggie Oke,
All to dislodge the Raven of her nest?
How have I wearied with many a stroke
The stately Walnut-tree, the while the rest
  Under the tree fell all for nuts at strife?
  For ylike to me was libertee and lyfe.

'And for I was in thilke same looser yeares,
(Whether the Muse so wrought me from my byrth,
Or I to much beleeved my shepherd peres,)
Somedele ybent to song and musicks mirth,   40
  A good old shephearde, Wrenock was his name,
  Made me by arte more cunning in the same.

'Fro thence I durst in derring-doe compare
With shepheards swayne what ever fedde in field;
And, if that Hobbinol right judgement bare,
To Pan his owne selfe pype I neede not yield:

15 sonet: song   17 cabinet: arbor

For, if the flocking Nymphes did follow Pan,
The wiser Muses after Colin ranne.

'But, ah! such pryde at length was ill repayde:
The shepheards God (perdie God was he none)   50
My hurtlesse pleasaunce did me ill upbraide;
My freedome lorne, my life he lefte to mone.
    Love they him called that gave me checkmate,
    But better mought they have behote him Hate.

'Tho gan my lovely Spring bid me farewel,
And Sommer season sped him to display
(For love then in the Lyons house did dwell)
The raging fyre that kindled at his ray.
    A comett stird up that unkindly heate,
    That reigned (as men sayd) in Venus seate.   60

'Forth was I ledde, not as I wont afore,
When choise I had to choose my wandring waye,
But whether luck and loves unbridled lore
Woulde leade me forth on Fancies bitte to playe:
    The bush my bedde, the bramble was my bowre,
    The Woodes can witnesse many a wofull
        stowre.

'Where I was wont to seeke the honey Bee,
Working her formall rowmes in wexen frame,
The grieslie Tode-stoole growne there mought I se,
And loathed Paddocks lording on the same: 70
    And where the chaunting birds luld me asleepe,
    The ghastlie Owle her grievous ynne doth keepe.

'Then as the springe gives place to elder time,
And bringeth forth the fruite of sommers pryde;
Also my age, now passed youngthly pryme,
To thinges of ryper reason selfe applyed,
    And learnd of lighter timber cotes to frame,
    Such as might save my sheepe and me fro shame.

'To make fine cages for the Nightingale,
And Baskets of bulrushes, was my wont: 80
Who to entrappe the fish in winding sale

54   behote: called   77   cotes: houses
70   Paddocks: toads   81   sale: net

Was better seene, or hurtful beastes to hont?
  I learned als the signes of heaven to ken,
    How Phœbe fayles, where Venus sittes, and when.

'And tryed time yet taught me greater thinges;
The sodain rysing of the raging seas,
The soothe of byrdes by beating of their winges,
The power of herbs, both which can hurt and ease,
  And which be wont t' enrage the restlesse sheepe,
  And which be wont to worke eternall sleepe.   90

'But, ah! unwise and witlesse Colin Cloute,
That kydst the hidden kinds of many a wede,
Yet kydst not ene to cure thy sore hart-roote,
Whose ranckling wound as yet does rifelye bleede.
  Why livest thou stil, and yet hast thy deathes wound?
  Why dyest thou stil, and yet alive art founde?

'Thus is my sommer worne away and wasted,
Thus is my harvest hastened all to rathe;
The eare that budded faire is burnt and blasted,
And all my hoped gaine is turnd to scathe: 100
  Of all the seede that in my youth was sowne
  Was nought but brakes and brambles to be mowne.

'My boughes with bloosmes that crowned were at firste,
And promised of timely fruite such store,
Are left both bare and barrein now at erst;
The flattring fruite is fallen to grownd before,
  And rotted ere they were halfe mellow ripe;
  My harvest, wast, my hope away dyd wipe.

'The fragrant flowres, that in my garden grewe,
Bene withered, as they had bene gathered long;   110
Theyr rootes bene dryed up for lacke of dewe,
Yet dewed with teares they han be ever among.
  Ah! who has wrought my Rosalind this spight,
  To spil the flowres that should her girlond dight?

'And I, that whilome wont to frame my pype
Unto the shifting of the shepheards foote,
Sike follies nowe have gathered as too ripe,
And cast hem out as rotten and unsoote.

87 soothe: prophecy   98 rathe: soon
92 kydst: knew

The loser Lasse I cast to please no more;
One if I please, enough is me therefore.   120

'And thus of all my harvest-hope I have
Nought reaped but a weedye crop of care;
Which, when I thought have thresht in swelling sheave,
Cockel for corne, and chaffe for barley, bare:
    Soone as the chaffe should in the fan be fynd,
    All was blowne away of the wavering wynd.

'So now my yeare drawes to his latter terme,
My spring is spent, my sommer burnt up quite;
My harveste hasts to stirre up Winter sterne,
And bids him clayme with rigorous rage hys right: 130
    So nowe he stormes with many a sturdy stoure;
    So now his blustring blast eche coste dooth scoure.

'The carefull cold hath nypt my rugged rynde,
And in my face deepe furrowes eld hath pight:
My head besprent with hoary frost I fynd,
And by myne eie the Crow his clawe dooth wright:
    Delight is layd abedde; and pleasure past;
    No sonne now shines; cloudes han all overcast.

'Now leave, ye shepheards boyes, your merry glee;
My Muse is hoarse and wearie of thys stounde,   140
Here will I hang my pype upon this tree:
Was never pype of reede did better sounde.
    Winter is come that blowes the bitter blaste,
    And after Winter dreerie death does hast.

'Gather together ye my little flocke,
My little flock, that was to me so liefe;
Let me, ah! lette me in your foldes ye lock,
Ere the breme Winter breede you greater griefe.
    Winter is come, that blowes the balefull breath,
    And after Winter commeth timely death.   150

'Adieu, delightes, that lulled me asleepe;
Adieu, my deare, whose love I bought so deare;
Adieu, my little Lambes and loved sheepe;
Adieu, ye Woodes, that oft my witnesse were:
    Adieu, good Hobbinoll, that was so true,
    Tell Rosalind, her Colin bids her adieu.'

125   fynd: refined   148   breme: cold

COLINS EMBLEME.

Vivitur ingenio: cætera mortis erunt.

Loe! I have made a Calender for every yeare,
That steele in strength, and time in durance, shall outweare;
And, if I marked well the starres revolution,
It shall continewe till the worlds dissolution,
To teach the ruder shepheard how to feede his sheepe,
And from the falsers fraude his folded flocke to keepe.
  Goe, lyttle Calender! thou hast a free passeporte;
Goe but a lowly gate emongste the meaner sorte:
Dare not to match thy pype with Tityrus his style.
Nor with the Pilgrim that the Ploughman playde awhyle;
But followe them farre off, and their high steppes adore:
The better please, the worse despise; I aske no more.

MERCE NON MERCEDE.

Mother Hubberds Tale

M OTHER HUBBERDS TALE appeared in a volume entitled
*Complaints. Containing sundrie small Poemes of the Worlds
Vanitie*, which was entered in the Stationers' Register December 29, 1590 and published in 1591. The collection includes
poems written years earlier as well as some of recent composition. There are passages in some of these poems that look
like attacks on the Queen's chief minister, William Cecil,
Lord Burghley, and no doubt for this reason the volume appears to have been suppressed.

A passionate exclamation in *Mother Hubberds Tale* (lines
892-918) complains bitterly of the state of a suitor who has the
Prince's grace, yet lacks that of her "peer." This suggests that
Cecil in some way interfered with the reward the Queen had
granted Spenser for the presentation of *The Faerie Queene*.
Since the dedication of the poem asserts that it was "long
sithens composed in the raw conceit of my youth," some
scholars have held that the whole poem is an assault upon
Cecil, and that the great man's wrath resulted in the poet's
"exile" to Ireland in 1580. I find it more likely that the passage in question was interpolated at some time after the presentation of *The Faerie Queene* in 1589 and that the poem as a
whole is to be read as a general satire.

"Prosopopoia" is a rhetorical term meaning "personification, representation in human form or with human attributes." Spenser evidently intends by it "beast fable." Such fables were often used for satiric purposes in the Middle Ages.

PROSOPOPOIA:

OR MOTHER HUBBERDS TALE

It was the month in which the righteous Maide,
That for disdaine of sinfull worlds upbraide
Fled back to heaven, whence she was first conceived,
Into her silver bowre the Sunne received;
And the hot Syrian Dog on him awayting,
After the chafed Lyons cruell bayting,
Corrupted had th' ayre with his noysome breath,
And powr'd on th' earth plague, pestilence, and death.
Emongst the rest a wicked maladie
Raign'd emongst men, that manie did to die,   10
Depriv'd of sense and ordinarie reason,
That it to Leaches seemed strange and geason.
My fortune was, mongst manie others moe,
To be partaker of their common woe;
And my weake bodie, set on fire with griefe,
Was rob'd of rest and naturall reliefe.
In this ill plight there came to visite mee
Some friends, who, sorie my sad case to see,
Began to comfort me in chearfull wise,
And meanes of gladsome solace to devise: 20
But seeing kindly sleep refuse to doe
His office, and my feeble eyes forgoe,
They sought my troubled sense how to deceave
With talke, that might unquiet fancies reave;

2 upbraide: reproach   24 reave: take away
12 geason: extraordinary

And, sitting all in seates about me round,
With pleasant tales (fit for that idle stound)
They cast in course to waste the wearie howres.
Some tolde of Ladies, and their Paramoures;
Some of brave Knights, and their renowned Squires;
Some of the Faeries and their strange attires;   30
And some of Giaunts, hard to be beleeved;
That the delight thereof me much releeved.
Amongst the rest a good old woman was,
Hight Mother Hubberd, who did farre surpas
The rest in honest mirth, that seem'd her well:
She, when her turne was come her tale to tell,
Tolde of a strange adventure, that betided
Betwixt the Foxe and th' Ape by him misguided;
The which, for that my sense it greatly pleased,
All were my spirite heavie and diseased,   40
Ile write in termes as she the same did say,
So well as I her words remember may.
No Muses aide me needes heretoo to call;
Base is the style, and matter meane withall.
  Whilome (said she) before the world was civill,
The Foxe and th' Ape, disliking of their evill
And hard estate, determined to seeke
Their fortunes farre abroad, lyeke with his lyeke,
For both were craftie and unhappie witted;
Two fellowes might no where be better fitted.   50
The Foxe, that first this cause of griefe did finde,
Gan first thus plaine his case with words unkinde.
'Neighbour Ape, and my Gossip eke beside,
(Both two sure bands in friendship to be tide)
To whom may I more trustely complaine
The evill plight that doth me sore constraine,
And hope thereof to finde due remedie?
Heare, then, my paine and inward agonie.
Thus manie yeares I now have spent and worne
In meane regard, and basest fortunes scorne,   60
Dooing my Countrey service as I might,
No lesse, I dare saie, than the prowdest wight;
And still I hoped to be up advaunced,
For my good parts; but still it has mischaunced.
Now therefore that no lenger hope I see,
But froward fortune still to follow mee,
And losels lifted up on high, where I did looke,
I meane to turne the next leafe of the booke:

26   stound: moment   52   unkinde: unnatural
49   unhappie witted: tricky

Yet, ere that anie way I doo betake,
I meane my Gossip privie first to make.'
'Ah! my deare Gossip, (answer'd then the Ape)   70
Deeply doo your sad words my wits awhape,
Both for because your griefe doth great appeare,
And eke because my selfe am touched neare:
For I likewise have wasted much good time,
Still wayting to preferment up to clime,
Whilest others alwayes have before me stept,
And from my beard the fat away have swept;
That now unto despaire I gin to growe,
And meane for better winde about to throwe.
Therefore to me, my trustie friend, aread   80
Thy councell: two is better than one head.'
'Certes (said he) I meane me to disguize
In some straunge habit, after uncouth wize;
Or like a Pilgrim, or a Lymiter,
Or like a Gipsen, or a Juggeler,
And so to wander to the worldës ende,
To seeke my fortune, where I may it mend:
For worse than that I have I cannot meete.
Wide is the world I wote, and everie streete   90
Is full of fortunes, and adventures straunge,
Continuallie subject unto chaunge.
Say, my faire brother now, if this device
Doth like you, or may you to like entice.'
'Surely (said th' Ape) it likes me wondrous well;
And would ye not poore fellowship expell,
My selfe would offer you t' accompanie
In this adventures chauncefull jeopardie:
For to wexe olde at home in idlenesse
Is disadventrous, and quite fortunelesse;   100
Abroad, where change is, good may gotten bee.'
    The Foxe was glad, and quickly did agree:
So both resolv'd, the morrow next ensuing,
So soone as day appeard to peoples vewing,
On their intended journey to proceede;
And over night whatso theretoo did neede
Each did prepare, in readines to bee.
The morrow next, so soone as one might see
Light out of heavens windowes forth to looke,
Both their habiliments unto them tooke,   110
And put themselves (a Gods name) on their way;
Whenas the Ape, beginning well to wey
This hard adventure, thus began t' advise.

72 awhape: terrify

'Now read, Sir Reynold, as ye be right wise,
What course ye weene is best for us to take,
That for our selves we may a living make.
Whether shall we professe some trade or skill,
Or shall we varie our device at will,
Even as new occasion appeares?
Or shall we tie our selves for certaine yeares   120
To anie service, or to anie place?
For it behoves, ere that into the race
We enter, to resolve first hereupon.'
'Now surely brother (said the Foxe anon)
Ye have this matter motioned in season;
For everie thing that is begun with reason
Will come by readie meanes unto his end,
But things miscounselled must needs miswend.
Thus therefore I advize upon the case,
That not to anie certaine trade or place,   130
Nor anie man, we should our selves applie;
For why should he that is at libertie
Make himselfe bond? sith then we are free borne,
Let us all servile base subjection scorne;
And as we bee sonnes of the world so wide,
Let us our fathers heritage divide,
And chalenge to our selves our portions dew
Of all the patrimonie, which a few
Now hold in hugger mugger in their hand,
And all the rest doo rob of good and land.   140
For now a few have all, and all have nought,
Yet all be brethren ylike dearly bought:
There is no right in this partition,
Ne was it so by institution
Ordained first, ne by the law of Nature,
But that she gave like blessing to each creture,
As well of worldly livelode as of life,
That there might be no difference nor strife,
Nor ought cald mine or thine: thrice happie then
Was the condition of mortall men.   150
That was the golden age of Saturne old,
But this might better be the world of gold;
For without golde now nothing wilbe got,
Therefore (if please you) this shalbe our plot:
We will not be of anie occupation;
Let such vile vassals, borne to base vocation,
Drudge in the world, and for their living droyle,
Which have no wit to live withouten toyle;

157 droyle: drudge

But we will walke about the world at pleasure
Like two free men, and make our ease our treasure.   160
Free men some beggers call, but they be free,
And they which call them so more beggers bee;
For they doo swinke and sweate to feed the other,
Who live like Lords of that which they doo gather,
And yet doo never thanke them for the same,
But as their due by Nature doo it clame.
Such will we fashion both our selves to bee,
Lords of the world; and so will wander free
Where so us listeth, uncontrol'd of anie:
Hard is our hap, if we (emongst so manie)   170
Light not on some that may our state amend;
Sildome but some good commeth ere the end.'
   Well seemd the Ape to like this ordinaunce;
Yet, well considering of the cirumstaunce,
As pausing in great doubt, awhile he staid,
And afterwards with grave advizement said:
'I cannot, my lief brother, like but well
The purpose of the complot which ye tell;
For well I wot (compar'd to all the rest
Of each degree) that Beggers life is best;   180
And they, that thinke themselves the best of all,
Oft-times to begging are content to fall.
But this I wot withall, that we shall ronne
Into great daunger, like to bee undone,
Thus wildly to wander in the worlds eye,
Withouten pasport or good warrantye,
For feare least we like rogues should be reputed,
And for eare-marked beasts abroad be bruted.
Therefore, I read that we our counsells call,
How to prevent this mischiefe ere it fall,   190
And how we may, with most securitie,
Beg amongst those that beggers doo defie.'
'Right well, deere Gossip, ye advized have,
(Said then the Foxe) but I this doubt will save;
For ere we farther passe I will devise
A pasport for us both in fittest wize,
And by the names of Souldiers us protect:
That now is thought a civile begging sect.
Be you the Souldier, for you likest are
For manly semblance, and small skill in warre: 200
I will but wayte on you, and, as occasion
Falls out, my selfe fit for the same will fashion.'

163   swinke: labor
188   eare-marked: marked as being owned by someone
192   defie: despise

The pasport ended, both they forward went;
The Ape clad Souldierlike, fit for th' intent,
In a blew jacket with a crosse of redd
And manie slits, as if that he had shedd
Much blood throgh many wounds therein receaved,
Which had the use of his right arme bereaved.
Upon his head an old Scotch cap he wore,
With a plume feather all to peeces tore: 210
His breeches were made after the new cut,
Al Portugese, loose like an emptie gut;
And his hose broken high above the heeling,
And his shooes beaten out with traveling.
But neither sword nor dagger he did beare;
Seemes that no foes revengement he did feare:
In stead of them a handsome bat he held,
On which he leaned, as one farre in elde.
Shame light on him, that through so false illusion,
Doth turne the name of Souldiers to abusion,   220
And that, which is the noblest mysterie,
Brings to reproach and common infamie!
Long they thus travailed, yet never met
Adventure which might them a working set;
Yet manie waies they sought, and manie tryed,
Yet for their purposes none fit espyed.
At last they chaunst to meet upon the way
A simple husbandman in garments gray;
Yet though his vesture were but meane and bace,
A good yeoman he was of honest place,   230
And more for thrift did care than for gay clothing:
Gay without good is good hearts greatest loathing.
The Foxe him spying, bad the Ape him dight
To play his part, for loe! he was in sight
That (if he er'd not,) should them entertaine,
And yeeld them timely profite for their paine.
Eftsoones the Ape himselfe gan up to reare,
And on his shoulders high his bat to beare,
As if good service he were fit to doo;
But little thrift for him he did it too: 240
And stoutly forward he his steps did straine,
That like a handsome swaine it him became.
    When as they nigh approached, that good man,
Seeing them wander loosly, first began
T' enquire of custome, what and whence they were?
To whom the Ape, 'I am a Souldiere,
That late in warres have spent my deerest blood,

221   mysterie: profession   240   thrift: profit

And in long service lost both limbs and good;
And now, constrain'd that trade to overgive,
I driven am to seeke some meanes to live: 250
Which might it you in pitie please t' afford,
I would be readie, both in deed and word,
To doo you faithfull service all my dayes.
This yron world (that same he weeping sayes)
Brings downe the stowtest hearts to lowest state;
For miserie doth bravest mindes abate,
And make them seeke for that they wont to scorne,
Of fortune and of hope at once forlorne.'
The honest man, that heard him thus complaine,
Was griev'd as he had felt part of his paine;   260
And, well dispos'd him some reliefe to showe,
Askt if in husbandrie he ought did knowe,
To plough, to plant, to reap, to rake, to sowe,
To hedge, to ditch, to thrash, to thetch, to mowe?
Or to what labour els he was prepar'd,
For husbands life is labourous and hard?
Whenas the Ape him hard so much to talke
Of labour, that did from his liking balke,
He would have slipt the coller handsomly,
And to him said: 'Good Sir, full glad am I,   270
To take what paines may anie living wight;
But my late maymed limbs lack wonted might
To doo their kindly services as needeth.
Scarce this right hand the mouth with diet feedeth,
So that it may no painfull worke endure,
Ne to strong labour can it selfe enure:
But if that anie other place you have,
Which askes small paines, but thriftines to save,
Or care to overlooke, or trust to gather,
Ye may me trust as your owne ghostly father.'   280
    With that the husbandman gan him avize,
That it for him were fittest exercise
Cattell to keep, or grounds to oversee;
And asked him, if he could willing bee
To keep his sheep, or to attend his swyne,
Or watch his mares, or take his charge of kyne?
'Gladly (said he) what ever such like paine
Ye put on me, I will the same sustaine;
But gladliest I of your fleecie sheepe
(Might it you please) would take on me the keep.   290
For ere that unto armes I me betooke,

264 thetch: thatch   280 ghostly: spiritual
273 kindly: natural

Unto my fathers sheepe I usde to looke,
That yet the skill thereof I have not loste:
Thereto right well this Curdog, by my coste,
(Meaning the Foxe) will serve my sheepe to gather,
And drive to follow after their Belwether.'
The Husbandman was meanly well content
Triall to make of his endevourment;
And, home him leading, lent to him the charge
Of all his flocke, with libertie full large,   300
Giving accompt of th' annuall increce
Both of their lambes, and of their woolly fleece.
Thus is this Ape become a shepheard swaine,
And the false Foxe his dog (God give them paine!)
For ere the yeare have halfe his course out-run,
And doo returne from whence he first begun,
They shall him make an ill accompt of thrift.
Now whenas Time, flying with wingës swift,
Expired had the terme, that these two javels
Should render up a reckning of their travels   310
Unto their master, which it of them sought,
Exceedingly they troubled were in thought,
Ne wist what answere unto him to frame,
Ne how to scape great punishment, or shame,
For their false treason and vile theeverie:
For not a lambe of all their flockes supply
Had they to shew; but, ever as they bred,
They slue them, and upon their fleshes fed;
For that disguised Dog lov'd blood to spill,
And drew the wicked Shepheard to his will.   320
So twixt them both they not a lambkin left,
And when lambes fail'd the old sheepes lives they reft;
That how t' acquite themselves unto their Lord
They were in doubt, and flatly set abord.
The Foxe then counsel'd th' Ape for to require
Respite till morrow t' answere his desire;
For times delay new hope of helpe still breeds.
The goodman granted, doubting nought their deeds,
And bad next day that all should readie be:
But they more subtill meaning had than he;   330
For the next morrowes meed they closely ment,
For feare of afterclaps, for to prevent:
And that same evening, when all shrowded were
In careles sleep, they without care or feare

297   meanly: moderately   324   abord: abroad, adrift (?)
309   javels: rascals   331   meed: payment
310   travels: labors

Cruelly fell upon their flock in folde,
And of them slew at pleasure what they wolde.
Of which whenas they feasted had their fill,
For a full complement of all their ill,
They stole away, and tooke their hastie flight,
Carried in clowdes of all-concealing night.   340
    So was the husbandman left to his losse,
And they unto their fortunes change to tosse:
After which sort they wandered long while,
Abusing manie through their cloaked guile,
That at the last they gan to be descryed
Of everie one, and all their sleights espyed.
So as their begging now them failed quyte,
For none would give, but all men would them wyte:
Yet would they take no paines to get their living,
But seeke some other way to gaine by giving,   350
Much like to begging, but much better named,
For manie beg which are thereof ashamed.
And now the Foxe had gotten him a gowne,
And th' Ape a cassocke sidelong hanging downe;
For they their occupation meant to change,
And now in other state abroad to range:
For, since their souldiers pas no better spedd,
They forg'd another, as for Clerkes booke-redd.
Who passing foorth, as their adventures fell,
Through manie haps, which needs not here to tell,   360
At length chaunst with a formall Priest to meete,
Whom they in civill manner first did greete,
And after askt an almes for Gods deare love.
The man straightway his choler up did move,
And with reproachfull tearmes gan them revile,
For following that trade so base and vile;
And askt what license, or what Pas they had?
'Ah! (said the Ape, as sighing wondrous sad)
Its an hard case, when men of good deserving
Must either driven be perforce to sterving,   370
Or asked for their pas by everie squib,
That list at will them to revile or snib:
And yet (God wote) small oddes I often see
Twixt them that aske, and them that asked bee.
Natheles, because you shall not us misdeeme,
But that we are as honest as we seeme,
Yee shall our pasport at your pleasure see,
And then ye will (I hope) well mooved bee.'
Which when the Priest beheld, he vew'd it nere,

348   wyte: blame   361   formall: in outward form

As if therein some text he studying were,
But little els (God wote) could thereof skill;
For read he could not evidence, nor will,
Ne tell a written word, ne write a letter,
Ne make one title worse, ne make one better:
Of such deep learning little had he neede,
Ne yet of Latine, ne of Greeke, that breede
Doubts mongst Divines, and difference of texts,
From whence arise diversitie of sects,
And hatefull heresies, of God abhor'd:
But this good Sir did follow the plaine word,   390
Ne medled with their controversies vaine;
All his care was, his service well to saine,
And to read Homelies upon holidayes;
When that was done, he might attend his playes:
An easie life, and fit high God to please.
   He, having overlookt their pas at ease,
Gan at the length them to rebuke againe,
That no good trade of life did entertaine,
But lost their time in wandring loose abroad;
Seeing the world, in which they bootles boad,   400
Had wayes enough for all therein to live;
Such grace did God unto his creatures give.
Said then the Foxe: 'Who hath the world not tride,
From the right way full eath may wander wide:
We are but Novices, new come abroad,
We have not yet the tract of anie troad,
Nor on us taken anie state of life,
But readie are of anie to make preife.
Therefore might please you, which the world have proved,
Us to advise, which forth but lately moved,   410
Of some good course that we might under-take;
Ye shall for ever us your bondmen make.'
The Priest gan wexe halfe proud to be so praide,
And thereby willing to affoord them aide;
'It seemes (said he) right well that ye be Clerks,
Both by your wittie words, and by your werks.
Is not that name enough to make a living
To him that hath a whit of Natures giving?
How manie honest men see ye arize
Daylie thereby, and grow to goodly prize;   420
To Deanes, to Archdeacons, to Commissaries,
To Lords, to Principalls, to Prebendaries?
All jolly Prelates, worthie rule to beare,
Who ever them envie: yet spite bites neare.

Why should ye doubt, then, but that ye likewise
Might unto some of those in time arise?
In the meane-time to live in good estate,
Loving that love, and hating those that hate;
Being some honest Curate, or some Vicker
Content with little in condition sicker.   430
'Ah! but (said th' Ape) the charge is wondrous great,
To feed mens soules, and hath an heavie threat.'
'To feede mens soules (quoth he) is not in man;
For they must feed themselves, doo what we can.
We are but charg'd to lay the meate before:
Eate they that list, we need to doo no more.
But God it is that feedes them with his grace,
The bread of life powr'd downe from heavenly place.
Therefore said he, that with the budding rod
Did rule the Jewes, *All shalbe taught of God*.   440
That same hath Jesus Christ now to him raught,
By whom the flock is rightly fed, and taught:
He is the Shepheard, and the Priest is hee;
We but his shepheard swaines ordain'd to bee.
Therefore herewith doo not your selfe dismay;
Ne is the paines so great, but beare ye may,
For not so great, as it was wont of yore,
It's now a dayes, ne halfe so streight and sore.
They whilome used duly everie day
Their service and their holie things to say,   450
At morne and even, besides their Anthemes sweete,
Their penie Masses, and their Complynes meete,
Their Diriges, their Trentals, and their shrifts,
Their memories, their singings, and their gifts.
Now all those needlesse works are laid away;
Now once a weeke, upon the Sabbath day,
It is enough to doo our small devotion,
And then to follow any merrie motion.
Ne are we tyde to fast, but when we list;
Ne to weare garments base of wollen twist,   460
But with the finest silkes us to aray,
That before God we may appeare more gay,
Resembling Aarons glorie in his place:
For farre unfit it is, that person bace
Should with vile cloaths approach Gods majestie,
Whom no uncleannes may approachen nie;
Or that all men, which anie master serve,
Good garments for their service should deserve;
But he that serves the Lord of hoasts most high,

430 sicker: secure   441 raught: granted

And that in highest place, t' approach him nigh,   470
And all the peoples prayers to present
Before his throne, as on ambassage sent
Both too and fro, should not deserve to weare
A garment better than of wooll or heare.
Beside, we may have lying by our sides
Our lovely Lasses, or bright shining Brides:
We be not tyde to wilfull chastitie,
But have the Gospell of free libertie.'
    By that he ended had his ghostly sermon,
The Foxe was well induc'd to be a Parson,   480
And of the Priest eftsoones gan to enquire,
How to a Benefice he might aspire?
'Marie, there (said the Priest) is arte indeed:
Much good deep learning one thereout may reed;
For that the ground-worke is, and end of all,
How to obtaine a Beneficiall.
First, therefore, when ye have in handsome wise
Your selfe attyred, as you can devise,
Then to some Noble-man your selfe applye,
Or other great one in the worldës eye,   490
That hath a zealous disposition
To God, and so to his religion.
There must thou fashion eke a godly zeale,
Such as no carpers may contrayre reveale;
For each thing fained ought more warie bee.
There thou must walke in sober gravitee,
And seeme as Saintlike as Saint Radegund:
Fast much, pray oft, looke lowly on the ground,
And unto everie one doo curtesie meeke:
These lookes (nought saying) doo a benefice seeke,   500
And be thou sure one not to lacke or long.
But if thee list unto the Court to throng,
And there to hunt after the hoped pray,
Then must thou thee dispose another way:
For there thou needs must learne to laugh, to lie,
To face, to forge, to scoffe, to companie,
To crouche, to please, to be a beetle-stock
Of thy great Masters will, to scorne, or mock.
So maist thou chaunce mock out a Benefice,
Unlesse thou canst one conjure by device,   510
Or cast a figure for a Bishoprick;
And if one could, it were but a schoole trick.

479 ghostly: spiritual   507 beetle-stock: handle of a
486 Beneficiall: letter of presenta-   sledge hammer
tion to a benefice

These be the wayes by which without reward
Livings in Court be gotten, though full hard;
For nothing there is done without a fee:
The Courtier needes must recompenced bee
With a Benevolence, or have in gage
The Primitias of your Parsonage:
Scarse can a Bishoprick forpas them by,
But that it must be gelt in privitie.   520
Doo not thou therefore seeke a living there,
But of more private persons seeke elswhere,
Whereas thou maist compound a better penie,
Ne let thy learning question'd be of anie.
For some good Gentleman, that hath the right
Unto his Church for to present a wight,
Will cope with thee in reasonable wise;
That if the living yerely doo arise
To fortie pound, that then his yongest sonne
Shall twentie have, and twentie thou hast wonne: 530
Thou hast it wonne, for it is of franke gift,
And he will care for all the rest to shift,
Both that the Bishop may admit of thee,
And that therein thou maist maintained bee.
This is the way for one that is unlern'd
Living to get, and not to be discern'd.
But they, that are great Clerkes, have nearer wayes,
For learning sake to living them to raise;
Yet manie eke of them (God wote) are driven
T' accept a Benefice in peeces riven.   540
How saist thou (friend) have I not well discourst
Upon this Common-place, (though plaine, not wourst?)
Better a short tale than a bad long shriving:
Needes anie more to learne to get a living?'
    'Now sure, and by my hallidome, (quoth he)
Ye a great master are in your degree:
Great thankes I yeeld you for your discipline,
And doo not doubt but duly to encline
My wits theretoo, as ye shall shortly heare.'
The Priest him wisht good speed, and well to fare: 550
So parted they, as eithers way them led.
But th' Ape and Foxe ere long so well them sped,
Through the Priests holesome counsell lately tought,
And throgh their owne faire handling wisely wroght,
That they a Benefice twixt them obtained;
And craftie Reynold was a Priest ordained,

518   Primitias: first fruits   531   franke: free
520   gelt: gelded   543   shriving: confession

And th' Ape his Parish Clarke procur'd to bee.
Then made they revell route and goodly glee;
But, ere long time had passed, they so ill
Did order their affaires, that th' evill will   560
Of all their Parishners they had constraind;
Who to the Ordinarie of them complain'd,
How fowlie they their offices abus'd,
And them of crimes and heresies accus'd,
That Pursivants he often for them sent;
But they neglected his commaundëment.
So long persisted obstinate and bolde,
Till at the length he published to holde
A Visitation, and them cyted thether:
Then was high time their wits about to geather.   570
What did they then, but made a composition
With their next neighbor Priest, for light condition,
To whom their living they resigned quight
For a few pence, and ran away by night.
   So passing through the Countrey in disguize,
They fled farre off, where none might them surprize;
And after that long straied here and there,
Through everie field and forrest farre and nere,
Yet never found occasion for their tourne,
But almost sterv'd did much lament and mourne.   580
At last they chaunst to meete upon the way
The Mule all deckt in goodly rich aray,
With bells and bosses that full lowdly rung,
And costly trappings that to ground downe hung.
Lowly they him saluted in meeke wise;
But he through pride and fatnes gan despise
Their meanesse; scarce vouchsafte them to requite.
Whereat the Foxe, deep groning in his sprite,
Said; 'Ah! sir Mule, now blessed be the day,
That I see you so goodly and so gay   590
In your attyres, and eke your silken hyde
Fil'd with round flesh, that everie bone doth hide.
Seemes that in fruitfull pastures ye doo live,
Or fortune doth you secret favour give.'
'Foolish Foxe (said the Mule) thy wretched need
Praiseth the thing that doth thy sorrow breed:
For well I weene, thou canst not but envie
My wealth, compar'd to thine owne miserie,
That art so leane and meagre waxen late,
That scarse thy legs uphold thy feeble gate.'   600
'Ay me! (said then the Foxe) whom evill hap

558   route: riot   562   Ordinarie: bishop

Unworthy in such wretchednes doth wrap,
And makes the scorne of other beasts to bee:
But read (faire Sir, of grace) from whence come yee;
Or what of tidings you abroad doo heare?
Newes may perhaps some good unweeting beare.'
'From royall Court I lately came (said he)
Where all the braverie that eye may see,
And all the happinesse that heart desire,
Is to be found: he nothing can admire,   610
That hath not seene that heavens portracture.
But tidings there is none, I you assure,
Save that which common is, and knowne to all,
That Courtiers, as the tide, doo rise and fall.'
'But tell us (said the Ape) we doo you pray,
Who now in Court doth beare the greatest sway,
That, if such fortune doo to us befall,
We make seeke favour of the best of all?'
'Marie, (said he) the highest now in grace
Be the wilde beasts, that swiftest are in chase;   620
For in their speedie course and nimble flight
The Lyon now doth take the most delight;
But chieflie joyes on foote them to beholde,
Enchaste with chaine and circulet of golde.
So wilde a beast so tame ytaught to bee,
And buxome to his bands, is joy to see;
So well his golden Circlet him beseemeth.
But his late chayne his Liege unmeete esteemeth;
For so brave beasts she loveth best to see
In the wilde forrest raunging fresh and free.   630
Therefore if fortune thee in Court to live,
In case thou ever there wilt hope to thrive,
To some of these thou must thy selfe apply;
Els as a thistle-downe in th' ayre doth flie,
So vainly shalt thou too and fro be tost,
And loose thy labour and thy fruitles cost.
And yet full few which follow them, I see,
For vertues bare regard advaunced bee,
But either for some gainfull benefit,
Or that they may for their owne turnes be fit.   640
Nath'les perhaps ye things may handle soe,
That ye may better thrive than thousands moe.'
    'But (said the Ape) how shall we first come in,
That after we may favour seeke to win?'
'How els (said he) but with a good bold face,
And with big words, and with a stately pace,

624   Enchaste: enclosed   626   buxome: obedient

That men may thinke of you in generall,
That to be in you which is not at all:
For not by that which is, the world now deemeth,
(As it was wont) but by that same that seemeth.   650
Ne do I doubt but that ye well can fashion
Your selves theretoo, according to occasion.
So fare ye well; good Courtiers may ye bee!'
So, proudlie neighing, from them parted hee.
Then gan this craftie couple to devize,
How for the Court themselves they might aguize;
For thither they themselves meant to addresse,
In hope to finde there happier successe.
So well they shifted, that the Ape anon
Himselfe had cloathed like a Gentleman,   660
And the slie Foxe, as like to be his groome,
That to the Court in seemly sort they come;
Where the fond Ape, himselfe uprearing hy
Upon his tiptoes, stalketh stately by,
As if he were some great Magnifico,
And boldlie doth amongst the boldest go;
And his man Reynold, with fine counterfesaunce,
Supports his credite and his countenaunce,
Then gan the Courtiers gaze on everie side,
And stare on him, with big lookes basen wide,   670
Wondring what mister wight he was, and whence:
For he was clad in strange accoustrements,
Fashion'd with queint devises, never seene
In Court before, yet there all fashions beene;
Yet he them in newfanglenesse did pas.
But his behaviour altogether was
Alla Turchesca, much the more admyr'd;
And his lookes loftie, as if he aspyr'd
To dignitie, and sdeign'd the low degree;
That all which did such strangenesse in him see   680
By secrete meanes gan of his state enquire,
And privily his servant thereto hire:
Who, throughly arm'd against such coverture,
Reported unto all, that he was sure
A noble Gentleman of high regard,
Which through the world had with long travel far'd,
And seene the manners of all beasts on ground;
Now here arriv'd, to see if like he found.
   Thus did the Ape at first him credit gaine,
Which afterwards he wisely did maintaine   690

670 basen wide: wide as a basin   683 coverture: dissimulation
671 mister: kind of

With gallant showe, and daylie more augment
Through his fine feates and Courtly complement;
For he could play, and daunce, and vaute, and spring,
And all that els pertaines to reveling,
Onely through kindly aptnes of his joynts.
Besides, he could doo manie other poynts.
The which in Court him served to good stead;
For he mongst Ladies could their fortunes read
Out of their hands, and merie leasings tell,
And juggle finely, that became him well.   700
But he so light was at legierdemaine,
That what he toucht came not to light againe;
Yet would he laugh it out, and proudly looke,
And tell them that they greatly him mistooke.
So would he scoffe them out with mockerie,
For he therein had great felicitie;
And with sharp quips joy'd others to deface,
Thinking that their disgracing did him grace;
So whilst that other like vaine wits he pleased,
And made to laugh, his heart was greatly eased.   71̃0
But the right gentle minde woulde bite his lip,
To heare the Javell so good men to nip;
For, though the vulgar yeeld an open eare,
And common Courtiers love to gybe and fleare
At everie thing which they heare spoken ill,
And the best speaches with ill meaning spill,
Yet the brave Courtier, in whose beauteous thought
Regard of honour harbours more than ought,
Doth loath such base condition, to backbite
Anies good name for envie or despite: 720
He stands on tearmes of honourable minde,
Ne will be carried with the common winde
Of Courts inconstant mutabilitie,
Ne after everie tattling fable flie;
But heares and sees the follies of the rest,
And thereof gathers for himselfe the best.
He will not creepe, nor crouche with fained face,
But walkes upright with comely stedfast pace,
And unto all doth yeeld due curtesie;
But not with kissed hand belowe the knee,   730
As that same Apish crue is wont to doo:
For he disdaines himselfe t' embase theretoo.
He hates fowle leasings, and vile flatterie,
Two filthie blots in noble gentrie;
And lothefull idlenes he doth detest,

699   leasings: lies

The canker worme of everie gentle brest;
The which to banish with faire exercise
Of knightly feates, he daylie doth devise:
Now menaging the mouthes of stubborne steedes,
Now practising the proofe of warlike deedes,   740
Now his bright armes assaying, now his speare,
Now the nigh aymed ring away to beare.
At other times he casts to sew the chace
Of swift wilde beasts, or runne on foote a race,
T' enlarge his breath, (large breath in armes most needfull)
Or els by wrestling to wex strong and heedfull,
Or his stiffe armes to stretch with Eughen bowe,
And manly legs, still passing too and fro,
Without a gowned beast him fast beside,
A vaine ensample of the Persian pride;   750
Who, after he had wonne th' Assyrian foe,
Did ever after scorne on foote to goe.
   Thus when this Courtly Gentleman with toyle
Himselfe hath wearied, he doth recoyle
Unto his rest, and there with sweete delight
Of Musicks skill revives his toyled spright;
Or els with Loves, and Ladies gentle sports,
The joy of youth, himselfe he recomforts;
Or lastly, when the bodie list to pause,
His minde unto the Muses he withdrawes: 760
Sweete Ladie Muses, Ladies of delight,
Delights of life, and ornaments of light!
With whom he close confers with wise discourse,
Of Natures workes, of heavens continuall course,
Of forreine lands, of people different,
Of kingdomes change, of divers gouvernment,
Of dreadfull battailes of renowmed Knights;
With which he kindleth his ambitious sprights
To like desire and praise of noble fame,
The onely upshot whereto he doth ayme: 770
For all his minde on honour fixed is,
To which he levels all his purposis,
And in his Princes service spends his dayes,
Not so much for to gaine, or for to raise
Himselfe to high degree, as for his grace,
And in his liking to winne worthie place,
Through due deserts and comely carriage,
In whatso please employ his personage,
That may be matter meete to gaine him praise:
For he is fit to use in all assayes,   780

740   proofe: experience

Whether for Armes and warlike amenaunce,
Or else for wise and civill governaunce.
For he is practiz'd well in policie,
And thereto doth his Courting most applie:
To learne the enterdeale of Princes strange,
To marke th' intent of Counsells, and the change
Of states, and eke of private men somewhile,
Supplanted by fine falshood and faire guile;
Of all the which he gathereth what is fit
T' enrich the storehouse of his powerfull wit,   790
Which through wise speaches and grave conference
He daylie eekes, and brings to excellence.
   Such is the rightfull Courtier in his kinde,
But unto such the Ape lent not his minde:
Such were for him no fit companions,
Such would descrie his lewd conditions;
But the yong lustie gallants he did chose
To follow, meete to whom he might disclose
His witlesse pleasance, and ill pleasing vaine.
A thousand wayes he them could entertaine,   800
With all the thriftles games that may be found;
With mumming and with masking all around,
With dice, with cards, with balliards farre unfit,
With shuttlecocks, misseeming manlie wit,
With courtizans, and costly riotize,
Whereof still somewhat to his share did rize:
Ne, them to pleasure, would he sometimes scorne
A Pandares coate (so basely was he borne).
Thereto he could fine loving verses frame,
And play the Poet oft. But ah! for shame,   810
Let not sweete Poets praise, whose onely pride
Is virtue to advaunce, and vice deride,
Be with the worke of losels wit defamed,
Ne let such verses Poetrie be named!
Yet he the name on him would rashly take,
Maugre the sacred Muses, and it make
A servant to the vile affection
Of such, as he depended most upon;
And with the sugrie sweete thereof allure
Chast Ladies eares to fantasies impure.   820
   To such delights the noble wits he led
Which him reliev'd, and their vaine humours fed
With fruitles follies and unsound delights.
But if perhaps into their noble sprights
Desire of honor or brave thought of armes

792 eekes: increases   813 losels: scoundrel's

Did ever creepe, then with his wicked charmes
And strong conceipts he would it drive away,
Ne suffer it to house there halfe a day.
And whenso love of letters did inspire
Their gentle wits, and kindle wise desire,   830
That chieflie doth each noble minde adorne,
Then he would scoffe at learning, and eke scorne
The Sectaries thereof, as people base
And simple men, which never came in place
Of worlds affaires, but, in darke corners mewd,
Muttred of matters as their bookes them shewd,
Ne other knowledge ever did attaine,
But with their gownes their gravitie maintaine.
From them he would his impudent lewde speach
Against Gods holie Ministers oft reach,   840
And mocke Divines and their profession.
What else then did he by progression,
But mocke high God himselfe, whom they professe?
But what car'd he for God, or godlinesse?
All his care was himselfe how to advaunce,
And to uphold his courtly countenaunce
By all the cunning meanes he could devise:
Were it by honest wayes, or otherwise,
He made small choyce: yet sure his honestie
Got him small gaines, but shameles flatterie,   850
And filthie brocage, and unseemly shifts,
And borowe base, and some good Ladies gifts:
But the best helpe, which chiefly him sustain'd,
Was his man Raynolds purchase which he gain'd.
For he was school'd by kinde in all the skill
Of close conveyance, and each practise ill
Of coosinage and cleanly knaverie,
Which oft maintain'd his masters braverie.
Besides, he usde another slipprie slight,
In taking on himselfe, in common sight,   860
False personages fit for everie sted,
With which he thousands cleanly coosined:
Now like a Merchant, Merchants to deceave,
With whom his credite he did often leave
In gage for his gay Masters hopelesse dett:
Now like a Lawyer, when he land would lett,
Or sell fee-simples in his Masters name.
Which he had never, nor ought like the same.
Then would he be a Broker, and draw in

851   brocage: pimping   857   coosinage: fraud
852   borowe: pledge, security

Both wares and money, by exchange to win: 870
Then would he seeme a Farmer, that would sell
Bargaines of woods, which he did lately fell,
Or corne, or cattle, or such other ware,
Thereby to coosin men not well aware:
Of all the which there came a secret fee,
To th' Ape, that he his countenaunce might bee.
   Besides all this, he us'd oft to beguile
Poore suters, that in Court did haunt some while;
For he would learne their busines secretly,
And then informe his Master hastely,   880
That he by meanes might cast them to prevent,
And beg the sute the which the other ment.
Or otherwise false Reynold would abuse
The simple Suter, and wish him to chuse
His Master, being one of great regard
In Court, to compas anie sute not hard,
In case his paines were recompenst with reason.
So would he worke the silly man by treason
To buy his Masters frivolous good will,
That had not power to doo him good or ill.   890
So pitifull a thing is Suters state!
Most miserable man, whom wicked fate
Hath brought to Court, to sue for had ywist,
That few have found, and manie one hath mist!
Full little knowest thou, that hast not tride,
What hell it is in suing long to bide:
To loose good dayes, that might be better spent;
To wast long nights in pensive discontent;
To speed to day, to be put back to morrow;
To feed on hope, to pine with feare and sorrow;   900
To have thy Princes grace, yet want her Peeres;
To have thy asking, yet waite manie yeeres;
To fret thy soule with crosses and with cares;
To eate thy heart through comfortlesse dispaires;
To fawne, to crowche, to waite, to ride, to ronne,
To spend, to give, to want, to be undonne.
Unhappie wight, borne to desastrous end,
That doth his life in so long tendance spend!
   Who ever leaves sweete home, where meane estate
In safe assurance, without strife or hate,   910
Findes all things needfull for contentment meeke,
And will to Court for shadowes vaine to seeke,
Or hope to gaine, himselfe will a daw trie:

874   coosin: cheat   893   had ywist: vain regret
888   silly: simple   913   trie: prove

That curse God send unto mine enemie!
For none but such as this bold Ape, unblest,
Can ever thrive in that unluckie quest;
Or such as hath a Reynold to his man,
That by his shifts his Master furnish can.
But yet this Foxe could not so closely hide
His craftie feates, but that they were descride   920
At length by such as sate in justice seate,
Who for the same him fowlie did entreate;
And having worthily him punished,
Out of the Court for ever banished.
And now the Ape wanting his huckster man,
That wont provide his necessaries, gan
To growe into great lacke, ne could upholde
His countenance in those his garments olde;
Ne new ones could he easily provide,
Though all men him uncased gan deride,   930
Like as a Puppit placed in a play,
Whose part once past all men bid take away:
So that he driven was to great distresse,
And shortly brought to hopelesse wretchednesse.
Then, closely as he might, he cast to leave
The Court, not asking any passe or leave;
But ran away in his rent rags by night,
Ne ever stayd in place, ne spake to wight,
Till that the Foxe, his copesmate he had found,
To whome complayning his unhappy stound,   940
At last againe with him in travell joynd,
And with him far'd some better chaunce to fynde.
   So in the world long time they wandered,
And mickle want and hardnesse suffered;
That them repented much so foolishly
To come so farre to seeke for misery,
And leave the sweetnes of contented home,
Though eating hipps, and drinking watry fome.
Thus as they them complayned too and fro,
Whilst through the forest rechlesse they did goe,   950
Lo! where they spide, how, in a gloomy glade,
The Lyon sleeping lay in secret shade,
His Crowne and Scepter lying him beside,
And having doft for heate his dreadfull hide:
Which when they sawe, the Ape was sore afrayde,
And would have fled with terror all dismayde.
But him the Foxe with hardy words did stay,

916   unluckie: ill-omened   939   copesmate: partner
930   uncased: revealed   940   stound: trouble

And bad him put all cowardize away:
For now was time (if ever they would hope)
To ayme their counsels to the fairest scope,   960
And them for ever highly to advaunce,
In case the good, which their owne happie chaunce
Them freely offred, they would wisely take.
Scarse could the Ape yet speake, so did he quake;
Yet, as he could, he askt how good might growe
Where nought but dread and death do seeme in show?
'Now, (sayd he) whiles the Lyon sleepeth sound,
May we his Crowne and Mace take from the ground,
And eke his skinne, the terror of the wood,
Wherewith we may our selves (if we thinke good)   970
Make Kings of Beasts, and Lords of forests all
Subject unto that powre imperiall.'
'Ah! but (sayd the Ape) who is so bold a wretch,
That dare his hardy hand to those outstretch,
When as he knowes his meede, if he be spide,
To be a thousand deathes, and shame beside?'
'Fond Ape! (sayd then the Foxe) into whose brest
Never crept thought of honor, nor brave gest,
Who will not venture life a King to be,
And rather rule and raigne in soveraign see,   980
Than dwell in dust inglorious and bace,
Where none shall name the number of his place?
One joyous howre in blisfull happines,
I chose before a life of wretchednes.
Be therefore counselled herein by me,
And shake off this vile harted cowardree.
If he awake, yet is not death the next,
For we may coulor it with some pretext
Of this, or that, that may excuse the cryme:
Else we may flye; thou to a tree mayst clyme,   990
And I creepe under ground, both from his reach:
Therefore be rul'd to doo as I doo teach.'
    The Ape, that earst did nought but chill and quake,
Now gan some courage unto him to take,
And was content to attempt that enterprise,
Tickled with glorie and rash covetise:
But first gan question, whether should assay
Those royall ornaments to steale away?
'Marie, that shall your selfe, (quoth he theretoo)
For ye be fine and nimble it to doo;   1000
Of all the beasts, which in the forrests bee,
Is not a fitter for this turne than yee:

978   gest: action   997   whether: which

Therefore, my owne deare brother, take good hart,
And ever thinke a Kingdome is your part.'
Loath was the Ape, though praised, to adventer,
Yet faintly gan into his worke to enter,
Afraid of everie leafe that stir'd him by,
And everie stick that underneath did ly,
Upon his tiptoes nicely he up went,
For making noyse, and still his eare he lent   1010
To everie sound that under heaven blew;
Now went, now stept, now crept, now backward drew,
That it good sport had been him to have eyde:
Yet at the last, (so well he him applyde)
Through his fine handling, and cleanly play,
He all those royall signes had stolne away,
And with the Foxes helpe them borne aside
Into a secret corner unespide.
Whither whenas they came they fell at words,
Whether of them should be the Lord of Lords: 1020
For th' Ape was stryfull, and ambicious;
And the Foxe guilefull, and most covetous;
That neither pleased was to have the rayne
Twixt them divided into even twaine,
But either (algates) would be Lords alone;
For Love and Lordship bide no paragone.
'I am most worthie, (said the Ape) sith I
For it did put my life in jeopardie:
Thereto I am in person and in stature
Most like a Man, the Lord of everie creature,   1030
So that it seemeth I was made to raigne,
And borne to be a Kingly soveraigne.'
'Nay (said the Foxe) Sir Ape, you are astray:
For though to steale the Diademe away
Were the worke of your nimble hand, yet I
Did first devise the plot by pollicie;
So that it wholly springeth from my wit:
For which also I claime my selfe more fit
Than you to rule; for government of state
Will without wisedome soone be ruinate.   1040
And where ye claime your selfe for outward shape
Most like a man, Man is not like an Ape
In his chiefe parts, that is, in wit and spirite:
But I therein most like to him doo merite,
For my slie wyles and subtill craftinesse,
The title of the Kingdome to possesse.
Nath'les (my brother) since we passed are

1009   nicely: delicately

Unto this point, we will appease our jarre;
And I with reason meete will rest content,
That ye shall have both crowne and government,   1050
Upon condition, that ye ruled bee
In all affaires, and counselled by mee;
And that ye let none other ever drawe
Your minde from me, but keepe this as a lawe:
And hereupon an oath unto me plight.'
    The Ape was glad to end the strife so light,
And thereto swore; for who would not oft sweare,
And oft unsweare, a Diademe to beare?
Then freely up those royall spoyles he tooke,
Yet at the Lyons skin he inly quooke;   1060
But it dissembled, and upon his head
The Crowne, and on his backe the skin he did,
And the false Foxe him helped to array.
Then, when he was all dight, he tooke his way
Into the forest, that he might be seene
Of the wilde beasts in his new glory sheene.
There the two first whome he encountred were
The Sheepe and th' Asse, who, striken both with feare,
At sight of him, gan fast away to flye;
But unto them the Foxe alowd did cry,   1070
And in the Kings name bad them both to stay,
Upon the payne that thereof follow may.
Hardly, naythles, were they restrayned so,
Till that the Foxe forth toward them did goe,
And there disswaded them from needlesse feare,
For that the King did favour to them beare;
And therefore dreadles bad them come to Corte,
For no wild beasts should do them any torte
There or abroad; ne would his majestye
Use them but well, with gracious clemencye,   1080
As whome he knew to him both fast and true.
So he perswaded them, with homage due
Themselves to humble to the Ape prostrate,
Who, gently to them bowing in his gate,
Receyved them with chearefull entertayne.
Thenceforth proceeding with his princely trayne,
He shortly met the Tygre, and the Bore,
Which with the simple Camell raged sore
In bitter words, seeking to take occasion
Upon his fleshly corpse to make invasion: 1090
But, soone as they this mock-King did espy,
Their troublous strife they stinted by and by,

1078   torte: wrong

Thinking indeed that it the Lyon was.
He then, to prove whether his powre would pas
As currant, sent the Foxe to them streightway,
Commaunding them their cause of strife bewray;
And, if that wrong on eyther side there were,
That he should warne the wronger to appeare
The morrow next at Court, it to defend;
In the mean-time upon the King t' attend.   1100
The subtile Foxe so well his message sayd,
That the proud beasts him readily obayd:
Whereby the Ape in wondrous stomack woxe,
Strongly encorag'd by the crafty Foxe;
That King indeed himselfe he shortly thought,
And all the Beasts him feared as they ought,
And followed unto his palaice hye;
Where taking Congé, each one by and by
Departed to his home in dreadful awe,
Full of the feared sight which late they sawe.   1110
    The Ape, thus seized of the Regall throne,
Eftsones by counsell of the Foxe alone,
Gan to provide for all things in assurance,
That so his rule might lenger have endurance.
First to his Gate he pointed a strong gard,
That none might enter but with issue hard:
Then, for the safegard of his personage,
He did appoint a warlike equipage
Of forreine beasts, not in the forest bred,
But part by land and part by water fed;   1120
For tyrannie is with strange ayde supported.
Then unto him all monstrous beasts resorted
Bred of two kindes, as Griffons, Minotaures,
Crocodiles, Dragons, Beavers, and Centaures:
With those himselfe he strengthened mightelie,
That feare he neede no force of enemie.
Then gan he rule and tyrannize at will,
Like as the Foxe did guide his graceless skill;
And all wylde beasts made vassals of his pleasures,
And with their spoyles enlarg'd his private treasures.   1130
No care of justice, nor no rule of reason,
No temperance, nor no regard of season,
Did thenceforth ever enter in his minde,
But crueltie, the signe of currish kinde,
And sdeignfull pride, and wilfull arrogaunce:
Such followes those whom fortune doth advaunce.
    But the false Foxe most kindly plaid his part;

1123   kindes: natures

For whatsoever mother-wit or arte
Could worke, he put in proofe: no practise slie,
No counterpoint of cunning policie, 1140
No reach, no breach, that might him profit bring,
But he the same did to his purpose wring.
Nought suffered he the Ape to give or graunt,
But through his hand must passe the Fiaunt.
All offices, all leases by him lept,
And of them all whatso he likte he kept.
Justice he solde injustice for to buy,
And for to purchase for his progeny.
Ill might it prosper that ill gotten was;
But, so he got it, little did he pas. 1150
He fed his cubs with fat of all the soyle,
And with the sweete of others sweating toyle;
He crammed them with crumbs of Benefices,
And fild their mouthes with meeds of malefices:
He cloathed them with all colours, save white,
And loded them with lordships and with might,
So much as they were able well to beare,
That with the weight their backs nigh broken were:
He chaffred Chayres in which Churchmen were set,
And breach of lawes to privie ferme did let: 1160
No statute so established might bee,
Nor ordinaunce so needfull, but that hee
Would violate, though not with violence,
Yet under colour of the confidence
The which the Ape repos'd in him alone,
And reckned him the kingdomes corner stone.
And ever, when he ought would bring to pas,
His long experience the platforme was:
And, when he ought not pleasing would put by,
The cloke was care of thrift, and husbandry, 1170
For to encrease the common treasures store;
But his owne treasure he encreased more,
And lifted up his loftie towres thereby,
That they began to threat the neighbour sky;
The whiles the Princes pallaces fell fast
To ruine (for what thing can ever last?)
And whilest the other Peeres, for povertie,
Were forst their auncient houses to let lie,
And their olde Castles to the ground to fall,
Which their forefathers, famous over-all, 1180
Had founded for the Kingdomes ornament,

1150 pas: care   1154   malefices: evil deeds
1154 meeds: rewards   1160   ferme: rent

And for their memories long moniment:
But he no count made of Nobilitie,
Nor the wilde beasts whom armes did glorifie,
The Realmes chiefe strength and girlond of the crowne.
All these through fained crimes he thrust adowne,
Or made them dwell in darknes of disgrace;
For none, but whom he list, might come in place.
    Of men of armes he had but small regard,
But kept them lowe, and streigned verie hard.   1190
For men of learning little he esteemed;
His wisdome he above their learning deemed.
As for the rascall Commons least he cared,
For not so common was his bountie shared:
Let God, (said he) if please, care for the manie,
I for my selfe must care before els anie.
So did he good to none, to manie ill,
So did he all the kingdome rob and pill,
Yet none durst speake, ne none durst of him plaine,
So great he was in grace, and rich through gaine.   1200
Ne would he anie let to have accesse
Unto the Prince, but by his owne addresse,
For all that els did come were sure to faile.
Yet would he further none but for availe;
For on a time the Sheepe, to whom of yore
The Foxe had promised of friendship store,
What time the Ape the kingdome first did gaine,
Came to the Court, her case there to complaine;
How that the Wolfe, her mortall enemie,
Had sithence slaine her Lambe most cruellie,   1210
And therefore crav'd to come unto the King,
To let him knowe the order of the thing.
'Soft, Gooddie Sheepe! (then said the Foxe) not soe:
Unto the King so rash ye may not goe;
He is with greater matter busied
Than a Lambe, or the Lambes owne mothers hed.
Ne, certes, may I take it well in part,
That ye my cousin Wolfe so fowly thwart,
And seeke with slaunder his good name to blot;
For there was cause, els doo it he would not: 1220
Therefore surcease, good Dame, and hence depart.'
So went the Sheepe away with heavie hart:
So many moe, so everie one was used,
That to give largely to the boxe refused.
    Now when high Jove, in whose almightie hand
The care of Kings and power of Empires stand,

1190   streigned: restrained   1193   rascall: base

Sitting one day within his turret hye,
From whence he vewes, with his black-lidded eye,
Whatso the heaven in his wide vawte containes,
And all that in the deepest earth remaines,   1230
The troubled kingdome of wilde beasts behelde,
Whom not their kindly Sovereigne did welde,
But an usurping Ape, with guile suborn'd,
Had all subverst, he sdeignfully it scorn'd
In his great heart, and hardly did refraine,
But that with thunder bolts he had him slaine,
And driven downe to hell, his dewest meed:
But, him avizing, he that dreadfull deed
Forbore, and rather chose with scornful shame
Him to avenge, and blot his brutish name   1240
Unto the world, that never after anie
Should of his race be voyd of infamie;
And his false counsellor, the cause of all,
To damne to death, or dole perpetuall,
From whence he never should be quit, nor stal'd.
Forthwith he Mercurie unto him cal'd,
And bad him flie with never-resting speed
Unto the forrest, where wilde beasts doo breed,
And there enquiring privily, to learne
What did of late chaunce to the Lyon stearne,   1250
That he rul'd not the Empire, as he ought?
And whence were all those plaints unto him brought
Of wronges, and spoyles, by salvage beasts committed?
Which done, he bad the Lyon be remitted
Into his seate, and those same treachours vile
Be punished for their presumptuous guile.
    The Sonne of Maia, soone as he receiv'd
That word, streight with his azure wings he cleav'd
The liquid clowdes, and lucid firmament;
Ne staid, till that he came with steep descent   1260
Unto the place where his prescript did showe.
There stouping, like an arrowe from a bowe,
He soft arrived on the grassie plaine,
And fairly paced forth with easie paine,
Till that unto the Pallace nigh he came.
Then gan he to himselfe new shape to frame;
And that faire face, and that Ambrosiall hew,
Which wonts to decke the Gods immortall crew
And beautefie the shinie firmament,
He doft, unfit for that rude rabblement.   1270
So, standing by the gates in strange disguize,

1232   kindly: natural   1245   stal'd: rescued

He gan enquire of some in secret wize,
Both of the King, and of his government,
And of the Foxe, and his false blandishment:
And evermore he heard each one complaine
Of foule abuses both in realme and raine;
Which yet to prove more true he meant to see,
And an ey-witnes of each thing to bee.
Tho on his head his dreadfull hat he dight,
Which maketh him invisible in sight,   1280
And mocketh th' eyes of all the lookers on,
Making them thinke it but a vision.
Through power of that he runnes through enemies swerds;
Through power of that he passeth through the herds
Of ravenous wilde beasts, and doth beguile
Their greedie mouthes of the expected spoyle;
Through power of that his cunning theeveries
He wonts to worke, that none the same espies;
And, through the power of that, he putteth on
What shape he list in apparition.   1290
That on his head he wore, and in his hand
He tooke Caduceus, his snakie wand,
With which the damned ghosts he governeth,
And furies rules, and Tartare tempereth.
With that he causeth sleep to seize the eyes,
And feare the harts of all his enemyes;
And, when him list, an universall night
Throughout the world he makes on everie wight;
As when his Syre with Alcumena lay.
    Thus dight, into the Court he tooke his way,   1300
Both through the gard, which never him descride,
And through the watchmen, who him never spide:
Thenceforth he past into each secrete part,
Whereas he saw, that sorely griev'd his hart,
Each place abounding with fowle injuries,
And fild with treasure rackt with robberies;
Each place defilde with blood of guiltles beasts,
Which had been slaine to serve the Apes beheasts:
Gluttonie, malice, pride, and covetize,
And lawlesnes raigning with riotize;   1310
Besides the infinite extortions,
Done through the Foxes great oppressions,
That the complaints thereof could not be tolde.
Which when he did with lothfull eyes beholde,
He would no more endure, but came his way,
And cast to seeke the Lion where he may,
That he might worke the avengement for this shame

On those two caytives, which had bred him blame.
And, seeking all the forrest busily,
At last he found, where sleeping he did ly,　　　　　1320
The wicked weed, which there the Foxe did lay,
From underneath his head he tooke away,
And then him waking, forced up to rize.
The Lion looking up gan him avize,
As one late in a traunce, what had of long
Become of him; for fantasie is strong.
'Arise, (said Mercurie) thou sluggish beast,
That here liest senseles, like the corpse deceast,
The whilste thy kingdome from thy head is rent,
And thy throne royall with dishonour blent:　　　　1330
Arise, and doo thyself redeeme from shame,
And be aveng'd on those that breed thy blame.'
　　Thereat enraged, soone he gan upstart,
Grinding his teeth, and grating his great hart;
And, rouzing up himselfe, for his rough hide
He gan to reach, but no where it espide.
Therewith he gan full terribly to rore,
And chafte at that indignitie right sore:
But when his Crowne and scepter both he wanted,
Lord! how he fum'd, and sweld, and rag'd, and panted;　1340
And threatned death, and thousand deadly dolours,
To them that had purloyn'd his Princely honours.
With that in hast, disroabed as he was,
He toward his owne Pallace forth did pas;
And all the way he roared as he went,
That all the forrest with astonishment
Thereof did tremble, and the beasts therein
Fled fast away from that so dreadfull din.
At last he came unto his mansion,
Where all the gates he found fast lockt anon,　　　1350
And manie warders round about them stood:
With that he roar'd alowd, as he were wood,
That all the Pallace quaked at the stound,
As if it quite were riven from the ground,
And all within were dead and hartles left:
And th' Ape himselfe, as one whose wits were reft,
Fled here and there, and everie corner sought,
To hide himselfe from his owne feared thought.
But the false Foxe, when he the Lion heard,
Fled closely forth, streightway of death afeard.　　1360
And to the Lion came, full lowly creeping,

1318　caytives: villains　　　1352　wood: mad
1330　blent: shamed

With fained face, and watrie eyne halfe weeping,
T' excuse his former treason and abusion,
And turning all unto the Apes confusion.
Nath'les the royall Beast forbore beleeving,
But bad him stay at ease till further preeving.
    Then, when he saw no entraunce to him graunted,
Roaring yet lowder that all harts it daunted,
Upon those gates with force he fiercely flewe,
And, rending them in pieces, felly slewe   1370
Those warders strange, and all that els he met.
But th' Ape still flying he no where might get:
From rowme to rowme, from beam to beame he fled
All breathles, and for feare now almost ded;
Yet him at last the Lyon spide, and caught,
And forth with shame unto his judgement brought.
Then all the beasts he caus'd assembled bee,
To heare their doome, and sad ensample see.
The Foxe, first Author of that treacherie,
He did uncase, and then away let flie: 1380
But th' Apes long taile (which then he had) he quight
Cut off, and both eares pared of their hight;
Since which all Apes but halfe their eares have left,
And of their tailes are utterlie bereft.
    So Mother Hubberd her discourse did end,
Which pardon me, if I amisse have pend;
For weake was my remembrance it to hold,
And bad her tongue that it so bluntly tolde.

1380 uncase: strip

Muiopotmos

MUIOPOTMOS, like *Mother Hubberds Tale,* formed part
of the volume of *Complaints* published in 1591 (see above,
page 492). The dedication to Lady Carey says nothing of the
date of its composition. There have been numerous attempts,
all of them I think unsuccessful, to find a topical allegory in
this poem.

MUIOPOTMOS:

OR THE FATE OF THE
BUTTERFLIE.

I SING OF DEADLY dolorous debate,
Stir'd up through wrathfull Nemesis despight,
Betwixt two mightie ones of great estate,
Drawne into armes, and proofe of mortall fight,

4 proofe: trial

Through prowd ambition and hart-swelling hate,
Whilest neither could the others greater might
And sdeignfull scorne endure; that from small jarre
Their wraths at length broke into open warre.

The roote whereof and tragicall effect,
Vouchsafe, O thou the mournfulst Muse of nyne!   10
That wontst the tragick stage for to direct,
In funerall complaints and waylfull tyne,
Reveale to me, and all the meanes detect,
Through which sad Clarion did at last decline
To lowest wretchednes: And is there then
Such rancour in the harts of mightie men?

Of all the race of silver-winged Flies
Which doo possesse the Empire of the aire,
Betwixt the centred earth and azure skies,
Was none more favourable, nor more faire,   20
Whilst heaven did favour his felicities,
Then Clarion, the eldest sonne and haire
Of Muscaroll; and in his fathers sight
Of all alive did seeme the fairest wight.

With fruitfull hope his aged breast he fed
Of future good, which his yong toward yeares,
Full of brave courage and bold hardyhed,
Above th' ensample of his equall peares,
Did largely promise, and to him fore-red,
(Whilst oft his heart, did melt in tender teares)   30
That he in time would sure prove such an one,
As should be worthie of his fathers throne.

The fresh yong flie, in whom the kindly fire
Of lustfull yongth began to kindle fast,
Did much disdaine to subject his desire
To loathsome sloth, or houres in ease to wast,
But joy'd to range abroad in fresh attire,
Through the wide compas of the ayrie coast;
And, with unwearied wings, each part t'inquire
Of the wide rule of his renowmed sire.   40

For he so swift and nimble was of flight,
That from this lower tract he dared to stie
Up to the clowdes, and thence with pineons light

12   tyne: sorrow   34   lustfull: passionate
33   kindly: natural   42   stie: rise

To mount aloft unto the Cristall skie,
To view the workmanship of heavens hight:
Whence, down descending, he along would flie
Upon the streaming rivers, sport to finde;
And oft would dare to tempt the troublous winde.

So on a Summers day, when season milde
With gentle calme the world had quieted,   50
And high in heaven Hyperions fierie childe
Ascending did his beames abroad dispred,
Whiles all the heavens on lower creatures smilde,
Yong Clarion, with vauntfull lustie-head,
After his guize did cast abroad to fare:
And theretoo gan his furnitures prepare.

His breastplate first, that was of substance pure,
Before his noble heart he firmely bound,
That mought his life from yron death assure,
And ward his gentle corpes from cruell wound;   60
For it by arte was framed to endure
The bit of balefull steele and bitter stownd,
No lesse than that which Vulcane made to shield
Achilles life from fate of Troyan field.

And then about his shoulders broad he threw
An hairie hide of some wilde beast, whom hee
In salvage forrest by adventure slew,
And reft the spoyle his ornament to bee;
Which, spredding all his backe, with dreadfull view
Made all that him so horrible did see   70
Thinke him Alcides with the Lyons skin,
When the Næmean Conquest he did win.

Upon his head his glistering Burganet,
The which was wrought by wonderous device
And curiously engraven, he did set:
The metall was of rare and passing price;
Not Bilbo steele, nor brasse from Corinth fet,
Nor costly Oricalche from strang Phœnice,
But such as could both Phœbus arrowes ward,
And th' hayling darts of heaven beating hard.   80

Therein two deadly weapons fixt he bore,
Strongly outlaunced towards either side,
Like two sharpe speares his enemies to gore:

60   corpes: body   62   stownd: stroke

Like as a warlike Brigandine, applyde
To fight, layes forth her threatfull pikes afore
The engines which in them sad death doo hyde:
So did this flie outstretch his fearefull hornes,
Yet so as him their terrour more adornes.

Lastly his shinie wings as silver bright,
Painted with thousand colours, passing farre   90
All Painters skill, he did about him dight:
Not halfe so manie sundrie colours arre
In Iris bowe; ne heaven doth shine so bright,
Distinguished with manie a twinckling starre;
Nor Junoes Bird in her ey-spotted traine
So many goodly colours doth containe.

Ne (may it be withouten perill spoken?)
The Archer God, the sonne of Cytheree,
That joyes on wretched lovers to be wroken,
And heaped spoyles of bleeding harts to see,   100
Beares in his wings so manie a changefull token.
Ah, my liege Lord! forgive it unto mee,
If ought against thine honour I have tolde;
Yet sure those wings were fairer manifolde.

Full many a Ladie faire, in Court full oft
Beholding them, him secretly envide,
And wisht that two such fannes, so silken soft
And golden faire, her Love would her provide;
Or that, when them the gorgeous Flie had doft,
Some one, that would with grace be gratifide,   110
From him would steale them privily away,
And bring to her so precious a pray.

Report is, that dame Venus, on a day
In spring, when flowres doo clothe the fruitful ground,
Walking abroad with all her Nymphes to play,
Bad her faire damzels, flocking her arownd,
To gather flowres her forhead to array:
Emongst the rest a gentle Nymph was found,
Hight Astery, excelling all the crewe
In curteous usage and unstained hewe;   120

Who, beeing nimbler joynted than the rest,
And more industrious, gathered more store
Of the fields honour than the others best;

99 wroken: revenged

Which they in secret harts envying sore,
Tolde Venus, when her as the worthiest
She praisd', that Cupide (as they heard before)
Did lend her secret aide, in gathering
Into her lap the children of the spring.

Whereof the Goddesse gathering jealous feare,
Not yet unmindfull how not long agoe   130
Her sonne to Psyche secrete love did beare,
And long it close conceal'd, till mickle woe
Thereof arose, and manie a rufull teare,
Reason with sudden rage did overgoe;
And, giving hastie credit to th' accuser,
Was led away of them that did abuse her.

Eftsoones that Damzell, by her heavenly might,
She turn'd into a winged Butterflie,
In the wide aire to make her wandring flight;
And all those flowres, with which so plenteouslie   140
Her lap she filled had, that bred her spight,
She placed in her wings, for memorie
Of her pretended crime, though crime none were:
Since which that flie them in her wings doth beare.

Thus the fresh Clarion, being readie dight,
Unto his journey did himself addresse,
And with good speed began to take his flight.
Over the fields, in his franke lustinesse,
And all the champain o're he soared light;
And all the countrey wide he did possesse,   150
Feeding upon their pleasures bounteouslie,
That none gainsaid, nor none did him envie.

The woods, the rivers, and the medowes green,
With his aire-cutting wings he measured wide,
Ne did he leave the mountaines bare unseene,
Nor the ranke grassie fennes delights untride.
But none of these, how ever sweete they beene,
Mote please his fancie, nor him cause t' abide:
His choicefull sense with every change doth flit:
No common things may please a wavering wit.   160

To the gay gardins his unstaid desire
Him wholly caried, to refresh his sprights:
There lavish Nature, in her best attire,
Powres forth sweete odors and alluring sights;

And Arte, with her contending, doth aspire
T' excell the naturall with made delights;
And all, that faire or pleasant may be found,
In riotous excesse doth there abound.

There he arriving round about doth flie,
From bed to bed, from one to other border,   170
And takes survey, with curious busie eye,
Of every flowre and herbe there set in order:
Now this, now that, he tasteth tenderly,
Yet none of them he rudely doth disorder,
Ne with his feete their silken leaves deface,
But pastures on the pleasures of each place.

And evermore, with most varietie
And change of sweetnesse, (for all change is sweete)
He casts his glutton sense to satisfie,
Now sucking of the sap of herbe most meete,   180
Or of the deaw which yet on them does lie,
Now in the same bathing his tender feete;
And then he pearcheth on some braunch thereby,
To weather him, and his moyst wings to dry.

And then againe he turneth to his play,
To spoyle the pleasures of that Paradise;
The wholesome Saulge, and Lavender still gray,
Ranke-smelling Rue, and Cummin good for eyes,
The Roses raigning in the pride of May,
Sharpe Isope, good for greene wounds remedies,   190
Faire Marigoldes, and Bees-alluring Thime
Sweet Marjoram, and Daysies decking prime:

Coole Violets, and Orpine growing still,
Embathed Balme, and chearfull Galingale,
Fresh Costmarie, and breathfull Camomill,
Dull Poppie, and drink-quickning Setuale,
Veyne-healing Verven, and hed-purging Dill,
Sound Savorie, and Bazil hartie-hale,
Fat Colworts, and comforting Perseline,
Colde Lettuce, and refreshing Rosmarine.   200

And whatso else of vertue good or ill
Grewe in this Gardin, fetcht from farre away,
Of everie one he takes, and tastes at will,
And on their pleasures greedily doth pray.
Then, when he hath both plaid and fed his fill,

In the warme Sunne he doth himselfe embay,
And there him rests in riotous suffisaunce
Of all his gladfulness, and kingly joyaunce.

What more felicitie can fall to creature
Then to enjoy delight with libertie,   210
And to be Lord of all the workes of Nature,
To raine in th' aire from th' earth to highest skie,
To feed on flowres and weeds of glorious feature,
To take what ever thing doth please the eie?
Who rests not pleased with such happines,
Well worthy he to taste of wretchednes.

But what on earth can long abide in state,
Or who can him assure of happie day,
Sith morning faire may bring fowle evening late,
And least mishap the most blisse alter may?   220
For thousand perills lie in close awaite
About us daylie, to worke our decay;
That none, except a God, or God him guide,
May them avoyde, or remedie provide.

And whatso heavens in their secret doome
Ordained have, how can fraile fleshly wight
Forecast, but it must needs to issue come?
The sea, the aire, the fire, the day, the night,
And th' armies of their creatures all and some
Do serve to them, and with importune might   230
Warre against us, the vassals of their will.
Who then can save what they dispose to spill?

Not thou, O Clarion! though fairest thou
Of all thy kinde, unhappie happie Flie,
Whose cruell fate is woven even now
Of Joves owne hand, to worke thy miserie.
Ne may thee help the manie hartie vow,
Which thy old Sire with sacred pietie
Hath powred forth for thee, and th' altars sprent:
Nought may thee save from heavens avengëment.   240

It fortuned (as heavens had behight)
That in this gardin, where yong Clarion
Was wont to solace him, a wicked wight,
The foe of faire things, th' author of confusion,
The shame of Nature, the bondslave of spight,

213   weeds: plants   239   sprent: sprinkled

Had lately built his hatefull mansion;
And, lurking closely, in awayte now lay,
How he might anie in his trap betray.

But when he spide the joyous Butterflie
In this faire plot dispacing too and fro,   250
Feareles of foes and hidden jeopardie,
Lord! how he gan for to bestirre him tho,
And to his wicked worke each part applie.
His heart did earne against his hated foe,
And bowels so with ranckling poyson swelde,
That scarce the skin the strong contagion helde.

The cause why he this Flie so maliced
Was (as in stories it is written found)
For that his mother, which him bore and bred,
The most fine-fingred workwoman on ground,   260
Arachne, by his means was vanquished
Of Pallas, and in her owne skill confound,
When she with her for excellence contended,
That wrought her shame, and sorrow never ended.

For the Tritonian goddesse, having hard
Her blazed fame which all the world had fil'd,
Came downe to prove the truth, and due reward
For her prais-worthie workmanship to yeild;
But the presumptuous Damzell rashly dar'd
The Goddesse selfe to chalenge to the field,   270
And to compare with her in curious skill
Of workes with loome, with needle, and with quill.

Minerva did the chalenge not refuse,
But deign'd with her the paragon to make:
So to their worke they sit, and each doth chuse
What storie she will for her tapet take.
Arachne figur'd how Jove did abuse
Europa like a Bull, and on his backe
Her through the sea did beare; so lively seene,
That it true Sea, and true Bull, ye would weene.   280

She seem'd still backe unto the land to looke,
And her play-fellowes aide to call, and feare
The dashing of the waves, that up she tooke
Her daintie feete, and garments gathered neare;

254   earne: yearn   276   tapet: tapestry
258   stories: histories

But(Lord!) how she in everie member shooke,
When as the land she saw no more appeare,
But a wilde wildernes of waters deepe:
Then gan she greatly to lament and weepe.

Before the Bull she pictur'd winged Love,
With his yong brother Sport, light fluttering   290
Upon the waves, as each had been a Dove;
The one his bowe and shafts, the other Spring
A burning Teade about his head did move,
As in their Syres new love both triumphing:
And manie Nymphes about them flocking round,
And manie Tritons which their hornes did sound.

And round about her worke she did empale
With a faire border wrought of sundrie flowres,
Enwoven with an Yvie-winding trayle:
A goodly worke, full fit for kingly bowres;   300
Such as Dame Pallas, such as Envie pale,
That al good things with venemous tooth devowres,
Could not accuse. Then gan the Goddesse bright
Her selfe likewise unto her worke to dight.

She made the storie of the olde debate
Which she with Neptune did for Athens trie:
Twelve Gods doo sit around in royall state,
And Jove in midst with awfull Majestie,
To judge the strife betweene them stirred late:
Each of the Gods, by his like visnomie   310
Eathe to be knowen; but Jove above them all,
By his great lookes and power Imperiall.

Before them stands the God of Seas in place,
Clayming that sea-coast Citie as his right.
And strikes the rockes with his three-forked mace;
Whenceforth issues a warlike steed in sight,
The signe by which he chalengeth the place;
That all the Gods, which saw his wondrous might,
Did surely deeme the victorie his due:
But seldome seene, forejudgment proveth true.   320

Then to her selfe she gives her Aegide shield,
And steelhed speare, and morion on her hedd,
Such as she oft is seene in warlicke field:
Then sets she forth, how with her weapon dredd

293   Teade: torch   297   empale: border

She smote the ground, the which streight foorth did yield
A fruitfull Olyve tree, with berries spredd,
That all the Gods admir'd: then, all the storie
She compast with a wreathe of Olyves hoarie.

Emongst these leaves she made a Butterflie,
With excellent device and wondrous slight,   330
Fluttring among the Olives wantonly,
That seem'd to live, so like it was in sight:
The velvet nap which on his wings doth lie,
The silken downe with which his backe is dight,
His broad outstretched hornes, his hayrie thies,
His glorious colours, and his glistering eies.

Which when Arachne saw, as overlaid
And mastered with workmanship so rare,
She stood astonied long, ne ought gainesaid;
And with fast fixed eyes on her did stare,   340
And by her silence, signe of one dismaid,
The victorie did yeeld her as her share:
Yet did she inly fret and felly burne,
And all her blood to poysonous rancor turne:

That shortly from the shape of womanhed,
Such as she was when Pallas she attempted,
She grew to hideous shape of dryrihed,
Pined with griefe of folly late repented:
Eftsoones her white streight legs were altered
To crooked crawling shankes, of marrowe empted;   350
And her faire face to fowle and loathsome hewe,
And her fine corpes to a bag of venim grewe.

This cursed creature, mindfull of that olde
Enfestred grudge, the which his mother felt,
So soone as Clarion he did beholde,
His heart with vengefull malice inly swelt;
And weaving straight a net with manie a fold
About the cave in which he lurking dwelt,
With fine small cords about it stretched wide,
So finely sponne that scarce they could be spide.   360

Not anie damzell, which her vaunteth most
In skillful knitting of soft silken twyne,
Nor anie weaver, which his worke doth boast
In dieper, in damaske, or in lyne,

331 wantonly: playfully, carelessly   364 dieper: a fabric
364 lyne: linen

Nor anie skil'd in workmanship embost,
Nor anie skil'd in loupes of fingring fine,
Might in their divers cunning ever dare
With this so curious networke to compare.

Ne doo I thinke, that that same subtil gin,
The which the Lemnian God framde craftily,   370
Mars sleeping with his wife to compasse in,
That all the Gods with common mockerie
Might laugh at them, and scorne their shamefull sin,
Was like to this. This same he did applie
For to entrap the careles Clarion,
That rang'd each where without suspition.

Suspition of friend, nor feare of foe
That hazarded his health, had he at all,
But walkt at will, and wandred too and fro,
In the pride of his freedome principall: 380
Little wist he his fatall future woe,
But was secure; the liker he to fall.
He likest is to fall into mischaunce,
That is regardles of his governaunce.

Yet still Aragnoll (so his foe was hight)
Lay lurking covertly him to surprise;
And all his gins, that him entangle might,
Drest in good order as he could devise.
At length, the foolish Flie, without foresight,
As he that did all daunger quite despise,   390
Toward those parts came flying carelesslie,
Where hidden was his hatefull enemie.

Who, seeing him, with secret joy therefore
Did tickle inwardly in everie vaine;
And his false hart, fraught with all treasons store,
Was fil'd with hope his purpose to obtaine:
Himselfe he close upgathered more and more
Into his den, that his deceitfull traine
By his there being might not be bewraid,
Ne anie noyse, ne anie motion made.   400

Like as a wily Foxe, that having spide
Where on a sunnie banke the Lambes doo play,
Full closely creeping by the hinder side,

380   principall: princely

Lyes in ambushment of his hoped pray,
Ne stirreth limbe; till, seeing readie tide,
He rusheth forth, and snatcheth quite away
One of the litle yonglings unawares:
So to his worke Aragnoll him prepares.

Who now shall give unto my heavie eyes
A well of teares, that all may overflow?   410
Or where shall I find lamentable cryes,
And mournfull tunes enough my griefe to show?
Helpe, O thou Tragick Muse! me to devise
Notes sad enough t' expresse this bitter throw:
For loe! the drerie stownd is now arrived,
That of all happines hath us deprived.

The luckles Clarion, whether cruell Fate
Or wicked Fortune faultles him misled,
Or some ungracious blast, out of the gate
Of Aeoles raine, perforce him drove on hed,   420
Was (O sad hap, and howre unfortunate!)
With violent swift flight forth caried
Into the cursed cobweb, which his foe
Had framed for his finall overthroe.

There the fond Flie, entangled, strugled long,
Himselfe to free thereout; but all in vaine:
For striving more, the more in laces strong
Himselfe he tide, and wrapt his wingës twaine
In lymie snares the subtill loupes among;
That in the ende he breathlesse did remaine,   430
And, all his yougthly forces idly spent,
Him to the mercy of th' avenger lent.

Which when the greisly tyrant did espie,
Like a grimme Lyon rushing with fierce might
Out of his den, he seized greedelie
On the resistles pray; and, with fell spight,
Under the left wing stroke his weapon slie
Into his heart, that his deepe-groning spright
In bloodie streames foorth fled into the aire,
His bodie left the spectacle of care.   440

414   throw: throe

Colin Clouts
Come Home Againe

LTHOUGH THE DEDICATION OF this poem to Sir Walter
Ralegh bears the date of December 27, 1591, it was not published until 1595 when it appeared in a volume together with a
group of elegies on Sir Philip Sidney by Spenser and other authors. One passage in the poem (lines 432-34), obviously interpolated after the rest had been written, refers to the death
of the Earl of Derby in 1594.

The voyage to England described in the poem apparently
alludes to Spenser's journey in company with Sir Walter (the
Shepherd of the Ocean) in October, 1589, to present the first
installment of *The Faerie Queene* to Queen Elizabeth. Ralegh
owned a great estate in Ireland not far from Spenser's Kilcolman. The two may indeed have read their poems to each
other, as this work suggests (see lines 56-179 below), but no
extant composition of Ralegh's has the "undersong" (refrain?)
that Spenser quotes.

In this edition, lines 380-583 are omitted. In that passage,
Colin praises notable English poets of the day, among them
Sidney, Samuel Daniel, and William Alabaster. Lucida then
asks him about the nymphs in Cynthia's retinue, and he re-

sponds with a celebration of Sidney's sister Mary, three ladies
of the noble family of Spencer with which the poet claimed
connection, and other gentlewomen.

COLIN CLOUTS COME HOME AGAINE.

THE SHEPHEARDS BOY (best knowen by that
    name)
That after Tityrus first sung his lay,
Laies of sweet love, without rebuke or blame,
Sate (as his custome was) upon a day,
Charming his oaten pipe unto his peres,
The shepheard swaines that did about him play:
Who all the while, with greedie listfull eares,
Did stand astonisht at his curious skill,
Like hartlesse deare, dismayd with thunders sound.
At last, when as he piped had his fill,   10
He rested him: and, sitting then around,
One of those groomes (a jolly groome was he,
As ever piped on an oaten reed,
And lov'd this shepheard dearest in degree,
Hight Hobbinol;) gan thus to him areed.
  'Colin, my liefe, my life, how great a losse
Had all the shepheards nation by thy lacke:
And I, poore swaine, of many, greatest crosse!
That, sith thy Muse first since thy turning backe
Was heard to sound as she was wont on hye,   20
Hast made us all so blessed and so blythe.
Whilest thou wast hence, all dead in dole did lie:
The woods were heard to waile full many a sythe,
And all their birds with silence to complaine:
The fields with faded flowers did seem to mourne,
And all their flocks from feeding to refraine:

9 hartlesse: timid

The running waters wept for thy returne,
And all their fish with languor did lament:
But now both woods and fields and floods revive,
Sith thou art come, their cause of meriment,   30
That us, late dead, has made againe alive:
But were it not too painfull to repeat
The passed fortunes, which to thee befell
In thy late voyage, we thee would entreat,
Now at thy leisure them to us to tell.'
   To whom the shepheard gently answered thus;
'Hobbin, thou temptest me to that I covet:
For of good passed newly to discus,
By dubble usurie doth twise renew it.
And since I saw that Angels blessed eie,   40
Her worlds bright sun, her heavens fairest light,
My mind, full of my thoughts satietie,
Doth feed on sweet contentment of that sight:
Since that same day in nought I take delight,
Ne feeling have in any earthly pleasure,
But in remembrance of that glorious bright,
My lifes sole blisse, my hearts eternall threasure,
Wake then, my pipe; my sleepie Muse, awake;
Till I have told her praises lasting long:
Hobbin desires, thou maist it not forsake;—   50
Harke then, ye jolly shepheards, to my song.'
   With that they all gan throng about him neare,
With hungrie eares to heare his harmonie:
The whiles their flocks, devoyd of dangers feare,
Did round about them feed at libertie.
   'One day (quoth he) I sat (as was my trade)
Under the foote of Mole, that mountaine hore,
Keeping my sheepe amongst the cooly shade
Of the greene alders by the Mullaes shore;
There a straunge shepheard chaunst to find me out,   60
Whether allured with my pipes delight,
Whose pleasing sound yshrilled far about,
Or thither led by chaunce, I know not right:
Whom when I asked from what place he came,
And how he hight, himselfe he did ycleepe
The Shepheard of the Ocean by name,
And said he came far from the main-sea deepe,
He, sitting me beside in that same shade,
Provoked me to plaie some pleasant fit;
And, when he heard the musicke which I made,   70
He found himselfe full greatly pleasd at it:

65   ycleepe: call   69   fit: strain of music

Yet, æmuling my pipe, he tooke in hond
My pipe, before that æmuled of many,
And plaid thereon; (for well that skill he cond;)
Himselfe as skilfull in that art as any.
He pip'd, I sung; and, when he sung, I piped;
By chaunge of turnes, each making other mery;
Neither envying other, nor envied,
So piped we, until we both were weary.'
   There interrupting him, a bonie swaine,   80
That Cuddy hight, him thus atweene bespake:
'And, should it not they readie course restraine,
I would request thee, Colin, for my sake,
To tell what thou didst sing, when he did plaie;
For well I weene it worth recounting was,
Whether it were some hymne, or morall laie,
Or carol made to praise thy loved lasse.'
   'Nor of my love, nor of my losse (quoth he,)
I then did sing, as then occasion fell:
For love had me forlorne, forlorne of me,   90
That made me in that desart chose to dwell.
But of my river Bregogs love I soong,
Which to the shiny Mulla he did beare,
And yet doth beare, and ever will, so long
As water doth within his bancks appeare.'
   'Of fellowship (said then that bony Boy)
Record to us that lovely lay againe:
The staie whereof shall nought these eares annoy,
Who all that Colin makes do covet faine.'
   'Heare then (quoth he) the tenor of my tale,   100
In sort as I it to that shepheard told:
No leasing new, nor Grandams fable stale,
But aunccient truth confirm'd with credence old.
   'Old father Mole, (Mole hight that mountain gray
That walls the Northside of Armulla dale)
He had a daughter fresh as floure of May,
Which gave that name unto that pleasant vale;
Mulla, the daughter of old Mole, so hight
The Nimph, which of that water course has charge,
That, springing out of Mole, doth run downe right   110
To Buttevant, where, spreading forth at large,
It giveth name unto that auncient Cittie,
Which Kilnemullah cleped is of old;
Whose ragged ruines breed great ruth and pittie
To travailers, which it from far behold.

72   æmuling: emulating   80 bonie: comely
74   cond: learned

Full faine she lov'd, and was belov'd full faine
Of her owne brother river, Bregog hight,
So hight because of this deceitfull traine,
Which he with Mulla wrought to win delight.
But her old sire more carefull of her good,   120
And meaning her much better to preferre,
Did thinke to match her with the neighbour flood,
Which Allo hight, Broad-water called farre;
And wrought so well with his continuall paine,
That he that river for his daughter wonne:
The dowre agreed, the day assigned plaine,
The place appointed where it should be doone.
Nath-lesse the Nymph her former liking held;
For love will not be drawne, but must be ledde;
And Bregog did so well her fancie weld,   130
That her good will he got her first to wedde.
But for her father, sitting still on hie,
Did warily still watch which way she went,
And eke from far observ'd, with jealous eie,
Which way his course the wanton Bregog bent;
Him to deceive, for all his watchfull ward,
The wily lover did devise this slight:
First into many parts his streame he shar'd,
That, whilest the one was watcht, the other might
Passe unespide to meete her by the way;   140
And then, besides, those little streames so broken
He under ground so closely did convay,
That of their passage doth appeare no token,
Till they into the Mullaes water slide.
So secretly did he his love enjoy
Yet not so secret, but it was descride,
And told her father by a shepheards boy,
Who, wondrous wroth, for that so foule despight,
In great avenge did roll downe from his hill
Huge mightie stones, the which encomber might   150
His passage, and his water-courses spill.
So of a River, which he was of old,
He none was made, but scattred all to nought;
And, lost among those rocks into him rold,
Did lose his name: so deare his love he bought.'
    Which having said, him Thestylis bespake;
'Now by my life this was a mery lay,
Worthie of Colin selfe, that did it make.
But read now eke, of friendship I thee pray,
What dittie did that other shepheard sing: 160

130   weld: manage

For I do covet most the same to heare,
As men use most to covet forreine thing.'
    'That shall I eke (quoth he) to you declare:
His song was all a lamentable lay
Of great unkindnesse, and of usage hard,
Of Cynthia the Ladie of the Sea,
Which from her presence faultlesse him debard.
And ever and anon, with singults rife,
He cryed out, to make his undersong;
Ah! my loves queene, and goddesse of my life,   170
Who shall me pittie, when thou doest me wrong?'
    Then gan a gentle bonylasse to speake,
That Marin hight; 'Right well be sure did plaine,
That could great Cynthiaes sore displeasure breake,
And move to take him to her grace againe.
But tell on further, Colin, as befell
Twixt him and thee, that thee did hence dissuade.'
    'When thus our pipes we both had wearied well,
(Quoth he) and each an end of singing made,
He gan to cast great lyking to my lore,   180
And great dislyking to my lucklesse lot,
That banisht had my selfe, like wight forlore,
Into that waste, where I was quite forgot.
The which to leave, thenceforth he counseld mee,
Unmeet for man, in whom was ought regardfull,
And wend with him, his Cynthia to see;
Whose grace was great, and bounty most rewardfull.
Besides her peerlesse skill in making well,
And all the ornaments of wondrous wit,
Such as all womankynd did far excell;   190
Such as the world admyr'd, and praised it:
So what with hope of good, and hate of ill,
He me perswaded forth with him to fare.
Nought tooke I with me, but mine oaten quill:
Small needments else need shepheard to prepare.
So to the sea we came; the sea, that is
A world of waters heaped up on hie,
Rolling like mountaines in wide wildernesse,
Horrible, hideous, roaring with hoarse crie.'
    'And is the sea (quoth Coridon) so fearfull?'   200
    'Fearful much more (quoth he) then hart can fear:
Thousand wyld beasts with deep mouthes gaping direfull
Therin stil wait poore passengers to teare.
Who life doth loath, and longs death to behold,

168 singults: sobs

Before he die, alreadie dead with feare,
And yet would live with heart halfe stonie cold,
Let him to sea, and he shall see it there.
And yet as ghastly dreadfull, as it seemes,
Bold men, presuming life for gaine to sell,
Dare tempt that gulf, and in those wandring stremes   210
Seek waies unknowne, waies leading down to hell.
For, as we stood there waiting on the strond,
Behold! an huge great vessell to us came,
Dauncing upon the waters back to lond,
As if it scornd the daunger of the same;
Yet was it but a wooden frame and fraile,
Glewed togither with some subtile matter.
Yet had it armes and wings, and head and taile,
And life to move it selfe upon the water.
Strange thing! how bold and swift the monster was,   220
That neither car'd for wynd, nor haile, nor raine,
Nor swelling waves, but thorough them did passe
So proudly, that she made them roare againe.
The same aboord us gently did receave,
And without harme us farre away did beare,
So farre that land, our mother, us did leave,
And nought but sea and heaven to us appeare.
Then hartlesse quite, and full of inward feare,
That shepheard I besought to me to tell,
Under what skie, or in what world we were,   230
In which I saw no living people dwell.
Who, me recomforting all that he might,
Told me that that same was the Regiment
Of a great shepheardesse, that Cynthia hight,
His liege, his Ladie, and his lifes Regent.—
   'If then (quoth I) a shepheardesse she bee,
Where be the flockes and heards, which she doth keep?
And where may I the hills and pastures see,
On which she useth for to feed her sheepe?'
   'These be the hills (quoth he) the surges hie,   240
On which faire Cynthia her heards doth feed:
Her heards be thousand fishes with their frie,
Which in the bosome of the billowes breed.
Of them the shepheard which hath charge in chief,
Is Triton, blowing loud his wreathed horne:
At sound whereof, they all for their relief
Wend too and fro at evening and at morne.
And Proteus eke with him does drive his heard
Of stinking Seales and Porcpisces together,

With hoary head and deawy dropping beard,   250
Compelling them which way he list and whether.
And, I among the rest, of many least,
Have in the Ocean charge to me assignd;
Where I will live or die at her beheast,
And serve and honour her with faithfull mind.
Besides an hundred Nymphs all heavenly borne,
And of immortall race, doo still attend
To wash faire Cynthiaes sheep, when they be shorne,
And fold them up, when they have made an end.
Those be the shepheards which my Cynthia serve   260
At sea, beside a thousand moe at land:
For land and sea my Cynthia doth deserve
To have in her commandëment at hand.'
    Thereat I wondred much, till, wondring more
And more, at length we land far off descryde:
Which sight much gladed me; for much afore
I feard, least land we never should have eyde:
Thereto our ship her course directly bent,
As if the way she perfectly had knowne.
We Lunday passe; by that same name is ment   270
An island, which the first to west was showne.
From thence another world of land we kend,
Floting amid the sea in jeopardie,
And round about with mightie white rocks hemd,
Against the seas encroching crueltie.
Those same, the shepheard told me, were the fields
In which dame Cynthia her landheards fed;
Faire goodly fields, then which Armulla yields
None fairer, nor more fruitfull to be red:
The first, to which we nigh approached, was   280
An high headland thrust far into the sea,
Like to an horne, whereof the name it has,
Yet seemed to be a goodly pleasant lea:
There did a loftie mount at first us greet,
Which did a stately heape of stones upreare,
That seemd amid the surges for to fleet,
Much greater then that frame, which us did beare;
There did our ship her fruitfull wombe unlade,
And put us all ashore on Cynthias land.
    'What land is that thou meanst, (then Cuddy sayd)   290
And is there other then whereon we stand?'
    'Ah! Cuddy (then quoth Colin) thous a fon,
That hast not seene least part of natures worke:
Much more there is unkend then thou doest kon,

251   whether: whither   292   fon: fool

And much more that does from mens knowledge lurke.
For that same land much larger is then this,
And other men and beasts and birds doth feed:
There fruitfull corne, faire trees, fresh herbage is,
And all things else that living creatures need.
Besides most goodly rivers there appeare,   300
No whit inferiour to thy Fanchins praise,
Or unto Allo, or to Mulla cleare:
Nought hast thou, foolish boy, seene in thy daies.'
   'But if that land be there (quoth he) as here,
And is theyr heaven likewise there all one?
And, if like heaven, be heavenly graces there,
Like as in this same world where we do wone?'
   'Both heaven and heavenly graces do much more
(Quoth he) abound in that same land then this:
For there all happie peace and plenteous store   310
Conspire in one to make contented blisse.
No wayling there nor wretchednesse is heard,
No bloodie issues nor no leprosies,
No griesly famine, nor no raging sweard,
No nightly bodrags, nor no hue and cries;
The shepheards there abroad may safely lie,
On hills and downes, withouten dread or daunger:
No ravenous wolves the good mans hope destroy,
Nor outlawes fell affray the forest raunger.
There learned arts do florish in great honor,   320
And Poets wits are had in peerlesse price:
Religion hath lay powre to rest upon her,
Advancing vertue and suppressing vice.
For end, all good, all grace there freely growes,
Had people grace it gratefully to use:
For God his gifts there plenteously bestowes,
But gracelesse men them greatly do abuse.'
   'But say on further (then said Corylas)
The rest of thine adventures, that betyded.'
   'Foorth on our voyage we by land did passe,   330
(Quoth he) as that same shepheard still us guyded,
Until that we to Cynthiaes presence came:
Whose glorie greater then my simple thought,
I found much greater then the former fame;
Such greatnes I cannot compare to ought:
But if I her like ought on earth might read,
I would her lyken to a crowne of lilies,
Upon a virgin brydes adorned head,
With Roses dight and Goolds and Daffadillies;

307   wone: dwell   315   bodrags: raids

Or like the circlet of a Turtle true,   340
In which all colours of the rainbow bee;
Or like faire Phebes garlond shining new,
In which all pure perfection one may see.
But vaine it is to thinke, by paragone
Of earthly things, to judge of things divine:
Her power, her mercy, and her wisdome, none
Can deeme, but who the Godhead can define.
Why then do I, base shepheard, bold and blind,
Presume the things so sacred to prophane?
More fit it is t' adore, with humble mind,   350
The image of the heavens in shape humane.'
    With that Alexis broke his tale asunder,
Saying; 'By wondring at thy Cynthiaes praise,
Colin, thy selfe thou mak'st us more to wonder,
And her upraising doest thy selfe upraise.
But let us heare what grace she shewed thee,
And how that shepheard strange thy cause advanced.'
    'The Shepheard of the Ocean (quoth he)
Unto that Goddess grace me first enhanced,
And to mine oaten pipe enclin'd her eare,   360
That she thenceforth therein gan take delight;
And it desir'd at timely houres to heare,
All were my notes but rude and roughly dight;
For not by measure of her owne great mynd,
And wondrous worth, she mott my simple song,
But joyd that country shepheard ought could fynd
Worth harkening to, emongst the learned throng.'
    'Why? (said Alexis then) what needeth shee
That is so great a shepheardesse her selfe,
And hath so many shepheards in her fee,   370
To heare thee sing, a simple silly Elfe?
Or be the shepheards which do serve her laesie,
That they list not their mery pipes applie?
Or be their pipes untunable and craesie,
That they cannot her honour worthylie?'
    'Ah! nay (said Colin) neither so, nor so:
For better shepheards be not under skie,
Nor better hable, when they list to blow
Their pipes aloud, her name to glorifie.

                    · · · · ·

    So having said, Aglaura him bespake:
'Colin, well worthie were those goodly favours

365   mott: measured   374   craesie: cracked
370   fee: service

Bestowd on thee, that so of them doest make,
And them requitest with thy thankfull labours.
But of great Cynthiaes goodness, and high grace,
Finish the storie which thou hast begunne.'
  'More eath (quoth he) it is in such a case   590
How to begin, then know how to have donne.
For everie gift, and everie goodly meed,
Which she on me bestowd, demaunds a day;
And everie day, in which she did a deed,
Demaunds a yeare it duly to display.
Her words were like a streame of honny fleeting,
The which doth softly trickle from the hive,
Hable to melt the hearers heart unweeting,
And eke to make the dead againe alive.
Her deeds were like great clusters of ripe grapes,   600
Which load the bunches of the fruitfull vine;
Offring to fall into each mouth that gapes,
And fill the same with store of timely wine.
Her lookes were like beames of the morning Sun,
Forth looking through the windowes of the East,
When first the fleecie cattell have begun
Upon the perled grasse to make their feast.
Her thoughts are like the fume of Franckincence,
Which from a golden Censer forth doth rise,
And throwing forth sweet odours mounts fro thence   610
In rolling globes up to the vauted skies.
There she beholds, with high aspiring thought,
The cradle of her owne creation,
Emongst the seats of Angels heavenly wrought
Much like an Angell in all forme and fashion.'
  'Colin, (said Cuddy then) thou hast forgot
Thy selfe, me seemes, too much, to mount so hie:
Such loftie flight base shepheard seemeth not,
From flocks and fields, to angels and to skie.'
  'True (answered he) but her great excellence   620
Lifts me above the measure of my might:
That, being fild with furious insolence,
I feele my selfe like one yrapt in spright.
For when I thinke of her, as oft I ought,
Then want I words to speake it fitly forth:
And, when I speake of her what I have thought,
I cannot thinke according to her worth:
Yet will I thinke of her, yet will I speake,
So long as life my limbs doth hold together;
And, when as death these vitall bands shall breake,   630

596 fleeting: floating   622 insolence: exultation

Her name recorded I will leave for ever.
Her name in every tree I will endosse,
That, as the trees do grow, her name may grow:
And in the ground each where will it engrosse,
And fill with stones, that all men may it know.
The speaking woods, and murmuring waters fall,
Her name Ile teach in knowen terms to frame:
And eke my lambs, when for their dams they call,
Ile teach to call for Cynthia by name.
And, long while after I am dead and rotten,   640
Amongst the shepheards daughters dancing rownd,
My layes made of her shall not be forgotten,
But sung by them with flowry gyrlonds crownd.
And ye, who so ye be, that shall survive,
When as ye heare her memory renewed,
Be witnesse of her bountie here alive,
Which she to Colin her poore shepheard shewed.'
    Much was the whole assembly of those heards
Moov'd at his speech, so feelingly he spake:
And stood awhile astonisht at his words,   650
Till Thestylis at last their silence brake,
Saying: 'Why Colin, since thou foundst such grace
With Cynthia and all her noble crew;
Why didst thou ever leave that happie place,
In which such wealth might unto thee accrew;
And back returnedst to this barrein soyle,
Where cold and care and penury do dwell,
Here to keep sheepe, with hunger and with toyle?
Most wretched he, that is and cannot tell.'
    'Happie indeed (said Colin) I him hold,   660
That may that blessed presence still enjoy,
Of fortune and of envy uncomptrold,
Which still are wont most happie states t'annoy:
But I, by that which little while I prooved,
Some part of those enormities did see,
The which in Court continually hooved,
And followd those which happie seemd to bee.
Therefore I, silly man, whose former dayes
Had in rude fields bene altogether spent,
Durst not adventure such unknowen wayes,   670
Nor trust the guile of fortunes blandishment;
But rather chose back to my sheep to tourne,
Whose utmost harnesse I before had tryde,
Then, having learnd repentance late, to mourne
Emongst those wretches which I there descryde.'

666 hooved: remained   668 silly: simple

'Shepheard, (said Thestylis) it seemes of spight
Thou speakest thus gainst their felicitie,
Which thou enviest, rather then of right
That ought in them blameworthie thou doest spie.'
'Cause have I none (quoth he) of cancred will   680
To quite them ill, that me demeand so well:
But selfe-regard of private good or ill
Moves me of each, so as I found, to tell
And eke to warne yong shepheards wandring wit,
Which, through report of that lives painted blisse,
Abandon quiet home to seeke for it,
And leave their lambes to losse, misled amisse.
For, sooth to say, it is no sort of life,
For shepheard fit to lead in that same place,
Where each one seeks with malice, and with strife,   690
To thrust downe other into foule disgrace,
Himselfe to raise: and he doth soonest rise
That best can handle his deceitfull wit
In subtil shifts, and finest sleights devise,
Either by slaundring his well-deemed name,
Through leasings lewd, and fained forgerie;
Or else by breeding him some blot of blame,
By creeping close into his secrecie;
To which him needs a guilefull hollow hart,
Masked with faire dissembling curtesie,   700
A filed toung, furnisht with tearmes of art,
No art of schoole, but Courtiers schoolery.
For arts of schoole have there small countenance,
Counted but toyes to busie ydle braines;
And there professours find small maintenance,
But to be instruments of others gaines.
Ne is there place for any gentle wit,
Unlesse to please it selfe it can applie;
But shouldred is, or out of doore quite shit,   710
As base, or blunt, unmeet for melodie.
For each mans worth is measured by his weed,
As harts by hornes, or asses by their eares:
Yet asses been not all whose eares exceed,
Nor yet all harts that hornes the highest beares;
For highest lookes have not the highest mynd,
Nor haughtie words most full of highest thoughts;
But are like bladders blowen up with wynd,
That being prickt do vanish into noughts.
Even such is all their vaunted vanitie,
Nought else but smoke, and fumeth soone away;   720

711   weed: attire

Such is their glorie that in simple eie
Seeme greatest, when their garments are most gay.
So they themselves for praise of fooles do sell,
And all their wealth for painting on a wall;
With price whereof they buy a golden bell,
And purchace highest rowmes in bowre and hall:
Whiles single Truth and simple Honestie
Do wander up and downe despys'd of all;
Their plaine attire such glorious gallantry
Disdaines so much, that none them in doth call.'   730
    'Ah! Colin, (then said Hobbinol) the blame
Which thou imputest, is too generall,
As if not any gentle wit of name
Nor honest mynd might there be found at all.
For well I wot, sith I my selfe was there,
To wait on Lobbin, (Lobbin well thou knewest,)
Full many worthie ones then waiting were,
As ever else in Princes Court thou vewest.
Of which among you many yet remaine,
Whose names I cannot readily now ghesse: 740
Those that poore Sutors papers do retaine,
And those that skill of medicine professe,
And those that do to Cynthia expound
The ledden of straunge languages in charge:
For Cynthia doth in sciences abound,
And gives to their professors stipends large.
Therefore unjustly thou doest wyte them all,
For that which thou mislikedst in a few.'
    'Blame is (quoth he) more blamelesse generall,
Then that which private errours doth pursew;   750
For well I wot, that there amongst them bee
Full many persons of right worthie parts,
Both for report of spotlesse honestie,
And for profession of all learned arts,
Whose praise hereby no whit impaired is,
Though blame do light on those that faultie bee;
For all the rest do most-what fare amis,
And yet their owne misfaring will not see:
For either they be puffed up with pride,
Or fraught with envie that their galls do swell,   760
Or they their dayes to ydlenesse divide,
Or drownded lie in pleasures wastefull well,
In which like Moldwarps nousling still they lurke,

744	ledden: speech	
745	sciences: branches of knowl-edge	
747	wyte: blame	
763	Moldwarps: moles	
763	nousling: burrowing	

Unmindfull of chiefe parts of manlinesse;
And do themselves, for want of other worke,
Vaine votaries of laesie Love professe,
Whose service high so basely that ensew,
That Cupid selfe of them ashamed is,
And, mustring all his men in Venus vew,
Denies them quite for servitors of his.'
  'And is Love then (said Corylas) once known   770
In Court, and his sweet lore professed there?
I weened sure he was our God alone,
And only woond in fields and forests here:'
  'Not so, (quoth he) Love most aboundeth there.
For all the walls and windows there are writ,
All full of love, and love, and love my deare,
And all their talke and studie is of it.
Ne any there doth brave or valiant seeme,
Unlesse that some gay Mistresse badge he beares: 780
Ne any one himselfe doth ought esteeme,
Unlesse he swim in love up to the eares.
But they of love, and of his sacred lere,
(As it should be) all otherwise devise,
Then we poore shepheards are accustomd here,
And him do sue and serve all otherwise:
For with lewd speeches, and licentious deeds,
His mightie mysteries they do prophane,
And use his ydle name to other needs.
But as a complement for courting vaine.   790
So him they do not serve as they professe,
But make him serve to them for sordid uses:
Ah! my dread Lord, that doest liege hearts possesse,
Avenge thy selfe on them for their abuses.
But we poore shepheards whether rightly so,
Or through our rudenesse into errour led,
Do make religion how we rashly go
To serve that God, that is so greatly dred;
For him the greatest of the Gods we deeme,
Borne without Syre or couples of one kynd;   800
For Venus selfe doth soly couples seeme,
Both male and female through commixture joynd:
So pure and spotlesse Cupid forth she brought,
And in the gardens of Adonis nurst:
Where growing he his owne perfection wrought,
And shortly was of all the Gods the first.
Then got he bow and shafts of gold and lead,
In which so fell and puissant he grew,

774   woond: dwelt   783   lere: lore

That Jove himselfe his powre began to dread,
And, taking up to heaven, him godded new.   810
From thence he shootes his arrowes every where
Into the world, at randon as he will,
On us fraile men, his wretched vassals here,
Like as himselfe us pleaseth save or spill.
So we him worship, so we him adore
With humble hearts to heaven uplifted hie,
That to true loves he may us evermore
Preferre, and of their grace us dignifie:
Ne is there shepheard, ne yet shepheards swaine,
What ever feeds in forest or in field,   820
That dare with evil deed or leasing vaine
Blaspheme his powre, or termes unworthie yield.'
    'Shepheard, it seemes that some celestiall rage
Of Love (quoth Cuddy) is breath'd into thy brest,
That powreth forth these oracles so sage
Of that high powre, wherewith thou art possest.
But never wist I till this present day,
Albe of love I alwayes humbly deemed,
That he was such an one as thou doest say,
And so religiously to be esteemed.   830
Well may it seeme, by this thy deep insight,
That of that God the Priest thou shouldest bee,
So well thou wot'st the mysterie of his might,
As if his godhead thou didst present see.'
    'Of loves perfection perfectly to speake,
Or of his nature rightly to define,
Indeed (said Colin) passeth reasons reach,
And needs his priest t' expresse his powre divine.
For long before the world he was ybore,
And bred above in Venus bosome deare: 840
For by his powre the world was made of yore,
And all that therein wondrous doth appeare.
For how should else things so far from attone,
And so great enemies as of them bee,
Be ever drawne together into one
And taught in such accordance to agree?
Through him the cold began to covet heat,
And water fire; the light to mount on hie,
And th' heavie downe to peize; the hungry t' eat,
And voydnesse to seeke full satietie.   850
So, being former foes, they wexed friends,
And gan by litle learne to love each other:

821 leasing: lie   849 peize: weigh
843 attone: in harmony

So, being knit, they brought forth other kynds
Out of the fruitfull wombe of their great mother.
Then first gan heaven out of darknesse dread
For to appeare, and brought forth chearfull day:
Next gan the earth to shew her naked head,
Out of deep waters which her drowned alway:
And, shortly after, everie living wight
Crept forth like wormes out of her slimie nature,   860
Soone as on them the Suns life-giving-light
Had powred kindly heat and formall feature,
Thenceforth they gan each one his like to love,
And like himselfe desire for to beget:
The Lyon chose his mate, the Turtle Dove
Her deare, the Dolphin his owne Dolphinet;
But man, that had the sparke of reasons might
More then the rest to rule his passion,
Chose for his love the fairest in his sight,
Like as himselfe was fairest by creation: 870
For beautie is the bayt which with delight
Doth man allure for to enlarge his kynd;
Beautie, the burning lamp of heavens light,
Darting her beames into each feeble mynd:
Against whose powre, nor God nor man can fynd
Defence, ne ward the daunger of the wound;
But, being hurt, seeke to be medicynd
Of her that first did stir that mortall stownd.
Then do they cry and call to love apace,
With praiers lowd importuning the skie,   880
Whence he them heares; and, when he list shew grace,
Does graunt them grace that otherwise would die.
So love is Lord of all the world by right,
And rules the creatures by his powrfull saw:
All being made the vassalls of his might,
Through secret sence which thereto doth them draw.
Thus ought all lovers of their lord to deeme,
And with chaste heart to honor him alway:
But who so else doth otherwise esteeme,
Are outlawes, and his lore do disobay.   890
For their desire is base, and doth not merit
The name of love, but of disloyall lust:
Ne mongst true lovers they shall place inherit,
But as Exuls out of his court be thrust.'
    So having said, Melissa spake at will;
'Colin, thou now full deeply hast divynd
Of Love and beautie; and, with wondrous skill,
Hast Cupid selfe depainted in his kynd,

To thee are all true lovers greatly bound.
That doest their cause so mightily defend: 900
But most, all wemen are thy debtors found,
That doest their bountie still so much commend.'
  'That ill (said Hobbinol) they him requite,
For having loved ever one most deare:
He is repayd with scorne and foule despite,
That yrkes each gentle heart which it doth heare.'
  'Indeed (said Lucid) I have often heard
Faire Rosalind of divers fowly blamed
For being to that swaine too cruell hard,
That her bright glorie else hath much defamed.   910
But who can tell what cause had that faire Mayd
To use him so that used her so well;
Or who with blame can justly her upbrayd
For loving not? for who can love compell?
And, sooth to say, it is foolhardie thing,
Rashly to wyten creatures so divine;
For demigods they be and first did spring
From heaven, though graft in frailnesse feminine.
And well I wote, that oft I heard it spoken,
How one, that fairest Helene did revile,   920
Through judgement of the gods to been ywroken,
Lost both his eyes and so remaynd long while,
Till he recanted had his wicked rimes,
And made amends to her with treble praise.
Beware therefore, ye groomes, I read betimes,
How rashly blame of Rosalind ye raise.'
  'Ah! shepheards, (then said Colin) ye ne weet
How great a guilt upon your heads ye draw,
To make so bold a doome, with words unmeet,
Of things celestiall which ye never saw.   930
For she is not like as the other crew
Of shepheards daughters which emongst you bee,
But of divine regard and heavenly hew,
Excelling all that ever ye did see.
Not then to her that scorned thing so base,
But to my selfe the blame that lookt so hie:
So hie her thoughts as she her selfe have place,
And loath each lowly thing with loftie eie.
Yet so much grace let her vouchsafe to grant
To simple swaine, sith her I may not love: 940
Yet that I may her honour paravant,
And praise her worth, though far my wit above.
Such grace shall be some guerdon for the griefe,

921 ywroken: avenged   941 paravant: preeminently

And long affliction which I have endured:
Such grace sometimes shall give me some reliefe,
And ease of paine which cannot be recured.
And ye, my fellow shepheards, which do see
And heare the languors of my too long dying,
Unto the world for ever witnesse bee,
That hers I die, nought to the world denying,   950
This simple trophé of her great conquest.'—
    So, having ended, he from ground did rise,
And after him uprose eke all the rest:
All loth to part, but that the glooming skies
Warnd them to draw their bleating flocks to rest.

Amoretti

[S E L E C T I O N S]

A N D

Epithalamion

THE AMORETTI AND THE EPITHALAMION were published in a single volume which was entered in the Stationers' Register on November 19, 1594, and appeared during the following year. The occasion of these poems was Spenser's courtship and marriage to Elizabeth Boyle. According to a stanza in the *Epithalamion* (lines 281 ff.) the wedding took place on St. Barnabas's Day, that is, June 11, although whether the event is to be dated 1594 or earlier remains uncertain. The publisher's note indicates that Spenser was in Ireland when the book appeared.

Of the eighty-nine sonnets in the original edition (really eighty-eight, since one is a duplicate of another) eleven are here reprinted.

The word "epithalamion" means "on the bed chamber." The most famous example of poems in this classical tradition is that of Catullus.

AMORETTI.

VIII

More then most faire, full of the living fire,
Kindled above unto the Maker neere;
No eies but joyes, in which al powers conspire,
That to the world naught else be counted deare;
Thrugh your bright beams doth not the blinded guest
Shoot out his darts to base affections wound;
But Angels come to lead fraile mindes to rest
In chast desires, on heavenly beauty bound.
You frame my thoughts, and fashion me within;
You stop my toung, and teach my hart to speake;
You calme the storme that passion did begin,
Strong thrugh your cause, but by your vertue weak.
  Dark is the world, where your light shined never;
  Well is he borne, that may behold you ever.

LXV

The doubt which ye misdeeme, fayre love, is vaine,
That fondly feare to loose your liberty;
When, loosing one, two liberties ye gayne,
And make him bond that bondage earst dyd fly.
Sweet be the bands, the which true love doth tye
Without constraynt, or dread of any ill:
The gentle birde feeles no captivity
Within her cage; but singes, and feeds her fill.
There pride dare not approch, nor discord spill
The league twixt them, that loyal love hath bound:
But simple truth, and mutuall good-will,
Seekes with sweet peace, to salve each others wound:
  There Fayth doth fearlesse dwell in brasen towre,
  And spotlesse Pleasure builds her sacred bowre.

LXVII

Lyke as a huntsman after weary chace,
Seeing the game from him escapt away,
Sits downe to rest him in some shady place,
With panting hounds beguiled of their pray:
So, after long pursuit and vaine assay,
When I all weary had the chace forsooke,

The gentle deare returnd the selfe-same way,
Thinking to quench her thirst at the next brooke:
There she, beholding me with mylder looke,
Sought not to fly, but fearelesse still did bide;
Till I in hand her yet halfe trembling tooke,
And with her owne goodwill hir fyrmely tyde.
    Strange thing, me seemd, to see a beast so wyld,
    So goodly wonne, with her owne will beguyld.

L X V I I I

Most glorious Lord of lyfe! that, on this day,
Didst make thy triumph over death and sin;
And, having harrowd hell, didst bring away
Captivity thence captive, us to win:
This joyous day, deare Lord, with joy begin;
And grant that we, for whom thou diddest dye,
Being with they deare blood clene washt from sin,
May live for ever in felicity!
And that thy love we weighing worthily,
May likewise love thee for the same againe;
And for thy sake, that all lyke deare didst buy,
With love may one another entertayne!
    So let us love, deare love, lyke as we ought:
    Love is the lesson which the Lord us taught.

L X X

Fresh Spring, the herald of loves mighty king,
In whose cote-armour richly are displayd
All sorts of flowers, the which on earth do spring,
In goodly colours gloriously arrayd;
Goe to my love, where she is carelesse layd,
Yet in her winters bowre not well awake;
Tell her the joyous time wil not be staid,
Unlesse she doe him by the forelock take;
Bid her therefore her selfe soone ready make,
To wayt on Love amongst his lovely crew;
Where every one, that misseth then her make,
Shall be by him amearst with penance dew.
    Make hast, therefore, sweet love, whilest it is prime;
    For none can call againe the passed time.

L X X I I

Oft, when my spirit doth spred her bolder winges,
In mind to mount up to the purest sky;
It down is weighed with thoght of earthly things,

LXX   13   prime: springtime
12   amearst: punished

And clogd with burden of mortality;
Where, when that soverayne beauty it doth spy,
Resembling heavens glory in her light,
Drawne with sweet pleasures bayt, it back doth fly,
And unto heaven forgets her former flight.
There my fraile fancy, fed with full delight,
Doth bath in blisse, and mantleth most at ease;
Ne thinks of other heaven, but how it might
Her harts desire with most contentment please.
    Hart need not wish none other happinesse,
    But here on earth to have such hevens blisse.

LXXVII

Was it a dreame, or did I see it playne;
A goodly table of pure yvory,
All spred with juncats, fit to entertayne
The greatest Prince with pompous roialty:
Mongst which, there in a silver dish did ly
Twoo golden apples of unvalewd price;
Far passing those which Hercules came by,
Or those which Atalanta did entice;
Exceeding sweet, yet voyd of sinfull vice;
That many sought, yet none could ever taste;
Sweet fruit of pleasure, brought from Paradice
By Love himselfe, and in his garden plaste.
    Her brest that table was, so richly spredd;
    My thoughts the guests, which would thereon have fedd.

LXXVIII

Lackyng my love, I go from place to place,
Lyke a young fawne, that late hath lost the hynd;
And seeke each where, where last I saw her face,
Whose ymage yet I carry fresh in mynd.
I seeke the fields with her late footing synd;
I seeke her bowre with her late presence deckt;
Yet nor in field nor bowre I her can fynd;
Yet field and bowre are full of her aspect:
But, when myne eyes I thereunto direct,
They ydly back returne to me agayne:
And, when I hope to see theyr trew objéct,
I fynd my selfe but fed with fancies vayne.
    Ceasse then, myne eyes, to seeke her selfe to see;
    And let my thoughts behold her selfe in mee.

LXXII
10 mantleth: stretches itself (as a
falcon does)

LXXVII
3   juncats: delicacies
LXXVIII
5   synd: signed

L X X X

After so long a race as I have run
Through Faery land, which those six books compile,
Give leave to rest me being halfe fordonne,
And gather to myselfe new breath awhile.
Then, as a steed refreshed after toyle,
Out of my prison I will breake anew;
And stoutly will that second worke assoyle,
With strong endevour and attention dew.
Till then give leave to me, in pleasant mew
To sport my muse, and sing my loves sweet praise;
The contemplation of whose heavenly hew,
My spirit to an higher pitch will rayse,
　　But let her prayses yet be low and meane,
　　Fit for the handmayd of the Faery Queene.

L X X X I V

The world that cannot deeme of worthy things,
When I doe praise her, say I doe but flatter:
So does the Cuckow, when the Mavis sings,
Begin his witlesse note apace to clatter.
But they that skill not of so heavenly matter,
All that they know not envy or admyre;
Rather then envy, let them wonder at her,
But not to deeme of her desert aspyre.
Deepe, in the closet of my parts entyre,
Her worth is written with a golden quill,
That me with heavenly fury doth inspire,
And my glad mouth with her sweet prayses fill.
　　Which when as Fame in her shrill trump shal thunder,
　　Let the world chose to envy or to wonder.

L X X X V I I I

Lyke as the Culver, on the bared bough,
Sits mourning for the absence of her mate;
And, in her songs, sends many a wishfull vow
For his returne that seemes to linger late:
So I alone, now left disconsolate,
Mourne to my selfe the absence of my love;
And, wandring here and there all desolate,
Seek with my playnts to match that mournful dove.
Ne joy of ought that under heaven doth hove
Can comfort me, but her owne joyous sight:

LXXX
3　fordonne: exhausted
7　assoyle: discharge

LXXXVIII
9　hove: linger

Whose sweet aspect both God and man can move,
In her unspotted pleasauns to delight.
Dark is my day, whyles her fayre light I mis,
And dead my life that wants such lively blis.

EPITHALAMION.

YE LEARNED SISTERS, which have oftentimes
Beene to me ayding, others to adorne,
Whom ye thought worthy of your gracefull rymes,
That even the greatest did not greatly scorne
To heare theyr names sung in your simple layes,
But joyed in theyr praise;
And when ye list your owne mishaps to mourne,
Which death, or love, or fortunes wreck did rayse,
Your string could soone to sadder tenor turne,
And teach the woods and waters to lament   10
Your dolefull dreriment:
Now lay those sorrowful complaints aside;
And, having all your heads with girland crownd,
Helpe me mine owne loves prayses to resound;
Ne let the same of any be envide:
So Orpheus did for his owne bride!
So I unto my selfe alone will sing;
The woods shall to me answer, and my Eccho ring.

Early, before the worlds light-giving lampe
His golden beame upon the hils doth spred,   20
Having disperst the nights unchearefull dampe,
Doe ye awake; and, with fresh lusty-hed,
Go to the bowre of my beloved love,
My truest turtle dove;
Bid her awake; for Hymen is awake,
And long since ready forth his maske to move,
With his bright Tead that flames with many a flake,
And many a bachelor to waite on him,

27 Tead: torch   27 flake: flash

In theyr fresh garments trim.
Bid her awake therefore, and soone her dight,   30
For lo! the wished day is come at last,
That shall, for all the paynes and sorrowes past,
Pay to her usury of long delight:
And, whylest she doth her dight,
Doe ye to her of joy and solace sing,
That all the woods may answer, and your eccho ring.

Bring with you all the Nymphes that you can heare
Both of the rivers and the forrests greene,
And of the sea that neighbours to her neare:
Al with gay girlands goodly wel beseene.   40
And let them also with them bring in hand
Another gay girland,
For my fayre love, of lillyes and of roses,
Bound truelove wize, with a blew silke riband.
And let them make great store of bridale poses,
And let them eeke bring store of other flowers,
To deck the bridale bowers.
And let the ground whereas her foot shall tread,
For feare the stones her tender foot should wrong,
Be strewed with fragrant flowers all along,   50
And diapred lyke the discolored mead.
Which done, doe at her chamber dore awayt,
For she will waken strayt;
The whiles doe ye this song unto her sing,
The woods shall to you answer, and your Eccho ring.

Ye Nymphes of Mulla, which with carefull heed
The silver scaly trouts doe tend full well,
And greedy pikes which use therein to feed;
(Those trouts and pikes all others doo excell;)
And ye likewise, which keepe the rushy lake,   60
Where none doo fishes take;
Bynd up the locks the which hang scatterd light,
And in his waters, which your mirror make,
Behold your faces as the christall bright,
That when you come whereas my love doth lie,
No blemish she may spie.
And eke, ye lightfoot mayds, which keepe the deere,
That on the hoary mountayne use to towre;
And the wylde wolves, which seeke them to devoure,
With your steele darts doo chace from comming neer;   70
Be also present heere,

51   diapred: variegated   51   discolored: many-colored

To helpe to decke her, and to help to sing,
That all the woods may answer, and your eccho ring.

Wake now, my love, awake! for it is time;
The Rosy Morne long since left Tithones bed,
All ready to her silver coche to clyme;
And Phœbus gins to shew his glorious hed.
Hark! how the cheerefull birds do chaunt theyr laies
And carroll of Loves praise.
The merry Larke hir mattins sings aloft;   80
The Thrush replyes; the Mavis descant playes:
The Ouzell shrills; the Ruddock warbles soft;
So goodly all agree, with sweet consent,
To this dayes merriment.
Ah! my deere love, why doe ye sleepe thus long,
When meeter were that ye should now awake,
T' awayt the comming of your joyous make,
And hearken to the birds love-learned song,
The deawy leaves among!
For they of joy and pleasance to you sing,   90
That all the woods them answer, and theyr eccho ring.

My love is now awake out of her dreames,
And her fayre eyes, like stars that dimmed were
With darksome cloud, now shew theyr goodly beams
More bright then Hesperus his head doth rere.
Come now, ye damzels, daughters of delight,
Helpe quickly her to dight:
But first come ye fayre houres, which were begot,
In Joves sweet paradice of Day and Night,
Which doe the seasons of the yeare allot,   100
And al, that ever in this world is fayre,
Doe make and still repayre:
And ye three handmayds of the Cyprian Queene,
The which doe still adorne her beauties pride,
Helpe to addorne my beautifullest bride:
And, as ye her array, still throw betweene
Some graces to be seene;
And, as ye use to Venus, to her sing,
The whiles the woods shal answer, and your eccho ring.

Now is my love all ready forth to come: 110
Let all the virgins therefore well awayt:
And ye fresh boyes, that tend upon her groome,
Prepare your selves; for he is comming strayt.

83   consent: harmony

Set all your things in seemely good aray,
Fit for so joyfull day:
The joyfulst day that ever sunne did see.
Faire Sun! shew forth thy favourable ray,
And let thy lifull heat not fervent be,
For feare of burning her sunshyny face,
Her beauty to disgrace.   120
O fayrest Phœbus! father of the Muse!
If ever I did honour thee aright,
Or sing the thing that mote thy mind delight,
Doe not thy servants simple boone refuse;
But let this day, let this one day, be myne;
Let all the rest be thine.
Then I thy soverayne prayses loud wil sing,
That all the woods shal answer, and theyr eccho ring.

Harke! how the Minstrils gin to shrill aloud
Their merry Musick that resounds from far,   130
The pipe, the tabor, and the trembling Croud.
That well agree withouten breach or jar.
But, most of all, the Damzels doe delite
When they their tymbrels smyte,
And thereunto doe daunce and carrol sweet,
That all the sences they doe ravish quite;
The whyles the boyes run up and downe the street,
Crying aloud with strong confused noyce,
As if it were one voyce,
Hymen, iö Hymen, Hymen, they do shout;   140
That even to the heavens theyr shouting shrill
Doth reach, and all the firmament doth fill;
To which the people standing all about,
As in approvance, doe thereto applaud,
And loud advaunce her laud;
And evermore they Hymen, Hymen sing,
That al the woods them answer, and theyr eccho ring.

Loe! where she comes along with portly pace,
Lyke Phœbe, from her chamber of the East,
Arysing forth to run her mighty race,   150
Clad all in white, that seemes a virgin best.
So well it her beseemes, that ye would weene
Some angell she had beene.
Her long loose yellow locks lyke golden wyre,
Sprinckled with perle, and perling flowres atweene,
Doe lyke a golden mantle her attyre;

118   lifull: life-giving   148   portly: stately

And, being crowned with a girland greene,
Seeme lyke some mayden Queene.
Her modest eyes, abashed to behold
So many gazers as on her do stare,   160
Upon the lowly ground affixed are;
Ne dare lift up her countenance too bold,
But blush to heare her prayses sung so loud,
So farre from being proud.
Nathlesse doe ye still loud her prayses sing,
That all the woods may answer, and your eccho ring.

Tell me, ye merchants daughters, did ye see
So fayre a creature in your towne before;
So sweet, so lovely, and so mild as she,
Adornd with beautyes grace and vertues store?   170
Her goodly eyes lyke Saphyres shining bright,
Her forehead yvory white,
Her cheekes lyke apples which the sun hath rudded,
Her lips lyke cherryes charming men to byte,
Her brest like to a bowle of creame uncrudded,
Her paps lyke lyllies budded,
Her snowie necke lyke to a marble towre;
And all her body like a pallace fayre,
Ascending up, with many a stately stayre,
To honors seat and chastities sweet bowre.   180
Why stand ye still ye virgins in amaze,
Upon her so to gaze,
Whiles ye forget your former lay to sing,
To which the woods did answer, and your eccho ring?

But if ye saw that which no eyes can see,
The inward beauty of her lively spright,
Garnisht with heavenly guifts of high degree,
Much more then would ye wonder at that sight,
And stand astonisht lyke to those which red
Medusaes mazeful hed.   190
There dwels sweet love, and constant chastity,
Unspotted fayth, and comely womanhood,
Regard of honour, and mild modesty;
There vertue raynes as Queene in royal throne,
And giveth lawes alone,
The which the base affections doe obay,
And yeeld theyr services unto her will;
Ne thought of thing uncomely ever may
Thereto approch to tempt her mind to ill.
Had ye once seene these her celestial threasures,   200

And unrevealed pleasures,
Then would ye wonder, and her prayses sing,
That al the woods should answer, and your echo ring.

Open the temple gates unto my love,
Open them wide that she may enter in,
And all the postes adorne as doth behove,
And all the pillours deck with girlands trim,
For to receyve this Saynt with honour dew,
That commeth in to you.
With trembling steps, and humble reverence,   210
She commeth in, before th' Almighties view;
Of her ye virgins learne obedience,
When so ye come into those holy places,
To humble your proud faces:
Bring her up to th' high altar, that she may
The sacred ceremonies there partake,
The which do endlesse matrimony make,
And let the roring Organs loudly play
The praises of the Lord in lively notes;
The whiles, with hollow throates,   220
The Choristers the joyous Antheme sing,
That al the woods may answere, and their eccho ring.

Behold, whiles she before the altar stands,
Hearing the holy priest that to her speakes,
And blesseth her with his two happy hands,
How the red roses flush up in her cheekes,
And the pure snow, with goodly vermill stayne
Like crimsin dyde in grayne:
That even th' Angels, which continually
About the sacred Altare doe remaine,   230
Forget their service and about her fly,
Ofte peeping in her face, that seems more fayre,
The more they on it stare.
But her sad eyes, still fastened on the ground,
Are governed with goodly modesty,
That suffers not one looke to glaunce awry,
Which may let in a little thought unsownd.
Why blush ye, love, to give to me your hand,
The pledge of all our band!
Sing, ye sweet Angels, Alleluya sing,   240
That all the woods may answere, and your eccho ring.

Now al is done: bring home the bride againe;
Bring home the triumph of our victory:

234   sad: serious

Bring home with you the glory of her gaine,
With joyance bring her and with jollity.
Never had man more joyfull day then this,
Whom heaven would heape with blis,
Make feast therefore now all this live-long day;
This day for ever to me holy is.
Poure out the wine without restraint or stay,   250
Poure not by cups, but by the belly full,
Poure out to all that wull,
And sprinkle all the postes and wals with wine,
That they may sweat, and drunken be withall.
Crowne ye God Bacchus with a coronall,
And Hymen also crowne with wreathes of vine;
And let the Graces daunce unto the rest,
For they can doo it best:
The whiles the maydens doe theyr carroll sing,
To which the woods shall answer, and theyr eccho ring.   260

Ring ye the bels, ye yong men of the towne,
And leave your wonted labors for this day:
This day is holy; doe ye write it downe,
That ye for ever it remember may.
This day the sunne is in his chiefest hight,
With Barnaby the bright,
From whence declining daily by degrees,
He somewhat loseth of his heat and light,
When once the Crab behind his back he sees.
But for this time it ill ordained was,   270
To chose the longest day in all the yeare,
And shortest night, when longest fitter weare:
Yet never day so long, but late would passe.
Ring ye the bels, to make it weare away,
And bonefiers make all day;
And daunce about them, and about them sing,
That all the woods may answer, and your eccho ring.

Ah! when will this long weary day have end,
And lende me leave to come unto my love?
How slowly do the houres theyr numbers spend?
How slowly does sad Time his feathers move?   280
Hast thee, O fayrest Planet, to thy home,
Within the Westerne fome:
Thy tyred steedes long since have need of rest.
Long though it be, at last I see it gloome,
And the bright evening-star with golden creast
Appeare out of the East.
Fayre childe of beauty! glorious lampe of love!

That all the host of heaven in rankes doost lead,
And guydest lovers through the nights dread,   290
How chearefully thou lookest from above,
And seemst to laugh atweene thy twinkling light,
As joying in the sight
Of these glad many, which for joy doe sing,
That all the woods them answer, and their echo ring!

Now ceasse, ye damsels, your delights fore-past;
Enough is it that all the day was youres:
Now day is doen, and night is nighing fast,
Now bring the Bryde into the brydall boures.
Now night is come, now soon her disaray.   300
And in her bed her lay;
Lay her in lillies and in violets,
And silken courteins over her display,
And odourd sheetes, and Arras coverlets.
Behold how goodly my faire love does ly,
In proud humility!
Like unto Maia, when as Jove her took
In Tempe, lying on the flowry gras,
Twixt sleepe and wake, after she weary was,
With bathing in the Acidalian brooke.   310
Now it is night, ye damsels may be gon,
And leave my love alone,
And leave likewise your former lay to sing:
The woods no more shall answere, nor your echo ring.

Now welcome, night! thou night so long expected,
That long daies labour doest at last defray,
And all my cares, which cruell Love collected,
Hast sumd in one, and cancelled for aye:
Spread thy broad wing over my love and me,
That no man may us see;   320
And in thy sable mantle us enwrap,
From feare of perill and foule horror free.
Let no false treason seeke us to entrap,
Nor any dread disquiet once annoy
The safety of our joy;
But let the night be calme, and quietsome,
Without tempestuous storms or sad afray:
Lyke as when Jove with fayre Alcmena lay,
When he begot the great Tirynthian groome:
Or lyke as when he with thy selfe did lie   330
And begot Majesty.

And let the mayds and yongmen cease to sing;
Ne let the woods them answer nor theyr eccho ring.

Let no lamenting cryes, nor dolefull teares,
Be heard all night within, nor yet without:
Ne let false whispers, breeding hidden feares,
Breake gentle sleepe with misconceived dout.
Let no deluding dreames, nor dreadfull sights,
Make sudden sad affrights;
Ne let house-fyres, nor lightnings helpelesse harmes,   340
Ne let the Pouke, nor other evill sprights,
Ne let mischivous witches with theyr charmes,
Ne let hob Goblins, names whose sence we see not,
Fray us with things that be not:
Let not the shriech Oule nor the Storke be heard,
Nor the night Raven, that still deadly yels;
Nor damned ghosts, cald up with mighty spels,
Nor griesly vultures, make us once affeard:
Ne let th' unpleasant Quyre of Frogs still croking
Make us to wish theyr choking.   350
Let none of these theyr drery accents sing;
Ne let the woods them answer, nor theyr eccho ring.

But let stil Silence trew night-watches keepe,
That sacred Peace may in assurance rayne,
And tymely Sleep, when it is tyme to sleepe,
May poure his limbs forth on your pleasant playne;
The whiles an hundred little winged loves,
Like divers-fethered doves,
Shall fly and flutter round about your bed,
And in the secret darke, that none reproves,   360
Their prety stealthes shal worke, and snares shal spread
To filch away sweet snatches of delight,
Conceald through covert night.
Ye sonnes of Venus, play your sports at will!
For greedy pleasure, carelesse of your toyes,
Thinks more upon her paradise of joyes,
Then what ye do, albe it good or ill.
All night therefore attend your merry play,
For it will soone be day:
Now none doth hinder you, that say or sing;   370
Ne will the woods now answer, nor your Eccho ring.

Who is the same, which at my window peepes?
Or whose is that faire face that shines so bright?
Is it not Cinthia, she that never sleepes,

But walkes about high heaven al the night?
O! fayrest goddesse, do thou not envy
My love with me to spy:
For thou likewise didst love, though now unthought,
And for a fleece of wooll, which privily
The Latmian shepherd once unto thee brought,   380
His pleasures with thee wrought.
Therefore to us be favorable now;
And sith of wemens labours thou hast charge,
And generation goodly dost enlarge,
Encline thy will t'effect our wishfull vow,
And the chast wombe informe with timely seed,
That may our comfort breed:
Till which we cease our hopefull hap to sing;
Ne let the woods us answere, nor our Eccho ring,

And thou, great Juno! which with awful might   390
The lawes of wedlock still dost patronize;
And the religion of the faith first plight
With sacred rites hast taught to solemnize:
And eeke for comfort often called art
Of women in their smart;
Eternally bind thou this lovely band,
And all thy blessings unto us impart.
And thou, glad Genius! in whose gentle hand
The bridale bowre and geniall bed remaine,
Without blemish or staine;   400
And the sweet pleasures of theyr loves delight
With secret ayde doest succour and supply,
Till they bring forth the fruitfull progeny;
Send us the timely fruit of this same night.
And thou, fayre Hebe! and thou, Hymen free!
Grant that it may so be.
Til which we cease your further prayse to sing;
Ne any woods shall answer, nor your Eccho ring.

And ye high heavens, the temple of the gods,
In which a thousand torches flaming bright   410
Doe burne, that to us wretched earthly clods
In dreadful darknesse lend desired light;
And all ye powers which in the same remayne,
More then we men can fayne!
Poure out your blessing on us plentiously,
And happy influence upon us raine,
That we may raise a large posterity,

399 geniall: generative

Which from the earth, which they may long possesse
With lasting happinesse,
Up to your haughty pallaces may mount; 420
And, for the guerdon of theyr glorious merit,
May heavenly tabernacles there inherit,
Of blessed Saints for to increase the count.
So let us rest, sweet love, in hope of this,
And cease till then our tymely joyes to sing:
The woods no more us answer, nor our eccho ring!

Song! made in lieu of many ornaments,
With which my love should duly have been dect
Which cutting off through hasty accidents,
Ye would not stay your dew time to expect, 430
But promist both to recompens;
Be unto her a goodly ornament,
And for short time an endlesse moniment.

420   haughty: noble

Prothalamion

T HE OCCASION OF THIS POEM, published in 1596, was the betrothal of the daughters of the Earl of Worcester to "two worthy gentlemen," Henry Guildford and William Petre. If there really was a Thames River ceremony of the kind described in the poem it must have taken place before Essex House in late summer or early autumn of 1596. The time of composition is limited by the return of the Earl of Essex from his victory at Cadiz in mid-August and the date of the wedding, November 8. One stanza of the poem (lines 127ff.) provides a rare bit of autobiography: Spenser tells us that he was born in London though of an ancient family rooted elsewhere, and that the Earl of Leicester, who once dwelt in Essex House, there gave him "gifts and goodly grace," since which time his case has been "friendless." The next stanza is filled with praise of the Earl of Essex and congratulations upon his great victory. Little more than two years later, Essex paid the costs of the poet's funeral.

"Prothalamion" is a word of Spenser's invention, evidently modeled on "Epithalamion."

PROTHALAMION.

OR A SPOUSALL VERSE

CALME WAS THE DAY, and through the trembling ayre
Sweete-breathing Zephyrus did softly play
A gentle spirit, that lightly did delay
Hot Titans beames, which then did glyster fayre;
When I, (whom sullein care,
Through discontent of my long fruitlesse stay
In Princes Court, and expectation vayne
Of idle hopes, which still doe fly away,
Like empty shaddowes, did afflict my brayne,)
Walkt forth to ease my payne   10
Along the shoare of silver streaming Themmes;
Whose rutty Bancke, he which his River hemmes
Was paynted all with variable flowers,
And all the meades adornd with daintie gemmes
Fit to decke maydens bowres,
And crowne their Paramours
Against the Brydale day, which is not long:
    Sweete Themmes! runne softly, till I end my Song.

There, in a Meadow, by the Rivers side,
A Flocke of Nymphes I chaunced to espy,   20
All lovely Daughters of the Flood thereby,
With goodly greenish locks, all loose untyde,
As each had bene a Bryde;
And each one had a little wicker basket,
Made of fine twigs, entrayled curiously,
In which they gathered flowers to fill their flasket,
And with fine Fingers cropt full feateously
The tender stalkes on hye.
Of every sort, which in that Meadow grew,
They gathered some; the Violet, pallid blew,   30
The little Dazie, that at evening closes,
The virgin Lillie, and the Primrose trew,
With store of vermeil Roses,

13   variable: varied   25   curiously: carefully
25   entrayled: interlaced   26   flasket: shallow basket

To decke their Bridegromes posies
Against the Brydale day, which was not long:
  Sweete Themmes! runne softly, till I end my **Song**.

With that I saw two Swannes of goodly hewe
Come softly swimming downe along the Lee;
Two fairer Birds I yet did never see;
The snow, which doth the top of Pindus strew,   **40**
Did never whiter shew,
Nor Jove himselfe, when he a Swan would be,
For love of Leda, whiter did appeare;
Yet Leda was (they say) as white as he,
Yet not so white as these, nor nothing neare;
So purely white they were,
That even the gentle streame, the which them bare,
Seem'd foule to them, and bad his billowes spare
To wet their silken feathers, least they might
Soyle their fayre plumes with water not so fayre,   **50**
And marre their beauties bright,
That shone as heavens light,
Against their Brydale day, which was not long:
  Sweete Themmes! runne softly, till I end my Song.

Eftsoones the Nymphes, which now had Flowers their fill,
Ran all in haste to see that silver brood,
As they came floating on the Christal Flood;
Whom when they sawe, they stood amazed still,
Their wondring eyes to fill;
Them seem'd they never saw a sight so fayre,   . **60**
Of Fowles, so lovely, that they sure did deeme
Them heavenly borne, or to be that same payre
Which through the Skie draw Venus silver Teeme;
For sure they did not seeme
To be begot of any earthly Seede,
But rather Angels, or of Angels breede;
Yet were they bred of Somers-heat, they say,
In sweetest Season, when each Flower and weede
The earth did fresh aray;
So fresh they seem'd as day,   **70**
Even as their Brydale day, which was not long:
  Sweete Themmes! runne softly, till I end my Song.

Then forth they all out of their baskets drew
Great store of Flowers, the honour of the field,
That to the sense did fragrant odours yeild,
All which upon those goodly Birds they threw

And all the Waves did strew,
That like old Peneus Waters they did seeme,
When downe along by pleasant Tempes shore,
Scattred with Flowres, through Thessaly they streeme,   80
That they appeare, through Lillies plenteous store,
Like a Brydes Chamber flore.
Two of those Nymphes, meane while, two Garlands bound
Of freshest Flowres which in that Mead they found,
The which presenting all in trim Array,
Their snowie Foreheads therewithall they crownd,
Whil'st one did sing this Lay,
Prepar'd against that Day,
Against their Brydale day, which was not long:
    Sweete Themmes! runne softly, till I end my Song.   90

'Ye gentle Birdes! the worlds faire ornament,
And heavens glorie, whom this happie hower
Doth leade unto your lovers blisfull bower,
Joy may you have, and gentle hearts content
Of your loves couplement;
And let faire Venus, that is Queene of love,
With her heart-quelling Sonne upon you smile,
Whose smile, they say, hath vertue to remove
All Loves dislike, and friendships faultie guile
For ever to assoile.   100
Let endlesse Peace your steadfast hearts accord,
And blessed Plentie wait upon your bord;
And let your bed with pleasures chast abound,
That fruitfull issue may to you afford,
Which may your foes confound,
And make your joyes redound
Upon your Brydale day, which is not long:
    Sweete Themmes! runne softlie, till I end my Song.'

So ended she; and all the rest around
To her redoubled that her undersong,   110
Which said their brydale daye should not be long:
And gentle Eccho from the neighbour ground
Their accents did resound.
So forth those joyous Birdes did passe along,
Adowne the Lee, that to them murmurde low,
As he would speake, but that he lackt a tong,
Yet did by signes his glad affection show,
Making his streame run slow.
And all the foule which in his flood did dwell

100   assoile: dispel

Gan flock about these twaine, that did excell 120
The rest, so far as Cynthia doth shend
The lesser starres. So they, enranged well,
Did on those two attend,
And their best service lend
Against their wedding day, which was not long:
   Sweete Themmes! run softly, till I end my Song.

At length they all to mery London came,
To mery London, my most kyndly Nurse,
That to me gave this Lifes first native sourse,
Though from another place I take my name, 130
An house of auncient fame:
There when they came, whereas those bricky towres
The which on Themmes brode aged backe doe ryde,
Where now the studious Lawyers have their bowers,
There whylome wont the Templer Knights to byde,
Till they decayd through pride:
Next whereunto there standes a stately place,
Where oft I gayned giftes and goodly grace
Of that great Lord, which therein wont to dwell,
Whose want too well now feeles my freendles case; 140
But ah! here fits not well
Olde woes, but joyes, to tell
   Against the bridale daye, which is not long:
   Sweete Themmes! runne softly, till I end my Song.

Yet therein now doth lodge a noble Peer,
Great Englands glory, and the Worlds wide wonder,
Whose dreadfull name late through all Spaine did thunder,
And Hercules two pillors standing neere
Did make to quake and feare:
Faire branch of Honor, flower of Chevalrie! 150
That fillest England with thy triumphes fame,
Joy have thou of thy noble victorie,
And endlesse happinesse of thine owne name
That promiseth the same;
That through thy prowesse, and victorious armes,
Thy country may be freed from forraine harmes;
And great Elisaes glorious name may ring
Through al the world, fil'd with thy wide Alarmes,
Which some brave muse may sing
To ages following, 160
Upon the Brydale day, which is not long:
   Sweete Themmes! runne softly till I end my Song.

121   shend: disgrace   137   place: palace

From those high Towers this noble Lord issuing,
Like Radiant Hesper, when his golden hayre
In th' Ocean billowes he hath bathed fayre,
Descended to the Rivers open vewing,
With a great traine ensuing.
Above the rest were goodly to bee seene
Two gentle Knights of lovely face and feature,
Beseeming well the bower of anie Queene,   170
With gifts of wit, and ornaments of nature,
Fit for so goodly stature,
That like the twins of Jove they seem'd in sight,
Which decke the Bauldricke of the Heavens bright;
They two, forth pacing to the Rivers side,
Received those two faire Brides, their Loves delight;
Which, at th' appointed tyde,
Each one did make his Bryde
Against their Brydale day, which is not long:
Sweete Themmes! runne softly, till I end my Song.   180
174 Bauldricke: girdle

Fowre Hymnes

The dedication of *Fowre Hymnes* was dated from Greenwich, September 1, 1596, and the work was published in that year. Spenser says that the first two hymns were written "in the greener times of my youth," and since they "too much pleased those of like age and disposition" he was moved "to amend, and by way of retractation to reform them, making instead of those two hymns of earthly or natural love and beauty two others of heavenly and celestial." Some scholars believe, nevertheless, that all four hymns were written at about the same time.

AN HYMNE IN HONOUR OF LOVE.

LOVE, THAT LONG SINCE hast to thy mighty powre
Perforce subdude my poore captived hart,
And, raging now therein with restlesse stowre,
Doest tyrannize in everie weaker part;
Faine would I seeke to ease my bitter smart
By any service I might do to thee,
Or ought that else might to thee pleasing bee.

And now t' asswage the force of this new flame,
And make thee more propitious in my need,
I meane to sing the praises of thy name,   10
And thy victorious conquests to areed,
By which thou madest many harts to bleed
Of mighty Victors, with wyde wounds embrewed,
And by thy cruell darts to thee subdewed.

Onely I feare my wits enfeebled late,
Through the sharpe sorrowes which thou hast me bred,
Should faint, and words should faile me to relate
The wondrous triumphs of thy great god-hed:
But, if thou wouldst vouchsafe to overspred
Me with the shadow of thy gentle wing,   20
I should enabled be thy actes to sing.

Come, then, O come, thou mightie God of Love,
Out of thy silver bowres and secret blisse,
Where thou doest sit in Venus lap above,
Bathing thy wings in her ambrosiall kisse,
That sweeter farre then any Nectar is;
Come softly, and my feeble breast inspire
With gentle furie, kindled of thy fire.

And ye, sweet Muses! which have often proved
The piercing points of his avengefull darts;   30

3 stowre: tumult   11 areed: proclaim

And ye, faire Nimphs! which oftentimes have loved
The cruell worker of your kindly smarts,
Prepare your selves, and open wide your harts
For to receive the triumph of your glorie,
That made you merie oft when ye were sorie.

And ye, faire blossomes of youths wanton breed,
Which in the conquests of your beautie bost,
Wherewith your lovers feeble eyes you feed,
But sterve their harts that needeth nourture most,
Prepare your selves to march amongst his host,   **40**
And all the way this sacred hymne do sing,
Made in the honor of your Soveraigne king.

GREAT GOD OF MIGHT, that reignest in the mynd,
And all the bodie to thy hest doest frame,
Victor of gods, subduer of mankynd,
That doest the Lions and fell Tigers tame,
Making their cruell rage thy scornefull game,
And in their roring taking great delight;
Who can expresse the glorie of thy might?

Or who alive can perfectly declare   **50**
The wondrous cradle of thine infancie,
When thy great mother Venus first thee bare,
Begot of Plentie and of Penurie,
Though elder then thine owne nativitie,
And yet a chyld, renewing still thy yeares,
And yet the eldest of the heavenly Peares?

For ere this worlds still moving mightie masse
Out of great Chaos ugly prison crept,
In which his goodly face long hidden was
From heavens view, and in deepe darknesse kept,   **60**
Love, that had now long time securely slept
In Venus lap, unarmed then and naked,
Gan reare his head, by Clotho being waked:

And, taking to him wings of his owne heate,
Kindled at first from heavens life-giving fyre,
He gan to move out of his idle seate;
Weakely at first, but after with desyre
Lifted aloft, he gan to mount up hyre,
And, like fresh Eagle, make his hardie flight
Through all that great wide wast, yet wanting light.   **70**

36   wanton: luxuriant

Yet wanting light to guide his wandring way,
His owne faire mother, for all creatures sake,
Did lend him light from her owne goodly ray;
Then through the world his way he gan to take,
The world, that was not till he did it make,
Whose sundrie parts he from themselves did sever
The which before had lyen confused ever.

The earth, the ayre, the water, and the fyre,
Then gan to raunge them selves in huge array,
And with contrary forces to conspyre   80
Each against other by all meanes they may,
Threatning their owne confusion and decay:
Ayre hated earth, and water hated fyre,
Till Love relented their rebellious yre.

He then them tooke, and, tempering goodly well
Their contrary dislikes with loved meanes,
Did place them all in order, and compell
To keepe them selves within their sundrie raines,
Together linkt with Adamantine chaines;
Yet so, as that in every living wight   90
They mixe themselves, and shew their kindly might.

So ever since they firmely have remained,
And duly well observed his beheast;
Through which now all these things that are contained
Within this goodly cope, both most and least,
Their being have, and dayly are increast
Through secret sparks of his infused fyre,
Which in the barraine cold he doth inspyre.

Thereby they all do live, and moved are
To multiply the likenesse of their kynd,   100
Whilest they seeke onely, without further care,
To quench the flame which they in burning fynd;
But man that breathes a more immortall mynd,
Not for lusts sake, but for eternitie,
Seekes to enlarge his lasting progenie;

For, having yet in his deducted spright
Some sparks remaining of that heavenly fyre,
He is enlumind with that goodly light,
Unto like goodly semblant to aspyre;
Therefore in choice of love he doth desyre   110

91 kindly: natural   95 cope: canopy

That seemes on earth most heavenly to embrace,
That same is Beautie, borne of heavenly race.

For sure of all that in this mortall frame
Contained is, nought more divine doth seeme,
Or that resembleth more th' immortall flame
Of heavenly light, then Beauties glorious beame.
What wonder then, if with such rage extreme
Fraile men, whose eyes seek heavenly things to see,
At sight thereof so much enravisht bee?

Which well perceiving, that imperious boy   120
Doth therwith tip his sharp empoisned darts,
Which glancing through the eyes with countenance coy
Rest not till they have pierst the trembling harts,
And kindled flame in all their inner parts,
Which suckes the blood, and drinketh up the lyfe,
Of carefull wretches with consuming griefe.

Thenceforth they playne, and make ful piteous mone
Unto the author of their balefull bane:
The daies they waste, the nights they grieve and grone,
Their lives they loath, and heavens light disdaine;   130
No light but that, whose lampe doth yet remaine
Fresh burning in the image of their eye,
They deigne to see, and seeing it still dye.

The whilst thou tyrant Love doest laugh and scorne
At their complaints, making their paine thy play,
Whylest they lye languishing like thrals forlorne,
The whyles thou doest triumph in their decay;
And otherwhyles, their dying to delay,
Thou doest emmarble the proud hart of her
Whose love before their life they doe prefer.   140

So hast thou often done (ay me, the more!)
To me thy vassall, whose yet bleeding hart
With thousand wounds thou mangled hast so sore,
That whole remaines scarse any little part;
Yet, to augment the anguish of my smart,
Thou hast enfrosen her disdainefull brest,
That no one drop of pitie there doth rest.

Why then do I this honor unto thee,
Thus to ennoble thy victorious name,

117   rage: passion

Since thou doest shew no favour unto mee,   150
Ne once move ruth in that rebellious Dame,
Somewhat to slacke the rigour of my flame?
Certes small glory doest thou winne hereby,
To let her live thus free, and me to dy.

But if thou be indeede, as men thee call,
The worlds great Parent, the most kind preserver
Of living wights, the soveraine Lord of all,
How falles it then that with thy furious fervour
Thou doest afflict as well the not-deserver,
As him that doeth thy lovely heasts despize,   160
And on thy subjects most doest tyrannize?

Yet herein eke thy glory seemeth more,
By so hard handling those which best thee serve,
That, ere thou doest them unto grace restore,
Thou mayest well trie if they will ever swerve,
And mayest them make it better to deserve,
And, having got it, may it more esteeme;
For things hard gotten men more dearely deeme.

So hard those heavenly beauties he enfyred
As things divine, least passions doe impresse,   170
The more of stedfast mynds to be admyred,
The more they stayed be on stedfastnesse;
But baseborne mynds such lamps regard the lesse,
Which at first blowing take not hastie fyre;
Such fancies feele no love, but loose desyre.

For love is Lord of truth and loialtie,
Lifting himselfe out of the lowly dust
On golden plumes up to the purest skie,
Above the reach of loathly sinfull lust,
Whose base affect through cowardly distrust   180
Of his weake wings dare not to heaven fly,
But like a moldwarpe in the earth doth ly.

His dunghill thoughts, which do themselves enure
To dirtie drosse, no higher dare aspyre,
Ne can his feeble earthly eyes endure
The flaming light of that celestiall fyre
Which kindleth love in generous desyre,

160 heasts: behests   182 moldwarpe: mole
180 affect: passion

And makes him mount above the native might
Of heavie earth, up to the heavens hight.

Such is the powre of that sweet passion,   190
That it all sordid basenesse doth expell,
And the refyned mynd doth newly fashion
Unto a fairer forme, which now doth dwell
In his high thought, that would it selfe excell,
Which he beholding still with constant sight,
Admires the mirrour of so heavenly light.

Whose image printing in his deepest wit,
He thereon feeds his hungrie fantasy,
Still full, yet never satisfyde with it;
Like Tantale, that in store doth sterved ly,   200
So doth he pine in most satiety;
For nought may quench his infinite desyre,
Once kindled through that first conceived fyre.

Thereon his mynd affixed wholly is,
Ne thinks on ought but how it to attaine;
His care, his joy, his hope, is all on this,
That seemes in it all blisses to containe,
In sight whereof all other blisse seemes vaine:
Thrise happie man! might he the same possesse,
He faines himselfe, and doth his fortune blesse.   210

And though he do not win his wish to end,
Yet thus farre happie he himselfe doth weene,
That heavens such happie grace did to him lend,
As thing on earth so heavenly to have seene
His harts enshrined saint, his heavens queene,
Fairer then fairest, in his fayning eye,
Whose sole aspect he counts felicitye.

Then forth he casts in his unquiet thought,
What he may do, her favour to obtaine;
What brave exploit, what perill hardly wrought   220
What puissant conquest, what adventurous paine,
May please her best, and grace unto him gaine;
He dreads no danger, nor misfortune feares,
His faith, his fortune, in his breast he beares.

Thou art his god, thou art his mightie guyde,
Thou, being blind, letst him not see his feares,
But cariest him to that which he hath eyde,

Through seas, through flames, through thousand swords and
    speares;
Ne ought so strong that may his force withstand,
With which thou armest his resistlesse hand.   230

Witnesse Leander in the Euxine waves,
And stout Æneas in the Trojane fyre,
Achilles preassing through the Phrygian glaives,
And Orpheus, daring to provoke the yre
Of damned fiends, to get his love retyre;
For both through heaven and hell thou makest way
To win them worship which to thee obay.

And if, by all these perils and these paynes,
He may but purchase lyking in her eye,
What heavens of joy then to himselfe he faynes!   240
Eftsoones he wypes quite out of memory
Whatever ill before he did aby:
Had it bene death, yet would he die againe,
To live thus happie as her grace to gaine.

Yet, when he hath found favour to his will,
He nathëmore can so contented rest,
But forceth further on, and striveth still
T' approch more neare, till in her inmost brest
He may embosomd bee and loved best;
And yet not best, but to be lov'd alone;   250
For love can not endure a Paragone.

The feare whereof, O how doth it torment
His troubled mynd with more then hellish paine!
And to his fayning fansie represent
Sights never seene, and thousand shadowes vaine,
To breake his sleepe, and waste his ydle braine:
Thou that hast never lov'd canst not beleeve
Least part of th' evils which poore lovers greeve.

The gnawing envie, the hart-fretting feare,
The vaine surmizes, the distrustfull showes,   260
The false reports that flying tales doe beare,
The doubts, the daungers, the delayes, the woes,
The fayned friends, the unassured foes,
With thousands more then any tongue can tell,
Doe make a lovers life a wretches hell.

230   resistlesse: irresistible   235   retyre: retirement

Yet is there one more cursed then they all,
That cancker-worme, that monster, Gelosie,
Which eates the hart and feedes upon the gall,
Turning all loves delight to miserie,
Through feare of loosing his felicitie.   270
Ah, Gods! that ever ye that monster placed
In gentle love, that all his joyes defaced!

By these, O Love! thou doest thy entrance make
Unto thy heaven, and doest the more endeere
Thy pleasures unto those which them partake,
As after stormes, when clouds begin to cleare,
The Sunne more bright and glorious doth appeare;
So thou thy folke, through paines of Purgatorie
Dost beare unto thy blisse, and heavens glorie.

There thou them placest in a Paradize   280
Of all delight and joyous happie rest,
Where they doe feede on Nectar heavenly-wize,
With Hercules and Hebe, and the rest
Of Venus dearlings, through her bountie blest;
And lie like Gods in yvorie beds arayd,
With rose and lillies over them displayd.

There with thy daughter Pleasure they doe play
Their hurtlesse sports, without rebuke or blame,
And in her snowy bosome boldly lay
Their quiet heads, devoyd of guilty shame,   290
After full joyance of their gentle game;
Then her they crowne their Goddesse and their Queene,
And decke with floures thy altars well beseene.

Ay me! deare Lord! that ever I might hope,
For all the paines and woes that I endure,
To come at length unto the wished scope
Of my desire, or might myselfe assure
That happie port for ever to recure!
Then would I thinke these paines no paines at all,
And all my woes to be but penance small.   300

Then would I sing of thine immortall praise
An heavenly Hymne, such as the Angels sing,
And thy triumphant name then would I raise
Bove all the gods, thee onely honoring,
My guide, my God, my victor, and my king:

286   displayd: spread out   298   recure: recover

Till then, dread Lord! vouchsafe to take of me
This simple song, thus fram'd in praise of thee.

AN HYMNE IN HONOUR OF BEAUTIE.

AH! WHITHER, LOVE! wilt thou now carrie mee?
What wontlesse fury dost thou now inspire
Into my feeble breast, too full of thee?
Whylest seeking to aslake thy raging fyre,
Thou in me kindlest much more great desyre,
And up aloft above my strength doest rayse
The wondrous matter of my fyre to prayse.

That as I earst, in praise of thine owne name,
So now in honour of thy Mother deare,
An honourable Hymne I eke should frame,   10
And, with the brightnesse of her beautie cleare,
The ravisht harts of gazefull men might reare
To admiration of that heavenly light,
From whence proceeds such soule-enchaunting might.

Therto do thou, great Goddesse! Queene of Beauty,
Mother of love, and of all worlds delight,
Without whose soverayne grace and kindly dewty
Nothing on earth seemes fayre to fleshly sight,
Doe thou vouchsafe with thy love-kindling light
T' illuminate my dim and dulled eyne,   20
And beautifie this sacred hymne of thyne:

That both to thee, to whom I meane it most,
And eke to her, whose faire immortall beame
Hath darted fyre into my feeble ghost,
That now it wasted is with woes extreame,
It may so please, that she at length will streame

24 ghost: spirit

Some deaw of grace into my withered hart,
After long sorrow and consuming smart.

WHAT TIME THIS WORLDS great workmaister did cast
To make al things such as we now behold,   30
It seemes that he before his eyes had plast
A goodly Paterne, to whose perfect mould
He fashiond them as comely as he could,
That now so faire and seemely they appeare,
As nought may be amended any wheare.

That wondrous Paterne, wheresoere it bee,
Whether in earth layd up in secret store,
Or else in heaven, that no man may it see
With sinfull eyes, for feare it to deflore,
Is perfect Beautie, which all men adore;   40
Whose face and feature doth so much excell
All mortall sence, that none the same may tell.

Thereof as every earthly thing partakes
Or more or lesse, by influence divine,
So it more faire accordingly it makes,
And the grosse matter of this earthly myne
Which clotheth it thereafter doth refyne,
Doing away the drosse which dims the light
Of that faire beame which therein is empight.

For, through infusion of celestiall powre,   50
The duller earth it quickneth with delight,
And life-full spirits privily doth powre
Through all the parts, that to the lookers sight
They seeme to please; that is thy soveraine might,
O Cyprian Queene! which flowing from the beame
Of thy bright starre, thou into them doest streame.

That is the thing which giveth pleasant grace
To all things faire, that kindleth lively fyre,
Light of thy lampe; which, shyning in the face,
Thence to the soule darts amorous desyre,   60
And robs the harts of those which it admyre;
Therewith thou pointest thy Sons poysned arrow,
That wounds the life, and wastes the inmost marrow.

How vainely then doe ydle wits invent,
That beautie is nought else but mixture made

39   deflore: deflower

Of colours faire, and goodly temp'rament
Of pure complexions, that shall quickly fade
And passe away, like to a sommers shade;
Or that it is but comely composition
Of parts well measurd, with meet disposition!   70

Hath white and red in it such wondrous powre,
That it can pierce through th' eyes unto the hart,
And therein stirre such rage and restlesse stowre,
As nought but death can stint his dolours smart?
Or can proportion of the outward part
Move such affection in the inward mynd,
That it can rob both sense, and reason blynd?

Why doe not then the blossomes of the field,
Which are arayd with much more orient hew,
And to the sense most daintie odours yield,   80
Worke like impression in the lookers vew?
Or why doe not faire pictures like powre shew,
In which oft-times we nature see of art
Exceld, in perfect limming every part?

But ah! beleeve me there is more then so,
That workes such wonders in the minds of men;
I, that have often prov'd, too well it know,
And who so list the like assayes to ken,
Shall find by tryall, and confesse it then,
That Beautie is not, as fond men misdeeme,   90
An outward shew of things that onely seeme.

For that same goodly hew of white and red,
With which the cheekes are sprinckled, shal decay,
And those sweete rosy leaves, so fairely spred
Upon the lips, shall fade and fall away
To that they were, even to corrupted clay:
That golden wyre, those sparckling stars so bright,
Shall turne to dust, and loose their goodly light.

But that faire lampe, from whose celestiall ray
That light proceedes, which kindleth lovers fire,   100
Shall never be extinguisht nor decay;
But, when the vitall spirits doe expyre,
Unto her native planet shall retyre;
For it is heavenly borne and can not die,
Being a parcell of the purest skie.

For when the soule, the which derived was,
At first, out of that great immortall Spright,
By whom all live to love, whilome did pas
Downe from the top of purest heavens hight
To be embodied here, it then tooke light   110
And lively spirits from that fayrest starre
Which lights the world forth from his firie carre.

Which powre retayning still or more or lesse,
When she in fleshly seede is eft enraced,
Through every part she doth the same impresse,
According as the heavens have her graced,
And frames her house, in which she will be placed,
Fit for her selfe, adorning it with spoyle
Of th' heavenly riches which she robd erewhyle.

Thereof it comes that these faire soules, which have   120
The most resemblance of that heavenly light,
Frame to themselves most beautifull and brave
Their fleshly bowre, most fit for their delight,
And the grosse matter by a soveraine might
Tempers so trim, that it may well be seene
A pallace fit for such a virgin Queene.

So every spirit, as it is most pure,
And hath in it the more of heavenly light,
So it the fairer bodie doth procure
To habit in, and it more fairely dight   130
With chearefull grace and amiable sight;
For of the soule the bodie forme doth take;
For soule is forme, and doth the bodie make.

Therefore where-ever that thou doest behold
A comely corpse, with beautie faire endewed,
Know this for certaine, that the same doth hold
A beauteous soule, with faire conditions thewed,
Fit to receive the seede of vertue strewed;
For all that faire is, is by nature good;
That is a signe to know the gentle blood.   140

Yet oft it falles that many a gentle mynd
Dwels in deformed tabernacle drownd,
Either by chaunce, against the course of kynd,
Or through unaptnesse in the substance fownd,
Which it assumed of some stubborne grownd,

135   corpse: body   137   thewed: trained

That will not yield unto her formes direction,
But is perform'd with some foule imperfection.

And oft it falles, (aye me, the more to rew!)
That goodly beautie, albe heavenly borne,
Is foule abusd, and that celestiall hew,   150
Which doth the world with her delight adorne,
Made but the bait of sinne, and sinners scorne,
Whilest every one doth seeke and sew to have it,
But every one doth seeke but to deprave it.

Yet nathëmore is that faire beauties blame,
But theirs that do abuse it unto ill:
Nothing so good, but that through guilty shame
May be corrupt, and wrested unto will:
Nathelesse the soule is faire and beauteous still,
How ever fleshes fault it filthy make;   160
For things immortall no corruption take.

But ye, faire Dames! the worlds deare ornaments
And lively images of heavens light,
Let not your beames with such disparagements
Be dimd, and your bright glorie darkned quight;
But, mindfull still of your first countries sight,
Doe still preserve your first informed grace,
Whose shadow yet shynes in your beauteous face.

Loath that foule blot, that hellish fiërbrand,
Disloiall lust faire beauties foulest blame,   170
That base affections, which your eares would bland
Commend to you by loves abused name,
But is indeede the bondslave of defame;
Which will the garland of your glorie marre,
And quench the light of your bright shyning starre.

But gentle Love, that loiall is and trew,
Will more illumine your resplendent ray,
And adde more brightnesse to your goodly hew,
From light of his pure fire; which, by like way
Kindled of yours, your likenesse doth display;   180
Like as two mirrours, by opposd reflexion,
Doe both expresse the faces first impression.

Therefore, to make your beautie more appeare,
It you behoves to love, and forth to lay

171 bland: soothe

That heavenly riches which in you ye beare,
That men the more admyre their fountaine may;
For else what booteth that celestiall ray,
If it in darknesse be enshrined ever,
That it of loving eyes be vewed never?

But, in your choice of Loves, this well advize,   190
That likest to your selves ye them select,
The which your forms first sourse may sympathize,
And with like beauties parts be inly deckt;
For, if you loosely love without respect,
It is no love, but a discordant warre,
Whose unlike parts amongst themselves do jarre.

For Love is a celestiall harmonie
Of likely harts composed of starres concent,
Which joyne together in sweete sympathie,
To worke ech others joy and true content,   200
Which they have harbourd since their first descent
Out of their heavenly bowres, where they did see
And know ech other here belov'd to bee.

Then wrong it were that any other twaine
Should in loves gentle band combyned bee
But those whom heaven did at first ordaine,
And made out of one mould the more t' agree;
For all, that like the beautie which they see,
Streight do not love; for Love is not so light   210
As streight to burne at first beholders sight.

But they, which love indeede, looke otherwise,
With pure regard and spotlesse true intent,
Drawing out of the object of their eyes
A more refyned forme, which they present
Unto their mind, voide of all blemishment;
Which it reducing to her first perfection,
Beholdeth free from fleshes frayle infection.

And then conforming it unto the light,
Which in it selfe it hath remaining still,
Of that first Sunne, yet sparckling in his sight,   220
Thereof he fashions in his higher skill
An heavenly beautie to his fancies will;
And, it embracing in his mind entyre,
The mirrour of his owne thought doth admyre.

192   sympathize: harmonize with   198   concent: harmony

Which seeing now so inly faire to be,
As outward it appeareth to the eye,
And with his spirits proportion to agree,
He thereon fixeth all his fantasie,
And fully setteth his felicitie;
Counting it fairer then it is indeede,   230
And yet indeede her fairenesse doth exceede.

For lovers eyes more sharply sighted bee
Then other mens, and in deare loves delight
See more then any other eyes can see,
Through mutuall receipt of beames bright,
Which carrie privie message to the spright,
And to their eyes that inmost faire display,
As plaine as light discovers dawning day.

Therein they see, through amorous eye-glaunces,
Armies of Loves still flying too and fro,   240
Which dart at them their litle fierie launces;
Whom having wounded, backe againe they go,
Carrying compassion to their lovely foe;
Who, seeing her faire eyes so sharpe effect,
Cures all their sorrowes with one sweete aspect.

In which how many wonders doe they reede
To their conceipt, that others never see!
Now of her smiles, with which their soules they feede,
Like Gods with Nectar in their bankets free;
Now of her lookes, which like to Cordials bee;   250
But when her words embássade forth she sends,
Lord, how sweete musicke that unto them lends!

Sometimes upon her forhead they behold
A thousand Graces masking in delight;
Sometimes within her eye-lids they unfold
Ten thousand sweet belgards, which to their sight
Doe seeme like twinckling starres in frostie night;
But on her lips, like rosy buds in May,
So many millions of chaste pleasures play.

All those, O Cytherea! and thousands more   260
Thy handmaides be, which do on thee attend,
To decke thy beautie with their dainties store,
That may it more to mortall eyes commend,
And make it more admyr'd of foe and frend;
256 belgards: glances

That in mens harts thou mayst thy throne enstall,
And spred thy lovely kingdome over-all.

Then Iö, tryumph! O great Beauties Queene,
Advance the banner of thy conquest hie,
That all this world, the which thy vassals beene,
May draw to thee, and with dew fëaltie   270
Adore the powre of thy great Majestie,
Singing this Hymne in honour of thy name,
Compyld by me, which thy poore liegeman am!

In lieu whereof graunt, O great Soveraine!
That she, whose conquering beautie doth captive
My trembling hart in her eternall chaine,
One drop of grace at length will to me give,
That I her bounden thrall by her may live,
And this same life, which first fro me she reaved,
May owe to her, of whom I it received.   280

And you, faire Venus dearling, my deare dread!
Fresh flowre of grace, great Goddesse of my life,
When your faire eyes these fearefull lines shal read,
Deigne to let fall one drop of dew reliefe,
That may recure my harts long pyning griefe,
And shew what wondrous powre your beauty hath,
That can restore a damned wight from death.

AN HYMNE OF
HEAVENLY LOVE.

Love, LIFT ME up upon thy golden wings,
From this base world unto thy heavens hight,
Where I may see those admirable things
Which there thou workest by thy soveraine might,
Farre above feeble reach of earthly sight,

281   dread: revered one

That I thereof an heavenly Hymne may sing
Unto the God of Love, high heavens king.

Many lewd layes (ah! woe is me the more!)
In praise of that mad fit which fooles call love,
I have in th' heat of youth made heretofore,
That in light wits did loose affection move;   10
But all those follies now I do reprove,
And turned have the tenor of my string,
The heavenly prayses of true love to sing.

And ye that wont with greedy vaine desire
To reade my fault, and, wondring at my flame,
To warme your selves at my wide sparckling fire,
Sith now that heat is quenched, quench my blame,
And in her ashes shrowd my dying shame;
For who my passed follies now pursewes,   20
Beginnes his owne, and my old fault renewes.

BEFORE THIS WORLDS GREAT FRAME, in which al things
Are now containd, found any being-place,
Ere flitting Time could wag his eyas wings
About that mightie bound which doth embrace
The rolling Spheres, and parts their houres by space,
That High Eternall Powre, which now doth move
In all these things, mov'd in it selfe by love.

It lov'd it selfe, because it selfe was faire;
(For faire is lov'd;) and of it selfe begot,
Like to it selfe his eldest sonne and heire,   30
Eternall, pure, and voide of sinfull blot,
The firstling of his joy, in whom no jot
Of loves dislike or pride was to be found,
Whom he therefore with equall honour crownd.

With him he raignd, before all time prescribed,
In endlesse glorie and immortall might,
Together with that third from them derived,
Most wise, most holy, most almightie Spright!
Whose kingdomes throne no thought of earthly wight   40
Can comprehend, much lesse my trembling verse
With equall words can hope it to reherse.

Yet, O most blessed Spirit! pure lampe of light,
Eternall spring of grace and wisedome trew,
Vouchsafe to shed into my barren spright

24 eyas: newly-fledged

Some little drop of thy celestiall dew,
That may my rymes with sweet infuse embrew,
And give me words equall unto my thought,
To tell the marveiles by thy mercie wrought.

Yet being pregnant still with powrefull grace,   50
And full of fruitfull love, that loves to get
Things like himselfe, and to enlarge his race,
His second brood, though not in powre so great,
Yet full of beautie, next he did beget
An infinite increase of Angels bright,
All glistring glorious in their Makers light.

To them the heavens illimitable hight
(Not this round heaven, which we from hence behold,
Adornd with thousand lamps of burning light,
And with ten thousand gemmes of shyning gold,)   60
He gave as their inheritance to hold,
That they might serve him in eternall blis,
And be partakers of those joyes of his.

There they in their trinall triplicities
About him wait, and on his will depend,
Either with nimble wings to cut the skies,
When he them on his messages doth send,
Or on his owne dread presence to attend,
Where they behold the glorie of his light,
And caroll Hymnes of love both day and night.   70

Both day, and night, is unto them all one;
For he his beames doth still to them extend,
That darknesse there appeareth never none;
Ne hath their day, ne hath their blisse, an end,
But there their termelesse time in pleasure spend;
Ne ever should their happinesse decay,
Had not they dar'd their Lord to disobay.

But pride, impatient of long resting peace,
Did puffe them up with greedy bold ambition,
That they gan cast their state how to increase   80
Above the fortune of their first condition,
And sit in Gods owne seat without commission:
The brightest Angell, even the Child of Light,
Drew millions more against their God to fight

Th' Almighty, seeing their so bold assay,
Kindled the flame of His consuming yre,

And with His onely breath them blew away
From heavens hight, to which they did aspyre,
To deepest hell, and lake of damned fyre,
Where they in darknesse and dread horror dwell,   90
Hating the happie light from which they fell.

So that next off-spring of the Makers love,
Next to Himselfe in glorious degree,
Degendering to hate, fell from above
Through pride, (for pride and love may ill agree)
And now of sinne to all ensample bee:
How then can sinfull flesh itselfe assure,
Sith purest Angels fell to be impure?

But that Eternall Fount of love and grace,
Still flowing forth His goodnesse unto all,   100
Now seeing left a waste and emptie place
In His wyde Pallace, through those Angels fall,
Cast to supply the same, and to enstall
A new unknowen Colony therein,
Whose root from earths base groundworke shold begin.

Therefore of clay, base, vile, and next to nought,
Yet form'd by wondrous skill, and by His might,
According to an heavenly patterne wrought,
Which He had fashiond in his wise foresight,
He man did make, and breathd a living spright   110
Into his face most beautifull and fayre,
Endewd with wisedomes riches, heavenly, rare.

Such He him made, that he resemble might
Himselfe, as mortall thing immortall could;
Him to be Lord of every living wight
He made by love out of His owne like mould,
In whom He might His mightie selfe behould;
For Love doth love the thing belov'd to see,
That like itselfe in lovely shape may bee.

But man, forgetfull of his Makers grace   12C
No lesse then Angels whom he did ensew,
Fell from the hope of promist heavenly place,
Into the mouth of death, to sinners dew,
And all his off-spring into thraldome threw,
Where they for ever should in bonds remaine
Of never-dead yet ever-dying paine;

121 ensew: follow

Till that great Lord of Love, which him at first
Made of meere love, and after liked well,
Seeing him lie like creature long accurst
In that deepe horror of despeyred hell,   130
Him, wretch, in doole would let no lenger dwell,
But cast out of that bondage to redeeme,
And pay the price, all were his debt extreeme.

Out of the bosome of eternall blisse,
In which he reigned with his glorious syre,
He downe descended, like a most demisse
And abject thrall, in fleshes fraile attyre,
That He for him might pay sinnes deadly hyre,
And him restore unto that happie state
In which he stood before his haplesse fate.   140

In flesh at first the guilt committed was,
Therefore in flesh it must be satisfyde;
Nor spirit, nor Angell, though they man surpas,
Could make amends to God for mans misguyde,
But onely man himselfe, who selfe did slyde:
So, taking flesh of sacred virgins wombe,
For mans deare sake he did a man become.

And that most blessed bodie, which was borne
Without all blemish or reprochfull blame,
He freely gave to be both rent and torne   150
Of cruell hands, who with despightfull shame
Revyling him, that them most vile became,
At length him nayled on a gallow-tree,
And slew the Just by most unjust decree.

O huge and most unspeakable impression
Of loves deepe wound, that pierst the piteous hart
Of that deare Lord with so entyre affection,
And, sharply launching every inner part,
Dolours of death into his soule did dart,
Doing him die that never it deserved,   160
To free his foes, that from his heast had swerved!

What hart can feele least touch of so sore launch,
Or thought can think the depth of so deare wound?
Whose bleeding sourse their streames yet never staunch
But stil do flow, and freshly still redound,
To heale the sores of sinfull soules unsound,

128 meere: perfect   158 launching: piercing
136 demisse: base   165 redound: flow

And clense the guilt of that infected cryme
Which was enrooted in all fleshly slyme.

O blessed Well of Love! O Floure of Grace!
O glorious Morning-Starre! O Lampe of Light!   170
Most lively image of thy Fathers face,
Eternall King of Glorie, Lord of Might,
Meeke Lambe of God, before all worlds behight,
How can we thee requite for all this good?
Or what can prize that thy most precious blood?

Yet nought thou ask'st in lieu of all this love,
But love of us, for guerdon of thy paine:
Ay me! what can us lesse then that behove?
Had he required life of us againe,
Had it beene wrong to aske his owne with gaine?   180
He gave us life, he it restored lost;
Then life were least, that us so litle cost.

But he our life hath left unto us free,
Free that was thrall, and blessed that was band;
Ne ought demaunds but that we loving bee,
As he himselfe hath lov'd us afore-hand,
And bound therto with an eternall band,
Him first to love that us so dearely bought,
And next our brethren, to his image wrought.

Him first to love great right and reason is,   190
Who first to us our life and being gave,
And after, when we fared had amisse,
Us wretches from the second death did save;
And last, the food of life, which now we have,
Even himselfe, in his deare sacrament,
To feede our hungry soules, unto us lent.

Then next, to love our brethren, that were made
Of that selfe mould, and that selfe Makers hand,
That we, and to the same againe shall fade,
Where they shall have like heritage of land,   200
How ever here on higher steps we stand,
Which also were with selfe-same price redeemed
That we, how ever of us light esteemed.

And were they not, yet since that loving Lord
Commaunded us to love them for his sake,
Even for his sake, and for his sacred word,
Which in his last bequest he to us spake,

We should them love, and with their needs partake;
Knowing that, whatsoere to them we give,
We give to him by whom we all doe live.   210

Such mercy he by his most holy reede
Unto us taught, and to approve it trew,
Ensampled it by his most righteous deede,
Shewing us mercie (miserable crew!)
That we the like should to the wretches shew,
And love our brethren; thereby to approve
How much, himselfe that loved us, we love.

Then rouze thy selfe, O Earth! out of thy soyle,
In which thou wallowest like to filthy swyne,
And doest thy mynd in durty pleasures moyle,   220
Unmindfull of that dearest Lord of thyne;
Lift up to him thy heavie clouded eyne,
That thou his soveraine bountie mayst behold,
And read, through love, his mercies manifold.

Beginne from first, where he encradled was
In simple cratch, wrapt in a wad of hay,
Betweene the toylefull Oxe and humble Asse,
And in what rags, and in how base aray,
The glory of our heavenly riches lay,
When him the silly Shepheards came to see,   230
Whom greatest Princes sought on lowest knee.

From thence reade on the storie of his life,
His humble carriage, his unfaulty wayes,
His cancred foes, his fights, his toyle, his strife,
His paines, his povertie, his sharpe assayes,
Through which he past his miserable dayes,
Offending none, and doing good to all,
Yet being malist both of great and small.

And looke at last, how of most wretched wights
He taken was, betrayd, and false accused;   240
How with most scornefull taunts, and fell despights,
He was revyld, disgrast, and foule abused;
How scourgd, how crownd, how buffeted, how brused;
And lastly, how twixt robbers crucifyde,
With bitter wounds through hands, through feet, and syde!

Then let thy flinty hart, that feeles no paine,
Empierced be with pittifull remorse,
And let thy bowels bleede in every vaine,

220   moyle: defile   230   silly: simple

At sight of his most sacred heavenly corse,
So torne and mangled with malicious forse;   250
And let thy soule, whose sins his sorrows wrought,
Melt into teares, and grone in grieved thought.

With sence whereof, whilest so thy softened spirit
Is inly toucht, and humbled with meeke zeale
Through meditation of his endlesse merit,
Lift up thy mind to th' Author of thy weale,
And to his soveraine mercie doe appeale;
Learne him to love that loved thee so deare,
And in thy brest his blessed image beare.

With all thy hart, with all thy soule and mind,   260
Thou must him love, and his beheasts embrace;
All other loves, with which the world doth blind
Weake fancies, and stirre up affections base,
Thou must renounce and utterly displace,
And give thy selfe unto him full and free,
That full and freely gave himselfe to thee.

Then shalt thou feele thy spirit so possest,
And ravisht with devouring great desire
Of his deare selfe, that shall thy feeble brest
Inflame with love, and set thee all on fire   270
With burning zeale, through every part entire,
That in no earthly thing thou shalt delight,
But in his sweet and amiable sight.

Thenceforth all worlds desire will in thee dye,
And all earthes glorie, on which men do gaze,
Seeme durt and drosse in thy pure-sighted eye,
Compar'd to that celestiall beauties blaze,
Whose glorious beames all fleshly sense doth daze
With admiration of their passing light,
Blinding the eyes, and lumining the spright.   280

Then shall thy ravisht soule inspired bee
With heavenly thoughts farre above humane skil,
And thy bright radiant eyes shall plainely see
Th' Idee of his pure glorie present still
Before thy face, that all thy spirits shall fill
With sweete enragement of celestiall love,
Kindled through sight of those faire things above.

AN HYMNE OF
HEAVENLY BEAUTIE.

RAPT WITH THE RAGE of mine own ravisht thought,
Through contemplation of those goodly sights,
And glorious images in heaven wrought,
Whose wondrous beauty, breathing sweet delights
Do kindle love in high conceipted sprights;
I faine to tell the things that I behold,
But feele my wits to faile, and tongue to fold.

Vouchsafe then, O thou most Almightie Spright!
From whom all guifts of wit and knowledge flow,
To shed into my breast some sparkling light   10
Of thine eternall Truth, that I may show
Some litle beames to mortall eyes below
Of that immortall beautie, there with thee,
Which in my weake distraughted mynd I see;

That with the glorie of so goodly sight
The hearts of men, which fondly here admyre
Faire seeming shewes, and feed on vaine delight,
Transported with celestiall desyre
Of those faire formes, may lift themselves up hyer,
And learne to love, with zealous humble dewty,   20
Th' eternall fountaine of that heavenly beauty.

Beginning then below, with th' easie vew
Of this base world, subject to fleshly eye,
From thence to mount aloft, by order dew,
To contemplation of th' immortall sky;
Of the soare faulcon so I learne to fly,
That flags awhile her fluttering wings beneath,
Till she her selfe for stronger flight can breath.

Then looke, who list thy gazefull eyes to feed
With sight of that is faire, looke on the frame   30
Of this wyde universe, and therein reed
26   soare faulcon: falcon of the first year

The endlesse kinds of creatures which by name
Thou canst not count, much lesse their natures aime;
All which are made with wondrous wise respect,
And all with admirable beautie deckt.

First, th' Earth, on adamantine pillers founded
Amid the Sea, engirt with brasen bands;
Then th' Aire still flitting, but yet firmely bounded
On everie side, with pyles of flaming brands,
Never consum'd, nor quencht with mortall hands;   40
And, last, that mightie shining christall wall,
Wherewith he hath encompassed this All.

By view whereof it plainly may appeare,
That still as every thing doth upward tend,
And further is from earth, so still more cleare
And faire it growes, till to his perfect end
Of purest beautie it at last ascend;
Ayre more then water, fire much more then ayre,
And heaven then fire, appeares more pure and fayre.

Looke thou no further, but affixe thine eye   50
On that bright shynie round still moving Masse,
The house of blessed God, which men call Skye,
All sowd with glistring stars more thicke then grasse,
Whereof each other doth in brightnesse passe,
But those two most, which, ruling night and day,
As King and Queene, the heavens Empire sway;

And tell me then, what hast thou ever seene
That to their beautie may compared bee,
Or can the sight that is most sharpe or keene
Endure their Captains flaming head to see?   60
How much lesse those, much higher in degree,
And so much fairer, and much more then these,
As these are fairer then the land and seas?

For farre above these heavens, which here we see,
Be others farre exceeding these in light,
Not bounded, not corrupt, as these same bee,
But infinite in largenesse and in hight,
Unmoving, uncorrupt, and spotlesse bright,
That need no Sunne t' illuminate their spheres,
But their owne native light farre passing theirs.   70

And as these heavens still by degrees arize,
Untill they come to their first Movers bound,

That in his mightie compasse doth comprize,
And carrie all the rest with him around;
So those likewise doe by degrees redound,
And rise more faire, till they at last arive
To the most faire, whereto they all do strive.

Faire is the heaven where happy soules have place,
In full enjoyment of felicitie,
Whence they doe still behold the glorious face   80
Of the Divine Eternall Majestie;
More faire is that, where those Idees on hie
Enraunged be, which Plato so admyred,
And pure Intelligences from God inspyred.

Yet fairer is that heaven, in which doe raine
The soveraine Powres and mightie Potentates,
Which in their high protections doe containe
All mortall Princes and imperiall States;
And fayrer yet, whereas the royall Seates
And heavenly Dominations are set,   90
From whom all earthly governance is fet.

Yet farre more faire be those bright Cherubins,
Which all with golden wings are overdight,
And those eternall burning Seraphins,
Which from their faces dart out fierie light;
Yet fairer then they both, and much more bright,
Be th' Angels and Archangels, which attend
On Gods owne person, without rest or end.

These thus in faire each other farre excelling,
As to the Highest they approch more neare,   100
Yet is that Highest farre beyond all telling,
Fairer then all the rest which there appeare,
Though all their beauties joynd together were;
How then can mortall tongue hope to expresse
The image of such endlesse perfectnesse?

Cease then, my tongue! and lend unto my mynd
Leave to bethinke how great that beautie is,
Whose utmost parts so beautifull I fynd;
How much more those essentiall parts of his,
His truth, his love, his wisedome, and his blis,   110
His grace, his doome, his mercy, and his might,
By which he lends us of himselfe a sight!

91   fet: fetched   108   utmost: outermost

Those unto all he daily doth display,
And shew himselfe in th' image of his grace,
As in a looking-glasse, through which he may
Be seene of all his creatures vile and base,
That are unable else to see his face,
His glorious face! which glistereth else so bright,
That th' Angels selves can not endure his sight.

But we, fraile wights! whose sight cannot sustaine   120
The Suns bright beames when he on us doth shyne,
But that their points rebutted backe againe
Are duld, how can we see with feeble eyne
The glory of that Majestie Divine,
In sight of whom both Sun and Moone are darke,
Compared to his least resplendent sparke?

The meanes, therefore, which unto us is lent
Him to behold, is on his workes to looke,
Which he hath made in beauty excellent,
And in the same, as in a brasen booke,   130
To reade enregistred in every nooke
His goodnesse, which his beautie doth declare;
For all thats good is beautifull and faire.

Thence gathering plumes of perfect speculation,
To impe the wings of thy high flying mynd,
Mount up aloft through heavenly contemplation,
From this darke world, whose damps the soule do blynd,
And, like the native brood of Eagles kynd,
On that bright Sunne of Glorie fixe thine eyes,
Clear'd from grosse mists of fraile infirmities.   140

Humbled with feare and awfull reverence,
Before the footestoole of his Majestie
Throw thy selfe downe, with trembling innocence,
Ne dare looke up with córruptible eye
On the dred face of that great Deity,
For feare, lest if he chaunce to looke on thee,
Thou turne to nought, and quite confounded be.

But lowly fall before his mercie seate,
Close covered with the Lambes integrity
From the just wrath of his avengefull threate   150
That sits upon the righteous throne on hy:
His throne is built upon Eternity,

135   impe: engraft feathers to improve the power of flight

More firme and durable then steele or brasse,
Or the hard diamond, which them both doth passe.

His scepter is the rod of Righteousnesse,
With which he bruseth all his foes to dust,
And the great Dragon strongly doth represse,
Under the rigour of his judgement just;
His seate is Truth, to which the faithfull trust,
From whence proceed her beames so pure and bright   160
That all about him sheddeth glorious light:

Light, farre exceeding that bright blazing sparke
Which darted is from Titans flaming head,
That with his beames enlumineth the darke
And dampish aire, whereby al things are red;
Whose nature yet so much is marvelled
Of mortall wits, that it doth much amaze
The greatest wisards which thereon do gaze.

But that immortall light, which there doth shine,
Is many thousand times more bright, more cleare,   170
More excellent, more glorious, more divine,
Through which to God all mortall actions here,
And even the thoughts of men, do plaine appeare;
For from th' Eternall Truth it doth proceed,
Through heavenly vertue which her beames doe breed.

With the great glorie of that wondrous light
His throne is all encompassed around,
And hid in his owne brightnesse from the sight
Of all that looke thereon with eyes unsound;
And underneath his feet are to be found   180
Thunder, and lightning, and tempestuous fyre,
The instruments of his avenging yre.

There in his bosome Sapience doth sit,
The soveraine dearling of the Deity,
Clad like a Queene in royall robes, most fit
For so great powre and peerelesse majesty,
And all with gemmes and jewels gorgeously
Adornd, that brighter then the starres appeare,
And make her native brightnes seem more cleare.

And on her head a crowne of purest gold   190
Is set, in signe of highest soveraignty;
And in her hand a scepter she doth hold,
With which she rules the house of God on hy,

And menageth the ever-moving sky,
And in the same these lower creatures all
Subjected to her powre imperiall.

Both heaven and earth obey unto her will,
And all the creatures which they both containe;
For of her fulnesse which the world doth fill
They all partake, and do in state remaine   200
As their great Maker did at first ordaine,
Through observation of her high beheast,
By which they first were made, and still increast.

The fairenesse of her face no tongue can tell;
For she the daughters of all wemens race,
And Angels eke, in beautie doth excell,
Sparkled on her from Gods owne glorious face,
And more increast by her owne goodly grace,
That it doth farre exceed all humane thought,
Ne can on earth compared be to ought.   210

Ne could that Painter (had he lived yet)
Which pictured Venus with so curious quill,
That all posteritie admyred it,
Have purtrayd this, for all his maistring skill;
Ne she her selfe, had she remained still,
And were as faire as fabling wits do fayne,
Could once come neare this beauty soverayne.

But had those wits, the wonders of their dayes,
Or that sweete Teian Poet, which did spend
His plenteous vaine in setting forth her prayse,   220
Seene but a glims of this which I pretend,
How wondrously would he her face commend,
Above that Idole of his fayning thought,
That all the world shold with his rimes be fraught!

How then dare I, the novice of his Art,
Presume to picture so divine a wight,
Or hope t' expresse her least perfections part,
Whose beautie filles the heavens with her light,
And darkes the earth with shadow of her sight?
Ah, gentle Muse! thou art too weake and faint   230
The pourtraict of so heavenly hew to paint.

Let Angels, which her goodly face behold
And see at will, her soveraigne praises sing,
And those most sacred mysteries unfold

Of that faire love of mightie heavens King;
Enough is me t' admyre so heavenly thing,
And, being thus with her huge love possest,
In th' only wonder of her selfe to rest,

But who so may, thrise happie man him hold,
Of all on earth whom God so much doth grace,   240
And lets his owne Beloved to behold;
For in the view of her celestiall face
All joy, all blisse, all happinesse, have place;
Ne ought on earth can want unto the wight
Who of her selfe can win the wishfull sight.

For she, out of her secret threasury
Plentie of riches forth on him will powre,
Even heavenly riches, which there hidden ly
Within the closet of her chastest bowre,
Th' eternall portion of her precious dowre,   250
Which mighty God hath given to her free,
And to all those which thereof worthy bee.

None thereof worthy be, but those whom shee
Vouchsafeth to her presence to receave,
And letteth them her lovely face to see,
Whereof such wondrous pleasures they conceave,
And sweete contentment, that it doth bereave
Their soule of sense, through infinite delight,
And them transport from flesh into the spright.

In which they see such admirable things,   260
As carries them into an extasy,
And heare such heavenly notes and carolings,
Of Gods high praise, that filles the brasen sky;
And feele such joy and pleasure inwardly,
That maketh them all worldly cares forget,
And onely thinke on that before them set.

Ne from thenceforth doth any fleshly sense,
Or idle thought of earthly things, remaine;
But all that earst seemed sweet seemes now offense,
And all that pleased earst now seemes to paine;   270
Their joy, their comfort, their desire, their gaine,
Is fixed all on that which now they see;
All other sights but fayned shadowes bee.

And that faire lampe, which useth to inflame
The hearts of men with selfe-consuming fyre
Thenceforth seemes fowle, and full of sinfull blame;
And all that pompe to which proud minds aspyre
By name of honor, and so much desyre,
Seemes to them basenesse, and all riches drosse,
And all mirth sadnesse, and all lucre losse.   280

So full their eyes are of that glorious sight,
And senses fraught with such satietie,
That in nought else on earth they can delight,
But in th' aspect of that felicitie,
Which they have written in their inward ey;
On which they feed, and in their fastened mynd
All happie joy and full contentment fynd.

Ah, then, my hungry soule! which long hast fed
On idle fancies of thy foolish thought,
And, with false beauties flattring bait misled,   290
Hast after vaine deceiptfull shadowes sought,
Which all are fled, and now have left thee nought
But late repentance through thy follies prief;
Ah! ceasse to gaze on matter of thy grief:

And looke at last up to that Soveraine Light,
From whose pure beams al perfect beauty springs,
That kindleth love in every godly spright
Even the love of God; which loathing brings
Of this vile world and these gay-seeming things;
With whose sweete pleasures being so possest,   300
Thy straying thoughts henceforth for ever rest.

A Brief Glossary of Words
Frequently Used by Spenser

abrade, abrayd: to awake, startle out of sleep or swoon
aggrate: to gratify, please
algate, algates: altogether, always, by all means, at all events,
    nevertheless
amate: to dismay, dishearten
apay: to repay, satisfy, please, requite
aread, areed: to counsel, proclaim, conjecture, judge
belive, bilive, bylive: promptly, quickly
blend: to blind, dazzle; to mingle, defile
blesse: to protect, preserve; to brandish
carefull: full of care, sorrowful
carle: churl
cheere: countenance, mood
cleep, clepe: to call, name
corage: spirit, nature
darraine, darrayne: to prepare (for battle), to wage war
earne: to yearn
embosse: to adorn; to cover, wrap; to press hard, drive to ex-
    tremity
envy (sb.): hatred, emulation
envy (v.): to grudge, be angry
fatal: ordained by fate
fere, feare: companion, mate
for thy: therefore, because
gentle: courteous, brave
gest: exploit
gride, gryde: pierce, transfix
impe: child, scion
kind: nature, fashion
kindly: natural, innate, characteristically
leasing: a lie
maine: force; ocean
mauger: inspite of, a curse on it!
mold, mould: form, structure, body

note, no'te: know not, cannot
raught: reached, handed, took, granted
reade, reede: to discern, discover, imagine, declare, name
rive, ryve: to split, pierce
sad: grave, sober, heavy
shend: to disgrace
silly: innocent, simple, harmless
sit: to befit
sleight, slight: artifice, trickery
stound: moment; blow, attack, noise; amazement, trouble, sorrow
stoure, stowre: strife, tumult; peril, crisis; fit, paroxysm
surquedry: arrogance, presumption
thrill: to pierce
travel, travell: labor
uncouth: unknown, strange
uneath: difficult, with difficulty
wanton: playful, wild
wite, wyte: to blame, reproach
wonne (sb.): dwelling, abode
wonne, wone (v.): to dwell; to be wont
wood: mad, frantic
yede, yeed: to go
yfere: in company

MODERN LIBRARY GIANTS

A series of sturdily bound and handsomely printed, full-sized library editions of books formerly available only in expensive sets. These volumes contain from 600 to 1,400 pages each.

THE MODERN LIBRARY GIANTS REPRESENT A
SELECTION OF THE WORLD'S GREATEST BOOKS

G88   O'HARA, JOHN: *49 Stories*
G55   O'NEILL, EUGENE: *Nine Plays*
G68   PAINE, TOM: *Selected Work*
G86   PASTERNAK, BORIS: *Doctor Zhivago*
G5   PLUTARCH: *Lives* (The Dryden Translation)
G40   POE, EDGAR ALLAN: *Complete Tales and Poems*
G29   PRESCOTT, WILLIAM H.: *The Conquest of Mexico* and *The Conquest of Peru*
G62   PUSHKIN: *Poems, Prose and Plays*
G65   RABELAIS: *Complete Works*
G12   SCOTT, SIR WALTER: *The Most Popular Novels* (Quentin Durward, Ivanhoe & Kenilworth)
G4   SHELLEY & KEATS: *Complete Poems*
G32   SMITH, ADAM: *The Wealth of Nations*
G61   SPAETH, SIGMUND: *A Guide to Great Orchestral Music*
G91   SPENSER, EDMUND: *Selected Poetry*
G75   STEVENSON, ROBERT LOUIS: *Selected Writings*
G53   SUE, EUGENE: *The Wandering Jew*
G42   TENNYSON: *The Poems and Plays*
G23   TOLSTOY, LEO: *Anna Karenina*
G1   TOLSTOY, LEO: *War and Peace*
G49   TWAIN, MARK: *Tom Sawyer* and *Huckleberry Finn*
G50   WHITMAN, WALT: *Leaves of Grass*
G83   WILSON, EDMUND: *The Shock of Recognition*

MISCELLANEOUS

G77   *An Anthology of Famous American Stories*
G54   *An Anthology of Famous British Stories*
G67   *Anthology of Famous English and American Poetry*
G81   *An Encyclopedia of Modern American Humor*
G47   *The English Philosophers from Bacon to Mill*
G16   *The European Philosophers from Descartes to Nietzsche*
G31   *Famous Science-Fiction Stories*
G85   *Great Ages and Ideas of the Jewish People*
G89   *Great Classical Myths*
G72   *Great Tales of Terror and the Supernatural*
G9   *Great Voices of the Reformation*
G87   *Medieval Epics*
G48   *The Metropolitan Opera Guide*
G46   *A New Anthology of Modern Poetry*
G69   *One Hundred and One Years' Entertainment*
G90   *Philosophies of Art and Beauty: Readings in Aesthetics from Plato to Heidegger*
G21   *Sixteen Famous American Plays*
G63   *Sixteen Famous British Plays*
G71   *Sixteen Famous European Plays*
G45   *Stoic and Epicurean Philosophers*
G22   *Thirty Famous One-Act Plays*
G66   *Three Famous Murder Novels, Before the Fact,* Francis Iles, *Trent's Last Case,* E. C. Bentley, *The House of the Arrow,* A. E. W. Mason
G10   *Twelve Famous Plays of the Restoration and Eighteenth Century* (1660–1820) Dryden, Congreve, Wycherley, Gay, etc.
G56   *The Wisdom of Catholicism*
G59   *The Wisdom of China and India*
G79   *The Wisdom of Israel*

The Best of the World's Best Books
COMPLETE LIST OF TITLES IN
THE MODERN LIBRARY